# ALA GUIDE TO
# ECONOMICS & BUSINESS
# REFERENCE

D1114455

# A L A   G U I D E   T O

# ECONOMICS & BUSINESS

# R E F E R E N C E

American Library Association

Chicago / 2011

© 2011 by the American Library Association. Any claim of copyright is subject to applicable limitations and exceptions, such as rights of fair use and library copying pursuant to Sections 107 and 108 of the U.S. Copyright Act. No copyright is claimed in content that is in the public domain, such as works of the U.S. government.

Printed in the United States of America

15  14  13  12  11      5  4  3  2

While extensive effort has gone into ensuring the reliability of the information in this book, the publisher makes no warranty, express or implied, with respect to the material contained herein.

ISBN: 978-0-8389-1024-5

*Library of Congress Cataloging-in-Publication Data*
ALA guide to economics & business reference / American Library Association. — 1st ed.
    p.    cm.
  ISBN 978-0-8389-1024-5 (alk. paper)
  1. Economics—Encyclopedias. 2. Industries—Encyclopedias. 3. Business—Encyclopedias.
I. American Library Association. II. Title: ALA guide to economics and business reference. III. Title: Guide to economics & business reference. IV. Title: Guide to economics and business reference.
  HB61.A423 2011
  016.33—dc22                                                    2011009721

Book design by Karen Sheets de Gracia in Helvetica and Times.
Composition by Publication Services, Inc.

♾This paper meets the requirements of ANSI/NISO Z39.48-1992 (Permanence of Paper).

ALA Editions also publishes its books in a variety of electronic formats. For more information, visit the ALA Store at www.alastore.ala.org and select eEditions.

# CONTENTS

# SERIES INTRODUCTION

**A**S THE PUBLISHER of the essential *Guide to Reference Books*, first printed more than a century ago, as well as *Reference Sources for Small and Medium-Sized Libraries* and *Fundamental Reference Sources*, the American Library Association has long been a source for authoritative bibliographies of the reference literature for practicing librarians, library educators, and reference service trainers. The ALA Guide to Reference series continues that tradition with expertly compiled, discipline-specific, annotated bibliographies of reference works. The volumes in the series draw their content from the successor to *Guide to Reference Books*, the online *Guide to Reference* (www.guidetoreference.org), and thus serve as snapshots of the evolving content of the online *Guide*.

Although compiled in North America for use largely in North American libraries serving institutions of higher education, the series volumes will also be valuable to public and school librarians, independent researchers, publishers, and book dealers, as well as librarians outside North America, for identifying sources that will answer questions, directing researchers, creating local instructional materials, educating and training LIS students and reference staff, and inventorying and developing reference collections. Because these guides provide a usably comprehensive, rather than exhaustive, repertory of sources as the foundation for reference and information services in today's North American higher education research settings, English-language works figure prominently. Works in other languages are included, however, as categories require them and as higher education curricula in North American colleges and universities suggest their inclusion.

The reader will find entries for works that are, for the most part, broadly focused; works on individual persons or works that are narrowly focused geographically or chronologically are not included. Selection criteria favored titles published in the last fifteen years; the reader will want to consult earlier printed bibliographies and indexes, such as the numerous print editions of *Guide to Reference Books*, for many earlier and still important works.

Together, the volumes in this series include works that can most usefully satisfy the vast majority of demands made on a reference service, while not altogether excluding "exotic" or little-known works that will meet only the unusual need. The hope is that the works included will directly meet 80 percent of the needs that librarians have for reference sources and, in the remaining 20 percent of cases, will lead to other works that will suffice.

Librarians today have a broader definition of that much-mooted and ambiguous term *reference work* than ever before. The volumes in this series therefore include the traditional array of encyclopedic, bibliographic, and compendious works as well as websites, search engines, and full-text databases. Because of current reference practice and user preferences, the bibliographies in the series include those online sources that have replaced their printed versions for most librarians under most circumstances. The annotations for such sources describe the relationships between online and print versions.

In addition to providing classified annotated bibliographies, every volume includes editors' guides that orient readers to each discipline, its scope and concerns, and the kinds of sources available for working in it. The editors' guides will be useful, therefore, to the generalist librarian and LIS student as background to the bibliographies or as intellectual frameworks for addressing reference questions.

We at ALA Publishing hope you find the series helpful and welcome your comments at guidetoreference@ala.org. To get the full benefit of the comprehensive compilation in a wide range of subject areas, we also encourage you to subscribe to the online *Guide*, where you have access to updated entries (especially current Web resources), annotations, and user comments.

# CONTRIBUTORS

**UNDER THE DIRECTION** of general editors Robert Kieft (2000–2009) and Denise Bennett (2009–), many librarians have contributed their time and their knowledge of reference literature to this series. A comprehensive list of these contributors appears under the About section of the online *Guide to Reference* (www.guidetoreference.org).

ALA GUIDE TO

# ECONOMICS & BUSINESS

## REFERENCE

# EDITOR'S GUIDE

**B**USINESS AND ECONOMICS are both diverse fields that can examine aspects of every discipline in the *Guide*. However, this section of the *Guide* attempts to focus on print and electronic sources that are key to economics and business reference.

Although many of the resources included in earlier editions are now available electronically, as free Internet resources are now relevant, print resources remain important. Many older key print resources from the last edition are now out of print, and though some have been replaced by new publications, a remarkable number of resources are simply gone. Though some of these are niche directories, which many will not mourn, there are some titles that would remain relevant if still in print, such as *Irwin Business and Investment Almanac*. Older print reference titles that remain useful have been included in this edition.

There are also far fewer bibliographies listed in this edition. This is not to imply that bibliographies are useless: however, few meaningful bibliographies in business and economics have been published recently. Where useful, they continue to be included, such as *Black Business and Economics: A Selected Bibliography* and *International Bibliography of Business History*.

Many indexes have been transformed into databases. However, print indexes are still listed, especially when the print version is easier to use or less costly than the electronic version.

Other changes include new sections, such as business law, electronic commerce, international business, and management of information systems; new areas, such as market research and various industries (agribusiness, biotechnology, leisure, pharmaceuticals, etc.); and new subcategories, such as organizations and associations, and Internet resources.

For those less familiar with these disciplines, *Strauss's Handbook of Business Information: A Guide for Librarians, Students, and Researchers* provides information on resources, as well as information on business itself, making it an invaluable source for foundational information. Each functional area of this category contains similar guides, which should assist in understanding these subdisciplines.

## —ELISABETH LEONARD, EDITOR

# 1 > BASIC INDUSTRY INFORMATION

## Financial Ratios

1    **Almanac of business and industrial financial ratios.** Leo Troy.
Englewood Cliffs, N.J.: Prentice-Hall. ISSN: 0747-9107.
338.740973                                                    HF5681.R25A45

Data come from nearly 5 million IRS tax returns. Table 1 reports operating
and financial information for all corporations. Table 2 reports operating
and financial information for all corporations with a net income. Also
includes 50 performance indicators. Covers 179 industries, arranged by
Standard Industrial Classification (SIC) code. The easiest ratio source to
use.

2    **Bank quarterly.** Sheshunoff Rating Services, Inc. Austin, Tex.:
Sheshunoff Rating Services.
332.10973021                                                  HG2401.B34

Data on liquidity, earnings, loan exposure, capital adequacy, and other
ratios for specific banks and savings and loans. Available online as
BankFocus.

3    **Best's aggregates and averages.** A. M. Best Company. Oldwick,
N.J.: A. M. Best, 1998–. ISSN: 1099-3592.
362.104258                                                    RA413.5.U5B476

Available for Property/Casualty, as well as Life/Health, with summary
data on the insurance industry. Includes balance sheet and summary of
operations, annual statements, quantitative analysis, insurance expenses,

time series, premiums written, industry underwriting, leading companies and groups (with assets, policyholders surplus, reserves, premiums written, underwriting gain/loss, net investment income, realized capital gains, underwriting expense ratio, etc.), rankings, and composite listings. Coverage is for Canada and the United States.

**4     Cost of capital quarterly.** Ibbotson Associates. Chicago: Ibbotson Associates, 1994–. ISSN: 1080-4021.

HC110.C3C67

Financial data for 300 industries, organized by SIC code, including several measures of cost of capital and cost of equity. Also gives industry betas, sales, profitability, capitalization, multiples, ratios, equity returns, and capital structure. Available online through Ibbotson Cost of Capital Center.

**5     Financial studies of the small business.** Winter Haven, Fla.: Financial Research Associates, 1976–. ISSN: 0363-8987.
658.15904                                                    HD2346.U5F55a

Uses data from 30,000 financial statements provided by certified public accounting firms to present financial data on U.S. small businesses. Arranged by industry, then by asset size. Gives current assets, fixed assets, liabilities and capital, income data, operating items such as advertising expense and rent, and ratios (current, quick, current assets/total assets, short term debt/total debt, short term debt/net worth, total debt/net worth, short term debt/total assets, long term debt/total assets, total debt/total assets, sales/receivables, average collection period, sales/inventory, sales/total assets, sales/net worth, pre-tax profit/total assets, pre-tax profit/net worth).

**6     RMA annual statement studies.** Robert Morris Associates. ill. Philadelphia: Robert Morris Associates, 1977–. ISSN: 1545-7699.
338                                                          HF5681.B2R6

Using 190,000 statements from member institutions, RMA presents 19 financial ratios (current, quick, times interest earned, etc.), with common-size balance sheet and income statement items sorted by asset and sales size. Five years of data. Contains 700 industries, arranged by NAICS code. Has useful definitions in the front, often necessary as formulas for ratios can vary.

# Indexes; Abstract Journals

7    **LexisNexis.** LexisNexis. [199?] Bethesda, Md.: LexisNexis.
http://www.lexisnexis.com/academic/.
Searchable full-text subscription database that includes approximately 350
U.S. and foreign newspapers, broadcast transcripts from the major radio and
TV networks, national and international wire services, campus newspapers,
polls and surveys, and over 600 newsletters. Non-English language news
sources available in Spanish, French, German, Italian, and Dutch. Dates of
coverage vary by individual source, with newspapers updated daily.

8    **The Wall Street Journal index.** Dow Jones. [New York]: Dow
Jones, 1957–. ISSN: 1042-9840.
332.05                                                          HG1.W26

Index coverage begins in 1955 and is based on the final Eastern edition of
the newspaper. Each issue has two parts: (1) corporate news indexed by
company name; (2) general news indexed by topic. Includes special sections for book reviews, personalities, deaths, and theater reviews. The last
section of the index includes the daily Dow Jones averages for each month
of the year. Since 1981, v. 1 includes *Barron's index*, a subject and corporate index to *Barron's business and financial weekly*. Since 1990, published
monthly with quarterly and annual cumulations. Former publication
frequency was monthly with annual cumulations. Annual cumulations
issued in 2 pts., 1980–2001.

Fully searchable page images of the complete *Wall Street Journal*
1889–1989 are available in ProQuest Historical Newspapers (Ann Arbor,
Mich.: ProQuest, 2001–). Searchable full text (although not original page
images) is also available in a number of other commercial database services, including ProQuest Newspapers (Ann Arbor, Mich.: ProQuest,
2001–), Factiva (794), and ABI/Inform Global (788).

# Overviews

9    **Business insights.** Datamonitor (Firm). [London?]: Reuters.
http://www.globalbusinessinsights.com/autologin.asp.
                                                                HF54.7

Reports on energy, consumer goods, finance, health care, and technology.
Reports, typically over 100 pages long, cover new product innovations,

marketing strategies, market drivers, key players, trends, forecast business opportunities, and industry interviews. International focus, especially strong for European coverage.

**10    Career guide to industries.** U.S. Department of Labor, Bureau of Labor Statistics. ill. Washington: Bureau of Labor Statistics, 1992–.
331.70205                                        HF5382.5.U5C316

Information on the nature of the industry, working conditions, employment, occupations within the industry, training and advancement, outlook, earnings, and sources of additional information. While this is similar to the *Occupational outlook handbook*, (22) it is organized by industry, of which there are 45, and has occupations not included in the *Handbook*. Also available online at http://www.bls.gov/oco/cg/.

**11    Forrester research.** Forrester Research. [1999–2003.] Cambridge, Mass.: Forrester. http://www.library.hbs.edu/forrester.htm.
HF5548.32T174

Nearly 17,000 original reports on technology's effect on business and the consumer in the United States, Canada, Europe, and Asia Pacific. Research is in two categories, technology and industry.

Topics in technology are application development, business intelligence, computing systems, consumer devices and access, content and collaboration, customer experience, enterprise applications, enterprise mobility, IT management, IT services, networking, portals and site technology, security, software infrastructure, and tech sector economics.

Topics in industry are brand strategy, brand tactics, consumer electronics, consumer products, customer insight, emerging marketing channels, energy and utilities, financial services, government, healthcare and life sciences, high tech, industry insight, manufacturing, marketing and advertising, marketing planning, media and entertainment, mobile services, professional services, relationship marketing, retail, telecommunications, television advertising, transportation and logistics, and travel.

Reports typically range from 3–20 pages, and some are available as videos.

**12    Global market information database.** Euromonitor. [1999–.] [London]: Euromonitor. http://www.gmid.euromonitor.com/.
HD2755.5.G56

Market reports, company profiles, and demographic, economic, and marketing statistics for 205 countries. Market reports are for 16 consumer markets (food and drink, tobacco, toys, etc.) and 14 industrial and service markets (accountancy, broadcasting, chemicals, property services, etc.).

Reports have market size, market sectors, share of market, marketing activity, research and development, corporate overview, distribution, consumer profiles, market forecasts, sector forecasts, sources, and definitions. Additional reports are available for market segments, such as baby food. Company profiles have background, recent news, competitive environment, and outlook. Consumer lifestyle reports and very useful marketing background analyze the consumer by country, gender, age, marital status, educational attainment, ethnicity, religion, home ownership, household profile, employment, income, health, eating and personal grooming habits, leisure activities, personal finance, communication, transport, and travel.

Search for data, which can be exported into Excel or browse for reports. Data are available from 1977 through 2016 and include inflation, exchange rates, GDP, GNI, government expenditures, government finance, income, labor, and money supply.

**13    A historical dictionary of American industrial language.** William H. Mulligan. xii, 332 p. New York: Greenwood Press, 1988. ISBN: 0313241716.

338.00321                                                        TS9.H57

Brief definitions drawn primarily from the period before World War I. An appendix lists terms by industry. Includes a list of contributors, bibliography, and index of institutions and people.

**14    Hoover's online.** Reference Press. 1996–. Austin, Tex.: Reference Press. http://www.hoovers.com/.

338.7                                                          HG4057

Nearly 18 million records describing public and private companies primarily in the United States, but including Canada, United Kingdom, Europe, and Asia/Pacific. Profiles have an overview, history, family tree, industry information, products/operations, top competitors, competitive landscape, top executives with biographies, news, significant developments, and financial data (summary; income statement; balance sheet; cash flow; historical financials such as five years of P/E and per share; stock quote;

interactive stock chart; market data; earnings estimates; this year's ratios for the company, industry, and market; SEC filings; and industry watch).

Covers 600 industries, organized into the following categories: Aerospace and Defense; Agriculture; Automotive and Transport; Banking; Beverages; Business Services; Charitable Organizations; Chemicals; Computer Hardware; Computer Services; Computer Software; Construction; Consumer Products Manufacturers; Consumer Services; Cultural Institutions; Education; Electronics; Energy and Utilities; Environmental Services and Equipment; Financial Services; Food; Foundations; Government; Health Care; Industrial Manufacturing; Insurance; Leisure; Media; Membership Organizations; Metals and Mining; Pharmaceuticals; Real Estate; Retail; Security Products and Services; Telecommunications Equipment; Telecommunications Services; and Transportation Services.

Coverage can be brief, but generally includes a fact sheet, overview, selected companies, industry watch with video interviews, news from the last 90 days, and web resources for terminology, associations, and organizations, and online publications. Includes Hoover's print publications (*Hoover's handbook of American business* [35], *Hoover's handbook of private companies* [36]).

**15    IBISWorld United States.** IBISWorld. New York: IBISWorld. http://www.ibisworld.com/.

HC103 .I247

700 reports on the following industries: agriculture, forestry, fishing and hunting; mining; utilities; construction; manufacturing; wholesale trade; retail trade; transportation and warehousing; information; finance and insurance; real estate and rental and leasing; professional, scientific, and technical services; administrative and support and waste management and remediation services; educational services; health care and social assistance; arts, entertainment, and recreation; accommodation and food services; and other services. Setting this database apart are reports on small industries, such as parking lots and garages.

Reports include industry definition; key statistics; segmentations (products and services segmentation, major market segments, industry concentration, geographic spread); market characteristics (market size, demand determinants, domestic and international markets, basis of competition, life cycle); industry conditions (barriers to entry, taxation, industry assistance, regulation and deregulation, cost structure, capital and labor intensity, technology and systems, industry volatility, globalization);

key factors (sensitivities and success factors); key competitors; and industry performance (current and historical).

16    **Industry research using the economic census: How to find it, how to use it.** Jennifer C. Boettcher, Leonard M. Gaines. xv, 305 p., ill., 1 map. Westport, Conn.: Greenwood Press, 2004. ISBN: 157356351X.

338.097300727                                              HC101.B594

Very useful guide to U.S. census concepts, methodology, terminology, and data sources, location of economic census resources. Appendixes for acronyms and initials, sample questionnaires, government print office, regional depository libraries, and state data centers. Available as an e-book.

17    **Investext plus.** Thomson Financial (Firm). [1998–.] [Boston?]: Thomson Financial. http://www.galegroup.com/.

Company and industry reports written by some 500 investment banks in North America, Europe, Asia/Pacific, Latin America, Africa, and the Middle East. Also contains research reports on 190 trade associations. Reports range from 1–100 pages long. Covers 10,000 publicly traded U.S. companies. Reports give earnings estimates, financials, business ratios, trends, forecasts, credit ratings, analysis, text of conference calls, and stock prices. Industry reports give background, financials, business ratios, trends, forecasts, analysis, and some brief company profiles. Formerly Research Bank Web. Coverage from 1982.

18    **Marketresearch.com academic.** Kalorama Information. 1999–. Bethesda, Md.: Kalorama Information. http://www.marketresearch. com/.

HF5415.2.K35

Market research reports from various sources (Icon Group, Kalorama, BizMiner, etc.) for Consumer Goods (apparel, cosmetics and personal care, house and home, pet services and supplies, travel services), Food and Beverage (alcoholic beverages, coffee and tea, soft drinks, confectionery, dairy products, food processing), Heavy Industry (energy, mining, utilities, construction, machines and parts, manufacturing, metals, paper and forest products, plastics, automotive, aviation & aerospace, logistics and shipping), Service Industries (accounting and finance, corporate services, banking and financial services, insurance), Public Sector (associations/nonprofits, education, government), Life Science (biotechnology, agriculture, genomics, proteomics, medical imaging, healthcare facilities, managed care, regulation and policy, cardiovascular devices, equipment and supplies, wound care, pharmaceuticals, diseases and conditions, prescription drugs, therapeutic area), Technology & Media (computer equipment, electronics, networks, e-commerce and IT outsourcing, software, telecommunications, wireless), and Demographics (age, lifestyle and economics, multicultural).

Reports range in length, with some over 300 pages long, and give a variety of information (definition of industry, consumer demographics, consumer shopping habits, spending patterns, sales, establishments, employment, forecasts, trends, market size, market share, and market segmentation). Some company information is also included.

**19   Mergent online.** Moody's Investors Service. 1998–. New York: Moody's Investors Service. http://www.mergent.com/.

HG4061

Provides a full source of information on company details, equity pricing, company financials, industry reports, news, and 58,000 annual reports. Reports can be created by searching company details (Synopsis, Financial Highlights, History, Joint Ventures, Business, Property, Subsidiary, Long Term Debt, and Capital Structure); research and news (Historic News, Institutional Holdings, and Insider Holdings); and financial statements (Income Statement, Balance Sheet, Cash Flows, and Profitability Ratios). Financials can be exported into Excel. More than 1,500 one-page equity reports for NYSE, NASDAQ, and AMEX companies, with quarterly financial results, analyses of future prospects, and operating ratios. Access to EDGAR filings from 1993 to present and data on 20,000 non-U.S.-based corporations. Industry reports, while brief, are international in scope. Includes the Mergent manuals, which were known as Moody's, except for the Municipal and Government Manual.

**20   Mintel reports.** Mintel International Group. London; Chicago: Mintel International Group. http://reports.mintel.com/.

HC240.9.C6

Marketing and consumer research reports focusing on the United States and Europe. Covers consumer goods and services, making this a good source of reports for market segments and consumer behavior, with reports like "Impact of celebrity chefs on cooking habits," "Nail color and care," and "MP3 players and other portable audio players," but not for business to business reports.

Market reports are available for automotive, beauty and personal, drink and tobacco, electronics, food and foodservice, health and medical, health and wellness, household, lifestyles, media, books and stationery, personal finances, retailing, technology, and travel. Reports include an executive summary, glossary, and sections on advertising and promotion, ownership and usage, attitudes and opinions, market drivers, market size and trends, market segmentation, future and forecast, and supply structure.

Consumer reports provide demographics, core needs and values, future trends, information on products currently targeted to the group, and advice on reaching and influencing the target audience. Consumer reports are available for financial lifestyles, general lifestyles, healthier lifestyles, and leisure lifestyles.

Marketing and promotion reports are for marketing and targeting, and promotions, incentives, and sponsorship. They include introduction and abbreviations, executive summary, background and market factors, challenges facing marketers, marketing segments, product development and pricing, and future trends.

Most data in Mintel can be downloaded into Excel. Reports cannot be viewed in their entirety and instead must be viewed in sections, making easy skimming or printing a report impossible.

21    North American industry classification system: United
      States, 2007. 2007 Rev. ed. United States. 1419 p. Lanham, Md.;
      Springfield, Va.: Bernan; National Technical Information Service,
      2007. ISBN: 0934213860.
338.0201273                                          HF1042.N67

The North American Industry Classification System (NAICS) is the replacement for Standard Industrial Classification (SIC) codes. This manual presents the 2007 and 2002 NAICS codes, industry definitions, and tables linking NAICS and SIC. Also available on CD-ROM and on the web (United States: U.S. Census Bureau, 199–).

22    Occupational outlook handbook. JIST Works, Inc. ill.
      Indianapolis, Ind.: JIST Works, 1987–. ISSN: 0082-9072.
331                                                  HF5381.U62

Gives information on employment trends and outlook in more than 800 occupations. Indicates nature of work, qualifications, earnings and working conditions, entry level jobs, information on the job market in each state, where to go for more information, etc. Available online at http://www.bls.gov/oco/. Similar information can be found in the *Career guide to industries* (000).

**23    STAT-USA Internet.** STAT-USA. [1994–.] [Washington, D.C.?]: STAT-USA, U.S. Dept. of Commerce. http://www.stat-usa.gov/.

382                                                                                    HF1379

Business and economic information compiled mainly from federal agencies. There are two main sections, "State of the Nation" and "Globus & NTDB."

"State of the Nation" concentrates on current U.S. information, with 2,500 files on general economic indicators (consumer price index, producer price index, gross domestic product, national income and product accounts), regional economic statistics (by NAICS sector, state personal income, metropolitan personal income) housing and construction (housing starts and building permits, new construction, new home sales), employment (employment cost index, local area employment and unemployment, weekly unemployment claims report), manufacturing and industry (retail sales, manufacturing inventories and sales, industrial production and capacity utilization, current industry reports), monetary statistics (interest rates, foreign exchange rates, bank credit), and economic policy (Beige Book, Treasury Statements).

"Globus & NTDB" is useful for current exchange rates (weekly, monthly, and annual), current and historical trade leads (United Nations trade leads, Defense Logistics Agency leads, FedBizOpps, commercial trade leads), international trade (Asia Development Bank, World Bank, Inter-American Development Bank, and European Bank Business Opportunities, country reports on terrorism, Country Studies Program reports, *International trade update newsletter, National trade estimates report on foreign trade barriers, World bank commodity price data*—"PinkSheets"—and *World factbook*), market and country research (*Country background notes, Country commercial guides, Industry sector analysis reports,* Global Agriculture Information Network [GAIN], *AgWorld attaché reports, International market insight (IMI) reports,* and Multilateral Development Bank), contacts (*NTDB global trade directory, National export directory,* Foreign Trade Offices), and current press releases (U.S. international trade in goods and services, FT900 supplemental tables, U.S. Export Sales—USDA, U.S. import and export price indexes, U.S. international transactions, and additional press releases).

# Statistics

24    Manufacturing and distribution U.S.A.: Industry analyses, statistics, and leading companies. Gale Group. ill. Detroit: Gale Group, 2000–. ISSN: 1529-7659.

338                                                                          HD9721.M3495

Industry analyses, statistics, and contact information for U.S. companies in the manufacturing, wholesaling, and retail industries. National and state profiles give leading establishments, employment, payroll, inputs, and outputs. Includes public and private companies. Also available as an e-book.

25    **Success by the numbers: Statistics for business development.** Ryan Womack, Reference and User Services Association. vii, 59 p., ill. Chicago: American Library Association; Reference and User Services Association, 2005. ISBN: 0838983278.

                                                                          HF54.56.S832

A guide to U.S. statistical resources, with information on how the data is gathered, as well as where to find it. Chapters on: Federal business statistics and the 2002 economic census; Finding Florida statistical resources and data; Demographics and marketing; Economic forecasts; Industry statistics; Financial statistics; Labor, employment, and wages statistics; and Trade statistics. State and national sources are provided and sources are both free and fee-based.

26    **Tablebase.** Gale Cengage Learning. [2001?–.] [s.l.]: Gale Cengage Learning. http://search.rdsinc.com/.

A terrific international statistical source for company, industry, and demographic information including market share, market size, market trends, price trends, rankings, sales forecasts, output and capacity, consumption, imports and exports, and shipments. Information comes from 900 trade publications, including *Accounting today, Adweek, Aftermarket business, Almanac of american employers, Beverage world, Chemical week, Datamonitor industry market research, Meed Middle East economic digest,* as well as reports, newsletters, and surveys.

27    **Yahoo! finance.** Yahoo! Inc., 2001. Sunnyvale, Calif.: Yahoo! Inc. http://finance.yahoo.com/.

A rich source of financial information, with company profiles, SEC filings, annual reports, stock quotes, news, analysis, conference call calendar, industry statistics and news, and information for the personal investor. The focus is on financial information about U.S. and Canadian companies and industries, but international information, such as indices and currency information, is also available, especially through the portals to Yahoo!Finance for other countries (linked from the bottom of the entry page). Historical quotes for stocks, bonds, and money markets are since 1970 and give daily, weekly, and monthly closing prices, and dividends. Occasionally links to fee-based information.

# 2 > COMPANY INFORMATION

## Biography

28    **Corporate eponymy: A biographical dictionary of the persons behind the names of major American, British, European, and Asian businesses.** Adrian Room. xx, 280 p. Jefferson, N.C.: McFarland, 1992. ISBN: 0899506798.

338.740922                                HC29.R66

Arranged alphabetically by name, with the origins of some 700 corporate names, brand, and trade names.

## Corporate Profiles

29    **The almanac of American employers.** Plunkett Research, Ltd. CD-ROMs. Houston, Tex.: Plunkett Research. ISSN: 1548-7369.

338                                     HF5382.75.U6

A comprehensive guide to the labor market in the U.S., with profiles of major companies, both private and public. Unique features include information on companies most likely to hire women and minorities, company hiring patterns (will hire MBAs, engineers, liberal arts majors, etc.), and company profiles that give textual information including corporate culture and plans for growth. Chapters on: Major Trends Affecting Job Seekers; Statistics (U.S. Employment Overview, U.S. Civilian Workforce Level: 1996–2006, Number of People Employed, U.S.: 1995–2006,

Unemployment Level of U.S. Labor Force: August 1996–2006, Top 10 Fastest Growing U.S. Occupations: 2000–2010, Top 10 U.S. Industries with the Fastest Growth of Wage and Salary Employment: 2004-2014, Jobs with the Largest Expected Employment Decreases from 2004-2014, Percent of U.S. Workers with Access to Retirement and Healthcare Benefits); Research: Seven Keys for Job Seekers (Financial Stability, Growth Plan, Research and Development Programs, Product Launch and Production, Marketing and Distribution Methods, Employee Benefits, Quality of Work Factors, Other Considerations); Important Contacts for Job Seekers; American Employers: Top 500; and Indexes (alphabetical, by headquarters location, by Regions, firms with operations outside the U.S., Firms Noted as Hot Spots for Advancement for Women and Minorities, and by Subsidiaries, Brand Names and Selected Affiliations). Also available online.

**30**  **The Bankers' almanac.** Reed Information Services Ltd. West Sussex, England: Reed Information Services, 1993–. ISSN: 1462-4125.

HG2984.B3

International coverage of over 4,000 banks, with information on executives, bank owners and their percentage of shares, bank correspondents, bank name changes, liquidations, balance sheet figures, profits and loss statements, world and country rankings, credit ratings, national bank and SWIFT codes. Also available, for a fee, at http://www.bankersalmanac.com/.

**31**  **BigCharts.** MarketWatch, Inc. 1998–. [San Francisco]: BigCharts. http://bigcharts.marketwatch.com/.

HG4638

Best known for historic stock quotes, BigCharts has information on over 50,000 symbols, including current information on all NYSE, NASDAQ, AMEX, and OTC stocks, all NASDAQ quoted mutual funds, as well as leading financial indexes and international exchanges. The current information includes company profiles, company financials, news, charts, analyst estimates, analysis, and intraday stock screeners. Historic quotes include open, closing, high and low prices, volume traded, split adjusted price, and adjustment factor since 1970.

**32**  **Business and company resource center.** Gale. 2000–. [Farmington Hills, Mich.]: Gale. http://www.gale.cengage.com/BusinessRC/.

HF54.7.B85B875x

A blend of articles from some 3,200 periodicals (journals, newspapers, and trade publications), investment reports (from Investext), company histories (from *International directory of company histories* [Chicago; Detroit: St. James Press, 1988–]), First Call consensus estimates, business rankings (from *Business rankings annual* [103]), and more. Search by company to find company profiles, rankings, financials, investment reports, articles, and histories. Search by industry to find industry associations, articles, and rankings. PROMT® (Predicast's Overview of Markets and Technology), Investext Plus (17), and Newsletters ASAP can be added onto the subscription.

**33**   **Corporateaffiliations.com.** LexisNexis Group. New York: LexisNexis. http://www.corporateaffiliations.com/.

Profiles nearly 200,000 public and private companies, with information on affiliates, subsidiaries, and divisions. Search by company type, location, title of executive, NAICS or SIC code, number of employees, sales revenue, ownership, fiscal year, stock exchange, earnings, assets, net worth, and liabilities. Profiles include contact information, very brief business description, year founded, number of employees, NAICS and SIC codes, names of top executives, outside service firms, and top competitors. Most useful for visual who-owns-whom hierarchies, linking to profiles for all companies in the hierarchy. While international in scope, coverage is best for the United States. Historical backfile is available, with coverage from 1993. Also available in print as the *Directory of corporate affiliations* and on CD-ROM as *Corporate affiliations plus.*

**34**   **Global market information database.** Euromonitor. [1999–.] [London]: Euromonitor. http://www.gmid.euromonitor.com/.

HD2755.5.G56

Market reports, company profiles, and demographic, economic, and marketing statistics for 205 countries. Market reports are for 16 consumer markets (food and drink, tobacco, toys, etc.) and 14 industrial and service markets (accountancy, broadcasting, chemicals, property services, etc.).

Reports have market size, market sectors, share of market, marketing activity, research and development, corporate overview, distribution, consumer profiles, market forecasts, sector forecasts, sources, and definitions. Additional reports are available for market segments, such as baby food. Company profiles have background, recent news, competitive

environment, and outlook. Consumer lifestyle reports and very useful marketing background analyze the consumer by country, gender, age, marital status, educational attainment, ethnicity, religion, home ownership, household profile, employment, income, health, eating and personal grooming habits, leisure activities, personal finance, communication, transport, and travel.

Search for data, which can be exported into Excel or browse for reports. Data are available from 1977 through 2016 and include inflation, exchange rates, GDP, GNI, government expenditures, government finance, income, labor, and money supply.

**35     Hoover's handbook of American business.** Gary Hoover. ill. Austin, Tex.: Reference Press, 1991–. ISSN: 1055-7202.

338.7402573                                          HG4057.A28617

Profiles 750 U.S. companies, about 50 of which are privately owned. In one to two pages, profiles discuss company history, major events, current strategy, and place in the industry. Lists top executives, contact information, domestic locations, number and type of international locations, products or services as a percentage of sales, competitors, and a brief snapshot of historical financials, with three financial ratios (debt ratio, return on equity, and current ratio). Indexed by industry, location of headquarters, and executive name. Available online through Hoovers Online (Austin, Tex.: Reference Press, 1996–).

**36     Hoover's handbook of private companies.** Austin, Tex.: Hoover's Business Press, 1997–. ISSN: 1555-3744.

338.7402573                                          HG4057.A28616

Covers 900 enterprises, including corporations, hospitals and health care organizations, charitable and membership organizations, mutual and cooperative organizations, joint ventures, government-owned corporations, and some major university systems. Information includes "A List-Lover's Compendium" with lists of the largest and fastest-growing companies; company profiles; and indexes: companies by industry, by headquarters, and by executive. Company profiles list top executives, locations, competitors, very brief historical financials covering 10 years (revenue, net income, net profit, number of employees, annual growth), current business profile and company history. Given how difficult basic financial information can be to find on private organizations, even the little information provided here can be useful.

37    **Hoover's online.** Reference Press. 1996–. Austin, Tex.: Reference
      Press. http://www.hoovers.com/.
338.7                                                          HG4057

Nearly 18 million records describing public and private companies primarily in the United States, but including Canada, United Kingdom,
Europe, and Asia/Pacific. Profiles have an overview, history, family tree,
industry information, products/operations, top competitors, competitive
landscape, top executives with biographies, news, significant developments, and financial data (summary; income statement; balance sheet;
cash flow; historical financials such as five years of P/E and per share;
stock quote; interactive stock chart; market data; earnings estimates;
this year's ratios for the company, industry, and market; SEC filings; and
industry watch).

Covers 600 industries, organized into the following categories: Aero-
space and Defense; Agriculture; Automotive and Transport; Banking; Bev-
erages; Business Services; Charitable Organizations; Chemicals; Computer
Hardware; Computer Services; Computer Software; Construction; Con-
sumer Products Manufacturers; Consumer Services; Cultural Institutions;
Education; Electronics; Energy and Utilities; Environmental Services and
Equipment; Financial Services; Food; Foundations; Government; Health
Care; Industrial Manufacturing; Insurance; Leisure; Media; Membership
Organizations; Metals and Mining; Pharmaceuticals; Real Estate; Retail;
Security Products and Services; Telecommunications Equipment; Tele-
communications Services; and Transportation Services.

Coverage can be brief, but generally includes a fact sheet, overview,
selected companies, industry watch with video interviews, news from the
last 90 days, and web resources for terminology, associations, and organizations, and online publications. Includes Hoover's print publications
(*Hoover's handbook of American business* [35], *Hoover's handbook of private
companies* [36]).

38    **Investext plus.** Thomson Financial (Firm). [1998–.] [Boston?]:
      Thomson Financial. http://www.galegroup.com/.

Company and industry reports written by some 500 investment banks in
North America, Europe, Asia/Pacific, Latin America, Africa, and the Middle East. Also contains research reports on 190 trade associations. Reports
range from 1–100 pages long. Covers 10,000 publicly traded U.S. companies. Reports give earnings estimates, financials, business ratios, trends,
forecasts, credit ratings, analysis, text of conference calls, and stock prices.

Industry reports give background, financials, business ratios, trends, forecasts, analysis, and some brief company profiles. Formerly Research Bank Web. Coverage from 1982.

**39    MarketLine business information centre.** MarketLine. London; New York: MarketLine. http://dbic.datamonitor.com/info/about/.

HD2709

Profiles of about 10,000 large companies, 3,000 industry segments, and 100 countries. Internat. in scope. Company profiles have business descriptions, history, major products and services, revenue analysis, key employees and biographies, locations and subsidiaries, company view (often taken from an annual report), SWOT analysis, and list of top competitors. Industry profiles are approx. 20 pages long, and are Datamonitor reports. They have an executive summary, market overview, market value, market segmentation, competitive landscape, leading companies, market forecast, and further reading. Country profiles are about 30 pages long, with information on the economy, politics and government, and macro-economic data.

The strength for this database is its international coverage of industry segments, with reports like "Beer in China." Company profiles are 45 percent United States, 35 percent European, 15 percent Asian, and 5 percent from the rest of world.

**40    Marketresearch.com academic.** Kalorama Information. 1999–. Bethesda, Md.: Kalorama Information. http://www.marketresearch.com/.

HF5415.2.K35

Market research reports from various sources (Icon Group, Kalorama, BizMiner, etc.) for Consumer Goods (apparel, cosmetics and personal care, house and home, pet services and supplies, travel services), Food and Beverage (alcoholic beverages, coffee and tea, soft drinks, confectionery, dairy products, food processing), Heavy Industry (energy, mining, utilities, construction, machines and parts, manufacturing, metals, paper and forest products, plastics, automotive, aviation & aerospace, logistics and shipping), Service Industries (accounting and finance, corporate services, banking and financial services, insurance), Public Sector (associations/nonprofits, education, government), Life Science (biotechnology, agriculture, genomics, proteomics, medical imaging, healthcare facilities, managed care, regulation and policy, cardiovascular devices, equipment and supplies, wound care, pharmaceuticals, diseases and conditions, prescription drugs, therapeutic area), Technology & Media (computer equipment, electronics, networks, e-commerce and IT outsourcing, software, telecommunications, wireless), and Demographics (age, lifestyle and economics, multicultural).

Reports range in length, with some over 300 pages long, and give a variety of information (definition of industry, consumer demographics, consumer shopping habits, spending patterns, sales, establishments, employment, forecasts, trends, market size, market share, and market segmentation). Some company information is also included.

**41**    **Mintel reports.** Mintel International Group. London; Chicago: Mintel International Group. http://reports.mintel.com/.

HC240.9.C6

Marketing and consumer research reports focusing on the United States and Europe. Covers consumer goods and services, making this a good source of reports for market segments and consumer behavior, with reports like "Impact of celebrity chefs on cooking habits," "Nail color and care," and "MP3 players and other portable audio players," but not for business to business reports.

Market reports are available for automotive, beauty and personal, drink and tobacco, electronics, food and foodservice, health and medical, health and wellness, household, lifestyles, media, books and stationery, personal finances, retailing, technology, and travel. Reports include an executive summary, glossary, and sections on advertising and promotion, ownership and usage, attitudes and opinions, market drivers, market size and trends, market segmentation, future and forecast, and supply structure.

Consumer reports provide demographics, core needs and values, future trends, information on products currently targeted to the group, and advice on reaching and influencing the target audience. Consumer reports are available for financial lifestyles, general lifestyles, healthier lifestyles, and leisure lifestyles.

Marketing and promotion reports are for marketing and targeting, and promotions, incentives, and sponsorship. They include introduction and abbreviations, executive summary, background and market factors, challenges facing marketers, marketing segments, product development and pricing, and future trends.

Most data in Mintel can be downloaded into Excel. Reports cannot be viewed in their entirety and instead must be viewed in sections, making easy skimming or printing a report impossible.

**42    Organization charts: Structures of 230 businesses, government agencies, and non-profit organizations.** 3rd ed. Nick Sternberg, Scott Heil. xi, 353 p., ill. Detroit: Gale Research, 2000. ISBN: 0787624527.

658.402                                                    HD38.O738

A unique collection of over 200 organization charts, showing how corporations are structured. "Organizations of many types, sizes, and from a variety of industries have been included: large and small, public and private, profit and non-profit, international and local."—*Pref.* This 3rd ed. contains some of the same corporations as the earlier editions, allowing comparison over time.

**43    Plunkett's airline, hotel, and travel industry almanac.** Jack W. Plunkett, Plunkett Research, Ltd. ill. Houston, Tex.: Plunkett Research, 2002–. ISSN: 1554-1215.

387.7                                         HE9803.A2P58; G155.U6P58

Data on 324 major companies, both public and private. Company profiles include types of business, brands and affiliates, contacts, employee benefits and top salaries, sales and profit numbers, growth plans, and competitive advantage. Especially useful for the industry trends, statistics and rankings (forecasts to 2020, top destinations worldwide, top airlines, top tourism nations, etc.) at the front of the volume and information on the main associations and organizations in the back of the volume. Most information is for the U.S., but some international coverage is provided. Available as an e-book.

**44    Yahoo! finance.** Yahoo! Inc. 2001. Sunnyvale, Calif.: Yahoo! Inc. http://finance.yahoo.com/.

A rich source of financial information, with company profiles, SEC filings, annual reports, stock quotes, news, analysis, conference call calendar, industry statistics and news, and information for the personal investor. The focus is on financial information about U.S. and Canadian companies and industries, but international information, such as indices and currency information, is also available, especially through the portals to Yahoo!Finance for other countries (linked from the bottom of the entry page). Historical quotes for stocks, bonds, and money markets are since

1970 and give daily, weekly, and monthly closing prices, and dividends. Occasionally links to fee-based information.

# Directories

**45** **American wholesalers and distributors directory.** Gale Research Inc. Detroit: Gale Research, 1992–. ISSN: 1061-2114.

381.2029473                                                            HF5421.A615

Lists 27,000 companies in the U.S. and Puerto Rico. Includes name and address, fax number, Standard Industrial Classification (SIC) code, principal product lines, total number of employees, estimated annual sales volume, and principal officers. Indexed by SIC code, state and city, and company name. Information can be hard to find for many of these privately held companies, making this a handy source. Available online as part of Gale Business Resources.

**46** **America's corporate finance directory.** New Providence, N.J.: National Register, 1994–. ISSN: 1080-1227.

338.7402573                                                            HG4057.A15647

Information on 4,500 public and private U.S. companies with revenue income or pension assets over $100,000,000 per year and large foreign subsidiaries located in the U.S. Also profiles financial executives and identifies business relationships between companies.

**47** **Bibliography of American directories through 1860.** Dorothea N. Spear. 389 p. Westport, Conn.: Greenwood Press, 1978; 1961. ISBN: 0313202516.

016.973025                                                       Z5771.2.S68; E154.5

Reprint of the 1961 publication. A geographical listing, with locations of 1,647 business directories, city and county directories, etc. Many annotations. Works listed are available in the microfilm collection City Directories of the United States (Woodbridge, Conn.: Research Publications, 1970–).

For a complementary overview and information on the usefulness and history of city directories, see City Directories of the United States of America (http://uscitydirectories.com/).

**48** **Bioscan.** Phoenix, Ariz.: Oryx Press, 1987–. ISSN: 0887-6207.

338.76208025                                                          HD9999.B44B56

Information on some 2,000 U.S. and foreign companies, giving contact information, company history, number of employees, facilities, very brief financial highlights (sales, net income, earnings per share, shares outstanding, total assets), business strategy, alliances, mergers and acquisitions, principal investors, and products in development, and products on the market. Available online through *BioWorld*.

**49    Brands and their companies.** Donna J. Wood, Susan L. Stetler.
Detroit: Gale Research, 1990–. ISSN: 1047-6407.
602.75                                                        T223.V4A25

Not sure what company is responsible for Night Owl? Don't even know what type of product it is? This is the source for answers. Alphabetically lists brand names, even for discontinued brands, and then lists the manufacturer or distributor. Brand names supplied by companies or found in print resources. Occasionally used by researchers interested in trademarks. Companion to *Companies and their brands* (50). Available in online form.

**50    Companies and their brands.** Donna J. Wood, Gale Group.
Detroit: Gale Research, 1990–. ISSN: 1047-6393.
602.75                                                       T223.V4A253

Alphabetical list of companies and the brand names attributed to them. Each entry is followed by the firm's address, telephone number, and list of trade names. Information is collected from print sources and from the individual companies. Companion to *Brands and their companies* (49).

**51    Corporateaffiliations.com.** LexisNexis Group. New York:
LexisNexis. http://www.corporateaffiliations.com/.

Profiles nearly 200,000 public and private companies, with information on affiliates, subsidiaries, and divisions. Search by company type, location, title of executive, NAICS or SIC code, number of employees, sales revenue, ownership, fiscal year, stock exchange, earnings, assets, net worth, and liabilities. Profiles include contact information, very brief business description, year founded, number of employees, NAICS and SIC codes, names of top executives, outside service firms, and top competitors. Most useful for visual who-owns-whom hierarchies, linking to profiles for all companies in the hierarchy. While international in scope, coverage is best for the United States. Historical backfile is available, with coverage from

1993. Also available in print as the *Directory of corporate affiliations* and on CD-ROM as *Corporate affiliations plus.*

**52    Corporate giving directory.** 29th ed. Information Today Inc. 1578
       p. Medford, N.J.: Information Today, 1991–. ISBN: 9781573872737.
361.765

Profiles of over 1,000 corporate charitable giving programs in the United States. Entries include cash, nonmonetary, and corporate sponsorship giving; matching gift and company-sponsored volunteer programs; corporate operating locations; geographic preferences; officers and directors; application procedures; and recently awarded grants data.

   "Approximately 21 percent of the companies featured in this edition cover difficult-to-research direct giving programs, which are often untapped sources of support"—*Introd.*

   14 indexes.

**53    Corporate magazines of the United States.** Sam G. Riley. xiii, 281
       p. New York: Greenwood Press, 1992. ISBN: 0313275696.
070.486                                                          PN4888.E6C67

Unique look at 324 corporate magazines. The publication, while dated, is still useful for historical research, especially as the earliest published magazine listed in it is from 1865. Fifty-one magazines are profiled, with history, significant contributors, and library or corporate holdings. Appendixes: Appendix A: chronology of corporate magazines profiled by year founded, Appendix B: location of magazines profiled by state, Appendix C: corporate magazines not profiled.

**54    CorpTech directory of technology companies.** U.S. ed. Corporate
       Technology Information Services. maps. Woburn, Mass.:
       Corporate Technology Information Services, 1995–.
338.7402573                                                      HG4057.A16

Describes more than 50,000 U.S. companies that manufacture or develop high-technology products. Company profiles generally include company name and address, telephone and fax numbers, executives and their departments (including research and development, marketing, purchasing, and personnel), type of ownership, date established, annual sales, number of employees, corporate history, and product codes. Indexed by firm and by product. A table converts SIC codes to CorpTech codes. Also available online and on CD-ROM.

**55    D and B million dollar directory: America's leading public and private companies.** Dun and Bradstreet, Inc. Bethlehem, Pa.: Dun and Bradstreet, 1997–. ISSN: 1093-4812.

338.740973                                                      HC102.D8

The first three volumes contain company entries. The fourth volume indexes companies by geography, and the fifth volume by industrial classification. Covers U.S. and Canadian public and private companies with sales of $1,000,000 or more. Entries include address and telephone number for headquarters, annual sales, number of employees, Standard Industrial Classification (SIC) codes, names and titles for top executives, and year established.

Also available as an online database, adding capabilities to search by executive name and to export records.

**56    Directory of American firms operating in foreign countries.** Juvenal L. Angel. New York: Uniworld Business Publications, 1955/56–. ISSN: 0070-5071.

338.88025                                                      HG4538.A1D5

Lists over 3,000 U.S. firms with more than 36,000 branches, subsidiaries, and affiliates in 196 countries. Pt. 1 is an alphabetical list of companies and lists by country foreign operations. Entries contain basic directory information, as well as names of key personnel, product information, and location of foreign branches, subsidiaries, and affiliates. Pt. 2 contains the directory information for the parent organizations with names and addresses for foreign branches, subsidiaries, and affiliates. Companion to *Directory of foreign firms operating in the United States* (58).

**57    Directory of corporate archives in the United States and Canada.** Gregory S. Hunter. 1997–. Chicago: Business Archives Section, Society of American Archivists. http://www.hunterinformation. com/corporat.htm.

Entries for locations of corporate historical records, with contact information, type of organization, hours of service, conditions of access, holdings, and total number of volumes. Some professional associations are included.

**58    Directory of foreign firms operating in the United States.** New York: Simon and Schuster, 1969–. ISSN: 0070-5543.

338.88873025                                                      HG4057.A21943

Lists some 3,500 foreign firms from 86 countries that own nearly 10,000 businesses in the U.S. Gives locations for the American headquarters and selected branches, subsidiaries or affiliates. Includes contact information. Pt. 1 is an alphabetical listing by American affiliate country, pt. 2 is an alphabetical listing by foreign firm, and pt. 3 is an alphabetical listing by American affiliate. Companion to the *Directory of American firms operating in foreign countries* (56).

**59    Directory of United States exporters.** New York: Journal of Commerce, 1990–. ISSN: 1057-6878.

HF3011.D63

Describes U.S. cargo shippers and the products they export. Gives contact information, SIC code, top executives, TEU's (Twenty-foot Equivalent Unit container size) and metric tonnage, estimated value, ports of exit, and products. Arranged by state and indexed by company and product (uses Harmonized Commodity Codes). Also provides contact information for: export assistance centers, U.S. and foreign commercial service international posts, trade commissions, foreign embassies and consulates, U.S. foreign trade zones, world ports, and banks and other financial services. Companion to *Directory of United States importers* (60).

**60    Directory of United States importers.** Journal of Commerce, Inc. ill. New York: Journal of Commerce, 1991–. ISSN: 1057-5111.

382.502573                                                      HF3012.D53

A geographical listing of importers to the U.S., indexed by products (Harmonized Commodity Codes) and industry (Standard Industrial Classification [SIC] codes). Gives contact information, SIC code, top executives, TEU's (Twenty-foot Equivalent Unit container size) and metric tonnage, estimated value, ports of exit, and products. Also provides contact information for: trade commissions, foreign embassies and consulates in the U.S., U.S. foreign trade zones, world ports, and banks and other financial services. Companion to the *Directory of United States exporters* (59).

**61    Harris U.S. manufacturers directory.** National ed. Harris InfoSource. Twinsburg, Ohio: Harris InfoSource, 2000–. ISSN: 1531-8273.

338                                                              HF5035.H37

Entries for U.S. companies include location, contact information, industry descriptions, Standard Industrial Classification (SIC) or NAICS codes, executive names, and size. Indexed by company name, geography, product or service category, and SIC code. Libraries receiving questions about local companies may want to invest in the regional and state directories also published by Harris. Available in an online version.

**62   Headquarters USA: A directory of contact information for headquarters and other central offices of major businesses and organizations nationwide.** Detroit: Omnigraphics, 1977–. ISSN: 1531-2909.

384.602573                                                                    E154.5.N37

Contains 114,500 entries listing central offices for businesses, professional organizations, government agencies, non-profits, military bases, sports teams, associations, industries, and political organizations. Minimal listings: name, mailing address, Web address, zip code, fax, stock exchange information, and phone or toll-free numbers. Useful conglomerate and subsidiaries section. Also available electronically as HQ Online.

**63   Hoover's handbook of private companies.** Austin, Tex.: Hoover's Business Press, 1997–. ISSN: 1555-3744.

338.7402573                                                                  HG4057.A28616

Covers 900 enterprises, including corporations, hospitals and health care organizations, charitable and membership organizations, mutual and cooperative organizations, joint ventures, government-owned corporations, and some major university systems. Information includes "A List-Lover's Compendium" with lists of the largest and fastest-growing companies; company profiles; and indexes: companies by industry, by headquarters, and by executive. Company profiles list top executives, locations, competitors, very brief historical financials covering 10 years. (revenue, net income, net profit, number of employees, annual growth), current business profile and company history. Given how difficult basic financial information can be to find on private organizations, even the little information provided here can be useful.

**64   Japan trade directory.** Nihon Bōeki Shinkōkai. 1982–. Tokyo: Japan External Trade Organization. http://jtd.weis.or.jp/.

382.029452                                                                    HF3823.J343

Lists 1,000 Japanese companies and associations involved in international trade, as well as 7,800 products. Gives contact information, representative, type of business, year established, capital, annual sales, number of employees, bank reference, product/service imported or exported. Also available in print and on CD-ROM.

**65**   **Major chemical and petrochemical companies of the world.**
Graham and Whiteside. London: Graham and Whiteside, 2000–.
ISSN: 1369-5444; ISBN: 1860991920.
658.0029; 661.804                                    HD9650.3

Lists over 7,000 companies, giving contact information, executive names, business description, brand names and trademarks, subsidiaries, principal bank, principal law firm, ticker symbol, date established, number of employees, auditors, and two years of very brief financial information (sales turnover, profit before tax, profit after tax, dividend per share, earnings per share, share capital, shareholders' equity).

**66**   **Major telecommunications companies of the world.** Graham and
Whiteside. London: Graham and Whiteside, 1998–. ISSN: 1369-5460.
Entries for 3,500 companies from around the world, giving contact information, executives' names, principal activities, parent company, subsidiaries, status (public/private), number of employees, and principal shareholders. Useful for libraries that do not have good international business directories.

**67**   **National directory of corporate giving.** Foundation Center. New
York: The Center, 1989–. ISSN: 1050-9852.
361.76502573                                         HV89.N26

Describes 3,736 firms that provided information to the Foundation Center or whose gift-giving activities were verified through public records. Entries, arranged alphabetically by company include general descriptions of the firms and their "giving mechanisms," types of programs funded, limitations (e.g., geographic, type of recipient), and relevant publications. Seven indexes: officers, donors, trustees, and administrators; geographic; international giving; type of support; subject; types of business; and corporation, foundation, and giving programs by name.

**68**   **National directory of corporate public affairs.** Columbia Books.
Washington: Columbia Books, 1983–. ISSN: 0749-9736.
659.28502573                                         HD59.N24

Lists more than 1,800 companies that maintain public affairs or government affairs programs. Includes home address and Washington, D.C. address, associated political action committees, contributions to candidates, corporate foundations and corporate giving programs (with annual grant total, geographic preference, primary interests), public affairs personnel, and publications. Personnel directory, indexes by geography and by industry.

**69**   **National directory of minority-owned business firms.** Business Research Services. Lombard, Ill.: Business Research Services, 1986–. ISSN: 0886-3881.

338.642202573                                         HD2346.U5N332

Includes complete address, contact name, minority type, date founded, trading area, business description, number of employees, and sales volume for 30,000 businesses.

**70**   **National minority and women-owned business directory.** Diversity Information Resources, Inc. ill. Minneapolis, Minn.: Diversity Information Resources, 2004–. ISSN: 1553-6025.

338                                              HD2358.5.U6T786

Contains 9,000 entries in 84 industries with contact information, URL, products/services, year established, minority type, number of employees, annual sales, and certification. Indexed by company.

**71**   **Plunkett's airline, hotel, and travel industry almanac.** Jack W. Plunkett, Plunkett Research, Ltd. ill. Houston, Tex.: Plunkett Research, 2002–. ISSN: 1554-1215.

387.7                                    HE9803.A2P58; G155.U6P58

Data on 324 major companies, both public and private. Company profiles include types of business, brands and affiliates, contacts, employee benefits and top salaries, sales and profit numbers, growth plans, and competitive advantage. Especially useful for the industry trends, statistics and rankings (forecasts to 2020, top destinations worldwide, top airlines, top tourism nations, etc.) at the front of the volume and information on the main associations and organizations in the back of the volume. Most information is for the U.S., but some international coverage is provided. Available as an e-book.

**72**   **ReferenceUSA.** infoUSA (Firm). Omaha, Neb.: infoUSA Inc. http://reference.infousa.com/.

HF5035

Data on 13 million U.S. businesses, 1 million Canadian businesses, 120 million U.S. households, 11 million Canadian residential households, and 683,000 U.S. health care providers. Most used for the ability to download customized lists of companies from searches by geography, size of business, sales volume, number of employees, and executive gender.

**73    Standard and Poor's register of corporations, directors, and executives.** ill. New York: Standard and Poor's. ISSN: 0361-3623.
332.67                                                                    HG4057.A4

Information on public and private corporations, with current address, financial and marketing information, and biographies for corporate executives and directors. Useful for identifying corporate relationships and executive's business connections. Vol. 1 lists firms, v. 2 lists executives, v. 3 provides indexes including Standard Industrial Classification (SIC) codes and geography. Also available through NetAdvantage.

**74    Ward's business directory of U.S. private and public companies.** Gale Research Inc. Detroit: Gale Research, 1990–. ISSN: 1048-8707.
338.7402573                                                               HG4057.A575

Vol. 1–3 list alphabetically over 100,000 public and private companies, describing type of company, number of employees, sales, officers, Standard Industrial Classification (SIC) codes, imports/exports, and parent/subsidiary information. Vol. 4 lists companies by zip code within states and ranks the top 1,000 private and top 1,000 public companies, including tabular analysis by state, revenue per employee, and SIC. Vol. 5 ranks companies by sales within SIC codes and contains names of chief executive officers. Most of the companies listed are privately held, making this source invaluable. Available online as part of Gale Business Sources.

**75    Who audits America.** Menlo Park, Calif.: Data Financial Press, 1976–. ISSN: 0149-0281.
657.4502573                                                               HF5616.U5W5

Organized by list of companies, auditor summary, national list, and state list. Useful for determining current and former auditors, especially for companies whose common shares are not traded. Appendixes for auditor codes, SIC codes, and state codes.

**76    World directory of trade and business journals.** Euromonitor PLC. London: Euromonitor PLC, 1996–.
Z7164.C81W67

Lists some 2,000 magazines, newsletters, and journals. Gives language, frequency, content, country coverage, format, publisher and contact information. Arranged into 80 industry categories, beginning with advertising and ending with wholesaling. Two indexes: A-Z index by country and publisher with publications, and A-Z index of journals by country. Especially useful for finding a source for news, organizational information, trends or statistics on a company or industry that is not gathered in a reference resource.

## Financial Filings

77 **Accounting research manager.** CCH Incorporated. [Riverwoods, Ill.]: CCH Inc. http://www.accountingresearchmanager.com/.

HF5626

Includes a dizzying array of authoritative and interpretive financial reporting literature. Divided into accounting, SEC, auditing, and government sections, each with standards, interpretations, and examples. The accounting section has documents from the Financial Accounting Standards Board (FASB), Emerging Issues Task Force (EITF), and International Accounting Standards Board (IASB). The SEC section includes Regulations S-X and S-K, Forms 10-K and 10-Q, SABs, Sarbanes-Oxley, Public Company Accounting Oversight Board (PCAOB), and Regulation S-B. The audit section includes AICPA, Public Company Accounting Oversight Board (PCAOB), U.S. Department of Housing and Urban Development, Office of Management and Budgets (OMB), and American Institute of Certified Public Accountants (AICPA). The government section includes GASB, GAO, and OMB.

Documents are color coded: white for authoritative, beige for interpretation, blue for proposed, and green for SEC. They also show amendments, deletions, or suspensions. SEC filings since 1994, available in Word, Adobe Acrobat, and Excel. Highlights current developments and events on the home page. An online tutorial and regularly scheduled live tutorials are available and recommended to master the database. Updated five times a day.

78 **Bankscope.** Bureau van Dijk Electronic Publishing. [199?–.] [Brussels, Belgium]: Bureau van Dijk Electronic Publishing. http:// scope.bvdep.com/.

Financial information on 25,000 public and private banks worldwide. Provides standardized reports, ratings, ownership data, financial analysis, security and price information, scanned images of the bank's annual or interim accounts, and country risk reports. Most data goes back eight years. Data sources include Fitch Ratings. Standardized reports contain detailed consolidated and/or unconsolidated balance sheet and income statement, as well as 36 pre-calculated ratios. Data can be downloaded to Excel. Also available on DVD-ROM or through WRDS (115).

**79    EDGAR database of corporate information.** U.S. Securities and Exchange Commission. Washington, D.C.: U.S. Securities and Exchange Commission. http://www.sec.gov/edgarhp.htm.

HG4028.B2E34

U.S. public company filings from 1993 through the present. Mutual fund filings since Feb. 6, 2006. Search by company name, fund name, ticker symbol, filing number, state, Standard Industrial Classification Code (SIC), and Ownership Forms. Mutual fund prospectuses, also known as 484 filings, also available. A beta version with full text searching for companies is available; useful for researchers interested in more than the numbers in a financial filing.

**80    EdgarScan.** PricewaterhouseCoopers Global Technology Centre. 2001–. Menlo Park, Calif.: PricewaterhouseCoopers Global Technology Centre. http://edgarscan.pwcglobal.com/servlets/edgarscan/.

005.74352.8

Access to SEC filings. The filing data have been normalized, which is not always what researchers are interested in. Especially useful for downloading financials into Excel.

**81    Foundation center 990 finder.** Foundation Center. New York: Foundation Center. http://foundationcenter.org/findfunders/990finder/.

Gives completed IRS forms 990 (Return of Organization Exempt from Income Tax) and 990PF (Return of Private Foundation) from 1993 to the present. The forms give revenue and expenses; information about officers, directors, trustees, foundation managers, highly paid employees, and contractors; summary of direct charitable activities; private operating foundations; and grants and contributions paid. Search by organization name, state, zip code, employer identification number (EIN), and year.

**82**   **Mergent online.** Moody's Investors Service. 1998–. New York: Moody's Investors Service. http://www.mergent.com/.

HG4061

Provides a full source of information on company details, equity pricing, company financials, industry reports, news, and 58,000 annual reports. Reports can be created by searching company details (Synopsis, Financial Highlights, History, Joint Ventures, Business, Property, Subsidiary, Long Term Debt, and Capital Structure); research and news (Historic News, Institutional Holdings, and Insider Holdings); and financial statements (Income Statement, Balance Sheet, Cash Flows, and Profitability Ratios). Financials can be exported into Excel. More than 1,500 one-page equity reports for NYSE, NASDAQ, and AMEX companies, with quarterly financial results, analyses of future prospects, and operating ratios. Access to EDGAR filings from 1993 to present and data on 20,000 non-U.S.-based corporations. Industry reports, while brief, are international in scope. Includes the Mergent manuals, which were known as Moody's, except for the Municipal and Government Manual.

**83**   **ProQuest historical annual reports.** ProQuest Information and Learning Company. 2006–. [Ann Arbor, Mich.]: ProQuest Information and Learning. http://il.proquest.com/products_pq/descriptions/pq_hist_annual_repts.shtml.

HG4028.B2P767

PDF copies of annual reports from 1884 to the present for nearly 850 U.S. companies. Most coverage begins before 1950. From the 222-page long report for Union Pacific Railway Company in 1884 to the 28-page long Dell Annual Report from 2005, this is a unique collection. Not all company coverage is complete, as reports for some years have not yet been located. In addition to the standard ProQuest search capabilities, companies can be browsed by year, name, or industry.

**84**   **Standard and Poor's research insight on the web.** Standard and Poor's Compustat Services. 2000s–. Englewood, Colo.: Standard and Poor's. http://www.researchinsightweb.com/.

Research Insight is the new interface to Compustat. An essential resource with the most recent 20 years of U.S. and Canadian financial statement data and monthly closing stock price data, six months of daily stock prices, and GlobalVantage, the most recent 10 years of financial data for companies in 80 countries. Not an easy database to use; complex screening is possible, which becomes easier from within Excel. Screening can be done for data items in financial reports. Choose from quarterly or annual financials, and from nearly every data item within a financial report. Over 100 preformatted reports are available (EVAntage, company highlights, cash flow statements, combined reports, common size statements, institutional holdings). Data is also available for geographic areas, industry composites, aggregates, and stock indexes, and about 7,000 inactive companies.

85   **Thomson one banker—analytics.** Thomson Financial (Firm). [2002–.] [New York]: Thomson Financial. http://banker. thomsonib.com/.

65,000 active and inactive global companies, with company financials, earnings estimates, analyst forecasts, market indices data, mergers and acquisitions, and corporate transaction data from 1998, and near real-time market data and stock quotes from Thomson Financial, Datastream advance (177), Extel, First Call, Worldscope, and Disclosure. Most data is a rolling ten years. Allows advanced screening and use of Excel to download and analyze data.

86   **Who audits America.** Menlo Park, Calif.: Data Financial Press, 1976–. ISSN: 0149-0281.

657.4502573                                                  HF5616.U5W5

Organized by list of companies, auditor summary, national list, and state list. Useful for determining current and former auditors, especially for companies whose common shares are not traded. Appendixes for auditor codes, SIC codes, and state codes.

87   **Yahoo! finance.** Yahoo! Inc. 2001. Sunnyvale, Calif.: Yahoo! Inc. http://finance.yahoo.com/.

A rich source of financial information, with company profiles, SEC filings, annual reports, stock quotes, news, analysis, conference call calendar, industry statistics and news, and information for the personal investor. The focus is on financial information about U.S. and Canadian companies and industries, but international information, such as indices and currency information, is also available, especially through the portals to Yahoo!Finance for other countries (linked from the bottom of the entry page). Historical quotes for stocks, bonds, and money markets are since 1970 and give daily, weekly, and monthly closing prices, and dividends. Occasionally links to fee-based information.

# Histories

88    A bibliography of British business histories. Francis Goodall.
638 p. Aldershot, [U.K.]; Brookfield, Vt.: Gower, 1987. ISBN:
0566053071.
016.338740941                                          Z7165.G8G59; HC253

The main section lists works alphabetically by author, giving full bibliographic information for each title and noting the presence of indexes or
illustrations, the name of the firm described, its primary SIC, and a code
for the source library. Preliminary pages include an essay on the nature,
new directions, and methodology of business history, the British standard
industrial classification, a bibliography of business history bibliographies,
libraries with business history collections, and a list of abbreviations.
Company name and SIC indexes.

89    Black business and economics: A selected bibliography. George
H. Hill. xvi, 351 p. New York: Garland, 1985. ISBN: 0824087879.
016.338642208996073                                    Z7164.C81H47; HD2346.U5

Gives citations to 100 books, 180 theses and dissertations, and articles
from popular periodicals written since 1885. Book citations, arranged by
author, are annotated. Government documents are listed by author, title,
or department, and are followed by topically arranged listings of dissertations, theses, journal and newspaper articles. About 2,268 citations in all.

90    Business incorporations in the United States, 1800–1943. George
Heberton Evans. viii, 184 p., ill. [New York]: National Bureau of
Economic Research, [1948].
338.7                                                  HD2785.E85

A look at business trends, cycles, and incorporations using statistical
analysis. Most useful for the tables, which include chronology of initial
state constitutional provisions that necessitated incorporation under general law; business incorporations, eight states, 1800–1875; incorporations,
United Kingdom, 1863–1937; monthly aggregate index of incorporations,
1860–1941; timing of cycles in total incorporations; and specific-cycle patterns in total incorporations.

91    Cases in corporate acquisitions, buyouts, mergers, and takeovers.
Gale Group. Detroit: Gale Group, 1999–. ISSN: 1526-5927.
658                                                    HD2746.5.C374

COMPANY INFORMATION | 37

Arranged alphabetically with 300 entries that are 3–5 pages long. Invaluable for capturing hard-to-find information in one easy-to-use source, but is not an annual. Covers major deals of the last century if one of the players was a U.S. company, summarizing background, the organizations involved, and the deal itself. Useful for the financials provided, and an explanation of the deal's effect on the companies involved and the industry as a whole. Indexed by company and industry.

**92** **Directory of corporate archives in the United States and Canada.**
Gregory S. Hunter. 1997–. Chicago: Business Archives Section, Society of American Archivists. http://www.hunterinformation. com/corporat.htm.

Entries for locations of corporate historical records, with contact information, type of organization, hours of service, conditions of access, holdings, and total number of volumes. Some professional associations are included.

**93** **Encyclopedia of American business history and biography.** Facts On File. ill. New York: Facts On File, 1988–. ISBN: 0816013713.

HE2751.R143

Combines biographical entries with articles discussing major companies, government and labor organizations, inventions, and legal decisions for various industries. The signed entries range in length from one-half to ten or more pages; most include photographs or other illustrations, and list publications and references, archives, and unpublished documents. Each volume is available separately. Volumes include: *The airline industry; The automobile industry, 1896–1920; The automobile industry, 1920–1980; Banking and finance to 1913; Banking and finance, 1913–1989; Iron and steel in the nineteenth century; Iron and steel in the twentieth century; Railroads in the nineteenth century; and Railroads in the age of regulation, 1900–1980.*

**94** **Encyclopedia of American business history.** Charles R. Geisst. New York: Facts On File, 2005. ISBN: 0816043507.

338.097303                                                                 HF3021.G44

Contains 400 entries on businesses and industries, business events, and leaders, as well as business and economic topics from 1776 to the present. Entries are cross-referenced and include recommended readings. Writing is accessible for students in high school, but coverage is complete enough to be useful to a much wider audience. Includes a chronology and 15 primary documents, including essays, legislative acts, and court judgments.

**95**   **Global companies in the twentieth century: Selected archival histories.** Malcolm McIntosh, Ruth Thomas. 9 v., ill., maps. London; New York: Routledge, 2001. ISBN: 0415181100.
338.88                                                                HD2755.5.G549

While *Global companies* examines a select set of companies (BBC, Levi Strauss and Co., Broken Hill Proprietary Company, Barclays, BP Amoco, Rio Tinto, Cable and Wireless, Marks and Spencer, and Royal Dutch/Shell), it does so thoroughly. Uses company archival documents to analyze how the companies have changed and adapted over time.

**96**   **A historical dictionary of American industrial language.** William H. Mulligan. xii, 332 p. New York: Greenwood Press, 1988. ISBN: 0313241716.
338.00321                                                             TS9.H57

Brief definitions drawn primarily from the period before World War I. An appendix lists terms by industry. Includes a list of contributors, bibliography, and index of institutions and people.

**97**   **United States business history, 1602–1988: A chronology.** Richard Robinson. xii, 643 p. New York: Greenwood Press, 1990. ISBN: 0313260958.
338.0973                                                              HC103.R595

"Designed to provide a basic calendar of representative events in the evolution of U.S. business."—*Pref.* Contains descriptive historical data, arranged by year, then under categories of general news and business news. Significant individuals, specific companies, inventions, trade unions, and key business, economic, and social developments are included. Brief bibliography; detailed index. Complemented by *Robinson's business history of the world: A chronology.*

## Indexes; Abstract Journals

**98**   **Business and company resource center.** Gale. 2000–. [Farmington Hills, Mich.]: Gale. http://www.gale.cengage.com/BusinessRC/.
HF54.7.B85B875x

A blend of articles from some 3,200 periodicals (journals, newspapers, and trade publications), investment reports (from Investext), company histories (from *International directory of company histories* [Chicago; Detroit: St. James Press, 1988–]), First Call consensus estimates, *business rankings (from Business rankings annual* [103]), and more. Search by company to find company profiles, rankings, financials, investment reports, articles, and histories. Search by industry to find industry associations, articles, and rankings. PROMT® (Predicast's Overview of Markets and Technology), Investext Plus (17), and Newsletters ASAP can be added onto the subscription.

**99    LexisNexis.** LexisNexis. [199?] Bethesda, Md.: LexisNexis. http://www.lexisnexis.com/academic/.

Searchable full-text subscription database that includes approximately 350 U.S. and foreign newspapers, broadcast transcripts from the major radio and TV networks, national and international wire services, campus newspapers, polls and surveys, and over 600 newsletters. Non-English language news sources available in Spanish, French, German, Italian, and Dutch. Dates of coverage vary by individual source, with newspapers updated daily.

**100    The Wall Street Journal index.** Dow Jones. [New York]: Dow Jones, 1957–. ISSN: 1042-9840.

332.05                                                                HG1.W26

Index coverage begins in 1955 and is based on the final Eastern edition of the newspaper. Each issue has two parts: (1) corporate news indexed by company name; (2) general news indexed by topic. Includes special sections for book reviews, personalities, deaths, and theater reviews. The last section of the index includes the daily Dow Jones averages for each month of the year. Since 1981, v. 1 includes Barron's index, a subject and corporate index to Barron's business and financial weekly. Since 1990, published monthly with quarterly and annual cumulations. Former publication frequency was monthly with annual cumulations. Annual cumulations issued in 2 pts., 1980–2001.

Fully searchable page images of the complete Wall Street Journal 1889–1989 are available in ProQuest Historical Newspapers (Ann Arbor, Mich.: ProQuest, 2001–). Searchable full text (although not original page images) is also available in a number of other commercial database services, including ProQuest Newspapers (Ann Arbor, Mich.: ProQuest, 2001–), Factiva (794), and ABI/Inform Global (788).

# Statistics

**101**    **Best's aggregates and averages.** A. M. Best Company. Oldwick, N.J.: A. M. Best, 1998–. ISSN: 1099-3592.

362.104258                                                      RA413.5.U5B476

Available for Property/Casualty, as well as Life/Health, with summary data on the insurance industry. Includes balance sheet and summary of operations, annual statements, quantitative analysis, insurance expenses, time series, premiums written, industry underwriting, leading companies and groups (with assets, policyholders surplus, reserves, premiums written, underwriting gain/loss, net investment income, realized capital gains, underwriting expense ratio, etc.), rankings, and composite listings. Coverage is for Canada and the United States.

**102**    **BigCharts.** MarketWatch, Inc. 1998–. [San Francisco]: BigCharts. http://bigcharts.marketwatch.com/.

HG4638

Best known for historic stock quotes, BigCharts has information on over 50,000 symbols, including current information on all NYSE, NASDAQ, AMEX, and OTC stocks, all NASDAQ quoted mutual funds, as well as leading financial indexes and international exchanges. The current information includes company profiles, company financials, news, charts, analyst estimates, analysis, and intraday stock screeners. Historic quotes include open, closing, high and low prices, volume traded, split adjusted price, and adjustment factor since 1970.

**103**    **Business rankings annual.** Business Library (Brooklyn Public Library). Detroit: Gale Research, 1989–. ISSN: 1043-7908.

338.74097305                                                      HG4050.B88

A collection of "top ten" lists extracted from newspapers, periodicals, directories, statistical annuals, and other publications, arranged alphabetically by subject. International in scope, content covers companies, products, services, and activities ranked by factors including assets, sales, revenue, production, employees, and market value. Each entry provides ranking criteria, first ten items in the original list, and source information including publication frequency.

**104**    **CRSP databases.** Chicago: Center for Research in Security Prices, 1989–.

One of the best sources for current and historical security data for the NYSE (daily from July 1962; monthly from Dec. 1925), AMEX (daily from July 1962; monthly from July 1962), and NASDAQ (daily from July 1972; monthly from Dec. 1972) Stock Markets. Data subsets include: CRSP U.S. Stock Database (NYSE, AMEX, NASD, S&P, annual/quarterly/ monthly/daily); CRSP U.S. Government Bond Fixed Term Index Series: monthly and daily; CRSP U.S. Treasury Risk-Free Rates File; and CRSP Fama-Bliss Discount Bond Files for prices and yields. Delivered by DVD or CD-ROM. Also available through Wharton Research Data Services (WRDS).

**105  Daily stock price record.** Standard and Poor's Corporation. New York: Standard and Poor's, 1993–. ISSN: 1072-3846.

332.632220973                                            HG4915.S665

Pt. 1 includes Standard and Poor's Indexes and the Dow Jones Averages. Pt. 2 includes information on daily volume, high, low, and closing prices for New York Stock Exchange, NASDAQ, Over the Counter, and American Stock Exchange stocks. Very useful as a historical source, especially for defunct stocks whose symbols and prices are difficult to find in other sources.

**106  D and B business rankings.** Dun and Bradstreet, Inc. Bethlehem, Pa.: Dun and Bradstreet, 1997–.

338.7402573                                             HG4057.A237

Ranks leading U.S. public and private businesses by annual sales volume and number of employees in five separate sections: alphabetically by company name, by state, by industry category, public businesses, and private businesses. Concluding sections cross-index division names with headquarter companies and list chief executives and other officers by function.

**107  Financial studies of the small business.** Winter Haven, Fla.: Financial Research Associates, 1976–. ISSN: 0363-8987.

658.15904                                              HD2346.U5F55a

Uses data from 30,000 financial statements provided by certified public accounting firms to present financial data on U.S. small businesses. Arranged by industry, then by asset size. Gives current assets, fixed assets, liabilities and capital, income data, operating items such as advertising expense and rent, and ratios (current, quick, current assets/total assets, short term debt/total debt, short term debt/net worth, total debt/net worth, short term debt/total assets, long term debt/total assets, total debt/total assets, sales/receivables, average collection period, sales/inventory, sales/total assets, sales/net worth, pre-tax profit/total assets, pre-tax profit/net worth).

**108**    **Global market information database.** Euromonitor. [1999–.]
[London]: Euromonitor. http://www.gmid.euromonitor.com/.
HD2755.5.G56

Market reports, company profiles, and demographic, economic, and marketing statistics for 205 countries. Market reports are for 16 consumer markets (food and drink, tobacco, toys, etc.) and 14 industrial and service markets (accountancy, broadcasting, chemicals, property services, etc.).

Reports have market size, market sectors, share of market, marketing activity, research and development, corporate overview, distribution, consumer profiles, market forecasts, sector forecasts, sources, and definitions. Additional reports are available for market segments, such as baby food. Company profiles have background, recent news, competitive environment, and outlook. Consumer lifestyle reports and very useful marketing background analyze the consumer by country, gender, age, marital status, educational attainment, ethnicity, religion, home ownership, household profile, employment, income, health, eating and personal grooming habits, leisure activities, personal finance, communication, transport, and travel.

Search for data, which can be exported into Excel or browse for reports. Data are available from 1977 through 2016 and include inflation, exchange rates, GDP, GNI, government expenditures, government finance, income, labor, and money supply.

**109**    **Ibbotson Associates' beta book publication.** Ibbotson Associates.
Chicago: Ibbotson Associates, 1996–. ISSN: 1087-6618.
332.041                                             HG4028.V3I23

Contains 60-month levered and unlevered beta calculations for 5,000 U.S. publicly traded companies. Betas are adjusted toward peer group average. Useful for Capital Assets Pricing Model (CAPM) calculations with data for the beta, Ibbotson beta, Fama-French beta. Data is used for modeling stock performance or pricing securities. Includes an overview of the beta estimation methodologies used.

110    **Market share reporter.** Gale Research Inc. Detroit: Gale Research,
       1991–. ISSN: 1052-9578.
380.105                                                          HF5410.M35
Market share statistics for over 4,000 companies and 2,300 products
and services. Compiled from periodicals and brokerage reports, and
arranged by Standard Industrial Classification (SIC) code. Indexed
by source, place name, product or service name, company, and brand
name. Includes the information from what was *World market share
reporter.*

111    **Mergerstat review.** Merrill Lynch Business Brokerage and
       Valuation. ill. Chicago: The Company, 1982–. ISSN: 1071-4065.
338.830973                                                      HD2746.5.M48
Review mergers and acquisitions. Pt. 1 is statistical analysis with aggregate announcements, composition of aggregate net merger and acquisition announcements, method of payment, P/E offered, divestitures,
publicly traded sellers, privately owned sellers, foreign sellers, aggressive
buyers, financial advisor ranking, legal advisor ranking, top managers,
and termination fees. Pt. 2 is industry analysis with highlights, industry
groups, spotlights giving industry activity for the two most active industries by Standard Industrial Classification (SIC) code, multiples (TIC/
EBITDA, P/E), premiums, composition, and cross-border activity. Pt. 3
is a geographical analysis with U.S. buyers and sellers by state, and foreign buyers and sellers. Pt. 4 is current year rosters with completed and
pending transactions with pricing disclosed, canceled transactions with
pricing disclosed, transactions with termination fees disclosed, and the
composition of the Mergerstat $1 billion club. Pt. 5 is a historical review
with a 25-year statistical review, record holders, 100 largest announcements in history, and largest announcements by industry. Pt. 6 lists
transactions by seller SIC code. There is also a glossary of terms. Also
available in online form.

112    **Standard and Poor's research insight on the web.** Standard and
       Poor's Compustat Services. 2000s–. Englewood, Colo.: Standard
       and Poor's. http://www.researchinsightweb.com/.
Research Insight is the new interface to Compustat. An essential resource
with the most recent 20 years of U.S. and Canadian financial statement
data and monthly closing stock price data, six months of daily stock

prices, and GlobalVantage, the most recent 10 years of financial data for companies in 80 countries. Not an easy database to use; complex screening is possible, which becomes easier from within Excel. Screening can be done for data items in financial reports. Choose from quarterly or annual financials, and from nearly every data item within a financial report. Over 100 preformatted reports are available (EVAntage, company highlights, cash flow statements, combined reports, common size statements, institutional holdings). Data is also available for geographic areas, industry composites, aggregates, and stock indexes, and about 7,000 inactive companies.

113 **Stock market encyclopedia.** Standard and Poor's Corporation. ill. New York: The Corporation, 1985–. ISSN: 0882-5467.

338.740973                                                 HG4057.A46

Lists S&P 500 plus 250 other leading public corporations. Two pages of information for each firm include summary of operations, current outlook and S&P forecast, 10 years of per-share data, and three-year balance sheet.

114 **Tablebase.** Gale Cengage Learning. [2001?–.] [s.l.]: Gale Cengage Learning. http://search.rdsinc.com/.
A terrific international statistical source for company, industry, and demographic information including market share, market size, market trends, price trends, rankings, sales forecasts, output and capacity, consumption, imports and exports, and shipments. Information comes from 900 trade publications, including *Accounting today, Adweek, Aftermarket business, Almanac of american employers, Beverage world, Chemical week, Datamonitor industry market research, Meed Middle East economic digest,* as well as reports, newsletters, and surveys.

115 **WRDS. Wharton School.** Philadelphia: The Wharton School, University of Pennsylvania. http://wrds.wharton.upenn.edu/.
Provides web access through a hosting service for a number of financial research databases, including Compustat (Englewood, Colo.: Standard and Poor's, 2000s–), CRSP (Center for Research in Securities Prices) (104), Dow Jones Averages, FDIC, Philadelphia Stock Exchange, Institutional Brokers Estimate System (New York: Institutional Brokers Estimate System, 1976–), BankScope (78), CSMAR China Stock Market databases, Eventus, First Call, and OptionMetrics.

# 3 > ECONOMIC CONDITIONS AND WORLD TRADE

## Atlases

116  **Atlas of the world economy.** Michael J. Freeman, Derek Howard Aldcroft. xv, 167 p., ill. New York: Simon and Schuster, 1991. ISBN: 0130507415.

330.904                                                    HC59.F734

While dated, still interesting for visuals of world economy. Broken into eight broad categories (population, agriculture, energy, industry, national income, transport and trade, labor, and multinationals), with introductory comments and some 250 maps, charts, tables, and graphs.

117  **The national economic atlas of China.** Chung-kuo k'o hsüeh yüan. 1 atlas, xvi, 314 p., col. maps. Hong Kong, [China]; New York: Oxford University Press, 1994. ISBN: 0195857364.

912.43                                                  G2306.G1K813

Translated work includes four handbooks of descriptive notes to maps bound separately in pockets. Maps illustrate China's resources, population, general economy, agriculture, industry, trade, social indicators, and regional economies. Comprehensive in nature and provides an excellent overview for anyone interested in studying the Chinese economy.

## Biography

118  **A biographical dictionary of dissenting economists.** 2nd ed. Philip Arestis, Malcolm C. Sawyer. xiv, 722 p. Cheltenham, U.K.; Northampton, Mass.: E. Elgar, 2000. ISBN: 1858985609.

330.0922B                                                   HB76.B5

A mix of biographical and autobiographical entries on nearly 100 international economists. Autobiographical entries include economists' statements about their principal contributions to the discipline. Contains biographical information, information on economic philosophies, and compact bibliographic information. Available as an e-book.

119  **Business cycles and depressions: An encyclopedia.** David Glasner, Thomas F. Cooley. xv, 779 p., ill. New York: Garland, 1997. ISBN: 0824009444.

338.54203                                                    HB3711.B936

Contains 327 essays about economists, theories, and historic events, with selective bibliographies. Biographies focus on an individual economist's contributions to understanding business cycles. Well written, with good international coverage.

120  **Dictionary of labour biography.** Joyce M. Bellamy, John Saville. v. 1–13. London; [Clifton], N.J.: Macmillan; A. M. Kelley, 1972–2007. ISBN: 0678070083.

331.0922                                                    HD8393.A1B44

Ambitious biographical dictionary that intends to include "not only the national personalities of the British labour movement but also the activists at regional and local level."—*Introd.* Indeed, "everyone who made a contribution, however modest, to any organisation or movement, provided that certain basic details of their career can be established," is to be included. The period of coverage is from 1790 to the present, excluding living persons. It is expected that 15 to 20 volumes will be required to treat figures down to 1914. Each volume is alphabetically arranged and includes biographies without regard to date of the biographee's activity. A consolidated index appears in each successive volume; a system of cross-references is also provided, referring to both earlier and later volumes. Vol. 6 includes a list of additions and corrections for v. 1–5. Online consolidated index (http://www.york.ac.uk/res/dlb/) currently unavailable but expected to reappear soon.

121  **Distinguished women economists.** James Cicarelli, Julianne Cicarelli. xxvi, 244 p. Westport, Conn.: Greenwood Press, 2003. ISBN: 0313303312.

330.0922                                                    HB76.C53

Contains 51 profiles of women selected from the 19th century to the present. Entries include an introduction, short biography, section on contributions to economics, and further reading. Most entries can be found in *A biographical dictionary of women economists* (716) or *Who's who in economics* (731). Available as an e-book.

122   Encyclopedia of the global economy: A guide for students
      and researchers. David E. O'Connor. 2 v., ill. Westport, Conn.:
      Greenwood Press, 2006. ISBN: 0313335842.
330.03                                                    HF1359O28

Over 150 entries briefly cover issues and key individuals related to the
global economy. Especially useful for the inclusion of tables, graphs, 59 key
primary documents, and statistical data located in v. 2. For historical perspective, see the *Timeline of key events in the global economy, 1776–2009.*
Also has a glossary of selected terms, a list of global economy websites, and
a selected bibliography. Available as an e-book.

123   **Fifty major economists.** Steven Pressman. xi, 207 p., ill. London;
      New York: Routledge, 1999. ISBN: 0415134803.
330.0922B                                                 HB76.P74

Profiles with biographical sketch, analysis of contributions, list of main
works, and further reading. Primary coverage is given to seminal economists. Glossary of economic terms. Also available as an e-book.

124   **Great economists before Keynes: An introduction to the lives and
      works of one hundred great economists of the past.** Mark Blaug.
      xi, 286 p., ports. Cambridge, [England]; New York: Cambridge
      University Press, 1986, 1988. ISBN: 0521367417.
330.0922B                                                 HB76.B54

Discusses the life, impact, and work of renowned economists, in 2–4 page
entries. Portraits included, where possible. Indexed by name and subject.

# Book Reviews

125   **H-net.** Michigan State University, National Endowment for the
      Humanities. 1995–. East Lansing, Mich.: Michigan State University.
      http://www.h-net.org/.
300.072; 001.3072; 370; 378.104; 700.072                  H85

Created to advance "research, teaching, learning, public outreach, and professional service within their own specialized areas of knowledge" (*About
H-net*), H-net is composed of discussion networks, scholarly reviews,
announcements, and a job guide.
     It serves diverse areas of interest in the social sciences and humanities,
including economics, history, maritime history, African studies, American
studies, and art history.

The reviews are from 1993 to the present and cover books and multimedia. H-net currently publishes about 1,000 reviews annually.

The job guide "posts academic position announcements in History and the Humanities, the Social Sciences, and Rhetoric and Composition, and serves a broad audience of administrators, faculty members, archivists, librarians, and other professionals in the humanities and social sciences" (*Introd. to Job Guide*); the positions can be searched or browsed, and an e-mail alert can be set up.

126 **The review of financial studies.** Oxford University Press. 1988–. New York: Oxford University Press and Society for Financial Studies. ISSN: 0893-9454. http://rfs.oxfordjournals.org/.

HG1.R45

One of the top journals in financial economics, it publishes theoretical and empirical research in financial economics. Sponsored by the Society for Financial Studies, with irregular, but lengthy book reviews. E-mail alerts can be set up for table of contents or to track topics and authors. Also available in print format.

# Dictionaries

127 **Dictionary of international economics terms.** John Owen Edward Clark. 300 p. London: Les50ns Professional Pub., 2006. ISBN: 0852976852.

330.03                                    HF1359.D4956

Defines concepts, jargon, and acronyms in economics, finance and business. Includes definitions such as accelerated depreciation, Andean Pact, coupon interest rate, marginal cost, shakeout, and X-inefficiency. Part of a series of dictionaries, which include: *Dictionary of international accounting terms, Dictionary of international banking and finance terms, Dictionary of international business terms, Dictionary of international insurance and finance terms,* and *Dictionary of international trade finance.* Some definitions are shared between the dictionaries in the series.

128 **Dictionary of international trade.** Jerry Martin Rosenberg. xii, 314 p. New York: Wiley, 1994. ISBN: 0471597325.

382.03                                    HF1373.R67

More than 4,000 entries define terms, simple to complex, sometimes offering more than one definition for an entry: "relatively simple for the layperson, more developed and technical for the specialist."—*Introd.* Contains cross-references. Includes an appendix of currency codes.

129 **Dictionary of international trade: Handbook of the global trade community includes 21 key appendixes.** 7th ed. Edward G. Hinkelman. 416 p., ill., maps. Novato, Calif.: World Trade Press, 2006. ISBN: 1885073739.

382.03                                                                                      HF1373.H55

An A-Z guide to terms on exporting, importing, banking, shipping, and other matters relating to international trade. Definitions make up half the book, with the other half devoted to appendixes. There are appendixes for: acronyms and abbreviations, country codes, international dialing guide, currencies of the world, business entities worldwide, weights and measures, ship illustrations, airplane illustrations, truck and trailer illustrations, railcar illustrations, guide to air freight containers, guide to ocean freight containers, world airports by IATA code, world airports by airport, seaports of the world, computer terms, guide to Incoterms 2000, guide to letters of credit, resources for international trade, top websites, guide to trade documentation, guide to international sourcing, key words in eight languages, global supply chain security, and maps of the world in color.

130 **Dictionary of trade policy terms.** 4th ed. Walter Goode World Trade Organization. xi, 437 p. Cambridge, U.K.; New York: Cambridge University Press, 2003. ISBN: 0521831083.

382.03                                                                                      HF1373.G66

Contains 2,000 entries on international organizations such as the WTO, and rules and issues for international trade. While some terminology dates back to 1947 when GATT (General Agreement on Tariffs and Trade) was formed, the dictionary focuses on current terms.

131 **Elsevier's dictionary of financial and economic terms: Spanish-English and English-Spanish.** Martha Uriona G. A., José Daniel Kwacz. 311 p. Amsterdam, [The Netherlands]; New York: Elsevier, 1996. ISBN: 0444822569.

332.03                                                                                      HG151.U75

Explanations and definitions for economics, finance and business, including jargon. Intended for practitioners.

132    **Historical dictionary of organized labor.** 2nd ed. J. C. Docherty. xlviii, 439 p., ill. Lanham, Md.: Scarecrow Press, 2004. ISBN: 0810849119.

331.8803                                                    HD4839.D58

Contains 400 entries on countries, national and international organizations, unions, and labor leaders. Begins with sections on abbreviations and acronyms, and a chronology starting in 1152 B.C. with tomb makers in Egypt and ending in 2003 with a general strike in Nigeria. Entries are typically two paragraphs long. Complemented by the *Historical dictionary of socialism*, by the same author, which covers political theories and parties.

133    **The new Palgrave dictionary of economics and the law.** Peter Newman. 3 v., ill. London; New York: Macmillan Reference; Stockton Press, 2004. ISBN: 033399755.

330.03                                                     K487.E3N49

Contains 399 signed articles with international coverage on the legal aspects of economics, such as airline deregulation and property rights. Includes statutes, treaties, directives, and cases. Written by 340 contributors from eight countries.

134    **World monetary units: An historical dictionary, country by country.** Howard M. Berlin. vii, 229 p. Jefferson, N.C.: McFarland, 2006. ISBN: 0786420804.

332.403                                                    HG216.B465

Chronologies, etymologies, and orthographic information for 203 countries and four confederations. Arranged by country. Appendixes for Foreign language number systems, Families of monetary units, Monetary abbreviations and symbols, ISO–4217 currency codes, and Central banks. References and index. Also useful is *Coins and currency: An historical encyclopedia* (138).

## Directories

135    **Directory of U.S. labor organizations.** Bureau of National Affairs. Washington: Bureau of National Affairs, 1982–. ISSN: 0734-6786.

331.8802573                                                HD6504.D64

Lists some 30,000 unions affiliated with AFL-CIO and other national, regional, state, and local affiliates. Gives the structure, leadership, and

ECONOMIC CONDITIONS AND WORLD TRADE

51

contact information for the unions. Index of unions by common name and by abbreviations; names and index of officers.

**136 Sustainable development policy directory.** W. Alan Strong, Lesley A. Hemphill. xi, 659 p. Oxford; Malden, Mass.: Blackwell, 2006. ISBN: 1405121505.

338.927025                                                          HC79.E5S773

Provides background information on sustainable development policy and actions in Europe (with a focus on the United Kingdom and Ireland) and internationally. Each chapter gives the main challenges of that topic, lists policy documents from the 1970s to the present (with the objectives of the policy, the contents of the document, and where available, the URLs for the documents). Chapters include: Biodiversity, Climate change, Construction, Energy, Environment, Planning, Pollution, Social issues, Sustainable development policy and practice, Transport, Urban development, Waste management, and Water. Available as an e-book.

## Encyclopedias

**137 Business cycles and depressions: An encyclopedia.** David Glasner, Thomas F. Cooley. xv, 779 p., ill. New York: Garland, 1997. ISBN: 0824009444.

338.54203                                                          HB3711.B936

Contains 327 essays about economists, theories, and historic events, with selective bibliographies. Biographies focus on an individual economist's contributions to understanding business cycles. Well written, with good international coverage.

**138 Coins and currency: An historical encyclopedia.** Mary Ellen Snodgrass. xii, 562 p., ill. Jefferson, N.C.: McFarland, 2003. ISBN: 0786414502.

737.403                                                             CJ59.S66

Contains 250 entries with historical commentary on coins and various other forms. Includes pictures of currency and biographical information about coin designers and creators of monetary systems. Entries are cross-referenced. Arranged alphabetically. Includes timeline, glossary, and bibliography. Also useful is *World monetary units: An historical dictionary, country by country* (134).

**139** Encyclopedia of international development. Tim Forsyth. xix, 826 p. Abingdon, [U.K.]; New York: Routledge, 2005. ISBN: 041525342X.

338.9003                                                        HD82.E547

Contains 600 entries on concepts, organizations, summits, policies, and leaders involved in international development. The authors take a wide view of the topic, including entries on religion, education, war, and reproductive rights. Entries are signed and include further reading.

**140** Encyclopedia of the developing world. Thomas M. Leonard. 3 v. New York: Routledge, 2006. ISBN: 1579583881.

909.0972403                                                    HC59.7.E52

Contains 800 entries by 251 authors, which include country descriptions, biographies, and topical definitions, such as "capitalist economic model." Entries are signed and include references and further readings. Country entries discuss location, temperature, history, and the economy. Biographical entries include educational background, professional accomplishments, and impact on the economy. Entries are 1–3 pages long.

**141** Encyclopedia of the global economy: A guide for students and researchers. David E. O'Connor. 2 v., ill. Westport, Conn.: Greenwood Press, 2006. ISBN: 0313335842.

330.03                                                          HF1359.O28

Over 150 entries briefly cover issues and key individuals related to the global economy. Especially useful for the inclusion of tables, graphs, 59 key primary documents, and statistical data located in v. 2. For historical perspective, see the *Timeline of key events in the global economy, 1776–2009.* Also has a glossary of selected terms, a list of global economy websites, and a selected bibliography. Available as an e-book.

**142** Encyclopedia of world poverty. Mehmet Odekon. 3 v., ill., maps. Thousand Oaks, Calif.: Sage Publications, 2006. ISBN: 1412918073.

362.503                                                         HV12.E54

Over 750 signed articles on the political, social, geographic, and economic characteristics of poverty in 191 countries. Where available, country rankings on the Human Development Index and the Human Poverty Index are given. Three appendixes: United Nations statistics on national poverty, World Trade organization statistics on national economics, and directory of poverty-relief organizations. Available as an e-book.

ECONOMIC CONDITIONS AND WORLD TRADE

143    **Encyclopedia of world trade: From ancient times to the present.**
Cynthia Clark Northrup. 4 v., ill., maps. Armonk, N.Y.: Sharpe
Reference, 2005. ISBN: 0765680580.
382.03                                                              HF1373.W67

With 450 entries, provides background to the development of world trade.
Signed entries vary in coverage and scope, but include the highlights. Some
entries are for an event, others for individuals, places, and even religions.
Also includes primary documents.

144    **Europa world plus.** Europa Publications Limited, Routledge,
Taylor & Francis Group. 2003–. New York: Routledge; Taylor &
Francis Group. http://www.europaworld.com/pub/about/.
                                                                   D443.E87

Economic and political information for more than 250 countries and territories. Includes *Europa world year book* (145) and the *Europa regional
surveys of the world* series:

- *Africa south of the Sahara* (London; New York: Routledge, 1971–)
- *Central and south-eastern Europe* (London: Europa Publications,
  2000–)
- *Eastern Europe, Russia and Central Asia* (London; New York: Rout-
  ledge, 2000–)
- *The Far East and Australasia* (London: Europa, 1969–)
- *The Middle East and North Africa* (991)
- *South America, Central America and the Caribbean* (London: Europa,
  1985–)
- *South Asia* (London; New York: Routledge, 2003–)
- *The USA and Canada* (London; New York: Routledge, 1989–)
- *Western Europe* (London; New York: Routledge, 1988–)

Country entries include country profile, geography, chronology, history,
economy, country statistics, government and politics directory, society and
media directory, business and commerce directory, and bibliography.

Unique to the online version is the comparative statistics section, which
generates five years of multinational statistics on area and population,
agriculture, industry, finance, external trade, and education in tables and
charts downloaded as an HTML table, comma-separated values and in tab-
separated values. The comparative statistics section uses different sources
than the country statistics section, making data comparisons possible.

145    **The Europa world year book.** Europa Publications Limited.
London: Europa Publications Limited, 1989–. ISSN: 0956-2273.
                                                        JN1.E85
Issued in two volumes, with v. 1 covering international organizations and
the first group of alphabetically arranged country entries and v. 2 the
remainder of the country entries. Information on the United Nations,
its agencies, and other international organizations followed by detailed
information about each country, arranged alphabetically in each volume,
giving an introductory survey, a statistical survey, the government, political parties, the constitution, judicial system, diplomatic representation,
religion, press, publishers, radio and television, finance, trade and industry, transport, and tourism. Vol. 1 ends with an index to international
organizations; v. 2 includes a country index.

Similar Europa publications are the *Regional surveys of the world*,
including *Africa south of the Sahara* (London; New York: Routledge,
1971–), *Central and south-eastern Europe* (London: Europa Publications, 2000–), *Eastern Europe, Russia, and Central Asia* (London; New
York: Routledge, 2000–), *The Far East and Australasia* (London: Europa,
1969–), *The Middle East and North Africa* (991), *South America, Central America, and the Caribbean* (London: Europa, 1985–), *South Asia*
(London; New York: Routledge, 2003–), *The USA and Canada* (London;
New York: Routledge, 1989–), and *Western Europe* (London; New York:
Routledge, 1988–). The electronic version of this resource, Europa World
Plus (144), includes both the year book and the regional surveys as well
as continual updates on recent elections, recent events, and a featured
country. It also provides the capability to search and create tables of
comparative statistics for the countries in the database.

146    **The Federal Reserve System: An encyclopedia.** R. W. Hafer.
xxxii, 451 p., ill. Westport, Conn.: Greenwood Press, 2005. ISBN:
0313328390.
332.11097303                                    HG2563.H235

Contains 250 well-written articles explaining the somewhat mysterious
Federal Reserve System, its structure, process, and policies. Entries also
cover people and key events related to the Federal Reserve. Appendixes
provide the text of The Federal Reserve Act, Federal Reserve Regulations,
and a list of the Membership of the Board of Governors: 1913–2004. Available as an e-book.

147 **Globalization: Encyclopedia of trade, labor, and politics.** Ashish K. Vaidya. 2 v., ill. Santa Barbara, Calif.: ABC-CLIO, 2006. ISBN: 1576078264.

JZ1318.G5816

Contains 94 entries about international trade since World War II, concentrating on the economic, business, legal, political and environmental aspects of international economic integration. Organized in four sections: basic trade and investment issues, impact of globalization in various economic sectors, roles of international blocs and agencies in furthering globalization, and social and political issues. Available as an e-book.

148 **History of world trade since 1450.** John J. MacCusker. 2 v. Detroit: Macmillan, 2006. ISBN: 002865840X.

Similar to *Encyclopedia of world trade: From ancient times to the present* (143), but more accessible for younger readers and with enough unique content to justify owning both sources. Over 400 signed entries, with cross-references and annotations for additional reading. Also available as an e-book.

149 **The Oxford encyclopedia of economic history.** Joel Mokyr, Oxford University Press. New York: Oxford University Press, 2003. ISBN: 0195105079.

330.03                                                                       HC15.O94

Authoritative five-volume set covering all aspects of economic history. Alphabetic arrangement of nearly 900 signed articles with bibliographies and cross-references. Major topics include geography, agriculture, production systems, business history, technology, demography, institutions, governments, markets, money, banking finance, labor, natural resources and the environment, and biographies. Separate listing of scholarly economic history internet sites. Index and topical outline of articles. Also available in online form.

150 **The Oxford encyclopedia of economic history.** Joel Mokyr, Oxford University Press. New York: Oxford University Press, 2005. ISBN: 0195187628.

HC15.O945x

Arranged alphabetically ("accounting and bookkeeping" to "zoos and other animal parks"), examines economic history from ancient to modern times. Contains 900 articles, ranging in length from 500–3,000 words, takes a global approach to: geography (cities, countries, regions); agriculture; production systems, business history, and technology; demography; institutions, governments, and markets; macroeconomic history and international economics; money, banking and finance; labor; natural resources and the environment; and biographies. Available online at Oxford Reference Online (Oxford; New York: Oxford University Press, 2002–).

## Guides and Handbooks

151　The economist numbers guide: The essentials of business numeracy. Richard Stutely. 237 p., ill. New York: Wiley, 1997. ISBN: 0471249548.

650.01513　　　　　　　　　　　　　　　　　　HF5695.S83

Introduction to numerical methods and quantitative techniques used in mathematics, statistics, business, accounting, and economics. Uses extensive examples, tables, and figures to explain in layman's terms. Appendix is a dictionary, with cross-references to the main section. Indexed.

152　Exporters' encyclopaedia. Dun's Marketing Services. maps. New York: Dun and Bradstreet International, 1982–. ISSN: 8755-013X.

382.602573　　　　　　　　　　　　　　　　　　HF3011.E9

Comprehensive world marketing guide for 220 world markets. Designed as a guide to possible markets and also as an instructional manual for some practicalities (e.g., shipping and insurance). Country profiles include communications, key contracts, trade regulations, documentation, marketing data, transportation, and business travel. Other sections cover U.S. ports, U.S. foreign trade zones, World Trade Center Association members, U.S. government agencies providing assistance to exporters, foreign trade organizations, foreign communications, and general export and shipping information.

153　Guide to foreign trade statistics. U.S. Dept. of Commerce, Bureau of the Census. Washington, D.C.: U.S. Dept. of Commerce, Bureau of the Census. ISSN: 0565-0933. http://purl.access.gpo.gov/GPO/ LPS72518/.

382.0973　　　　　　　　　　　　　　　　　　HF105.B73a

Guide to various sources of foreign trade statistics from the U.S. government. Most useful for definitions and links to relevant sources. Earlier editions available in print.

154   **Handbook of United States economic and financial indicators.**
Rev. ed. Frederick M. O'Hara, F. M. O'Hara. x, 395 p. Westport,
Conn.: Greenwood Press, 2000. ISBN: 0313274509.
330.973                                                    HC106.8.O47

Definitions for 284 economic and financial indicators, with calculations,
derivations, use, and publishers. Appendixes for nonquantitative indicators, key to printed sources, compilers of indicators, key to electronic
sources, and general reading. Available as an e-book.

155   **The index of economic freedom.** Heritage Foundation. maps.
Washington: The Heritage Foundation, 1995–. ISSN: 1095-7308.
338.9005                                                    HB95.I48

Uses 50 independent variables to rank 161 countries, including Hong
Kong, on the level of government involvement in the economy. The more
that a government is involved in constraint in the production, distribution, or consumption of goods and services, the less freedom the editors
believe is present. In addition to the score, 2-p. long country profiles
discuss trade policy, fiscal burden, government intervention, monetary
policy, foreign investment, banking and finance, wages and prices, property rights, regulation, and informal market. The 2007 ed. adds a chapter
on regions. The current version is available for free at http://www.heri-
tage.org/research/.

156   **The secrets of economic indicators: Hidden clues to future
economic trends and investment opportunities.** Bernard
Baumohl. xxi, 366 p., ill. Upper Saddle River, N.J.: Wharton
School, 2005. ISBN: 013145501X.
338.54                                                      HB3730.B38

Information on the indicators with the greatest influence on markets,
indicators that are best for forecasting the economy, data sources, and
information on interpreting economic indicators. Includes frequency of
publication, release times, and revisions. Focus is primarily on U.S. indicators, but includes international economic indicators. Available as an
e-book.

157   **Sustainable development policy directory.** W. Alan Strong, Lesley
A. Hemphill. xi, 659 p. Oxford; Malden, Mass.: Blackwell, 2006.
ISBN: 1405121505.
338.927025                                                  HC79.E5S773

Provides background information on sustainable development policy and actions in Europe (with a focus on the United Kingdom and Ireland) and internationally. Each chapter gives the main challenges of that topic, lists policy documents from the 1970s to the present (with the objectives of the policy, the contents of the document, and where available, the URLs for the documents). Chapters include: Biodiversity, Climate change, Construction, Energy, Environment, Planning, Pollution, Social issues, Sustainable development policy and practice, Transport, Urban development, Waste management, and Water. Available as an e-book.

## Indexes; Abstract Journals

158    SourceOECD. Organisation for Economic Co-operation and Development. [Paris, France]: OECD. http://new.sourceoecd.org/. A subscription database containing OECD books, reports, working papers, serials, and statistical databases on economic and social topics, as well as the environment, energy, and technological development. Focuses mainly on the 30 OECD member states and major nonmember developing countries.

Serials include journals; the OECD Factbook (Paris: OECD, 2005–) and other statistical works; and titles that forecast and analyze trends, such as the OECD Economic Outlook (Paris: Organisation for Economic Co-operation and Development, 1967–), *African economic outlook* (Paris: African Development Bank, Development Centre of the Organisation for Economic Co-operation and Development, 2002–), International Migration Outlook (Paris: Organisation for Economic Co-operation and Development, 2006–), and OECD-FAO Agricultural Outlook (Paris: Organisation for Economic Co-operation and Development; Food and Agriculture Organization, 2005–).

Current, themed databases include the OECD Economic Outlook Database (Paris: Organisation for Economic Co-operation and Development, 2002–), SourceOECD Main Economic Indicators (Paris: Organisation for Economic Co-operation and Development, 2002–), Banking Statistics, Education Statistics, Globalisation, Indicators of Industry and Services, Insurance, International Development, International Direct Investment Statistics, International Migration Statistics, the ITCS International Trade by Commodity Database, Monthly Statistics of International Trade, the National Accounts Database, OECD Health Data, OECD Statistics on International Trade in Services, the Revenue Statistics of OECD Member Countries Database, the Science and Technology Database, the Social Expenditure Database, Structural and Demographic Business Statistics, Taxing Wages Statistics, and the Telecommunications Database. Statistical databases of the International Energy Agency are also available via this source. OECD.Stat enables users to query multiple databases simultaneously and to export search results in several formats.

Also incorporates Future Trends, an index of published and unpublished sources in more than a dozen languages covering issues affecting the public and private sectors. Glossary.

## Internet Resources

**159** **Country briefings.** Economist.com. [199?–.] London: Economist Newspaper. http://www.economist.com/countries/.

909.83                                                              HC59.15

News from *The economist* (151) print edition, country profiles, forecasts, statistics, political outlook, economic policy outlook, economic forecast, and economic structure for 60 countries. Ten key economic statistics can be downloaded into Excel (GDP per head, GDP, government consumption, budget balance, consumer prices, public debt, labour costs per hour, recorded unemployment, current-account balance, and foreign-exchange reserves). Links to some subscription-based materials and free external related websites, such as governmental and news websites.

**160** **Economic history services.** EH.Net. 2004–. [Oxford, Ohio]: EH.Net. http://eh.net/.

HC21.E25

Owned by the Economic History Association and intended primarily for economic historians, historians of economics, economists, and historians, EH.net has research abstracts and book reviews, course syllabi, directory of economic historians, Encyclopedia of Economic and Business History, historical economic data sets (such as Global Financial Data, 1880–1913 and historic labor statistics), links to economic history websites, and a section called "How Much Is That?".

"How Much Is That?" gives comparative values of money, including five ways to compare the worth of a U.S. dollar, 1790–2005; the price of gold for 1257–2005; annual Consumer Price Index for the United States for 1774–2005; the purchasing power of the British pound, 1264–2005;

annual real and nominal GDP for the United States, 1790–2005; annual real and nominal GDP for the United Kingdom, 1086–2005; interest rate series for the United Kingdom and the United States, 1790–2001; and daily closing values of the Dow Jones Industrial Average (DJIA) from 1896.

161 **Penn world table.** Alan W. Heston, Robert Summers, Bettina Aten, University of Pennsylvania. 2006. Philadelphia: Center for International Comparisons of Production, Income and Prices, University of Pennsylvania. http://pwt.econ.upenn.edu/php_site/ pwt62/pwt62_form.php.
International data on "purchasing power parity and national income accounts converted to international prices for 188 countries for some or all of the years 1950–2004."—*About PWT.* Variables are Population, Exchange Rate, Purchasing Power, Parity over GDP, Real Gross Domestic Product per Capita, Consumption Share of CGPD, Government Share of CGDP, Investment Share of CGDP, Price Level of Gross Domestic Product, Price Level of Consumption, Price Level of Government, Price Level of Investment, Openness in Current Prices, Ratio of GNP to GDP, CGDP Relative to the United States, Real GDP per Capita (Constant Prices: Laspeyres), Real GDP per capita (Constant Prices: Chain Series), Real GDP Chain per Equivalent Adult, Real GDP Chain per Worker, Real Gross Domestic Income (RGDPL Adjusted for Terms of Trade Changes), Openness in Constant Prices, Consumption Share of RGDPL, Government Share of RGDPL, Investment Share of RGDPL, Growth Rate of Real GDP per Capita (Constant Prices: Chain Series). Data is based on World Development Indicators and National Accounts of OECD countries. Data can be downloaded as SAS and comma separated values (.csv).

162 **Statistical sites on the World Wide Web.** U.S. Bureau of Labor Statistics. Washington: U.S. Bureau of Labor Statistics. http://www. bls.gov/bls/other.htm.
Links to official government statistical offices all over the world, including more than 130 countries and some international agencies. Also links to sites of nearly 70 U.S. federal statistical agencies. Excellent starting point for researchers.

163 **United Nations common database (UNCDB).** United Nations Statistic Division. New York: United Nations Statistic Division. http://unstats.un.org/unsd/cdb/cdb_help/cdb_quick_start.asp.

Provides socioeconomic data from 55 sources on 274 countries and areas, with coverage from 1948–2050. Allows comparison of data from 10 countries at a time, and data can be downloaded to Excel. Formerly a fee-based database but now free.

Covers 31 topics: agriculture, forestry, and fishing; communication and culture; construction; development assistance; economically active/not economically active population; education and learning; energy; environment; financial statistics; health, health services, impairment, disabilities, nutrition; households and families, marital status, fertility; human settlements, housing, geographical distribution of population; income, consumption and wealth; industrial production; international finance; international tourism; international trade; millennium development goals (MDG); mining and quarrying; national accounts; population composition and change; prices; public order and safety; science and technology, intellectual property; services industries; social security and welfare services; socioeconomic groups and social mobility; statistical yearbook; transport; and women and men.

164  **VIBES.** Jeanie M. Welch, J. Murrey Atkins Library (University of North Carolina at Charlotte). [199?–.] Charlotte, N.C.: University of North Carolina at Charlotte, J. Murrey Atkins Library. http://library.uncc.edu/vibes/.
025.04; 382; 330; 650

Links to over 3,000 free Internet sources with international business and economic information in English. Organized into three categories: comprehensive, regional, and national. Coverage includes agricultural and forest products; banking and finance (includes insurance); business news, business practices and company information (includes labor); country information; emerging markets; foreign exchange rates; foreign stock markets; international electronic commerce; international statistics (general and economic); international tourism; international trade law; marketing and advertising; patents (includes other intellectual property); petroleum, energy, mining, and construction; portals (web meta pages with several international links); taxation in foreign countries (includes social security); trade issues and statistics; and business and economics for Africa, Asia-Pacific, Eastern Europe, Western Europe, Latin America and the Caribbean, Middle East, and NAFTA (U.S., Canada, and Mexico).

# Periodicals

165   **American economic review.** American Economic Association. ill. Princeton, N.J.: American Economic Association, 1911–. ISSN: 0002-8282.

HB1.E26

Articles and shorter papers on a variety of economic topics. Each May issue is devoted to the papers and proceedings of the annual meeting of the American Economic Association. Archived in JSTOR.

166   **Econometrica: Journal of the Econometric Society.** Econometric Society. ports., diagrs. Chicago: Econometric Society, University of Chicago, 1933–. ISSN: 0012-9682.

330.5                                                                                           HB1.E2

Includes articles on a wide range of economic topics, but *Econometrica* looks to publish articles that unify the theoretical-quantitative and the empirical-quantitative approaches to economics. At least one co-author must be a member of the Econometric Society. Archived in JSTOR.

167   **The economist.** ill. London: Economist Newspaper, 1843–. ISSN: 0013-0613.

330.05                                                                                       HG11.E2

Coverage of political, economic, and business events, world leaders, and science and technology. Economic and financial indicators (output, prices and jobs, *The economist* commodity-price index, GDP growth forecasts, trade, exchange rates, budget balances and interest rates, markets, and stock markets), and emerging market indicators (overview, child mortality, economy, financial markets) are published regularly. Regular book reviews. Full access available for a fee at http://www.economist.com/and through various aggregator databases.

168   **World development report.** World Bank. ill., maps. [New York]: Oxford University Press, 1978–. ISSN: 0163-5085.

330.91724                                                                              HC59.7.W659

Each report presents an overview and analysis of a currently relevant international economic development issue such as youth, or investment climate. The statistical portion presents selected social, economic, and demographic data for some 180 countries. Also available online through the World Bank at http://econ.worldbank.org/wdrs/.

169   **World economic and social survey.** United Nations. New York:
United Nations, 1955–.

330.9005                                                                          HC59.A169

Analysis and economic data for long-term social and economic development issues. Chapters on the global outlook, international trade, financial
flows to developing countries, regional developments and outlooks, and
statistical tables. Includes a lengthy bibliography. Online from 1998 at the
U.N.'s website (http://www.un.org/esa/policy/publications/papers.htm).

170   **World economic outlook: A survey by the staff of the**
**International Monetary Fund.** International Monetary Fund.
ill. Washington: The International Monetary Fund, 1980–. ISSN:
0256-6877.

338.544309048                                                                  HC10.W7979

Reviews world economic conditions with short- to mid-term economic
projections. Over half the publication consists of expository chapters, supplemented by tables and charts, that discuss industrial countries, developing countries, and economies in transition. The statistical appendix has
43 tables, giving output, inflation, financial policies, foreign trade, current
account transactions and financing, external debt and debt service, and
flow of funds summary. Available online from 1993 on the IMF website
(http://www.imf.org/external/ns/cs.aspx?id=29/).

# Reviews of Research and Trends

171   **Advances in entrepreneurship, firm emergence, and growth.**
Jerome A. Katz. ill. Amsterdam, [The Netherlands]; Boston:
Elsevier/JAI Press, 1993–. ISSN: 1074-7540.

658.42105                                                                        HB615.A377

Brings together studies relating to the impact of entrepreneurial activities
on U.S. economic development. These research findings are relevant to
the academic and business communities; especially pertinent to practicing entrepreneurs. Annual. Volumes cover all aspects of entrepreneurship,
from entrepreneurial education to the impact of government regulation.
Vol. 10 to be published in 2007. Available in online form.

172   **World development report.** World Bank. ill., maps. [New York]:
Oxford University Press, 1978–. ISSN: 0163-5085.

330.91724                                                                        HC59.7.W659

Each report presents an overview and analysis of a currently relevant international economic development issue such as youth, or investment climate. The statistical portion presents selected social, economic, and demographic data for some 180 countries. Also available online through the World Bank at http://econ.worldbank.org/wdrs/.

**173** **World economic and social survey.** United Nations. New York: United Nations, 1955–.
330.9005                                                HC59.A169

Analysis and economic data for long-term social and economic development issues. Chapters on the global outlook, international trade, financial flows to developing countries, regional developments and outlooks, and statistical tables. Includes a lengthy bibliography. Online from 1998 at the U.N.'s website (http://www.un.org/esa/policy/publications/papers.htm).

## Statistics

**174** **Balance of payments statistics.** International Monetary Fund. Washington: International Monetary Fund, 1981–. ISSN: 0252-3035.
382.170212                                              HG3882.B34

Continues, in part, *Balance of payments yearbook* (1947–80), which has data back to 1938. Includes information on 56 countries, organized into three parts: country tables; world and regional tables; and methodologies, compilation practices, and data sources. Contains detailed balance of payments and international investment position data, i.e., information about transactions in goods, services, and income between an economy and the rest of the world; changes in ownership in that country's monetary gold; special drawing rights (SDRs); and claims and liabilities to the rest of the world. Often used to help determine a country's short-term market potential. Also available on CD-ROM and in various aggregator services.

**175** **Bulletin of labour statistics.** International Labour Office. ill. Geneva, [Switzerland]: The Office, 1965–. ISSN: 0007-4950.
331.0212                                                HD4826.I53

Monthly and quarterly international labor data, including level of employment, numbers and percentages unemployed, average number of hours worked, average earnings or wage rates, and consumer prices. Covers 190 countries. Supplements the *Yearbook of labour statistics* (202).

**176** **The complete economic and demographic data source: CEDDS.** Woods and Poole Economics. Washington: Woods and Poole Economics, 1984–. ISSN: 1044-2545.

330.9730021                                                                     HC101.C616

Based on results of the Woods and Poole regional forecasting model of every county in the United States. Vol. 1 (1992) summarizes the results of the 1992 forecast, points out trends in regional economies, describes the database and methodology, and presents statistical tables that rank states, statistical areas, and counties in terms of population, employment, and income historically and over the forecast period up to 2015. The remainder of v. 1 and the whole of v. 2 and 3 present detailed statistical tables for counties in each state, in alphabetical order by state.

**177** **Datastream advance.** Datastream. London: Datastream International, 1995–.

A wide array of current and historic global market and economic data. Covers 700 topics, with data going back 20 years Includes: global and sector indexes, exchange-traded derivatives, investment research, fixed income and equity securities, current and historical fundamental data, foreign exchange and money markets data, real-time financial news from Dow Jones, closing prices for OTC bond instruments, forecast and historical economics data, and interest and exchange rates. Data can easily be compared and downloaded to Excel, Word, or PowerPoint.

**178** **Direction of trade statistics.** International Monetary Fund. 13 v. Washington: International Monetary Fund, 1981–1994. ISSN: 0252-306X.

382.0212                                                                     HF1016.I652a

Presents tables on the value of imports and exports to their most important trading partners for about 156 countries. A yearbook provides similar data for about 186 countries, the world, and major areas. Methodology is included in the periodic *Guide to direction of trade statistics.* Prior to 1960, data was contained in *International financial statistics.* Also available on CD-ROM and in various aggregators.

**179** **EIU.com.** Economist Intelligence Unit (Great Britain). 2005–. [London?]: Economist Intelligence Unit. http://www.eiu.com/.

Covers political, economic, and business information for 201 countries. Access to Economist Intelligence Unit publications: *Country finance, Country commerce, Country monitor, Business Africa, Business Asia, Business China, Business Eastern Europe, Business Europe, Business India intelligence, Business Latin America,* and *Business Middle East.* Country reports similar to Political Risk Yearbook (192), but with more frequent updates. Key data include GDP, forecast GDP, exports, imports, inflation, exchange rates, interest rates, consumer and producer prices, deposit rate, lending rate, money market rate, select commodity prices, and select industry data. Many numbers can be downloaded into Excel. Archives available from 1992.

180   **FAO statistical yearbook = Annuaire statistique de la FAO = Anuario estadístico de la FAO = Liang nong zu zhi tong ji nian jian.** Food and Agriculture Organization of the United Nations. Rome: Food and Agriculture Organization of the United Nations, 2004–. ISSN: 1812-0571.

HD1421.F367

Profiles food and agriculture in 155 countries. Data is by topic or by country. Country tables begin with a socio-economic overview, then an overview of agricultural sectors, followed by details of agricultural resources, production, trade, prices, food consumption, and nutritional status. Combines *FAO bulletin of statistics, FAO yearbook: Production, FAO yearbook: Trade,* and *FAO yearbook: Fertilizer.*

  Also available online at http://www.fao.org/docrep/009/a0490m/a0490m00.htm with related data in FAOSTAT (180).

181   **Global development finance.** World Bank. 2 v. Washington: World Bank, 1997–. ISSN: 1020-5454.

336.3435091724                                HJ8899.W672

External debt and financial flow data for 136 countries. Vol. 1 is *Analysis and outlook,* with financial flows to developing countries. Vol. 2 is *Summary and country tables* and includes summary data for regions and income groups. Indicators include external debt stocks and flows, major economic aggregates, key debt ratios, average terms of new commitments, and currency composition of long-term debt. Also available online and on CD-ROM, with data from 1970.

182   **Global financial data.** Global Financial Data. [2003–.] Los Angeles: Global Financial Data. http://www.globalfinancialdata.com/.

20,000 financial and economic data series for some 200 countries, dating from the 1600s to the present. Categories are daily stock market data from 1962 (open, high, low, close, volume, available in split adjusted or unadjusted format); state, national, and international real estate market data from 1830 (includes Median New Home Prices—United States, Winans International U.S. Real Estate Index—Price Only, Austria ATX Real Estate Index, Shanghai SE Real Estate Index); international bond indices from 1862; central bank interest yields; commercial paper yields; commodity indices; commodity prices; consumer price indices; U.S and European corporate bond yields, some from 1857; international deposit rates; international exchange rates, some from 1660; futures contracts; government bond yields; gross domestic product; international interbank interest rates from the 1980s; interest rate swaps from 1988 (United States, Europe, Japan); U.S. intraday data, daily from January 1933 to May 2007; international lending rates, some from 1934; overnight and call money rates, some from 1857 (monthly, weekly, daily); international population; sector indices (consumer discretionary, consumer staples, energy, finance, health care, industrials, information technology, materials, telecommunications, transports, utilities), stock indices—preferred stocks; stock indices—composites; stock indices—size and style; stock market—AMEX; stock market—NASDAQ; stock market—NYSE; stock market—OTC; stocks (capitalization, volume, dividend yields and P/E ratios, technical indicators); total return indices—bills; total return indices—bonds; total return indices—stocks; international treasury bill yields; international unemployment rates, some from 1890; and international wholesale price indices.

**183    Global market information database.** Euromonitor. [1999–.] [London]: Euromonitor. http://www.gmid.euromonitor.com/.

HD2755.5.G56

Market reports, company profiles, and demographic, economic, and marketing statistics for 205 countries. Market reports are for 16 consumer markets (food and drink, tobacco, toys, etc.) and 14 industrial and service markets (accountancy, broadcasting, chemicals, property services, etc.).

Reports have market size, market sectors, share of market, marketing activity, research and development, corporate overview, distribution, consumer profiles, market forecasts, sector forecasts, sources, and definitions. Additional reports are available for market segments, such as baby food. Company profiles have background, recent news, competitive

environment, and outlook. Consumer lifestyle reports and very useful marketing background analyze the consumer by country, gender, age, marital status, educational attainment, ethnicity, religion, home ownership, household profile, employment, income, health, eating and personal grooming habits, leisure activities, personal finance, communication, transport, and travel.

Search for data, which can be exported into Excel or browse for reports. Data are available from 1977 through 2016 and include inflation, exchange rates, GDP, GNI, government expenditures, government finance, income, labor, and money supply.

**184   Government finance statistics yearbook.** International Monetary Fund. Washington: International Monetary Fund, 1977–. ISSN: 02507374.

336.0212                                                                      HJ101.G68

Provides detailed tables for each country on revenue, grants, expenditure, lending minus repayments, financing, and debt of central governments. Also includes data on state and local governments. Annual time series beginning in 1972. Documentation can be found in supplements and *Government finance statistics manual.* Also available online and on CD-ROM.

**185   Harmonized tariff schedule of the United States.** U.S. International Trade Commission. [1987–.] Washington, D.C.: International Trade Commission. ISSN: 1066-0925. http://www. usitc.gov/tata/hts/bychapter/index.htm.

343.73056; 347.30356                                               KF6654.599.U55

Approximately 5,000 six- to ten-digit product-based numbers arranged into over 95 chapters. The schedule classifies imported merchandise for rate of duty and for statistical purposes and is used by most countries. Three statistical appendixes are Schedule C, Classification of Country and Territory Designations for U.S. Import Statistics; International Standard Country Codes; and Customs District and Port Codes.

**186   IMD world competitiveness yearbook.** IMD International. ill. Lausanne, Switzerland: IMD, 2002–. ISSN: 1026-2628.

337.05                                                                        HF1414.W67

Ranks and analyzes how a nation's business and economic environment affects the competitiveness of enterprises. Provides data for 55 national and regional economies within 323 criteria, grouped into four categories:

economic performance, government efficiency, business efficiency, and infrastructure. Country profiles include current challenges, competitiveness landscape, peer rankings, improvements, declines, strengths, weaknesses, government efficiency, business efficiency, and infrastructure. Data is gathered from international, regional, and national organizations, private institutes, and a survey conducted by the publisher. Also available online and on CD-ROM.

187 **International marketing data and statistics.** London: Euromonitor, 1975/76–. ISSN: 0308-2938.
382.09                                                                  HA42.I56

Demographic trends and forecasts and economic statistics for 161 non-European countries. Includes 24 years of data on cultural indicators, consumer market sizes and expenditures, labor force, foreign trade, health, energy, environment, IT and telecommunications, literacy and education, crime, retailing, travel and tourism, and consumer prices. Sources include the International Monetary Fund, United Nations, national statistical offices and national trade associations. Companion volume to *European marketing data and statistics* (663).

188 **Inter-university consortium for political and social research.** University of Michigan. [1997–.] Ann Arbor, Mich.: Institute for Social Research, University of Michigan. http://www.icpsr. umich.edu/.

Archive of international social science data, with a large collection of economic data. Thematic collections are Census Enumerations; Community and Urban Studies; Conflict, Aggression, Violence, Wars; Economic Behavior and Attitudes; Education; Elites and Leadership; Geography and Environment; Government Structures, Policies, and Capabilities; Health Care and Facilities; Instructional Packages; International Systems; Legal Systems; Legislative and Deliberative Bodies; Mass Political Behavior and Attitudes; Organizational Behavior; Social Indicators; Social Institutions and Behavior; Publication-Related Archive; and External Data Resources. Data, which can be downloaded for SAS, SPSS, and STATA, are available to the 500 member institutions, but some is also available to the public.

189 **MarketLine business information centre.** MarketLine. London; New York: MarketLine. http://dbic.datamonitor.com/info/about/.
HD2709

Profiles of about 10,000 large companies, 3,000 industry segments, and 100 countries. Internat. in scope. Company profiles have business descriptions, history, major products and services, revenue analysis, key employees and biographies, locations and subsidiaries, company view (often taken from an annual report), SWOT analysis, and list of top competitors. Industry profiles are approx. 20 pages long, and are Datamonitor reports. They have an executive summary, market overview, market value, market segmentation, competitive landscape, leading companies, market forecast, and further reading. Country profiles are about 30 pages long, with information on the economy, politics and government, and macroeconomic data.

The strength of this database is its international coverage of industry segments, with reports like "Beer in China." Company profiles are 45 percent United States, 35 percent European, 15 percent Asian, and 5 percent from the rest of world.

**190** **National accounts statistics.** United Nations. New York: United Nations, 1985–.

339.3                                                                      HC79.I5N387

Detailed national accounts estimates from 170–200 countries and areas. Data gathered from national statistical services and national and international source publications. This source is invaluable for providing data since 1950. Prepared by The Statistical Offices of the United Nations Secretariat. Continues *Yearbook of national accounts statistics (1957–81)*, which superseded *Statistics of national income and expenditure (1952–57)*. Also available through the National Accounts Main Aggregates database (http://unstats.un.org/unsd/snaama/Introduction.asp/), with data from 1970 to the present.

**191** **Penn world table.** Alan W. Heston, Robert Summers, Bettina Aten, University of Pennsylvania. 2006. Philadelphia: Center for International Comparisons of Production, Income and Prices, University of Pennsylvania. http://pwt.econ.upenn.edu/php_site/pwt62/pwt62_form.php.

International data on "purchasing power parity and national income accounts converted to international prices for 188 countries for some or all of the years 1950–2004."—*About PWT*. Variables are Population, Exchange Rate, Purchasing Power, Parity over GDP, Real Gross Domestic Product per Capita, Consumption Share of CGPD, Government

Share of CGDP, Investment Share of CGDP, Price Level of Gross Domestic Product, Price Level of Consumption, Price Level of Government, Price Level of Investment, Openness in Current Prices, Ratio of GNP to GDP, CGDP Relative to the United States, Real GDP per Capita (Constant Prices: Laspeyres), Real GDP per capita (Constant Prices: Chain Series), Real GDP Chain per Equivalent Adult, Real GDP Chain per Worker, Real Gross Domestic Income (RGDPL Adjusted for Terms of Trade Changes), Openness in Constant Prices, Consumption Share of RGDPL, Government Share of RGDPL, Investment Share of RGDPL, Growth Rate of Real GDP per Capita (Constant Prices: Chain Series). Data is based on World Development Indicators and National Accounts of OECD countries. Data can be downloaded as SAS and comma separated values (.csv).

192   **Political risk yearbook online.** PRS Group. 1999–. East Syracuse,
      N.Y.: PRS Group. https://www.prsgroup.com/prsgroup_
      shoppingcart/pc-48-7-political-risk-yearbook.aspx.
Political and economic risk analysis for 106 countries. Reports are PDF files with a country forecast (highlights, current data, comments and analysis, forecast scenarios, political players), and country conditions (investment climate, climate for trade including political violence and legal framework, background on geography, history, social conditions, government, political conditions, and environmental trends). Includes forecasts for GDP growth, current account, inflation, political turmoil, investment and trade restrictions, and domesic and international economic problems. Also has statistics for foreign direct investment flows by source country and sector.

193   Sourceoecd. Organisation for Economic Co-operation and
      Development. [Paris, France]: OECD. http://new.sourceoecd.org/.
A subscription database containing OECD books, reports, working papers, serials, and statistical databases on economic and social topics, as well as the environment, energy, and technological development. Focuses mainly on the 30 OECD member states and major nonmember developing countries.

Serials include journals; the OECD Factbook (Paris: OECD, 2005–) and other statistical works; and titles that forecast and analyze trends, such as the OECD Economic Outlook (Paris: Organisation for Economic Co-operation and Development, 1967–), *African economic outlook* (Paris:

African Development Bank, Development Centre of the Organisation for Economic Co-operation and Development, 2002–), International Migration Outlook (Paris: Organisation for Economic Co-operation and Development, 2006–), and OECD-FAO Agricultural Outlook (Paris: Organisation for Economic Co-operation and Development; Food and Agriculture Organization, 2005–).

Current, themed databases include the OECD Economic Outlook Database (Paris: Organisation for Economic Co-operation and Development, 2002–), SourceOECD Main Economic Indicators (Paris: Organisation for Economic Co-operation and Development, 2002–), Banking Statistics, Education Statistics, Globalisation, Indicators of Industry and Services, Insurance, International Development, International Direct Investment Statistics, International Migration Statistics, the ITCS International Trade by Commodity Database, Monthly Statistics of International Trade, the National Accounts Database, OECD Health Data, OECD Statistics on International Trade in Services, the Revenue Statistics of OECD Member Countries Database, the Science and Technology Database, the Social Expenditure Database, Structural and Demographic Business Statistics, Taxing Wages Statistics, and the Telecommunications Database. Statistical databases of the International Energy Agency are also available via this source. OECD.Stat enables users to query multiple databases simultaneously and to export search results in several formats.

Also incorporates Future Trends, an index of published and unpublished sources in more than a dozen languages covering issues affecting the public and private sectors. Glossary.

**194  Statistical yearbook: Annuaire statistique.** United Nations. 37 v.
New York: United Nations. ISSN: 0082-8459.

310.5                                                              HA12.5.U63

A summary of international statistics to continue the *Statistical yearbook of the League of Nations*. Covers population, agriculture, mining, manufacturing, finance, trade, social statistics, education, etc., of the various countries of the world, the tables usually covering a number of years. References are given to sources. A world summary was introduced beginning with v. 15 (1963), summarizing tables appearing in various chapters. The *Monthly bulletin of statistics online* (New York: U.N. Statistical Div., Dept. of Economic and Social Development, 1992–) complements this resource by providing current information.

195  **Sustainable development policy directory.** W. Alan Strong, Lesley A. Hemphill. xi, 659 p. Oxford; Malden, Mass.: Blackwell, 2006. ISBN: 1405121505.

338.927025                                                      HC79.E5S773

Provides background information on sustainable development policy and actions in Europe (with a focus on the United Kingdom and Ireland) and internationally. Each chapter gives the main challenges of that topic, lists policy documents from the 1970s to the present (with the objectives of the policy, the contents of the document, and where available, the URLs for the documents). Chapters include: Biodiversity, Climate change, Construction, Energy, Environment, Planning, Pollution, Social issues, Sustainable development policy and practice, Transport, Urban development, Waste management, and Water. Available as an e-book.

196  **United Nations common database (UNCDB).** United Nations Statistic Division. New York: United Nations Statistic Division. http://unstats.un.org/unsd/cdb/cdb_help/cdb_quick_start.asp. Provides socioeconomic data from 55 sources on 274 countries and areas, with coverage from 1948–2050. Allows comparison of data from 10 countries at a time, and data can be downloaded to Excel. Formerly a fee-based database but now free.

Covers 31 topics: agriculture, forestry, and fishing; communication and culture; construction; development assistance; economically active/not economically active population; education and learning; energy; environment; financial statistics; health, health services, impairment, disabilities, nutrition; households and families, marital status, fertility; human settlements, housing, geographical distribution of population; income, consumption and wealth; industrial production; international finance; international tourism; international trade; millennium development goals (MDG); mining and quarrying; national accounts; population composition and change; prices; public order and safety; science and technology, intellectual property; services industries; social security and welfare services; socioeconomic groups and social mobility; statistical yearbook; transport; and women and men.

197  **World development indicators.** World Bank. CD-ROM, ill. Washington: The World Bank, 1978–. ISSN: 1029-4325.

330.9005                                                        HC59.15.W656

Data compiled annually for 152 economies with populations of more than

1 million, including Taiwan, China, 56 economies with populations between 30,000 and 1 million, and smaller economies of World Bank members. Organized in six sections: World view, People, Environment, Economy, States and markets, and Global links. Data back to 1960, from national statistical organizations, the World Bank, and other authoritative sources. Especially useful since data can be scaled, ranged against a particular year, viewed by percentage change, charted, and exported. Also available online.

**198    World development report.** World Bank. ill., maps. [New York]: Oxford University Press, 1978–. ISSN: 0163-5085.
330.91724                                                     HC59.7.W659

Each report presents an overview and analysis of a currently relevant international economic development issue such as youth, or investment climate. The statistical portion presents selected social, economic, and demographic data for some 180 countries. Also available online through the World Bank at http://econ.worldbank.org/wdrs/.

**199    World economic and social survey.** United Nations. New York: United Nations, 1955–.
330.9005                                                      HC59.A169

Analysis and economic data for long-term social and economic development issues. Chapters on the global outlook, international trade, financial flows to developing countries, regional developments and outlooks, and statistical tables. Includes a lengthy bibliography. Online from 1998 at the U.N.'s website (http://www.un.org/esa/policy/publications/papers.htm).

**200    World economic outlook: A survey by the staff of the International Monetary Fund.** International Monetary Fund. ill. Washington: The International Monetary Fund, 1980–. ISSN: 0256-6877.
338.544309048                                                 HC10.W7979

Reviews world economic conditions with short- to mid-term economic projections. Over half the publication consists of expository chapters, supplemented by tables and charts, that discuss industrial countries, developing countries, and economies in transition. The statistical appendix has 43 tables, giving output, inflation, financial policies, foreign trade, current account transactions and financing, external debt and debt service, and flow of funds summary. Available online from 1993 on the IMF website (http://www.imf.org/external/ns/cs.aspx?id=29/).

201  **WRDS.** Wharton School. Philadelphia: The Wharton School,
University of Pennsylvania. http://wrds.wharton.upenn.edu/.
Provides web access through a hosting service for a number of financial
research databases, including Compustat (Englewood, Colo.: Standard
and Poor's, 2000s–), CRSP (Center for Research in Securities Prices)
(104), Dow Jones Averages, FDIC, Philadelphia Stock Exchange, Institutional Brokers Estimate System (New York: Institutional Brokers Estimate
System, 1976–), BankScope (78), CSMAR China Stock Market databases,
Eventus, First Call, and OptionMetrics.

202  **Yearbook of labour statistics.** International Labour Office.
Geneva, [Switzerland]: International Labour Office, 1936–. ISSN:
0084-3857.

331.29                                          HD4826.I63

Summarizes labor statistics on the economically active population of 184
countries and territories. Covers consumer price indexes, employment,
wages and hours of work, occupational injuries, strikes and lockouts, and
household income and expenditures. In English, French, and Spanish.
Updated by *Bulletin of labor statistics* (Geneva, [Switzerland]: The Office,
1965–) (Geneva, 1965–, quarterly). The *Retrospective edition on population census*, 1945–89 (Geneva, [Switzerland]: International Labour Office,
1990), combines and adjusts data from previous yearbooks with some new
data derived from recent or previously unpublished censuses.

# 4 > FUNCTIONAL AREAS OF BUSINESS

203  **IBISWorld United States.** IBISWorld. New York: IBISWorld.
http://www.ibisworld.com/.

HC103.I247

700 reports on the following industries: agriculture, forestry, fishing and
hunting; mining; utilities; construction; manufacturing; wholesale trade;
retail trade; transportation and warehousing; information; finance and
insurance; real estate and rental and leasing; professional, scientific, and

technical services; administrative and support and waste management and remediation services; educational services; health care and social assistance; arts, entertainment, and recreation; accommodation and food services; and other services. Setting this database apart are reports on small industries, such as parking lots and garages.

Reports include industry definition; key statistics; segmentations (products and services segmentation, major market segments, industry concentration, geographic spread); market characteristics (market size, demand determinants, domestic and international markets, basis of competition, life cycle); industry conditions (barriers to entry, taxation, industry assistance, regulation and deregulation, cost structure, capital and labor intensity, technology and systems, industry volatility, globalization); key factors (sensitivities and success factors); key competitors; and industry performance (current and historical).

# Accounting and Taxation

## Accounting Practices

**204  Accounting research manager.** CCH Incorporated. [Riverwoods, Ill.]: CCH Inc. http://www.accountingresearchmanager.com/.

HF5626

Includes a dizzying array of authoritative and interpretive financial reporting literature. Divided into accounting, SEC, auditing, and government sections, each with standards, interpretations, and examples. The acccounting section has documents from the Financial Accounting Standards Board (FASB), Emerging Issues Task Force (EITF), and International Accounting Standards Board (IASB). The SEC section includes Regulations S-X and S-K, Forms 10-K and 10-Q, SABs, Sarbanes-Oxley, Public Company Accounting Oversight Board (PCAOB), and Regulation S-B. The audit section includes AICPA, Public Company Accounting Oversight Board (PCAOB), U.S. Department of Housing and Urban Development, Office of Management and Budgets (OMB), and American Institute of Certified Public Accountants (AICPA). The government section includes GASB, GAO, and OMB.

Documents are color coded: white for authoritative, beige for interpretation, blue for proposed, and green for SEC. They also show amendments, deletions, or suspensions. SEC filings since 1994, available in Word, Adobe Acrobat, and Excel. Highlights current developments and events on the home page. An online tutorial and regularly scheduled live tutorials are available and recommended to master the database. Updated five times a day.

**205    CCH tax research network.** CCH Incorporated. Chicago: CCH, [2006–.].
Organized into fully searchable libraries: Accounting/Auditing, Federal, State, Financial and estate, Special entities, Pension and payroll, International, and Perform Plus II. Each library is organized into sub-sections that include Current features and journals; CCH explanations and analysis; Treatises; Primary sources; Practice aids; Archives; and Topical indexes. Perhaps most used for federal tax materials, but also addresses state taxes (has all State Tax Reporters), sales tax, financial and estate planning, business entities, international (treaties), tax forms, practice aids, and calculators for accountants.

The Federal library includes legislative materials, Federal Tax Code, Federal Tax Regulations, Cases, Tax Court and other trial court cases, U.S. Circuit Courts of Appeal, U.S. Supreme Court, IRS Publications (*Revenue rulings, Revenue procedures, IRS notices, IRS announcements, Letter rulings, IRS positions,* and *Internal revenue manual*), Standard Federal Tax Reporter, Federal Estate/Gift Tax Reporter, and Federal Excise Tax Reporter.

Search includes citation, check citator, news, and a thesaurus.

**206    Comperio.** PricewaterhouseCoopers. 2004–. New York: PricewaterhouseCoopers. http://www.pwc.com/Extweb/aboutus. nsf/docid/58B3A4A2F1C2053680256E2800357A82.
Full text of global financial reporting and accounting literature for Australia, Belgium, Canada, Ireland, Italy, Luxembourg, Netherlands, New Zealand, United Kingdom, and United States. Also has international documents, with International Financial Reporting Standards, International Accounting Standards, IFRS Exposure Drafts, Checklists, Practice Aids, and Interpretations, SIC Interpretations, International Standards on Auditing, IFAC Code of Ethics, International Public Sector Accounting Standards, and even the occasional text of a speech.

For the United States, it includes American Institute of Certified Public Accountants (AICPA) Professional Standards, Statements of Position Practice Bulletins, Issues Papers, Audit and Accounting Guides, Audit Risk Alerts, COSO Report, and Exposure Drafts and Response Letters; Financial Accounting Standards Board (FASB) Statements and Interpretations, Technical Bulletins, Accounting Research Bulletins, APB Opinions and

Statements, Implementations Guides, Special Reports, Exposure Drafts; GASB documents; Securities and Exchange Commission (SEC) Securities Act of 1933, Securities Exchange Act of 1934, Investment Advisor's Act of 1940, Investment Company Act of 1940; PricewaterhouseCoopers SEC Volume; Emerging Issues Task Force (EITF) Abstracts, Minutes, and Issues Summaries; Independence Standards Board (ISB) Standards and Interpretations; Derivatives Implementation Group (DIG) Issues and Discussion; PricewaterhouseCoopers Guidance and Interpretations, Accounting and Reporting Manual, Montgomery's Auditing, Twelfth Edition, Accounting and Auditing DataLines, and Implementation Guides.

Search by organization (like Australian Accounting Standards Board), territory, topic (ranges from assurance to strategic monitoring risk), document type (ranges from best practice to news and views), and publication. Optimized for Internet Explorer.

**207**  **RIA checkpoint.** RIA Group. [1998–.] [Mt. Kisco, N.Y.]: RIA Group. http://ria.thomson.com/integratedsolutions/.
Integrates RIA tax and accounting publications that provide primary tax documents and secondary analysis into one online resource with the federal tax code (from 1990), regulations, committee reports, rulings (1954 to present), Internal Revenue Bulletins (1996 to present), WG&L tax treatises and journals, IBFD Materials, state tax guides and laws, and federal tax case histories (1860 to present).

Sections of Checkpoint are Tax News, Federal Tax Library, State and Local Tax Library, International Tax Library, Pensions and Benefits Library, Estate Planning Library, Payroll Library, WG&L Financial Reporting and Management (FRM) Library, Accounting and Auditing Library, Checkpoint Archives, and Continuing Professional Education (CPE). Major publications and primary documents are *RIA daily updates, the BNA daily tax report, Federal tax coordinator* (265), *United States tax reporter, Federal tax handbook, Tax planning and practice guides, Federal income taxation of corporations and shareholders, WG&L tax dictionary, RIA worldwide tax law, Comtax news* (2001–5), *International taxes weekly newsletter* (1999–2006), *WG&L international transfer pricing treatises, RIA's executive compensation analysis, ERISA, DOL and PBGC regulations and committee reports*, SEC compliance documents, GAAP compliance documents, AICPA documents (Professional Standards, Technical Practice Aids, Audit and Accounting Guides), FASB documents (Original Pronouncements, Original Pronouncements as amended including Implementation Guides and FASB Staff Positions, Current Text, Emerging Issues Task Force,

Derivative Instruments and Hedging Activities, Exposure Drafts, Business Reporting Research Project, FASB Reports, Action Alerts, Proposed Documents, Topical Index), GASB documents (Original Pronouncements, Implementation Guides, Exposure Drafts, Topical Index), IASB (IASC Foundation Constitution, Standards, Interpretations, Implementation Guidance for IFRS and IAS, Proposal Stage Documents, News, Glossary), PCAOB documents (Advance PCAOB, Final Releases, Proposals, Final and Proposed Rules, Auditing Standards, Interim Auditing Standards, Interim Attestation Standards, Interim Quality Control Standards, Interim Ethics Standards, Interim Independence Standards, Registration System, Ethics Code), *Advance Sarbanes-Oxley cases* (2003 to present), and the *Handbook of accounting and auditing* (Boston: Warren, Gorham, and Lamont, 1982–).

Many of these resources are also available through Westlaw, CCH's Accounting Research Manager (77) or Tax Research Network (205).

## *Accounting Standards*

208   **Accounting and tax.** Bell and Howell Information and Learning. 2000. [Ann Arbor, Mich.]: Proquest Information and Learning. http://www.proquest.com/en-US/catalogs/databases/detail/pq_accounting_tax.shtml.

HF5635

Comprehensive coverage of accounting and tax, with nearly 500 sources, including top accounting journals like the *Accounting review* (257) and the *Journal of accounting research* (260). Has accounting standards from FASB, GASB, and IASB, with International Financial Reporting Standards, SIC Interpretations, IFRC Interpretations, pronouncements, statements, technical bulletins, interpretations, board opinions, American Institute of Certified Public Accountants (AICPA) Interpretations, and Emerging Issues Task Force (EITF) abstracts. A handy glossary of terms appears within the text of the FASB, GASB, and IASB documents. Other features include links to related standards and SmartView, a split screen displaying the table of contents and the text of the standards.

209   **Accounting standards.** Financial Accounting Standards Board. Stamford, Conn.: Financial Accounting Standards Board, 1982–. ISSN: 0888-7896.

657.0218                                                              HF5616.U5F537

The Financial Accounting Standards Board is recognized by the Securities and Exchange Commission and the American Institute of Certified Public Accountants as the designated authority for U.S. private sector accounting standards. While the full text of Standards, Concepts, Interpretations, Technical Bulletins, and EITF abstracts is also available through the FASB website at http://www.fasb.org/st/, the website provides no indexing or searching. FASB standards are also available in online services including Accounting research manager (77) and Comperio (206).

**210    AICPA online.** American Institute of Certified Public Accountants. 1998–. New York: American Institute of Certified Public Accountants. http://www.aicpa.org/.
"The American Institute of Certified Public Accountants is the national, professional organization for all Certified Public Accountants."—*AICPA Mission.* Includes professional resources; conferences, publications, CPE, and the AICPA library; magazines and newsletters; information on becoming a CPA; career development and workplace issues; consumer information; AICPA Media Center; and information on legislative activities and state licensing issues impacting CPAs. The professional resources area has the AICPA Code of Professional Conduct and Ethics Code, AICPA standards (Statements on Auditing Standards SAS 1–114, Statements on Standards for Attestation Engagements SSARS 1-14, Statements on Quality Control Standards 2, 3, and 5), and links to FASB, IASB, IFAC, GASB, SEC, the GAO, FASAB, and PCAOB websites.

**211    Codification of auditing standards.** American Institute of Certified Public Accountants. New York: American Institute of Certified Public Accountants, 2004–.

HF5667.C566

Presents American Institute of Certified Public Accountants (AICPA) auditing and attestation standards (*Statements on auditing standards*), as well as interpretations and amendments, which are applicable to nonissuers. Arranged by subject.

**212    Comperio.** PricewaterhouseCoopers. 2004–. New York: PricewaterhouseCoopers. http://www.pwc.com/Extweb/aboutus. nsf/docid/58B3A4A2F1C2053680256E2800357A82.
Full text of global financial reporting and accounting literature for Australia, Belgium, Canada, Ireland, Italy, Luxembourg, Netherlands, New

Zealand, United Kingdom, and United States. Also has international documents, with International Financial Reporting Standards, International Accounting Standards, IFRS Exposure Drafts, Checklists, Practice Aids, and Interpretations, SIC Interpretations, International Standards on Auditing, IFAC Code of Ethics, International Public Sector Accounting Standards, and even the occasional text of a speech.

For the United States, it includes American Institute of Certified Public Accountants (AICPA) Professional Standards, Statements of Position Practice Bulletins, Issues Papers, Audit and Accounting Guides, Audit Risk Alerts, COSO Report, and Exposure Drafts and Response Letters; Financial Accounting Standards Board (FASB) Statements and Interpretations, Technical Bulletins, Accounting Research Bulletins, APB Opinions and Statements, Implementations Guides, Special Reports, Exposure Drafts; GASB documents; Securities and Exchange Commission (SEC) Securities Act of 1933, Securities Exchange Act of 1934, Investment Advisor's Act of 1940, Investment Company Act of 1940; PricewaterhouseCoopers SEC Volume; Emerging Issues Task Force (EITF) Abstracts, Minutes, and Issues Summaries; Independence Standards Board (ISB) Standards and Interpretations; Derivatives Implementation Group (DIG) Issues and Discussion; PricewaterhouseCoopers Guidance and Interpretations, Accounting and Reporting Manual, Montgomery's Auditing, Twelfth Edition, Accounting and Auditing DataLines, and Implementation Guides.

Search by organization (like Australian Accounting Standards Board), territory, topic (ranges from assurance to strategic monitoring risk), document type (ranges from best practice to news and views), and publication. Optimized for Internet Explorer.

213    **Financial accounting research system for Windows.** Financial
       Accounting Standards Board. CD ROMs. New York: Wiley, 1990–.
       ISSN: 1551-126X.
657                                                          HF5679

Gives the text of FASB and AICPA pronouncements (FASB Statements, interpretations, technical bulletins, concepts statements, AICPA accounting interpretations and terminology bulletins). Especially useful for the text of superseded pronouncements.

214    **IAS plus.** Deloitte and Touche. 2007–. Hong Kong: Deloitte
       Touche Tohmatsu. http://www.iasplus.com/.
It's all about the international accounting standards at IAS Plus. Organized into IFRS News, Standards (summaries of IFRS 1–8, IAS 1–41),

Interpretations (summaries of documents issued by the International Financial Reporting Interpretations Committee), IASB Agenda, IASB Structure, Newsletter, Financials (IFRS Financial Statements, Disclosure Checklist, Compliance Questionnaire), links to 200 websites about International Financial Reporting Standards (including governmental and regulatory organizations, international organizations, securities exchanges, professional accountancy organizations, standard-setting bodies), Countries-Regions (table showing the country requirements for use of International Financial Reporting Standards as the primary GAAP, as used by domestic listed and unlisted companies), and Resources (odds and ends such as information on the International Valuation Standards Committee, IFAD Activities, IFAC Public Sector Committee, IFRS Reference Materials, Comment Letters to IASB, and tools like a 14-year calendar), and a currency converter.

**215    RIA checkpoint.** RIA Group. [1998–.] [Mt. Kisco, N.Y.]: RIA Group. http://ria.thomson.com/integratedsolutions/.
Integrates RIA tax and accounting publications that provide primary tax documents and secondary analysis into one online resource with the federal tax code (from 1990), regulations, committee reports, rulings (1954 to present), Internal Revenue Bulletins (1996 to present), WG&L tax treatises and journals, IBFD Materials, state tax guides and laws, and federal tax case histories (1860 to present).

Sections of Checkpoint are Tax News, Federal Tax Library, State and Local Tax Library, International Tax Library, Pensions and Benefits Library, Estate Planning Library, Payroll Library, WG&L Financial Reporting and Management (FRM) Library, Accounting and Auditing Library, Checkpoint Archives, and Continuing Professional Education (CPE). Major publications and primary documents are *RIA daily updates, the BNA daily tax report, Federal tax coordinator* (265), *United States tax reporter, Federal tax handbook, Tax planning and practice guides, Federal income taxation of corporations and shareholders, WG&L tax dictionary, RIA worldwide tax law, Comtax news* (2001–5), *International taxes weekly newsletter* (1999–2006), *WG&L international transfer pricing treatises, RIA's executive compensation analysis, ERISA, DOL and PBGC regulations and committee reports,* SEC compliance documents, GAAP compliance documents, AICPA documents (Professional Standards, Technical Practice Aids, Audit and Accounting Guides), FASB documents (Original Pronouncements, Original Pronouncements as amended including Implementation Guides and FASB Staff Positions, Current Text, Emerging Issues Task Force, Derivative Instruments and Hedging Activities, Exposure Drafts, Business Reporting Research Project,

FASB Reports, Action Alerts, Proposed Documents, Topical Index), GASB documents (Original Pronouncements, Implementation Guides, Exposure Drafts, Topical Index), IASB (IASC Foundation Constitution, Standards, Interpretations, Implementation Guidance for IFRS and IAS, Proposal Stage Documents, News, Glossary), PCAOB documents (Advance PCAOB, Final Releases, Proposals, Final and Proposed Rules, Auditing Standards, Interim Auditing Standards, Interim Attestation Standards, Interim Quality Control Standards, Interim Ethics Standards, Interim Independence Standards, Registration System, Ethics Code), *Advance Sarbanes-Oxley cases* (2003 to present), and the *Handbook of accounting and auditing* (Boston: Warren, Gorham, and Lamont, 1982–).

Many of these resources are also available through Westlaw, CCH's Accounting Research Manager (77) or Tax Research Network (205).

## Book Reviews

216 **Business information alert.** Alert Publications. Chicago: Alert Publications, 1989–. ISSN: 1042-0746.

025                                                        HF5001

Contains reviews of print and electronic business resources, and news, trends, and tips for business researchers. Also available through various aggregator databases.

217 **Journal of business and finance librarianship.** ill. Binghamton, N.Y.: Haworth Press, 1990–. ISSN: 0896-3568.

027.6905                                                     Z675.B8

Reviews of books, databases, and websites written by librarians for librarians. "The immediate focus of the journal is practice-oriented articles, but it also provides an outlet for new empirical studies on business librarianship and business information. Aside from articles, this journal offers valuable statistical and meeting reports, literature and media reviews, Website reviews, and interviews."—*About.*

## CPA Examination Guides

218 **AICPA online.** American Institute of Certified Public Accountants. 1998–. New York: American Institute of Certified Public Accountants. http://www.aicpa.org/.

"The American Institute of Certified Public Accountants is the national, professional organization for all Certified Public Accountants."—*AICPA Mission*. Includes professional resources; conferences, publications, CPE, and the AICPA library; magazines and newsletters; information on becoming a CPA; career development and workplace issues; consumer information; AICPA Media Center; and information on legislative activities and state licensing issues impacting CPAs. The professional resources area has the AICPA Code of Professional Conduct and Ethics Code, AICPA standards (Statements on Auditing Standards SAS 1-114, Statements on Standards for Attestation Engagements SSARS 1-14, Statements on Quality Control Standards 2, 3, and 5), and links to FASB, IASB, IFAC, GASB, SEC, the GAO, FASAB, and PCAOB websites.

## Dictionaries

219   **A dictionary of accounting.** 3rd ed. Gary Owen, Jonathan Law.
408 p. Oxford: Oxford University Press, 2005. ISBN: 0192806270.
HF5621.D53

This inexpensive dictionary has 3,500 definitions of terms, concepts, and jargon for management accounting, financial reporting, taxation, auditing, corporate finance, and accounting organizations. Some definitions include examples, which aid in clarity: the entry for "liquid ratio" defines the ratio, provides alternate names for the ratio, explains why the ratio is used, gives the formula for calculating it, and then goes through an example. Relevant web links are included. Written for accounting students and professionals. No index, but good cross-references. Also available through Oxford Reference Online (Oxford; New York: Oxford University Press, 2002–).

220   **The handbook of international financial terms.** Peter Moles,
Nicholas Terry. 2005. [New York]: Oxford University Press. http://www.oxfordreference.com/.
HG3881.M578

8,500 brief definitions on finance and accounting, including international stock exchanges, option strategies, and laws. Some definitions include examples. Also available in print.

221   **The international dictionary of accounting acronyms.** Library
ed. Thomas W. Morris. viii, 155 p. Chicago: Glenlake; Fitzroy
Dearborn, 1998. ISBN: 1884964567.
657.03                                                         HF5621.M67

Contains 2,000 currently used acronyms from accounting and related disciplines, with brief explanation of the acronym's meaning. Appendix for monetary units, with country, currency, and symbols. Alphabetically arranged with no index. Available as an e-book.

222  **Kohler's dictionary for accountants.** 6th ed. Eric Louis Kohler, William W. Cooper, Yuji Ijiri. xi, 574 p. Englewood Cliffs, N.J.: Prentice-Hall, 1983. ISBN: 0135166586.
657.0321                                                          HF5621.K6

The classic dictionary for accounting and still a relevant resource. Contains explanations and definitions for 2,600 terms. Kohler was chair of the American Institute of Accountants' Committee on Terminology, which may explain why his definitions are so meaningful. Accounting has changed since publication in 1983, so no collection should rely solely upon this source, but many will find entries here easier to understand than those in other newer dictionaries.

## Directories

223  **Who audits America.** Menlo Park, Calif.: Data Financial Press, 1976–. ISSN: 0149-0281.
657.4502573                                                   HF5616.U5W5

Organized by list of companies, auditor summary, national list, and state list. Useful for determining current and former auditors, especially for companies whose common shares are not traded. Appendixes for auditor codes, SIC codes, and state codes.

## Encyclopedias

224  **Encyclopedia of business and finance.** 2nd ed. Burton S. Kaliski. Macmillan Reference. Detroit: Macmillan Reference, 2007. ISBN: 0028660617.
650.03                                                          HF1001.E466

Written for the novice but useful for anyone seeking background information on management, marketing, management information systems (MIS), and finance. The 310 essays include graphs, tables, photographs, and recommended readings. Alphabetically arranged entries range from the history of computing to green marketing and the Sarbanes-Oxley Act. Also available online.

225   **Encyclopedia of management.** 5th ed. Marilyn M. Helms. xxix, 1003 p., ill. Detroit: Thomson Gale, 2006. ISBN: 0787665568.
658.00322; 658.003                                              HD30.15.E49

Covers 18 functional areas: corporate planning and strategic management, emerging topics in management, entrepreneurship, financial management and accounting, general management, human resources management, innovation and technology, international management, leadership, legal issues, management science and operations, management information systems, performance measures and assessment, personal growth and development for managers, production and operations management, quality management and total quality management, supply chain management, and training and development. Contains 350 essays written by academics and business professionals. Almost all essays are new or revised from the 2000 ed. Arranged alphabetically, entries are 3–5 pages long, with cross-references and recommended reading lists. Available as an e-book.

226   **The encyclopedia of taxation and tax policy.** 2nd ed. Joseph J. Cordes, Robert D. Ebel, Jane Gravelle. Urban Institute. xvii, 499 p., ill. Washington: Urban Institute Press, 2005. ISBN: 0877667527.
HJ2305.E53

Alphabetically arranged, with over 200 essays on tax policy, tax structure, tax compliance, and tax administration, with some coverage of public finance. Written by tax professionals, academicians, and administrators, almost all of whom are members of the National Tax Association. Entries are brief, but cover definitions, background, and relevance. Most entries include recommended readings. The 2nd ed. adds 45 new entries and updates entries with legislative changes.

## Guides and Handbooks

227   **Accountants' handbook.** 10th ed. D. R. Carmichael, Paul Rosenfield. 2 v., ill. Hoboken, N.J.: Wiley, 2003. ISBN: 047126993X.
657                                                             HF5621.A22

An authoritative handbook written by financial executives, financial analysts, partners in accounting firms, and faculty. Covers accounting standards and organizations, financial statements (presentation, analysis, areas), specialized industries, compensation and benefits, special areas of accounting, and topics in auditing and management information systems. Kept up-to-date with annual supplements. Available as an e-book.

228 **Accounting desk book: The accountant's everyday instant answer book.** 14th ed. Tom Plank. Chicago: Commerce Clearing House, 2005. ISBN: 0808089889.

Organized by topical area (information systems, standards, statement of cash flows, cost accounting, etc.). Useful for practitioners or advanced accounting students who are looking for guidance on the application of accounting standards, rules, and guidelines. Includes information on international accounting standards.

229 **AICPA audit and accounting manual: Nonauthoritative technical practice aids.** American Institute of Certified Public Accountants. Chicago: Commerce Clearing House, 1979–. ISSN: 1535-6264.

657                                                                                          HF5667.A4

Intended for the practitioner, but useful for students. Explains practices, techniques, and procedures. Includes practice aids, sample letters, and internal control checklists.

230 **Business ratios and formulas: A comprehensive guide.** Steven M. Bragg. xvii, 334 p., ill. Hoboken, N.J.: Wiley, 2002. ISBN: 0471396435.

650.01513                                                                               HF5691.B73

A wonderful guide to the world of business ratios with definitions, formulas, examples, and cautions for nearly 200 measures. "Cautions" explain when another measure would be better suited, as well as how a measure can be misunderstood. Designed for managers, but useful for anyone who must calculate and understand business ratios. Available as an e-book.

231 **The economist numbers guide: The essentials of business numeracy.** Richard Stutely. 237 p., ill. New York: Wiley, 1997. ISBN: 0471249548.

650.01513                                                                               HF5695.S83

Introduction to numerical methods and quantitative techniques used in mathematics, statistics, business, accounting, and economics. Uses extensive examples, tables, and figures to explain in layman's terms. Appendix is a dictionary, with cross-references to the main section. Indexed.

232 **Federal accounting handbook: Policies, standards, procedures, practices.** 2nd ed. Cornelius E. Tierney. Hoboken, N.J.: Wiley, 2007. ISBN: 9780471739289.

657.83500973                                                                          HJ9801.T528

Written in accessible language for anyone interested in federal accounting. Pt. 1 focuses on financial management in the federal government, with chapters on legislation and policy, the Chief Financial Officers Act of 1990, the federal budget, accounting events, budgetary and proprietary accounting practices, the Department of the Treasury, federal financial and information systems, and federal financial statements. Pt. 2 focuses on accounting practices for federal activities and transactions, with chapters on pay, leave and allowances, contracts, expenditures, receipts, reimbursements and refunds, assets, liabilities, net entity position, nonappropriated fund activities, and grants. The appendix concentrates on federal government and the Sarbanes-Oxley Act of 2002.

**233    Mathematical formulas for economists.** 3rd ed. Bernd Luderer. New York: Springer, 2006. ISBN: 9783540469018.

Defines formulas used in economics, finance, and accounting, including definitions for the notations used in formulas. Gives basic formulas, as well as alternate formulas. Prior knowledge of the usage is necessary, as context is not provided.

**234    RIA checkpoint.** RIA Group. [1998–.] [Mt. Kisco, N.Y.]: RIA Group. http://ria.thomson.com/integratedsolutions/.

Integrates RIA tax and accounting publications that provide primary tax documents and secondary analysis into one online resource with the federal tax code (from 1990), regulations, committee reports, rulings (1954 to present), Internal Revenue Bulletins (1996 to present), WG&L tax treatises and journals, IBFD Materials, state tax guides and laws, and federal tax case histories (1860 to present).

Sections of Checkpoint are Tax News, Federal Tax Library, State and Local Tax Library, International Tax Library, Pensions and Benefits Library, Estate Planning Library, Payroll Library, WG&L Financial Reporting and Management (FRM) Library, Accounting and Auditing Library, Checkpoint Archives, and Continuing Professional Education (CPE). Major publications and primary documents are *RIA daily updates, the BNA daily tax report, Federal tax coordinator (265), United States tax reporter, Federal tax handbook, Tax planning and practice guides, Federal income taxation of corporations and shareholders, WG&L tax dictionary, RIA worldwide tax law, Comtax news* (2001–5), *International taxes weekly newsletter* (1999–2006), *WG&L international transfer pricing treatises, RIA's executive compensation analysis, ERISA, DOL and PBGC regulations and committee reports,* SEC compliance documents, GAAP compliance documents, AICPA documents

(Professional Standards, Technical Practice Aids, Audit and Accounting Guides), FASB documents (Original Pronouncements, Original Pronouncements as amended including Implementation Guides and FASB Staff Positions, Current Text, Emerging Issues Task Force, Derivative Instruments and Hedging Activities, Exposure Drafts, Business Reporting Research Project, FASB Reports, Action Alerts, Proposed Documents, Topical Index), GASB documents (Original Pronouncements, Implementation Guides, Exposure Drafts, Topical Index), IASB (IASC Foundation Constitution, Standards, Interpretations, Implementation Guidance for IFRS and IAS, Proposal Stage Documents, News, Glossary), PCAOB documents (Advance PCAOB, Final Releases, Proposals, Final and Proposed Rules, Auditing Standards, Interim Auditing Standards, Interim Attestation Standards, Interim Quality Control Standards, Interim Ethics Standards, Interim Independence Standards, Registration System, Ethics Code), *Advance Sarbanes-Oxley cases* (2003 to present), and the *Handbook of accounting and auditing* (Boston: Warren, Gorham, and Lamont, 1982–).

Many of these resources are also available through Westlaw, CCH's Accounting Research Manager (77) or Tax Research Network (205).

**235    TRANSACC: Transnational accounting.** 2nd ed. Dieter Ordelheide. KPMG7. 4 v. Basingstoke, [U.K.]: Palgrave, 2001. ISBN: 1561592463.

An invaluable source for accounting practices for individual and group accounts in 21 countries, for rules from the European Union, and for International Accounting Standards. Most covered countries are European, but includes the United States, Argentina, Australia, Canada, and Japan. The 2nd ed. added Argentina, Finland, Italy, Norway and Portugal. In addition to lengthy entries on individual countries, two reference matrices provide a comparative glance across countries: one for recognition and valuation rules, the other for principles of consolidation. Each matrix provides International Accounting Standards, and refers to the relevant section in the set. Glossary defines 500 terms in English with translations into 11 other languages.

**236    The ultimate accountants' reference: Including GAAP, IRS and SEC regulations, leases, and more.** 2nd ed. Steven M. Bragg. Hoboken, N.J.: Wiley, 2006. ISBN: 9780471771555.
657.0973                                                    HF5616.U5B713

Intended for the practicing accountant, but also useful for students. Provides good background information for accounting topics. Organized into chapters on the role and structure of accounting, accounting rules and regulations, accounting reports, balance sheet and income statement, accounting management, accounting topics, and appendixes. Appendixes with a sample chart of accounts, interest tables, formulas and explanations for ratios, dictionary of terms, and due diligence checklist. Available as an e-book.

## Indexes; Abstract Journals

237 **Accounting and tax.** Bell and Howell Information and Learning. 2000. [Ann Arbor, Mich.]: Proquest Information and Learning. http://www.proquest.com/en-US/catalogs/databases/detail/pq_ accounting_tax.shtml.

HF5635

Comprehensive coverage of accounting and tax, with nearly 500 sources, including top accounting journals like the *Accounting review* (257) and the *Journal of accounting research* (260). Has accounting standards from FASB, GASB, and IASB, with International Financial Reporting Standards, SIC Interpretations, IFRC Interpretations, pronouncements, statements, technical bulletins, interpretations, board opinions, American Institute of Certified Public Accountants (AICPA) Interpretations, and Emerging Issues Task Force (EITF) abstracts. A handy glossary of terms appears within the text of the FASB, GASB, and IASB documents. Other features include links to related standards and SmartView, a split screen displaying the table of contents and the text of the standards.

238 **Accounting and tax index.** UMI. Ann Arbor, Mich.: UMI, 1992–. ISSN: 1063-0287.
016.657 Z7164.C81A224; HF5635

Abstracts for over 1,000 publications, including books, journals, government documents, and professional reports. International in scope. Sometimes awkward to use: e.g., the issuing body and standard number of a standard are needed to locate articles about the standard. That said, this is the main print index for accounting. Also available through Dialog.

239 **Accounting articles.** Commerce Clearing House. Chicago: Commerce Clearing House, 1965–.
016.657 Z7164.C81C78; HF563

Unique coverage of major accounting and taxation articles and books, as well as some coverage of finance and financial services. Organized by subject. Author index.

240    **Bibliography of works on accounting by American authors.**
Harry C. Bentley, Ruth S. Leonard. Mansfield Centre, Conn.:
Martino, 2005. ISBN: 1578985439.
016.657                                                    Z7164.C81B5; HF5635
Reprint of a 1934 bibliography of 1,500 books on accounting and bookkeeping published from 1796 to 1934. Some citations include an annotation.

241    **Rutgers accounting research center.** Rutgers Accounting Research
Center. Newark, N.J.: Rutgers Accounting Research Center. http://
raw.rutgers.edu/.
HF5625.7
Links to online resources for accounting and finance. Categories are Big Five, Professional Associations (state, U.S., and international), Journals and Publications, Education, Finance (major stock exchanges, stock quotes, currency converter, financial services), Professors, Taxation (tax analysis, tax associations, tax services), Audit and Law (audit agencies and associations, auditing software), Government, EDGAR, FASB, International, Publishers, Software, Other Sites, and Entertainment. Also links to the Rutgers Accounting Research Directory, with an index to accounting articles publ. since 1963.

## International Accounting Resources

242    **CCH tax research network.** CCH Incorporated. Chicago: CCH,
[2006–.].
Organized into fully searchable libraries: Accounting/Auditing, Federal, State, Financial and estate, Special entities, Pension and payroll, International, and Perform Plus II. Each library is organized into sub-sections that include Current features and journals; CCH explanations and analysis; Treatises; Primary sources; Practice aids; Archives; and Topical indexes. Perhaps most used for federal tax materials, but also addresses state taxes (has all State Tax Reporters), sales tax, financial and estate planning, business entities, international (treaties), tax forms, practice aids, and calculators for accountants.
The Federal library includes legislative materials, Federal Tax Code, Federal Tax Regulations, Cases, Tax Court and other trial court cases, U.S. Circuit Courts of Appeal, U.S. Supreme Court, IRS Publications (*Revenue rulings, Revenue procedures, IRS notices, IRS announcements, Letter rulings, IRS positions*, and *Internal revenue manual*), Standard Federal Tax Reporter, Federal Estate/Gift Tax Reporter, and Federal Excise Tax Reporter.
Search includes citation, check citator, news, and a thesaurus.

243 **Comperio.** PricewaterhouseCoopers. 2004–. New York: PricewaterhouseCoopers. http://www.pwc.com/Extweb/aboutus. nsf/docid/58B3A4A2F1C2053680256E2800357A82.
Full text of global financial reporting and accounting literature for Australia, Belgium, Canada, Ireland, Italy, Luxembourg, Netherlands, New Zealand, United Kingdom, and United States. Also has international documents, with International Financial Reporting Standards, International Accounting Standards, IFRS Exposure Drafts, Checklists, Practice Aids, and Interpretations, SIC Interpretations, International Standards on Auditing, IFAC Code of Ethics, International Public Sector Accounting Standards, and even the occasional text of a speech.

For the United States, it includes American Institute of Certified Public Accountants (AICPA) Professional Standards, Statements of Position Practice Bulletins, Issues Papers, Audit and Accounting Guides, Audit Risk Alerts, COSO Report, and Exposure Drafts and Response Letters; Financial Accounting Standards Board (FASB) Statements and Interpretations, Technical Bulletins, Accounting Research Bulletins, APB Opinions and Statements, Implementations Guides, Special Reports, Exposure Drafts; GASB documents; Securities and Exchange Commission (SEC) Securities Act of 1933, Securities Exchange Act of 1934, Investment Advisor's Act of 1940, Investment Company Act of 1940; PricewaterhouseCoopers SEC Volume; Emerging Issues Task Force (EITF) Abstracts, Minutes, and Issues Summaries; Independence Standards Board (ISB) Standards and Interpretations; Derivatives Implementation Group (DIG) Issues and Discussion; PricewaterhouseCoopers Guidance and Interpretations, Accounting and Reporting Manual, Montgomery's Auditing, Twelfth Edition, Accounting and Auditing DataLines, and Implementation Guides.

Search by organization (like Australian Accounting Standards Board), territory, topic (ranges from assurance to strategic monitoring risk), document type (ranges from best practice to news and views), and publication. Optimized for Internet Explorer.

244 **Deloitte international tax and business guides.** Deloitte Touche Tohmatsu. 2007–. [New York]: Deloitte Touche Tohmatsu, Economist Intelligence Unit. http://www.deloittetaxguides.com/.
Information on laws and regulations for doing business in 50 countries, with coverage of investment climate (economic structure, banking and financing, foreign trade), business and regulatory environment (registration and licensing, price controls, monopolies and restraint of trade,

intellectual property, mergers and acquisitions, accounting standards), foreign investment (foreign investment incentives and restrictions, exchange controls), choice of business entity (principal forms of doing business, establishing a branch, setting up a company), corporate and individual taxation (taxable income and rates, capital gains, foreign income and tax treaties, transfer pricing, turnover and other indirect taxes and duties, tax compliance and administration), employment law (employees' rights and remuneration, wages and benefits, termination of employment), and entry requirements. Snapshots are available for 100 countries, giving country profiles, with economic indicators, tax rates, business forms, and labor environment.

245 **The handbook of international financial terms.** Peter Moles, Nicholas Terry. 2005. [New York]: Oxford University Press. http://www.oxfordreference.com/.

HG3881.M578

8,500 brief definitions on finance and accounting, including international stock exchanges, option strategies, and laws. Some definitions include examples. Also available in print.

246 **IAS plus.** Deloitte and Touche. 2007–. Hong Kong: Deloitte Touche Tohmatsu. http://www.iasplus.com/.

It's all about the international accounting standards at IAS Plus. Organized into IFRS News, Standards (summaries of IFRS 1–8, IAS 1–41), Interpretations (summaries of documents issued by the International Financial Reporting Interpretations Committee), IASB Agenda, IASB Structure, Newsletter, Financials (IFRS Financial Statements, Disclosure Checklist, Compliance Questionnaire), links to 200 websites about International Financial Reporting Standards (including governmental and regulatory organizations, international organizations, securities exchanges, professional accountancy organizations, standard-setting bodies), Countries-Regions (table showing the country requirements for use of International Financial Reporting Standards as the primary GAAP, as used by domestic listed and unlisted companies), and Resources (odds and ends such as information on the International Valuation Standards Committee, IFAD Activities, IFAC Public Sector Committee, IFRS Reference Materials, Comment Letters to IASB, and tools like a 14-year calendar), and a currency converter.

247 **International accounting/financial reporting standards guide.** New York: Aspen, 2004–. ISSN: 1550-7181.

657                                                     HF5626.M55

Information and commentary on reporting standards issued by the International Accounting Standards Board (IASB). Organized into three parts: pt.1 is an overview of the IASB, pt. 2 provides commentary on general standards, pt. 3 gives industry standards (agriculture, banks and other financial institutions, and insurance contracts). Each year's edition covers new International Financials Reporting Standards (IFRS's) and amendments to standards. Practice pointers are weaved into the text and explain how to apply the standards. Formerly *Miller international accounting/ financial reporting standards guide*. Also available through Tax Research NetWork (205) and Accounting Research Manager (77).

**248   RIA checkpoint.** RIA Group. [1998–.] [Mt. Kisco, N.Y.]: RIA Group. http://ria.thomson.com/integratedsolutions/.

Integrates RIA tax and accounting publications that provide primary tax documents and secondary analysis into one online resource with the federal tax code (from 1990), regulations, committee reports, rulings (1954 to present), Internal Revenue Bulletins (1996 to present), WG&L tax treatises and journals, IBFD Materials, state tax guides and laws, and federal tax case histories (1860 to present).

Sections of Checkpoint are Tax News, Federal Tax Library, State and Local Tax Library, International Tax Library, Pensions and Benefits Library, Estate Planning Library, Payroll Library, WG&L Financial Reporting and Management (FRM) Library, Accounting and Auditing Library, Checkpoint Archives, and Continuing Professional Education (CPE). Major publications and primary documents are *RIA daily updates, the BNA daily tax report, Federal tax coordinator* (265), *United States tax reporter, Federal tax handbook, Tax planning and practice guides, Federal income taxation of corporations and shareholders, WG&L tax dictionary, RIA worldwide tax law, Comtax news* (2001–5), *International taxes weekly newsletter* (1999–2006), *WG&L international transfer pricing treatises, RIA's executive compensation analysis, ERISA, DOL and PBGC regulations and committee reports,* SEC compliance documents, GAAP compliance documents, AICPA documents (Professional Standards, Technical Practice Aids, Audit and Accounting Guides), FASB documents (Original Pronouncements, Original Pronouncements as amended including Implementation Guides and FASB Staff Positions, Current Text, Emerging Issues Task Force, Derivative Instruments and Hedging Activities, Exposure Drafts, Business Reporting Research Project, FASB Reports, Action Alerts, Proposed Documents, Topical Index), GASB documents (Original Pronouncements, Implementation Guides, Exposure Drafts, Topical Index), IASB (IASC Foundation Constitution, Standards,

Interpretations, Implementation Guidance for IFRS and IAS, Proposal Stage Documents, News, Glossary), PCAOB documents (Advance PCAOB, Final Releases, Proposals, Final and Proposed Rules, Auditing Standards, Interim Auditing Standards, Interim Attestation Standards, Interim Quality Control Standards, Interim Ethics Standards, Interim Independence Standards, Registration System, Ethics Code), *Advance Sarbanes-Oxley cases* (2003 to present), and the *Handbook of accounting and auditing* (Boston: Warren, Gorham, and Lamont, 1982–).

Many of these resources are also available through Westlaw, CCH's Accounting Research Manager (77) or Tax Research Network (205).

## Internet Resources

249  **Deloitte international tax and business guides.** Deloitte Touche Tohmatsu. 2007–. [New York]: Deloitte Touche Tohmatsu, Economist Intelligence Unit. http://www.deloittetaxguides.com/.
Information on laws and regulations for doing business in 50 countries, with coverage of investment climate (economic structure, banking and financing, foreign trade), business and regulatory environment (registration and licensing, price controls, monopolies and restraint of trade, intellectual property, mergers and acquisitions, accounting standards), foreign investment (foreign investment incentives and restrictions, exchange controls), choice of business entity (principal forms of doing business, establishing a branch, setting up a company), corporate and individual taxation (taxable income and rates, capital gains, foreign income and tax treaties, transfer pricing, turnover and other indirect taxes and duties, tax compliance and administration), employment law (employees' rights and remuneration, wages and benefits, termination of employment), and entry requirements. Snapshots are available for 100 countries, giving country profiles, with economic indicators, tax rates, business forms, and labor environment.

250  **Ernst and Young.** Ernst and Young. 2007. London: Ernst and Young. http://www.ey.com/global/content.nsf/International/Industry_Overview/.
Ernst and Young provides "accounting and auditing, tax reporting and operations, tax advisory, business risk services, technology and security risk services, transaction advisory, and human capital services." The site is useful for articles on financial management, corporate governance, initial public offerings (IPOs), and industry reports (asset management, automotive, banking and capital markets, biotechnology, consumer products,

insurance, media and entertainment, mining and metals, oil and gas, pharmaceuticals, real estate and construction, hospitality and leisure, technology, telecommunications, utilities).

**251  IAS plus.** Deloitte and Touche. 2007–. Hong Kong: Deloitte Touche Tohmatsu. http://www.iasplus.com/.
It's all about the international accounting standards at IAS Plus. Organized into IFRS News, Standards (summaries of IFRS 1–8, IAS 1–41), Interpretations (summaries of documents issued by the International Financial Reporting Interpretations Committee), IASB Agenda, IASB Structure, Newsletter, Financials (IFRS Financial Statements, Disclosure Checklist, Compliance Questionnaire), links to 200 websites about International Financial Reporting Standards (including governmental and regulatory organizations, international organizations, securities exchanges, professional accountancy organizations, standard-setting bodies), Countries-Regions (table showing the country requirements for use of International Financial Reporting Standards as the primary GAAP, as used by domestic listed and unlisted companies), and Resources (odds and ends such as information on the International Valuation Standards Committee, IFAD Activities, IFAC Public Sector Committee, IFRS Reference Materials, Comment Letters to IASB, and tools like a 14-year calendar), and a currency converter.

**252  Rutgers accounting research center.** Rutgers Accounting Research Center. Newark, N.J.: Rutgers Accounting Research Center. http://raw.rutgers.edu/.

HF5625.7

Links to online resources for accounting and finance. Categories are Big Five, Professional Associations (state, U.S., and international), Journals and Publications, Education, Finance (major stock exchanges, stock quotes, currency converter, financial services), Professors, Taxation (tax analysis, tax associations, tax services), Audit and Law (audit agencies and associations, auditing software), Government, EDGAR, FASB, International, Publishers, Software, Other Sites, and Entertainment. Also links to the Rutgers Accounting Research Directory, with an index to accounting articles publ. since 1963.

## *Organizations and Associations*

**253  AICPA online.** American Institute of Certified Public Accountants. 1998–. New York: American Institute of Certified Public Accountants. http://www.aicpa.org/.

"The American Institute of Certified Public Accountants is the national, professional organization for all Certified Public Accountants."—*AICPA Mission.* Includes professional resources; conferences, publications, CPE, and the AICPA library; magazines and newsletters; information on becoming a CPA; career development and workplace issues; consumer information; AICPA Media Center; and information on legislative activities and state licensing issues impacting CPAs. The professional resources area has the AICPA Code of Professional Conduct and Ethics Code, AICPA standards (Statements on Auditing Standards SAS 1–114, Statements on Standards for Attestation Engagements SSARS 1-14, Statements on Quality Control Standards 2, 3, and 5), and links to FASB, IASB, IFAC, GASB, SEC, the GAO, FASAB, and PCAOB websites.

**254    American Accounting Association.** American Accounting Association, Rutgers Accounting Research Center. [Newark, N.J.]: Rutgers Accounting Research Center. http://aaahq.org/.
Founded in 1916, the Association's purpose is to "influence ways of thinking about professional practice, education, business issues and standard setting."—*Mission and Shared Values*
    Includes information on Association journals (*The accounting review, Issues in accounting education, Accounting horizons*), faculty development resources, awards, a placement service, links to other accounting sites and assoications, and a discussion forum.

**255    IAS plus.** Deloitte and Touche. 2007–. Hong Kong: Deloitte Touche Tohmatsu. http://www.iasplus.com/.
It's all about the international accounting standards at IAS Plus. Organized into IFRS News, Standards (summaries of IFRS 1–8, IAS 1–41), Interpretations (summaries of documents issued by the International Financial Reporting Interpretations Committee), IASB Agenda, IASB Structure, Newsletter, Financials (IFRS Financial Statements, Disclosure Checklist, Compliance Questionnaire), links to 200 websites about International Financial Reporting Standards (including governmental and regulatory organizations, international organizations, securities exchanges, professional accountancy organizations, standard-setting bodies), Countries-Regions (table showing the country requirements for use of International Financial Reporting Standards as the primary GAAP, as used by domestic listed and unlisted companies), and Resources (odds and ends such as information on the International Valuation Standards Committee, IFAD Activities, IFAC Public

Sector Committee, IFRS Reference Materials, Comment Letters to IASB, and tools like a 14-year calendar), and a currency converter.

256  **Rutgers accounting research center.** Rutgers Accounting Research Center. Newark, N.J.: Rutgers Accounting Research Center. http://raw.rutgers.edu/.

HF5625.7

Links to online resources for accounting and finance. Categories are Big Five, Professional Associations (state, U.S., and international), Journals and Publications, Education, Finance (major stock exchanges, stock quotes, currency converter, financial services), Professors, Taxation (tax analysis, tax associations, tax services), Audit and Law (audit agencies and associations, auditing software), Government, EDGAR, FASB, International, Publishers, Software, Other Sites, and Entertainment. Also links to the Rutgers Accounting Research Directory, with an index to accounting articles publ. since 1963.

## Periodicals

257  **The accounting review.** American Accounting Association. Sarasota, Fla.: American Accounting Association, 1926–. ISSN: 0001-4826.

HF5601.A6

Published by the American Accounting Association, with research articles in all areas of accounting for a primary audience of academicians and graduate students. A typical issue has articles on reporting incentives in European firms, the value of cash flow news on SEC filings, the evolution of stock option accounting, the influence of venture capitalists on IPO earnings, the existence and extent of abnormal accrual anomaly, and the effects of regulations on auditor-provided tax services. Most articles have a U.S. bent, but some occasionally venture into international topics.

258  **Harvard business review.** ill. Boston: Graduate School of Business Administration, Harvard University. ISSN: 0017-8012.

330.904                                                                 HF5001.H3

Articles, best practices, book reviews, and case studies on communication, finance and accounting, global business, innovation and entrepreneurship, leadership, management, organizational development, sales and marketing, strategy and execution, and technology and operations. Also available online, through Business Source Elite (791).

259 **Journal of accounting and economics.** University of Rochester. ill. Amsterdam, [The Netherlands]: North-Holland, 1979–. ISSN: 0165-4101.

HF5601.J724

Articles that apply economic theory to accounting, including discussions of the role of accounting within the firm, in capital markets, and in financial contracts. Intended audience is academicians and accounting practioners. Available in online form.

260 **Journal of accounting research.** London School of Economics and Political Science. ill. Chicago; [London]: Institute of Professional Accounting, Graduate School of Business, University of Chicago; London School of Economics and Political Science, University of London, 1963–. ISSN: 0021-8456.

657.05                                                                                                     HF5601.J75

Publishes theoretical, empirical, and clinical research in all areas of accounting. Four regular issues plus one conference issue (published in May) covering the previous year's annual accounting research conference from the Institute of Professional Accounting at the University of Chicago's Graduate School of Business. Typical articles cover international accounting standards, insider trading and voluntary disclosure, stock returns, ownership concentration in privatized firms, the press as a watchdog for accounting fraud, and auditors' responses to political connections in Malaysia.

## *Reviews of Research and Trends*

261 **Accounting trends and techniques.** American Institute of Certified Public Accountants. [New York]: American Institute of Certified Public Accountants, 1945/47–. ISSN: 1531-4340.

HF5681.B2A35

Annual survey of accounting practices. Used to analyze accounting information disclosed in stockholders' reports. Organized around the financial statement (balance sheet, income statement, statement of cash flows), including information from the independent auditors' report. Includes appendix for the 600 companies surveyed, plus index for companies, pronouncements, and subjects.

**262  More than a numbers game: A brief history of accounting.**
Thomas A. King. Hoboken, N.J.: John Wiley & Sons, 2006. ISBN:
9780470008737.
657.0973                                                    HF5616.U5K53
With chapters on double entry, railroads, taxes, costs, disclosure, standards, science, inflation, volatility, intangibles, debt, options, earnings,
and SOX (Sarbanes-Oxley), this is an engaging glimpse at the events that
have shaped modern U.S. accounting. Especially useful for the context it
provides. Available as an e-book.

## Tax Guides

**263  International accounting/financial reporting standards guide.**
New York: Aspen, 2004–. ISSN: 1550-7181.
657                                                          HF5626.M55
Information and commentary on reporting standards issued by the International Accounting Standards Board (IASB). Organized into three parts:
pt.1 is an overview of the IASB, pt. 2 provides commentary on general
standards, pt. 3 gives industry standards (agriculture, banks and other
financial institutions, and insurance contracts). Each year's edition covers
new International Financials Reporting Standards (IFRS's) and amendments to standards. Practice pointers are woven into the text and explain
how to apply the standards. Formerly *Miller international accounting/
financial reporting standards guide.* Also available through Tax Research
NetWork (205) and Accounting Research Manager (77).

## Tax Services

**264  CCH tax research network.** CCH Incorporated. Chicago: CCH,
[2006–.].
Organized into fully searchable libraries: Accounting/Auditing, Federal,
State, Financial and estate, Special entities, Pension and payroll, International, and Perform Plus II. Each library is organized into sub-sections that
include Current features and journals; CCH explanations and analysis;
Treatises; Primary sources; Practice aids; Archives; and Topical indexes.
Perhaps most used for federal tax materials, but also addresses state taxes
(has all State Tax Reporters), sales tax, financial and estate planning, business entities, international (treaties), tax forms, practice aids, and calculators for accountants.

The Federal library includes legislative materials, Federal Tax Code, Federal Tax Regulations, Cases, Tax Court and other trial court cases, U.S. Circuit Courts of Appeal, U.S. Supreme Court, IRS Publications (*Revenue rulings, Revenue procedures, IRS notices, IRS announcements, Letter rulings, IRS positions,* and *Internal revenue manual*), Standard Federal Tax Reporter, Federal Estate/Gift Tax Reporter, and Federal Excise Tax Reporter. Search includes citation, check citator, news, and a thesaurus.

**265   Federal tax coordinator.** 2nd [ed.] Research Institute of America. New York: Research institute of America, 1984–. ISSN: 10603343.

HJ3252.F4

Easy to understand analysis of tax laws (income, gift, estate, and excise), regulations, IRS rulings, and releases, as well as text of the Internal Revenue Code and Treasury Regulations. Arranged by subject, with a good index. Updated weekly. Similar to *CCH Standard federal tax reporter* (267). Available through RIA Checkpoint (207) and Westlaw.

**266   RIA checkpoint.** RIA Group. [1998–.] [Mt. Kisco, N.Y.]: RIA Group. http://ria.thomson.com/integratedsolutions/.
Integrates RIA tax and accounting publications that provide primary tax documents and secondary analysis into one online resource with the federal tax code (from 1990), regulations, committee reports, rulings (1954 to present), Internal Revenue Bulletins (1996 to present), WG&L tax treatises and journals, IBFD Materials, state tax guides and laws, and federal tax case histories (1860 to present).

Sections of Checkpoint are Tax News, Federal Tax Library, State and Local Tax Library, International Tax Library, Pensions and Benefits Library, Estate Planning Library, Payroll Library, WG&L Financial Reporting and Management (FRM) Library, Accounting and Auditing Library, Checkpoint Archives, and Continuing Professional Education (CPE). Major publications and primary documents are *RIA daily updates, the BNA daily tax report, Federal tax coordinator* (265), *United States tax reporter, Federal tax handbook, Tax planning and practice guides, Federal income taxation of corporations and shareholders, WG&L tax dictionary, RIA worldwide tax law, Comtax news* (2001–5), *International taxes weekly newsletter* (1999–2006), *WG&L international transfer pricing treatises, RIA's executive compensation analysis, ERISA, DOL and PBGC regulations and committee reports,* SEC compliance documents, GAAP compliance documents, AICPA documents (Professional Standards, Technical Practice Aids, Audit and Accounting Guides), FASB documents (Original Pronouncements,

Original Pronouncements as amended including Implementation Guides and FASB Staff Positions, Current Text, Emerging Issues Task Force, Derivative Instruments and Hedging Activities, Exposure Drafts, Business Reporting Research Project, FASB Reports, Action Alerts, Proposed Documents, Topical Index), GASB documents (Original Pronouncements, Implementation Guides, Exposure Drafts, Topical Index), IASB (IASC Foundation Constitution, Standards, Interpretations, Implementation Guidance for IFRS and IAS, Proposal Stage Documents, News, Glossary), PCAOB documents (Advance PCAOB, Final Releases, Proposals, Final and Proposed Rules, Auditing Standards, Interim Auditing Standards, Interim Attestation Standards, Interim Quality Control Standards, Interim Ethics Standards, Interim Independence Standards, Registration System, Ethics Code), *Advance Sarbanes-Oxley cases* (2003 to present), and the *Handbook of accounting and auditing* (Boston: Warren, Gorham, and Lamont, 1982–).

Many of these resources are also available through Westlaw, CCH's Accounting Research Manager (77) or Tax Research Network (205).

**267   Standard federal tax reporter.** Commerce Clearing House.
Chicago: Commerce Clearing House, 1945–. ISSN: 0162-3494.
343.7304; 347.3034                                    KF6285.C67

The best known tax service, with analysis and primary documents for federal tax law (such as personal income, corporate income, business expenses and deductions, mergers and acquisitions, employee benefit plans, tax accounting, exempt organizations, capital gains and losses). Primary documents include: Internal Revenue code sections, regulations and proposed regulations, and excerpts of committee reports. Most used for CCH explanations of federal tax law and the annotations of cases and rulings that go back to 1913. Arranged by code section, with four topical indexes, each in a separate volume: in the *Index* volume; in *Internal Revenue Code*, v. 1; and the cumulative index in the *New Matters* volume. Updated weekly. Available through CCH Tax Research Network (205) and LexisNexis. Similar to RIA's *Federal tax coordinator, 2nd ed.* (265).

# Business Law

## Book Reviews

**268   Journal of business and finance librarianship.** ill. Binghamton,
N.Y.: Haworth Press, 1990–. ISSN: 0896-3568.
027.6905                                              Z675.B8

Reviews of books, databases, and websites written by librarians for librarians. "The immediate focus of the journal is practice-oriented articles, but it also provides an outlet for new empirical studies on business librarianship and business information. Aside from articles, this journal offers valuable statistical and meeting reports, literature and media reviews, Website reviews, and interviews."—*About*

## Dictionaries

**269** **A dictionary of human resource management.** Edmund Heery, Mike Noon. xxvii, 449 p. Oxford; New York: Oxford University Press, 2001. ISBN: 0198296185.
658.3003                                                    HF5549.A23D53

Written for students and those new to human resources. Includes jargon (such as *dumb-sizing*) and legal terms (such as *duty of care*). Appendixes for classification of key terms, abbreviations, and acronyms. No index. Available in online form.

**270** **A handbook of business law terms.** Bryan A. Garner, David W. Schultz. iii, 637 p. St. Paul, Minn.: West Group, 1999. ISBN: 0314239359.
346.730703                                                    KF390.B84H36

Clear definitions for more than 3,000 words and phrases in business law. Useful for both students and business practitioners.

**271** **The new Palgrave dictionary of economics and the law.** Peter Newman. 3 v., ill. London; New York: Macmillan Reference; Stockton Press, 2004. ISBN: 033399755.
330.03                                                    K487.E3N49

Contains 399 signed articles with international coverage on the legal aspects of economics, such as airline deregulation and property rights. Includes statutes, treaties, directives, and cases. Written by 340 contributors from eight countries.

## Encyclopedias

**272** **Affirmative action: An encyclopedia.** James A. Beckman. 2 v., 1074 p., ill. Westport, Conn.: Greenwood Press, 2004. ISBN: 1573565199.
331.133097303                                                    HF5549.5.A34A426

Entries on affirmative action from legal, political science, historical, and sociological perspectives. Contributors are both academics and practitioners, providing a balanced perspective. Appendixes include full text of *Gratz v. Bollinger* and *Grutter v. Bollinger.* Selective bibliography and index. Available as an e-book.

**273  Encyclopedia of law and economics.** Boudewijn Bouckaert, Gerrit de Geest. 5 v. Cheltenham, England; Northampton, Mass.: Edward Elgar, 2000. ISBN: 185898565X.

330                                                                   K48.E3E53

Written by more than 350 legal scholars. Contains more than 400 signed entries on legal systems around the world, as well as on legal concepts. Country profiles include legal history, court structure, and impact of the legal system on the country. Entries include references, a bibliography, and cases, where applicable; entries can be lengthy.

In five volumes: v. 1, *The history and methodology of law and economics*; v. 2, *Civil law and economics*; v. 3, *The regulation of contracts*; v. 4, *The economics of public and tax law*; v. 5, *The economics of crime and litigation.* Also available online at http://encyclo.findlaw.com/.

**274  Encyclopedia of management.** 5th ed. Marilyn M. Helms. xxix, 1003 p., ill. Detroit: Thomson Gale, 2006. ISBN: 0787665568.

658.00322; 658.003                                              HD30.15.E49

Covers 18 functional areas: corporate planning and strategic management, emerging topics in management, entrepreneurship, financial management and accounting, general management, human resources management, innovation and technology, international management, leadership, legal issues, management science and operations, management information systems, performance measures and assessment, personal growth and development for managers, production and operations management, quality management and total quality management, supply chain management, and training and development. Contains 350 essays written by academics and business professionals. Almost all essays are new or revised from the 2000 ed. Arranged alphabetically, entries are 3–5 pages long, with cross-references and recommended reading lists. Available as an e-book.

**275  The encyclopedia of taxation and tax policy.** 2nd ed. Joseph J. Cordes, Robert D. Ebel, Jane Gravelle, Urban Institute. xvii, 499 p., ill. Washington: Urban Institute Press, 2005. ISBN: 0877667527.

HJ2305.E53

Alphabetically arranged, with over 200 essays on tax policy, tax structure, tax compliance, and tax administration, with some coverage of public finance. Written by tax professionals, academicians, and administrators, almost all of whom are members of the National Tax Association. Entries are brief, but cover definitions, background, and relevance. Most entries include recommended readings. The 2nd ed. adds 45 new entries and updates entries with legislative changes.

276 **Encyclopedia of white-collar crime.** Jurg Gerber, Eric L. Jensen. Westport, Conn.: Greenwood Press, 2006. ISBN: 0313335249.
364.168097303                                                                HV6768.E65

More than 500 entries giving history, definitions, law, investigations, prosecutions, biographical sketches, and events. Arranged in 17 topics: business fraud and crimes, companies, consumers, countries and regions, criminology and justice, financial and securities fraud, government, laws, medical and healthcare fraud, people, political scandals, pollution, products, regulation, scams and swindles, war profiteering, and work-related crimes. Includes cross-references, further readings, and a chronology of events.

277 **McCarthy's desk encyclopedia of intellectual property.** 3rd ed. J. Thomas McCarthy, Roger E. Schechter, David J. Franklyn. xxi, 736 p. Washington: Bureau of National Affairs, 2004. ISBN: 1570184011.

KF2976.4.M38

Definitions for 800 words, phrases, conventions and statutes in the areas of patents, trademarks, copyright, trade secrets, entertainment, and computer law. McCarthy is a professor at the University of San Francisco School of Law. Arranged alphabetically, with references to relevant cases and statutes. Appendixes list the superintendents and commissioners of patents and trademarks from 1802 to the present, the assistant commissioners of trademarks from 1953 to the present, annual patent applications filed and issued between 1790 and 1994, annual trademark registrations and renewals between 1870 and 1994, and the registers of copyrights from 1897 to the present.

## Guides and Handbooks

278 **BNA labor and employment law library.** Bureau of National Affairs (Washington, D.C.). [1999–.] [Washington, D.C.]: Bureau of National Affairs. http://laborandemploymentlaw.bna.com/.

Cases, summaries of developments, manuals, and explanations of state and federal laws in areas like arbitration, collective bargaining, wages and hours, fair employment, disability, and employee rights. Includes Labor-Management Relations with Decisions from 1984, Fair Employment Practices from 1965, Individual Employment Rights from 1986, BNA's *Labor relations reporter*, *HR policy handbook*, and *Client letters, Checklists, and Forms*.

**279    The business guide to legal literacy: What every manager should know about the law.** Hanna Hasl-Kelchner. xii, 372 p., ill. San Francisco: Jossey-Bass, 2006. ISBN: 0787982555.
346.7307                                                                    KF390.B84H37

Uses real-life stories to increase understanding about how the law impacts business. Written by a corporate lawyer who taught business law to MBA students at Duke University. Pt. 1 addresses legal risk; pt. 2, actions that employees should take; and pt. 3, actions that organizations should take. Appendixes include a legal primer. Written for managers, but useful for anyone trying to grasp legal risks.

**280    Collective bargaining negotiations and contracts.** Bureau of National Affairs. loose-leaf. Washington: Bureau of National Affairs, 1945–. ISSN: 0010-079X.
                                                                       KF3408.A8C644

Information on preparing and conducting contract negotiations, with sample clauses, cost of living, and consumer price information.

**281    The employer's legal handbook.** 7th ed. Fred Steingold, Amy Delpo. 1 v. (various pagings), ill. Berkeley, Calif.: Nolo, 2005. ISBN: 1413301835.
344.7301                                                                    KF3455.Z9S74

Practical coverage of hiring, personnel practices, wages and hours, employee benefits, taxes, family and medical leave, health and safety, illegal discrimination, workers with disabilities, termination, employee privacy, independent contractors, unions, lawyers and legal research. Appendixes for: labor departments and agencies, state drug and alcohol testing laws, state laws on employee arrest and conviction records, state laws on access to personnel records, state minimum wage laws for tipped and regular employees, state meal and rest breaks, state health insurance continuation laws, state family and medical leave laws, right-to-know laws (hazardous chemicals), state laws prohibiting discrimination in employment, agencies that enforce laws prohibiting discrimination in employment, and state laws that control final paychecks. Available as an e-book.

**282 Handbook of organizational justice.** Jerald Greenberg, Jason Colquitt. xxvi, 647 p., ill. Mahwah, N.J.: Lawrence Erlbaum Associates, 2005. ISBN: 0805842039.

658.314                                                             HD6971.3.H36

Provides historical perspective and summary of current research. Articles cover consequences of treatment and justice in the workplace, cross-cultural differences, and the development of organizational justice. Looks at organizational justice from the perspective of the public's perception of fairness in organizations. Author and subject indexes.

**283 The law of securities regulation.** Rev. 5th ed. Thomas Lee Hazen. xxxvii, 927 p. St. Paul, Minn.: Thomson/West, 2006. ISBN: 9780314172457.

KF1439.H39

Annual introduction and overview to U.S. securities laws. Five ch. on the Securities Act of 1933, with other chapters on state blue sky laws, market regulation, civil liability, shareholder suffrage, market manipulation, the Public Utility Holding Act of 1935, debt securities and the Trust Indenture Act of 1939, federal regulation of investment companies and the Investment Company Act of 1940, the Investment Advisers Act of 1940, and overviews of related laws. Appendix on securities research using Westlaw.

**284 Understanding international business and financial transactions.** 2nd ed. Jerold A. Friedland. xix, 359 p., ill. Newark, N.J.: LexisNexis, 2005. ISBN: 0820563390.

346.7307                                                             KF390.B8F75

Chapters on Money, currency and finance international trade; Rules of international trade; United States trade law; International sales; Operating in foreign markets; and Taxation of international transactions. Friedland, a law professor at DePaul, presents a solid overview of international business law.

## Indexes; Abstract Journals

**285 BNA labor and employment law library.** Bureau of National Affairs (Washington, D.C.). [1999–.] [Washington, D.C.]: Bureau of National Affairs. http://laborandemploymentlaw.bna.com/.

Cases, summaries of developments, manuals, and explanations of state and federal laws in areas like arbitration, collective bargaining, wages and hours, fair employment, disability, and employee rights. Includes Labor-Management Relations with Decisions from 1984, Fair Employment Practices from 1965, Individual Employment Rights from 1986, BNA's *Labor relations reporter*, *HR policy handbook*, and *Client letters, Checklists, and Forms.*

## Internet Resources

286   **Code of federal regulations.** U.S. National Archives and Records Administration, Office of the Federal Register. Washington: National Archives and Records Administration, Office of the Federal Register. ISSN: 1946-4975. http://www.gpoaccess.gov/cfr/about.html.

342                                                                                           KF70

Cited as *CFR.* Supersedes *Code of federal regulations of the United States of America . . .* (1st ed., 1938).

A subject arrangement of administrative agency rules and regulations, in paper format consisting of more than 200 paperback volumes revised and reissued each year on a staggered, quarterly basis. Arranged in a subject scheme of 50 titles divided into chapters, each of which contains the regulations of a specific agency. A list in the back of each volume lists the title and chapter of each agency's regulations. Title 3 contains presidential documents, including proclamations and executive orders. An "Index and finding aids" volume provides access by agency name and subject.

New rules as they are promulgated appear in the daily *Federal register* (294). Each issue has a cumulative table for the month, noting which parts of the *CFR* are affected by new regulations. An index by agency is published monthly and cumulates references since the beginning of the year.

Free electronic access to the *CFR* and the *Federal register* is available from the website of the Government Printing Office (GPO). The *CFR* is available at permanent URL http://purl.access.gpo.gov/GPO/LPS494 both in HTML and PDF formats. The *Federal register* is available at http://purl.access.gpo.gov/GPO/LPS1756. The GPO also makes available the *e-CFR*, which keeps the text of the *CFR* fully updated with the new rules published in the *Federal register*. The *e-CFR* is usually only 2-3 days behind; the currency is indicated in bold red type at the top of the home page.

An electronic version of the *CFR* in PDF format, complete back to its earliest publication in 1938, is available on HeinOnline (Buffalo, N.Y.: W. S. Hein), as is the *Federal register.*

287    **Deloitte international tax and business guides.** Deloitte Touche Tohmatsu. 2007–. [New York]: Deloitte Touche Tohmatsu, Economist Intelligence Unit. http://www.deloittetaxguides.com/. Information on laws and regulations for doing business in 50 countries, with coverage of investment climate (economic structure, banking and financing, foreign trade), business and regulatory environment (registration and licensing, price controls, monopolies and restraint of trade, intellectual property, mergers and acquisitions, accounting standards), foreign investment (foreign investment incentives and restrictions, exchange controls), choice of business entity (principal forms of doing business, establishing a branch, setting up a company), corporate and individual taxation (taxable income and rates, capital gains, foreign income and tax treaties, transfer pricing, turnover and other indirect taxes and duties, tax compliance and administration), employment law (employees' rights and remuneration, wages and benefits, termination of employment), and entry requirements. Snapshots are available for 100 countries, giving country profiles, with economic indicators, tax rates, business forms, and labor environment.

288    **Federal deposit insurance corporation.** Federal Deposit Insurance Corporation. [1996–.] [Washington, D.C.]: Federal Deposit Insurance Corporation. http://www.fdic.gov/.

HG2441

The site is organized into: Deposit Insurance, Consumer Protection, Industry Analysis, Regulation & Examinations, Asset Sales, and News & Events. Includes Call Reports and Thrift Financial Reports from 1998 to the present; an institution directory for federally insured institutions; Summary of Deposits; Quarterly Banking Profile from December 31, 1994; statistics on banking and depository institutions; and laws and regulations.

289    **Harmonized tariff schedule of the United States.** U.S. International Trade Commission. [1987–.] Washington, D.C.: International Trade Commission. ISSN: 1066-0925. http://www. usitc.gov/tata/hts/bychapter/index.htm.

343.73056; 347.30356                                                KF6654.599.U55

Approximately 5,000 six- to ten-digit product-based numbers arranged into over 95 chapters. The schedule classifies imported merchandise for rate of duty and for statistical purposes and is used by most countries. Three statistical appendixes are Schedule C, Classification of Country and Territory Designations for U.S. Import Statistics; International Standard Country Codes; and Customs District and Port Codes.

290    **LLRX.com.** Sabrina I. Pacifici Law Library Resource Xchange. 1996–. [Silver Spring, Md.]: Law Library Resource XChange. http://www.llrx.com/.
A guide to legal resources, especially court rules, forms, and dockets, this site also has pathfinders, presentations, and articles with tips on legal research, information management, government resources, and competitive intelligence.

## *Organizations and Associations*

291    **American bar association, section of business law.** American Bar Association. Chicago: American Bar Association. http://www. abanet.org/buslaw/home.shtml.
Includes news, program materials, publications (*Business law today, The business lawyer*, and various monographs), event calendar, and committee links.

292    **Association of corporate counsel.** Association of Corporate Counsel. 1997–. Washington, D.C.: Association of Corporate Counsel. http://www.acc.com/.
Intended for in-house counsel, the site offers research (virtual library with legal forms, statistics and surveys, compliance and ethics), education, member directory, ACC publications (*ACC docket, European and Canadian briefings*), public policy, and career resources.

## *Periodicals*

293    **Annual review of banking and financial law.** Boston University. Newark, N.J.: LexisNexis, 2003–. ISSN: 1544-4627.
346                                                           K1.N53
Edited by law students at Boston University's Morin Center for Banking and Financial Law, with articles written by professors and practitioners. Topics include banking, securities, financial services, and administrative and general corporate law.

294 **Federal register.** U.S. National Archives and Records
Administration, Office of the Federal Register. Washington, D.C.:
National Archives and Records Administration, Office of the Federal
Register. ISSN: 0097-6326. http://www.gpoaccess.gov/fr/index.html.
353.005                                                        KF70

Official repository for the daily publication of all newly adopted rules and
regulations, proposed rules, and notices of federal agencies and organizations, executive orders, and other presidential documents. When a regulation is codified, it is part of the *Code of federal regulations* (286). As many
federal rules, codes, and regulations affect business establishments, this is a
necessary resource. For example, information on business rates and terms,
trademarks, or even the *Federal register* notice describing changes adopted
for NAICS 2007.

Online access to issues 1994 (v. 59) through the most current. Issues
prior to 1994 available at Federal depository libraries.

Subscriber access to the complete digitized *Federal register*, from its
earliest date of publication, is available from HeinOnline (Buffalo, N.Y.:
W. S. Hein).

## Reviews of Research and Trends

295 **American business law journal.** Academy of Legal Studies in
Business. Malden, Mass.: Blackwell, 1963–. ISSN: 0002-7766.
346.730705; 347.306705                                          K1.M4

Covers the full range of business law topics. Published by the Academy
of Legal Studies in Business, an association of business and corporate law
educators who teach outside of law schools. Intended for students and
professors. Available online.

## Topical Law Services

296 **BNA labor and employment law library.** Bureau of National
Affairs (Washington, D.C.). [1999–.] [Washington, D.C.]: Bureau
of National Affairs. http://laborandemploymentlaw.bna.com/.

Cases, summaries of developments, manuals, and explanations of state and
federal laws in areas like arbitration, collective bargaining, wages and hours,
fair employment, disability, and employee rights. Includes Labor-Management Relations with Decisions from 1984, Fair Employment Practices from
1965, Individual Employment Rights from 1986, BNA's *Labor relations
reporter, HR policy handbook,* and *Client letters, checklists, and forms.*

**297** **BNA's bankruptcy law reporter.** Bureau of National Affairs. loose-leaf. [Washington, D.C.]: Bureau of National Affairs, 1989–. ISSN: 1044-7474.

346.7307805            KF1507.B63

Covers state and federal bankruptcy law, with filings, forms, motions, decisions, and legislation. Also available online.

**298** **CCH tax research network.** CCH Incorporated. Chicago: CCH, [2006–.].

Organized into fully searchable libraries: Accounting/Auditing, Federal, State, Financial and estate, Special entities, Pension and payroll, International, and Perform Plus II. Each library is organized into sub-sections that include Current features and journals; CCH explanations and analysis; Treatises; Primary sources; Practice aids; Archives; and Topical indexes. Perhaps most used for federal tax materials, but also addresses state taxes (has all State Tax Reporters), sales tax, financial and estate planning, business entities, international (treaties), tax forms, practice aids, and calculators for accountants.

The Federal library includes legislative materials, Federal Tax Code, Federal Tax Regulations, Cases, Tax Court and other trial court cases, U.S. Circuit Courts of Appeal, U.S. Supreme Court, IRS Publications (*Revenue rulings, Revenue procedures, IRS notices, IRS announcements, Letter rulings, IRS positions,* and *Internal revenue manual*), Standard Federal Tax Reporter, Federal Estate/Gift Tax Reporter, and Federal Excise Tax Reporter.

Search includes citation, check citator, news, and a thesaurus.

**299** **Contemporary corporation forms.** 2nd ed. Aspen Law and Business. 5 v., loose-leaf, ill., forms. New York: Aspen Law and Business, 1998–. ISBN: 1567066623.

346.730660269            KF1411.C662

Compiles 500 actual documents from law firms, intended to serve as templates. Targets all types of corporations and even those interested in forming a corporation. Forms cover shareholder agreements, warrants, options, dividends, spin-offs, mergers and acquisitions, initial public offerings, bylaws, and more. Forms are cross-referenced with relevant state corporation law.

**300** **Federal tax coordinator.** 2nd [ed.] Research Institute of America. New York: Research institute of America, 1984–. ISSN: 10603343.

HJ3252.F4

Easy to understand analysis of tax laws (income, gift, estate, and excise), regulations, IRS rulings, and releases, as well as text of the Internal Revenue Code and Treasury Regulations. Arranged by subject, with a good index. Updated weekly. Similar to *CCH standard federal tax reporter* (267). Available through RIA Checkpoint (207) and Westlaw.

**301    RIA checkpoint.** RIA Group. [1998–.] [Mt. Kisco, N.Y.]: RIA Group. http://ria.thomson.com/integratedsolutions/.
Integrates RIA tax and accounting publications that provide primary tax documents and secondary analysis into one online resource with the federal tax code (from 1990), regulations, committee reports, rulings (1954 to present), Internal Revenue Bulletins (1996 to present), WG&L tax treatises and journals, IBFD Materials, state tax guides and laws, and federal tax case histories (1860 to present).

Sections of Checkpoint are Tax News, Federal Tax Library, State and Local Tax Library, International Tax Library, Pensions and Benefits Library, Estate Planning Library, Payroll Library, WG&L Financial Reporting and Management (FRM) Library, Accounting and Auditing Library, Checkpoint Archives, and Continuing Professional Education (CPE). Major publications and primary documents are *RIA daily updates, the BNA daily tax report, Federal tax coordinator* (265), *United States tax reporter, Federal tax handbook, Tax planning and practice guides, Federal income taxation of corporations and shareholders, WG&L tax dictionary, RIA worldwide tax law, Comtax news* (2001–5), *International taxes weekly newsletter* (1999–2006), *WG&L international transfer pricing treatises, RIA's executive compensation analysis, ERISA, DOL and PBGC regulations and committee reports*, SEC compliance documents, GAAP compliance documents, AICPA documents (Professional Standards, Technical Practice Aids, Audit and Accounting Guides), FASB documents (Original Pronouncements, Original Pronouncements as amended including Implementation Guides and FASB Staff Positions, Current Text, Emerging Issues Task Force, Derivative Instruments and Hedging Activities, Exposure Drafts, Business Reporting Research Project, FASB Reports, Action Alerts, Proposed Documents, Topical Index), GASB documents (Original Pronouncements, Implementation Guides, Exposure Drafts, Topical Index), IASB (IASC Foundation Constitution, Standards, Interpretations, Implementation Guidance for IFRS and IAS, Proposal Stage Documents, News, Glossary), PCAOB documents (Advance PCAOB, Final Releases, Proposals, Final and Proposed Rules, Auditing Standards, Interim Auditing Standards, Interim Attestation Standards, Interim Quality Control Standards, Interim Ethics Standards, Interim Independence Standards,

Registration System, Ethics Code), *Advance Sarbanes-Oxley cases* (2003 to present), and the *Handbook of accounting and auditing* (Boston: Warren, Gorham, and Lamont, 1982–).

Many of these resources are also available through Westlaw, CCH's Accounting Research Manager (77) or Tax Research Network (205).

**302   Standard federal tax reporter.** Commerce Clearing House. Chicago: Commerce Clearing House, 1945–. ISSN: 0162-3494.
343.7304; 347.3034                                    KF6285.C67

The best known tax service, with analysis and primary documents for federal tax law (such as personal income, corporate income, business expenses and deductions, mergers and acquisitions, employee benefit plans, tax accounting, exempt organizations, capital gains and losses). Primary documents include: Internal Revenue code sections, regulations and proposed regulations, and excerpts of committee reports. Most used for CCH explanations of federal tax law and the annotations of cases and rulings that go back to 1913. Arranged by code section, with four topical indexes, each in a separate volume: in the *Index* volume; in *Internal Revenue Code*, v. 1; and the cumulative index in the *New Matters* volume. Updated weekly. Available through CCH Tax Research NetWork (205) and LexisNexis. Similar to RIA's *federal tax coordinator, 2nd ed.* (265).

**303   Trade regulation reporter.** 13th ed. Commerce Clearing House. 7 v., loose-leaf, ill. Chicago: Commerce Clearing House, 1988–.
343.7308; 347.3038                                    KF1606.5.T7

Coverage of U.S. antitrust cases and pending consent decrees. Includes the text of court decisions for government and private antitrust litigation, relevant antitrust legislation and regulations, summaries of federal and state statutes, advisory material, policy pronouncements, and case settlements. Available in online form.

# Electronic Commerce

## *Dictionaries*

**304   Dictionary of e-business: A definitive guide to technology and business terms.** 2nd ed. Francis Botto. ix, 368 p., ill. Chichester, England; Hoboken, N.J.: Wiley, 2003. ISBN: 0470844701.
658.84                                    HF5548.32.B67

Definitions and some short articles explain terms and concepts related to electronic commerce and the Internet. Available as an e-book.

## Directories

**305**  **Plunkett's e-commerce and Internet business almanac.** Jack W. Plunkett, Plunkett Research, Ltd., ill. Houston, Tex.: Plunkett Research, 2000–. ISSN: 1548-5447.

004                                                                    HF5548.325.U6P59

Like all the Plunkett almanacs, contains data on 300 major companies. Company profiles include types of business, brands and affiliates, contacts, employee benefits and top salaries, sales and profit numbers, growth plans, and competitive advantage. Especially useful for the industry statistics and rankings at the front of the volume. Also contains a glossary of key words and phrases. Available as an e-book.

## Encyclopedias

**306**  **Desktop encyclopedia of telecommunications.** 3rd ed. Nathan J. Muller. xx, 1250 p., ill. New York: McGraw-Hill, 2002. ISBN: 0071381481.

621.38203                                                                    TK5102.M85

Written for nontechnical professionals, the *Encyclopedia* explains local and wide-area networking, equipment and services, network applications, regulations, standards, industry trends, and covers industry organizations. Articles can be thorough, with information on the evolution of a technology or a regulation. The second edition is available as an e-book through NetLibrary.

**307**  **Encyclopedia of e-commerce, e-government, and mobile commerce.** Mehdi Khosrowpour. Hershey, Pa.: Idea Group Reference, 2006. ISBN: 1591407990.

381.14203                                                                    HF5548.32.E52

Nearly 200 contributions from over 300 authors from around the world. Alphabetically arranged by topic, with good cross-references. Topics include e-collaboration technologies and applications, e-commerce technologies and applications, e-commerce management and social issues, e-government technologies and applications, e-government management and social issues, e-healthcare technologies and applications, e-learning technologies and applications, e-technologies security and privacy, mobile commerce technologies and applications, mobile commerce management and social issues, virtual communities and enterprises, and web portals and services. Available as an e-book.

**308    Encyclopedia of wireless telecommunications.** Francis Botto. 1 v. (various pagings), ill. Boston: McGraw-Hill, 2002. ISBN: 0071390251.

621.38203                                    TK5103.2.B68

While no print source can keep up with the pace of technological advances, this source provides a solid background on architectures, devices and handsets, free space communications technology, globalization, infrastructure, LAN technologies, local communication technologies (Bluetooth, Piano, IrDA, etc.), principles of radio and light, services and products, e-business, and standards and protocols.

**309    Gale encyclopedia of e-commerce.** Jane A. Malonis. 2 v., xx, 863 p. Detroit: Gale Group, Thomson Learning, 2002. ISBN: 0787656607.

381.1                                          HF5548.32.G35

Contains 470 entries on e-commerce, including profiles of individuals, organizations, and companies, coverage of significant events, a timeline of the development of e-commerce, and topics like encryption, internet metrics, and scalability. Available as an e-book.

## *Guides and Handbooks*

**310    Gale e-commerce sourcebook.** Detroit: Gale, 2003–. ISSN: 1542-1120.

381                                            HF5548.32.G347

Organized into three sections: "How To" topics, directory information, and top 250 e-commerce companies worldwide. "How To" contains information for start-ups (business plans financing). The directory lists companies, services, and government agencies related to e-commerce, with contact information and organizational background for each entry. Index includes organization and personal names, industry terms and subject terms. Available as an e-book.

**311    Handbook of quantitative supply chain analysis: Modeling in the e-business era.** David Simchi-Levi, S. David Wu, Zuo-Jun Shen. xiii, 817 p., ill. Boston: Kluwer, 2004. ISBN: 1402079524.

658.70151                                      HD38.5.H355

Includes trends, theory, and practice. Organized into five parts: emerging paradigms for supply chain analysis; auctions and bidding; supply chain coordinations in e-business; multi-channel coordination; and network design, IT, and financial services. Strong coverage of game theory as it applies to supply chains.

## Indexes; Abstract Journals

312   **Web marketing today.** Wilson Internet Services. 1995–. Rocklin, Calif.: Wilson Internet Services. ISSN: 1094-8112. http://www. wilsonweb.com/wmt/.
384

Index to nearly 17,000 articles and other resources for web marketing and e-commerce. Categories for Industry Case Studies, Business to Business (B2B), Online Transactions, E-Commerce Environmental Design, Store-Building "Cart" Software, Website Promotion, Business Site Environ-mental Design, Paid Advertising, E-Mail Marketing, Miscellaneous Web Marketing, and Local Web Marketing. Access is a mix of fee and free.

## Internet Resources

313   **ClickZ stats.** INT Media Group. [2006–.] Darien, Conn.: INT Media Group. http://www.clickz.com/showPage.html?page=stats.
HF5548.32.C931

A treasure trove of statistics and trends about 22 different sectors of internet marketing, including advertising, business to business, broad-band, demographics, education, e-mail and spam, entertainment, finance, geographics, government/politics, hardware, health care, professional, retailing, search tools, security, small/medium enterprises, software and IT, traffic patterns, and wireless. Some data back to 1999. Because ClickZ links to outside sources, some URLs can lead to broken links.

314   **E-stats.** U.S. Bureau of the Census. [2001–.] [Washington, D.C.]: U.S. Bureau of the Census. http://www.census.gov/eos/www/ ebusiness614.htm.
Invaluable free Census Bureau resource presenting e-commerce data on shipments, sales, and revenue from multiple Census Bureau surveys of NAICS industries accounting for 70 percent of U.S. economic activity (not included are "agriculture, mining, utilities, construction, agents, brokers, electronic markets in wholesale trade, and approximately one-third of

service-related industries"). Some tables are available in Excel. Also provides research papers and reports.

**315** **Federal communications commission.** U.S. Superintendent of Documents. 2007. Washington, D.C.: U.S. Government Printing Office, Superintendent of Documents. http://www.fcc.gov/.
The FCC was founded in 1923 and regulates interstate and international communications by radio, television, wire, satellite and cable. The website contains a treasure trove of information, including reports, statistics, trends, rules and regulations, and more. Examples include annual reports on cable industry prices, periodic reviews of the radio industry, the statistics of communications common carriers, statistical trends in telephony, local and long distance telephone industries, local telephone competition and broadband deployment, telephone industry infrastructure and service quality, federal-state joint board monitoring reports, telephone numbering facts, and international traffic data.

**316** **Web marketing today.** Wilson Internet Services. 1995–. Rocklin, Calif.: Wilson Internet Services. ISSN: 1094-8112. http://www.wilsonweb.com/wmt/.

384

Index to nearly 17,000 articles and other resources for web marketing and e-commerce. Categories for Industry Case Studies, Business to Business (B2B), Online Transactions, E-Commerce Environmental Design, Store-Building "Cart" Software, Website Promotion, Business Site Environmental Design, Paid Advertising, E-Mail Marketing, Miscellaneous Web Marketing, and Local Web Marketing. Access is a mix of fee and free.

## *Organizations and Associations*

**317** **Federal communications commission.** U.S. Superintendent of Documents. 2007. Washington, D.C.: U.S. Government Printing Office, Superintendent of Documents. http://www.fcc.gov/.
The FCC was founded in 1923 and regulates interstate and international communications by radio, television, wire, satellite and cable. The website contains a treasure trove of information, including reports, statistics, trends, rules and regulations, and more. Examples include annual reports on cable industry prices, periodic reviews of the radio industry, the statistics of communications common carriers, statistical trends in telephony, local and long distance telephone industries, local telephone competition

and broadband deployment, telephone industry infrastructure and service quality, federal-state joint board monitoring reports, telephone numbering facts, and international traffic data.

## Periodicals

**318**  **eMarketer.** eMarketer (Organization). 1999–. New York: eMarketer. http://www.emarketer.com/.
Aggregates data from 2,800 sources, with summaries in reports and articles. Sources include Accenture, ACNielsen, *Advertising age* (573), Harris Poll, Juniper Research, Jupitermedia, Mediamark Research Inc. (MRI), Rand Corporation, Pew Internet & American Life Project, Red Hat, Red Herring, as well as various advertising and marketing associations. The data is searchable, making this a good source for online marketing and e-commerce statistics.

**319**  **Technology review.** Massachusetts Institute of Technology. 1998–. Cambridge, Mass.: Association of Alumni and Alumnae of the Massachusetts Institute of Technology. ISSN: 1099-274X. http://www.technologyreview.com/.
620                                                                                                     T171.M47
Covers trends and developments in business technology, especially as they effect the energy, nanotech, biotech, and infotech industries. Includes annual list of the top emerging technologies. For many years, it included an annual R&D Scorecard, published each fall, which now is useful for tracking historical research and development expenditures.

## Reviews of Research and Trends

**320**  **FACCTS.** Faulkner Information Services. 1995–. Pennsauken, N.J.: Faulkner Information Services. ISSN: 1082-7471. http://www.faulkner.com/showcase/faccts.htm.
005                                                                                                     QA76.753
Over 1,200 reports on trends, issues, market conditions, implementation guides, companies, products, and services in information technology. Arranged into 14 categories: enterprise data networking, broadband, information security, electronic government, electronic business, content management, IT asset management, application development, Website management, converging communications, telecom and global network

services, mobile business strategies, wireless communications, and Internet strategies. Especially useful for the up-to-date technology trend reports.

321    **Jupiterresearch.** Jupiter Communications. New York: Jupiter Communications. http://www.jupiterresearch.com/bin/item.pl/ home.

Combines proprietary primary research with secondary research to give trends, statistics, forecasts, and best practices on information technology and its effects on industries and consumers. In seven categories: Personal Technologies; Marketing & Media; Web Technologies & Operations; European Focus; Industry Focus; Jupiter Data (statistics); and Hot Topics.

# Entrepreneurship

## *Small Business*

### BIOGRAPHY

322    **American inventors, entrepreneurs, and business visionaries.**
Charles W. Carey. xxi, 410 p., ill. New York: Facts On File, 2002.
ISBN: 0816045593.
338.092273                                                   CT214.C29

Profiles nearly 300 Americans from the seventeenth through twentieth centuries. Not all individuals are well known or achieved business success, making this a richer resource than the typical biographical source. Entries of 1–2 pages cover birth and death dates, life and innovations, with brief bibliographies. Indexes for invention, industry, and birth year. Available as an e-book.

323    **The guru guide to entrepreneurship: A concise guide to the best ideas from the world's top entrepreneurs.** Joseph H. Boyett, Jimmie T. Boyett. xvi, 370 p. New York: Wiley, 2001. ISBN: 0471390844.
658.421                                                       HB615.B685

Compiles the views of 70 entrepreneurs on basic questions relating to establishing and running your own business. The authors have synthesized ideas from more than 250 books and over 2,500 articles. These expert opinions are organized around six themes that cover the following issues: traits essential for entrepreneurial success, finding ideas for businesses, raising money, attracting customers, keeping customers, and managing people. An appendix includes biographical sketches of each of the 70 entrepreneurs profiled. Available as an e-book.

**324    So who the heck was Oscar Mayer?** Doug Gelbert. 400 p., ill. New York: Barricade Books, 1996. ISBN: 1569800820.
338.0092273B                                                      HC102.5.A2G45

Gelbert reveals the person and story behind 200 well-known brand names. Brief biographical sketches (averaging one to two pages in length) are cleverly categorized under themes such as "In the Kitchen," "From the Bottle," "In the Closet," and "At the Game." Not only fun to read but thoroughly researched.

**325    United States entrepreneurs and the companies they built: An index to biographies in collected works.** Wahib Nasrallah. 366 p. Westport, Conn.: Praeger, 2003. ISBN: 0313323321.
016.338092273                                    Z7164.C81N237; HC102.5.A2

Citations for biographies of 1,700 people, using 120 sources. Organized by name of entrepreneur. No annotations are provided. Indexed by corporation. Available as an e-book.

## BOOK REVIEWS

**326    Business information alert.** Alert Publications. Chicago: Alert Publications, 1989–. ISSN: 1042-0746.
025                                                                      HF5001

Contains reviews of print and electronic business resources, and news, trends, and tips for business researchers. Also available through various aggregator databases.

**327    Harvard business review.** ill. Boston: Graduate School of Business Administration, Harvard University. ISSN: 0017-8012.
330.904                                                                  HF5001.H3

Articles, best practices, book reviews, and case studies on communication, finance and accounting, global business, innovation and entrepreneurship, leadership, management, organizational development, sales and marketing, strategy and execution, and technology and operations. Also available online, through Business Source Elite (791).

**328    Journal of business and finance librarianship.** ill. Binghamton, N.Y.: Haworth Press, 1990–. ISSN: 0896-3568.
027.6905                                                                  Z675.B8

Reviews of books, databases, and websites written by librarians for librarians. "The immediate focus of the journal is practice-oriented articles, but it also provides an outlet for new empirical studies on business librarianship and business information. Aside from articles, this journal offers valuable statistical and meeting reports, literature and media reviews, website reviews, and interviews."—*About*

## DIRECTORIES

329　American wholesalers and distributors directory. Gale Research Inc. Detroit: Gale Research, 1992–. ISSN: 1061-2114.
381.2029473　　　　　　　　　　　　　　　　　HF5421.A615

Lists 27,000 companies in the U.S. and Puerto Rico. Includes name and address, fax number, Standard Industrial Classification (SIC) code, principal product lines, total number of employees, estimated annual sales volume, and principal officers. Indexed by SIC code, state and city, and company name. Information can be hard to find for many of these privately held companies, making this a handy source. Available online as part of Gale Business Resources.

330　America's corporate finance directory. New Providence, N.J.: National Register, 1994–. ISSN: 1080-1227.
338.7402573　　　　　　　　　　　　　　　　　HG4057.A15647

Information on 4,500 public and private U.S. companies with revenue income or pension assets over $100,000,000 per year and large foreign subsidiaries located in the U.S. Also profiles financial executives and identifies business relationships between companies.

331　Bond's franchise guide. Source Book Publications. ill. Oakland, Calif.: Source Book Publications, 1995–. ISSN: 1089-8794.
381.1302573　　　　　　　　　　　　　　HF5429.235.U5S66

Profiles for 1,000 franchises, which include background, capital requirements, initial training and other start-up assistance provided, franchisee evaluation criteria, and specific areas of geographic criteria. Index.

332　Consultants and consulting organizations directory: A reference guide to more than 26,000 firms and individuals engaged in consultation for business, industry, and government. 29th ed. Julie A. Gough. 2 v. Detroit: Thomson/Gale, 2006. ISBN: 0787679437.

Organized into 14 general fields of consulting. Entries give contact information, brief description of activities, mergers and former names, geographic area served, and where possible, annual consulting revenue.

**333  The corporate finance sourcebook.** New Providence, N.J.:
National Register, 1979–. ISSN: 0163-3031.
332.02573                                          HG4057.A1565

Directory of firms involved in capital investments and financial services (e.g., venture capital, private lenders, commercial and financial factors, business intermediaries, leasing companies and corporate real estate, commercial, U.S.-based foreign, and investment banks and trusts, securities analysts and CPA/auditing firms). Entries include personnel, financial information, type of investor or service, minimum investment, funds available, average number of deals completed annually, industry preferences, and exit criteria. Indexed by name of company, personnel, and geography.

**334  D and B consultants directory.** Dun and Bradstreet Corporation.
Bethlehem, Pa.: Dun and Bradstreet, 1997–. ISSN: 1524-9743.
658.4602573                                          HD69.C6D86

Provides information on more than 30,000 of the largest consulting firms in the U.S., with profiles arranged alphabetically. Companies are cross-referenced geographically and by consulting activity.

**335  The directory of venture capital and private equity firms,**
**domestic and international.** Millerton, N.Y.: Grey House, 2002–.
ISSN: 1549-702X.
332                                          HG4751.F582

With over 3,000 entries, this surpasses *Galante's venture capital and private equity directory* (Wellesley, Mass.: Asset Alternatives, 1997–) for coverage of venture capital firms. Includes contact information, mission statement, industry group and geographic preferences, average and minimum investments and investment criteria. Particularly useful for finding portfolio companies, and educational and professional history of key executives. Available as an online database.

**336  National minority and women-owned business directory.**
Diversity Information Resources, Inc. ill. Minneapolis, Minn.:
Diversity Information Resources, 2004–. ISSN: 1553-6025.
338                                          HD2358.5.U6T786

Contains 9,000 entries in 84 industries with contact information, URL, products/services, year established, minority type, number of employees, annual sales, and certification. Indexed by company.

**337** **Small business sourcebook.** Gale Research Company. Detroit: Gale Research, 1983–. ISSN: 0883-3397.

658.02207073                                                    HD2346.U5S66

Vol. 1 is organized by state and gives small business profiles that include sources of information for about 350 different types of businesses, e.g., start-up information, primary associations, statistical sources, trade periodicals, trade shows, and conventions. Vol. 2 contains sources for general topics common to the operation of any small business (funding, consultants, sources of supply, etc.). It also contains directories and descriptions of sources of assistance offered by state organizations and federal government agencies, a glossary, and master index.

## ENCYCLOPEDIAS

**338** **Encyclopedia of management.** 5th ed. Marilyn M. Helms. xxix, 1003 p., ill. Detroit: Thomson Gale, 2006. ISBN: 0787665568.

658.00322; 658.003                                                HD30.15.E49

Covers 18 functional areas: corporate planning and strategic management, emerging topics in management, entrepreneurship, financial management and accounting, general management, human resources management, innovation and technology, international management, leadership, legal issues, management science and operations, management information systems, performance measures and assessment, personal growth and development for managers, production and operations management, quality management and total quality management, supply chain management, and training and development. Contains 350 essays written by academics and business professionals. Almost all essays are new or revised from the 2000 ed. Arranged alphabetically, entries are 3–5 pages long, with cross-references and recommended reading lists. Available as an e-book.

**339** **Encyclopedia of small business.** 3rd ed. Arsen Darnay, Monique D. Magee, Kevin Hillstrom. Detroit: Thomson Gale, 2007. ISBN: 0787691127.

658.022                                                          HD62.7.H553

Over 600 entries on the basics of creating, owning and operating a small business, with articles on financial planning, business plans, marketing, sales, exporting, business law, and tax planning. Articles are 1–3 pages long, with cross-references and bibliographies. Also available as an e-book.

**340 Small business resource center.** Gale Group. 2006–. [Farmington Hills, Mich.]: Gale Group. http://www.galegroup.com/ SmallBusiness/about.htm.

HF54.56

Combines reference sources, journals, trade magazines, and books relevant to students or individuals interested in small businesses or entrepreneurship. Includes books like *Franchising for dummies* (2006) and *Entrepreneur and small business problem solver* (2005), as well as reference books like the *Business plans handbook* (344) series, the *Encyclopedia of business information sources* (2006) (778), *Encyclopedia of business and finance* (2007) (224), and the *Encyclopedia of small business* (2002). Trade magazines and journals include *Black enterprise, Direct marketing, Entrepreneur, Financial management, Journal of small business management, Kiplinger business forecasts, Quarterly journal of business and economics, Small business economics,* and *The tax adviser.*

## GUIDES AND HANDBOOKS

**341 Accounting and finance for your small business.** 2nd ed. Steven M. Bragg, E. James Burton. xv, 296 p., ill. Hoboken, N.J.: Wiley, 2006. ISBN: 0471771562.

658 HD31.B852

Contains information on tasks that should be accomplished before starting a business, and tasks and tips for operating an existing small business. Techniques and strategies for accounting, taxes, finance, and reporting. Also available as an e-book.

**342 Anatomy of a business plan: A step-by-step guide to building a business and securing your company's future.** 6th ed. Linda Pinson. x, 292 p. Chicago: Dearborn Trade, 2005. ISBN: 0793191920.

658.4012 HD30.28.P5

Walks through the components of a business plan, explaining the purpose of each section and the ways to write it. Includes forms and three complete business plans. Available as an e-book.

343    The Blackwell handbook of entrepreneurship. Donald L. Sexton, Hans Landström, Blackwell Publishers. xxiv, 468 p., ill. Oxford; Malden, Mass.: Blackwell Business; Nova Southeastern University, 2000. ISBN: 0631215735.

658.421                                                    HB615.B617

Summarizes the scholarly literature on entrepreneurship and identifies gaps in entrepreneurship research. International in scope, comparing and contrasting American and European models of entrepreneurship. Of use to graduate students and researchers in the growing subfield of entrepreneurship scholarship.

344    Business plans handbook: A compilation of actual business plans developed by small businesses throughout North America. Gale Research Inc. Detroit: Gale Research, 1995–. ISSN: 1084-4473.

658.401205                                                 HD62.7.B865

Real examples of company business plans across industries. Useful for entrepreneurs looking for capital and for students writing mock business plans. Lists of small business organizations, agencies, and consultants, glossary of small business terms, and a bibliography. Available as e-books in Gale Virtual Reference Library (Farmington HIills, Mich.: Gale Cengage Learning, 2002–).

345    The guru guide to entrepreneurship: A concise guide to the best ideas from the world's top entrepreneurs. Joseph H. Boyett, Jimmie T. Boyett. xvi, 370 p. New York: Wiley, 2001. ISBN: 0471390844.

658.421                                                    HB615.B685

Compiles the views of 70 entrepreneurs on basic questions relating to establishing and running your own business. The authors have synthesized ideas from more than 250 books and over 2,500 articles. These expert opinions are organized around six themes that cover the following issues: traits essential for entrepreneurial success, finding ideas for businesses, raising money, attracting customers, keeping customers, and managing people. An appendix includes biographical sketches of each of the 70 entrepreneurs profiled. Available as an e-book.

346    Small business resource center. Gale Group. 2006–. [Farmington Hills, Mich.]: Gale Group. http://www.galegroup.com/ SmallBusiness/about.htm.

HF54.56

Combines reference sources, journals, trade magazines, and books relevant to students or individuals interested in small businesses or entrepreneurship. Includes books like *Franchising for dummies* (2006) and *Entrepreneur and small business problem solver* (2005), as well as reference books like the *Business plans handbook* (344) series, the *Encyclopedia of business information sources* (2006) (778), *Encyclopedia of business and finance* (2007) (224), and the *Encyclopedia of small business* (2002). Trade magazines and journals include *Black enterprise, Direct marketing, Entrepreneur, Financial management, Journal of small business management, Kiplinger business forecasts, Quarterly journal of business and economics, Small business economics,* and *The tax adviser.*

**347    Vault Reports guide to starting your own business.** Jonathan
         Reed Aspatore, H. S. Hamadeh, Samer Hamadeh, Vault Reports.
         296 p., ill. Boston: Houghton Mifflin, 1998. ISBN: 0395861705.
658.041                                                            HD62.5.A85

Provides sound advice on all stages of establishing your own business, from developing a plan to filing tax forms. Aspatore has written several books on entrepreneurship including a handbook for students who want to start businesses while in college. Vault Reports, a company specializing in career advice, always offers an insider's perspective on the issue at hand. Aspatore achieves this through the inclusion of interviews with entrepreneurs from a wide range of industries. Readers will also find the sample business plan useful.

**348    Venture capital: The definitive guide for entrepreneurs, investors,**
         **and practitioners.** Joel Cardis. xv, 320 p., ill. New York: Wiley,
         2001. ISBN: 0471398136.
658.15224                                                          HG4751.V476

Detailed guide to venture capital clearly explains what venture capitalists look for and includes an insider's perspective on this type of start-up funding for entrepreneurs. The content is useful to small business owners in need of seed money in the range of $500,000 to growing companies hoping to secure funding in the $20 million range. Pt. 1 outlines the homework that entrepreneurs need to do before they seek funding. Pt. 2 focuses on getting funded. Multiple appendixes are included: checklists, sample agreements, a listing of online entrepreneurial resources, and a directory of venture capital resources for women and minorities.

## INDEXES; ABSTRACT JOURNALS

349    **Small business resource center.** Gale Group. 2006–. [Farmington
Hills, Mich.]: Gale Group. http://www.galegroup.com/
SmallBusiness/about.htm.

HF54.56

Combines reference sources, journals, trade magazines, and books relevant
to students or individuals interested in small businesses or entrepreneurship. Includes books like *Franchising for dummies* (2006) and *Entrepreneur
and small business problem solver* (2005), as well as reference books like the
*Business plans handbook* (344) series, the *Encyclopedia of business information sources* (2006) (778), *Encyclopedia of business and finance* (2007)
(224), and the *Encyclopedia of small business* (2002). Trade magazines and
journals include *Black enterprise, Direct marketing, Entrepreneur, Financial
management, Journal of small business management, Kiplinger business forecasts, Quarterly journal of business and economics, Small business economics,*
and *The tax adviser.*

350    **United States entrepreneurs and the companies they built: An
index to biographies in collected works.** Wahib Nasrallah. 366 p.
Westport, Conn.: Praeger, 2003. ISBN: 0313323321.

016.338092273                        Z7164.C81N237; HC102.5.A2

Citations for biographies of 1,700 people, using 120 sources. Organized by
name of entrepreneur. No annotations are provided. Indexed by corporation. Available as an e-book.

## INTERNET RESOURCES

351    **Entrepreneur.com.** Entrepreneur.com (Firm). 2000–. [s.l.]:
Entrepreneur.com, Inc. http://www.entrepreneur.com/.

Gives clear how-to advice in all the areas of concern to a small business
owner. Sections are: Starting a Business (how-to guides, business plans);
Money (financing, money management, payments and collections, tax
center, personal finance, financial calculators); Marketing (marketing
basics, finding customers, market research, branding); Sales (finding prospects, sales techniques, presentations, closing the sale, customer service);
Advertising (how-to guides, ads by type); Franchises (how to buy, top
franchises); Biz Opportunities (buying, network, kiosks); Home Based

(self-assessment, home-based ideas, home-based basics, work/life balance, growth options); Biz E-Business (eBay center, e-business ideas, getting started, getting traffic, operations, search optimization, site design); Management (operations, insurance, legal issues, leadership, family business, women's center); Human Resources (hiring, compensation and benefits, employment law, managing employees); Technology (news and trends, product reviews, software guide, managing technology); and Work/Life (health and fitness, personal finance, work/life balance, success stories). Also has a small business encyclopedia.

352    **International franchise association.** International Franchise Association. [1998–.] [Washington, D.C.]: International Franchise Association. http://www.franchise.org/.
Includes lists for over 1,000 franchise opportunities, searchable by category, level of desired investment, and type of franchise. Also contains advice for getting started and a supplier directory.

353    **Kauffman eventuring.** Ewing Marion Kauffman Foundation. Kansas City, Mo.: Ewing Marion Kauffman Foundation. http://www.eventuring.org/.
Advice and resources for entrepreneurs. Sections on Finance and Accounting (funding sources, accounting, financial management), People/HR (recruiting, compensation and benefits, staff management, external human resources), Sales and Marketing (sales, marketing, competitive analysis, global markets), Products and Services (research and development, pricing, intellectual property, customer service, market analysis), Operations (facilities, production, delivery and distribution, vendors, technology, legal), and The Entrepreneur (strategy, growth strategies, partners, personal development, culture, leadership, exit planning, giving to entrepreneurship).

354    **Small business economic trends.** NFIB Education Foundation. 1993–. Washington, D.C.: NFIB Education Foundation. http://www.nfib.com/page/sbet/.
Monthly report with economic indicators such as optimism, earnings, sales, prices, employment, compensation, credit conditions, inventories, and capital outlays. Information comes from a survey of members of the National Federation of Independent Business. Online from 10/03/2001.

355 **The small business economy.** U.S. Government Printing Office. 2004–. Washington, D.C.: U.S. Government Printing Office. ISSN: 1932-3573. http://purl.access.gpo.gov/GPO/LPS1196/.
338.7                                                      HD2346.U5S78
Annual review, including small business trends, demographics, financing, federal procurement, women in business, regulations, and data. Data includes U.S. Business Counts and Turnover Measures for 1980–2005, Macroeconomic Indicators for 1995–2005, Business Turnover by State, Opening and Closing Establishments for 1992–2005, and Characteristics of Self-Employed Individuals for 1995–2004.

## ORGANIZATIONS AND ASSOCIATIONS

356 **U.S. small business administration.** U.S. Small Business Administration. [1997?–.] Washington, D.C.: U.S. Small Business Administration. http://www.sbaonline.sba.gov/.
658.02                                                      HD2346.U5
This well-known agency offers information on topics such as starting, financing, and managing a business. Includes forms, regulations, loan information, and SBA resources by region and state.

## PERIODICALS

357 **Business week.** ill. New York: McGraw-Hill, 1929–. ISSN: 0007-7135.
65011                                                      HF5001.B89
A good source for current news on companies and industries, the impact of the economy on business, investing, and markets. Various special issues cover most innovative companies, investment outlook, top global companies, best employers, and report on philanthropy with top corporate givers. Much of the print content is available for free at http://www.businessweek.com/.

358 **Financial studies of the small business.** Winter Haven, Fla.: Financial Research Associates, 1976–. ISSN: 0363-8987.
658.15904                                                      HD2346.U5F55a
Uses data from 30,000 financial statements provided by certified public accounting firms to present financial data on U.S. small businesses. Arranged by industry, then by asset size. Gives current assets, fixed assets, liabilities and capital, income data, operating items such as advertising expense and rent,

and ratios (current, quick, current assets/total assets, short term debt/total debt, short term debt/net worth, total debt/net worth, short term debt/total assets, long term debt/total assets, total debt/total assets, sales/receivables, average collection period, sales/inventory, sales/total assets, sales/net worth, pre-tax profit/total assets, pre-tax profit/net worth).

**359  Harvard business review.** ill. Boston: Graduate School of Business
Administration, Harvard University. ISSN: 0017-8012.
330.904                                                                          HF5001.H3

Articles, best practices, book reviews, and case studies on communication, finance and accounting, global business, innovation and entrepreneurship, leadership, management, organizational development, sales and marketing, strategy and execution, and technology and operations. Also available online, through Business Source Elite (791).

**360  Kosmont-Rose Institute cost of doing business survey.** Kosmont
Companies. Claremont, Calif.; Los Angeles: Rose Institute;
Kosmont, 2003–. ISSN: 1558-1055.
338                                                                          HC107.C23K67

Contains data about fees, taxes, costs, and incentives for 398 cities. Includes rankings. Used to compare the costs of locating in particular communities.

**361  Small business economic trends.** NFIB Education Foundation.
1993–. Washington, D.C.: NFIB Education Foundation. http://
www.nfib.com/page/sbet/.

Monthly report with economic indicators such as optimism, earnings, sales, prices, employment, compensation, credit conditions, inventories, and capital outlays. Information comes from a survey of members of the National Federation of Independent Business. Online from 10/03/2001.

**362  The small business economy.** U.S. Government Printing Office.
2004–. Washington, D.C.: U.S. Government Printing Office. ISSN:
1932-3573. http://purl.access.gpo.gov/GPO/LPS1196/.
338.7                                                                          HD2346.U5S78

Annual review, including small business trends, demographics, financing, federal procurement, women in business, regulations, and data. Data includes U.S. Business Counts and Turnover Measures for 1980–2005, Macroeconomic Indicators for 1995–2005, Business Turnover by State,

Opening and Closing Establishments for 1992–2005, and Characteristics of Self-Employed Individuals for 1995–2004.

## REVIEWS OF RESEARCH AND TRENDS

363 **Advances in entrepreneurship, firm emergence, and growth.** Jerome A. Katz. ill. Amsterdam, [The Netherlands]; Boston: Elsevier/JAI Press, 1993–. ISSN: 1074-7540.

658.42105                                                   HB615.A377

Brings together studies relating to the impact of entrepreneurial activities on U.S. economic development. These research findings are relevant to the academic and business communities; especially pertinent to practicing entrepreneurs. Annual. Volumes cover all aspects of entrepreneurship, from entrepreneurial education to the impact of government regulation. Vol. 10 to be published in 2007. Available in online form.

364 **Advances in the study of entrepreneurship, innovation, and economic growth.** ill. Greenwich, Conn.: JAI Press, 1986–. ISSN: 1048-4736.

338.0405                                                    HB615.A38

Edited papers from top researchers, useful as summaries. Papers were presented at the Colloquium on Entrepreneurship Education and Technology Transfer, organized by the McGuire Center for Entrepreneurship at the University of Arizona. Available in online form.

# Finance and Investments

## *Biography*

365 **Who's who in finance and business.** Marquis Who's Who. New Providence, N.J.: Marquis Who's Who, 2005–. ISSN: 1930-3262.

338                                           HF3023.A2W5; HC29.W46

Over 24,000 entries on executives in the U.S. and in 100 other countries and territories. Also has entries for administrators and professors in the top business schools in the U.S., Canada, and Mexico. Continues: 1936–59, *Who's who in commerce and industry;* 1961–1968/69, *World who's who in commerce and industry;* 1970/71, *World's who's who in commerce and industry;* and 1972/73–2003, *Who's who in finance and industry.* Included in Marquis Who's Who on the Web (United States: U.S. Census Bureau, 199–).

## Book Reviews

366   **Business information alert.** Alert Publications. Chicago: Alert
Publications, 1989–. ISSN: 1042-0746.
025                                                                      HF5001
Contains reviews of print and electronic business resources, and news,
trends, and tips for business researchers. Also available through various
aggregator databases.

367   **Journal of business and finance librarianship.** ill. Binghamton,
N.Y.: Haworth Press, 1990–. ISSN: 0896-3568.
027.6905                                                                 Z675.B8
Reviews of books, databases, and websites written by librarians for librarians. "The immediate focus of the journal is practice-oriented articles, but
it also provides an outlet for new empirical studies on business librarianship and business information. Aside from articles, this journal offers
valuable statistical and meeting reports, literature and media reviews,
website reviews, and interviews."—*About*

368   **The review of financial studies.** Oxford University Press. 1988–.
New York: Oxford University Press and Society for Financial
Studies. ISSN: 0893-9454. http://rfs.oxfordjournals.org/.
                                                                         HG1.R45
One of the top journals in financial economics, it publishes theoretical and
empirical research in financial economics. Sponsored by the Society for
Financial Studies, with irregular, but lengthy book reviews. E-mail alerts
can be set up for table of contents or to track topics and authors. Also
available in print format.

## Dictionaries

369   **Barron's finance and investment handbook.** 7th ed. John Downes,
Jordan Elliot Goodman. xii, 1396 p., ill. Hauppauge, N.Y.: Barron's
Educational Series, 2006. ISBN: 9780764159923.
332.678                                                                  HG173.D66
Presents a wide array of background information on financial institutions, finance, and investing. Arranged in five parts. Pt 1: 30 investment
opportunities (from annuities to zero coupon bonds), pt. 2: how to read
an annual report and a quarterly report, pt. 3: how to read the financial
pages and ticker tape, pt. 4: dictionary of finance and investment (about

800 pages), and pt. 5: finance and investing ready reference (sources of information and assistance in the U.S. and Canada, lists of major financial institutions and mutual funds, historical data on various stock exchanges and other financial data, and lists for publicly traded companies on the NYSE and NASDAQ 100). Appendixes for currencies of the world, abbreviations and acronyms, and selected further readings. Available as an e-book.

**370    Business ratios and formulas: A comprehensive guide.** Steven M. Bragg. xvii, 334 p., ill. Hoboken, N.J.: Wiley, 2002. ISBN: 0471396435.

650.01513                                        HF5691.B73

A wonderful guide to the world of business ratios with definitions, formulas, examples, and cautions for nearly 200 measures. "Cautions" explain when another measure would be better suited, as well as how a measure can be misunderstood. Designed for managers, but useful for anyone who must calculate and understand business ratios. Available as an e-book.

**371    Common stock newspaper abbreviations and trading symbols.** Howard R. Jarrell. x, 413 p., [1] leaf of plates, ill. Metuchen, N.J.: Scarecrow Press, 1989. ISBN: 0810822555.

332.63220973                                      HG4636.J37

Lists Associated Press abbreviations, primary stock exchange/market on which traded, and ticker symbols for more than 6,300 companies selling common stock on the New York or American Stock Exchanges, or traded in the 6,300 companies selling common stock on the New York or American Stock Exchanges, or traded in the over-the-counter National Association of Securities Dealers Automated Quotations (NASDAQ) market. Separate sections provide access by company name, AP newspaper abbreviation, and ticker symbol. A 1991 supplement covers some 2,400 changes and new listings that occurred after the original volume was compiled. Available as an e-book.

**372    Derivatives dictionary.** The William Margrabe Group, Inc. 1996–2002. Westchester County, N.Y.: The William Margrabe Group, Inc. http://www.margrabe.com/Dictionary.html.

Definitions can be very terse, but at its best, the online dictionary gives definitions with examples, applications, and importance to pricing and risk management.

373   **Dictionary of finance and investment terms.** 7th ed. John
Downes, Jordan Elliot Goodman. viii, 832 p., ill. Hauppauge, N.Y.:
Barron's, 2006. ISBN: 9780764134166.
332.03                                                                                    HG151.D69
A basic financial dictionary, with some 5,000 definitions on stocks, bonds,
mutual funds, banking, tax laws, financial markets, and related fields. Includes
a list of financial abbreviations and acronyms. Available in online form.

374   **Dictionary of financial abbreviations.** John Paxton. New York:
Fitzroy Dearborn, 2002. ISBN: 1579583970.
332.03                                                                                    HG151.3.P38
Every discipline has a unique set of abbreviations. This dictionary defines
over 4,000 abbreviations and acronyms for finance, including international institutions, regulatory bodies, trade unions and associations, and
currencies. Most entries are about a paragraph long, but where needed,
there are lengthier explanations.

375   **Elsevier's banking dictionary in seven languages: English,
American, French, Italian, Spanish, Portuguese, Dutch, and
German.** 3rd rev. and enl. ed. Julio Ricci. 359 p. Amsterdam, [The
Netherlands]; New York: Elsevier, 1990. ISBN: 0444880674.
A polyglot dictionary for banking and finance arranged on an English-
language base with equivalent terms in the other languages. The third
revision of Elsevier's banking dictionary in seven languages, adding Portuguese to the list of languages. More than 2,400 terms; indexed by terms
in the other languages.

376   **The futures markets dictionary.** George Steinbeck, Rosemary
Erickson. xv, 191 p., ill. New York: New York Institute of Finance,
1988. ISBN: 0133458776.
332.644                                                                                  HG6024.A3S75
Describes key words and phrases used in the commodities, options,
forwards, and actuals markets. Explains how to read futures quotations.
Many definitions contain examples, illustrations, and cross-references.

377   **The handbook of international financial terms.** Peter Moles,
Nicholas Terry. 2005. [New York]: Oxford University Press. http://
www.oxfordreference.com/.
                                                                                          HG3881.M578

8,500 brief definitions on finance and accounting, including international stock exchanges, option strategies, and laws. Some definitions include examples. Also available in print.

378 **International dictionary of finance.** 4th ed. Graham Bannock, W. A. P. Manser. vi, 287 p. London: Profile Books, 2003. ISBN: 1861974787.

332.03                                                                                    HG151.B274

Covers international finance, as well as domestic finance in various countries. Concentrates on the U.S. and the United Kingdom. Includes foreign language terms. Definitions range from one word to one-half page in length, depending on the complexity of the concept.

379 **Investorwords.com.** WebFinance, Inc. 1997–. [Fairfax, Va.]: WebFinance, Inc. http://www.investorwords.com/.

HG151

Over 6,000 definitions on subjects like accounting, banking, bonds, brokerages, currencies, dividends, earnings, economics, forex, futures, insurance, investor relations, IPOs, law/estate planning, lending/credit, mergers/acquisitions, mutual funds, options, public companies, real estate, retirement, stocks, strategies, taxes, technical analysis, trading, and venture capital. Definitions seem to be intended for the general public as well as for advanced investors.

380 **Language of trade.** Merritt R. Blakeslee, Carlos A. Garcia, U.S. Dept. of State, Office of International Information Programs. [2000]. [Washington, D.C.]: U.S. Dept. of State, Office of International Information Programs. http://usinfo.state.gov/products/pubs/trade/.

Contains a glossary of trade terminology, a list of acronyms used in international trade, and a chronology of major events in international trade since 1916. Most glossary entries are a short paragraph in length and include links to other entries. The glossary and acronyms are also cross-linked. Also available in print edition.

381 **The new Palgrave dictionary of money and finance.** Peter Newman, Murray Milgate, John Eatwell. 3 v., ill. London; New York: Macmillan Press; Stockton Press, 1992. ISBN: 156159041X.

332.03                                                                                    HG151.N48

With 1,008 well-written articles on banking, monetary theory, finance, and financial economics, this serves as an indispensable reference source. Includes abbreviations and acronyms. Articles are signed and most include a bibliography.

**382 Online trader's dictionary: The most up-to-date and authoritative compendium of financial terms.** R. J. Shook. 508 p. Franklin Lakes, N.J.: Career Press, 2002. ISBN: 1564145670.
332.63203 HG4515.95.S48

Nearly 7,000 terms on investing and the Internet. Includes lesser-known phrases such as *casino society*, as well as better-known phrases like *best-of-breed*. All definitions are short, but are written for the novice and expert alike.

**383 Wall Street words: An A to Z guide to investment terms for today's investor.** 3rd ed. David Logan Scott. Boston: Houghton Mifflin, 2003. ISBN: 0618176519.
332.603 HG4513.S37

Contains definitions of 4,500 terms, 100 of which are supplemented by case studies. Also features 50 investment tips from experts, typical examples of technical analysis chart patterns, and a brief bibliography. Available online through Credo Reference (London; Boston: Credo Reference).

**384 Webster's new world finance and investment dictionary.** Barbara Etzel. viii, 369 p., ill. Indianapolis, Ind.: Wiley, 2003. ISBN: 0764526359.
332.03 HG151.E89

Contains 3,500 international financial terms from accounting, finance, banking, economics, investing, financial markets, real estate, and securities, briefly described. Available online through Credo Reference (London; Boston: Credo Reference).

## Directories

**385 America's corporate finance directory.** New Providence, N.J.: National Register, 1994–. ISSN: 1080-1227.
338.7402573 HG4057.A15647

Information on 4,500 public and private U.S. companies with revenue income or pension assets over $100,000,000 per year and large foreign subsidiaries located in the U.S. Also profiles financial executives and identifies business relationships between companies.

**386**   **Annual guide to stocks.** Financial Information, Inc. Jersey City, N.J.: Financial Information, 1997–.

HG4512.R4

International coverage of listed and unlisted stocks, with place of incorporation, par value, CUSIP number, transfer agent, transfer charge, dividend disbursing agent, capital structure, and dividends. Companion to the *Directory of obsolete securities: Annual guide to stocks* (391), which annually compiles information on defunct corporations.

**387**   **Bank for international settlements.** Bank for International Settlements. [Basle, Switzerland]: Bank for International Settlements. http://www.bis.org/.

HG1811

Includes a directory of central bank websites; speeches by central bankers; working papers; banking statistics from central banks in 40 countries; securities statistics; derivatives statistics, including Herfindahl indices; effective exchange rates for 52 economies, with data since 1964; foreign exchange statistics; external debt statistics; and payment statistics from 1993 to the present.

**388**   **The bond buyer's municipal marketplace: Directory.** National ed. Thomson Financial Publishing. ill. Skokie, Ill.: Thomson Financial, 1993–. ISSN: 1079-2260.

332.6323302573                                                  HG4907.B67

Lists municipal bond firms and professionals (dealers, underwriters, financial advisers, public fund managers, municipal derivatives specialists, bond attorneys, tax controversy representation, credit enhancers, corporate trust departments, arbitrage rebate, rating agencies, and municipal issuers). Ranks underwriters, financial advisers, bond counsels, leading credit enhancers and credit issuers, and corporate trust departments. Available online.

**389**   **The corporate finance sourcebook.** New Providence, N.J.: National Register, 1979–. ISSN: 0163-3031.

332.02573                                                       HG4057.A1565

Directory of firms involved in capital investments and financial services (e.g., venture capital, private lenders, commercial and financial factors, business intermediaries, leasing companies and corporate real estate, commercial, U.S.-based foreign, and investment banks and trusts, securities analysts and CPA/auditing firms). Entries include personnel, financial information, type of investor or service, minimum investment, funds available, average number of deals completed annually, industry preferences, and exit criteria. Indexed by name of company, personnel, and geography.

**390    Credit union directory.** National Credit Union Administration. Alexandria, Va.: National Credit Union Administration. http:// purl.access.gpo.gov/GPO/LPS208.

Information from NCUA on U.S. credit unions, except "state-chartered natural person credit unions that are either uninsured or covered by private insurance corporations."—*Pref.* Gives charter number, address, name of CEO/manager, telephone number, assets, loans, net worth ratio, percent share growth, percent loan growth, loans/assets ratio, investments/ assets ratio, number of members, and number of full-time employees. Also includes national statistics.

**391    Directory of obsolete securities.** Jersey City, N.J.: Financial Information, 1970–. ISSN: 0085-0551.

332.67                                                                                                  HG4961.D56

Used to identify old stock certificates. Records are chronological, with details of the final action rendering the security obsolete. Companion to the *Annual guide to stocks* (386).

**392    Directory of world futures and options: A guide to international futures and options exchanges and products.** M. J. M. Robertson. 1 v. (various pagings). New York: Prentice Hall, 1990. ISBN: 0132178788.

332.645                                                                                              HG6024.A3R63

Arranged by regions of the world. Each entry contains stock exchange directory information, a brief history of the exchange, a description of what futures and options contracts are available, and details of how each commodity is traded. Includes where trades are quoted, if available. Indexed by exchange name, category, and product type. Glossary.

**393    The money market directory of small pension funds: Assets, $1–$25 million.** Money Market Directories. 7 v. [Charlottesville, Va.]: Money Market Directories, 2000–2006. ISSN: 1936-3346.

332                                                                                                    HG4509.M6533

Lists 51,000 organizations with tax-exempt funds (corporate, hospital, union, and government plan sponsors), giving contact information, names of benefit officers, tax exempt fund type, total assets and asset allocations, and service provider information.

**394 Morningstar.com.** [Chicago]: Morningstar. http://library. morningstar.com/.

Reports and screening for more than 8,000 stocks and 12,000 mutual funds. Mutual fund reports give a snapshot; data interpreter; analyst report to make sense of the data; stewardship grade (rates corporate culture, board quality, manager incentives, fees, and regulatory issues); three-, five-, and ten-year Morningstar rating; ten years of performance returns; seven years of quarterly returns; seven years of investor returns; tax analysis; risk measures; portfolio; management; fees and expenses; and purchase information, including minimum investments and brokerage availability. Stock reports give a snapshot, quote, analyst report, Morningstar rating, data interpreter, valuation ratios (price/earnings, price/book, price/sales, price/cash flows, and dividend yield percentage calculated for the stock, industry, S&P 500, and stock's five-year average), ten years of basic financial statements and two years of quarterly sales and income, key ratios, charts, five years of dividends, splits, and returns, owners and estimates, and links to the SEC filings. Analyst reports are available for only 1,000 stocks and 2,000 mutual funds, and are archived from 2001 for stocks and from 1993 for mutual funds. Includes an investment glossary and training courses.

**395 Nelson Information's directory of investment managers.** Nelson Information, Inc. Port Chester, N.Y.: Nelson Information, 2001–. ISSN: 1933-7558.

332.602573             HG4907.N44

Detailed profiles of some 1,700 money management firms listed alphabetically with up to 18 categories of data (e.g., investment specialties, decision-making process, fees, professional staff). Separate sections list firms geographically and by total assets managed, organization type, and area of specialization. With seven indexes, the most unique are those for minority and women-owned firms. *World's best money managers* (Port Chester, N.Y.: Nelson Publications, 1995–) provides a ranked list of money managers. Also available on CD-ROM.

**396 Nelson Information's directory of investment research.** Nelson Information, Inc. Port Chester, N.Y.: Nelson Information, 1975–. ISSN: 1553-2755.

332.6202573             HG4907.N43

Through several name changes, this remains one of the top directories. Lists more than 22,000 U.S. corporations, 750 investment research firms, and approx. 5,500 non-U.S. corporations that are covered by at least one investment analyst. For each corporation there is summary financial and corporate data and the investment research firms that provide coverage. For research firms it lists service offered, key executives, and financial data.

**397** **North American financial institutions directory.** North American ed. Thomson Financial Publishing. maps. Skokie, Ill.: Thomson Financial, 2000–. ISSN: 1529-1367.

332.10257                                                           HG1536.P635

Covers Canada, the U.S., Central America, the Caribbean, and Mexico. Entries vary in length from very brief to extensive, the latter providing information about branches and corporate and financial structure. A separate section lists banks by name and gives ranked lists of banks, commercial banks, savings and loan banks, and credit unions. Includes directories of associations, the Federal Reserve System, pertinent government organizations (e.g., the Secret Service), and a limited directory of the largest international banks.

**398** **Registered investment advisors edirectory.** Money Market Directories, Inc. Charlottesville, Va.: Standard & Poor's. http://www.mmdwebaccess.com/RIA.htm.

Lists 17,000 firms and their investment and mutual fund advisors, with information on type of accounts handled, investment style, and strategy. Also ranks advisors by assets managed. Formerly available in print as the *Directory of registered investment advisors.*

**399** **The savings directory.** Accuity. ill., maps. Duluth, Ga.: Accuity, 2005–. ISSN: 1931-8839.

332.3202573                                                         HG2150.U18

Lists savings and loans institutions by state and city, then gives type of charter, type of institution, membership code, type of insurance for deposits, type of ownership, year established, number of employees, officers, brief financial data, routing number, mortgage portfolios, and other operational information. Also available in LexisNexis.

**400** **Thomson bank directory.** 5 v. Thomson Financial Publishing. maps. Skokie, Ill.: Thomson Financial, 2000–. ISSN: 1529-1375.

332.102573                                                          HG2441.R3

The best known bank directory, it provides information primarily for U.S. banks, but coverage includes international banks and government banking agencies and officials. Information includes national routing codes, personnel, basic financials, credit ratings, standard settlement instructions, and industry statistics and rankings. Also available through various aggregator databases. A similar resource, with much wider international coverage, is the *World bank directory* (Skokie, Ill.: Accuity, 2005–).

## Encyclopedias

**401**  **Encyclopedia of retirement and finance.** Lois A. Vitt, E. Craig MacBean, Jürg K. Siegenthaler, Institute for Socio-Financial Studies. 2 v., ill. Westport, Conn.: Greenwood Press, 2003. ISBN: 0313324956.

305.2603                                                          HQ1064.U5E524

Contains 175 articles about financial issues affecting the elderly or retired individuals. Articles are written by a variety of scholars, many of whom are not writing from a business perspective, making this a holistic approach. Available as an e-book.

**402**  **The encyclopedia of taxation and tax policy.** 2nd ed. Joseph J. Cordes, Robert D. Ebel, Jane Gravelle, Urban Institute. xvii, 499 p., ill. Washington: Urban Institute Press, 2005. ISBN: 0877667527.

HJ2305.E53

Alphabetically arranged, with over 200 essays on tax policy, tax structure, tax compliance, and tax administration, with some coverage of public finance. Written by tax professionals, academicians, and administrators, almost all of whom are members of the National Tax Association. Entries are brief, but cover definitions, background, and relevance. Most entries include recommended readings. The 2nd ed. adds 45 new entries and updates entries with legislative changes.

**403**  **The encyclopedia of technical market indicators.** 2nd ed. Robert W. Colby. xii, 820 p., ill. New York: McGraw-Hill, 2003. ISBN: 0070120579.

332.632220973                                                    HG4915.C56

Detailed information on over 100 indicators for sophisticated investors or advanced finance students. Essays focus on methods of evaluating technical market indicators, and there are descriptions of stock market performance (e.g., advance/decline divergence oscillator, confidence index, presidential election cycle), arranged alphabetically. Entries vary in length:

most occupy at least half a page. Charts, graphs, and other ill. are frequent. Appendix of indicator interpretation definitions, index.

**404   The Federal Reserve System: An encyclopedia.** R. W. Hafer. xxxii, 451 p., ill. Westport, Conn.: Greenwood Press, 2005. ISBN: 0313328390.
332.11097303                                                          HG2563.H235

Contains 250 well-written articles explaining the somewhat mysterious Federal Reserve System, its structure, process, and policies. Entries also cover people and key events related to the Federal Reserve. Appendixes provide the text of The Federal Reserve Act, Federal Reserve Regulations, and a list of the Membership of the Board of Governors: 1913–2004. Available as an e-book.

**405   The international encyclopedia of mutual funds, closed-end funds, and real estate investment trusts.** Peter Madlem, Thomas K. Sykes. 367 p. Chicago: Glenlake; Fitzroy Dearborn, 2000. ISBN: 1579580866.
332.6327                                                              HG4530.M227

Over 5,000 entries in two section: mutual funds (how they operate, how to invest, categories) and closed-end funds (what they are, regulations, discounts, rights offerings, and categories). Good background information for investors. Available as an e-book.

**406   Swaps/financial derivatives: Products, pricing, applications, and risk management.** 3rd ed. Satyajit Das. 4 v., ill., charts. Singapore: Wiley, 2004. ISBN: 0470821094.
332.6457                                                              HG6024.A3D375

Explains the role and function of swaps and derivatives, as well as the derivatives themselves, in a way useful to an advanced student or to practitioner. Includes description of interest rates, yield curve modeling, options pricing, volatility, determination and behavior of swap spreads, risk management principles, market risk, credit risk, derivative trading, exotic options, new derivative markets, and the structure and evolution of derivative markets.

**407   The world financial system.** 2nd ed. Robert D. Fraser, Christopher Long. xii, 508 p. Harlow, Essex, U.K.; Detroit: Longman Current Affairs, 1992. ISBN: 0582096529.
332.042                                                               HG3881.F7118

Pt. 1 discusses the evolution of the world financial system, developments such as the Marshall Plan, the formation of the International Monetary Fund (IMF), and currency movements, with statistical tables and texts of significant agreements excerpted or printed in their entirety. Pt. 2, International economic organizations, lists over 50 organizations grouped geographically under four headings (general, monetary, developmental, and trade), with extensive discussion of the organization's background, objectives, membership, and structure, in addition to standard directory information. Index.

## Factbooks

408  **China securities market investment yearbook.** GTA Securities Research Institute. ill. Hong Kong, [China]: GTA Securities Research Institute, 2005–.

HG5781.C494

Provides a review of China's securities market from 1990–2004, and gives data from 2004. Chapters include: China securities market overview, 1990–2004; statistics for SSE and SZSE index; stock market monthly statistics, 2004; rankings for 2004; transition statistics, 2004; China fund market 1998–2004; statistics of delisted securities, 1990–2004; securities law; company law; historical exchange rate, 1990–2004; and major securities agencies in China.

409  **The CRB commodity yearbook.** Commodity Research Bureau (U.S.). ill. New York: Wiley, 1994–. ISSN: 1076–2906.

332.6328                                    HF1041.C56

Provides background information and statistical data on 100 domestic and international agricultural and industrial commodities, and on financial and stock index futures. Includes seasonal patterns and historical data from the prior ten years, with some tables going back 100 years. Organized alphabetically by commodity, with articles on each commodity that describe the commodity and give pricing trends and factors affecting price. Data sources are primarily U.S. official publications, with some from U.N., trade association, and international organization publications. Includes feature articles discussing current issues. Also available on CD-ROM.

410  **The financial services fact book.** Insurance Information Institute. ill. New York: Insurance Information Institute [and] Financial Services Roundtable, 2002–. ISSN: 1537-6257.

658                                         HG181.F643465

Current information on insurance, banking, securities, and the financial services industry as a whole. Includes statistics on U.S. savings, investment and debt ownership, consumer fraud and identity theft, convergence of financial services companies, IT spending, and the growth of online commerce. The most current Fact book is available at http://www.financialservicesfacts.org/financial/.

**411    Securities industry fact book.** Securities Industry Association. New York: SIA, 1993–. ISSN: 1933–7043.

Information on capital markets, the securities industry, market activity, investor participation, global markets, and savings and investment. Good for finding statistics on corporate underwriting and private placements, capital raised for U.S. business, initial public offerings by state, total U.S. mergers and acquisitions, securities industry employment by firm category, securities industry profitability, pre-tax profit margins and return on equity, stock market capitalization, stock exchange activity, compound annual rates of return by decade for stocks, bonds and treasuries, and value of international securities offerings. Some data goes back to 1965.

**412    Thorndike encyclopedia of banking and financial tables.** [4th] ed. [David] [Thorndike], [A.S. Pratt and Sons], Thomson Financial Publishing. Arlington, Va.; [Skokie, Ill.]: A.S. Pratt and Sons; [Thomson Financial], [2007].

Tables for loan payment and amortization, compound interest and annuity, simple interest, savings and withdrawals, installment loans, and investment. A companion Yearbook (Boston: Warren, Gorham, and Lamont) is also published.

## Guides and Handbooks

**413    Barron's finance and investment handbook.** 7th ed. John Downes, Jordan Elliot Goodman. xii, 1396 p., ill. Hauppauge, N.Y.: Barron's Educational Series, 2006. ISBN: 9780764159923.

332.678                                                                      HG173.D662006

Presents a wide array of background information on financial institutions, finance, and investing. Arranged in five parts. Pt 1: 30 investment opportunities (from annuities to zero coupon bonds), pt. 2: how to read an annual report and a quarterly report, pt. 3: how to read the financial pages and ticker tape, pt. 4: dictionary of finance and investment (about 800 pages), and pt. 5: finance and investing ready reference (sources of information and assistance in the U.S. and Canada, lists of major financial institutions and mutual funds, historical data on various stock exchanges and other financial data, and lists for publicly traded companies on the NYSE and NASDAQ 100). Appendixes for currencies of the world, abbreviations and acronyms, and selected further readings. Available as an e-book.

**414   Business ratios and formulas: A comprehensive guide.** Steven M. Bragg. xvii, 334 p., ill. Hoboken, N.J.: Wiley, 2002. ISBN: 0471396435.

650.01513                                                    HF5691.B73

A wonderful guide to the world of business ratios with definitions, formulas, examples, and cautions for nearly 200 measures. "Cautions" explain when another measure would be better suited, as well as how a measure can be misunderstood. Designed for managers, but useful for anyone who must calculate and understand business ratios. Available as an e-book.

**415   Cases in corporate acquisitions, buyouts, mergers, and takeovers.** Gale Group. Detroit: Gale Group, 1999–. ISSN: 1526-5927.

658                                                          HD2746.5.C374

Arranged alphabetically with 300 entries that are 3–5 pages long. Invaluable for capturing hard-to-find information in one easy-to-use source, but is not an annual. Covers major deals of the last century if one of the players was a U.S. company, summarizing background, the organizations involved, and the deal itself. Useful for the financials provided, and an explanation of the deal's effect on the companies involved and the industry as a whole. Indexed by company and industry.

**416   Commodities price locator.** Karen J. Chapman. xxx, 135 p. Phoenix: Oryx Press, 1989. ISBN: 0897743660.

016.332644                                                  Z7164.C83C46; HF1040.7

More than 150 government, trade, financial, and other serials that publish commodities price information are listed alphabetically by commodity and briefly annotated. An appendix lists databases (none of which appear in the main list) that contain commodities prices. The emphasis is on cash ("spot") prices paid for commodities received rather than on commodities futures prices, which are not covered. While dated, much of the information is still of use.

**417   Commodity futures trading: Bibliography.** Chicago Board of Trade. Chicago: Chicago Board of Trade, 1967–1995.

016.3326328                                                 Z7164.C83C64; HG6046

In three sections: (1) books, monographs, and material provided by commodity exchanges; (2) resource material, i.e., scholarly journal articles and government publications; (3) trade, or popular press articles. Each section is subdivided by specific topics or commodity. No index.

**418    The economist numbers guide: The essentials of business numeracy.** Richard Stutely. 237 p., ill. New York: Wiley, 1997. ISBN: 0471249548.

650.01513                                                        HF5695.S83

Introduction to numerical methods and quantitative techniques used in mathematics, statistics, business, accounting, and economics. Uses extensive examples, tables, and figures to explain in layman's terms. Appendix is a dictionary, with cross-references to the main section. Indexed.

**419    The handbook of European fixed income securities.** Frank J. Fabozzi, Moorad Choudhry. xiv, 1010 p., ill. New York: Wiley, 2003. ISBN: 0471430390.

332.632044

A well-written guide to European financial markets, including government and corporate bond market instruments and institutions. In five sections. Section 1: background to fixed income securities, bondholder and shareholder value, bond pricing and yield measures, measuring interest rate risk. Section 2: Euro government bond market, Eurobond market, German Pfandbrief and European covered bonds market, inflation linked bonds, United Kingdom gilts market, European repo market, mortgage backed securities, credit card and auto consumer loan ABS, and structured credit. Section 3: interest rate futures and options, pricing options on interest rate instruments, interest rate swaps, credit derivatives, and credit default swaps. Section 4: portfolio management for fixed incomes, portfolio strategies, and analysis and evaluation of corporate bonds. Section 5 covers legal considerations. Available as an e-book.

**420    The law of securities regulation.** Rev. 5th ed. Thomas Lee Hazen. xxxvii, 927 p. St. Paul, Minn.: Thomson/West, 2006. ISBN: 9780314172457.

KF1439.H39

Annual introduction and overview to U.S. securities laws. Five ch. on the Securities Act of 1933, with other chapters on state blue sky laws, market regulation, civil liability, shareholder suffrage, market manipulation, the Public Utility Holding Act of 1935, debt securities and the

Trust Indenture Act of 1939, federal regulation of investment companies and the Investment Company Act of 1940, the Investment Advisers Act of 1940, and overviews of related laws. Appendix on securities research using Westlaw.

**421    Mathematical formulas for economists.** 3rd ed. Bernd Luderer. New York: Springer, 2006. ISBN: 9783540469018.
Defines formulas used in economics, finance, and accounting, including definitions for the notations used in formulas. Gives basic formulas, as well as alternate formulas. Prior knowledge of the usage is necessary, as context is not provided.

**422    Money and exchange in Europe and America, 1600–1775: A handbook.** John J. McCusker, Institute of Early American History and Culture. xi, 367 p., ill. Chapel Hill, N.C.: University of North Carolina Press, 1978. ISBN: 0807812846.
332.450212                                                                  HG219.M33
Explains the economic role of money in colonial America. "Aims to provide sufficient information of a technical and statistical nature to allow the reader to convert a sum stated in one money into its equivalent in another."—*p. 3*. Conversion tables.

**423    Morningstar.com.** [Chicago]: Morningstar. http://library.morningstar.com/.
Reports and screening for more than 8,000 stocks and 12,000 mutual funds. Mutual fund reports give a snapshot; data interpreter; analyst report to make sense of the data; stewardship grade (rates corporate culture, board quality, manager incentives, fees, and regulatory issues); three-, five-, and ten-year Morningstar rating; ten years of performance returns; seven years of quarterly returns; seven years of investor returns; tax analysis; risk measures; portfolio; management; fees and expenses; and purchase information, including minimum investments and brokerage availability. Stock reports give a snapshot, quote, analyst report, Morningstar rating, data interpreter, valuation ratios (price/earnings, price/book, price/sales, price/cash flows, and dividend yield percentage calculated for the stock, industry, S&P 500, and stock's five-year average), ten years of basic financial statements and two years of quarterly sales and income, key ratios, charts, five years of dividends, splits, and returns, owners and estimates, and links to the SEC filings. Analyst reports are available for only 1,000 stocks and 2,000 mutual funds, and are archived from 2001 for

stocks and from 1993 for mutual funds. Includes an investment glossary and training courses.

**424 MRI bankers' guide to foreign currency.** Monetary Research International. ill. Houston, Tex.: Monetary Research International, 1991–. ISSN: 1055-3851.

769.55024332            HG353.M75

Describes the currency of more than 220 countries. Includes exchange restrictions, current exchange rates, and information on where the currency is used. Used most for the color images of paper notes and traveler's checks.

**425 Stock trader's almanac.** Yale Hirsch, Jeffrey Hirsch. Hoboken, N.J.: Wiley, 1967–. ISSN: 1553-4812.

Most used for the annotated calendar noting daily historical trading tendencies. A bull or bear appears on days with significant historical directional tendencies. Unusual in that it covers the best performing months or days.

## Indexes; Abstract Journals

**426 Banking information index.** American Bankers Association. Ann Arbor, Mich.: UMI, 1994–. ISSN: 1075-282X.

016.3321            Z7164.F5A53; HG1501

Indexes over 200 periodicals of interest to the financial services industry, especially banking. Also available through Banking Information Source (427).

**427 Banking information source.** ProQuest Information and Learning Company. Ann Arbor, Mich.: ProQuest Information and Learning. http://il.proquest.com/products_pq/descriptions/pq_banking_info. shtml.

Indexes nearly 450 journals and trade publications in banking and finance, many of which also appear in full-text. Indexing is from ABA's *Banking information index* (426) and FINIS (Financial Industry Information Service). About half of the publications are unique to Banking Information Source and not covered in ABI/Inform Global (788) or Complete. These unique titles include: *ABA bank directors briefing, ABA trust & investments, American banker, American bankruptcy law journal, Bank accounting & finance, Bank of America journal of applied corporate finance, Compliance reporter, Credit union journal, Financial adviser, Financial markets, Institutions & instruments, Private asset management, School of Bank Marketing papers, Stonier Graduate School of Banking theses,* and *Internal revenue bulletin.* Coverage is from 1971 to the present. Also available through Dialog (Stamford, Conn.: Thomson Corporation, 2002–).

**428**  **The Wall Street Journal index.** Dow Jones. [New York]: Dow Jones, 1957–. ISSN: 1042-9840.

332.05                                                                          HG1.W26

Index coverage begins in 1955 and is based on the final Eastern edition of the newspaper. Each issue has two parts: (1) corporate news indexed by company name; (2) general news indexed by topic. Includes special sections for book reviews, personalities, deaths, and theater reviews. The last section of the index includes the daily Dow Jones averages for each month of the year. Since 1981, v. 1 includes *Barron's index,* a subject and corporate index to *Barron's business and financial weekly.* Since 1990, published monthly with quarterly and annual cumulations. Former publication frequency was monthly with annual cumulations. Annual cumulations issued in 2 pts., 1980–2001.

Fully searchable page images of the complete *Wall Street Journal* 1889–1989 are available in ProQuest Historical Newspapers (Ann Arbor, Mich.:ProQuest, 2001–). Searchable full text (although not original page images) is also available in a number of other commercial database services, including ProQuest Newspapers (Ann Arbor, Mich.: ProQuest, 2001–), Factiva (794), and ABI/Inform Global (788).

## Internet Resources

**429**  **American association of individual investors.** American Association of Individual Investors. 2002–. Chicago: American Association of Individual Investors. http://www.aaii.com/.

HG4930.I49

The Association was founded in 1978 to support individual investors. The site has seven sections, each with articles: portfolio management; personal finance; stocks (stock screener, shadow stock portfolio, DRPs, classroom); bonds (review of bond websites, classroom); mutual funds (fund portfolio, exchange traded funds, guides, classroom); investing basics (guides, classroom, top investing sites); and research (quotes, S&P research, fund screener, investor surveys). Some resources are available only to members.

**430    American finance association.** American Finance Association. 1998–. Berkeley, Calif.: American Finance Association. http://www. afajof.org/.
The Association was founded in 1939 to serve the interests of those interested in finance and financial economics. The site has a history of finance, Worldwide Directory of Finance Faculty, news, jobs, and *The journal of finance*, one of the top journals in the field (membership required for some content).

**431    American management association.** American Management Association. 1997–. New York: American Management Association. http://www.amanet.org/.
Founded in 1923 to provide "a full range of management development and educational services to individuals, companies and government agencies worldwide, including 486 of the Fortune 500 companies."—*About AMA*. The website has information on seminars, corporate solutions, government solutions, events, books and self-study, e-learning, and membership.

**432    Bank for international settlements.** Bank for International Settlements. [Basle, Switzerland]: Bank for International Settlements. http://www.bis.org/.

HG1811

Includes a directory of central bank websites; speeches by central bankers; working papers; banking statistics from central banks in 40 countries; securities statistics; derivatives statistics, including Herfindahl indices; effective exchange rates for 52 economies, with data since 1964; foreign exchange statistics; external debt statistics; and payment statistics from 1993 to the present.

**433    Better investing.** National Association of Investors Corp. 2007–. Madison Heights, Mich.: National Association of Investors Corp. http://www.better-investing.org/.
Founded in 1951 to "empower our members to make better investment decisions by providing unbiased, objective education, tools and support, and a proven investment methodology."—*About*. The site supports this mission with tools and resources (publications, courses, online tools, data services, research, events), personal finance (budget, banking, credit, financial planning, fun money, frugal marketplace, insurance), and investment clubs.

**434    BigCharts.** MarketWatch, Inc. 1998–. [San Francisco]: BigCharts. http://bigcharts.marketwatch.com/.

HG4638

Best known for historic stock quotes, BigCharts has information on over 50,000 symbols, including current information on all NYSE, NASDAQ, AMEX, and OTC stocks, all NASDAQ quoted mutual funds, as well as leading financial indexes and international exchanges. The current information includes company profiles, company financials, news, charts, analyst estimates, analysis, and intraday stock screeners. Historic quotes include open, closing, high and low prices, volume traded, split adjusted price, and adjustment factor since 1970.

**435  Credit union directory.** National Credit Union Administration. Alexandria, Va.: National Credit Union Administration. http://purl.access.gpo.gov/GPO/LPS208.

Information from NCUA on U.S. credit unions, except "state-chartered natural person credit unions that are either uninsured or covered by private insurance corporations."—*Pref.* Gives charter number, address, name of CEO/manager, telephone number, assets, loans, net worth ratio, percent share growth, percent loan growth, loans/assets ratio, investments/assets ratio, number of members, and number of full-time employees. Also includes national statistics.

**436  Derivatives dictionary.** The William Margrabe Group, Inc. 1996–2002. Westchester County, N.Y.: The William Margrabe Group, Inc. http://www.margrabe.com/Dictionary.html.

Definitions can be very terse, but at its best, the online dictionary gives definitions with examples, applications, and importance to pricing and risk management.

**437  Economic history services.** EH.Net. 2004–. [Oxford, Ohio]: EH.Net. http://eh.net/.

HC21.E25

Owned by the Economic History Association and intended primarily for economic historians, historians of economics, economists, and historians, EH.net has research abstracts and book reviews, course syllabi, directory of economic historians, Encyclopedia of Economic and Business History, historical economic data sets (such as Global Financial Data, 1880–1913 and historic labor statistics), links to economic history websites, and a section called "How Much Is That?"

"How Much Is That?" gives comparative values of money, including five ways to compare the worth of a U.S. dollar, 1790–2005; the price of gold for 1257–2005; annual Consumer Price Index for the United States for 1774–2005; the purchasing power of the British pound, 1264–2005; annual real and nominal GDP for the United States, 1790–2005; annual real and nominal GDP for the United Kingdom, 1086–2005; interest rate series for the United Kingdom and the United States, 1790–2001; and daily closing values of the Dow Jones Industrial Average (DJIA) from 1896.

438    **Ernst and Young.** Ernst and Young. 2007. London: Ernst and Young. http://www.ey.com/global/content.nsf/International/Industry_Overview/.

Ernst and Young provides "accounting and auditing, tax reporting and operations, tax advisory, business risk services, technology and security risk services, transaction advisory, and human capital services." The site is useful for articles on financial management, corporate governance, initial public offerings (IPOs), and industry reports (asset management, automotive, banking and capital markets, biotechnology, consumer products, insurance, media and entertainment, mining and metals, oil and gas, pharmaceuticals, real estate and construction, hospitality and leisure, technology, telecommunications, utilities).

439    **Federal deposit insurance corporation.** Federal Deposit Insurance Corporation. [1996–.] [Washington, D.C.]: Federal Deposit Insurance Corporation. http://www.fdic.gov/.

HG2441

The site is organized into: Deposit Insurance, Consumer Protection, Industry Analysis, Regulation & Examinations, Asset Sales, and News & Events. Includes Call Reports and Thrift Financial Reports from 1998 to the present; an institution directory for federally insured institutions; Summary of Deposits; Quarterly Banking Profile from December 31, 1994; statistics on banking and depository institutions; and laws and regulations.

440    **Investorwords.com.** WebFinance, Inc. 1997–. [Fairfax, Va.]: WebFinance, Inc. http://www.investorwords.com/.

HG151

Over 6,000 definitions on subjects like accounting, banking, bonds, brokerages, currencies, dividends, earnings, economics, forex, futures, insurance, investor relations, IPOs, law/estate planning, lending/credit, mergers/acquisitions, mutual funds, options, public companies, real estate, retirement, stocks, strategies, taxes, technical analysis, trading, and venture capital. Definitions seem to be intended for the general public as well as for advanced investors.

441 **Rutgers accounting research center.** Rutgers Accounting Research Center. Newark, N.J.: Rutgers Accounting Research Center. http:// raw.rutgers.edu/.

HF5625.7

Links to online resources for accounting and finance. Categories are Big Five, Professional Associations (state, U.S., and international), Journals and Publications, Education, Finance (major stock exchanges, stock quotes, currency converter, financial services), Professors, Taxation (tax analysis, tax associations, tax services), Audit and Law (audit agencies and associations, auditing software), Government, EDGAR, FASB, International, Publishers, Software, Other Sites, and Entertainment. Also links to the Rutgers Accounting Research Directory, with an index to accounting articles publ. since 1963.

442 **Yahoo! finance.** Yahoo! Inc. 2001. Sunnyvale, Calif.: Yahoo! Inc. http://finance.yahoo.com/.

A rich source of financial information, with company profiles, SEC filings, annual reports, stock quotes, news, analysis, conference call calendar, industry statistics and news, and information for the personal investor. The focus is on financial information about U.S. and Canadian companies and industries, but international information, such as indices and currency information, is also available, especially through the portals to Yahoo!Finance for other countries (linked from the bottom of the entry page). Historical quotes for stocks, bonds, and money markets are since 1970 and give daily, weekly, and monthly closing prices, and dividends. Occasionally links to fee-based information.

## Organizations and Associations

443 **American association of individual investors.** American Association of Individual Investors. 2002–. Chicago: American Association of Individual Investors. http://www.aaii.com/.

HG4930.I49

The Association was founded in 1978 to support individual investors. The site has seven sections, each with articles: portfolio management; personal finance; stocks (stock screener, shadow stock portfolio, DRPs, classroom); bonds (review of bond websites, classroom); mutual funds (fund portfolio, exchange traded funds, guides, classroom); investing basics (guides, classroom, top investing sites); and research (quotes, S&P research, fund screener, investor surveys). Some resources are available only to members.

**444    American finance association.** American Finance Association. 1998–. Berkeley, Calif.: American Finance Association. http://www. afajof.org/.
The Association was founded in 1939 to serve the interests of those interested in finance and financial economics. The site has a history of finance, World-wide Directory of Finance Faculty, news, jobs, and *The journal of finance*, one of the top journals in the field (membership required for some content).

**445    Bank for international settlements.** Bank for International Settlements. [Basle, Switzerland]: Bank for International Settlements. http://www.bis.org/.

HG1811

Includes a directory of central bank websites; speeches by central bankers; working papers; banking statistics from central banks in 40 countries; securities statistics; derivatives statistics, including Herfindahl indices; effective exchange rates for 52 economies, with data since 1964; foreign exchange statistics; external debt statistics; and payment statistics from 1993 to the present.

**446    Better investing.** National Association of Investors Corp. 2007–. Madison Heights, Mich.: National Association of Investors Corp. http://www.better-investing.org/.
Founded in 1951 to "empower our members to make better investment decisions by providing unbiased, objective education, tools and support, and a proven investment methodology."—*About.* The site supports this mission with tools and resources (publications, courses, online tools, data services, research, events), personal finance (budget, banking, credit, financial planning, fun money, frugal marketplace, insurance), and investment clubs.

**447    Federal deposit insurance corporation.** Federal Deposit Insurance Corporation. [1996–.] [Washington, D.C.]: Federal Deposit Insurance Corporation. http://www.fdic.gov/.

HG2441

The site is organized into: Deposit Insurance, Consumer Protection, Industry Analysis, Regulation & Examinations, Asset Sales, and News & Events. Includes Call Reports and Thrift Financial Reports from 1998 to the present; an institution directory for federally insured institutions; Summary of Deposits; Quarterly Banking Profile from December 31, 1994; statistics on banking and depository institutions; and laws and regulations.

# Periodicals

**448**   Barron's. ill. Chicopee, Mass.: Dow Jones, 1994–. ISSN: 1077-8039.
Microfilm 5413

Reports on stocks, bonds, mutual fund and hedge fund performance; also reviews and ranks brokers and fund managers. Some information also available at the magazine's website at http://online.barrons.com/public/main/.

**449**   **Harvard business review.** ill. Boston: Graduate School of Business Administration, Harvard University. ISSN: 0017-8012.
330.904                                                    HF5001.H3

Articles, best practices, book reviews, and case studies on communication, finance and accounting, global business, innovation and entrepreneurship, leadership, management, organizational development, sales and marketing, strategy and execution, and technology and operations. Also available online, through Business Source Elite (791).

**450**   **The review of financial studies.** Oxford University Press. 1988–.
New York: Oxford University Press and Society for Financial Studies. ISSN: 0893-9454. http://rfs.oxfordjournals.org/.
HG1.R45

One of the top journals in financial economics, it publishes theoretical and empirical research in financial economics. Sponsored by the Society for Financial Studies, with irregular, but lengthy book reviews. E-mail alerts can be set up for table of contents or to track topics and authors. Also available in print format.

# Statistics

**451**   **Bank for international settlements.** Bank for International Settlements. [Basle, Switzerland]: Bank for International Settlements. http://www.bis.org/.
HG1811

Includes a directory of central bank websites; speeches by central bankers; working papers; banking statistics from central banks in 40 countries; securities statistics; derivatives statistics, including Herfindahl indices; effective exchange rates for 52 economies, with data since 1964; foreign exchange statistics; external debt statistics; and payment statistics from 1993 to the present.

**452    BigCharts.** MarketWatch, Inc. 1998–. [San Francisco]: BigCharts. http://bigcharts.marketwatch.com/.

HG4638

Best known for historic stock quotes, BigCharts has information on over 50,000 symbols, including current information on all NYSE, NASDAQ, AMEX, and OTC stocks, all NASDAQ quoted mutual funds, as well as leading financial indexes and international exchanges. The current information includes company profiles, company financials, news, charts, analyst estimates, analysis, and intraday stock screeners. Historic quotes include open, closing, high and low prices, volume traded, split adjusted price, and adjustment factor since 1970.

**453    Cost of capital quarterly.** Ibbotson Associates. Chicago: Ibbotson Associates, 1994–. ISSN: 1080-4021.

HC110.C3C67

Financial data for 300 industries, organized by SIC code, including several measures of cost of capital and cost of equity. Also gives industry betas, sales, profitability, capitalization, multiples, ratios, equity returns, and capital structure. Available online through Ibbotson Cost of Capital Center.

**454    The CRB commodity yearbook.** Commodity Research Bureau (U.S.). ill. New York: Wiley, 1994–. ISSN: 1076-2906.

332.6328                                                    HF1041.C56

Provides background information and statistical data on 100 domestic and international agricultural and industrial commodities, and on financial and stock index futures. Includes seasonal patterns and historical data from the prior ten years, with some tables going back 100 years. Organized alphabetically by commodity, with articles on each commodity that describe the commodity and give pricing trends and factors affecting price. Data sources are primarily U.S. official publications, with some from U.N., trade association, and international organization publications. Includes feature articles discussing current issues. Also available on CD-ROM.

**455    CRSP databases.** Chicago: Center for Research in Security Prices, 1989–.

One of the best sources for current and historical security data for the NYSE (daily from July 1962; monthly from Dec. 1925), AMEX (daily from July 1962; monthly from July 1962), and NASDAQ (daily from July 1972; monthly from Dec. 1972) Stock Markets. Data subsets include: CRSP U.S.

Stock Database (NYSE, AMEX, NASD, S&P, annual/quarterly/monthly/ daily); CRSP U.S. Government Bond Fixed Term Index Series: monthly and daily; CRSP U.S. Treasury Risk-Free Rates File; and CRSP Fama-Bliss Discount Bond Files for prices and yields. Delivered by DVD or CD-ROM. Also available through Wharton Research Data Services (WRDS).

**456  Datastream advance.** Datastream. London: Datastream International, 1995–.

A wide array of current and historic global market and economic data. Covers 700 topics, with data going back 20 years. Includes: global and sector indexes, exchange-traded derivatives, investment research, fixed income and equity securities, current and historical fundamental data, foreign exchange and money markets data, real-time financial news from Dow Jones, closing prices for OTC bond instruments, forecast and historical economics data, and interest and exchange rates. Data can easily be compared and downloaded to Excel, Word, or PowerPoint.

**457  The Dow Jones averages, 1885–1995.** Phyllis S. Pierce. 1 v. (unpaged), ill. Chicago: Irwin Professional, 1996. ISBN: 0786309741. 332.632220973                                                                    HG4915.D6434

Chronology of the development of the Dow Jones Averages. Presents daily figures, beginning with the 14-stock average (combining railroads and industrials) in 1885 and ending with 1995 daily averages for industrials, transportation, utilities, and bonds. Supersedes earlier volumes.

**458  Federal Reserve bulletin.** Board of Governors of the Federal Reserve System. Washington: G.P.O., 1915–. ISSN: 0014-9209. 332.110973                                                                       HG2401.A5

The most complete current information, including statistics, on financial conditions in the United States. Includes bank asset quality, bank assets and liabilities, bank structure data, business finance, exchange rates, flow of funds accounts, household finance, industrial activity, interest rates, and money stock and reserve balances. Also reports on financial developments in foreign countries. No longer published quarterly in print. Current *Bulletins* are available at: http://www.federalreserve.gov/pubs/bulletin/default.htm.

**459  Global financial data.** Global Financial Data. [2003–.] Los Angeles: Global Financial Data. http://www.globalfinancialdata.com/.

20,000 financial and economic data series for some 200 countries, dating from the 1600s to the present. Categories are daily stock market data from 1962 (open, high, low, close, volume, available in split adjusted or unadjusted format); state, national, and international real estate market data from 1830 (includes Median New Home Prices—United States, Winans International U.S. Real Estate Index—Price Only, Austria ATX Real Estate Index, Shanghai SE Real Estate Index); international bond indices from 1862; central bank interest yields; commercial paper yields; commodity indices; commodity prices; consumer price indices; U.S and European corporate bond yields, some from 1857; international deposit rates; international exchange rates, some from 1660; futures contracts; government bond yields; gross domestic product; international interbank interest rates from the 1980s; interest rate swaps from 1988 (United States, Europe, Japan); U.S. intraday data, daily from January 1933 to May 2007; international lending rates, some from 1934; overnight and call money rates, some from 1857 (monthly, weekly, daily); international population; sector indices (consumer discretionary, consumer staples, energy, finance, health care, industrials, information technology, materials, telecommunications, transports, utilities), stock indices—preferred stocks; stock indices—composites; stock indices—size and style; stock market—AMEX; stock market—NASDAQ; stock market—NYSE; stock market—OTC; stocks (capitalization, volume, dividend yields and P/E ratios, technical indicators); total return indices—bills; total return indices—bonds; total return indices—stocks; international treasury bill yields; international unemployment rates, some from 1890; and international wholesale price indices.

**460    Ibbotson Associates' beta book publication.** Ibbotson Associates. Chicago: Ibbotson Associates, 1996–. ISSN: 1087-6618.

332.041                                                         HG4028.V3I23

Contains 60-month levered and unlevered beta calculations for 5,000 U.S. publicly traded companies. Betas are adjusted toward peer group average. Useful for Capital Assets Pricing Model (CAPM) calculations with data for the beta, Ibbotson beta, Fama-French beta. Data is used for modeling stock performance or pricing securities. Includes an overview of the beta estimation methodologies used.

**461    Investment companies yearbook.** CDA/Wiesenberger. Rockville, Md.: CDA/Wiesenberger, 1993–2001. ISSN: 1068-9958.

332                                                             HG4530.I5

A comprehensive source on mutual funds and investment companies. The first two parts contain general information on the use and selection of mutual funds to meet specific investment objectives. Pt. 3 contains single-page entries for mutual funds, including for each a description of its objective; composition of its portfolio; list of directors, investment manager(s), and other key personnel; a ten-year financial/statistical history; address and telephone; whether or not there is a sales charge; special services offered; and states in which the fund is qualified for sale. Pt. 4 covers closed-end and variable annuity funds. Contains a glossary and index by fund name.

**462 Mergerstat review.** Merrill Lynch Business Brokerage and Valuation. ill. Chicago: The Company, 1982–. ISSN: 1071-4065. 338.830973                                                    HD2746.5.M48

Review mergers and acquisitions. Pt. 1 is statistical analysis with aggregate announcements, composition of aggregate net merger and acquisition announcements, method of payment, P/E offered, divestitures, publicly traded sellers, privately owned sellers, foreign sellers, aggressive buyers, financial advisor ranking, legal advisor ranking, top managers, and termination fees. Pt. 2 is industry analysis with highlights, industry groups, spotlights giving industry activity for the two most active industries by Standard Industrial Classification (SIC) code, multiples (TIC/EBITDA, P/E), premiums, composition, and cross-border activity. Pt. 3 is a geographical analysis with U.S. buyers and sellers by state, and foreign buyers and sellers. Pt. 4 is current year rosters with completed and pending transactions with pricing disclosed, canceled transactions with pricing disclosed, transactions with termination fees disclosed, and the composition of the Mergerstat $1 billion club. Pt. 5 is a historical review with a 25-year statistical review, record holders, 100 largest announcements in history, and largest announcements by industry. Pt. 6 lists transactions by seller SIC code. There is also a glossary of terms. Also available in online form.

**463 Morningstar.com.** [Chicago]: Morningstar. http://library. morningstar.com/.

Reports and screening for more than 8,000 stocks and 12,000 mutual funds. Mutual fund reports give a snapshot; data interpreter; analyst report to make sense of the data; stewardship grade (rates corporate culture, board quality, manager incentives, fees, and regulatory issues); three-, five-, and ten-year Morningstar rating; ten years of performance returns; seven years of quarterly returns; seven years of investor returns; tax analysis; risk measures; portfolio; management; fees and expenses; and purchase information, including minimum investments and brokerage availability. Stock reports give a snapshot, quote, analyst report, Morningstar rating, data interpreter, valuation ratios (price/earnings, price/book, price/sales, price/cash flows, and dividend yield percentage calculated for the stock, industry, S&P 500, and stock's five-year average), ten years of basic financial statements and two years of quarterly sales and income, key ratios, charts, five years of dividends, splits, and returns, owners and estimates, and links to the SEC filings. Analyst reports are available for only 1,000 stocks and 2,000 mutual funds, and are archived from 2001 for stocks and from 1993 for mutual funds. Includes an investment glossary and training courses.

**464    National accounts statistics.** United Nations. New York: United
Nations, 1985–.
339.3                                                    HC79.I5N387

Detailed national accounts estimates from 170–200 countries and areas. Data gathered from national statistical services and national and international source publications. This source is invaluable for providing data since 1950. Prepared by The Statistical Offices of the United Nations Secretariat. Continues *Yearbook of national accounts statistics (1957–81)*, which superseded *Statistics of national income and expenditure (1952–57)*. Also available through the National Accounts Main Aggregates database (http://unstats.un.org/unsd/snaama/Introduction.asp/), with data from 1970 to the present.

**465    Natural resource commodities: A century of statistics, prices,
output, consumption, foreign trade, and employment in the
United States, 1870–1973.** Robert S. Manthy, Joan R. Tron,
Resources for the Future. xiii, 240 p., graphs. Baltimore: Johns
Hopkins University Press, 1978. ISBN: 0801821428.
333                                                      HF1052.M35

An update of Resources for the Future's *Trends in natural resource commodities* by Neal Potter and Francis Christy, Jr. (1962). In five sections: (1) methodology; (2) highlights; (3) detailed agricultural, mineral, and forest commodity summaries, emphasizing the post-1950 period; (4) individual data series for 200 natural resources commodities, from 1870 to 1973; (5) documented sources and explanatory notes for the data tables.

466    SourceOECD. Organisation for Economic Co-operation and
       Development. [Paris, France]: OECD. http://new.sourceoecd.org/.
A subscription database containing OECD books, reports, working papers,
serials, and statistical databases on economic and social topics, as well as the
environment, energy, and technological development. Focuses mainly on
the 30 OECD member states and major nonmember developing countries.
       Serials include journals; the OECD Factbook (Paris: OECD, 2005–)
and other statistical works; and titles that forecast and analyze trends,
such as the OECD Economic Outlook (Paris: Organisation for Economic
Co-operation and Development, 1967–), *African economic outlook* (Paris:
African Development Bank, Development Centre of the Organisation
for Economic Co-operation and Development, 2002–), International
Migration Outlook (Paris: Organisation for Economic Co-operation and
Development, 2006–), and OECD-FAO Agricultural Outlook (Paris:
Organisation for Economic Co-operation and Development; Food and
Agriculture Organization, 2005–).
       Current, themed databases include the OECD Economic Out-
look Database (Paris: Organisation for Economic Co-operation and
Development, 2002–), SourceOECD Main Economic Indicators (Paris:
Organisation for Economic Co-operation and Development, 2002–),
Banking Statistics, Education Statistics, Globalisation, Indicators of
Industry and Services, Insurance, International Development, Interna-
tional Direct Investment Statistics, International Migration Statistics,
the ITCS International Trade by Commodity Database, Monthly Sta-
tistics of International Trade, the National Accounts Database, OECD
Health Data, OECD Statistics on International Trade in Services, the
Revenue Statistics of OECD Member Countries Database, the Science
and Technology Database, the Social Expenditure Database, Structural
and Demographic Business Statistics, Taxing Wages Statistics, and the
Telecommunications Database. Statistical databases of the International
Energy Agency are also available via this source. OECD.Stat enables users
to query multiple databases simultaneously and to export search results
in several formats.
       Also incorporates Future Trends, an index of published and unpub-
lished sources in more than a dozen languages covering issues affecting the
public and private sectors. Glossary.

467    **Standard and Poor's research insight on the web.** Standard and
       Poor's Compustat Services. 2000s–. Englewood, Colo.: Standard
       and Poor's. http://www.researchinsightweb.com/.

Research Insight is the new interface to Compustat. An essential resource with the most recent 20 years of U.S. and Canadian financial statement data and monthly closing stock price data, six months of daily stock prices, and GlobalVantage, the most recent 10 years of financial data for companies in 80 countries. Not an easy database to use; complex screening is possible, which becomes easier from within Excel. Screening can be done for data items in financial reports. Choose from quarterly or annual financials, and from nearly every data item within a financial report. Over 100 preformatted reports are available (EVAntage, company highlights, cash flow statements, combined reports, common size statements, institutional holdings). Data is also available for geographic areas, industry composites, aggregates, and stock indexes, and about 7,000 inactive companies.

**468    Stock market encyclopedia.** Standard and Poor's Corporation. ill.
New York: The Corporation, 1985–. ISSN: 0882-5467.
338.740973                                                      HG4057.A46

Lists S&P 500 plus 250 other leading public corporations. Two pages of information for each firm include summary of operations, current outlook and S&P forecast, 10 yrs. of per-share data, and three-year balance sheet.

**469    Stock trader's almanac.** Yale Hirsch, Jeffrey Hirsch. Hoboken, N.J.:
Wiley, 1967–. ISSN: 1553-4812.

Most used for the annotated calendar noting daily historical trading tendencies. A bull or bear appears on days with significant historical directional tendencies. Unusual in that it covers the best performing months or days.

**470    Success by the numbers: Statistics for business development.**
Ryan Womack, Reference and User Services Association. vii, 59 p., ill. Chicago: American Library Association; Reference and User Services Association, 2005. ISBN: 0838983278.
                                                      HF54.56.S832

A guide to U.S. statistical resources, with information on how the data is gathered, as well as where to find it. Chapters on: Federal business statistics and the 2002 economic census; Finding Florida statistical resources and data; Demographics and marketing; Economic forecasts; Industry statistics; Financial statistics; Labor, employment, and wages statistics; and Trade statistics. State and national sources are provided and sources are both free and fee-based.

471    **Thomson one banker—analytics.** Thomson Financial (Firm).
[2002–.] [New York]: Thomson Financial. http://banker.
thomsonib.com/.
65,000 active and inactive global companies, with company financials,
earnings estimates, analyst forecasts, market indices data, mergers and
acquisitions, and corporate transaction data from 1998, and near real-
time market data and stock quotes from Thomson Financial, Datastream
advance (177), Extel, First Call, Worldscope, and Disclosure. Most data is a
rolling ten years. Allows advanced screening and use of Excel to download
and analyze data.

472    **The value of a dollar: Colonial era to the Civil War, 1600–1865.**
Scott Derks, Tony Smith. 436 p., ill. Millerton, N.Y.: Grey House,
2005. ISBN: 1592370942.
338.520973                                              HB235.U6D47
Similar to *The value of a dollar, 1860–2004* (473), each chapter covers a
different period of time. Each chapter includes background, historical
snapshots, currency, selected incomes, services and fees, financial rates and
exchanges, commodities, selected prices, and miscellany. Slave trades are
included through chapter four, 1800–1824. Useful for historical research,
as well as an interesting glimpse into history.

473    **The value of a dollar: Prices and incomes in the United States,**
**1860–2004.** 3rd ed. Scott Derks. xvii, 664 p., ill. Millerton, N.Y.:
Grey House, 2004. ISBN: 1592370748.
338.520973                                              HB235.U6V35
Illustrates trends in prices. Each chapter covers a different period of time
and includes background, historical snapshots, currency, selected incomes,
services and fees, financial rates and exchanges, commodities, selected
prices, and miscellany. Also has composite consumer price index with the
value of an 1860 dollar from 1860–2003. Data is by city, county, or state.
For earlier information, see *The value of a dollar: Colonial era to the Civil
War, 1600–1865* (472).

474    **WRDS.** Wharton School. Philadelphia: The Wharton School,
University of Pennsylvania. http://wrds.wharton.upenn.edu/.
Provides web access through a hosting service for a number of financial
research databases, including Compustat (Englewood, Colo.: Standard
and Poor's, 2000s–), CRSP (Center for Research in Securities Prices)

(104), Dow Jones Averages, FDIC, Philadelphia Stock Exchange, Institutional Brokers Estimate System (New York: Institutional Brokers Estimate System, 1976–), BankScope (78), CSMAR China Stock Market databases, Eventus, First Call, and OptionMetrics.

**475  Yahoo! finance.** Yahoo! Inc. 2001. Sunnyvale, Calif.: Yahoo! Inc. http://finance.yahoo.com/.

A rich source of financial information, with company profiles, SEC filings, annual reports, stock quotes, news, analysis, conference call calendar, industry statistics and news, and information for the personal investor. The focus is on financial information about U.S. and Canadian companies and industries, but international information, such as indices and currency information, is also available, especially through the portals to Yahoo!Finance for other countries (linked from the bottom of the entry page). Historical quotes for stocks, bonds, and money markets are since 1970 and give daily, weekly, and monthly closing prices, and dividends. Occasionally links to fee-based information.

# International Business

## *Book Reviews*

**476  Business information alert.** Alert Publications. Chicago: Alert Publications, 1989–. ISSN: 1042-0746.

025                                                                      HF5001

Contains reviews of print and electronic business resources, and news, trends, and tips for business researchers. Also available through various aggregator databases.

**477  Harvard business review.** ill. Boston: Graduate School of Business Administration, Harvard University. ISSN: 0017-8012.

330.904                                                              HF5001.H3

Articles, best practices, book reviews, and case studies on communication, finance and accounting, global business, innovation and entrepreneurship, leadership, management, organizational development, sales and marketing, strategy and execution, and technology and operations. Also available online, through Business Source Elite (791).

**478  Journal of business and finance librarianship.** ill. Binghamton, N.Y.: Haworth Press, 1990–. ISSN: 0896-3568.

027.6905                                                              Z675.B8

Reviews of books, databases, and websites written by librarians for librarians. "The immediate focus of the journal is practice-oriented articles, but it also provides an outlet for new empirical studies on business librarianship and business information. Aside from articles, this journal offers valuable statistical and meeting reports, literature and media reviews, Website reviews, and interviews."—*About*

## Dictionaries

479    **Dictionary of international business terms.** 3rd ed. John J. Capela, Stephen Hartman. ix, 626 p. Hauppauge, N.Y.: Barron's, 2004. ISBN: 0764124455.

382.03                                                                  HD62.4.C36

Nearly 5,000 terse definitions of business and economics terms. Appendixes with abbreviations, acronyms, contacts for major foreign markets, and U.S. Customs officers, regions, and districts. 2000 edition available as an e-book.

480    **Dictionary of international economics terms.** John Owen, Edward Clark. 300 p. London: Les50ns Professional Pub, 2006. ISBN: 0852976852.

330.03                                                                  HF1359.D4956

Defines concepts, jargon, and acronyms in economics, finance and business. Includes definitions such as accelerated depreciation, Andean Pact, coupon interest rate, marginal cost, shakeout, and X-inefficiency. Part of a series of dictionaries, which include: *Dictionary of international accounting terms*, *Dictionary of international banking and finance terms*, *Dictionary of international business terms*, *Dictionary of international insurance and finance terms*, and *Dictionary of international trade finance*. Some definitions are shared between the dictionaries in the series.

481    **Dictionary of international trade: Handbook of the global trade community includes 21 key appendixes.** 7th ed. Edward G. Hinkelman. 416 p., ill., maps. Novato, Calif.: World Trade Press, 2006. ISBN: 1885073739.

382.03                                                                  HF1373.H55

An A-Z guide to terms on exporting, importing, banking, shipping, and other matters relating to international trade. Definitions make up half the book, with the other half devoted to appendixes. There are appendixes for: acronyms and abbreviations, country codes, international dialing guide, currencies of the world, business entities worldwide, weights and measures, ship illustrations, airplane illustrations, truck and trailer illustrations, railcar illustrations, guide to air freight containers, guide to ocean freight containers, world airports by IATA code, world airports by airport, seaports of the world, computer terms, guide to Incoterms 2000, guide to letters of credit, resources for international trade, top websites, guide to trade documentation, guide to international sourcing, key words in eight languages, global supply chain security, and maps of the world in color.

**482  Elsevier's dictionary of financial and economic terms: Spanish-English and English-Spanish.** Martha Uriona G. A., José Daniel Kwacz. 311 p. Amsterdam, [The Netherlands]; New York: Elsevier, 1996. ISBN: 0444822569.

332.03                                                                HG151.U75

Explanations and definitions for economics, finance and business, including jargon. Intended for practitioners.

**483  The handbook of international financial terms.** Peter Moles, Nicholas Terry. 2005. [New York]: Oxford University Press. http://www.oxfordreference.com/.

HG3881.M578

8,500 brief definitions on finance and accounting, including international stock exchanges, option strategies, and laws. Some definitions include examples. Also available in print.

**484  International dictionary of finance.** 4th ed. Graham Bannock, W. A. P. Manser. vi, 287 p. London: Profile Books, 2003. ISBN: 1861974787.

332.03                                                                HG151.B274

Covers international finance, as well as domestic finance in various countries. Concentrates on the U.S. and the United Kingdom. Includes foreign language terms. Definitions range from one word to one-half page in length, depending on the complexity of the concept.

**485  Language of trade.** Merritt R. Blakeslee, Carlos A. Garcia, U.S. Dept. of State, Office of International Information Programs. [2000]. [Washington, D.C.]: U.S. Dept. of State, Office of International Information Programs. http://usinfo.state.gov/products/pubs/trade/. Contains a glossary of trade terminology, a list of acronyms used in international trade, and a chronology of major events in international trade since 1916. Most glossary entries are a short paragraph in length and include links to other entries. The glossary and acronyms are also cross-linked. Also available in print edition.

## *Directories*

486 The directory of trade and professional associations in the European Union: = Répertoire de. associations professionnelles et commerciales dans l'Union européenne. Euroconfidential. London; New York: Europa, 1994–. ISSN: 1742-4011.

HD2429.E88D57

Gives contact information and publications for 750 associations in the European Union. Also gives contact information for 11,700 national member organizations and the Chambers of Commerce in Europe. Indexes for: acronyms and abbreviations, full names, keywords, and Standard Industrial Classification (SIC) codes.

487 Japan trade directory. Nihon Bōeki Shinkōkai. 1982–. Tokyo: Japan External Trade Organization. http://jtd.weis.or.jp/.
382.029452                                             HF3823.J343

Lists 1,000 Japanese companies and associations involved in international trade, as well as 7,800 products. Gives contact information, representative, type of business, year established, capital, annual sales, number of employees, bank reference, product/service imported or exported. Also available in print and on CD-ROM.

488 Major chemical and petrochemical companies of the world. Graham and Whiteside. London: Graham and Whiteside, 2000–. ISSN: 1369-5444; ISBN: 1860991920.
658.0029; 661.804                                        HD9650.3

Lists over 7,000 companies, giving contact information, executive names, business description, brand names and trademarks, subsidiaries, principal bank, principal law firm, ticker symbol, date established, number of employees, auditors, and two years of very brief financial information (sales turnover, profit before tax, profit after tax, dividend per share, earnings per share, share capital, shareholders' equity).

489 World directory of trade and business journals. Euromonitor PLC. London: Euromonitor PLC, 1996–.

Z7164.C81W67

Lists some 2,000 magazines, newsletters, and journals. Gives language, frequency, content, country coverage, format, publisher and contact information. Arranged into 80 industry categories, beginning with advertising and ending with wholesaling. Two indexes: A-Z index by country and publisher with publications, and A-Z index of journals by country. Especially useful for finding a source for news, organizational information, trends or statistics on a company or industry that is not gathered in a reference resource.

## Encyclopedias

**490   Biographical dictionary of management.** Morgen Witzel. 2 v.
Bristol, [U.K.]: Thoemmes, 2001. ISBN: 1855068710.
658.00922

Contains 600 entries on leaders and scholars from around the world, who have made major contributions to business from the beginning of civilization to modern times. Written by some 50 international scholars, who note the work, scholarship, and contributions each individual has produced.

**491   Encyclopedia of Japanese business and management.** Allan Bird.
xix, 500 p. London; New York: Routledge, 2002. ISBN: 0415189454.
650.0952                                                              HF1001.E467

Written for the specialist and student alike, with articles on economics, finance, management, government institutions, history, human resource management, industries, companies, social entities, business personalities, industrial relations, Japanese business overseas, manufacturing, marketing, and research and development. The encyclopedia is a good mix of expected information (history of the labor movement) and the unexpected (such as the article on office ladies, young, single women in clerical jobs). Entries range between 150 and 2,000 words in length. Entries are signed and some have recommended further reading. Available as an e-book.

**492   Encyclopedia of management.** 5th ed. Marilyn M. Helms. xxix,
1003 p., ill. Detroit: Thomson Gale, 2006. ISBN: 0787665568.
658.00322; 658.003                                                    HD30.15.E49

Covers 18 functional areas: corporate planning and strategic management, emerging topics in management, entrepreneurship, financial management and accounting, general management, human resources management, innovation and technology, international management, leadership, legal issues, management science and operations, management information systems, performance measures and assessment, personal growth and development for managers, production and opera-tions management, quality management and total quality management, supply chain management, and training and development. Contains 350 essays written by academics and business professionals. Almost all essays are new or revised from the 2000 ed. Arranged alphabetically, entries are 3–5 pages long, with cross-references and recommended reading lists. Available as an e-book.

**493    Global companies in the twentieth century: Selected archival histories.** Malcolm McIntosh, Ruth Thomas. 9 v., ill., maps. London; New York: Routledge, 2001. ISBN: 0415181100.
338.88                                                                HD2755.5.G549

While *Global companies* examines a select set of companies (BBC, Levi Strauss and Co., Broken Hill Proprietary Company, Barclays, BP Amoco, Rio Tinto, Cable and Wireless, Marks and Spencer, and Royal Dutch/ Shell), it does so thoroughly. Uses company archival documents to analyze how the companies have changed and adapted over time.

**494    International encyclopedia of business and management.** 2nd ed. Malcolm Warner, John P. Kotter. 8 v., xvii, 7160 p., ill. London: Thomson Learning, 2002. ISBN: 1861521618.

Contains 750 entries, intended to clarify international management and management education topics for students and faculty in higher education. Interdisciplinary in scope, including concepts from psychology, sociology, mathematics, computer engineering, political science, and economics.

## Guides and Handbooks

**495    A bibliography of British business histories.** Francis Goodall. 638 p. Aldershot, [U.K.]; Brookfield, Vt.: Gower, 1987. ISBN: 0566053071.
016.338740941                                           Z7165.G8G59; HC253

The main section lists works alphabetically by author, giving full biblio-graphic information for each title and noting the presence of indexes or illustrations, the name of the firm described, its primary SIC, and a code for the source library. Preliminary pages include an essay on the nature, new directions, and methodology of business history, the British standard industrial classification, a bibliography of business history bibliographies, libraries with business history collections, and a list of abbreviations. Company name and SIC indexes.

**496** **The Blackwell handbook of cross-cultural management.** Martin J. Gannon, Karen L. Newman. xxiii, 509 p., ill. Oxford; Malden, Mass.: Blackwell Business, 2002. ISBN: 0631214305.

658.049                                                                                    HD62.4.B58

Overview of theory and research findings. Organized into six sections: pt. 1: Frameworks for cross-cultural management; pt. 2: Strategy, structure, and inter-organizational relationships; pt 3: Managing human resources across cultures; pt. 4: Motivation, rewards, and leadership behavior; pt. 5: Interpersonal processes; and pt. 6: Corporate culture and values.

**497** **Craighead's international business, travel, and relocation guide to. countries.** Gale Research Inc. maps. Detroit: Gale Research, 1991–. ISSN: 1058-3904.

910.202                                                                                   HF5549.5.E45D56

Guide to the political, economic and business environment, and everyday life in 84 countries. Entries are by country and include business customs and protocols, gift-giving, work ethic, employment conditions, power structure and hierarchy, attitude toward foreigners, tips for establishing a business presence, and even information on establishing a social life and finding a home. Similar to the *PriceWaterhouseCoopers guides* (New York: PriceWaterhouseCoopers, 1975–).

**498** **Exporters' encyclopaedia.** Dun's Marketing Services. maps. New York: Dun and Bradstreet International, 1982–. ISSN: 8755-013X.

382.602573                                                                                HF3011.E9

Comprehensive world marketing guide for 220 world markets. Designed as a guide to possible markets and also as an instructional manual for some practicalities (e.g., shipping and insurance). Country profiles include communications, key contracts, trade regulations, documentation, marketing data, transportation, and business travel. Other sections cover U.S. ports, U.S. foreign trade zones, World Trade Center Association members, U.S. government agencies providing assistance to exporters, foreign trade organizations, foreign communications, and general export and shipping information.

**499** **Global business etiquette: A guide to international communication and customs.** Jeanette S. Martin, Lillian H. Chaney. 178 p. Westport, Conn.: Praeger, 2006. ISBN: 0275988155.

395.52                                                                                     HF5389.M375

Designed to orient the business traveler to local customs. Chapters include: travel customs and tips; language, greetings, introductions, and business cards; socializing; gestures and other nonverbal communicators; dress and appearance; cultural attitudes and behaviors; dining and tipping customs; conversational customs and manners; and oral and written communication customs and etiquette. Concentrates on the customs of the United States' top ten trading partners. Available as an e-book.

**500    International business information: How to find it, how to use it.** 2nd ed. Ruth A. Pagell, Michael Halperin. xvii, 445 p., ill. New York; Chicago: AMACOM; Glenlake, 1999. ISBN: 0814405770.
016.33                                                        HF54.5.P33

"Describes key international business publications and databases, and provides the subject background needed to understand them."—*Pref.* While dated, many of the resources are still applicable. Most sources are English-language directories, yearbooks, reports, and electronic files that describe companies, industries, markets, and international transactions. Extensively illustrated with examples and tables. Appendixes, title and subject index.

**501    International business information on the web: Searcher magazine's guide to sites and strategies for global business research.** Sheri R. Lanza, Barbara Quint. xxiii, 396 p., ill., map. Medford, N.J.: CyberAge Books, 2001. ISBN: 0910965463.
025.0665                                                     HF54.56.L364

Annotated guide mostly to free Internet resources for international business research, with sections on the World, Western Europe, Central and Eastern Europe, Latin America and the Caribbean, the Middle East and North Africa, Sub-Saharan Africa, Mexico and Canada, and Asia and the Pacific. Available as an e-book.

**502    Kiss, bow, or shake hands: The bestselling guide to doing business in more than 60 countries.** 2nd ed. Terri Morrison, Wayne A. Conaway. xiii, 593 p., ill. Avon, Mass.: Adams Media, 2006. ISBN: 1593373686.
395.52                                                        HF5389.M67

A welcome update to the 1995 ed., serving as a guide to business etiquette for anyone engaged in international business. Entries are about ten pages long, beginning with a brief cultural quiz, and then adding background information, tips on doing business in that country, political context, language, cultural orientation (negotiation style, cognitive styles, value system), and business practices (punctuality, appointments, local time, entertainment). Appendixes for: titles and forms of address, contacts and resources, holidays, and international electric adapters.

**503   The Oxford handbook of international business.** Alan M. Rugman, Thomas L. Brewer. xviii, 877 p., ill. New York: Oxford University Press, 2001. ISBN: 0199241821.
658.848                                                          HF1379.O996

Written by academics, the *Handbook* provides background into international business. Organized into five parts. Pt. 1: History and theory of the multinational enterprise, Pt. 2: The political and policy environment, Pt. 3: Strategy for MNEs (multi-national enterprises), Pt. 4: Managing the MNE, and Pt. 5: Regional studies. Available in online form.

**504   Russia, all 89 regions: Trade and investment guide.** 1029 p., maps. [New York; Moscow]: CTEC Pub., LLC, 2003–. ISBN: 0974347817.
330.947                                                          HF5192.2.A3

Economic, investment, and trade information for the various regions. Entries are by region and have general background, economic potential (including gross regional product by industry), trade opportunities (including main goods, imports and exports), investment opportunities (including sector analysis and data for capital investment by industry), and specific investment projects.

## Internet Resources

**505   Academy of international business.** Academy of International Business. 1995. East Lansing, Mich.: Academy of International Business. http://aib.msu.edu/.

This internat. assoc. was founded in 1959. The assoc. strives to be the "leading global community of scholars for the creation and dissemination of knowledge about international business and policy issues."—*About* The website includes events, a career center, publications (*Journal of international business studies, AIB insights, AIB newsletter,* conference proceedings), and links to online resources (announcements, course content, academic publishers, paper depositories, journals, professional organizations, and mailing lists).

506    Deloitte international tax and business guides. Deloitte Touche
       Tohmatsu. 2007–. [New York]: Deloitte Touche Tohmatsu,
       Economist Intelligence Unit. http://www.deloittetaxguides.com/.
Information on laws and regulations for doing business in 50 countries,
with coverage of investment climate (economic structure, banking and
financing, foreign trade), business and regulatory environment (registration and licensing, price controls, monopolies and restraint of trade, intellectual property, mergers and acquisitions, accounting standards), foreign
investment (foreign investment incentives and restrictions, exchange
controls), choice of business entity (principal forms of doing business,
establishing a branch, setting up a company), corporate and individual
taxation (taxable income and rates, capital gains, foreign income and tax
treaties, transfer pricing, turnover and other indirect taxes and duties, tax
compliance and administration), employment law (employees' rights and
remuneration, wages and benefits, termination of employment), and entry
requirements. Snapshots are available for 100 countries, giving country
profiles, with economic indicators, tax rates, business forms, and labor
environment.

507    VIBES. Jeanie M. Welch, J. Murrey Atkins Library (University of
       North Carolina at Charlotte). [199?–.] Charlotte, N.C.: University
       of North Carolina at Charlotte, J. Murrey Atkins Library. http://
       library.uncc.edu/vibes/.
025.04; 382; 330; 650

Links to over 3,000 free Internet sources with international business
and economic information in English. Organized into three categories:
comprehensive, regional, and national. Coverage includes agricultural
and forest products; banking and finance (includes insurance); business
news, business practices and company information (includes labor);
country information; emerging markets; foreign exchange rates; foreign stock markets; international electronic commerce; international
statistics (general and economic); international tourism; international
trade law; marketing and advertising; patents (includes other intellectual
property); petroleum, energy, mining, and construction; portals (web
meta pages with several international links); taxation in foreign countries (includes social security); trade issues and statistics; and business
and economics for Africa, Asia-Pacific, Eastern Europe, Western Europe,
Latin America and the Caribbean, Middle East, and NAFTA (U.S., Canada,
and Mexico).

## Organizations and Associations

508 **Academy of international business.** Academy of International Business. 1995. East Lansing, Mich.: Academy of International Business. http://aib.msu.edu/.
This internat. assoc. was founded in 1959. The assoc. strives to be the the "leading global community of scholars for the creation and dissemination of knowledge about international business and policy issues."—*About* The website includes events, a career center, publications (*Journal of international business studies, AIB insights, AIB newsletter,* conference proceedings), and links to online resources (announcements, course content, academic publishers, paper depositories, journals, professional organizations, and mailing lists).

## Periodicals

509 **Harvard business review.** ill. Boston: Graduate School of Business Administration, Harvard University. ISSN: 0017-8012.
330.904                                                                                  HF5001.H3
Articles, best practices, book reviews, and case studies on communication, finance and accounting, global business, innovation and entrepreneurship, leadership, management, organizational development, sales and marketing, strategy and execution, and technology and operations. Also available online, through Business Source Elite (791).

## Statistics

510 **The Arab world competitiveness report 2005.** Augusto Lopez-Claros, World Economic Forum. xiv, 352 p. New York: Palgrave MacMillan, 2005. ISBN: 1403948011.
320.9174927
Discussion of the economic issues facing the Arab world, with articles and statistics. Pt. 1 contains articles on reform, competitiveness, labor markets, politics, economic freedom, and women in the Arab world. Pt. 2 contains country profiles for Algeria, Bahrain, Egypt, Jordan, Kuwait, Lebanon, Libya, Libyan Arab Jamahiriya, Morocco, Oman, Qatar, Saudi Arabia, Syria, Syrian Arab Republic, Tunisia, United Arab Emirates, and Yemen. Profiles include key economic indicators, human development indicators, infrastructure and technology diffusion indicators, economic

trends, export profiles, and competitiveness rankings. Pt. 3 contains data tables, compiling data for all the countries, with coverage of the macro-economic climate, infrastructure and technology diffusion indicators, human resources (education, labor, and health), infrastructure, public institutions, domestic competition, cluster development, environment, and company operations and strategy.

**511   Consumer Europe.** London: Euromonitor Publications Limited, 1976–2004/2005. ISSN: 0308-4353.

381.094                                                                            HD7022.C68

Market-size time series for last five years and forecasted time series for upcoming five years for over 330 consumer markets, as well as economic, demographic, lifestyle, and purchasing data and analysis. Also lists manufacturer and brand shares for major consumer goods sectors. Covers Austria, Belgium, Denmark, Finland, France, Germany, Greece, Ireland, Italy, Netherlands, Norway, Portugal, Spain, Sweden, Switzerland, Turkey, and the United Kingdom.

**512   Global market share planner.** 2nd ed. Euromonitor PLC. London; Chicago: Euromonitor PLC; Euromonitor International, 2002–. ISBN: 1842643916.

Market share data for 30 consumer markets in 52 countries. Company information includes contact information, executive names, organizational structure and subsidiaries, turnover, market share performance, net and operating performance, margins, assets, earnings per share, SWOT analysis, distribution strategies, business development strategies, and brand names. In six volumes: *Major market share tracker* (v. 1), *World leading global brand owners* (v. 2), *Major market share companies: Americas* (v. 3), *Major market share companies: Western Europe* (v. 4), *Major market share companies: Asia-Pacific* (v. 5), and *Major market share companies: Eastern Europe, Middle East and Africa* (v. 6).

**513   Harmonized tariff schedule of the United States.** U.S. International Trade Commission. [1987–.] Washington, D.C.: International Trade Commission. ISSN: 1066-0925. http://www. usitc.gov/tata/hts/bychapter/index.htm.

343.73056; 347.30356                                                   KF6654.599.U55

Approximately 5,000 six- to ten-digit product-based numbers arranged into over 95 chapters. The schedule classifies imported merchandise for rate of duty and for statistical purposes and is used by most countries. Three statistical appendixes are Schedule C, Classification of Country and Territory Designations for U.S. Import Statistics; International Standard Country Codes; and Customs District and Port Codes.

**514   Latin American market planning report.** Strategy Research Corporation. ill. Miami: Strategy Research, 1996–. ISSN: 1083-6950.
380.1098021                                      HC130.C6.L38

Consumer information for 18 countries, Puerto Rico, and 70 metropolitan markets. The latest published is 2003, but still contains valuable information. Organized into topics: business environment, population and demography, buying power, consumer profile, country profiles, and summary tables.

**515   Russia, all 89 regions: Trade and investment guide.** 1029 p., maps. [New York; Moscow]: CTEC Pub., LLC, 2003–. ISBN: 0974347817.
330.947                                           HF5192.2.A3

Economic, investment, and trade information for the various regions. Entries are by region and have general background, economic potential (including gross regional product by industry), trade opportunities (including main goods, imports and exports), investment opportunities (including sector analysis and data for capital investment by industry), and specific investment projects.

# Management

## *Biography*

**516   Biographical dictionary of management.** Morgen Witzel. 2 v. Bristol, [U.K.]: Thoemmes, 2001. ISBN: 1855068710.
658.00922

Contains 600 entries on leaders and scholars from around the world, who have made major contributions to business from the beginning of civilization to modern times. Written by some 50 international scholars, who note the work, scholarship, and contributions each individual has produced.

**517   Encyclopedia of American women in business: From colonial times to the present.** Carol Krismann. 2 v., 692 p. Westport, Conn.: Greenwood Press, 2005. ISBN: 0313327572.
338.0922                                          HD6054.4.U6K753

Contains 426 alphabetically-arranged entries, including 327 biographies. Also covers topics like affirmative action and civil rights law. Appendixes for *Fortune* magazine's 50 most powerful women in American business, 1998–2003; *Working woman's* top 30 women business owners, 1997-2001; businesswomen by ethnic/cultural heritage; businesswomen by historical period; businesswomen by profession; and women in Junior Achievement's Global Business Hall of Fame. Good cross-references, bibliography, and index.

**518** **The encyclopedia of the history of American management.** Morgen Witzel. xvii, 564 p. Bristol, [U.K.]: Thoemmes Continuum, 2005. ISBN: 1843711311.

HC102.5.A2E53

Contains 260 biographical entries, ranging from 600–2,500 words on business leaders and academicians. Entries include "work, writings, ideas, and contribution to the history of management."—*How to use.* Bibliographies are given for each entry. Especially useful for those who do not own *The biographical dictionary of management* (490), from which these entries are culled.

## Book Reviews

**519** **Administrative science quarterly.** Cornell University, Johnson Graduate School of Management, Cornell University. Ithaca, N.Y.: Graduate School of Business and Public Administration, Cornell University. ISSN: 0001-8392.

658.05                                                                    HD28.A25

Includes reviews of new books on organizational studies and management. Theoretical and empirical articles from doctoral students and established scholars on organizational studies, including organizational behavior, sociology, psychology, strategic management, economics, public administration, and industrial relations.

**520** **Business information alert.** Alert Publications. Chicago: Alert Publications, 1989–. ISSN: 1042-0746.

025                                                                        HF5001

Contains reviews of print and electronic business resources, and news, trends, and tips for business researchers. Also available through various aggregator databases.

**521** **Harvard business review.** ill. Boston: Graduate School of Business Administration, Harvard University. ISSN: 0017-8012.

330.904                                                                  HF5001.H3

Articles, best practices, book reviews, and case studies on communication, finance and accounting, global business, innovation and entrepreneurship, leadership, management, organizational development, sales and marketing, strategy and execution, and technology and operations. Also available online, through Business Source Elite (791).

**522    Journal of business and finance librarianship.** ill. Binghamton, N.Y.: Haworth Press, 1990–. ISSN: 0896-3568.

027.6905                                                                 Z675.B8

Reviews of books, databases, and websites written by librarians for librarians. "The immediate focus of the journal is practice-oriented articles, but it also provides an outlet for new empirical studies on business librarianship and business information. Aside from articles, this journal offers valuable statistical and meeting reports, literature and media reviews, Website reviews, and interviews."—*About*

## Dictionaries

**523    A dictionary of human resource management.** Edmund. Heery, Mike Noon. xxvii, 449 p. Oxford; New York: Oxford University Press, 2001. ISBN: 0198296185.

658.3003                                                        HF5549.A23D53

Written for students and those new to human resources. Includes jargon (such as *dumb-sizing*) and legal terms (such as *duty of care*). Appendixes for classification of key terms, abbreviations, and acronyms. No index. Available in online form.

## Encyclopedias

**524    The Blackwell encyclopedia of management.** 2nd ed. Cary L. Cooper, Chris Argyris, William H. Starbuck, Blackwell Publishing Ltd. 13 v., ill. Malden, Mass.: Blackwell, 2005. ISBN: 0631233172.

658.003                                                         HD30.15.B455

Over 6,500 alphabetically-arranged entries on the theory and practice of management. This 2nd ed. contains 30 percent new material. Covers major subjects, including business ethics, cross-cultural management, marketing, finance, management information systems, organizational learning and knowledge, organizational behavior, human resource management, strategic management, operations, and entrepreneurship. Available as an e-book.

525   Encyclopedia of business and finance. 2nd ed. Burton S. Kaliski. Macmillan Reference. Detroit: Macmillan Reference, 2007. ISBN: 0028660617.

650.03                                                        HF1001.E466

Written for the novice but useful for anyone seeking background information on management, marketing, management information systems (MIS), and finance. The 310 essays include graphs, tables, photographs, and recommended readings. Alphabetically-arranged entries range from the history of computing to green marketing and the Sarbanes-Oxley Act. Also available online.

526   Encyclopedia of leadership. George R. Goethals, Georgia Jones Sorenson, James MacGregor Burns. 4 v., xlvi, 1927 p., ill., maps. Thousand Oaks, Calif.: Sage Publications, 2004. ISBN: 076192597X.

658.409203                                                   HD57.7.E53

Contains 400 articles that deal with biographical studies, case studies, gender issues, and leadership theories, concepts, and practices. Wide coverage of social science and historical themes. Well written by experts such as Warren Bennis. Four appendixes: bibliography of significant books on leadership, directory of leadership programs, primary sources: presidential speeches on foreign policy and war, and primary sources: sacred texts.

527   The encyclopedia of leadership: A practical guide to popular leadership theories and techniques. Murray Hiebert, Bruce Klatt. xxxi, 479 p., ill. New York: McGraw-Hill, 2001. ISBN: 0071363084.

658.4092                                                     HD57.7.H525

Quick reference guide to over 200 business leadership principles, theories, tools, and techniques. Each explanation of a theory or tool is followed by an exercise or worksheet. Leadership concepts are grouped into 15 sections, such as leading change and critical thinking. Cross-references.

528   Encyclopedia of management. 5th ed. Marilyn M. Helms. xxix, 1003 p., ill. Detroit: Thomson Gale, 2006. ISBN: 0787665568.

658.00322; 658.003                                           HD30.15.E49

Covers 18 functional areas: corporate planning and strategic management, emerging topics in management, entrepreneurship, financial management and accounting, general management, human resources management, innovation and technology, international management, leadership, legal issues, management science and operations, management information systems, performance measures and assessment, personal growth and development for managers, production and operations management, quality management and total quality management, supply chain management, and training and development. Contains 350 essays written by academics and business professionals. Almost all essays are new or revised from the 2000 ed. Arranged alphabetically, entries are 3–5 pages long, with cross-references and recommended reading lists. Available as an e-book.

529    **Encyclopedia of operations research and management science.** 2nd ed. Saul I. Gass, Carl M. Harris. xxxviii, 917 p., ill. Boston: Kluwer Academic, 2000. ISBN: 079237827X.

658.403403                                                          T57.6.E53

Brief entries on the theories, economics, and mathematics involved in operations management. Written for advanced students or practitioners. Available as an e-book.

530    **International encyclopedia of business and management.** 2nd ed. Malcolm Warner, John P. Kotter. 8 v., xvii, 7160 p., ill. London: Thomson Learning, 2002. ISBN: 1861521618.

Contains 750 entries, intended to clarify international management and management education topics for students and faculty in higher education. Interdisciplinary in scope, including concepts from psychology, sociology, mathematics, computer engineering, political science, and economics.

## Guides and Handbooks

531    **The AMA style guide for business writing.** American Management Association. ix, 326 p., ill. New York: AMACOM, 1996. ISBN: 0814402976.

808.06665                                                          HF5726.A49

Used as a desk reference, this handbook is intended as a guideline for business writing, such as that in memos, budgets, planning documents, annual reports, and manuals. Available as an e-book.

532    **The Blackwell handbook of cross-cultural management.** Martin J. Gannon, Karen L. Newman. xxiii, 509 p., ill. Oxford; Malden, Mass.: Blackwell Business, 2002. ISBN: 0631214305.

658.049                                                          HD62.4.B58

Overview of theory and research findings. Organized into six sections: pt. 1: Frameworks for cross-cultural management; pt. 2: Strategy, structure, and inter-organizational relationships; pt. 3: Managing human resources across cultures; pt. 4: Motivation, rewards, and leadership behavior; pt. 5: Interpersonal processes; and pt. 6: Corporate culture and values.

**533   BNA labor and employment law library.** Bureau of National Affairs (Washington, D.C.). [1999–.] [Washington, D.C.]: Bureau of National Affairs. http://laborandemploymentlaw.bna.com/.
Cases, summaries of developments, manuals, and explanations of state and federal laws in areas like arbitration, collective bargaining, wages and hours, fair employment, disability, and employee rights. Includes Labor-Management Relations with Decisions from 1984, Fair Employment Practices from 1965, Individual Employment Rights from 1986, BNA's *labor relations reporter, HR policy handbook,* and *Client letters, checklists, and forms.*

**534   Business grammar, style, and usage: A desk reference for articulate and polished business writing and speaking.** Alicia Abell. Boston: Aspatore, 2003. ISBN: 158762026X.
428.202465                                          PE1479.B87P36
General guidelines, rules for grammar and punctuation, guidelines for style, and information on avoiding common mistakes in business writing.

**535   Handbook of organizational justice.** Jerald Greenberg, Jason Colquitt. xxvi, 647 p., ill. Mahwah, N.J.: Lawrence Erlbaum Associates, 2005. ISBN: 0805842039.
658.314                                             HD6971.3.H36
Provides historical perspective and summary of current research. Articles cover consequences of treatment and justice in the workplace, cross-cultural differences, and the development of organizational justice. Looks at organizational justice from the perspective of the public's perception of fairness in organizations. Author and subject indexes.

**536   A primer on organizational behavior.** 5th ed. James L. Bowditch, Anthony F. Buono. xiii, 433 p., ill. New York: Wiley, 2001. ISBN: 0471384534.
658.4                                               HD58.7.B69

Provides an overview of topics and theories in organizational behavior, and serves as an introduction to basic terms and concepts. Includes bibliographical references and indexes.

## Indexes; Abstract Journals

537    **International abstracts in operations research.** International Federation of Operational Research Societies. Houndmills, Basingstoke, Hampshire, [U.K.]: Palgrave Press, 1961–. ISSN: 0020-580X.

658.4034                                                                    Q500.I5

Unique content with abstracts from over 180 journals covering operations and management science. Coverage begins in 1989. Also available as IAOR Online.

## Organizations and Associations

538    **American management association.** American Management Association. 1997–. New York: American Management Association. http://www.amanet.org/.

Founded in 1923 to provide "a full range of management development and educational services to individuals, companies and government agencies worldwide, including 486 of the Fortune 500 companies."—*About AMA.* The website has information on seminars, corporate solutions, government solutions, events, books and self-study, e-learning, and membership.

539    **Professional ethics and insignia.** 2nd ed. John P. Stierman, Jane Clapp. xii, 445 p., ill. Lanham, Md.: Scarecrow Press, 2000. ISBN: 0810836203.

061.3                                                                    HD6504.A194

An unusual collection of 222 statements for various occupations. Taken verbatim from the professional associations. Alphabetically arranged by association with good indexing by profession.

## Periodicals

540    **Academy of Management journal.** Academy of Management. Ada, Ohio: Academy of Management, 1957–. ISSN: 0001-4273.

658.05                                                                    HD28.A24

Articles on management theory and practice, with empirical research results and theoretical considerations. Occasional thematic special issues. Topics include organizational behavior, human resources, strategy, and organizational theory. Recent articles are indexed on the Academy of Management website (http://www.aomonline.org/).

**541 Administrative science quarterly.** Cornell University, Johnson Graduate School of Management, Cornell University. Ithaca, N.Y.: Graduate School of Business and Public Administration, Cornell University. ISSN: 0001-8392.

658.05                                                                    HD28.A25

Includes reviews of new books on organizational studies and management. Theoretical and empirical articles from doctoral students and established scholars on organizational studies, including organizational behavior, sociology, psychology, strategic management, economics, public administration, and industrial relations.

**542 Handbook of business strategy.** ill. New York: Faulkner and Gray, 1993–. ISSN: 1077-5730.

658                                                                    HD30.28.H3663

An annual collection of articles written by top business strategists. Valuable as a good review of what is capturing the interest of business, as well as for the recommendations made by each author. Organized into: globalization, markets and marketing, strategic management, leadership, human resource development, technology and processing, and corporate and customer communications. Available in online form.

**543 Harvard business review.** ill. Boston: Graduate School of Business Administration, Harvard University. ISSN: 0017-8012.

330.904                                                                    HF5001.H3

Articles, best practices, book reviews, and case studies on communication, finance and accounting, global business, innovation and entrepreneurship, leadership, management, organizational development, sales and marketing, strategy and execution, and technology and operations. Also available online, through Business Source Elite (791).

**544 MIT Sloan management review.** Sloan School of Management. ill. Cambridge, Mass.: Sloan Management Review Association, MIT Sloan School of Management, 1998–. ISSN: 1532-9194.

658.005                                                                    HD28.I14

Articles written for business executives on all areas of management, with special attention to corporate strategy, leadership, management of technology, and innovation. Authors are academicians and practitioners. Available in online form: email alerts are available through the journal's website, as are abstracts of recent articles.

## Reviews of Research and Trends

545  **International journal of management reviews.** Blackwell Publishers. Oxford; Malden, Mass.: Blackwell Publishers, 1999–. ISSN: 1460-8545.

HD28.I5253

Provides literature surveys and reviews on accounting, entrepreneurship, management, marketing, strategy, and technology management. Issues have 3–4 articles, which range in length from 20 to 30 pages.

# Management of Information Systems

## Book Reviews

546  **AI magazine.** American Association for Artificial Intelligence. ill. La Canada, Calif.: American Association for Artificial Intelligence, 1980–. ISSN: 0738-4602.

001.53505                                                                Q334.A5

Intended to provide current research and literature on artificial intelligence, this quarterly publication has book reviews, news, reports from conferences, articles, a calendar of events, and a regular column called "AI in the News." Includes coverage of informatics, robotics, automation, innovation, and human cognition. Available in online form through aggregators.

547  **European journal of information systems: An official journal of the Operational Research Society.** Operational Research Society. ill. Birmingham, [England]: Operational Research Society, 1991–. ISSN: 0960-085X.

658.4038011                                                              T58.5.E82

Articles, case studies, and book reviews on information systems from a European perspective. Some content is available for free at the publisher's website (http://www.palgrave-journals.com/ejis/index.html). The journal has a high impact factor and focuses on "technology, development, implementation, strategy, management and policy."—*About the journal*

**548    European journal of operational research.** Association of European Operational Research Societies. ill. Amsterdam, [The Netherlands]: North-Holland, 1977–. ISSN: 0377-2217.
001.424                                                          T57.6.E92

Articles, editorials, case studies, and book reviews on operations management and research. Organized into eight sections: continuous optimization; discrete optimization; production, manufacturing, and logistics; stochastics and statistics; decision support; computing, artificial intelligence, and information management; O.R. applications; and interfaces with other disciplines.

## Dictionaries

**549    The Blackwell encyclopedic dictionary of management information systems.** Gordon Bitter Davis. viii, 263 p., ill. Malden, Mass.: Blackwell Business, 1999. ISBN: 1557869480.
658.4038011                                              HF5548.2.B524

An A-Z dictionary, written by academics, and edited by an MIS professor at the University of Minnesota. Entries range in scope from short definitions to longer essays. While now dated, provides a solid background for MIS theory. Available as an e-book.

**550    The call center dictionary: The complete guide to call center and customer support technology solutions.** Rev. ed. Madeline Bodin, Keith Dawson. 227 p., ill. New York: CMP Books, 2002. ISBN: 1578200954.
658.812                                                    HF5548.2.B625

Over 1,200 entries that explain the technology involved, and how the technology affects service. Includes some images. Available as an e-book.

## Directories

**551    Directory of top computer executives.** East ed. Applied Computer Research. Phoenix: Applied Computer Research, 1985–. ISSN: 1936-4202.
338.4.700402574                                      HD9696.C63U516313

Lists information technology information for companies with minimum gross revenues of $50 million or a minimum of 250 employees in manufacturing and service, banking, diversified finance, insurance, retail, transportation, utilities, education, health service, federal government, state government, and local government. Entries give company name, contact information, top computer executive names, subsidiary divisions, type of industry, second level manager names, major computer systems used, number of PCs deployed throughout the organization, and number of information system employees. Arranged geographically and indexed by company name and industry classification. Available in print and PDF editions for the Eastern U.S., Western U.S., and Canada. Also available online.

## Encyclopedias

552  **Encyclopedia of business and finance.** 2nd ed. Burton S. Kaliski, Macmillan Reference. Detroit: Macmillan Reference, 2007. ISBN: 0028660617.

650.03                                                    HF1001.E466

Written for the novice but useful for anyone seeking background information on management, marketing, management information systems (MIS), and finance. The 310 essays include graphs, tables, photographs, and recommended readings. Alphabetically arranged entries range from the history of computing to green marketing and the Sarbanes-Oxley Act. Also available online.

553  **Encyclopedia of information systems.** Hossein Bidgoli. 1–4 v., ill. Amsterdam, [The Netherlands]; Boston: Academic Press, 2003–. ISBN: 0122272404.

004.03                                                    QA76.15.E516

Contains 200 peer-reviewed articles and 2,000 glossary entries on applications, artificial intelligence, data communications, database design and utilization, hardware and software, international issues, management support systems, office automation and end-user computing, social, legal, and organizational issues, systems analysis and design, and theories, methodologies, and foundations. Articles include an overview of the topic and further reading. Available in online form.

554  **Encyclopedia of management.** 5th ed. Marilyn M. Helms. xxix, 1003 p., ill. Detroit: Thomson Gale, 2006. ISBN: 0787665568.

658.00322; 658.003                                        HD30.15.E49

Covers 18 functional areas: corporate planning and strategic management, emerging topics in management, entrepreneurship, financial management and accounting, general management, human resources management, innovation and technology, international management, leadership, legal issues, management science and operations, management information systems, performance measures and assessment, personal growth and development for managers, production and operations management, quality management and total quality management, supply chain management, and training and development. Contains 350 essays written by academics and business professionals. Almost all essays are new or revised from the 2000 ed. Arranged alphabetically, entries are 3–5 pages long, with cross-references and recommended reading lists. Available as an e-book.

## *Indexes; Abstract Journals*

555 **ACM guide to computing literature.** Association for Computing Machinery. 2001–. New York: Association for Computing Machinery. http://portal.acm.org/guide.cfm.

QA76

Provides free bibliographic access to the computing literature of the ACM (Association for Computing Machinery) and more than 3,000 other publishers. The database contains more than 750,000 records describing books, journal articles, conference proceedings, doctoral dissertations, master's theses, and technical reports. The free access allows use of the basic search and the browse functions of the Guide. Use of the advanced search function is restricted to ACM professionals, students, and Special Interest Group members. The ACM also sells access to the full text of its literature via the ACM Portal (556).

556 **ACM portal.** Association for Computing Machinery. 2001–. New York: Association for Computing Machinery. http://portal.acm. org/dl.cfm.

QA76

Provides browsable and searchable access to the full text of literature of the ACM (Association for Computing Machinery). Literature includes journals, magazines, transactions, proceedings, newsletters, and oral histories. Also includes publications of the SIG's (Special Interest Groups) and affiliated organizations. In comparison, the free ACM Guide to Computing Literature (555) provides a low-budget alternative for bibliographic access only.

557    **Infotech trends.** Data Analysis Group. 1999. Cloverdale, Calif.:
Data Analysis Group. http://www.infotechtrends.com/.
Indexes 65 periodicals (*Business week, Computer world, PC week, KM world,
Forbes, Internet week*) with coverage of computers, computer peripherals,
software, storage, the Internet, and communications equipment. Includes
forecast sales and shipments, market share, installed base, and industry
trends. Coverage begins in 1984. Results can be downloaded to Excel.

558    **Internet and personal computing abstracts.** Information Today.
2000–. Medford, N.J.: Information Today. ISSN: 1529-7705.
016.00416                                                    QA75.5.M5
Abstracts and indexing for 400 trade journals, magazines, and a small
number of journals. Titles include *CIO, Information resources management
journal, IT professional, Linux journal, PC world, Social science computer
review, Technology review,* and *Wired.* Coverage from 1980s to present.
Includes product and vendor guides, software and hardware reviews, and
developments in business and industry, education, and personal computing. Not all periodicals are indexed fully. Available through EBSCO or
Information Today, Inc.

## Internet Resources

559    **Technology review.** Massachusetts Institute of Technology. 1998–.
Cambridge, Mass.: Association of Alumni and Alumnae of the
Massachusetts Institute of Technology. ISSN: 1099-274X. http://
www.technologyreview.com/.
620                                                          T171.M47
Covers trends and developments in business technology, especially as they
affect the energy, nanotech, biotech, and infotech industries. Includes
annual list of the top emerging technologies. For many years, it included
an annual R&D Scorecard, published each fall, which now is useful for
tracking historical research and development expenditures.

## Periodicals

560    **AI magazine.** American Association for Artificial Intelligence. ill.
La Canada, Calif.: American Association for Artificial Intelligence,
1980–. ISSN: 0738-4602.
001.53505                                                    Q334.A5

Intended to provide current research and literature on artificial intelligence, this quarterly publication has book reviews, news, reports from conferences, articles, a calendar of events, and a regular column called "AI in the News." Includes coverage of informatics, robotics, automation, innovation, and human cognition. Available in online form through aggregators.

**561    European journal of information systems: An official journal of the Operational Research Society.** Operational Research Society. ill. Birmingham, [England]: Operational Research Society, 1991–. ISSN: 0960-085X.

658.4038011                                                    T58.5.E82

Articles, case studies, and book reviews on information systems from a European perspective. Some content is available for free at the publisher's website (http://www.palgrave-journals.com/ejis/index.html). The journal has a high impact factor and focuses on "technology, development, implementation, strategy, management and policy."—*About the journal*

**562    European journal of operational research.** Association of European Operational Research Societies. ill. Amsterdam, [The Netherlands]: North-Holland, 1977–. ISSN: 0377-2217.

001.424                                                       T57.6.E92

Articles, editorials, case studies, and book reviews on operations management and research. Organized into eight sections: continuous optimization; discrete optimization; production, manufacturing, and logistics; stochastics and statistics; decision support; computing, artificial intelligence, and information management; O.R. applications; and interfaces with other disciplines.

**563    Technology review.** Massachusetts Institute of Technology. 1998–. Cambridge, Mass.: Association of Alumni and Alumnae of the Massachusetts Institute of Technology. ISSN: 1099-274X. http://www.technologyreview.com/.

620                                                           T171.M47

Covers trends and developments in business technology, especially as they affect the energy, nanotech, biotech, and infotech industries. Includes annual list of the top emerging technologies. For many years, it included an annual R&D Scorecard, published each fall, which now is useful for tracking historical research and development expenditures.

# Reviews of Research and Trends

**564** **Business insights.** Datamonitor (Firm). [London?]: Reuters. http://www.globalbusinessinsights.com/autologin.asp.

HF54.7

Reports on energy, consumer goods, finance, health care, and technology. Reports, typically over 100 pages long, cover new product innovations, marketing strategies, market drivers, key players, trends, forecast business opportunities, and industry interviews. International focus, especially strong for European coverage.

**565** **FACCTS.** Faulkner Information Services. 1995–. Pennsauken, N.J.: Faulkner Information Services. ISSN: 1082-7471. http://www. faulkner.com/showcase/faccts.htm.

005 QA76.753

Over 1,200 reports on trends, issues, market conditions, implementation guides, companies, products, and services in information technology. Arranged into 14 categories: enterprise data networking, broadband, information security, electronic government, electronic business, content management, IT asset management, application development, website management, converging communications, telecom and global network services, mobile business strategies, wireless communications, and Internet strategies. Especially useful for the up-to-date technology trend reports.

**566** **Gartneradvisory intraweb.** Gartner Group. 2000–. [Stamford, Conn.]: Gartner Group. http://www.gartner.com/.

The database is made from Gartner Research and Advisory Services, Datapro, and Dataquest Research. Especially useful for reports that discuss strategy within the IT industry. Also has company profiles, trends, developments, and product reports.

**567** **Information systems: The state of the field.** John Leslie King, Kalle Lyytinen. Hoboken, N.J.: Wiley, 2006. ISBN: 0470017775.

658.4038011 T58.6.I487

Examines the evolution of the information systems discipline. The 11 essays and eight commentaries are well grounded, combining information from 30 years of literature from the field and the expertise of the authors. Available as an e-book.

568   **Jupiterresearch.** Jupiter Communications. New York: Jupiter Communications. http://www.jupiterresearch.com/bin/item.pl/home. Combines proprietary primary research with secondary research to give trends, statistics, forecasts, and best practices on information technology and its effects on industries and consumers. In seven categories: Personal Technologies; Marketing & Media; Web Technologies & Operations; European Focus; Industry Focus; Jupiter Data (statistics); and Hot Topics.

## Marketing, Advertising, and Public Relations

## *Biography*

569   **The ad men and women: A biographical dictionary of advertising.** Edd Applegate. xvii, 401 p. Westport, Conn.: Greenwood Press, 1994. ISBN: 0313278016.
659.1092273B                                                     HF5810.AA3

Provides difficult-to-find information on copywriters, art directors, and others. Biographical essays on more than 50 individuals who played a prominent role in advertising in 19th and 20th century America. Bibliographies accompanying entries are particularly rich sources of information, listing works by the individual, works about the individual, and notable clients and campaigns.

570   **Entrepreneurs, the men and women behind famous brand names and how they made it.** Joseph J. Fucini, Suzy Fucini. xviii, 297 p., ill., ports. Boston: G.K. Hall, 1985. ISBN: 0816187088.
338.040922B                                                     HC29.F83

Burpee's seeds, Gillette razors, Jacuzzi spas, Calvin Klein jeans, Phillip's Milk of Magnesia, and Reynold's Wrap are among 225 products bearing the names of their founders. Chronicles the history of these products and the individuals behind them. While some of these entrepreneurs have been forgotten, their stories remain fascinating reading. Provides substantive 3–4 page biographical profiles for 50 individuals, and shorter biographical entries for 175 men and women. Well researched and includes an extensive bibliography.

571   **Made in America: The true stories behind the brand names that built a nation.** Berkley ed. John Gove. xiii, 303 p., ill., ports. New York: Berkley Books, 2001. ISBN: 0425178838.
338.7092273                                                     HC102.5.G64

**FUNCTIONAL AREAS OF BUSINESS**

Chef Boyardee, Dinty Moore, Uncle Ben's, and Welch's are all recognizable brand names, but few of us know the history behind these products. This engaging compendium brings together 74 biographical sketches (from 2 to 8 pages in length) of the individuals behind familiar brand names. A useful bibliography rounds out this compact work.

572 **So who the heck was Oscar Mayer?** Doug Gelbert. 400 p., ill. New York: Barricade Books, 1996. ISBN: 1569800820.
338.0092273B                                    HC102.5.A2G45

Gelbert reveals the person and story behind 200 well-known brand names. Brief biographical sketches (averaging one to two pages in length) are cleverly categorized under themes such as "In the Kitchen," "From the Bottle," "In the Closet," and "At the Game." Not only fun to read but thoroughly researched.

## Book Reviews

573 **Advertising age.** Advertising Publications. ill. Chicago: Crain Communications, 1930–. ISSN: 0001-8899.
659.105                                        HF5801.A276

Essential trade publication tracking news and trends in advertising, marketing, brand management, and sales promotion. Articles on advertising campaigns often provide unique market share data. In addition to providing current industry news, this weekly is a rich source of statistical data, as it often includes reports on special markets. There are also special reports on leading marketers, technology, top agencies, and award winning campaigns. Partially available online as http://Adage.com/ and available online through aggregators.

574 **Business information alert.** Alert Publications. Chicago: Alert Publications, 1989–. ISSN: 1042-0746.
025                                                  HF5001

Contains reviews of print and electronic business resources, and news, trends, and tips for business researchers. Also available through various aggregator databases.

575 **Harvard business review.** ill. Boston: Graduate School of Business Administration, Harvard University. ISSN: 0017-8012.
330.904                                          HF5001.H3

Articles, best practices, book reviews, and case studies on communication, finance and accounting, global business, innovation and entrepreneurship, leadership, management, organizational development, sales and marketing, strategy and execution, and technology and operations. Also available online, through Business Source Elite (791).

**576    JMR: Journal of marketing research.** American Marketing Association. ill. Chicago: American Marketing Association, 1964–. ISSN: 0022-2437.

658.8305                                                HF5415.2.J66

As the title indicates, articles are on marketing research. The intended audience is technically oriented research analysts, educators, and statisticians. Available in online form. A regular "New books in review" column provides 1–3 book reviews in each issue, with texts of reviews freely available on the journal's website. Also available on the website are tables of contents back to 2002.

**577    Journal of business and finance librarianship.** ill. Binghamton, N.Y.: Haworth Press, 1990–. ISSN: 0896-3568.

027.6905                                                Z675.B8

Reviews of books, databases, and websites written by librarians for librarians. "The immediate focus of the journal is practice-oriented articles, but it also provides an outlet for new empirical studies on business librarianship and business information. Aside from articles, this journal offers valuable statistical and meeting reports, literature and media reviews, Website reviews, and interviews."—*About*

**578    Journal of marketing.** American Marketing Association. ill. Chicago: American Marketing Association, 1936–. ISSN: 0022-2429.

658.8005                                                HF5415.A2J6

One of the top marketing journals, self-identified as being closely aligned with management practices. International in scope, with a focus on marketing practice and theory. Regular book reviews. Intended audience is marketing managers, consumers, or public policy makers. Tables of contents are available through the journal's website back to 2002. Also available online through aggregators.

**579    The journal of product innovation management.** Product Development and Management Association. ill. New York: North-Holland, 1984–. ISSN: 0737-6782.

658.57505                                                HF5415.153.J68

Articles and book reviews on product innovation, development, and marketing. Some issues review up to four books, with reviews ranging 2–3 pages in length.

**580   Journal of the Academy of Marketing Science.** Academy of Marketing Science. Amsterdam, The Netherlands: Springer, 1973–. ISSN: 0092-0703.

658.8005                                                                    HF5415.A319a

Articles, book and software reviews, and reports on legal decisions and regulatory actions affecting marketing internationally. Annual index in the last issue of each volume.

## Dictionaries

**581   Advertising slogans of America.** Harold S. Sharp. xi, 543 p. Metuchen, N.J.: Scarecrow Press, 1984. ISBN: 0810816814.

659.1322                                                                    HF6135.S53

Fifteen thousand slogans used by 6,000 companies and organizations. Slogans, organizations, and products appear alphabetically.

**582   The dictionary of marketing.** Rona Ostrow, Sweetman R. Smith. 258 p., ill. New York: Fairchild Publications, 1988. ISBN: 0870055739.

380.10321                                                                   HF5415.O76

Some 3,000 non-technical definitions, with etymologies, charts, graphs, and cross-references.

**583   Dictionary of marketing communications.** Norman A. Govoni. 249 p. Thousand Oaks, Calif.: Sage, 2004. ISBN: 0761927700.

380.103                                                                     HF5412.G68

Some 4,000 definitions of advertising, sales promotion, public relations, direct marketing, and e-marketing terms and concepts. Written by a business professor prompted by the needs of students in his marketing classes.

**584   Dictionary of social and market research.** Wolfgang J. Koschnick. 416 p., ill. Hampshire, England; Brookfield, Vt.: Gower, 1996. ISBN: 056607611X.

658.8303                                                                    HF5415.2.K627

Contains 2,500 entries used to answer questions for students and practitioners as they conduct social and market research. Entries range from a brief sentence to 2 pages long, giving formulas, graphs, and explanations, rather than limiting all entries to terse definitions.

585   **Marketing: The encyclopedic dictionary.** David Mercer. 422 p., ill. Oxford; Malden, Mass.: Blackwell, 1999. ISBN: 0631191070.
658.8003                                                    HF5412.M47

Intended for practitioners, but useful for undergraduate and MBA students. Contains definitions for thousands of marketing terms, as well as longer discussions of topics. No index, but good cross-references.

586   **Trade name origins.** Adrian Room. 217 p. Lincolnwood, Ill.: NTC Pub. Group, 1997. ISBN: 084420904X.
929.9503                                                    T324.R68

A witty examination of the origin of some 700 well-known trade names, with an analysis of the process of choosing a new trade name. Prior editions had titles *Dictionary of trade name origins* and *NTC's dictionary of trade name origins.*

## Directories

587   **The advertising red books.** LexisNexis. New Providence, N.J.: LexisNexis, 2003–.
                                                    HF5805.S786

Covers 6,600 worldwide agency parent companies, 5,750 U.S. publicly traded companies, the top 2,000 global companies, and the 300 largest U.S. private companies. Use to find information on both advertisers and agencies. Data for agencies includes contact information, year founded, number of employees, gross billings by media, NAICS and SIC codes, names of key personnel, and names of accounts. For advertisers, information includes contact information, year founded, number of employees, NAICS and SIC codes, month budget is set, media expenditures, and brands. Where possible, the name and email address for the marketing director for the advertiser is included. Available online and on CD-ROM.

588   **The adweek directory.** ASM Communications. New York: ASM Communications, 1998–. ISSN: 1528-3291.
659                                                    HF6182.U5A387

Listing of ad agencies, public relations firms, media buying services, and specialized marketing companies. Entries include contact information, U.S. affiliates/branch offices, services offered, fields served, employees, year founded, key personnel, and major accounts. Also ranks agencies nationally and regionally, with revenue and percentage change from prior year, billings and percentage change from prior year.

**589    Brands and their companies.** Donna J. Wood, Susan L. Stetler. Detroit: Gale Research, 1990–. ISSN: 1047-6407.
602.75                                                                    T223.V4A25

Not sure what company is responsible for Night Owl? Don't even know what type of product it is? This is the source for answers. Alphabetically lists brand names, even for discontinued brands, and then lists the manufacturer or distributor. Brand names supplied by companies or found in print resources. Occasionally used by researchers interested in trademarks. Companion to *Companies and their brands* (591). Available in online form.

**590    The brandweek directory.** ASM Communications. ill. New York: ASM Communications, 1998–. ISSN: 1530-616X.
338.761659102573                                                          HF6182.U5A39

Lists the top 2,000 brands by media spending, with contact information, ultimate parent organization, product/service category, media expenditures, lead advertising agency, additional agencies, and key personnel. Also provides the complete list of "superbrands" by industry category.

**591    Companies and their brands.** Donna J. Wood, Gale Group. Detroit: Gale Research, 1990–. ISSN: 1047-6393.
602.75                                                                    T223.V4A253

Alphabetical list of companies and the brand names attributed to them. Each entry is followed by the firm's address, telephone number, and list of trade names. Information is collected from print sources and from the individual companies. Companion to *Brands and their companies* (589).

**592    The direct marketing market place.** Hilary House Publishers. Hewlett Harbor, N.Y.: Hilary House, 1980–. ISSN: 0192-3137.
381                                                                       HF5415.1.D57

A source similar in purpose and format to *Literary market place* for the direct marketing field. Classified sections list 8,700 direct marketers of products and services (principally through mail order catalogs), service firms and suppliers, creative and consulting services, associations and events, awards, etc. Primarily U.S. listings, with a chapter on Canadian and foreign firms. Gives names, addresses, and telephone numbers for companies and individuals, number of employees, advertising budget related to direct marketing, and gross sales or billing. Also provides an overview of advertising expenditures by medium and market for four years, with a forecast for future expenditures. Indexes of individuals and companies. Some issues have title: *Direct marketing marketplace.*

**593    Green book.** American Marketing Association. ill. New York: New York Chapter, American Marketing Assoc., 2000. ISSN: 8756534X.
658.83025                                                                    HF5415.2.G69

Useful for locating market research companies in the U.S. and abroad. Vol. 1 covers market research companies and services; v. 2 covers focus group companies, facilities, and services. *Green book* also publishes an online directory (http://www.greenbook.org/) with access to about 400 companies included in the print volumes. The print directory provides information on approximately 2,300 companies.

**594    Internet resources and services for international marketing and advertising: A global guide.** James R. Coyle. xiii, 352 p. Westport, Conn.: Oryx Press, 2002. ISBN: 1573564079.
658.848                                                                        HF1416.C69

More than 2,000 commercial, organizational, and academic websites (including e-journals) relating to marketing and advertising for more than 150 countries and regions, selected by a marketing and advertising professor at a leading U.S. business school. Priority is given to English-language sites that are free or that provide substantive free information in part. Strengths of this resource are rigor in identifying sites for inclusion, broad coverage, and availability of multiple indexes by site title, website sponsor, country, and subject.

**595    Market guide.** The Editor and Publisher Company. maps, tables. New York: The Editor and Publisher, 1924–. ISSN: 0362-1200.
658.8                                                                          HF5905.E38

Individual market surveys of nearly 1,400 U.S. and Canadian cities where a daily newspaper is published. Arranged by state and city, with data in 16 categories such as population, households, climate, principal industries, military installations, and newspapers. Includes U.S. retail census data. *Better living index* ranks cities by cost of living, crime data, and education statistics.

**596**  **O'Dwyer's directory of public relations firms.** J.R. O'Dwyer Co. New York: J.R. O'Dwyer, 1969–. ISSN: 0078-3374.
338.761659202573                                        HM263.O37

Lists almost 3,000 U.S. and international public relations firms and public relations departments of advertising agencies. Entries generally include contact information, an indication of specialties, date founded, number of employees, list of major clients, name of the president/director, and list of other key staff. Multiple access points include a geographical index, a specialties index, and a cross-index to client companies of firms profiled. Rankings in this directory (such as ranking firms by net fees) are a popular feature.

**597**  **SRDS business publication advertising source.** Standard Rate and Data Service. Des Plaines, Ill.: SRDS, 1995–. ISSN: 1529-6490.
659                                                       HF5905.S723

Provides advertising rates for 9,000 trade publications, listed in 220 subject areas. Publication entries give total circulation; publisher's positioning statement; contact information; commission and cash discount; general rate policy; black/white rates; color rates; rates for covers and inserts; bleed information; special advertising positions; and classified, mail order, and specialty rates.

**598**  **SRDS consumer magazine advertising source.** Standard Rate and Data Service. ill. Des Plaines, Ill.: SRDS, 1995–. ISSN: 1086-8208.
659.102573                                                HF5905.S725

Lists 2,900 magazines, organized by interest (affluence, teen, gaming). Entries give publication frequency, contact information, editorial profile, executives, commission and cash discount, advertising rates, billed, special position, classified/mail order/specialty rates, special issue rates, general requirements, issue and closing dates, and circulation. Use for planning advertising costs and timing. Also available online.

## *Encyclopedias*

**599**  **The Advertising Age encyclopedia of advertising.**
John McDonough, Karen Egolf, Museum of Broadcast

Communications. 3 v., xxiii, 1873 p., 72 p. of plates, ill. New York: Fitzroy Dearborn, 2003. ISBN: 1579581722.

659.103 HF5803.A38

The first comprehensive reference work on the history of advertising. A collaborative effort undertaken by *Advertising age* (the profession's most important trade publication), the Museum of Broadcast Communications, and Duke University's Hartman Center for Sales, Advertising, and Marketing History. Profiles more than 120 advertising agencies, over 160 major advertisers, brands, and campaigns, and the lives of almost 50 prominent men and women. Includes thematic essays covering advertising theory, strategy, and practice (e.g., market research, psychographics, demographics, ethics, sex in advertising). Inclusion of more than 500 illustrations (including color reproductions of ads) makes this a visually appealing and fun resource. Exhaustive index and useful appendixes, including those providing chronological listings of top agencies and top advertisers.

**600 All-American ads: 1900–1919.** Jim Heimann. 638 p. Koln, [Germany]; Los Angeles: Taschen, 2005. ISBN: 3822825123.

NC998.5.A1A45

The first in a series presenting reproductions of print advertising. Each volume in the series covers a different decade: available volumes now cover every decade up through the 1980s.

**601 Encyclopedia of business and finance.** 2nd ed. Burton S. Kaliski. Macmillan Reference. Detroit: Macmillan Reference, 2007. ISBN: 0028660617.

650.03 HF1001.E466

Written for the novice but useful for anyone seeking background information on management, marketing, management information systems (MIS), and finance. The 310 essays include graphs, tables, photographs, and recommended readings. Alphabetically-arranged entries range from the history of computing to green marketing and the Sarbanes-Oxley Act. Also available online.

**602 Encyclopedia of major marketing campaigns.** 2nd ed. Thomas Riggs. xxii, 2063 p., ill. Detroit: Gale Group, 2006. ISBN: 078763042X.

659.10973 HF5837.E53

Covers nearly 500 major campaigns from 1999–2005. In 2–5 pages, gives an overview and historic context, information about the target market, expected outcomes, competition, marketing strategy and development hurdles, and the outcome of the campaign. Includes references to pertinent articles. Useful for learning why a campaign did, or did not, work. Arranged alphabetically by company name. Available as an e-book. The 1st ed. covers 500 major campaigns from the 20th century.

**603**   **Encyclopedia of public relations.** Robert L. Heath. 2 v., ill. Thousand Oaks, Calif.: Sage, 2005. ISBN: 0761927336.
659.203                                                                                                          HD59.E48

While there is discussion where to place public relations (communications or business), there is no doubt the impact PR can have on business and industry. In two volumes this encyclopedia explores the theories, practices, and ethical guidelines that are employed in public relations. Entries are arranged alphabetically, covering the broad topics of crisis communications and management, cyberspace, ethics, global public relations, history, jargon, management, media, news, organizations, practitioners, relations, reports, research, and theories and models. Entries are typically 2–4 pages long, signed, and include a bibliography. Appendixes include: Public Relations Society of America code of ethics; International Association of Business Communicators code of ethics; Milestones in the history of public relations; Public relations education for the 21st century: a port of entry; Corporate annual report: an evolution, with American Bell Telephone Company's annual report from 1881 and the AT&T 2002 annual report; Public Relations Society of America local chapters; Public relations online resources; Where to study public relations; and Dictionary of public relations measurement. Available as an e-book.

**604**   **The IEBM encyclopedia of marketing.** Michael John Baker. xiii, 865 p., ill. London: International Thomson Business, 1999. ISBN: 1861523041.
658.003                                                                                                          HF5415.B272

Contains 63 articles by world renowned marketing experts like Philip Kotler, Gordon Foxall, and John O'Shaughnessy that provide thorough explanations of selected marketing theories, techniques, and practices. Index.

**605**   **The international encyclopedia of marketing.** Michael Thomas, Stanley J. Paliwoda, European Marketing Confederation. 372 p., ill. Oxford: Butterworth-Heinemann, 1997. ISBN: 0750635010.
658.8003                                                                                                        HF5415.N58513

Intended for practitioners. Mainly a European focus, but with terms and topics that apply internationally. Divided into 19 sections that cover the range of marketing areas (marketing research, business to business marketing, services marketing, retail marketing, etc.). References and index.

## Guides and Handbooks

**606** **Advertising organizations and publications: A resource guide.**
John Philip Jones. xviii, 346 p., ill. Thousand Oaks, Calif.: Sage Publications, 2000. ISBN: 0761912363.

659.1                                          HF5813.U6.A654

Profiles 77 advertising and marketing communications organizations and publications, describing purpose and contact information. Primary focus is the U.S.

**607** **Exporters' encyclopaedia.** Dun's Marketing Services. maps. New York: Dun and Bradstreet International, 1982–. ISSN: 8755-013X.

382.602573                                          HF3011.E9

Comprehensive world marketing guide for 220 world markets. Designed as a guide to possible markets and also as an instructional manual for some practicalities (e.g., shipping and insurance). Country profiles include communications, key contracts, trade regulations, documentation, marketing data, transportation, and business travel. Other sections cover U.S. ports, U.S. foreign trade zones, World Trade Center Association members, U.S. government agencies providing assistance to exporters, foreign trade organizations, foreign communications, and general export and shipping information.

**608** **Handbook of marketing.** Barton A. Weitz, Robin Wensley. xix, 582 p., ill. London; Thousand Oaks, [Calif.]: Sage, 2002. ISBN: 0761956824.

658.8                                          HF5415.H18665

Synthesizes the body of research relating to: the role of marketing in society, the history of research about marketing as a discipline, the role of marketing in the firm, marketing strategy, marketing activities, and marketing management. Includes chapters examining important special topics (e.g., global marketing, marketing in business markets, services marketing, the impact of the Internet on marketing). Written for graduate students in marketing.

609  Handbook of marketing scales: Multi-item measures for marketing and consumer behavior research. 2nd ed. William O. Bearden, Richard G. Netemeyer. xiv, 537 p. Thousand Oaks, Calif.: Sage Publications, 1999. ISBN: 076191000X.

658.83                                                                    HF5415.3.B323

Presents 134 marketing and consumer behavior scales with definitions, background on the scale's development, relevance to marketing, estimates of reliability and validity, and references to the scale in scholarly literature. Scales are indexed by title and author.

610  Handbook of relationship marketing. Jagdish N. Sheth, Atul Parvatiyar. xvi, 660 p., ill. Thousand Oaks, Calif.: Sage Publications, 2000. ISBN: 0761918108.

658.8                                                                     HF5415.55.H36

Collection of scholarly articles serves as a handbook on relationship marketing, so named because of its focus on the relationship between buyers, sellers, suppliers, and other key players in the marketing process. Since there are few textbooks solely on relationship marketing, this handbook serves as a core resource on the underlying theory and development of this subdiscipline. Each chapter contains extensive references making this a rich bibliographic resource on this topic. Thorough index enhances this work's value as a reference tool.

611  Handbook of services marketing and management. Teresa A. Swartz, Dawn Iacobucci. ix, 521 p., ill. Thousand Oaks, Calif.: Sage Publications, 2000. ISBN: 0761916113.

658                                                                       HD9980.5.H36

Anthology introduces services marketing. This unique handbook meets the need for a comprehensive source providing theoretical and practical information on topics relating to the service economy. Useful to upper-level students, researchers, and managers in a myriad of service industries.

612  The international handbook of market research techniques. 2nd ed. Robin Birn, Market Research Society. xxvi, 594 p., ill. London: Kogan Page in association with MRS, 2002. ISBN: 0749438657.

658.83                                                                    HF5415.2.H284

Essays on preparation, data collection, communications, advertising and media, analysis, and presentation of results. Intended for practitioners and students.

**613** **Marketing information: A strategic guide for business and finance libraries.** Wendy Diamond, Michael R. Oppenheim. xxvi, 342 p. Binghamton, N.Y.: Haworth Information Press, 2004. ISBN: 0789021129.

658.83                                                    HF5415.2.D49

Information about sources to use in marketing research. Use to discover where to look for: industry scans; companies, brands, and competitors; market research reports; demographic, geographic, and lifestyle sources; demographic niches; advertising and media planning; public relations; sales management, sales promotion, and retail; direct marketing and e-commerce; international marketing; product development, packaging, pricing, and place; social marketing; nonprofit organizations; services marketing; and legal/ethical issues. Available as an e-book.

**614** **Marketing metrics: 50+ metrics every executive should master.** Paul Farris. xvi, 359 p., ill. Upper Saddle River, N.J.: Wharton School, 2006. ISBN: 0131873709.

658.83                                                    HF5415.2.M35543

Particularly well-written guide to marketing metrics, from metrics for promotional strategy, advertising, customer perceptions and loyalty, market share, competitors' power, products, to metrics for portfolios, channels, and pricing strategies. A good source for definitions of metrics, such as share of wallet, as well as for coverage of why, when, and how to employ a metric. Available as an e-book.

**615** **Marketing scales handbook: A compilation of multi-item measures.** Gordon C. Bruner, Paul J. Hensel, Karen E. James. 4 v. Chicago: American Marketing Association, 1992–2005. ISBN: 0877572267.

658.83028                                                 HF5415.3.B785

Nearly 1,200 multi-item measurement scales taken from seven leading marketing journals. Volumes include scales published in different years (1980–1989, 1990–1993, 1994–1997, and 1998–2001). Describes origin of the scale, how the scale was measured, past results, psychometric characteristics, and possible research use.

## Indexes; Abstract Journals

**616**  The bibliography of marketing research methods. 3rd ed. John R. Dickinson, Marketing Science Institute. xi, 1025 p. Lexington, Mass.: Lexington Books, 1990. ISBN: 0669216976.
016.65883                                    Z7164.M18D52; HF5415.2
Contains 14,000 entries on market research, data collection, and data analysis drawn from marketing journals, handbooks, and conference proceedings, and from related disciplines. Entries are grouped by subject. Not annotated. Author and subject indexes.

**617**  Essential readings in marketing. Leigh McAlister, Ruth N. Bolton, Ross Rizley, Marketing Science Institute. 196 p. Cambridge, Mass.: Marketing Science Institute, 2006. ISBN: 0965711455.
Abstracts of research articles in various areas of marketing, with brief essays at the beginning of each chapter explaining the topic. Chapters include: New products, growth, and innovation; Branding and brand equity; Metrics linking marketing to financial performance; Managing relationships with customers and organizations; The role of marketing; Research tools; Marketing mix; Customer insight; and Strategy.

**618**  Market research abstracts. Market Research Society. London: Market Research Society. ISSN: 0025-3596. http://www.warc.com/ContentAndPartners/MRA.asp.
658.8305                                          HF5415.2.M328
Detailed abstracts for articles in international journals, including *Journal of consumer research*, *Journal of marketing*, *Journal of marketing research*, *British journal of sociology*, and *Journal of the American statistical association*, with coverage from 1963.

**619**  Web marketing today. Wilson Internet Services. 1995–. Rocklin, Calif.: Wilson Internet Services. ISSN: 1094-8112. http://www.wilsonweb.com/wmt/.
384
Index to nearly 17,000 articles and other resources for web marketing and e-commerce. Categories for Industry Case Studies, Business to Business (B2B), Online Transactions, E-Commerce Environmental Design, Store-Building "Cart" Software, Website Promotion, Business Site Environmental Design, Paid Advertising, E-Mail Marketing, Miscellaneous

Web Marketing, and Local Web Marketing. Access is a mix of fee and free.

## Internet Resources

620    **Ad*Access.** John W. Hartman, Center for Sales, Advertising, and Marketing History. 1999. Durham, N.C.: Duke University. http:// scriptorium.lib.duke.edu/adaccess.

HF5813.U6

Images of 7,000 advertisements printed in U.S. and Canadian newspapers and magazines between 1911 and 1955. Browse in five categories (beauty and hygiene, radio, television, transportation, and World War II) or search by words in the headline or in information about the ad, such as name of company, product, artist, program, or publication.

621    **Advertising world.** University of Texas at Austin, Department of Advertising. 1997–. Austin, Tex.: University of Texas at Austin. http://advertising.utexas.edu/world.

A portal with links to websites, organized into 83 categories from account planning to word-of-mouth advertising. Best for hard-to-find examples of Internet sites on topics such as children's advertising, environmental claims, subliminal messages, and unconventional media. Sites can be submitted by anyone but are reviewed by the University of Texas Department of Advertising.

622    **American factfinder.** U.S. Census Bureau. [1999–.] Washington, D.C.: U.S. Census Bureau. http://factfinder.census.gov/.

317.3                         HA181

U.S. population, housing, economic, and geographic data from the Economic Census, the American Community Survey, the 1990 Census, Census 2000 and the latest Population Estimates. Details range from national, state, county, county subdivision, census tract, block group, place, consolidated city, congressional district, American Indian and Alaska Native areas, metropolitan areas, urbanized area, region, and division. With maps, statistical data, geographic comparison tables, useful for researchers in various areas of business and economics.

Marketers find it useful for demographics; economists enjoy the easy search for Economic Census data, data from the Survey of Business Owners, Business Expenses Survey, Nonemployer Statistics, Annual Survey of Manufacturers, and County Business Patterns.

623    **American marketing association.** American Marketing
       Association. [2001–.] Chicago: American Marketing Association.
       http://www.marketingpower.com/.
The Association supports marketing professionals in the U.S. and Canada.
The website has membership information, resources for members, AMA
publications (*Marketing news, Journal of public policy & marketing, Marketing management, Marketing research, Marketing health services, Journal of marketing, Journal of marketing research, Journal of international marketing*), best practices, case studies, webcasts, hot topics, dictionary of
marketing terms, careers, and tools (marketing templates, project management, statistics resources, ROI enhancers).

624    **ClickZ stats.** INT Media Group. [2006–.] Darien, Conn.: INT
       Media Group. http://www.clickz.com/showPage.html?page=stats.
                                                        HF5548.32.C931
A treasure trove of statistics and trends about 22 different sectors of
internet marketing, including advertising, business to business, broadband, demographics, education, e-mail and spam, entertainment, finance,
geographics, government/politics, hardware, health care, professional,
retailing, search tools, security, small/medium enterprises, software and IT,
traffic patterns, and wireless. Some data back to 1999. Because ClickZ links
to outside sources, some URLs can lead to broken links.

625    **Knowthis.com.** Paul Christ. [West Chester, Pa.?]: KnowThis.com.
       http://www.knowthis.com/.
135 categories and content including tutorials, articles, forums, links to
associations, online groups, and research reports, make finding information and reading about marketing easy. A great first stop for background
information. Editor Paul Christ is an MBA/PhD professor at West Chester
University.

626    **VIBES.** Jeanie M. Welch, J. Murrey Atkins Library (University of
       North Carolina at Charlotte). [199?–.] Charlotte, N.C.: University
       of North Carolina at Charlotte, J. Murrey Atkins Library. http://
       library.uncc.edu/vibes/.
025.04; 382; 330; 650

Links to over 3,000 free Internet sources with international business
and economic information in English. Organized into three categories:
comprehensive, regional, and national. Coverage includes agricultural

and forest products; banking and finance (includes insurance); business news, business practices and company information (includes labor); country information; emerging markets; foreign exchange rates; foreign stock markets; international electronic commerce; international statistics (general and economic); international tourism; international trade law; marketing and advertising; patents (includes other intellectual property); petroleum, energy, mining, and construction; portals (web meta pages with several international links); taxation in foreign countries (includes social security); trade issues and statistics; and business and economics for Africa, Asia-Pacific, Eastern Europe, Western Europe, Latin America and the Caribbean, Middle East, and NAFTA (U.S., Canada, and Mexico).

627 **Web marketing today.** Wilson Internet Services. 1995–. Rocklin, Calif.: Wilson Internet Services. ISSN: 1094-8112. http://www. wilsonweb.com/wmt/.
384

Index to nearly 17,000 articles and other resources for web marketing and e-commerce. Categories for Industry Case Studies, Business to Business (B2B), Online Transactions, E-Commerce Environmental Design, Store-Building "Cart" Software, Website Promotion, Business Site Environmental Design, Paid Advertising, E-Mail Marketing, Miscellaneous Web Marketing, and Local Web Marketing. Access is a mix of fee and free.

## Market Research

628 **Business insights.** Datamonitor (Firm). [London?]: Reuters. http://www.globalbusinessinsights.com/autologin.asp.
HF54.7

Reports on energy, consumer goods, finance, health care, and technology. Reports, typically over 100 pages long, cover new product innovations, marketing strategies, market drivers, key players, trends, forecast business opportunities, and industry interviews. International focus, especially strong for European coverage.

629 **Forrester research.** Forrester Research. [1999–2003.] Cambridge, Mass.: Forrester. http://www.library.hbs.edu/forrester.htm.
HF5548.32T174

Nearly 17,000 original reports on technology's effect on business and the consumer in the United States, Canada, Europe, and Asia Pacific. Research is in two categories, technology and industry.

Topics in technology are application development, business intelligence, computing systems, consumer devices and access, content and collaboration, customer experience, enterprise applications, enterprise mobility, IT management, IT services, networking, portals and site technology, security, software infrastructure, and tech sector economics.

Topics in industry are brand strategy, brand tactics, consumer electronics, consumer products, customer insight, emerging marketing channels, energy and utilities, financial services, government, healthcare and life sciences, high tech, industry insight, manufacturing, marketing and advertising, marketing planning, media and entertainment, mobile services, professional services, relationship marketing, retail, telecommunications, television advertising, transportation and logistics, and travel.

Reports typically range from 3–20 pages, and some are available as videos.

**630    Global market information database.** Euromonitor. [1999–.] [London]: Euromonitor. http://www.gmid.euromonitor.com/.

HD2755.5.G56

Market reports, company profiles, and demographic, economic, and marketing statistics for 205 countries. Market reports are for 16 consumer markets (food and drink, tobacco, toys, etc.) and 14 industrial and service markets (accountancy, broadcasting, chemicals, property services, etc.).

Reports have market size, market sectors, share of market, marketing activity, research and development, corporate overview, distribution, consumer profiles, market forecasts, sector forecasts, sources, and definitions. Additional reports are available for market segments, such as baby food. Company profiles have background, recent news, competitive environment, and outlook. Consumer lifestyle reports and very useful marketing background analyze the consumer by country, gender, age, marital status, educational attainment, ethnicity, religion, home ownership, household profile, employment, income, health, eating and personal grooming habits, leisure activities, personal finance, communication, transport, and travel.

Search for data, which can be exported into Excel or browse for reports. Data are available from 1977 through 2016 and include inflation, exchange rates, GDP, GNI, government expenditures, government finance, income, labor, and money supply.

**631    IBISWorld United States.** IBISWorld. New York: IBISWorld. http://www.ibisworld.com/.

HC103.I247

700 reports on the following industries: agriculture, forestry, fishing and hunting; mining; utilities; construction; manufacturing; wholesale trade; retail trade; transportation and warehousing; information; finance and insurance; real estate and rental and leasing; professional, scientific, and technical services; administrative and support and waste management and remediation services; educational services; health care and social assistance; arts, entertainment, and recreation; accommodation and food services; and other services. Setting this database apart are reports on small industries, such as parking lots and garages.

Reports include industry definition; key statistics; segmentations (products and services segmentation, major market segments, industry concentration, geographic spread); market characteristics (market size, demand determinants, domestic and international markets, basis of competition, life cycle); industry conditions (barriers to entry, taxation, industry assistance, regulation and deregulation, cost structure, capital and labor intensity, technology and systems, industry volatility, globalization); key factors (sensitivities and success factors); key competitors; and industry performance (current and historical).

**632    Magazine dimensions.** Media Dynamics, Inc. New York: Media Dynamics, 1993–. ISSN: 1074-7419.

659.132                                                    HF6105.U5M23

Statistical information mixed with narrative, providing a picture of the magazine industry. Chapters include: General dimensions (history of magazines from 1740–2006, trends in magazines published and ad revenues, changing face of editorial content, magazine CPM's), Magazine audiences (audience definitions, circulation trends, subscriber profiles, reader profiles by magazine, total audience by magazine, website audiences, reading diet by genre, median age and income trends, reader-per-copy, reach and frequency, and accumulation patterns), and Qualitative factors (reader attitudes and intensity of exposure, location and timing of reading, advertising receptivity, comparison to TV), and Information sources (circulation audits, subscriber/panel studies, syndicated audience/marketing research).

633   **Marketresearch.com academic.** Kalorama Information. 1999–.
Bethesda, Md.: Kalorama Information. http://www.marketresearch.
com/.

HF5415.2.K35

Market research reports from various sources (Icon Group, Kalorama,
BizMiner, etc.) for Consumer Goods (apparel, cosmetics and personal
care, house and home, pet services and supplies, travel services), Food and
Beverage (alcoholic beverages, coffee and tea, soft drinks, confectionery,
dairy products, food processing), Heavy Industry (energy, mining, utilities, construction, machines and parts, manufacturing, metals, paper and
forest products, plastics, automotive, aviation & aerospace, logistics and
shipping), Service Industries (accounting and finance, corporate services,
banking and financial services, insurance), Public Sector (associations/
nonprofits, education, government), Life Science (biotechnology, agriculture, genomics, proteomics, medical imaging, healthcare facilities, managed care, regulation and policy, cardiovascular devices, equipment and
supplies, wound care, pharmaceuticals, diseases and conditions, prescription drugs, therapeutic area), Technology & Media (computer equipment,
electronics, networks, e-commerce and IT outsourcing, software, telecommunications, wireless), and Demographics (age, lifestyle and economics,
multicultural).

Reports range in length, with some over 300 pages long, and give a
variety of information (definition of industry, consumer demographics, consumer shopping habits, spending patterns, sales, establishments,
employment, forecasts, trends, market size, market share, and market segmentation). Some company information is also included.

634   **Mintel reports.** Mintel International Group. London; Chicago:
Mintel International Group. http://reports.mintel.com/.

HC240.9.C6

Marketing and consumer research reports focusing on the United States
and Europe. Covers consumer goods and services, making this a good
source of reports for market segments and consumer behavior, with
reports like "Impact of celebrity chefs on cooking habits," "Nail color and
care," and "MP3 players and other portable audio players," but not for
business to business reports.

Market reports are available for automotive, beauty and personal, drink
and tobacco, electronics, food and foodservice, health and medical, health
and wellness, household, lifestyles, media, books and stationery, personal

finances, retailing, technology, and travel. Reports include an executive summary, glossary, and sections on advertising and promotion, ownership and usage, attitudes and opinions, market drivers, market size and trends, market segmentation, future and forecast, and supply structure.

Consumer reports provide demographics, core needs and values, future trends, information on products currently targeted to the group, and advice on reaching and influencing the target audience. Consumer reports are available for financial lifestyles, general lifestyles, healthier lifestyles, and leisure lifestyles.

Marketing and promotion reports are for marketing and targeting, and promotions, incentives, and sponsorship. They include introduction and abbreviations, executive summary, background and market factors, challenges facing marketers, marketing segments, product development and pricing, and future trends.

Most data in Mintel can be downloaded into Excel. Reports cannot be viewed in their entirety and instead must be viewed in sections, making easy skimming or printing a report impossible.

635    **MRI+.** Mediamark Research, Inc. 1999–. [New York]: Mediamark Research, Inc. http://www.mriplus.com/.

HF5415.3M436x

Demographic information about users of consumer products and about the audiences of print and broadcast media. Includes age, household income, education, employment status/occupation, race within region, marital status, county size, marketing region, household size, and Hispanic origin. Use to determine which consumers are most likely to use a product and what media those consumers read or watch. Reports can be exported to Excel. MRI+ has an interactive cost worksheet to help determine the price of an advertising campaign. Available on CD-ROM as *Mediamark reporter*.

636    **The retail market research yearbook.** Richard K. Miller and Associates. Loganville, Ga.: Richard K. Miller and Associates, 2005–. ISSN: 1930-966X.

381

An overview of the retail market, with information on companies, consumers, and resources for each retail industry segment. Chapters include: Market summary; Current and future trends; Industry profile; Department stores; Discount stores and supercenters; Warehouse clubs; Supermarkets;

Variety and dollar stores; Drug stores; Apparel; Footwear; Jewelry; Health, beauty, and cosmetics; Consumer electronics; Home decor and furnishings; Home centers and hardware; Housewares and home textiles; Book stores; Music and video; Office products; Sporting goods; Toys and video games; Pet supplies; Crafts and fabrics; Photography; Closeout and off-price chains; Convenience stores; Military post exchanges; Resale and thrift stores; E-commerce; Catalog and mail-order retail; Television home shopping; Christmas holiday shopping; Back-to-school; Holiday markets; and The bridal and wedding market.

**637    SRDS tv and cable source.** Standard Rate and Data Service. maps. Wilmette, Ill.: Standard Rate and Data Service, 1994–. ISSN: 1071-4596.

Lists broadcast, cable, syndicated and alternative television outlets, organized by state. Entries give contact information, executives, corporate owner, system background, coverage, insertion networks, traffic specifications, and special features. Each market includes a profile, with sales rankings by merchandise, SQAD cost per point levels, top daily newspapers and newspaper groups, metro radio stations by county, and a demographic profile of the market. Also available online.

**638    STAT-USA Internet.** STAT-USA. [1994–.] [Washington, D.C.?]: STAT-USA, U.S. Dept. of Commerce. http://www.stat-usa.gov/.

382                                                                    HF1379

Business and economic information compiled mainly from federal agencies. There are two main sections, "State of the Nation" and "Globus & NTDB."

"State of the Nation" concentrates on current U.S. information, with 2,500 files on general economic indicators (consumer price index, producer price index, gross domestic product, national income and product accounts), regional economic statistics (by NAICS sector, state personal income, metropolitan personal income) housing and construction (housing starts and building permits, new construction, new home sales), employment (employment cost index, local area employment and unemployment, weekly unemployment claims report), manufacturing and industry (retail sales, manufacturing inventories and sales, industrial production and capacity utilization, current industry reports), monetary statistics (interest rates, foreign exchange rates, bank credit), and economic policy (Beige Book, Treasury Statements).

"Globus & NTDB" is useful for current exchange rates (weekly, monthly, and annual), current and historical trade leads (United Nations trade leads, Defense Logistics Agency leads, FedBizOpps, commercial trade leads), international trade (Asia Development Bank, World Bank, Inter-American Development Bank, and European Bank Business Opportunities, country reports on terrorism, Country Studies Program reports, *International trade update newsletter, National trade estimates report on foreign trade barriers, World bank commodity price data*— "PinkSheets"—and *World factbook*), market and country research (*Country background notes, Country commercial guides, Industry sector analysis reports*, Global Agriculture Information Network [GAIN], *AgWorld attaché reports, International market insight (IMI) reports*, and Multilateral Development Bank), contacts (*NTDB global trade directory, National export directory*, Foreign Trade Offices), and current press releases (U.S. international trade in goods and services, FT900 supplemental tables, U.S. Export Sales—USDA, U.S. import and export price indexes, U.S. international transactions, and additional press releases).

## Organizations and Associations

639   **American marketing association.** American Marketing Association. [2001–.] Chicago: American Marketing Association. http://www.marketingpower.com/.
The Association supports marketing professionals in the U.S. and Canada. The website has membership information, resources for members, AMA publications (*Marketing news, Journal of public policy & marketing, Marketing management, Marketing research, Marketing health services, Journal of marketing, Journal of marketing research, Journal of international marketing*), best practices, case studies, webcasts, hot topics, dictionary of marketing terms, careers, and tools (marketing templates, project management, statistics resources, ROI enhancers).

## Periodicals

640   **Advertising age.** Advertising Publications. ill. Chicago: Crain Communications, 1930–. ISSN: 0001-8899.
659.105                                                      HF5801.A276
Essential trade publication tracking news and trends in advertising, marketing, brand management, and sales promotion. Articles on advertising

campaigns often provide unique market share data. In addition to providing current industry news, this weekly is a rich source of statistical data, as it often includes reports on special markets. There are also special reports on leading marketers, technology, top agencies, and award winning campaigns. Partially available online as http://Adage.com/ and available online through aggregators.

**641  American demographics.** American Demographics, Inc. ill. Stamford, Conn.: Cowles Business Media, 1979–2004. ISSN: 01634089.

301.32973                                                        HB3505.A66

This trade periodical has been an indispensable source for demographic and consumer trends, and corresponding market niches for products and services. Issues often contain articles that do an excellent job of analyzing census data, especially for business implications. Use for finding historical information.

**642  eMarketer.** eMarketer (Organization). 1999–. New York: eMarketer. http://www.emarketer.com/.

Aggregates data from 2,800 sources, with summaries in reports and articles. Sources include Accenture, ACNielsen, *Advertising age,* Harris Poll, Juniper Research, Jupitermedia, Mediamark Research Inc. (MRI), Rand Corporation, Pew Internet & American Life Project, Red Hat, Red Herring, as well as various advertising and marketing associations. The data is searchable, making this a good source for online marketing and e-commerce statistics.

**643  Harvard business review.** ill. Boston: Graduate School of Business Administration, Harvard University. ISSN: 0017-8012.

330.904                                                         HF5001.H3

Articles, best practices, book reviews, and case studies on communication, finance and accounting, global business, innovation and entrepreneurship, leadership, management, organizational development, sales and marketing, strategy and execution, and technology and operations. Also available online, through Business Source Elite.

**644  JMR: Journal of marketing research.** American Marketing Association. ill. Chicago: American Marketing Association, 1964–. ISSN: 0022-2437.

658.8305                                                       HF5415.2.J66

As the title indicates, articles are on marketing research. The intended audience is technically oriented research analysts, educators, and statisticians. Available in online form. A regular "New books in review" column provides 1–3 book reviews in each issue, with texts of reviews freely available on the journal's website. Also available on the website are tables of contents back to 2002.

645   **Journal of marketing.** American Marketing Association. ill. Chicago: American Marketing Association, 1936–. ISSN: 0022-2429.

658.8005                                                      HF5415.A2J6

One of the top marketing journals, self-identified as being closely aligned with management practices. International in scope, with a focus on marketing practice and theory. Regular book reviews. Intended audience is marketing managers, consumers, or public policy makers. Tables of contents are available through the journal's website back to 2002. Also available online through aggregators.

646   **The journal of product innovation management.** Product Development and Management Association. ill. New York: North-Holland, 1984–. ISSN: 0737-6782.

658.57505                                                 HF5415.153.J68

Articles and book reviews on product innovation, development, and marketing. Some issues review up to four books, with reviews ranging 2–3 pages in length.

647   **Journal of the Academy of Marketing Science.** Academy of Marketing Science. Amsterdam, The Netherlands: Springer, 1973–. ISSN: 0092-0703.

658.8005                                                    HF5415.A319a

Articles, book and software reviews, and reports on legal decisions and regulatory actions affecting marketing internationally. Annual index in the last issue of each volume.

## Reviews of Research and Trends

648   **The bibliography of marketing research methods.** 3rd ed. John R. Dickinson, Marketing Science Institute. xi, 1025 p. Lexington, Mass.: Lexington Books, 1990. ISBN: 0669216976.

016.65883                                        Z7164.M18D52; HF5415.2

Contains 14,000 entries on market research, data collection, and data analysis drawn from marketing journals, handbooks, and conference proceedings, and from related disciplines. Entries are grouped by subject. Not annotated. Author and subject indexes.

**649    Essential readings in marketing.** Leigh McAlister, Ruth N. Bolton, Ross Rizley, Marketing Science Institute. 196 p. Cambridge, Mass.: Marketing Science Institute, 2006. ISBN: 0965711455.

Abstracts of research articles in various areas of marketing, with brief essays at the beginning of each chapter explaining the topic. Chapters include: New products, growth, and innovation; Branding and brand equity; Metrics linking marketing to financial performance; Managing relationships with customers and organizations; The role of marketing; Research tools; Marketing mix; Customer insight; and Strategy.

## Statistics

**650    Ad $ summary.** TNS Media Intelligence, Media Watch, Competitive Media Reporting, Leading National Advertisers. ill. New York: TNS Media Intelligence, 1973–. ISSN: 0190-7166.

659                                                                                        HF5801

Information on brands that spend over $250,000 annually in advertising; especially useful for finding information on the types of media spending on a brand. Ranks companies by media spending. Data found here are often used to calculate share of voice.

**651    Advertising age.** Advertising Publications. ill. Chicago: Crain Communications, 1930–. ISSN: 0001-8899.

659.105                                                                              HF5801.A276

Essential trade publication tracking news and trends in advertising, marketing, brand management, and sales promotion. Articles on advertising campaigns often provide unique market share data. In addition to providing current industry news, this weekly is a rich source of statistical data, as it often includes reports on special markets. There are also special reports on leading marketers, technology, top agencies, and award winning campaigns. Partially available online as http://Adage.com/ and available online through aggregators.

**652    Advertising ratios and budgets.** Schonfeld and Associates. Lincolnshire, Ill: Schonfeld and Associates.

HF5801.A344

Information for one year of advertising budgets for thousands of companies in hundreds of industries. Organized by SIC. Annual. Ratios include ad-to-sales and ad-to-gross margin. Also provides budget forecasts and growth rates. Useful for comparing ad spending, as well as for estimating advertising budgets.

**653    The adweek directory.** ASM Communications. New York: ASM Communications, 1998–. ISSN: 1528-3291.
659                                                                           HF6182.U5A387

Listing of ad agencies, public relations firms, media buying services, and specialized marketing companies. Entries include contact information, U.S. affiliates/branch offices, services offered, fields served, employees, year founded, key personnel, and major accounts. Also ranks agencies nationally and regionally, with revenue and percentage change from prior year, billings and percentage change from prior year.

**654    ClickZ stats.** INT Media Group. [2006–.] Darien, Conn.: INT Media Group. http://www.clickz.com/showPage.html?page=stats.
                                                                           HF5548.32.C931

A treasure trove of statistics and trends about 22 different sectors of internet marketing, including advertising, business to business, broadband, demographics, education, e-mail and spam, entertainment, finance, geographics, government/politics, hardware, health care, professional, retailing, search tools, security, small/medium enterprises, software and IT, traffic patterns, and wireless. Some data back to 1999. Because ClickZ links to outside sources, some URLs can lead to broken links.

**655    Company/brand$.** Leading National Advertisers, Inc. New York: Leading National Advertisers. ISSN: 8756-1220.

Use to find the advertising expenditures in ten media formats (magazines, Sunday magazines, newspapers, outdoor, network TV, spot TV, syndicated TV, cable TV, network radio, and national spot radio) for U.S. companies. Similar to the *Advertising age* occasional report (http://adage.com/images/random/lna2005.pdf).

**656    Consumer Europe.** London: Euromonitor Publications Limited, 1976–2004/2005. ISSN: 0308-4353.
381.094                                                                    HD7022.C68

Market-size time series for last five years and forecasted time series for upcoming five years for over 330 consumer markets, as well as economic, demographic, lifestyle, and purchasing data and analysis. Also lists manufacturer and brand shares for major consumer goods sectors. Covers Austria, Belgium, Denmark, Finland, France, Germany, Greece, Ireland, Italy, Netherlands, Norway, Portugal, Spain, Sweden, Switzerland, Turkey, and the United Kingdom.

**657**   **Consumer Latin America.** Euromonitor Publications Limited. ill. London: Euromonitor Publications Limited, 1993–. ISSN: 1359-0979.

HC121.C667

Market-size time series for last five years and forecasted time series for upcoming five years for over 330 consumer markets in six Latin American countries (Argentina, Brazil, Chile, Colombia, Mexico, and Venezuela), as well as economic, demographic, lifestyle, and purchasing data and analysis. Also lists manufacturer and brand shares for major consumer goods sectors.

**658**   **Consumer Middle East.** Euromonitor PLC. London: Euromonitor PLC, 1998–.

658.834C7583                                      HC415.15.Z9C616

Market-size time series for last five years and forecasted time series for upcoming five years for over 330 consumer markets, as well as economic, demographic, lifestyle, and purchasing data and analysis. Also lists manufacturer and brand shares for major consumer goods sectors. Covers Algeria, Egypt, Israel, Jordan, Kuwait, Morocco, Saudi Arabia, Tunisia, Turkey, United Arab Emirates, with information on political structure, main industries, and the economy. Tables rank per capita consumer market sizes by country.

**659**   **Consumer USA.** Euromonitor Publications Limited. London: Euromonitor Publications Limited, 1988–. ISSN: 0952-9543.

339.47097305                                      HC101.C744

Market-size time series for last five years and forecasted time series for upcoming five years for over 330 consumer markets, as well as economic, demographic, lifestyle, and purchasing data and analysis. Also lists manufacturer and brand shares for major consumer goods sectors.

**660**   **Demographics USA.** County ed. Market Statistics. ill., maps. New York: Market Statistics, 1993–.

HF5415.1.D46

Demographic and economic data, consumer expenditure data, retail sales and number of establishments by store group, establishments and employment data, and occupation data. Projections for categories such as population, households, and retail sales. Especially useful for the *Effective buying income and buying power index.* Also available in ZIP code ed.

**661**  **The direct marketing market place.** Hilary House Publishers. Hewlett Harbor, N.Y.: Hilary House, 1980–. ISSN: 0192-3137.
381                                                                          HF5415.1.D57

A source similar in purpose and format to *Literary market place* for the direct marketing field. Classified sections list 8,700 direct marketers of products and services (principally through mail order catalogs), service firms and suppliers, creative and consulting services, associations and events, awards, etc. Primarily U.S. listings, with a chapter on Canadian and foreign firms. Gives names, addresses, and telephone numbers for companies and individuals, number of employees, advertising budget related to direct marketing, and gross sales or billing. Also provides an overview of advertising expenditures by medium and market for four years, with a forecast for future expenditures. Indexes of individuals and companies. Some issues have title: *Direct marketing marketplace.*

**662**  **eMarketer.** eMarketer (Organization). 1999–. New York: eMarketer. http://www.emarketer.com/.

Aggregates data from 2,800 sources, with summaries in reports and articles. Sources include Accenture, ACNielsen, *Advertising age* (573), Harris Poll, Juniper Research, Jupitermedia, Mediamark Research Inc. (MRI), Rand Corporation, Pew Internet & American Life Project, Red Hat, Red Herring, as well as various advertising and marketing associations. The data is searchable, making this a good source for online marketing and e-commerce statistics.

**663**  **European marketing data and statistics.** European Research Consultants. London: European Research Consultants, 1962–. ISSN: 0071-2930.
338.094                                                                      HA1107.E87

Demographic trends and forecasts, and economic statistics for 44 European countries. Includes 24 years of data on advertising, cultural indicators, consumer market sizes and expenditures, labor force, foreign trade, health, energy, environment, IT and telecommunications, literacy and education, crime, retailing, travel and tourism, and consumer prices. Sources include the International Monetary Fund, United Nations, national statistical offices, and national trade associations. Companion volume to *International marketing data and statistics* (187).

**664    Global market share planner.** 2nd ed. Euromonitor PLC. London; Chicago: Euromonitor PLC; Euromonitor International, 2002–. ISBN: 1842643916.

Market share data for 30 consumer markets in 52 countries. Company information includes contact information, executive names, organizational structure and subsidiaries, turnover, market share performance, net and operating performance, margins, assets, earnings per share, SWOT analysis, distribution strategies, business development strategies, and brand names. In six volumes: *Major market share tracker* (v. 1), *World leading global brand owners* (v. 2), *Major market share companies: Americas* (v. 3), *Major market share companies: Western Europe* (v. 4), *Major market share companies: Asia-Pacific* (v. 5), and *Major market share companies: Eastern Europe, Middle East and Africa* (v. 6).

**665    International marketing data and statistics.** London: Euromonitor, 1975/76–. ISSN: 0308-2938.

382.09                                                                                    HA42.I56

Demographic trends and forecasts and economic statistics for 161 non-European countries. Includes 24 years of data on cultural indicators, consumer market sizes and expenditures, labor force, foreign trade, health, energy, environment, IT and telecommunications, literacy and education, crime, retailing, travel and tourism, and consumer prices. Sources include the International Monetary Fund, United Nations, national statistical offices and national trade associations. Companion volume to *European marketing data and statistics* (663).

**666    Jupiterresearch.** Jupiter Communications. New York: Jupiter Communications. http://www.jupiterresearch.com/bin/item.pl/ home.

Combines proprietary primary research with secondary research to give trends, statistics, forecasts, and best practices on information technology and its effects on industries and consumers. In seven categories: Personal Technologies; Marketing & Media; Web Technologies & Operations; European Focus; Industry Focus; Jupiter Data (statistics); and Hot Topics.

**667**   **Latin American market planning report.** Strategy Research
Corporation. ill. Miami: Strategy Research, 1996–. ISSN: 1083-
6950.
380.1098021                                        HC130.C6.L38

Consumer information for 18 countries, Puerto Rico, and 70 metropolitan markets. The latest published is 2003, but still contains valuable
information. Organized into topics: business environment, population
and demography, buying power, consumer profile, country profiles, and
summary tables.

**668**   **The lifestyle market analyst.** Standard Rate and Data Service. ill.
Wilmette, Ill.: Standard Rate and Data Service, 1989–. ISSN: 1067-
182X.
658.834097305                                   HF5415.33.U6L54

Profiles 210 regional markets, 60 lifestyles, and 40 consumer segments.
Data is based on census data and surveys of 15 million households. Use to
find information on regional buying power, consumer demographics, consumer interests by location, and magazines that these consumers read.

**669**   **Marketer's guide to media.** Nielsen Business Media. New
York: Nielsen Business Media, 1978–. ISSN: 1061-7159; ISBN:
9781891204494.
338.4                                          HF5826.5; HF5805

This annual neatly packages statistics for all the major types of media
(including but not limited to television, radio, newspapers, magazines,
online services, and outdoor advertising). Among the types of data collected are audience demographics, audience estimates, media rates, and
data on specific markets such as Hispanics and teens. Data are often used
as the basis for projecting trends. Title varies.

**670**   **Market guide.** The Editor and Publisher Company. maps, tables.
New York: The Editor and Publisher, 1924–. ISSN: 0362-1200.
658.8                                                HF5905.E38

Individual market surveys of nearly 1,400 U.S. and Canadian cities where a
daily newspaper is published. Arranged by state and city, with data in 16 categories such as population, households, climate, principal industries, military
installations, and newspapers. Includes U.S. retail census data. *Better living
index* ranks cities by cost of living, crime data, and education statistics.

671 **Market research handbook: Manuel statistique pour études de marché.** Canada Statistics Canada. ill. Ottawa, Canada: Dominion Bureau of Statistics, Merchandising and Services Division = Bureau fédéral de la statistique, Division du commerce et des services, [1969]–. ISSN: 0590-9325.

658.83971           HC111.A19

Annual summary of Canadian national and international trade statistics. Includes data for national and 25 metropolitan markets, with demographic and economic projections. Organized into 11 sections: user's guide, population, labor market and income, consumer expenditures, housing and household characteristics, macroeconomic and financial statistics, international trade, business and industry statistics, census metropolitan areas and census agglomerations, glossary and alphabetic index. Current edition available for free online at http://www.statcan.ca/english/ads/63-224-XPB/toc.htm.

672 **Market share reporter.** Gale Research Inc. Detroit: Gale Research, 1991–. ISSN: 1052-9578.

380.105           HF5410.M35

Market share statistics for over 4,000 companies and 2,300 products and services. Compiled from periodicals and brokerage reports, and arranged by Standard Industrial Classification (SIC) code. Indexed by source, place name, product or service name, company, and brand name. Includes the information from what was *World market share reporter.*

673 **MRI+.** Mediamark Research, Inc. 1999–. [New York]: Mediamark Research, Inc. http://www.mriplus.com/.

          HF5415.3M436x

Demographic information about users of consumer products and about the audiences of print and broadcast media. Includes age, household income, education, employment status/occupation, race within region, marital status, county size, marketing region, household size, and Hispanic origin. Use to determine which consumers are most likely to use a product and what media those consumers read or watch. Reports can be exported to Excel. MRI+ has an interactive cost worksheet to help determine the price of an advertising campaign. Available on CD-ROM as *Mediamark reporter.*

674 **Radio dimensions.** Media Dynamics, Inc. ill. New York: Media Dynamics, 2005–. ISSN: 1931-4795.

659           HF6146.R3R323

Uses data from MRI, Simmons, Scarborough Research, and Radio Recall to show who listens to radio. Augmented by narratives that give context to the data. Chapters on: History of radio, Radio basics (trends in ownership, radio's penetration from 1925-present, ad revenue and profits from 1935-present), Radio audiences (Arbitron's PPM, average number of stations listened to per week, listening trends, daypart audiences, radio usage, internet radio, satellite radio), Reach and frequency patterns, SQAD's CPP estimates, and Qualitative factors.

**675    The sourcebook of zip code demographics.** Census ed. CACI, Inc. Arlington, Va.: CACI Marketing Systems, 1991–. ISSN: 1063-1224.
317.305                                                                  HA203.S67

Statistics on income, age, ethnicity, education, and employment for every zip code in the U.S. Includes dominant lifestyle segmentation, dominant industry, as well as purchasing potential for selected products and services, such as apparel, footwear, groceries, furniture, and financial services. Useful for determining market potential and existing competition in an area.

**676    SRDS business publication advertising source.** Standard Rate and Data Service. Des Plaines, Ill.: SRDS, 1995–. ISSN: 1529-6490.
659                                                                      HF5905.S723

Provides advertising rates for 9,000 trade publications, listed in 220 subject areas. Publication entries give total circulation; publisher's positioning statement; contact information; commission and cash discount; general rate policy; black/white rates; color rates; rates for covers and inserts; bleed information; special advertising positions; and classified, mail order, and specialty rates.

**677    SRDS tv and cable source.** Standard Rate and Data Service. maps. Wilmette, Ill.: Standard Rate and Data Service, 1994–. ISSN: 1071-4596.

Lists broadcast, cable, syndicated and alternative television outlets, organized by state. Entries give contact information, executives, corporate owner, system background, coverage, insertion networks, traffic specifications, and special features. Each market includes a profile, with sales rankings by merchandise, SQAD cost per point levels, top daily newspapers and newspaper groups, metro radio stations by county, and a demographic profile of the market. Also available online.

678 **Statistical abstract of the United States.** U.S. Dept. of the
Treasury, Bureau of Statistics, U.S. Dept. of Commerce and
Labor, Bureau of Statistics, U.S. Bureau of Foreign and Domestic
Commerce, U.S. Bureau of the Census, U.S. Census Bureau. ill.
Washington: U.S. G.P.O., 1878–. ISSN: 0081-4741.

317.3                                                                    HA202

A single-volume work presenting quantitative summary statistics on the
political, social, and economic organization of the United States. Statistics
given in the tables cover a period of several years. Indispensable in any
library: it serves not only as a first source for statistics of national importance but also as a guide to further information, as references are given to
the sources of all tables. Includes a table of contents arranged by broad
subject areas and a detailed alphabetical index. Also available online from
the Census Bureau at http://www.census.gov/compendia/statab/.
Supplement: *County and city data book* (1020).

679 **Success by the numbers: Statistics for business development.**
Ryan Womack, Reference and User Services Association. vii, 59 p.,
ill. Chicago: American Library Association; Reference and User
Services Association, 2005. ISBN: 0838983278.

HF54.56.S832

A guide to U.S. statistical resources, with information on how the data is
gathered, as well as where to find it. Chapters on: Federal business statistics and the 2002 economic census; Finding Florida statistical resources
and data; Demographics and marketing; Economic forecasts; Industry
statistics; Financial statistics; Labor, employment, and wages statistics; and
Trade statistics. State and national sources are provided and sources are
both free and fee-based.

680 **Tablebase.** Gale Cengage Learning. [2001?–.] [s.l.]: Gale Cengage
Learning. http://search.rdsinc.com/.

A terrific international statistical source for company, industry, and demographic information including market share, market size, market trends,
price trends, rankings, sales forecasts, output and capacity, consumption,
imports and exports, and shipments. Information comes from 900 trade
publications, including *Accounting today, Adweek, Aftermarket business,
Almanac of american employers, Beverage world, Chemical week, Datamonitor industry market research, Meed Middle East economic digest,* as well as
reports, newsletters, and surveys.

681   **Who buys what.** Euromonitor International. 2 v., 953 p. London:
Euromonitor International, 2006. ISBN: 1842643827.

HC79.C6.W56

Data on consumer purchasing from 35 developed and emerging countries,
presented in 1,200 tables. Data for 66 sectors, broken into lifestyle-age groups
(Boomers, Gen Y, Gen X, tweens, etc.), income groups, educational attainment, and gender. Valuable for sector data that can be difficult to find.

## Operations Management

## *Book Reviews*

682   **Business information alert.** Alert Publications. Chicago: Alert
Publications, 1989–. ISSN: 1042-0746.

025                                                               HF5001

Contains reviews of print and electronic business resources, and news,
trends, and tips for business researchers. Also available through various
aggregator databases.

683   **European journal of operational research.** Association of
European Operational Research Societies. ill. Amsterdam, [The
Netherlands]: North-Holland, 1977–. ISSN: 0377-2217.

001.424                                                          T57.6.E92

Articles, editorials, case studies, and book reviews on operations management and research. Organized into eight sections: continuous optimization; discrete optimization; production, manufacturing, and logistics;
stochastics and statistics; decision support; computing, artificial intelligence, and information management; O.R. applications; and interfaces
with other disciplines.

684   **Harvard business review.** ill. Boston: Graduate School of Business
Administration, Harvard University. ISSN: 0017-8012.

330.904                                                          HF5001.H3

Articles, best practices, book reviews, and case studies on communication,
finance and accounting, global business, innovation and entrepreneurship,
leadership, management, organizational development, sales and marketing, strategy and execution, and technology and operations. Also available
online, through Business Source Elite (791).

685 **Journal of business and finance librarianship.** ill. Binghamton, N.Y.: Haworth Press, 1990–. ISSN: 0896-3568.

027.6905                                                                        Z675.B8

Reviews of books, databases, and websites written by librarians for librarians. "The immediate focus of the journal is practice-oriented articles, but it also provides an outlet for new empirical studies on business librarianship and business information. Aside from articles, this journal offers valuable statistical and meeting reports, literature and media reviews, Website reviews, and interviews."—*About*

686 **The journal of product innovation management.** Product Development and Management Association. ill. New York: North-Holland, 1984–. ISSN: 0737-6782.

658.57505                                                               HF5415.153.J68

Articles and book reviews on product innovation, development, and marketing. Some issues review up to four books, with reviews ranging 2–3 pages in length.

687 **SIAM review.** Society for Industrial and Applied Mathematics. ill. Philadelphia: Society for Industrial and Applied Mathematics, [1959–.]. ISSN: 0036-1445.

519                                                                             QA1.S2

One of the leading journals in the field, *SIAM review* is presented in five sections: Survey and Review, Problems and Techniques, SIGEST, Education, and Book Reviews. The book review section is quite lengthy, with up to 25 reviews. Reviews are signed and have references.

## Dictionaries

688 **The Blackwell encyclopedic dictionary of operations management.** Nigel Slack. viii, 256 p., ill. Cambridge, Mass.: Blackwell, 1999. ISBN: 0631210822.

658.5003                                                                     TS155.B525

Brief entries on the basics of operations management, such as total quality management (TQM), bottlenecks, and benchmarking. Available as an e-book.

# Directories

**689** **Manufacturing and distribution U.S.A.: Industry analyses, statistics, and leading companies.** Gale Group. ill. Detroit: Gale Group, 2000–. ISSN: 1529-7659.

338                                                                 HD9721.M3495

Industry analyses, statistics, and contact information for U.S. companies in the manufacturing, wholesaling, and retail industries. National and state profiles give leading establishments, employment, payroll, inputs, and outputs. Includes public and private companies. Also available as an e-book.

# Encyclopedias

**690** **Encyclopedia of management.** 5th ed. Marilyn M. Helms. xxix, 1003 p., ill. Detroit: Thomson Gale, 2006. ISBN: 0787665568.

658.00322; 658.003                                                  HD30.15.E49

Covers 18 functional areas: corporate planning and strategic management, emerging topics in management, entrepreneurship, financial management and accounting, general management, human resources management, innovation and technology, international management, leadership, legal issues, management science and operations, management information systems, performance measures and assessment, personal growth and development for managers, production and operations management, quality management and total quality management, supply chain management, and training and development. Contains 350 essays written by academics and business professionals. Almost all essays are new or revised from the 2000 ed. Arranged alphabetically, entries are 3–5 pages long, with cross-references and recommended reading lists. Available as an e-book.

**691** **Encyclopedia of operations research and management science.** 2nd ed. Saul I. Gass, Carl M. Harris. xxxviii, 917 p., ill. Boston: Kluwer Academic, 2000. ISBN: 079237827X.

658.403403                                                          T57.6.E53

Brief entries on the theories, economics, and mathematics involved in operations management. Written for advanced students or practitioners. Available as an e-book.

692   **Encyclopedia of optimization.** Christodoulos A. Floudas, P. M. (Panos M.) Pardalos. 6 v. Dordrecht, [The Netherlands]; London: Kluwer Academic, 2001. ISBN: 0792369327.

519.303                                                                QA402.5.E53

Articles on all areas of optimization, including operations, engineering, mathematics, and computer science. Written by more than 400 authors, with entries ranging from 4–10 pages in length. Available as an e-book.

## Guides and Handbooks

693   **Handbook of quantitative supply chain analysis: Modeling in the e-business era.** David Simchi-Levi, S. David Wu, Zuo-Jun Shen. xiii, 817 p., ill. Boston: Kluwer, 2004. ISBN: 1402079524.

658.70151                                                              HD38.5.H355

Includes trends, theory, and practice. Organized into five parts: emerging paradigms for supply chain analysis; auctions and bidding; supply chain coordinations in e-business; multi-channel coordination; and network design, IT, and financial services. Strong coverage of game theory as it applies to supply chains.

694   **Operations research calculations handbook.** Dennis Blumenfeld. 199 p., ill. Boca Raton, [Fla.]: CRC Press, 2001. ISBN: 0849321271.

658.4034                                                                T57.6B57

Over 250 results and formulas used in systems modeling and systems behavior. There are chapters on means and variances, discrete probability distributions, continuous probability distributions, probability relationships, stochastic processes, Markov chain results, queuing theory results, production systems modeling, inventory control, distance formulas for logistics analysis, linear programming formulations including transportation problems, solution methods, calculus results, matrices, summations, and interest formulas.

695   **The supply management handbook.** 7th ed. Joseph L. Cavinato, Anna E. Flynn, Ralph G. Kauffman. xiv, 945 p., ill. New York: McGraw-Hill, 2006. ISBN: 0071445137.

658.7                                                                  HD39.5.P873

Formerly *The purchasing handbook* and written by three business professors, discusses topics like: next-generation supply methodologies, social responsibility, logistics, and supply management. Includes impact of technology on supply management.

## Indexes; Abstract Journals

**696  Inspec.** Institution of Engineering and Technology. London: Institution of Engineering and Technology. http://www.theiet.org/publishing/inspec/index.cfm.
Index to the literature on physics, electrical engineering, electronics, control theory and technology, computing, and control engineering. Made up of four subfiles: *Series A, Physics abstracts; Series B, Electrical and electronics abstracts; Series C, Computer and control abstracts; Series D, Information technology.* This database is available online from several vendors. Coverage starts in 1898 (when it was called *Science abstracts*), and database contains over 9 million records.

**697  International abstracts in operations research.** International Federation of Operational Research Societies. Houndmills, Basingstoke, Hampshire, [U.K.]: Palgrave Press, 1961–. ISSN: 0020-580X.
658.4034                                                   Q500.I5
Unique content with abstracts from over 180 journals covering operations and management science. Coverage begins in 1989. Also available as IAOR Online.

**698  MathSciNet.** American Mathematical Society. [1990?]–. Providence, R.I.: American Mathematical Society. http://www.ams.org/mathscinet/.
                                                           QA1
Subscription/fee-based database is the online version of the print resources *Mathematical reviews* and *Current mathematical publications.* MathSciNet is a comprehensive, searchable index of mathematics literature from 1940 to the present. Includes a few bibliographic entries for retrodigitized items back to the 1800s. Updated continuously. Contains reference lists, bibliographic citations and mathematical reviews to over 2 million items. The full text of the review is available, even the very short ones, from the MathSciNet entry. If the review or bibliography refers to other items in the database, they are also linked. Full text of the articles still need to be accessed through link resolvers and your subscriptions (either personal or institutional).

Reviewers are members of the research mathematics community and make this a vital resource for mathematics. MathSciNet overlaps a great deal with *Zentralblatt MATH* (Heidelberg, Germany: Springer-Verlag, 1990?–) and despite changes to both, MathSciNet is still easier to use.

MathSciNet uses a sophisticated and highly reliable author name authority control.

Access to either MathSciNet or *Zentralblatt MATH* is essential for any library serving a university-level mathematics department or a sizeable group of research mathematicians. Heavily used as well by statisticians, engineers, physicists, and others doing research involving advanced mathematics.

> **699** **Operations research/management science.** Executive Sciences Institute. Whippany, N.J.: Executive Sciences Institute, [1961]–. ISSN: 0030-3658.
>
> 001                                                          HD28.O645
>
> Abstracts for 150 journals, arranged by subject, with an annual index in the December issue. Particularly useful, as lengthy summaries contain research results. Coverage from 1961.

## *Internet Resources*

> **700** **American productivity and quality center.** APQC. 2003–. Houston, Tex.: APQC. http://www.apqc.org/portal/apqc/site.
>
> The organization is devoted to benchmarking and best-practice research. The site includes best-practice studies, professional development, survey hosting, success profiles, and a knowledge base. The knowledge base is for finding best practices, books, case studies, measures and metrics, newsletters, presentations, surveys/questionnaires, and white papers. Many services are for members only.

> **701** **Manufacturing.net.** Advantage Business Media. 2000s–. [s.l.]: Reed Business Information. http://www.manufacturing.net/.
>
> Covers manufacturing for aerospace, automotive, chemical, food, material handling, pharmaceuticals, and utilities. Includes design and development; case studies; electrical and electronics; energy; environmental; facilities and operations; labor relations; manufacturing technology; materials; quality control; safety; and supply chain management. Has international focus.

> **702** **MathSciNet.** American Mathematical Society. [1990?]–. Providence, R.I.: American Mathematical Society. http://www.ams. org/mathscinet/.

QA1

Subscription/fee based database is the online version of the print resources *Mathematical reviews* and *Current mathematical publications*. MathSciNet is a comprehensive, searchable index of mathematics literature from 1940 to the present. Includes a few bibliographic entries for retrodigitized items back to the 1800s. Updated continuously. Contains reference lists, bibliographic citations and mathematical reviews to over 2 million items. The full text of the review is available, even the very short ones, from the MathSci-Net entry. If the review or bibliography refers to other items in the database, they are also linked. Full text of the articles still need to be accessed through link resolvers and your subscriptions (either personal or institutional). Reviewers are members of the research mathematics community and make this a vital resource for mathematics. MathSciNet overlaps a great deal with *Zentralblatt MATH* (Heidelberg, Germany: Springer-Verlag, 1990?–) and despite changes to both, MathSciNet is still easier to use.

MathSciNet uses a sophisticated and highly reliable author name authority control.

Access to either MathSciNet or *Zentralblatt MATH* is essential for any library serving a university-level mathematics department or a sizeable group of research mathematicians. Heavily used as well by statisticians, engineers, physicists, and others doing research involving advanced mathematics.

## *Organizations and Associations*

**703** **American productivity and quality center.** APQC. 2003–.
Houston, Tex.: APQC. http://www.apqc.org/portal/apqc/site.
The organization is devoted to benchmarking and best-practice research. The site includes best-practice studies, professional development, survey hosting, success profiles, and a knowledge base. The knowledge base is for finding best practices, books, case studies, measures and metrics, newsletters, presentations, surveys/questionnaires, and white papers. Many services are for members only.

**704** **INFORMS online.** Institute for Operations Research and the Management Sciences. Linthicum, Md.: Institute for Operations Research and the Management Sciences. http://www.informs.org/.
The institute serves professionals, students, and academics interested in operations research, and is the publisher of two of the top journals in the field, *Operations research* and *Management science*. The website includes INFORMS Meetings Database (conference presentations), Member Directory, Press Releases, Expert List, Publications, Awards, Scholarships, Education, Careers, and Resources (including a comprehensive list of operations research resources).

705 **Production and operations management.** Production and Operations Management Society. 1992–. Baltimore: Production and Operations Management Society. http://www.poms.org/.

TS155.A1P683

Has information on society membership, its publications (*Production and operations management* and *POMS chronicle*), meetings, research, education, placement, and colleges.

## Periodicals

706 **European journal of operational research.** Association of European Operational Research Societies. ill. Amsterdam, [The Netherlands]: North-Holland, 1977–. ISSN: 0377-2217.

001.424                                                                  T57.6.E92

Articles, editorials, case studies, and book reviews on operations management and research. Organized into eight sections: continuous optimization; discrete optimization; production, manufacturing, and logistics; stochastics and statistics; decision support; computing, artificial intelligence, and information management; O.R. applications; and interfaces with other disciplines.

707 **Harvard business review.** ill. Boston: Graduate School of Business Administration, Harvard University. ISSN: 0017-8012.

330.904                                                                  HF5001.H3

Articles, best practices, book reviews, and case studies on communication, finance and accounting, global business, innovation and entrepreneurship, leadership, management, organizational development, sales and marketing, strategy and execution, and technology and operations. Also available online, through Business Source Elite (791).

708 **The journal of product innovation management.** Product Development and Management Association. ill. New York: North-Holland, 1984–. ISSN: 0737-6782.

658.57505                                                                HF5415.153.J68

Articles and book reviews on product innovation, development, and marketing. Some issues review up to four books, with reviews ranging 2–3 pages in length.

ECONOMICS & BUSINESS

709    **SIAM review.** Society for Industrial and Applied Mathematics.
ill. Philadelphia: Society for Industrial and Applied Mathematics,
[1959–.]. ISSN: 0036-1445.

519                                                                  QA1.S2

One of the leading journals in the field, *SIAM review* is presented in five
sections: Survey and Review, Problems and Techniques, SIGEST, Education, and Book Reviews. The book review section is quite lengthy, with up
to 25 reviews. Reviews are signed and have references.

# 5 > GENERAL WORKS

## Biography

710    **African-American business leaders: A biographical dictionary.**
John N. Ingham, Lynne B. Feldman. xiv, 806 p. Westport, Conn.:
Greenwood Press, 1994. ISBN: 0313272530.

338.64208996073                                              HC102.5.A2I52

Lengthy biographies for 123 African-American business leaders, with information on many individuals who do not appear in standard biographical
sources. Each essay concludes with references list, some with primary sources.
Includes bibliographic references and indexes. Available as an e-book.

711    **American business leaders: From colonial times to the present.**
Neil A. Hamilton. 2 v., 791 p., ports. Santa Barbara, Calif.: ABC-
CLIO, 1999. ISBN: 1576070026.

338.092272B                                                 HC102.5.A2H36

Some 400 short entries with information on significant dates, family, education, discussion of entrepreneurial efforts, and brief bibliography. Arranged
alphabetically, but with an index by industry. Available as an e-book.

712    **American inventors, entrepreneurs, and business visionaries.**
Charles W. Carey. xxi, 410 p., ill. New York: Facts On File, 2002.
ISBN: 0816045593.

338.092273                                                     CT214.C29

Profiles nearly 300 Americans from the seventeenth through twentieth centuries. Not all individuals are well known or achieved business success, making this a richer resource than the typical biographical source. Entries of 1–2 pages cover birth and death dates, life and innovations, with brief bibliographies. Indexes for invention, industry, and birth year. Available as an e-book.

713 **A to Z of American women business leaders and entrepreneurs.** Victoria Sherrow. xx, 252 p., ill. New York: Facts On File, 2002. ISBN: 0816045569.

338.0082092273B         HD6054.4.U6S5

Contains 135 profiles of well-known women throughout U.S. history. Entries of 1–2 pages cover accomplishments, with a bit on each woman's life, and suggested further reading. A more complete source is *Encyclopedia of American women in business: From colonial times to the present* (517).

714 **Biographical dictionary of American business leaders.** John N. Ingham. 4 v., xvi, 2026 p. Westport, Conn.: Greenwood Press, 1983. ISBN: 0313213623.

338.0922B         HC102.5.A2I53

835 entries, with information on 1,159 leaders from colonial times to the early 1980s. Appendixes by industry, company, birthplace and date, ethnic background and religion, place of business activity, and sex. Partially updated by *Contemporary American business leaders: A biographical dictionary* (718).

715 **The biographical dictionary of British economists.** Donald Rutherford. 2 v., xxv, 1330 p. Bristol, [U.K.]: Thoemmes, 2004. ISBN: 1843710307.

330.092241         HB76.B52

Covers 600 economists who lived before the 21st century, with a focus on those in the 20th century. Entries include well-known economists such as Friedrich Engels, but many are for lesser-known figures.

716 **A biographical dictionary of women economists.** Robert W. Dimand, Mary Ann Dimand, Evelyn L. Forget. xxviii, 491 p. Cheltenham, U.K.; Northampton, Mass.: Edward Elgar, 2000. ISBN: 1852789646.

330.0820922B         HB76.B535

124 profiles of deceased or retired female economists from around the world. Entries include biographical information, as well as information about the contributions made and the significance of those contributions. No index.

**717 Business leader profiles for students.** Gale Research Inc. ill. Farmington Hills, Mich.: Gale Research, 1999–. ISSN: 1520-9296.

650                                                HC102.5.A2B79

About 200 profiles, which range from 1,250 to 2,500 words in length. Entries include an overview, personal life, career, details, a chronology, social and economic impact, and a bibliography. Photographs are often included. Also available as an e-book.

**718 Contemporary American business leaders: A biographical dictionary.** John N. Ingham, Lynne B. Feldman. xxxv, 788 p. New York: Greenwood Press, 1990. ISBN: 0313257434.

338.0922B                                HC102.5.A2I534

Contains 116 biographies of the major U.S. leaders from 1945–1989. Emphasizes business decisions made rather than personal lives. Entries are several pages long, with bibliographies. Appendixes include industry, company, place of business, place of birth, and black and women leaders. Indexed. Considered a companion to the *Biographical dictionary of American business leaders* (714).

**719 Directory of members.** American Economic Association. Nashville, Tenn.: American Economic Association. ISSN: 1066-3568. http://www.lbmchost.com/aea/search.asp.

330.06073                                    HB1.A59a

Search for individuals by name, field, institution, employer, alma mater, or geographic location.

**720 Distinguished Asian American business leaders.** Naomi Hirahara. viii, 242 p., ports. Westport, Conn.: Greenwood Press, 2003. ISBN: 1573563447.

338.0973092395                             HC102.5.A2H56

Contains 96 profiles with education and career highlights, and the story of how they succeeded. Entries include further reading. Appendix for distinguished Asian American business leaders by field.

721 **Distinguished women economists.** James Cicarelli, Julianne Cicarelli. xxvi, 244 p. Westport, Conn.: Greenwood Press, 2003. ISBN: 0313303312.

330.0922                                                                              HB76.C53

Contains 51 profiles of women selected from the 19th century to the present. Entries include an introduction, short biography, section on contributions to economics, and further reading. Most entries can be found in *A biographical dictionary of women economists* (716) or *Who's who in economics* (731). Available as an e-book.

722 **Encyclopedia of American women in business: From colonial times to the present.** Carol Krismann. 2 v., 692 p. Westport, Conn.: Greenwood Press, 2005. ISBN: 0313327572.

338.0922                                                                      HD6054.4.U6K753

Contains 327 brief entries on American businesswomen and nearly 100 entries on topics related to their lives, such as affirmative action, child care, and civil rights. Coverage begins in the 18th century. Appendixes for *Fortune* 50 most powerful women in American business, 1998–2003; *Working woman* top 30 woman-owned businesses, 1997–2001; businesswomen by ethnic group; businesswomen by historical periods; businesswomen by profession; and women in Junior Achievement's national business hall of fame. Good cross-references, bibliography, and index.

723 **Fifty major economists.** Steven Pressman. xi, 207 p., ill. London; New York: Routledge, 1999. ISBN: 0415134803.

330.0922B                                                                              HB76.P74

Profiles with biographical sketch, analysis of contributions, list of main works, and further reading. Primary coverage is given to seminal economists. Glossary of economic terms. Also available as an e-book.

724 **Great economists before Keynes: An introduction to the lives and works of one hundred great economists of the past.** Mark Blaug. xi, 286 p., ports. Cambridge, [England]; New York: Cambridge University Press, 1986, 1988. ISBN: 0521367417.

330.0922B                                                                              HB76.B54

Discusses the life, impact, and work of renowned economists, in 2–4 page entries. Portraits included, where possible. Indexed by name and subject.

725 **Great economists since Keynes: An introduction to the lives and works of one hundred modern economists.** 2nd ed. Mark Blaug.

xiii, 312 p., ill. Cheltenham, U.K.; Northampton, Mass.: Edward Elgar, 1998. ISBN: 1858986923.

330.0922B                                                                          HB76.B55

Blaug, a well known economic historian, describes the careers and contributions of key economists, with biographical and academic information, list of major works, photographs, and illustrations. Indexed by name and subject.

**726   Historical encyclopedia of American women entrepreneurs: 1776 to the present.** Jeannette M. Oppedisano. xii, 283 p., ports. Westport, Conn.: Greenwood Press, 2000. ISBN: 0313306478.

338.04082092273B                                                                   HF3023.A2O64

Eminently readable narratives that bring 100 women to life. Entries are short (2–3 pages) and include references. Index includes personal names, company names, and industries.

**727   International directory of business biographies.** Neil Schlager, Schlager Group. 4 v., ill. Detroit: St. James Press, 2005. ISBN: 1558625542.

338.0922                                                                           HC29.I57

Profiles over 600 business leaders. International in scope, with almost half the profiles on non-U.S. figures. Includes information on education, awards, family, career path, leadership style, impact, and business strategies. Four indexes (nationality, geographic, company and industry, and name) assist in locating information. Available as an e-book.

**728   Leadership library on the Internet.** Leadership Directories, Inc. 2002–. New York: Leadership Directories, Inc. http://www.leadershipdirectories.com/.

                                                                                   CT210

Profiles 400,000 individuals in the United States, including in government, business, professional, and nonprofit organizations. Includes contact information, education, religion, political affiliations, date and place of birth, and professional highlights.

**729   The new Palgrave: A dictionary of economics.** John Eatwell, Murray Milgate, Peter K. Newman. 4 v., ill. London; New York; Tokyo: Macmillan; Stockton Press; Maruzen, 1987. ISBN: 0333372352.

330.0321                                                                           HB61.N49

Successor to *Palgrave's dictionary of political economy*, first published 1894–96. A sophisticated encyclopedic coverage of modern economic thought, with nearly 2,000 signed entries written by more than 900 prominent economists, historians, philosophers, mathematicians, and statisticians. Articles present diverse philosophies, ideologies, and methodologies and discuss their origin, historical development, and philosophical foundation. The 700 biographical entries exclude living economists born after 1915. Bibliographies accompany most entries. Appendixes list contributors and biographies included in the earlier edition of *Palgrave* but omitted here, and show subject entries classified under 53 fields of study. Analytical subject index.

**730** **Standard and Poor's register of corporations, directors, and executives.** ill. New York: Standard and Poor's. ISSN: 0361-3623.
332.67 HG4057.A4

Information on public and private corporations, with current address, financial and marketing information, and biographies for corporate executives and directors. Useful for identifying corporate relationships and executive's business connections. Vol. 1 lists firms, v. 2 lists executives, v. 3 provides indexes including Standard Industrial Classification (SIC) codes and geography. Also available through NetAdvantage.

**731** **Who's who in economics.** 3rd ed. Mark Blaug. xx, 1235 p. Cheltenham, U.K.; Northampton, Mass.: Edward Elgar, 1999. ISBN: 1858988861.
330.0922B HB76.W47

Profiles 1,000 living and 500 deceased economists. Brief entries include date and place of birth, education, current and past posts, offices and honors, editorial positions, major publications, and contributions. Living economists were selected on the basis of number of citations in 200 economics journals between 1984 and 1996. Available as an e-book.

**732** **Who's who in finance and business.** Marquis Who's Who. New Providence, N.J.: Marquis Who's Who, 2004–. ISSN: 1930-3262.
338.00922B HF3023.A2W5

Brief coverage of business executives in the U.S., Canada, and Mexico. Particularly useful for finding senior U.S. executives by revenue, presidents of U.S. chambers of commerce, executives of the largest minority-owned businesses, the largest Mexican and Canadian industrial firms, and administrators and professors from the top business schools in the U.S., Mexico, and Canada. Formerly *Who's who in commerce and industry* and then *Who's who in finance and industry*. Available online.

**733 Who's who in finance and business.** Marquis Who's Who. New
Providence, N.J.: Marquis Who's Who, 2005–. ISSN: 1930-3262.
338                                   HF3023.A2W5; HC29.W46
Over 24,000 entries on executives in the U.S. and in 100 other countries and territories. Also has entries for administrators and professors in the top business schools in the U.S., Canada, and Mexico. Continues: 1936–59, *Who's who in commerce and industry*; 1961–1968/69, *World who's who in commerce and industry*; 1970/71, *World's who's who in commerce and industry*; and 1972/73–2003, *Who's who in finance and industry*. Included in Marquis Who's Who on the Web (United States: U.S. Census Bureau, 199–).

# Book Reviews

**734 Business information alert.** Alert Publications. Chicago: Alert
Publications, 1989–. ISSN: 1042-0746.
025                                          HF5001
Contains reviews of print and electronic business resources, and news, trends, and tips for business researchers. Also available through various aggregator databases.

**735 Economic history services.** EH.Net. 2004–. [Oxford, Ohio]:
EH.Net. http://eh.net/.

                                             HC21.E25
Owned by the Economic History Association and intended primarily for economic historians, historians of economics, economists, and historians, EH.net has research abstracts and book reviews, course syllabi, directory of economic historians, Encyclopedia of Economic and Business History, historical economic data sets (such as Global Financial Data, 1880–1913 and historic labor statistics), links to economic history websites, and a section called "How Much Is That?".

"How Much Is That?" gives comparative values of money, including five ways to compare the worth of a U.S. dollar, 1790–2005; the price of gold for 1257–2005; annual Consumer Price Index for the United States for 1774–2005; the purchasing power of the British pound, 1264–2005; annual real and nominal GDP for the United States, 1790–2005; annual real and nominal GDP for the United Kingdom, 1086–2005; interest rate series for the United Kingdom and the United States, 1790–2001; and daily closing values of the Dow Jones Industrial Average (DJIA) from 1896.

**736    The economist.** ill. London: Economist Newspaper, 1843–. ISSN: 0013-0613.

330.05                                                                      HG11.E2

Coverage of political, economic, and business events, world leaders, and science and technology. Economic and financial indicators (output, prices and jobs, *The economist* commodity-price index, GDP growth forecasts, trade, exchange rates, budget balances and interest rates, markets, and stock markets), and emerging market indicators (overview, child mortality, economy, financial markets) are published regularly. Regular book reviews. Full access available for a fee at http://www.economist.com/and through various aggregator databases.

**737    Harvard business review.** ill. Boston: Graduate School of Business Administration, Harvard University. ISSN: 0017-8012.

330.904                                                                     HF5001.H3

Articles, best practices, book reviews, and case studies on communication, finance and accounting, global business, innovation and entrepreneurship, leadership, management, organizational development, sales and marketing, strategy and execution, and technology and operations. Also available online, through Business Source Elite (791).

**738    H-net.** Michigan State University, National Endowment for the Humanities. 1995–. East Lansing, Mich.: Michigan State University. http://www.h-net.org/.

300.072; 001.3072; 370; 378.104; 700.072                                    H85

Created to advance "research, teaching, learning, public outreach, and professional service within their own specialized areas of knowledge" (*About H-net*), H-net is composed of discussion networks, scholarly reviews, announcements, and a job guide.

It serves diverse areas of interest in the social sciences and humanities, including economics, history, maritime history, African studies, American studies, and art history.

The reviews are from 1993 to the present and cover books and multimedia. H-net currently publishes about 1,000 reviews annually.

The job guide "posts academic position announcements in History and the Humanities, the Social Sciences, and Rhetoric and Composition, and serves a broad audience of administrators, faculty members, archivists, librarians, and other professionals in the humanities and social sciences"—*Introd. to Job Guide.* The positions can be searched or browsed, and an e-mail alert can be set up.

**739    Journal of business and finance librarianship.** ill. Binghamton, N.Y.: Haworth Press, 1990–. ISSN: 0896-3568.

027.6905                                                                                     Z675.B8

Reviews of books, databases, and websites written by librarians for librarians. "The immediate focus of the journal is practice-oriented articles, but it also provides an outlet for new empirical studies on business librarianship and business information. Aside from articles, this journal offers valuable statistical and meeting reports, literature and media reviews, Website reviews, and interviews."—*About*

## Dictionaries

**740    The Chartered Management Institute dictionary of business and management.** Chartered Management Institute. ix, 660 p. London: Bloomsbury, 2003. ISBN: 0747562369.

658.003

Easy to read definitions for 6,000 international business terms, people, and phrases. Ranges from slang, "herding cats," to management tools, "vertical linkage analysis."

**741    A dictionary of business.** 3rd ed., New ed. Oxford University Press. 545 p., ill. Oxford; New York: Oxford University Press, 2002. ISBN: 0198603975.

650.03                                                                                     HF1001.C63

For business students and practitioners, with short definitions of terms and jargon in all fields of business, with more selective coverage of economics and law.

**742    A dictionary of business and management.** 4th ed. Oxford University Press. 562 p. Oxford; New York: Oxford University Press, 2006. ISBN: 0192806483.

650.03                                                                                     HF1001.C63

Contains 6,500 entries relating to business strategy, marketing, taxation, accounting, operations management, investment, banking and international finance. Non-American terms and phrases are defined, such as *zaibatsu* and *badges of trade*, but readers should be aware that common phrases, such as balance sheet, are often defined with a British bent. Also available through Oxford Reference Online (Oxford; New York: Oxford University Press, 2002–).

743    **Dictionary of business terms.** Jae K. Shim. vi, 441 p. Mason, Ohio: Thomson, 2006. ISBN: 0324205457.

650.03                                                          HF1001.S5247

A good general dictionary, covering all areas of business and written in language accessible to the general public, as well as to the business student. Definitions often include charts, graphs, or formulas.

744    **Dictionary of international business terms.** 3rd ed. John J. Capela, Stephen Hartman. ix, 626 p. Hauppauge, N.Y.: Barron's, 2004. ISBN: 0764124455.

382.03                                                          HD62.4.C36

Nearly 5,000 terse definitions of business and economics terms. Appendixes with abbreviations, acronyms, contacts for major foreign markets, and U.S. Customs officers, regions, and districts. 2000 edition available as an e-book.

745    **Dictionary of international economics terms.** John Owen, Edward Clark. 300 p. London: Les50ns Professional Pub., 2006. ISBN: 0852976852.

330.03                                                          HF1359.D4956

Defines concepts, jargon, and acronyms in economics, finance and business. Includes definitions such as accelerated depreciation, Andean Pact, coupon interest rate, marginal cost, shakeout, and X-inefficiency. Part of a series of dictionaries, which include: *Dictionary of international accounting terms*, *Dictionary of international banking and finance terms*, *Dictionary of international business terms*, *Dictionary of international insurance and finance terms*, and *Dictionary of international trade finance*. Some definitions are shared between the dictionaries in the series.

746    **An eponymous dictionary of economics: A guide to laws and theorems named after economists.** Julio Segura, Carlos Rodríguez Braun. Cheltenham, U.K.; Northampton, Mass.: Edward Elgar Pub., 2004. ISBN: 1843760290.

330.03                                                          HB61.E66

Over 300 thorough entries for well-known (Adam Smith's problem) and lesser-known eponyms (Schmeidler's lemma), written by more than 200 authors. Available as an e-book.

**747    A historical dictionary of American industrial language.** William H. Mulligan. xii, 332 p. New York: Greenwood Press, 1988. ISBN: 0313241716.

338.00321                                                                TS9.H57

Brief definitions drawn primarily from the period before World War I. An appendix lists terms by industry. Includes a list of contributors, bibliography, and index of institutions and people.

# Directories

**748    Business week's guide to the best business schools.** New York: McGraw-Hill, 1990–.

Ranks business schools using surveys measuring student and recruiter satisfaction. Names top full-time and part-time programs, and top international programs. Tables list test scores, employment outcomes, costs, and more. Also available for a fee through http://www.businessweek.com/. A similar ranking is available through the *Wall Street Journal* (New York: Dow Jones, 1959–).

**749    Cabell's directory of publishing opportunities in accounting, economics, and finance.** David W. E. Cabell, Deborah L. English. 2 v. Beaumont, Tex.: Cabell, 1994–. ISSN: 1532-5911.

330.13                                                                    H1.C22

Covers periodicals in accounting, economics, finance, management, and marketing, with information on circulation data, publication guidelines, where to submit, journal acceptance rate, review information, manuscript topics and guidelines, format, length, and style guidelines. Indexes by acceptance rate, review process, number of external reviewers, and by sub-discipline, for example, accounting education, accounting theory and practice, econometrics, fiscal policy, insurance, technology/innovation, and direct marketing. Each directory is available individually or online (Beaumont, Texas: Cabell Pub., 2004–).

**750    Consultants and consulting organizations directory: A reference guide to more than 26,000 firms and individuals engaged in**

consultation for business, industry, and government. 29th ed. Julie A. Gough. 2 v. Detroit: Thomson/Gale, 2006. ISBN: 0787679437.

Organized into 14 general fields of consulting. Entries give contact information, brief description of activities, mergers and former names, geographic area served, and where possible, annual consulting revenue.

**751    Directory of members.** American Economic Association. Nashville, Tenn.: American Economic Association. ISSN: 1066-3568. http://www.lbmchost.com/aea/search.asp.

330.06073                                                    HB1.A59a

Search for individuals by name, field, institution, employer, alma mater, or geographic location.

**752    The directory of trade and professional associations in the European Union: = Répertoire de. associations professionnelles et commerciales dans l'Union européenne.** Euroconfidential. London; New York: Europa, 1994–. ISSN: 1742-4011.

HD2429.E88D57

Gives contact information and publications for 750 associations in the European Union. Also gives contact information for 11,700 national member organizations and the Chambers of Commerce in Europe. Indexes for: acronyms and abbreviations, full names, keywords, and Standard Industrial Classification (SIC) codes.

**753    Directory of U.S. labor organizations.** Bureau of National Affairs. Washington: Bureau of National Affairs, 1982–. ISSN: 0734-6786.

331.8802573                                                  HD6504.D64

Lists some 30,000 unions affiliated with AFL-CIO and other national, regional, state, and local affiliates. Gives the structure, leadership, and contact information for the unions. Index of unions by common name and by abbreviations; names and index of officers.

**754    Economics departments, institutes and research centers in the world.** Christian Zimmermann, University of Connecticut, Department of Economics. [1995–.] Storrs, Conn.: University of Connecticut, Department of Economics. http://edirc.repec.org/.

Free index to over 10,000 nonprofit institutions employing economists (including institutes, think tanks, academic research centers, finance ministries, central banks, and statistical offices) in 226 countries and territories. Organized by country, areas, fields, and functions. Prepared by a faculty member at the University of Connecticut.

**755   Grad school rankings.** PhDs.org. 1997–2008. [s.l.]: PhDs.org. http://www.phds.org/rankings/economics/.
Terrific resource for determining which graduate program is the right fit. Weight criteria like educational quality, faculty reputation and activity, program size, funding measures, and program composition to arrive at a list of top-ranked schools. Based on National Research Council data.

**756   National trade and professional associations of the United States.** Craig Colgate, John J. Russell. Washington: Columbia Books, 1966–. ISSN: 0734-354X.
061.3                                                                HD2425.D53
Entries for more than 7,200 trade and professional associations and labor unions, with directory information, historical notes, membership information, and lists of publications and annual meetings. Separate directory lists association management companies with the names of the organizations they manage. Indexes: subject, geography, budget size, executive name, and acronyms. Companion publication: *State and regional associations of the United States* (759).

**757   Peterson's graduate programs in business, education, health, information studies, law and social work.** Peterson's (Firm). ill. Princeton, N.J.: Peterson's, 1997–. ISSN: 1088-9442.
378.15530257                                                         L901.P459
The standard guide to graduate schools, with information on programs offered; degree requirements; number and gender of faculty; number, gender, and ethnicity of students; average student age; percentage of students accepted; entrance requirements; application deadlines; application fee; costs; and financial aid. Also available online.

**758   SI.** SI, Special Issues. 2001–. Houston, Tex.: SI, Special Issues. http://specialissues.com/.
Many useful business statistics and industry surveys are hidden away in special issues of trade publications, newsletters, and journals. SI indexes nearly 3,500 trade magazines, reporting on the content of their special issues and websites. Entries include a monthly listing of special reports

(linking to the online content where possible), contact information for the publisher, and any special content that is available on a magazine's accompanying website, including archives, special reports, indexes, etc. Search by publication, subject, or keyword. Coverage from 2000 to the present. Some information is available for free from a sample database. Subscribers also receive a newsletter reviewing magazines.

**759    State and regional associations of the United States.** Washington, D.C.: Columbia Books, 1989–. ISSN: 1044-324X.

380.102573                                                                      HD2425.S68

Lists 8,000 major trade associations, professional societies, and labor organizations that have state or regional memberships. Fraternal, patriotic, charitable, hobby, and small organizations are excluded, making SRA significantly smaller than the *Encyclopedia of associations*, which includes all types of nonprofit groups. Entries include address, telephone, fax, president, number of members and of staff, and, when available, annual budget, historical note, publ., and annual meetings. Arranged geographically with the following indexes: subject, budget, executive, acronym, and management firm.

For associations with national memberships, consult the companion directory: *National trade and professional associations of the United States* (756). Both titles are available online at http://www.associationexecs.com/.

**760    The Wall Street Journal guide to the top business schools.** Wall Street Journal. New York: Simon and Schuster, 2002–. ISSN: 1544-2977.

650.13; 650.0711                                                                HF1101.W35

Ranks business schools using recruiter surveys. Lists include top-ranked national, regional, and international programs, top schools for major industries, by academic discipline, for recruiting women, for recruiting minorities, and for recruiting MBAs with high ethical standards. Detailed profiles of full-time programs are included, with the school's ranking, admissions process, test scores, the industries and companies most likely to hire graduates, and expected first-year salaries. Some of the information is available through the *Wall Street Journal* (New York: Dow Jones, 1959–) and the Journal Online (http://online.wsj.com/public/us/). Similar to *Business week's guide to the best business schools* (748).

**761    World directory of business information websites.** Euromonitor PLC. London: Euromonitor PLC, 1998–.

HF54.56.W67

Nearly 4,000 entries of free and fee-based websites. Includes a brief description, URL, publisher's name, email address, statistical coverage, charging structure, and country coverage.

**762  World directory of trade and business journals.** Euromonitor PLC. London: Euromonitor PLC, 1996–.

Z7164.C81W67

Lists some 2,000 magazines, newsletters, and journals. Gives language, frequency, content, country coverage, format, publisher and contact information. Arranged into 80 industry categories, beginning with advertising and ending with wholesaling. Two indexes: A-Z index by country and publisher with publications, and A-Z index of journals by country. Especially useful for finding a source for news, organizational information, trends or statistics on a company or industry that is not gathered in a reference resource.

**763  Yearbook of international organizations online.** Union of International Associations. 2000–. Brussels, Belgium: Union of International Associations. http://www.uia.be/node/52.

314.2                                                           JX1904

A subscription database made up of four components:

At its core is International Organizations Online (Beaumont, Tex.: Cabell Pub., 2004–), a guide to more than 60,000 international nongovernmental organizations (INGOs) and intergovernmental organizations (IGOs) and selected subsidiary bodies. Covers all known IGOs, but the inclusion of NGOs is dependent on numerous criteria. Entries range from a few words in length to more than 10,000.

Biography Profiles Online (Beaumont, Tex.: Cabell Pub., 2004–) consists of biographical entries on more than 20,000 individuals holding or having held significant positions in organizations profiled in International Organizations Online (Beaumont, Tex.: Cabell Pub., 2004–).

Statistics Online contains graphs and detailed tables on various aspects of IGOs and INGOs, such as their geographic distribution, fields of activity, dates founded, structure, language use, publishing output, and interrelationships. Periods covered vary; one time series begins in 312 CE.

Bibliography Online consists of bibliographic references to titles mentioned in International Organizations Online (Beaumont, Tex.: Cabell Pub., 2004–) and to studies on IGOs and INGOs by scholars throughout the social sciences. Its value to users having access to such databases as WorldCat (Dublin, Ohio: OCLC Online Computer Library Center) and Worldwide Political Science Abstracts (Bethesda, Md.: Cambridge Scientific Abstracts, 2001–) is questionable.

Issued annually in print as the *Yearbook of international organizations* and on CD-ROM as the *Yearbook plus of international organizations and biographies* (München, Germany; New Providence, N.J.: K. G. Saur, 1996–).

## Encyclopedias

**764   Economic history services.** EH.Net. 2004–. [Oxford, Ohio]: EH.Net. http://eh.net/.

HC21.E25

Owned by the Economic History Association and intended primarily for economic historians, historians of economics, economists, and historians, EH.net has research abstracts and book reviews, course syllabi, directory of economic historians, Encyclopedia of Economic and Business History, historical economic data sets (such as Global Financial Data, 1880–1913 and historic labor statistics), links to economic history websites, and a section called "How Much Is That?"

"How Much Is That?" gives comparative values of money, including five ways to compare the worth of a U.S. dollar, 1790–2005; the price of gold for 1257–2005; annual Consumer Price Index for the United States for 1774–2005; the purchasing power of the British pound, 1264–2005; annual real and nominal GDP for the United States, 1790–2005; annual real and nominal GDP for the United Kingdom, 1086–2005; interest rate series for the United Kingdom and the United States, 1790–2001; and daily closing values of the Dow Jones Industrial Average (DJIA) from 1896.

**765   Encyclopedia of American business history.** Charles R. Geisst. New York: Facts On File, 2005. ISBN: 0816043507.

338.097303                                                                     HF3021.G44

Contains 400 entries on businesses and industries, business events, and leaders, as well as business and economic topics from 1776 to the present. Entries are cross-referenced and include recommended readings. Writing is accessible for students in high school, but coverage is complete enough to be useful to a much wider audience. Includes a chronology and 15 primary documents, including essays, legislative acts, and court judgments.

**766   Encyclopedia of business and finance.** 2nd ed. Burton S. Kaliski Macmillan Reference. Detroit: Macmillan Reference, 2007. ISBN: 0028660617.

650.03                                                                         HF1001.E466

Written for the novice but useful for anyone seeking background information on management, marketing, management information systems (MIS), and finance. The 310 essays include graphs, tables, photographs, and recommended readings. Alphabetically-arranged entries range from the history of computing to green marketing and the Sarbanes-Oxley Act. Also available online.

**767    International encyclopedia of business and management.** 2nd ed. Malcolm Warner, John P. Kotter. 8 v., xvii, 7160 p., ill. London: Thomson Learning, 2002. ISBN: 1861521618.
Contains 750 entries, intended to clarify international management and management education topics for students and faculty in higher education. Interdisciplinary in scope, including concepts from psychology, sociology, mathematics, computer engineering, political science, and economics.

**768    The new Palgrave: A dictionary of economics.** John Eatwell, Murray Milgate, Peter K. Newman. 4 v., ill. London; New York; Tokyo: Macmillan; Stockton Press; Maruzen, 1987. ISBN: 0333372352.
330.0321                                                      HB61.N49
Successor to *Palgrave's dictionary of political economy*, first published 1894–96. A sophisticated encyclopedic coverage of modern economic thought, with nearly 2,000 signed entries written by more than 900 prominent economists, historians, philosophers, mathematicians, and statisticians. Articles present diverse philosophies, ideologies, and methodologies and discuss their origin, historical development, and philosophical foundation. The 700 biographical entries exclude living economists born after 1915. Bibliographies accompany most entries. Appendixes list contributors and biographies included in the earlier edition of *Palgrave* but omitted here, and show subject entries classified under 53 fields of study. Analytical subject index.

**769    The Oxford encyclopedia of economic history.** Joel Mokyr, Oxford University Press. New York: Oxford University Press, 2003. ISBN: 0195105079.
330.03                                                        HC15.O94
Authoritative five-volume set covering all aspects of economic history. Alphabetic arrangement of nearly 900 signed articles with bibliographies and cross-references. Major topics include geography, agriculture, production systems, business history, technology, demography, institutions,

governments, markets, money, banking finance, labor, natural resources and the environment, and biographies. Separate listing of scholarly economic history Internet sites. Index and topical outline of articles. Also available in online form.

770  **The Oxford encyclopedia of economic history.** Joel Mokyr, Oxford University Press. New York: Oxford University Press, 2005. ISBN: 0195187628.

HC15.O945x

Arranged alphabetically ("accounting and bookkeeping" to "zoos and other animal parks"), examines economic history from ancient to modern times. Contains 900 articles, ranging in length from 500–3,000 words, takes a global approach to: geography (cities, countries, regions); agriculture; production systems, business history, and technology; demography; institutions, governments, and markets; macroeconomic history and international economics; money, banking and finance; labor; natural resources and the environment; and biographies. Available online at Oxford Reference Online (Oxford; New York: Oxford University Press, 2002–).

771  **Routledge encyclopedia of international political economy.** R. J. Barry Jones. 3 v. New York: Routledge, 2001. ISBN: 0415243505.
337.03                                                                    HF1359.R68

Explanations for a wide range of issues, developments, people, terms, organizations, and concepts about the global political economy. Includes brief biographical sketches. Intended for students, scholars, and practitioners. Entries are signed and followed by suggested readings. Available as an e-book.

## Guides and Handbooks

772  **The basic business library: Core resources.** 4th ed. Rashelle S. Karp, Bernard S. Schlessinger. ix, 288 p. Westport, Conn.: Greenwood Press, 2002. ISBN: 1573565121.
016.02769                                                                  Z675.B8B37

In two parts: (1) core list of printed reference sources (with critical annotations); (2) business reference sources and services: essays. Essays include electronic resources in various business disciplines, as well as "Acquisitions and Collection Development in Business Libraries" and "Marketing the Business Library." Indexed. Available as an e-book.

**773** **Black business and economics: A selected bibliography.** George
H. Hill. xvi, 351 p. New York: Garland, 1985. ISBN: 0824087879.
016.338642208996073                                    Z7164.C81H47; HD2346.U5

Gives citations to 100 books, 180 theses and dissertations, and articles
from popular periodicals written since 1885. Book citations, arranged by
author, are annotated. Government documents are listed by author, title,
or department, and are followed by topically-arranged listings of dissertations, theses, journal and newspaper articles. About 2,268 citations in all.

**774** **Business information: How to find it, how to use it.** 2nd ed.
Michael R. Lavin. xi, 499 p., ill. Phoenix: Oryx Press, 1992. ISBN:
0897746430.
650.072                                                       HF5356.L36

Along with Daniel's *Business information sources* (775), a classic and still
relevant guide. Combines descriptions of major business publications and
databases. Detailed coverage of major business sources. Bibliographies,
title and subject indexes.

**775** **Business information sources.** Rev. ed. Lorna M. Daniels. xvi,
673 p. Berkeley, Calif.: University of California Press, 1985. ISBN:
0520053354.
016.33                                              Z7164.C81D16; HF5351

One of a handful of classic guides to business information that still provide a useful approach to business (also see Lavin's *Business information:
How to find it, how to use it* [774]). Chapters 1–9 discuss basic reference
sources; chapters 10–20 discuss more specific areas such as corporate
finance and banking. Indexed.

**776** **Codes of professional responsibility: Ethics standards in
business, health, and law.** 4th ed. Rena A. Gorlin. xvii, 1149 p.
Washington: Bureau of National Affairs, 1999. ISBN: 1570181489.
174                                                          BJ1725.C57

Collects some 60 codes of ethics or similar documents ("statements of
principles," "ethical guidelines," etc.) of North American organizations
within the three domains listed in the subtitle. Construing these domains
broadly, it embraces, e.g., professions such as engineering, computing, and
journalism under "business," and mental health and social work under
"health." Also includes directory of U.S. and worldwide organizations and
programs concerned with professional responsibility and an extensive

guide to information resources including periodicals, reference works, and websites. Indexes of issues, professions, and organizations. Serving a similar function for the U.K., *Professional codes of conduct in the United Kingdom*, 2nd ed. (London; New York: Mansell, 1996), presents an even broader range of codes, numbering around 200 reproduced in full plus summary descriptions of some 300 more.

An extensive web-based collection, "Codes of Ethics Online," is among the resources offered at the Center for the Study of Ethics in the Profession at IIT website (http://ethics.iit.edu/), which also provides links to other ethics centers and the catalog of CSEP's extensive library—a virtual bibliography of the field of professional ethics.

777    **Economists' mathematical manual.** 4th ed. Knut Sydsæter, Arne Strøm, Peter Berck. 225 p., ill. Berlin: Springer, 2005. ISBN: 3540260889.

330.0151                                                    HB135.B467

Mathematical formulas, results, and theorems commonly used in economics. Coverage includes game theory and statistical concepts and distributions. Useful for any student or researcher in economics.

778    **Encyclopedia of business information sources.** Paul Wasserman, Gale Research Company. Detroit: Gale Research, 1970–. ISSN: 0071-0210.

016.33                                           Z7164.C81E93; HF5351

Comprehensive source for print and electronic sources. Arranged alphabetically by subject, then by type of resource. Not all entries are annotated.

779    **Guide to economic indicators.** 4th ed. Norman Frumkin. xx, 283 p., ill. Armonk, N.Y.: M.E. Sharpe, 2006. ISBN: 0765616467.

330.9730021                                                  HC103.F9

Completely updated, with over 60 economic indicators. Entries have definitions, availability, methodology, accuracy, relevance, and recent trends for each indicator. This edition added indicators for unemployment, housing, and energy.

780    **H-net.** Michigan State University, National Endowment for the Humanities. 1995–. East Lansing, Mich.: Michigan State University. http://www.h-net.org/.

300.072; 001.3072; 370; 378.104; 700.072                          H85

Created to advance "research, teaching, learning, public outreach, and professional service within their own specialized areas of knowledge" (*AboutH-net*), H-net is composed of discussion networks, scholarly reviews, announcements, and a job guide.

It serves diverse areas of interest in the social sciences and humanities, including economics, history, maritime history, African studies, American studies, and art history.

The reviews are from 1993 to the present and cover books and multimedia. H-net currently publishes about 1,000 reviews annually.

The job guide "posts academic position announcements in History and the Humanities, the Social Sciences, and Rhetoric and Composition, and serves a broad audience of administrators, faculty members, archivists, librarians, and other professionals in the humanities and social sciences" (*Introd. to Job Guide*); the positions can be searched or browsed, and an e-mail alert can be set up.

**781    International bibliography of business history.** Francis Goodall, T. R. Gourvish, Steven Tolliday. xvi, 668 p. London; New York: Routledge, 1997. ISBN: 0415086418.

016.3387                                                    Z7164.C81G595; HF1008

Selective bibliography of business history in the U.S., Europe, Japan, and the "rest of the world." Annotations are critical and explain the nature and content of each work. Arranged by industry, with an index for authors and for firms mentioned in each work.

**782    Mathematical formulas for economists.** 3rd ed. Bernd Luderer. New York: Springer, 2006. ISBN: 9783540469018.

Defines formulas used in economics, finance, and accounting, including definitions for the notations used in formulas. Gives basic formulas, as well as alternate formulas. Prior knowledge of the usage is necessary, as context is not provided.

**783    Peterson's graduate programs in business, education, health, information studies, law and social work.** Peterson's (Firm). ill. Princeton, N.J.: Peterson's, 1997–. ISSN: 1088-9442.

378.15530257                                                    L901.P459

The standard guide to graduate schools, with information on programs offered; degree requirements; number and gender of faculty; number, gender, and ethnicity of students; average student age; percentage of students accepted; entrance requirements; application deadlines; application fee; costs; and financial aid. Also available online.

784 **Strauss's handbook of business information: A guide for librarians, students, and researchers.** 2nd ed. Rita W. Moss, Diane Wheeler Strauss. xvii, 455 p., ill. Westport, Conn.: Libraries Unlimited, 2004. ISBN: 1563085208.

016.33                                         Z7164.C81S7796; HF1010

Excellent introduction to basic business concepts and resources. Follows the basic organization of the first edition. Divided into two parts. The first part discusses formats, introducing various resources, and the second part is fields, providing background information on functional areas of business. Appendixes for acronyms, government agencies, business information published by government agencies, key economic indicators, and representative websites.

785 **Success by the numbers: Statistics for business development.** Ryan Womack, Reference and User Services Association. vii, 59 p., ill. Chicago: American Library Association; Reference and User Services Association, 2005. ISBN: 0838983278.

                                         HF54.56.S832

A guide to U.S. statistical resources, with information on how the data is gathered, as well as where to find it. Chapters on: Federal business statistics and the 2002 economic census; Finding Florida statistical resources and data; Demographics and marketing; Economic forecasts; Industry statistics; Financial statistics; Labor, employment, and wages statistics; and Trade statistics. State and national sources are provided and sources are both free and fee-based.

786 **United States business history, 1602–1988: A chronology.** Richard Robinson. xii, 643 p. New York: Greenwood Press, 1990. ISBN: 0313260958.

338.0973                                         HC103.R595

"Designed to provide a basic calendar of representative events in the evolution of U.S. business."—*Pref.* Contains descriptive historical data, arranged by year, then under categories of general news and business news. Significant individuals, specific companies, inventions, trade unions, and key business, economic, and social developments are included. Brief bibliography; detailed index. Complemented by *Robinson's business history of the world: A chronology.*

787  **Using the financial and business literature.** Thomas P. Slavens. xiv, 655 p. New York: Marcel Dekker, 2004. ISBN: 0824753186.
016.33                                                                     HG173.S585

Lists resources that assist with general business, company, industry, and marketing research. Pt. 1 covers electronic resources and pt. 2 covers print resources. Each section is arranged alphabetically by topic, which range from disciplines like accounting, to subjects like African Americans in business. Entries cover publisher information, URLs (where relevant), and general content of the resource. Also available as an e-book.

## Indexes; Abstract Journals

788  **ABI/Inform global.** 2004. Ann Arbor, Mich.: Proquest. http://www. il.proquest.com/products_pq/descriptions/abi_inform_global.shtml. Comprehensive indexing and abstracting of business periodicals, some economics periodicals, as well as other periodicals related to business. ABI/Inform Global includes over 2,770 publications, with more than 1,800 available in full text. Includes 14,000 business dissertations, the *Wall Street Journal*, and *EIU viewsWire*. Coverage is from 1923 to present. ABI/Inform Complete includes 3,700 periodicals and 14,000 business dissertations. ABI/Inform Research has over 1,750 journals, with more than 1,200 available in full text. ABI/Inform Select has over 510 journals, with more than 410 available in full text.

H. W. Wilson Company's Wilson Business Full Text (New York: H. W. Wilson) and its predecessors (http://www.hwwilson.com/Databases/business.htm) began indexing the business literature in 1913. Wilson Business Full Text covers a more selective array of titles than ABI (indexing 1982–, full text 1995–) and is suitable for a non-specialist audience. Often held in libraries as part of Wilson Omni File Full Text Mega (Bronx, N.Y.: H. W. Wilson Company).

789  **Abstracts of working papers in economics: The official journal of the AWPE database.** Cambridge University Press. New York: Cambridge University Press, 1986–. ISSN: 0951-0079.
330.05                                                                     HB1.A27

Indexes and abstracts of over 100 working paper series from universities and research organizations. Each issue covers about 550 working papers.

Entries are alphabetical by author and include abstracts, bibliographic information, web links, and contact information for obtaining the paper. Includes indexes for series, keywords, issuing institution, and permuted titles. Formerly available through EconLit.

**790   Business dateline.** OCLC. [Dublin, Ohio]: OCLC. http://firstsearch.oclc.org/.

HF54.7

Indexes articles on regional business activities. Especially useful for coverage of local firms, products and executives. Available through multiple vendors.

**791   Business source elite.** EBSCO Publishing. Ipswich, Mass.: EBSCO. ISSN: 1092-9754. http://www.ebsco.com/home/.

338

Comprehensive indexing of over 1,100 business peridicals, including *Harvard business review* and more than 10,000 Datamonitor company profiles. Over 1,000 journals are full text. Backfiles from 1985. Business Source Complete indexes more than 3,600 periodicals with over 2,700 full text, including market research reports and case studies. Coverage from 1886 to present.

**792   Econlit.** American Economic Association. 1990–. Newton Lower Falls, Mass.: SilverPlatter Information Services. http://www.econlit.org/.

Z7164.E2; Z7164.E2.E266

Comprehensive index of and abstracts for economics literature from around the world, including journal articles, books, book reviews, collective volume articles, dissertations, and working papers. Includes the *Journal of economic literature* and *Index of economic articles in journals and collective volumes*. Most references are to English language publ. Coverage since 1969 available online in multiple platforms.

**793   EconPapers.** Handelshögskolan i Stockholm. [Stockholm]: Stockholm School of Economics, Economic Research Institute. http://econpapers.hhs.se.

HB171

Search engine for RePEc: Research Papers in Economics (Helsinki, Finland: University of Helsinki, Department of Economics, Faculty of Social

Sciences, 1994–), which contains over 450,000 working papers, 200,000 journal articles, and 1,400 software items. More than 340,000 of the items are available online. Many of the working papers are available through EconLit (792) as well.

**794  Factiva.** Dow Jones & Co. [2000–.] New York: Dow Jones and Reuters. http://www.factiva.com/.

Covers international business news using over 1,000 global and local newspapers, more than 3,000 journals and magazines, and more than 30,000 company reports. Content is in 22 languages.

**795  International bibliography of economics.** Fondation nationale des sciences politiques. Paris: UNESCO, 1955–. ISSN: 0085-204X.

016.33                                                                              Z7164.E2I58

An extensive and unique international list of books, selected chapters from multi-authored books, pamphlets, 715 current journals, 200 defunct journals, and official government publications that deal with economic history, methodology and theory, international and domestic economic policy, the production of goods and services, prices and markets, money and finance, social economics and public economy. Best for its international coverage, as more than half the journals covered are published outside the U.S. or U.K. Some records date back to 1951. Subject indexes in English and French. Available on CD-ROM. Online access through several vendors.

**796  ISI web of science.** Thomson Reuters. 2002. Philadelphia: Thomson Reuters. http://www.thomsonreuters.com/ products_services/scientific/Web_of_Science.

Web of Science is the citation indexing component of ISI's suite of databases, now unified under the name ISI Web of Knowledge (Philadelphia: Thomson Reuters, 2002–). Includes the Science Citation Index, the Social Sciences Citation Index (Stamford, Conn.?: Thomson Reuters), and the Arts and Humanities Citation Index (Stamford, Conn.?: Thomson Reuters). Allows for searches of a cited reference as well as general search options. Includes the ability to search for "related records" that have similar common citations, even though the items do not actually cite each other. Coverage currently goes back to 1900.

**797  LexisNexis.** LexisNexis. [199?] Bethesda, Md.: LexisNexis. http:// www.lexisnexis.com/academic/.

Searchable full-text subscription database that includes approximately 350 U.S. and foreign newspapers, broadcast transcripts from the major radio and TV networks, national and international wire services, campus newspapers, polls and surveys, and over 600 newsletters. Non-English language news sources available in Spanish, French, German, Italian, and Dutch. Dates of coverage vary by individual source, with newspapers updated daily.

**798** **SI.** SI, Special Issues. 2001–. Houston, Tex.: SI, Special Issues. http://specialissues.com/.
Many useful business statistics and industry surveys are hidden away in special issues of trade publications, newsletters, and journals. SI indexes nearly 3,500 trade magazines, reporting on the content of their special issues and websites. Entries include a monthly listing of special reports (linking to the online content where possible), contact information for the publisher, and any special content that is available on a magazine's accompanying website, including archives, special reports, indexes, etc. Search by publication, subject, or keyword. Coverage from 2000 to the present. Some information is available for free from a sample database. Subscribers also receive a newsletter reviewing magazines.

**799** **The Wall Street Journal index.** Dow Jones. [New York]: Dow Jones, 1957–. ISSN: 1042-9840.
332.05                                                        HG1.W26

Index coverage begins in 1955 and is based on the final Eastern edition of the newspaper. Each issue has two parts: (1) corporate news indexed by company name; (2) general news indexed by topic. Includes special sections for book reviews, personalities, deaths, and theater reviews. The last section of the index includes the daily Dow Jones averages for each month of the year. Since 1981, v. 1 includes *Barron's index*, a subject and corporate index to *Barron's business and financial weekly*. Since 1990, published monthly with quarterly and annual cumulations. Former publication frequency was monthly with annual cumulations. Annual cumulations issued in 2 pts., 1980–2001.

Fully searchable page images of the complete *Wall Street Journal* 1889–1989 are available in ProQuest Historical Newspapers (Ann Arbor, Mich.: ProQuest, 2001–). Searchable full text (although not original page images) is also available in a number of other commercial database services, including ProQuest Newspapers (Ann Arbor, Mich.: ProQuest, 2001–), Factiva (794), and ABI/Inform Global (788).

# Periodicals

**800**  **Business journals of the United States.** William Harvey Fisher. ix, 318 p. New York: Greenwood Press, 1991. ISBN: 0313252920.

016.33005                                        Z7164.C81B978; HF5001

Surveys over 100 business serials to create an overview of business publishing in the U.S. during the 19th and 20th cent. Serials are compared and important articles, special issues, and features are mentioned. Useful for historic research, especially for information on where the journal is indexed, availability of microfilm copy or reprints, types of libraries where located, and bibliographic notes. Some information, such as availability, may have changed since publication, but this is a valuable starting point.

**801**  **Business week.** ill. New York: McGraw-Hill, 1929–. ISSN: 0007-7135.

65011                                                        HF5001.B89

A good source for current news on companies and industries, the impact of the economy on business, investing, and markets. Various special issues cover most innovative companies, investment outlook, top global companies, best employers, and report on philanthropy with top corporate givers. Much of the print content is available for free at http://www.businessweek.com/.

**802**  **Corporate magazines of the United States.** Sam G. Riley. xiii, 281 p. New York: Greenwood Press, 1992. ISBN: 0313275696.

070.486                                                      PN4888.E6C67

Unique look at 324 corporate magazines. The publication, while dated, is still useful for historical research, especially as the earliest published magazine listed in it is from 1865. Fifty-one magazines are profiled, with history, significant contributors, and library or corporate holdings. Appendixes: Appendix A: chronology of corporate magazines profiled by year founded, Appendix B: location of magazines profiled by state, Appendix C: corporate magazines not profiled.

**803**  **The economist.** ill. London: Economist Newspaper, 1843–. ISSN: 0013-0613.

330.05                                                        HG11.E2

Coverage of political, economic, and business events, world leaders, and science and technology. Economic and financial indicators (output, prices and jobs, *The economist* commodity-price index, GDP growth forecasts, trade, exchange rates, budget balances and interest rates, markets, and stock markets), and emerging market indicators (overview, child mortality, economy, financial markets) are published regularly. Regular book reviews. Full access available for a fee at http://www.economist.com/and through various aggregator databases.

**804  Harvard business review.** ill. Boston: Graduate School of Business Administration, Harvard University. ISSN: 0017-8012.

330.904                                                                      HF5001.H3

Articles, best practices, book reviews, and case studies on communication, finance and accounting, global business, innovation and entrepreneurship, leadership, management, organizational development, sales and marketing, strategy and execution, and technology and operations. Also available online, through Business Source Elite (791).

## Quotations

**805  A dictionary of business quotations.** Simon R. James, R. H. Parker. x, 172 p. New York: Simon and Schuster, 1990. ISBN: 0132101548.

PN6084.B87D54

Covers more than 215 topics. Setting this book of quotations apart from the rest are the quotes that business leaders have made about themselves. Author/source and keyword indexes.

**806  The Elgar dictionary of economic quotations.** Charles R. McCann, Edward Elgar Publishing. xi, 315 p. Cheltenham, U.K.: Edward Elgar, 2003. ISBN: 1840648201.

330.21                                                                      PN6084.E36E44

Quotes from economists, as well as jurists, politicians, religious leaders, scientists, and others. Authoritative quotes intended for use in supporting economic arguments, but that also provide insight into how economists view diverse topics such as altruism, competition, corruption, equality, free trade, human nature, and taxes. Arranged alphabetically by author, making the index invaluable.

**807  The Wiley book of business quotations.** Henry Ehrlich. xviii, 430 p. New York: Wiley, 1998. ISBN: 0471182079.

650                                                                      PN6084.B87W55

Over 5,000 quotations from speeches and articles. Organized in 44 categories such as management, success, and geographical area. Brief context for each quote provided. Indexed by name and organization.

## Reviews of Research and Trends

**808  Business history.** David J. Jeremy, Geoffrey Tweedale. 4 v., ill. London: SAGE, 2005. ISBN: 1412902630.

338.0904                                                HF499.B855

Compiles 30 years of journal articles to provide a picture of the major international business developments of the 20th cent. Organized by parts into business environment, business organization, global business, entrepreneurs and management, and ethics and environment.

## Statistics

**809  Business statistics of the United States.** Cornelia J. Strawser. ill. Lanham, Md.: Bernan Press, 1996–. ISSN: 1086-8488.

338.12                                                  HC101.A13122

Compiles data from other sources. Part I contains economic data; pt. II, industry profiles; pt. III, historical data. Highlights are more than 150 tables, 30 years of annual data and four years of monthly data, and information by ciy, state, region, and country. A good general source to start with, if the *Statistical abstract of the United States* (678) does not have what is needed. Available as an e-book.

**810  The economist.** ill. London: Economist Newspaper, 1843–. ISSN: 0013-0613.

330.05                                                  HG11.E2

Coverage of political, economic, and business events, world leaders, and science and technology. Economic and financial indicators (output, prices and jobs, *The economist* commodity-price index, GDP growth forecasts, trade, exchange rates, budget balances and interest rates, markets, and stock markets), and emerging market indicators (overview, child mortality, economy, financial markets) are published regularly. Regular book reviews. Full access available for a fee at http://www.economist.com/and through various aggregator databases.

**811  EIU country data.** Bureau van Dijk Electronic Publishing. 2002–. [s.l.]: Bureau van Dijk. http://countrydata.bvdep.com/ip/.

HB3730

Annual, quarterly, and monthly economic indicators and forecasts. 278 series from 1980 to the present for 117 countries and 40 regional aggregates (e.g., ASEAN, Australasia, Balkans, Economies in Transition, Sub-Saharan Africa, Oil Exporters, Central America). Series have seven general categories: gross domestic product, fiscal and monetary indicators, demographics and income, foreign payments, external debt stock, external debt service, and external trade. Key forecast series include real GDP growth, GDP per head, consumer price inflation, exchange rate and current-account balance/GDP, with forecasts to 2030.

812    **Inter-university consortium for political and social research.** University of Michigan. [1997–.] Ann Arbor, Mich.: Institute for Social Research, University of Michigan. http://www.icpsr.umich. edu/.

Archive of international social science data, with a large collection of economic data. Thematic collections are Census Enumerations; Community and Urban Studies; Conflict, Aggression, Violence, Wars; Economic Behavior and Attitudes; Education; Elites and Leadership; Geography and Environment; Government Structures, Policies, and Capabilities; Health Care and Facilities; Instructional Packages; International Systems; Legal Systems; Legislative and Deliberative Bodies; Mass Political Behavior and Attitudes; Organizational Behavior; Social Indicators; Social Institutions and Behavior; Publication-Related Archive; and External Data Resources. Data, which can be downloaded for SAS, SPSS, and STATA, are available to the 500 member institutions, but some is also available to the public.

813    **United States business history, 1602–1988: A chronology.** Richard Robinson. xii, 643 p. New York: Greenwood Press, 1990. ISBN: 0313260958.

338.0973                                                                HC103.R595

"Designed to provide a basic calendar of representative events in the evolution of U.S. business."—*Pref.* Contains descriptive historical data, arranged by year, then under categories of general news and business news. Significant individuals, specific companies, inventions, trade unions, and key business, economic, and social developments are included. Brief bibliography; detailed index. Complemented by *Robinson's business history of the world: A chronology.*

**814**  The value of a dollar: Colonial era to the Civil War, 1600–1865.
Scott Derks, Tony Smith. 436 p., ill. Millerton, N.Y.: Grey House,
2005. ISBN: 1592370942.

338.520973                                           HB235.U6D47

Similar to *The value of a dollar, 1860–2004* (815), each chapter covers a
different period of time. Each chapter includes background, historical
snapshots, currency, selected incomes, services and fees, financial rates and
exchanges, commodities, selected prices, and miscellany. Slave trades are
included through chapter four, 1800–1824. Useful for historical research,
as well as an interesting glimpse into history.

**815**  The value of a dollar: Prices and incomes in the United States,
1860–2004. 3rd ed. Scott Derks. xvii, 664 p., ill. Millerton, N.Y.:
Grey House, 2004. ISBN: 1592370748.

338.520973                                           HB235.U6V35

Illustrates trends in prices. Each chapter covers a different period of time
and includes background, historical snapshots, currency, selected incomes,
services and fees, financial rates and exchanges, commodities, selected
prices, and miscellany. Also has composite consumer price index with the
value of an 1860 dollar from 1860–2003. Data is by city, county, or state.
For earlier information, see *The value of a dollar: Colonial era to the Civil
War, 1600–1865* (000).

# 6 > OCCUPATIONS AND CAREERS

## Directories

**816**  The career guide: Dun's employment opportunities directory.
Dun's Marketing Services. Parsippany, N.J.: Dun's Marketing
Services, 1984–. ISSN: 0740-7289.

331.128                                              HF5382.5.U5D86

Lists 10,000 U.S. companies. Entries give contact information, annual sales, names of executives, and educational specialties the companies seek. Indexed by state and city, industry, branch location, and disciplines hired.

**817   Consultants and consulting organizations directory: A reference guide to more than 26,000 firms and individuals engaged in consultation for business, industry, and government.** 29th ed. Julie A. Gough. 2 v. Detroit: Thomson/Gale, 2006. ISBN: 0787679437.

Organized into 14 general fields of consulting. Entries give contact information, brief description of activities, mergers and former names, geographic area served, and where possible, annual consulting revenue.

**818   D and B consultants directory.** Dun and Bradstreet Corporation. Bethlehem, Pa.: Dun and Bradstreet, 1997–. ISSN: 1524-9743.
658.4602573                                             HD69.C6D86

Provides information on more than 30,000 of the largest consulting firms in the U.S., with profiles arranged alphabetically. Companies are cross-referenced geographically and by consulting activity.

**819   The directory of executive recruiters.** Fitzwilliam, N.H.: Kennedy Information, 1971–. ISSN: 0090-6484.
658.3111                                             HF5549.5.R44D58

Lists over 16,000 recruiters, with contact information, summary of the firm's specialty, key contacts, salary minimum, and targeted functions and industries. Indexed by function, industry, and specialty.

**820   The guide to national professional certification programs.** 3rd ed. Phillip A. Barnhart. xv, 403, 42, 9 p. Amherst, Mass.; Boca Raton, Fla.: HRD Press; CRC Press, 2001. ISBN: 0874256321.
331.70202573                                             HD3630.U7B36

Gives contact information, information on the program (inception, number certified, organizational affiliation, online availability), education/experience requirements, examination requirements, and covers the recertification process. Indexed by sponsor, certification program, and occupation/area of interest.

**821   Job hunter's sourcebook.** Gale Research Inc. Detroit: Gale Research, 1991–. ISSN: 1053-1874.
331.128097305                                  HF5382.75.U6J63; HF5382.7.J62

A guide to sources useful for more than 200 occupations. Organized into two parts: Pt. 1, Sources of job-hunting information by professions and occupations; pt. 2, Sources of essential job-hunting information. Sources include help-wanted ads in various periodicals (including trade and professional journals, as well as sources like *National business employment weekly*), placement and referral services, employer directories and networking lists, handbooks and manuals, employment agencies, websites, and trade shows.

**822    The National job bank.** B. Adams. Brighton, Mass.: B. Adams, 1983–. ISSN: 1051-4872.

331.12802573                                                                    HF5382.5.U5N34

Arranged by state; within state listings, public and private firms are listed by industry. Entries give directory information, contact persons, and brief business descriptions. Entries may indicate typical job classifications, projected hiring activity, and training programs. Regional directories that follow the same format are also available.

**823    Riley guide.** Margaret F. Dikel. 1998–2007. [Rockville, Md.]: [Margaret F. Dikel]. http://www.rileyguide.com/.

Links to various websites with information on how to job search; before you search; where to search; resumes and cover letters; research and target employers and locations; network, interview, and negotiate; and salary guides and guidance. It includes an A–Z index and an area for recruiters and employers. Most of the sites listed are free, but fee-based resources are also included.

# Encyclopedias

**824    Encyclopedia of career development.** Jeffrey H. Greenhaus, Gerard A. Callanan. 2 v., ill. Thousand Oaks, Calif.: Sage Publications, 2006. ISBN: 1412905370.

331.70203                                                                       HF5381.E5165

Some 300 practical and theoretical entries, covering such diverse topics as academic advising, hostile work environment, mentoring, and pay for performance reward systems. Organized in 10 themes: theoretical perspectives on careers, social context of careers, evolution and development of careers, decision making and career development, variations in career patterns and success, career development initiatives, legislative and regulatory mandates, assessment areas and techniques, job search and organizational recruiting, and professional associations. Entries range from 1–6 pages in length, giving background and analysis on topics. Written for students, academics, and practitioners. Complete with cross-references, further readings, and references.

**825  Encyclopedia of careers and vocational guidance.** 13th ed. Neil Romanosky, J.G. Ferguson Publishing Company. 5 v., ill. New York: Ferguson, 2005. ISBN: 081606055X.

331.702                                                                      HF5381.E52

An overview of careers, with advice on preparing for and searching for a position. Career entries describe educational and training requirements, duties, salaries, and prospects. Each volume contains a complete index of the job titles. Vol. 1 (*Career guidance and field profiles*) describes 93 industries, their historical backgrounds, employment statistics, products, structure, and career patterns and outlooks. Vols. 2–5 discuss 741 jobs arranged in 14 broad categories (e.g., professional, clerical, machine trades). Appendixes list organizations that assist in training and job placement for disabled and other special groups and provide information on internships, apprenticeships, and training programs.

## Guides and Handbooks

**826  The almanac of American employers.** Plunkett Research, Ltd. CD-Roms. Houston, Tex.: Plunkett Research. ISSN: 1548-7369.

338                                                                          HF5382.75.U6

A comprehensive guide to the labor market in the U.S., with profiles of major companies, both private and public. Unique features include information on companies most likely to hire women and minorities, company hiring patterns (will hire MBAs, engineers, liberal arts majors, etc.), and company profiles that give textual information including corporate culture and plans for growth. Chapters on: Major Trends Affecting Job Seekers; Statistics (U.S. Employment Overview, U.S. Civilian Workforce Level: 1996–2006, Number of People Employed, U.S.: 1995–2006, Unemployment Level of U.S. Labor Force: August 1996–2006, Top 10 Fastest Growing U.S. Occupations: 2000–2010, Top 10 U.S. Industries with the Fastest Growth of Wage and Salary Employment: 2004–2014, Jobs with the Largest Expected Employment Decreases from 2004–2014, Percent of U.S. Workers with Access to Retirement and Healthcare Benefits); Research: Seven Keys for Job Seekers (Financial Stability, Growth Plan, Research and Development Programs, Product Launch and Production, Marketing and Distribution Methods, Employee Benefits, Quality of Work Factors, Other Considerations); Important Contacts for Job Seekers; American Employers: Top 500; and Indexes (alphabetical, by headquarters location, by Regions, firms with operations outside the U.S., Firms Noted as Hot Spots for Advancement for Women and Minorities, and by Subsidiaries, Brand Names and Selected Affiliations). Also available online.

**827 The American almanac of jobs and salaries.** New York: Avon, 1982–.

331.7020973                                         HD8038.U5A68

A survey of mostly white collar occupations. Especially useful for new graduates is the section on starting salaries. Some historical data.

**828 Best career and education Websites: A quick guide to online job search.** 5th ed. Anne Wolfinger, Rachel Singer Gordon. viii, 198 p., ill. Indianapolis, Ind.: JIST Works, 2007. ISBN: 159357312X.

025.06331702                                        HF5382.75.U6W65

Contains 340 annotated entries for websites on mentoring, training, certification, and job searching. Includes professional associations and megasites, as well as sites for jobs within specific states. Available as an e-book.

**829 Career guide to industries.** U.S. Department of Labor, Bureau of Labor Statistics. ill. Washington: Bureau of Labor Statistics, 1992–.

331.70205                                           HF5382.5.U5C316

Information on the nature of the industry, working conditions, employment, occupations within the industry, training and advancement, outlook, earnings, and sources of additional information. While this is similar to the *Occupational outlook handbook,* (22) it is organized by industry, of which there are 45, and has occupations not included in the *Handbook.* Also available online at http://www.bls.gov/oco/cg/.

**830 Career information center.** 9th ed. v. 5–13, ill. New York: MacMillan Reference, 2007. ISSN: 1082-703X; ISBN: 0028656377.

331.702                                             HF5382.5.U5C32

For use in finding career information. The 13 relatively thin volumes present some 650 occupational profiles and more than 3,000 jobs. Each volume covers a broad field (e.g., health, construction) with an overview of its job market, followed by entries for individual careers that describe work characteristics, entry procedures, advancement possibilities and employment outlook, working conditions, earnings, and benefits. Appendixes in each volume list further reading and offer a directory of institutions offering training and an index by occupation. The last volume has an index covering the entire work and presenting employment trends.

**831** **Collective bargaining negotiations and contracts.** Bureau of National Affairs. loose-leaf. Washington: Bureau of National Affairs, 1945–. ISSN: 0010-079X.

KF3408.A8C644

Information on preparing and conducting contract negotiations, with sample clauses, cost of living, and consumer price information.

**832** **Job choices for business and liberal arts students.** 4th ed. National Association of Colleges and Employers. ill. Bethlehem, Pa.: National Association of Colleges and Employers, 2003–. ISSN: 0069-5734.

331.702                                                    HF5382.5.U5J59

Lists employers, with information on desired qualifications and benefits offered, and contact information. Also has articles on resume writing, interviewing, and networking. Other similar titles from this publisher are *Job choices for science, engineering, and technology students* and *Job choices: Diversity edition.*

**833** **Jobs and careers abroad.** Deborah Penrith. ill. Oxford, [England]; Guilford, Conn.: Vacation Work Publications; Globe Pequot Press, 2005–. ISSN: 0143-3482.

Information on finding international jobs. Contains chapters on finding jobs, rules and regulations for working abroad, learning the language, chapters on specific careers, and a section on employment in different regions (Western Europe, Eastern and Central Europe, the Americas, Australasia, Asia, Middle East and North Africa, and Africa). Appendixes for further reading, worldwide living standards, and company classifications.

**834** **Occupational outlook handbook.** JIST Works, Inc. ill. Indianapolis, Ind.: JIST Works, 1987–. ISSN: 0082-9072.

331                                                         HF5381.U62

Gives information on employment trends and outlook in more than 800 occupations. Indicates nature of work, qualifications, earnings and working conditions, entry level jobs, information on the job market in each state, where to go for more information, etc. Available online at http://www.bls.gov/oco/. Similar information can be found in the *Career guide to industries* (10).

**835 What color is your parachute?.** Richard Nelson Bolles. ill. Berkeley, Calif.: Ten Speed Press, 1971–. ISSN: 8755-4658.

650.1405                                                          HF5382.7.B64

Perhaps the best-known guide to discovering the career that is right for you, with tips on finding a job and on interviewing. The book is supplemented by a website (http://www.jobhuntersbible.com/).

## Internet Resources

**836 Aboutjobs.com.** AboutJobs.com, Inc. 1990s–. [Sagamore Beach, Mass.]: AboutJobs.com, Inc. http://www.aboutjobs.com/.

Links to InternJobs.com, OverseasJobs.com, ResortJobs.com, and SummerJobs.com. The sites are good for new college graduates and high school students.

**837 H-net.** Michigan State University, National Endowment for the Humanities. 1995–. East Lansing, Mich.: Michigan State University. http://www.h-net.org/.

300.072; 001.3072; 370; 378.104; 700.072                          H85

Created to advance "research, teaching, learning, public outreach, and professional service within their own specialized areas of knowledge"— *About H-net.* H-net is composed of discussion networks, scholarly reviews, announcements, and a job guide.

It serves diverse areas of interest in the social sciences and humanities, including economics, history, maritime history, African studies, American studies, and art history.

The reviews are from 1993 to the present and cover books and multimedia. H-net currently publishes about 1,000 reviews annually.

The job guide "posts academic position announcements in History and the Humanities, the Social Sciences, and Rhetoric and Composition, and serves a broad audience of administrators, faculty members, archivists, librarians, and other professionals in the humanities and social sciences"—*Introd. to Job Guide.* The positions can be searched or browsed, and an e-mail alert can be set up.

**838   Monster jobs.** Monster (Firm). 2007. New York: Monster. http://www.monster.com/.
A rich source for advice on interviewing, resume writing, as well as a place to search for jobs and post a resume. Has articles, sample resumes and cover letters, information on job fairs, and a section on career advice.

**839   National compensation survey.** U.S. Dept. of Labor, Bureau of Labor Statistics. 1998–. Washington, D.C.: Bureau of Labor Statistics. http://www.bls.gov/ncs/home.htm.

HD4976.A735N38

Summarizes wages, earnings, and hours for cities, regions, and the nation. "Wage data are shown by industry, occupational group, full-time and part-time status, union and nonunion status, establishment size, time and incentive status, and job level." —*Summary.* Also includes benefits and the Employment Cost Index, which is released quarterly.

**840   Riley guide.** Margaret F. Dikel. 1998–2007. [Rockville, Md.]: [Margaret F. Dikel]. http://www.rileyguide.com/.
Links to various websites with information on how to job search; before you search; where to search; resumes and cover letters; research and target employers and locations; network, interview, and negotiate; and salary guides and guidance. It includes an A–Z index and an area for recruiters and employers. Most of the sites listed are free, but fee-based resources are also included.

**841   Salary.com.** Salary.com. 2000–. Wellesley, Mass.: Salary.com. http://salary.com/.
HD4961
Useful for the various tools: salary report, college tuition planner, benefits calculator, job listings, cost of living wizard, performance self-test, and job assessor.

## Periodicals

**842   The American almanac of jobs and salaries.** New York: Avon, 1982–.
331.7020973                                                   HD8038.U5A68

A survey of mostly white collar occupations. Especially useful for new graduates is the section on starting salaries. Some historical data.

**843** **Job choices for business and liberal arts students.** 4th ed. National Association of Colleges and Employers. ill. Bethlehem, Pa.: National Association of Colleges and Employers, 2003–. ISSN: 0069-5734.

331.702                                          HF5382.5.U5J59

Lists employers, with information on desired qualifications and benefits offered, and contact information. Also has articles on resume writing, interviewing, and networking. Other similar titles from this publisher are *Job choices for science, engineering, and technology students* and *Job choices: Diversity edition.*

**844** **National compensation survey.** U.S. Dept. of Labor, Bureau of Labor Statistics. 1998–. Washington, D.C.: Bureau of Labor Statistics. http://www.bls.gov/ncs/home.htm.

HD4976.A735N38

Summarizes wages, earnings, and hours for cities, regions, and the nation. "Wage data are shown by industry, occupational group, full-time and part-time status, union and nonunion status, establishment size, time and incentive status, and job level." —*Summary.* Also includes benefits and the Employment Cost Index, which is released quarterly.

**845** **Occupational outlook handbook.** JIST Works, Inc. ill. Indianapolis, Ind.: JIST Works, 1987–. ISSN: 0082-9072.

331                                              HF5381.U62

Gives information on employment trends and outlook in more than 800 occupations. Indicates nature of work, qualifications, earnings and working conditions, entry level jobs, information on the job market in each state, where to go for more information, etc. Available online at http://www.bls.gov/oco/. Similar information can be found in the *Career guide to industries* (000).

**846** **What color is your parachute?.** Richard Nelson Bolles. ill. Berkeley, Calif.: Ten Speed Press, 1971–. ISSN: 8755-4658.

650.1405                                         HF5382.7.B64

Perhaps the best-known guide to discovering the career that is right for you, with tips on finding a job and on interviewing. The book is supplemented by a website (http://www.jobhuntersbible.com/).

## Statistics

847    The American almanac of jobs and salaries. New York: Avon,
1982–.
331.7020973                                                  HD8038.U5A68

A survey of mostly white collar occupations. Especially useful for new
graduates is the section on starting salaries. Some historical data.

848    American salaries and wages survey. Gale Research Inc. Detroit:
Gale Research, 1991–. ISSN: 1055-7628.
331.2973021                                                   HD4973.A67

Data on some 4,000 occupations, with information on salaries by state and
major metropolitan area. Gives a low, mid, and high wage offered. Useful
for salary negotiations.

849    National compensation survey. U.S. Dept. of Labor, Bureau
of Labor Statistics. 1998–. Washington, D.C.: Bureau of Labor
Statistics. http://www.bls.gov/ncs/home.htm.
HD4976.A735N38

Summarizes wages, earnings, and hours for cities, regions, and the nation.
"Wage data are shown by industry, occupational group, full-time and
part-time status, union and nonunion status, establishment size, time and
incentive status, and job level." —*Summary*. Also includes benefits and the
Employment Cost Index, which is released quarterly.

# 7 > REGIONAL ECONOMIC RESOURCES

## Africa

850    Africa development indicators. United Nations Development
Programme, World Bank. ill. New York; Washington: United
Nations Development Programme; World Bank, 1992–. ISSN:
1020-2927.
330.960021                                                   HC800.A1A356

Indicators for national accounts (value added in agriculture, industry and services, total consumption, gross private and public investment, GDP, resource balance); prices and exchange rates (GDP deflator, consumer price index, official exchange rate, SDR exchange rate index, currency conversion factor, parallel market exchange rate, ratio of parallel markets to official exchange rates, real effective exchange rate index); money and banking (domestic credit, credit to the private sector and the government, net foreign assets, growth of money supply, discount rate and real discount rate, commercial bank lending rate and commercial bank deposit rate); external sector (balance of payments, prices, and commodity trade); external debt and related flows (amortization, interest payments, debt and debt payments, and debt and debt service ratios); government finance (debt and surplus, expenditure, revenue, grants, foreign financing, taxes, and revenue); agriculture (nominal producer prices, food price index, food production index, nonfood production index, food production per capita index, volume of food output, by major food crop, value of agricultural exports, cereal production, crop production index, fertilizer use, fertilizer imports, area under permanent crops, agricultural yields, by major crop, and incidence of drought); power, communications, and transportation (electric power consumption per capita, energy production and use, telephone, radio, and television availability, personal computers and internet use, vehicle ownership, roads, railroads, airplanes); doing business (cost of starting and closing a business, registering property, contract enforcement, investor protection); labor force and employment (number and structure of the labor force); aid flows, social indicators (poverty, income distribution, literacy, survival, education, economic opportrnities); environmental indicators; Heavily Indebted Poor Countries (HIPC) initiative; household welfare (by individual country); privatization of public enterprises.

Companion CD-ROM, World Bank Africa Database, has time series from 1970. Also available online (Beaumont, Tex.: Cabell Pub., 2004–).

**851**  **Africa development indicators.** World Bank Group. 2007–. Washington: World Bank Group. http://publications.worldbank. org/ADI/.

HC800.A1

The most extensive statistical database on the 53 countries of Africa. Contains more than 940 time series on population, births, and deaths; migration and refugees; health; social topics, including education, literacy, health care, sanitation and access to potable water, contraception, crime and corruption, poverty and income, and gender equality; Internet access; ownership of computers, cell phones, and vehicles; prices and expenditures; the labor force and employment; the environment, natural resources, and energy and water use; agriculture, manufacturing, and the service sector; GDP; exports and imports; balance of payments; development assistance and external debt; government finance; investment; money and banking; transportation and communication infrastructure; political stability; and governance.

The longest time series begin in 1960; some cover only the last few years. Data availability varies from one country to another.

The search for statistical series seeks exact phrases and is sensitive to punctuation. Therefore, one cannot retrieve "population, total" by entering "population total". Search results may be charted and mapped. Continuously updated.

Available via subscription. Also issued annually in print *Africa development indicators* (850) and on CD-ROM.

852   **African development report.** African Development Bank. Abidjan, Ivory Coast: African Development Bank, [1989?]–.
330.96005                                                    HC800.A1A354

An annual thematic publication. Part I includes general overview essays, financial statistics, regional profiles, and outlooks. Part II provides interpretative essays and a bibliography. Part III presents economic and social statistics. The data represent all 53 countries that are members of the African Development Bank.

853   **African statistical yearbook: Annuaire statistique pour l'Afrique.** United Nations. [Addis Ababa], [Ethiopia]: Economic Commission for Africa, United Nations, 1974–. ISSN: 0252-5488.
330.9600212                                                    HA1955.U5

African nations are arranged in alphabetical order, with tables grouped in nine chapters: population and employment, national accounts, agriculture and fishing, industry, transport and communications, foreign trade, prices, finance, and social statistics.

854   **The Arab world competitiveness report 2005.** Augusto Lopez-Claros, World Economic Forum. xiv, 352 p. New York: Palgrave MacMillan, 2005. ISBN: 1403948011.
320.9174927

Discussion of the economic issues facing the Arab world, with articles and statistics. Pt. 1 contains articles on reform, competitiveness, labor markets, politics, economic freedom, and women in the Arab world. Pt. 2 contains country profiles for Algeria, Bahrain, Egypt, Jordan, Kuwait, Lebanon, Libya, Libyan Arab Jamahiriya, Morocco, Oman, Qatar, Saudi Arabia, Syria, Syrian Arab Republic, Tunisia, United Arab Emirates, and Yemen. Profiles include key economic indicators, human development indicators, infrastructure and technology diffusion indicators, economic trends, export profiles, and competitiveness rankings. Pt. 3 contains data tables, compiling data for all the countries, with coverage of the macroeconomic climate, infrastructure and technology diffusion indicators, human resources (education, labor, and health), infrastructure, public institutions, domestic competition, cluster development, environment, and company operations and strategy.

**855   Country briefings.** Economist.com. [199?–.] London: Economist Newspaper. http://www.economist.com/countries/.
909.83                                                              HC59.15

News from *The economist* (151) print edition, country profiles, forecasts, statistics, political outlook, economic policy outlook, economic forecast, and economic structure for 60 countries. Ten key economic statistics can be downloaded into Excel (GDP per head, GDP, government consumption, budget balance, consumer prices, public debt, labour costs per hour, recorded unemployment, current-account balance, and foreign-exchange reserves). Links to some subscription-based materials and free external related websites, such as governmental and news websites.

**856   EIU.com.** Economist Intelligence Unit (Great Britain). 2005–.
[London?]: Economist Intelligence Unit. http://www.eiu.com/.
Covers political, economic, and business information for 201 countries. Access to Economist Intelligence Unit publications: *Country finance, Country commerce, Country monitor, Business Africa, Business Asia, Business China, Business Eastern Europe, Business Europe, Business India intelligence, Business Latin America,* and *Business Middle East.* Country reports similar to Political Risk Yearbook (192), but with more frequent updates. Key data include GDP, forecast GDP, exports, imports, inflation, exchange rates, interest rates, consumer and producer prices, deposit rate, lending rate, money market rate, select commodity prices, and select industry data. Many numbers can be downloaded into Excel. Archives available from 1992.

857    **EIU country data.** Bureau van Dijk Electronic Publishing. 2002–.
       [s.l.]: Bureau van Dijk. http://countrydata.bvdep.com/ip/.

                                                                    HB3730

Annual, quarterly, and monthly economic indicators and forecasts.
278 series from 1980 to the present for 117 countries and 40 regional
aggregates (e.g., ASEAN, Australasia, Balkans, Economies in Transition,
Sub-Saharan Africa, Oil Exporters, Central America). Series have seven
general categories: gross domestic product, fiscal and monetary indicators, demographics and income, foreign payments, external debt stock,
external debt service, and external trade. Key forecast series include real
GDP growth, GDP per head, consumer price inflation, exchange rate and
current-account balance/GDP, with forecasts to 2030.

858    **Europa world plus.** Europa Publications Limited, Routledge,
       Taylor & Francis Group. 2003–. New York: Routledge; Taylor &
       Francis Group. http://www.europaworld.com/pub/about/.

                                                                    D443.E87

Economic and political information for more than 250 countries and territories. Includes *Europa world year book* (145) and the *Europa regional
surveys of the world* series:

- *Africa south of the Sahara* (London; New York: Routledge, 1971–)
- *Central and south-eastern Europe* (London: Europa Publications,
  2000–)
- *Eastern Europe, Russia and Central Asia* (London; New York: Rout-
  ledge, 2000–)
- *The Far East and Australasia* (London: Europa, 1969–)
- *The Middle East and North Africa* (991)
- *South America, Central America and the Caribbean* (London: Europa,
  1985–)
- *South Asia* (London; New York: Routledge, 2003–)
- *The USA and Canada* (London; New York: Routledge, 1989–)
- *Western Europe* (London; New York: Routledge, 1988–)

Country entries include country profile, geography, chronology, history,
economy, country statistics, government and politics directory, society and
media directory, business and commerce directory, and bibliography.

  Unique to the online version is the comparative statistics section, which
generates five years of multinational statistics on area and population,
agriculture, industry, finance, external trade, and education in tables and
charts downloaded as an HTML table, comma-separated values and in tab-

separated values. The comparative statistics section uses different sources than the country statistics section, making data comparisons possible.

**859    Foreign government resources on the web.** University of Michigan. [Ann Arbor, Mich.]: Documents Center, University of Michigan Library. http://www.lib.umich.edu/govdocs/foreign.html.

ZA5050

Websites of foreign governments arranged by region, then by country. For each country, links to main home page and websites of major agencies. Also contains links to sites compiling background information, embassy listings, constitutions and other legal material, news, and statistics, either for countries worldwide or in a particular region.

**860    Global development finance.** World Bank. 2 v. Washington: World Bank, 1997–. ISSN: 1020-5454.

336.3435091724                                                    HJ8899.W672

External debt and financial flow data for 136 countries. Vol. 1 is *Analysis and outlook*, with financial flows to developing countries. Vol. 2 is *Summary and country tables* and includes summary data for regions and income groups. Indicators include external debt stocks and flows, major economic aggregates, key debt ratios, average terms of new commitments, and currency composition of long-term debt. Also available online and on CD-ROM, with data from 1970.

**861    The index of economic freedom.** Heritage Foundation. maps. Washington: The Heritage Foundation, 1995–. ISSN: 1095-7308.

338.9005                                                          HB95.I48

Uses 50 independent variables to rank 161 countries, including Hong Kong, on the level of government involvement in the economy. The more that a government is involved in constraint in the production, distribution, or consumption of goods and services, the less freedom the editors believe is present. In addition to the score, 2-page long country profiles discuss trade policy, fiscal burden, government intervention, monetary policy, foreign investment, banking and finance, wages and prices, property rights, regulation, and informal market. The 2007 ed. adds a chapter on regions. The current version is available for free at http://www.heritage.org/research/.

**862    International historical statistics: Africa, Asia and Oceania, 1750–2000.** 4th ed. B. R. Mitchell. xix, 1113 p., 29 cm. Houndmills,

REGIONAL ECONOMIC SOURCES

Basingstokes, Hampshire, [U.K.]; New York: Palgrave Macmillan, 2003. ISBN: 0333994124; 9780333994122.

310                                                                     HA4675

Gives key economic and social indicators in this companion to the author's *International historical statistics: The Americas* (904). Official and unofficial statistical sources were used to provide comparative data for the included countries. Data for more than two centuries are arranged in ten sections that cover population and vital statistics, labor force, agriculture, industry, external trade, transport, and communications.

863    **Inter-university consortium for political and social research.** University of Michigan. [1997–.] Ann Arbor, Mich.: Institute for Social Research, University of Michigan. http://www.icpsr.umich. edu/.

Archive of international social science data, with a large collection of economic data. Thematic collections are Census Enumerations; Community and Urban Studies; Conflict, Aggression, Violence, Wars; Economic Behavior and Attitudes; Education; Elites and Leadership; Geography and Environment; Government Structures, Policies, and Capabilities; Health Care and Facilities; Instructional Packages; International Systems; Legal Systems; Legislative and Deliberative Bodies; Mass Political Behavior and Attitudes; Organizational Behavior; Social Indicators; Social Institutions and Behavior; Publication-Related Archive; and External Data Resources. Data, which can be downloaded for SAS, SPSS, and STATA, are available to the 500 member institutions, but some is also available to the public.

864    **NationMaster.com.** 2003–. NationMaster.com. http://www. nationmaster.com/index.php.

HA154

Uses data from government and international organizations to present comparative statistics between nations. Some of the topics covered include economy, education, health issues, immigration, industry, labor, taxation, and transportation. Data is displayed in easy-to-read graphs. The source of the data is also cited. This is a companion to StateMaster.com (Brooklyn, N.Y.: StateMaster.com, 2006–).

865    **Political risk yearbook online.** PRS Group. 1999–. East Syracuse, N.Y.: PRS Group. https://www.prsgroup.com/prsgroup_ shoppingcart/pc-48-7-political-risk-yearbook.aspx.

Political and economic risk analysis for 106 countries. Reports are PDF files with a country forecast (highlights, current data, comments and analysis, forecast scenarios, political players), and country conditions (investment climate, climate for trade including political violence and legal framework, background on geography, history, social conditions, government, political conditions, and environmental trends). Includes forecasts for GDP growth, current account, inflation, political turmoil, investment and trade restrictions, and domestic and international economic problems. Also has statistics for foreign direct investment flows by source country and sector.

**866    SourceOECD.** Organisation for Economic Co-operation and Development. [Paris, France]: OECD. http://new.sourceoecd.org/. A subscription database containing OECD books, reports, working papers, serials, and statistical databases on economic and social topics, as well as the environment, energy, and technological development. Focuses mainly on the 30 OECD member states and major nonmember developing countries.

Serials include journals; the OECD Factbook (Paris: OECD, 2005–) and other statistical works; and titles that forecast and analyze trends, such as the OECD Economic Outlook (Paris: Organisation for Economic Co-operation and Development, 1967–), *African economic outlook* (Paris: African Development Bank, Development Centre of the Organisation for Economic Co-operation and Development, 2002–), International Migration Outlook (Paris: Organisation for Economic Co-operation and Development, 2006–), and OECD-FAO Agricultural Outlook (Paris: Organisation for Economic Co-operation and Development; Food and Agriculture Organization, 2005–).

Current, themed databases include the OECD Economic Outlook Database (Paris: Organisation for Economic Co-operation and Development, 2002–), SourceOECD Main Economic Indicators (Paris: Organisation for Economic Co-operation and Development, 2002–), Banking Statistics, Education Statistics, Globalisation, Indicators of Industry and Services, Insurance, International Development, International Direct Investment Statistics, International Migration Statistics, the ITCS International Trade by Commodity Database, Monthly Statistics of International Trade, the National Accounts Database, OECD Health Data, OECD Statistics on International Trade in Services, the Revenue Statistics of OECD Member Countries Database, the Science and Technology Database, the Social Expenditure Database, Structural and Demographic Business Statistics, Taxing Wages Statistics, and the Telecommunications Database. Statistical databases of the International Energy Agency are also available via this source. OECD.Stat enables users to query multiple databases simultaneously and to export search results in several formats.

Also incorporates Future Trends, an index of published and unpublished sources in more than a dozen languages covering issues affecting the public and private sectors. Glossary.

**867 Statistical sites on the World Wide Web.** U.S. Bureau of Labor Statistics. Washington: U.S. Bureau of Labor Statistics. http://www. bls.gov/bls/other.htm.

Links to official government statistical offices all over the world, including more than 130 countries and some international agencies. Also links to sites of nearly 70 U.S. federal statistical agencies. Excellent starting point for researchers.

**868 STAT-USA Internet.** STAT-USA. [1994–.] [Washington, D.C.?]: STAT-USA, U.S. Dept. of Commerce. http://www.stat-usa.gov/.

382                                                                 HF1379

Business and economic information compiled mainly from federal agencies. There are two main sections, "State of the Nation" and "Globus & NTDB."

"State of the Nation" concentrates on current U.S. information, with 2,500 files on general economic indicators (consumer price index, producer price index, gross domestic product, national income and product accounts), regional economic statistics (by NAICS sector, state personal income, metropolitan personal income) housing and construction (housing starts and building permits, new construction, new home sales), employment (employment cost index, local area employment and unemployment, weekly unemployment claims report), manufacturing and industry (retail sales, manufacturing inventories and sales, industrial production and capacity utilization, current industry reports), monetary statistics (interest rates, foreign exchange rates, bank credit), and economic policy (Beige Book, Treasury Statements).

"Globus & NTDB" is useful for current exchange rates (weekly, monthly, and annual), current and historical trade leads (United Nations trade leads, Defense Logistics Agency leads, FedBizOpps, commercial trade leads), international trade (Asia Development Bank, World Bank, Inter-American Development Bank, and European Bank Business Opportunities, country reports on terrorism, Country Studies Program reports, *International trade update newsletter, National trade estimates report on foreign trade barriers, World bank commodity price data*—"PinkSheets"—and *World factbook*), market and country research (*Country background notes, Country commercial guides, Industry sector analysis reports*, Global Agriculture Information Network [GAIN], *AgWorld attaché reports, International market insight (IMI) reports*, and Multilateral Development Bank), contacts (*NTDB global trade directory, National export directory*, Foreign Trade Offices), and current press releases (U.S. international trade in goods and services, FT900 supplemental tables, U.S. Export Sales—USDA, U.S. import and export price indexes, U.S. international transactions, and additional press releases).

**869  United Nations common database (UNCDB).** United Nations Statistic Division. New York: United Nations Statistic Division. http://unstats.un.org/unsd/cdb/cdb_help/cdb_quick_start.asp. Provides socioeconomic data from 55 sources on 274 countries and areas, with coverage from 1948–2050. Allows comparison of data from 10 countries at a time, and data can be downloaded to Excel. Formerly a fee-based database but now free.

Covers 31 topics: agriculture, forestry, and fishing; communication and culture; construction; development assistance; economically active/not economically active population; education and learning; energy; environment; financial statistics; health, health services, impairment, disabilities, nutrition; households and families, marital status, fertility; human settlements, housing, geographical distribution of population; income, consumption and wealth; industrial production; international finance; international tourism; international trade; millennium development goals (MDG); mining and quarrying; national accounts; population composition and change; prices; public order and safety; science and technology, intellectual property; services industries; social security and welfare services; socioeconomic groups and social mobility; statistical yearbook; transport; and women and men.

**870  VIBES.** Jeanie M. Welch, J. Murrey Atkins Library (University of North Carolina at Charlotte). [199?–.] Charlotte, N.C.: University of North Carolina at Charlotte, J. Murrey Atkins Library. http://library.uncc.edu/vibes/. 025.04; 382; 330; 650

Links to over 3,000 free Internet sources with international business and economic information in English. Organized into three categories: comprehensive, regional, and national. Coverage includes agricultural and forest products; banking and finance (includes insurance); business news, business practices and company information (includes labor); country information; emerging markets; foreign exchange rates; foreign stock markets; international electronic commerce; international statistics (general and economic); international tourism; international trade law; marketing and advertising; patents (includes other intellectual property); petroleum, energy, mining, and construction; portals (web meta pages with several international links); taxation in foreign countries (includes social security); trade issues and statistics; and business and economics for Africa, Asia-Pacific, Eastern Europe, Western Europe, Latin America and the Caribbean, Middle East, and NAFTA (U.S., Canada, and Mexico).

## Asia

871    **Asia yearbook.** ill. [Hong Kong]: Review Publishing Co., 1973–2001. ISSN: 1023-4365.

330.95042                                                           HC411.F19

Overview of economic and political events in the previous year. Brief articles on trade, currencies, communications, energy, transportation, the environment, and population issues. Following these articles are sections on each Asian country with a brief background on political events, foreign relations, population, and the economy. Includes maps, charts, and illustrations.

872    **China's provincial statistics, 1949–1989.** Tien-tung Hseh, Qiang Li, Shu-chéng Liu. xxiii, 595 p. Boulder, Colo.: Westview Press, 1993. ISBN: 0813387329.

330.95105021                                            HC427.92.C45145648

Divided into two parts. In pt. 1, statistics are under individual provinces. Pt. 2 covers autonomous regions and municipalities. Over 15 key components are covered, such as national income, investment, consumption, public finance, trade, labor, education, and population. Appendixes provide explanatory notes on key variables with separate English alphabetical and Chinese phonetical indexes.

873    **China statistical yearbook.** English ed. China Statistical Information & Consultancy Service Centre, International Centre

for the Advancement of Science & Technology, University of Illinois at Chicago. Hong Kong, [China]; Beijing, [China]: International Centre for the Advancement of Science & Technology; China Statistical Information & Consultancy Service Centre, 1988–. ISSN: 1052-9225.

315.105                                    HA4631.S83

Arranged in 25 sections covering demographics, finance and economics, industry and commerce, trade and tourism, education, and culture and health. Publication is available on the Internet at http://www.stats.gov.cn/tjsj/ndsj/2006/indexeh.htm.

**874   Country briefings.** Economist.com. [199?–.] London: Economist Newspaper. http://www.economist.com/countries/.

909.83                                    HC59.15

News from *The economist* (151) print edition, country profiles, forecasts, statistics, political outlook, economic policy outlook, economic forecast, and economic structure for 60 countries. Ten key economic statistics can be downloaded into Excel (GDP per head, GDP, government consumption, budget balance, consumer prices, public debt, labour costs per hour, recorded unemployment, current-account balance, and foreign-exchange reserves). Links to some subscription-based materials and free external related websites, such as governmental and news websites.

**875   Economic and social survey of Asia and the Pacific.** United Nations; Economic and Social Commission for Asia and the Pacific. Bangkok, [Thailand]: United Nations, 1974–. ISSN: 0252-5704.

330.95042                                    HC411.E357

Examines policy issues impacting the region, global and regional economic developments, macroeconomic performance, and poverty reduction strategies. Full of tables with economic data. Also available as a PDF from http://unescap.org/pdd/publications/survey2005/index.asp/.

**876   EIU.com.** Economist Intelligence Unit (Great Britain). 2005–. [London?]: Economist Intelligence Unit. http://www.eiu.com/. Covers political, economic, and business information for 201 countries. Access to Economist Intelligence Unit publications: *Country finance, Country commerce, Country monitor, Business Africa, Business Asia, Business China, Business Eastern Europe, Business Europe, Business India intelligence, Business Latin America,* and *Business Middle East.* Country reports similar to Political Risk Yearbook (192), but with more frequent updates. Key data include GDP, forecast GDP, exports, imports, inflation, exchange rates, interest rates, consumer and producer prices, deposit rate, lending rate, money market rate, select commodity prices, and select industry data. Many numbers can be downloaded into Excel. Archives available from 1992.

877  **EIU country data.** Bureau van Dijk Electronic Publishing. 2002–.
      [s.l.]: Bureau van Dijk. http://countrydata.bvdep.com/ip/.
                                                                    HB3730

Annual, quarterly, and monthly economic indicators and forecasts. 278 series from 1980 to the present for 117 countries and 40 regional aggregates (e.g., ASEAN, Australasia, Balkans, Economies in Transition, Sub-Saharan Africa, Oil Exporters, Central America). Series have seven general categories: gross domestic product, fiscal and monetary indicators, demographics and income, foreign payments, external debt stock, external debt service, and external trade. Key forecast series include real GDP growth, GDP per head, consumer price inflation, exchange rate and current-account balance/GDP, with forecasts to 2030.

878  **Europa world plus.** Europa Publications Limited, Routledge,
      Taylor & Francis Group. 2003–. New York: Routledge; Taylor & Francis Group. http://www.europaworld.com/pub/about/.
                                                                    D443.E87

Economic and political information for more than 250 countries and territories. Includes *Europa world year book* (145) and the *Europa regional surveys of the world* series:

- *Africa south of the Sahara* (London; New York: Routledge, 1971–)
- *Central and south-eastern Europe* (London: Europa Publications, 2000–)
- *Eastern Europe, Russia and Central Asia* (London; New York: Routledge, 2000–)
- *The Far East and Australasia* (London: Europa, 1969–)
- *The Middle East and North Africa* (991)
- *South America, Central America and the Caribbean* (London: Europa, 1985–)
- *South Asia* (London; New York: Routledge, 2003–)
- *The USA and Canada* (London; New York: Routledge, 1989–)
- *Western Europe* (London; New York: Routledge, 1988–)

ECONOMICS & BUSINESS

Country entries include country profile, geography, chronology, history, economy, country statistics, government and politics directory, society and media directory, business and commerce directory, and bibliography.

Unique to the online version is the comparative statistics section, which generates five years of multinational statistics on area and population, agriculture, industry, finance, external trade, and education in tables and charts downloaded as an HTML table, comma-separated values and in tab-separated values. The comparative statistics section uses different sources than the country statistics section, making data comparisons possible.

**879**   **Foreign government resources on the web.** University of Michigan. [Ann Arbor, Mich.]: Documents Center, University of Michigan Library. http://www.lib.umich.edu/govdocs/foreign.html.

ZA5050

Websites of foreign governments arranged by region, then by country. For each country, links to main home page and websites of major agencies. Also contains links to sites compiling background information, embassy listings, constitutions and other legal material, news, and statistics, either for countries worldwide or in a particular region.

**880**   **Global development finance.** World Bank. 2 v. Washington: World Bank, 1997–. ISSN: 1020-5454.

336.3435091724                                        HJ8899.W672

External debt and financial flow data for 136 countries. Vol. 1 is *Analysis and outlook,* with financial flows to developing countries. Vol. 2 is *Summary and country tables* and includes summary data for regions and income groups. Indicators include external debt stocks and flows, major economic aggregates, key debt ratios, average terms of new commitments, and currency composition of long-term debt. Also available online and on CD-ROM, with data from 1970.

**881**   **The index of economic freedom.** Heritage Foundation. maps. Washington: The Heritage Foundation, 1995–. ISSN: 1095-7308.

338.9005                                                HB95.I48

Uses 50 independent variables to rank 161 countries, including Hong Kong, on the level of government involvement in the economy. The more that a government is involved in constraint in the production, distribution, or consumption of goods and services, the less freedom the editors believe is present. In addition to the score, 2-page long country profiles discuss trade policy, fiscal burden, government intervention, monetary policy, foreign investment, banking and finance, wages and prices, property rights, regulation, and informal market. The 2007 ed. adds a chapter on regions. The current version is available for free at http://www.heritage .org/research/.

882 **International historical statistics: Africa, Asia and Oceania, 1750–2000.** 4th ed. B. R. Mitchell. xix, 1113 p, 29 cm. Houndmills, Basingstokes, Hampshire, [U.K.]; New York: Palgrave Macmillan, 2003. ISBN: 0333994124; 9780333994122.

310                                                                 HA4675

Gives key economic and social indicators in this companion to the author's *International historical statistics: the Americas* (904). Official and unofficial statistical sources were used to provide comparative data for the included countries. Data for more than two centuries are arranged in ten sections that cover population and vital statistics, labor force, agriculture, industry, external trade, transport, and communications.

883 **Key indicators of developing Asian and Pacific countries.** Economics and Development Resource Center. Manila, Philippines; Hong Kong, [China]: ADB; Oxford University Press, 1970–. ISSN: 0116-3000.

HC411

Presents economic and financial statistics from 1998–2005 for Asian and Pacific countries. Each year's publication also has a specific focus (*Measuring policy effectiveness in health and education, Labor markets in Asia: Promoting full, productive, and decent employment, Poverty in Asia: Measurement, estimates, and prospects*, etc.). Categories for data include: poverty, inequality, and human development; education indicators; environment indicators; health and nutrition indicators; mortality and reproductive health; population; population by age group; labor and employment by gender and economic activity; land use; agriculture production; total and per capita GNI; shares of major sectors in GDP; expenditure shares in GDP; domestic saving, capital formation, and resource gap; growth rates of GDP and major sectors; inflation rates; growth rates of merchandise exports and imports; foreign trade indicators; direction of trade: merchandise exports and imports; government finance indicators; money supply indicators; foreign direct investment, net inflows; international reserves indicators; external debt and debt service payments; debt indicators; official flows from all sources to DMC's; net private flows from all sources to DMC's; and aggregate net resource flows from all sources to DMC's. Also available online.

**884** **The national economic atlas of China.** Chung-kuo k'o hsüeh yüan. 1 atlas, xvi, 314 p., col. maps. Hong Kong, [China]; New York: Oxford University Press, 1994. ISBN: 0195857364.

912.43                                                    G2306.G1K813

Translated work includes four handbooks of descriptive notes to maps bound separately in pockets. Maps illustrate China's resources, population, general economy, agriculture, industry, trade, social indicators, and regional economies. Comprehensive in nature and provides an excellent overview for anyone interested in studying the Chinese economy.

**885** **Nationmaster.com.** 2003–. NationMaster.com. http://www. nationmaster.com/index.php.

HA154

Uses data from government and international organizations to present comparative statistics between nations. Some of the topics covered include economy, education, health issues, immigration, industry, labor, taxation, and transportation. Data is displayed in easy-to-read graphs. The source of the data is also cited. This is a companion to StateMaster.com (Brooklyn, N.Y.: StateMaster.com, 2006–).

**886** **Political risk yearbook online.** PRS Group. 1999–. East Syracuse, N.Y.: PRS Group. https://www.prsgroup.com/prsgroup_ shoppingcart/pc-48-7-political-risk-yearbook.aspx.

Political and economic risk analysis for 106 countries. Reports are PDF files with a country forecast (highlights, current data, comments and analysis, forecast scenarios, political players), and country conditions (investment climate, climate for trade including political violence and legal framework, background on geography, history, social conditions, government, political conditions, and environmental trends). Includes forecasts for GDP growth, current account, inflation, political turmoil, investment and trade restrictions, and domesic and international economic problems. Also has statistics for foreign direct investment flows by source country and sector.

**887** **Russia, all 89 regions: Trade and investment guide.** 1029 p., maps. [New York; Moscow]: CTEC Pub., LLC, 2003–. ISBN: 0974347817.

330.947                                                    HF5192.2.A3

Economic, investment, and trade information for the various regions. Entries are by region and have general background, economic potential (including gross regional product by industry), trade opportunities (including main goods, imports and exports), investment opportunities (including sector analysis and data for capital investment by industry), and specific investment projects.

**888    SourceOECD.** Organisation for Economic Co-operation and Development. [Paris, France]: OECD. http://new.sourceoecd.org/. A subscription database containing OECD books, reports, working papers, serials, and statistical databases on economic and social topics, as well as the environment, energy, and technological development. Focuses mainly on the 30 OECD member states and major nonmember developing countries.

Serials include journals; the OECD Factbook (Paris: OECD, 2005–) and other statistical works; and titles that forecast and analyze trends, such as the OECD Economic Outlook (Paris: Organisation for Economic Co-operation and Development, 1967–), *African economic outlook* (Paris: African Development Bank, Development Centre of the Organisation for Economic Co-operation and Development, 2002–), International Migration Outlook (Paris: Organisation for Economic Co-operation and Development, 2006–), and OECD-FAO Agricultural Outlook (Paris: Organisation for Economic Co-operation and Development; Food and Agriculture Organization, 2005–).

Current, themed databases include the OECD Economic Outlook Database (Paris: Organisation for Economic Co-operation and Development, 2002–), SourceOECD Main Economic Indicators (Paris: Organisation for Economic Co-operation and Development, 2002–), Banking Statistics, Education Statistics, Globalisation, Indicators of Industry and Services, Insurance, International Development, International Direct Investment Statistics, International Migration Statistics, the ITCS International Trade by Commodity Database, Monthly Statistics of International Trade, the National Accounts Database, OECD Health Data, OECD Statistics on International Trade in Services, the Revenue Statistics of OECD Member Countries Database, the Science and Technology Database, the Social Expenditure Database, Structural and Demographic Business Statistics, Taxing Wages Statistics, and the Telecommunications Database. Statistical databases of the International Energy Agency are also available via this source. OECD.Stat enables users to query multiple databases simultaneously and to export search results in several formats.

Also incorporates Future Trends, an index of published and unpublished sources in more than a dozen languages covering issues affecting the public and private sectors. Glossary.

**889    Statistical sites on the World Wide Web.** U.S. Bureau of Labor Statistics. Washington: U.S. Bureau of Labor Statistics. http://www.bls.gov/bls/other.htm.
Links to official government statistical offices all over the world, including more than 130 countries and some international agencies. Also links to sites of nearly 70 U.S. federal statistical agencies. Excellent starting point for researchers.

**890    Statistical yearbook: Annuaire statistique.** United Nations. 37 v. New York: United Nations. ISSN: 0082-8459.
310.5                                                         HA12.5.U63
A summary of international statistics to continue the *Statistical yearbook of the League of Nations.* Covers population, agriculture, mining, manufacturing, finance, trade, social statistics, education, etc., of the various countries of the world, the tables usually covering a number of years. References are given to sources. A world summary was introduced beginning with v. 15 (1963), summarizing tables appearing in various chapters. The *Monthly bulletin of statistics online* (New York: U.N. Statistical Div., Dept. of Economic and Social Development, 1992–) complements this resource by providing current information.

**891    STAT-USA Internet.** STAT-USA. [1994–.] [Washington, D.C.?]: STAT-USA, U.S. Dept. of Commerce. http://www.stat-usa.gov/.
382                                                          HF1379
Business and economic information compiled mainly from federal agencies. There are two main sections, "State of the Nation" and "Globus & NTDB."
  "State of the Nation" concentrates on current U.S. information, with 2,500 files on general economic indicators (consumer price index, producer price index, gross domestic product, national income and product accounts), regional economic statistics (by NAICS sector, state personal income, metropolitan personal income) housing and construction (housing starts and building permits, new construction, new home sales), employment (employment cost index, local area employment and unemployment, weekly unemployment claims report), manufacturing

and industry (retail sales, manufacturing inventories and sales, industrial production and capacity utilization, current industry reports), monetary statistics (interest rates, foreign exchange rates, bank credit), and economic policy (Beige Book, Treasury Statements).

"Globus & NTDB" is useful for current exchange rates (weekly, monthly, and annual), current and historical trade leads (United Nations trade leads, Defense Logistics Agency leads, FedBizOpps, commercial trade leads), international trade (Asia Development Bank, World Bank, Inter-American Development Bank, and European Bank Business Opportunities, country reports on terrorism, Country Studies Program reports, *International trade update newsletter, National trade estimates report on foreign trade barriers, World bank commodity price data*—"PinkSheets"—and *World factbook*), market and country research (*Country background notes, Country commercial guides, Industry sector analysis reports,* Global Agriculture Information Network [GAIN], *AgWorld attaché reports, International market insight (IMI) reports,* and Multilateral Development Bank), contacts (*NTDB global trade directory, National export directory,* Foreign Trade Offices), and current press releases (U.S. international trade in goods and services, FT900 supplemental tables, U.S. Export Sales—USDA, U.S. import and export price indexes, U.S. international transactions, and additional press releases).

**892    Taiwan yearbook.** Taipei, Taiwan: Government Information Office. http://www.gio.gov.tw/.

Overview of Taiwan in narrative and statistical format; 22 sections provide details on history, government, national defense, foreign relations, education, economics, environmental protection, science and technology, relations with China, and other important aspects of Taiwan. Also includes a "Who's Who in Taiwan" section with prominent leaders across the political spectrum and from all walks of life. Continues the print version of *Republic of China yearbook (Boston: Warren, Gorham, and Lamont).*

**893    United Nations common database (UNCDB).** United Nations Statistic Division. New York: United Nations Statistic Division. http://unstats.un.org/unsd/cdb/cdb_help/cdb_quick_start.asp.

Provides socioeconomic data from 55 sources on 274 countries and areas, with coverage from 1948–2050. Allows comparison of data from 10 countries at a time, and data can be downloaded to Excel. Formerly a fee-based database but now free.

Covers 31 topics: agriculture, forestry, and fishing; communication and culture; construction; development assistance; economically active/ not economically active population; education and learning; energy; environment; financial statistics; health, health services, impairment, disabilities, nutrition; households and families, marital status, fertility; human settlements, housing, geographical distribution of population; income, consumption and wealth; industrial production; international finance; international tourism; international trade; millennium development goals (MDG); mining and quarrying; national accounts; population composition and change; prices; public order and safety; science and technology, intellectual property; services industries; social security and welfare services; socioeconomic groups and social mobility; statistical yearbook; transport; and women and men.

**894   VIBES.** Jeanie M. Welch, J. Murrey Atkins Library (University of North Carolina at Charlotte). [199?–.] Charlotte, N.C.: University of North Carolina at Charlotte, J. Murrey Atkins Library. http://library.uncc.edu/vibes/.
025.04; 382; 330; 650

Links to over 3,000 free Internet sources with international business and economic information in English. Organized into three categories: comprehensive, regional, and national. Coverage includes agricultural and forest products; banking and finance (includes insurance); business news, business practices and company information (includes labor); country information; emerging markets; foreign exchange rates; foreign stock markets; international electronic commerce; international statistics (general and economic); international tourism; international trade law; marketing and advertising; patents (includes other intellectual property); petroleum, energy, mining, and construction; portals (web meta pages with several international links); taxation in foreign countries (includes social security); trade issues and statistics; and business and economics for Africa, Asia-Pacific, Eastern Europe, Western Europe, Latin America and the Caribbean, Middle East, and NAFTA (U.S., Canada, and Mexico).

# Canada

**895   The Canada year book.** Census and Statistics Office (Canada). ill. (some fold., some col.), maps (some fold., some col.). Ottawa, [Canada]: Census and Statistics Office, 1906–. ISSN: 0068-8142.
317.1                                                                      HA744.S81

Subtitle (varies): *Statistical annual of the resources, demography, institutions and social and economic conditions of Canada.* Some volumes cover two years. Volumes for 1905–71 issued by the agency under its earlier name, Canada, Bureau of Statistics. Presents official data on history, constitution and government, institutions, population, production, industry, trade, transportation, finance, labor, administration, and general social and economic conditions. Current year books are available in print only. The first century of *Canada year books*, 1867–1967, are available free online at http://www65.statcan.gc.ca/acyb_r000-eng.htm.

**896    Canadian almanac and directory.** maps (part fold.). Toronto: Grey House Canada, 1848–. ISSN: 0068-8193.
971.0025                                                            AY414.C2

162nd ed., 2008. Previous title: *Canadian almanac and legal and court directory.*

Contains reliable legal, commercial, governmental, statistical, astronomical, departmental, ecclesiastical, financial, educational, and general information with charts and color photographs plus election results. Also available in online form.

**897    Canadian economic observer. Historical statistical supplement: L'Observateur économique canadien. Supplément statistique historique.** Statistics Canada. Ottawa, [Canada]: Statistics Canada, 1988–. ISSN: 0838-0236.
330.9710021                                                  HC111.C1976

Annual data for all series reported monthly in the *Canadian economic observer*, including national accounts, prices, international and domestic trade, labor, and financial markets. Provincial detail given for employment earnings, retail trade, housing, and consumer price indexes. Available in online form.

**898    CANSIM, Canadian socio-economic information management system.** Statistics Canada. 1979–. Ottawa, [Canada]: Statistics Canada (Statistique Canada). ISSN: 0706-0858. http://cansim2. statcan.ca/.
016.3171                                                        HA37.C24c

Over 35 million time series on Canadian economic, social, financial, and monetary issues. Includes agriculture, construction and housing, demography, domestic trade, health and social conditions, energy, environment and natural resources, finance, household expenditures, international trade, justice, labor, manufacturing, prices and price indexes, service industries, national accounts, transportation, travel and tourism, education, and culture. Daily updates.

**899 Country briefings.** Economist.com. [199?–.] London: Economist Newspaper. http://www.economist.com/countries/.
909.83                                                          HC59.15

News from *The economist* (151) print edition, country profiles, forecasts, statistics, political outlook, economic policy outlook, economic forecast, and economic structure for 60 countries. Ten key economic statistics can be downloaded into Excel (GDP per head, GDP, government consumption, budget balance, consumer prices, public debt, labour costs per hour, recorded unemployment, current-account balance, and foreign-exchange reserves). Links to some subscription-based materials and free external related websites, such as governmental and news websites.

**900 EIU.com.** Economist Intelligence Unit (Great Britain). 2005–. [London?]: Economist Intelligence Unit. http://www.eiu.com/.

Covers political, economic, and business information for 201 countries. Access to Economist Intelligence Unit publications: *Country finance, Country commerce, Country monitor, Business Africa, Business Asia, Business China, Business Eastern Europe, Business Europe, Business India intelligence, Business Latin America,* and *Business Middle East.* Country reports similar to Political Risk Yearbook (192), but with more frequent updates. Key data include GDP, forecast GDP, exports, imports, inflation, exchange rates, interest rates, consumer and producer prices, deposit rate, lending rate, money market rate, select commodity prices, and select industry data. Many numbers can be downloaded into Excel. Archives available from 1992.

**901 EIU country data.** Bureau van Dijk Electronic Publishing. 2002–. [s.l.]: Bureau van Dijk. http://countrydata.bvdep.com/ip/.
HB3730

Annual, quarterly, and monthly economic indicators and forecasts. 278 series from 1980 to the present for 117 countries and 40 regional aggregates (e.g., ASEAN, Australasia, Balkans, Economies in Transition, Sub-Saharan Africa, Oil Exporters, Central America). Series have seven general categories: gross domestic product, fiscal and monetary indicators, demographics and income, foreign payments, external debt stock, external debt service, and external trade. Key forecast series include real GDP growth, GDP per head, consumer price inflation, exchange rate and current-account balance/GDP, with forecasts to 2030.

902   **Europa world plus.** Europa Publications Limited, Routledge, Taylor & Francis Group. 2003–. New York: Routledge; Taylor & Francis Group. http://www.europaworld.com/pub/about/.

D443.E87

Economic and political information for more than 250 countries and territories. Includes *Europa world year book* (145) and the *Europa regional surveys of the world* series:

- *Africa south of the Sahara* (London; New York: Routledge, 1971–)
- *Central and south-eastern Europe* (London: Europa Publications, 2000–)
- *Eastern Europe, Russia and Central Asia* (London; New York: Routledge, 2000–)
- *The Far East and Australasia* (London: Europa, 1969–)
- *The Middle East and North Africa* (991)
- *South America, Central America and the Caribbean* (London: Europa, 1985–)
- *South Asia* (London; New York: Routledge, 2003–)
- *The USA and Canada* (London; New York: Routledge, 1989–)
- *Western Europe* (London; New York: Routledge, 1988–)

Country entries include country profile, geography, chronology, history, economy, country statistics, government and politics directory, society and media directory, business and commerce directory, and bibliography.

Unique to the online version is the comparative statistics section, which generates five years of multinational statistics on area and population, agriculture, industry, finance, external trade, and education in tables and charts downloaded as an HTML table, comma-separated values and in tab-separated values. The comparative statistics section uses different sources than the country statistics section, making data comparisons possible.

903   **The index of economic freedom.** Heritage Foundation. maps. Washington: The Heritage Foundation, 1995–. ISSN: 1095-7308.
338.9005                                                                      HB95.I48

Uses 50 independent variables to rank 161 countries, including Hong Kong, on the level of government involvement in the economy. The more that a government is involved in constraint in the production, distribution, or consumption of goods and services, the less freedom the editors believe is present. In addition to the score, 2-page long country profiles discuss trade policy, fiscal burden, government intervention, monetary policy, foreign investment, banking and finance, wages and prices, property rights, regulation, and informal market. The 2007 ed. adds a chapter on regions. The current version is available for free at http://www.heritage.org/research/.

**904** **International historical statistics: The Americas, 1750–2000.** 5th ed. B. R. Mitchell. xv, 830 p. Houndmills, Basingstoke, Hampshire, [England]; New York: Palgrave Macmillan, 2003. ISBN: 0333994108.

317                                                    HA175.M55

A companion to the author's *International historical statistics: Europe* and *International historical statistics: Africa and Asia.* Presents comparative statistics for 26 North, Central, and South American countries from the early 19th century to the late 20th century for most. Tables are grouped in 11 broad subject areas.

**905** **Inter-university consortium for political and social research.** University of Michigan. [1997–.] Ann Arbor, Mich.: Institute for Social Research, University of Michigan. http://www.icpsr.umich.edu/.

Archive of international social science data, with a large collection of economic data. Thematic collections are Census Enumerations; Community and Urban Studies; Conflict, Aggression, Violence, Wars; Economic Behavior and Attitudes; Education; Elites and Leadership; Geography and Environment; Government Structures, Policies, and Capabilities; Health Care and Facilities; Instructional Packages; International Systems; Legal Systems; Legislative and Deliberative Bodies; Mass Political Behavior and Attitudes; Organizational Behavior; Social Indicators; Social Institutions and Behavior; Publication-Related Archive; and External Data Resources. Data, which can be downloaded for SAS, SPSS, and STATA, are available to the 500 member institutions, but some is also available to the public.

**906** **Market research handbook: Manuel statistique pour études de marché.** Canada Statistics Canada. v, ill. Ottawa, Canada: Dominion Bureau of Statistics, Merchandising and Services

Division = Bureau fédéral de la statistique, Division du commerce et des services, [1969]–. ISSN: 0590-9325.

658.83971                                                    HC111.A19

Annual summary of Canadian national and international trade statistics. Includes data for national and 25 metropolitan markets, with demographic and economic projections. Organized into 11 sections: user's guide, population, labor market and income, consumer expenditures, housing and household characteristics, macroeconomic and financial statistics, international trade, business and industry statistics, census metropolitan areas and census agglomerations, glossary and alphabetic index. Current edition available for free online at http://www.statcan.ca/english/ads/63-224-XPB/toc.htm.

**907  NationMaster.com.** 2003–. NationMaster.com. http://www.nationmaster.com/index.php.

HA154

Uses data from government and international organizations to present comparative statistics between nations. Some of the topics covered include economy, education, health issues, immigration, industry, labor, taxation, and transportation. Data is displayed in easy-to-read graphs. The source of the data is also cited. This is a companion to StateMaster.com (Brooklyn, N.Y.: StateMaster.com, 2006–).

**908  Political risk yearbook online.** PRS Group. 1999–. East Syracuse, N.Y.: PRS Group. https://www.prsgroup.com/prsgroup_shoppingcart/pc-48-7-political-risk-yearbook.aspx.

Political and economic risk analysis for 106 countries. Reports are PDF files with a country forecast (highlights, current data, comments and analysis, forecast scenarios, political players), and country conditions (investment climate, climate for trade including political violence and legal framework, background on geography, history, social conditions, government, political conditions, and environmental trends). Includes forecasts for GDP growth, current account, inflation, political turmoil, investment and trade restrictions, and domesic and international economic problems. Also has statistics for foreign direct investment flows by source country and sector.

**909  SourceOECD.** Organisation for Economic Co-operation and Development. [Paris, France]: OECD. http://new.sourceoecd.org/.

A subscription database containing OECD books, reports, working papers, serials, and statistical databases on economic and social topics, as well as the environment, energy, and technological development. Focuses mainly on the 30 OECD member states and major nonmember developing countries.

Serials include journals; the OECD Factbook (Paris: OECD, 2005–) and other statistical works; and titles that forecast and analyze trends, such as the OECD Economic Outlook (Paris: Organisation for Economic Co-operation and Development, 1967–), *African economic outlook* (Paris: African Development Bank, Development Centre of the Organisation for Economic Co-operation and Development, 2002–), International Migration Outlook (Paris: Organisation for Economic Co-operation and Development, 2006–), and OECD-FAO Agricultural Outlook (Paris: Organisation for Economic Co-operation and Development; Food and Agriculture Organization, 2005–).

Current, themed databases include the OECD Economic Outlook Database (Paris: Organisation for Economic Co-operation and Development, 2002–), SourceOECD Main Economic Indicators (Paris: Organisation for Economic Co-operation and Development, 2002–), Banking Statistics, Education Statistics, Globalisation, Indicators of Industry and Services, Insurance, International Development, International Direct Investment Statistics, International Migration Statistics, the ITCS International Trade by Commodity Database, Monthly Statistics of International Trade, the National Accounts Database, OECD Health Data, OECD Statistics on International Trade in Services, the Revenue Statistics of OECD Member Countries Database, the Science and Technology Database, the Social Expenditure Database, Structural and Demographic Business Statistics, Taxing Wages Statistics, and the Telecommunications Database. Statistical databases of the International Energy Agency are also available via this source. OECD.Stat enables users to query multiple databases simultaneously and to export search results in several formats.

Also incorporates Future Trends, an index of published and unpublished sources in more than a dozen languages covering issues affecting the public and private sectors. Glossary.

**910    Statistical sites on the World Wide Web.** U.S. Bureau of Labor Statistics. Washington: U.S. Bureau of Labor Statistics. http://www.bls.gov/bls/other.htm.

Links to official government statistical offices all over the world, including more than 130 countries and some international agencies. Also links to sites of nearly 70 U.S. federal statistical agencies. Excellent starting point for researchers.

911　**STAT-USA Internet.** STAT-USA. [1994–.] [Washington, D.C.?]:
STAT-USA, U.S. Dept. of Commerce. http://www.stat-usa.gov/.
382　　　　　　　　　　　　　　　　　　　　　　　　　　HF1379
Business and economic information compiled mainly from federal agencies.
There are two main sections, "State of the Nation" and "Globus & NTDB."
"State of the Nation" concentrates on current U.S. information,
with 2,500 files on general economic indicators (consumer price index,
producer price index, gross domestic product, national income and
product accounts), regional economic statistics (by NAICS sector, state
personal income, metropolitan personal income) housing and construction (housing starts and building permits, new construction, new home
sales), employment (employment cost index, local area employment and
unemployment, weekly unemployment claims report), manufacturing
and industry (retail sales, manufacturing inventories and sales, industrial
production and capacity utilization, current industry reports), monetary
statistics (interest rates, foreign exchange rates, bank credit), and economic
policy (Beige Book, Treasury Statements).

"Globus & NTDB" is useful for current exchange rates (weekly,
monthly, and annual), current and historical trade leads (United Nations
trade leads, Defense Logistics Agency leads, FedBizOpps, commercial
trade leads), international trade (Asia Development Bank, World Bank,
Inter-American Development Bank, and European Bank Business Opportunities, country reports on terrorism, Country Studies Program reports,
*International trade update newsletter, National trade estimates report on for-
eign trade barriers, World bank commodity price data*—"PinkSheets"—and
*World factbook*), market and country research (*Country background notes,
Country commercial guides, Industry sector analysis reports*, Global Agriculture Information Network [GAIN], *AgWorld attaché reports, International market insight (IMI) reports*, and Multilateral Development Bank),
contacts (*NTDB global trade directory, National export directory*, Foreign
Trade Offices), and current press releases (U.S. international trade in
goods and services, FT900 supplemental tables, U.S. Export Sales—USDA,
U.S. import and export price indexes, U.S. international transactions, and
additional press releases).

912　**United Nations common database (UNCDB).** United Nations
Statistic Division. New York: United Nations Statistic Division.
http://unstats.un.org/unsd/cdb/cdb_help/cdb_quick_start.asp.

Provides socioeconomic data from 55 sources on 274 countries and areas, with coverage from 1948–2050. Allows comparison of data from 10 countries at a time, and data can be downloaded to Excel. Formerly a fee-based database but now free.

Covers 31 topics: agriculture, forestry, and fishing; communication and culture; construction; development assistance; economically active/not economically active population; education and learning; energy; environment; financial statistics; health, health services, impairment, disabilities, nutrition; households and families, marital status, fertility; human settlements, housing, geographical distribution of population; income, consumption and wealth; industrial production; international finance; international tourism; international trade; millennium development goals (MDG); mining and quarrying; national accounts; population composition and change; prices; public order and safety; science and technology, intellectual property; services industries; social security and welfare services; socioeconomic groups and social mobility; statistical yearbook; transport; and women and men.

**913 VIBES.** Jeanie M. Welch, J. Murrey Atkins Library (University of North Carolina at Charlotte). [199?–.] Charlotte, N.C.: University of North Carolina at Charlotte, J. Murrey Atkins Library. http://library.uncc.edu/vibes/.

025.04; 382; 330; 650

Links to over 3,000 free Internet sources with international business and economic information in English. Organized into three categories: comprehensive, regional, and national. Coverage includes agricultural and forest products; banking and finance (includes insurance); business news, business practices and company information (includes labor); country information; emerging markets; foreign exchange rates; foreign stock markets; international electronic commerce; international statistics (general and economic); international tourism; international trade law; marketing and advertising; patents (includes other intellectual property); petroleum, energy, mining, and construction; portals (web meta pages with several international links); taxation in foreign countries (includes social security); trade issues and statistics; and business and economics for Africa, Asia-Pacific, Eastern Europe, Western Europe, Latin America and the Caribbean, Middle East, and NAFTA (U.S., Canada, and Mexico).

# Central and Latin America

**914    Anuario estadístico de América Latina: Statistical yearbook for Latin America.** United Nations. 8 v. Santiago, Chile: United Nations, Economic Commission for Latin America. ISSN: 0251-9445.

300.8s318                                                    JX1977.A2subser

Socioeconomic statistics for Latin America, organized into four sections: 1. Social statistics, 2. Economic statistics, 3. Statistics on natural resources and the environment, 4. Technical notes. Statistics are generally for ten years, but also include forecasts. Current edition available for download at the ECLAC website; however, "The printed version of the *Yearbook* contains a selection of tables which seek to provide statistical information from the regional perspective, with emphasis on the international comparability of data such as national accounts statistics in dollars."—*Introd.*

**915    Anuario estadístico de América Latina y el Caribe = Statistical yearbook for Latin America and the Caribbean.** United Nations, Economic Commission for Latin America and the Caribbean. 1986–. [Santiago, Chile]: Economic Commission for Latin America and the Caribbean. ISSN: 1014-0697. http://websie.eclac.cl/anuario_estadistico/anuario_2008/eng/index.asp.

More than 130 indicators summarize the past and present social and economic development of 33 Latin American and Caribbean countries. Some historical data series begin in 1950. Includes technical notes with definitions, methodology, information sources, and comments on each indicator. Great for relatively current Latin American data. Print version is available but has fewer detailed indicators.

**916    Consumer Latin America.** Euromonitor Publications Limited. ill. London: Euromonitor Publications Limited, 1993–. ISSN: 1359-0979.

HC121.C667

Market-size time series for last five years and forecasted time series for upcoming five years for over 330 consumer markets in six Latin American countries (Argentina, Brazil, Chile, Colombia, Mexico, and Venezuela), as well as economic, demographic, lifestyle, and purchasing data and analysis. Also lists manufacturer and brand shares for major consumer goods sectors.

**917**  **Country briefings.** Economist.com. [199?–.] London: Economist Newspaper. http://www.economist.com/countries/.

909.83                                                               HC59.15

News from *The economist* (151) print edition, country profiles, forecasts, statistics, political outlook, economic policy outlook, economic forecast, and economic structure for 60 countries. Ten key economic statistics can be downloaded into Excel (GDP per head, GDP, government consumption, budget balance, consumer prices, public debt, labour costs per hour, recorded unemployment, current-account balance, and foreign-exchange reserves). Links to some subscription-based materials and free external related websites, such as governmental and news websites.

**918**  **Economic and social progress in Latin America.** Inter-American Development Bank. ill. Washington: Inter-American Development Bank, 1972–. ISSN: 0095-2850.

330.98003                                                          HC125.I514

Reviews economic and political progress in Latin America, with development, economics, and finance data. Available online in English and Spanish (http://www.iadb.org/res/ipes/2007/previous.cfm?language=English/) from 1997 to the present.

**919**  **Economic survey of Latin America and the Caribbean.** United Nations. ill. Santiago, Chile: United Nations, 1984–. ISSN: 0257-2184.

330.980005                                                         HC161.U525

Presents a summary of the international economy, details the regional economy, outlines economic policy, domestic performance, and the economic conditions of each country in the region. With a lengthy statistical appendix, this is a rich source of data.

**920**  **EIU.com.** Economist Intelligence Unit (Great Britain). 2005–. [London?]: Economist Intelligence Unit. http://www.eiu.com/.

Covers political, economic, and business information for 201 countries. Access to Economist Intelligence Unit publications: *Country finance, Country commerce, Country monitor, Business Africa, Business Asia, Business China, Business Eastern Europe, Business Europe, Business India intelligence, Business Latin America,* and *Business Middle East.* Country reports similar to Political Risk Yearbook (192), but with more frequent updates.

Key data include GDP, forecast GDP, exports, imports, inflation, exchange rates, interest rates, consumer and producer prices, deposit rate, lending rate, money market rate, select commodity prices, and select industry data. Many numbers can be downloaded into Excel. Archives available from 1992.

**921** **EIU country data.** Bureau van Dijk Electronic Publishing. 2002–. [s.l.]: Bureau van Dijk. http://countrydata.bvdep.com/ip/.

HB3730

Annual, quarterly, and monthly economic indicators and forecasts. 278 series from 1980 to the present for 117 countries and 40 regional aggregates (e.g., ASEAN, Australasia, Balkans, Economies in Transition, Sub-Saharan Africa, Oil Exporters, Central America). Series have seven general categories: gross domestic product, fiscal and monetary indicators, demographics and income, foreign payments, external debt stock, external debt service, and external trade. Key forecast series include real GDP growth, GDP per head, consumer price inflation, exchange rate and current-account balance/GDP, with forecasts to 2030.

**922** **Europa world plus.** Europa Publications Limited, Routledge, Taylor & Francis Group. 2003–. New York: Routledge; Taylor & Francis Group. http://www.europaworld.com/pub/about/.

D443.E87

Economic and political information for more than 250 countries and territories. Includes *Europa world year book* (145) and the *Europa regional surveys of the world* series:

- *Africa south of the Sahara* (London; New York: Routledge, 1971–)
- *Central and south-eastern Europe* (London: Europa Publications, 2000–) *Eastern Europe, Russia and Central Asia* (London; New York: Routledge, 2000–)
- *The Far East and Australasia* (London: Europa, 1969–)
- *The Middle East and North Africa* (991)
- *South America, Central America and the Caribbean* (London: Europa, 1985–)
- *South Asia* (London; New York: Routledge, 2003–)
- *The USA and Canada* (London; New York: Routledge, 1989–)
- *Western Europe* (London; New York: Routledge, 1988–)

Country entries include country profile, geography, chronology, history, economy, country statistics, government and politics directory,

ECONOMICS & BUSINESS

society and media directory, business and commerce directory, and bibliography.

Unique to the online version is the comparative statistics section, which generates five years of multinational statistics on area and population, agriculture, industry, finance, external trade, and education in tables and charts downloaded as an HTML table, comma-separated values and in tab-separated values. The comparative statistics section uses different sources than the country statistics section, making data comparisons possible.

**923  Foreign government resources on the web.** University of Michigan. [Ann Arbor, Mich.]: Documents Center, University of Michigan Library. http://www.lib.umich.edu/govdocs/foreign.html. ZA5050

Websites of foreign governments arranged by region, then by country. For each country, links to main home page and websites of major agencies. Also contains links to sites compiling background information, embassy listings, constitutions and other legal material, news, and statistics, either for countries worldwide or in a particular region.

**924  Global development finance.** World Bank. 2 v. Washington: World Bank, 1997–. ISSN: 1020-5454.
336.3435091724                                                    HJ8899.W672

External debt and financial flow data for 136 countries. Vol. 1 is *Analysis and outlook*, with financial flows to developing countries. Vol. 2 is *Summary and country tables* and includes summary data for regions and income groups. Indicators include external debt stocks and flows, major economic aggregates, key debt ratios, average terms of new commitments, and currency composition of long-term debt. Also available online and on CD-ROM, with data from 1970.

**925  HAPI online.** UCLA Latin American Center. Los Angeles: UCLA Latin American Center. http://hapi.gseis.ucla.edu.

The online version of *HAPI: Hispanic American periodicals index* (Los Angeles: UCLA Latin American Center Publications, University of California, [1970?]–). As of 2006, HAPI covered more than 275 peer-reviewed journals with content on Latin America, the Caribbean, Brazil, and U.S. Latinos. Historically, more than 500 periodicals have been indexed. Includes citations to articles, book reviews (through 2001), documents, and original literary works. Initially, indexing began with 1975, but a retrospective project bridged the gap with the cessation of

*Index to Latin American periodical literature, 1929–1960* (Boston: G. K. Hall, 1962). The database has a thesaurus and provides links to some full text.

926   **The index of economic freedom.** Heritage Foundation. maps.
Washington: The Heritage Foundation, 1995–. ISSN: 1095-7308.
338.9005                                                              HB95.I48

Uses 50 independent variables to rank 161 countries, including Hong Kong, on the level of government involvement in the economy. The more that a government is involved in constraint in the production, distribution, or consumption of goods and services, the less freedom the editors believe is present. In addition to the score, 2-page long country profiles discuss trade policy, fiscal burden, government intervention, monetary policy, foreign investment, banking and finance, wages and prices, property rights, regulation, and informal market. The 2007 ed. adds a chapter on regions. The current version is available for free at http://www.heritage.org/research/.

927   **International historical statistics: The Americas, 1750–2000.** 5th
ed. B. R. Mitchell. xv, 830 p. Houndmills, Basingstoke, Hampshire,
[England]; New York: Palgrave Macmillan, 2003. ISBN:
0333994108.
317                                                                  HA175.M55

A companion to the author's *International historical statistics: Europe* and *International historical statistics: Africa and Asia.* Presents comparative statistics for 26 North, Central, and South American countries from the early 19th century to the late 20th century for most. Tables are grouped in 11 broad subject areas.

928   **Inter-university consortium for political and social research.**
University of Michigan. [1997–.] Ann Arbor, Mich.: Institute for
Social Research, University of Michigan. http://www.icpsr.umich.
edu/.

Archive of international social science data, with a large collection of economic data. Thematic collections are Census Enumerations; Community and Urban Studies; Conflict, Aggression, Violence, Wars; Economic Behavior and Attitudes; Education; Elites and Leadership; Geography and Environment; Government Structures, Policies, and Capabilities; Health Care and Facilities; Instructional Packages; International Systems; Legal Systems; Legislative and Deliberative Bodies; Mass Political Behavior and Attitudes; Organizational Behavior;

Social Indicators; Social Institutions and Behavior; Publication-Related Archive; and External Data Resources. Data, which can be downloaded for SAS, SPSS, and STATA, are available to the 500 member institutions, but some is also available to the public.

**929    LANIC.** Latin American Network Information Center. 2001–. Austin, Tex.: Latin American Network Information Center. http://lanic.utexas.edu/.

AP63

Excellent directory of online resources from and about Latin America. Arranged both by country and by topic, provides links to resources on the economy, education, culture, arts, libraries, social sciences, environment, etc. The Media and Communications subsection of the site includes listings of academic journals and magazines, many of them electronic. Hosts a variety of digital projects, such as the Government Documents Archive, the Open Archives Portal to Latin American gray literature in the social sciences, and LAPTOC (Latin American Periodicals Tables of Contents) (Austin, Tex.: Latin American Network Information Center), which provides a searchable database to the tables of contents of more than 800 periodicals.

**930    Latin American market planning report.** Strategy Research Corporation. ill. Miami: Strategy Research, 1996–. ISSN: 1083-6950.

380.1098021                                           HC130.C6.L38

Consumer information for 18 countries, Puerto Rico, and 70 metropolitan markets. The latest published is 2003, but still contains valuable information. Organized into topics: business environment, population and demography, buying power, consumer profile, country profiles, and summary tables.

**931    Nationmaster.com.** 2003–. NationMaster.com. http://www.nationmaster.com/index.php.

HA154

Uses data from government and international organizations to present comparative statistics between nations. Some of the topics covered include economy, education, health issues, immigration, industry, labor, taxation, and transportation. Data is displayed in easy-to-read graphs. The source of the data is also cited. This is a companion to StateMaster.com (Brooklyn, N.Y.: StateMaster.com, 2006–).

932 **Oxford Latin American economic history database.** Pablo
Astorga, Ame Berges, E. V. K. Fitzgerald, University of Oxford. 2002.
[Oxford]: Oxford University. http://www2.qeh.ox.ac.uk/oxlad/.
HC125
Funded by the Inter-American Development Bank, with statisti-
cal series for economic and social indicators for 20 countries from
1900–2000. Includes Population and Demographics; Labour Force;
Industry; Transport and Communications Infrastructure; Exter-
nal Trade; Finance; National Accounts; Nominal Exchange Rate;
Consumer and Producer Price Indices; and Commodity Price Indices and
Weighted Commodity Price Indices.

933 *Political risk yearbook online.* PRS Group. 1999–. East Syracuse,
N.Y.: PRS Group. https://www.prsgroup.com/prsgroup_
shoppingcart/pc-48-7-political-risk-yearbook.aspx.
Political and economic risk analysis for 106 countries. Reports are PDF
files with a country forecast (highlights, current data, comments and
analysis, forecast scenarios, political players), and country conditions
(investment climate, climate for trade including political violence and
legal framework, background on geography, history, social conditions,
government, political conditions, and environmental trends). Includes
forecasts for GDP growth, current account, inflation, political turmoil,
investment and trade restrictions, and domesic and international economic problems. Also has statistics for foreign direct investment flows by
source country and sector.

934 **SourceOECD.** Organisation for Economic Co-operation and
Development. [Paris, France]: OECD. http://new.sourceoecd.org/.
A subscription database containing OECD books, reports, working papers,
serials, and statistical databases on economic and social topics, as well as the
environment, energy, and technological development. Focuses mainly on
the 30 OECD member states and major nonmember developing countries.
Serials include journals; the OECD Factbook (Paris: OECD, 2005–)
and other statistical works; and titles that forecast and analyze trends,
such as the OECD Economic Outlook (Paris: Organisation for Economic
Co-operation and Development, 1967–), *African economic outlook* (Paris:
African Development Bank, Development Centre of the Organisation
for Economic Co-operation and Development, 2002–), International
Migration Outlook (Paris: Organisation for Economic Co-operation and

Development, 2006–), and OECD-FAO Agricultural Outlook (Paris: Organisation for Economic Co-operation and Development; Food and Agriculture Organization, 2005–).

Current, themed databases include the OECD Economic Outlook Database (Paris: Organisation for Economic Co-operation and Development, 2002–), SourceOECD Main Economic Indicators (Paris: Organisation for Economic Co-operation and Development, 2002–), Banking Statistics, Education Statistics, Globalisation, Indicators of Industry and Services, Insurance, International Development, International Direct Investment Statistics, International Migration Statistics, the ITCS International Trade by Commodity Database, Monthly Statistics of International Trade, the National Accounts Database, OECD Health Data, OECD Statistics on International Trade in Services, the Revenue Statistics of OECD Member Countries Database, the Science and Technology Database, the Social Expenditure Database, Structural and Demographic Business Statistics, Taxing Wages Statistics, and the Telecommunications Database. Statistical databases of the International Energy Agency are also available via this source. OECD.Stat enables users to query multiple databases simultaneously and to export search results in several formats.

Also incorporates Future Trends, an index of published and unpublished sources in more than a dozen languages covering issues affecting the public and private sectors. Glossary.

**935   Statistical sites on the World Wide Web.** U.S. Bureau of Labor Statistics. Washington: U.S. Bureau of Labor Statistics. http://www.bls.gov/bls/other.htm.

Links to official government statistical offices all over the world, including more than 130 countries and some international agencies. Also links to sites of nearly 70 U.S. federal statistical agencies. Excellent starting point for researchers.

**936   Statistical yearbook: Annuaire statistique.** United Nations. 37 v. New York: United Nations. ISSN: 0082-8459.

310.5                                                                HA12.5.U63

A summary of international statistics to continue the *Statistical yearbook of the League of Nations.* Covers population, agriculture, mining, manufacturing, finance, trade, social statistics, education, etc., of the various countries of the world, the tables usually covering a number of years. References are given to sources. A world summary was introduced beginning with v. 15 (1963), summarizing tables appearing in various chapters. The *Monthly bulletin of statistics online* (New York: U.N. Statistical Div., Dept. of Economic and Social Development, 1992–) complements this resource by providing current information.

**937** **STAT-USA Internet.** STAT-USA. [1994–.] [Washington, D.C.?]: STAT-USA, U.S. Dept. of Commerce. http://www.stat-usa.gov/.
382                                                                      HF1379

Business and economic information compiled mainly from federal agencies. There are two main sections, "State of the Nation" and "Globus & NTDB."

"State of the Nation" concentrates on current U.S. information, with 2,500 files on general economic indicators (consumer price index, producer price index, gross domestic product, national income and product accounts), regional economic statistics (by NAICS sector, state personal income, metropolitan personal income) housing and construction (housing starts and building permits, new construction, new home sales), employment (employment cost index, local area employment and unemployment, weekly unemployment claims report), manufacturing and industry (retail sales, manufacturing inventories and sales, industrial production and capacity utilization, current industry reports), monetary statistics (interest rates, foreign exchange rates, bank credit), and economic policy (Beige Book, Treasury Statements).

"Globus & NTDB" is useful for current exchange rates (weekly, monthly, and annual), current and historical trade leads (United Nations trade leads, Defense Logistics Agency leads, FedBizOpps, commercial trade leads), international trade (Asia Development Bank, World Bank, Inter-American Development Bank, and European Bank Business Opportunities, country reports on terrorism, Country Studies Program reports, *International trade update newsletter, National trade estimates report on foreign trade barriers, World bank commodity price data*—"PinkSheets"—and *World factbook*), market and country research (*Country background notes, Country commercial guides, Industry sector analysis reports,* Global Agriculture Information Network [GAIN], *AgWorld attaché reports, International market insight (IMI) reports,* and Multilateral Development Bank), contacts (*NTDB global trade directory, National export directory,* Foreign Trade Offices), and current press releases (U.S. international trade in goods and services, FT900 supplemental tables, U.S. Export Sales—USDA, U.S. import and export price indexes, U.S. international transactions, and additional press releases).

**938**    **United Nations common database (UNCDB).** United Nations
Statistic Division. New York: United Nations Statistic Division.
http://unstats.un.org/unsd/cdb/cdb_help/cdb_quick_start.asp.
Provides socioeconomic data from 55 sources on 274 countries and areas,
with coverage from 1948–2050. Allows comparison of data from 10 countries at a time, and data can be downloaded to Excel. Formerly a fee-based
database but now free.

Covers 31 topics: agriculture, forestry, and fishing; communication
and culture; construction; development assistance; economically active/
not economically active population; education and learning; energy; environment; financial statistics; health, health services, impairment, disabilities, nutrition; households and families, marital status, fertility; human
settlements, housing, geographical distribution of population; income,
consumption and wealth; industrial production; international finance;
international tourism; international trade; millennium development goals
(MDG); mining and quarrying; national accounts; population composition and change; prices; public order and safety; science and technology, intellectual property; services industries; social security and welfare
services; socioeconomic groups and social mobility; statistical yearbook;
transport; and women and men.

**939**    **VIBES.** Jeanie M. Welch, J. Murrey Atkins Library (University of
North Carolina at Charlotte). [199?–.] Charlotte, N.C.: University
of North Carolina at Charlotte, J. Murrey Atkins Library. http://
library.uncc.edu/vibes/.
025.04; 382; 330; 650

Links to over 3,000 free Internet sources with international business
and economic information in English. Organized into three categories:
comprehensive, regional, and national. Coverage includes agricultural
and forest products; banking and finance (includes insurance); business
news, business practices and company information (includes labor);
country information; emerging markets; foreign exchange rates; foreign
stock markets; international electronic commerce; international statistics
(general and economic); international tourism; international trade law;
marketing and advertising; patents (includes other intellectual property);
petroleum, energy, mining, and construction; portals (web meta pages
with several international links); taxation in foreign countries (includes
social security); trade issues and statistics; and business and economics for
Africa, Asia-Pacific, Eastern Europe, Western Europe, Latin America and
the Caribbean, Middle East, and NAFTA (U.S., Canada, and Mexico).

# Europe

**940   Consumer Eastern Europe.** Euromonitor PLC. London: Euromonitor PLC, 1992–. ISSN: 0967-3601.

HC244.Z9C6138

Market-size time series for last five years and forecasted time series for upcoming five years for over 330 consumer markets, as well as economic, demographic, lifestyle, and purchasing data and analysis. Also lists manufacturer and brand shares for major consumer goods sectors. Covers Bulgaria, Czech Republic, Hungary, Poland, Romania, Russia, Slovakia, and the Ukraine, with an overview and information on political structure, main industries, and the economy.

**941   Consumer Europe.** London: Euromonitor Publications Limited, 1976–2004/2005. ISSN: 0308-4353.

381.094                           HD7022.C68

Market-size time series for last five years and forecasted time series for upcoming five years for over 330 consumer markets, as well as economic, demographic, lifestyle, and purchasing data and analysis. Also lists manufacturer and brand shares for major consumer goods sectors. Covers Austria, Belgium, Denmark, Finland, France, Germany, Greece, Ireland, Italy, Netherlands, Norway, Portugal, Spain, Sweden, Switzerland, Turkey, and the United Kingdom.

**942   Country briefings.** Economist.com. [199?–.] London: Economist Newspaper. http://www.economist.com/countries/.

909.83                            HC59.15

News from *The economist* (151) print edition, country profiles, forecasts, statistics, political outlook, economic policy outlook, economic forecast, and economic structure for 60 countries. Ten key economic statistics can be downloaded into Excel (GDP per head, GDP, government consumption, budget balance, consumer prices, public debt, labour costs per hour, recorded unemployment, current-account balance, and foreign-exchange reserves). Links to some subscription-based materials and free external related websites, such as governmental and news websites.

**943   EIU.com.** Economist Intelligence Unit (Great Britain). 2005–. [London?]: Economist Intelligence Unit. http://www.eiu.com/.

Covers political, economic, and business information for 201 countries. Access to Economist Intelligence Unit publications: *Country finance, Country commerce, Country monitor, Business Africa, Business Asia, Business China, Business Eastern Europe, Business Europe, Business India intelligence, Business Latin America,* and *Business Middle East.* Country reports similar to Political Risk Yearbook (192), but with more frequent updates. Key data include GDP, forecast GDP, exports, imports, inflation, exchange rates, interest rates, consumer and producer prices, deposit rate, lending rate, money market rate, select commodity prices, and select industry data. Many numbers can be downloaded into Excel. Archives available from 1992.

**944  EIU country data.** Bureau van Dijk Electronic Publishing. 2002–. [s.l.]: Bureau van Dijk. http://countrydata.bvdep.com/ip/.

HB3730

Annual, quarterly, and monthly economic indicators and forecasts. 278 series from 1980 to the present for 117 countries and 40 regional aggregates (e.g., ASEAN, Australasia, Balkans, Economies in Transition, Sub-Saharan Africa, Oil Exporters, Central America). Series have seven general categories: gross domestic product, fiscal and monetary indicators, demographics and income, foreign payments, external debt stock, external debt service, and external trade. Key forecast series include real GDP growth, GDP per head, consumer price inflation, exchange rate and current-account balance/GDP, with forecasts to 2030.

**945  Europa world plus.** Europa Publications Limited, Routledge, Taylor & Francis Group. 2003–. New York: Routledge; Taylor & Francis Group. http://www.europaworld.com/pub/about/.

D443.E87

Economic and political information for more than 250 countries and territories. Includes *Europa world year book* (145) and the *Europa regional surveys of the world* series:

- *Africa south of the Sahara* (London; New York: Routledge, 1971–)
- *Central and south-eastern Europe* (London: Europa Publications, 2000–)
- *Eastern Europe, Russia and Central Asia* (London; New York: Routledge, 2000–)
- *The Far East and Australasia* (London: Europa, 1969–)
- *The Middle East and North Africa* (991)

- *South America, Central America and the Caribbean* (London: Europa, 1985–)
- *South Asia* (London; New York: Routledge, 2003–)
- *The USA and Canada* (London; New York: Routledge, 1989–)
- *Western Europe* (London; New York: Routledge, 1988–)

Country entries include country profile, geography, chronology, history, economy, country statistics, government and politics directory, society and media directory, business and commerce directory, and bibliography.

Unique to the online version is the comparative statistics section, which generates five years of multinational statistics on area and population, agriculture, industry, finance, external trade, and education in tables and charts downloaded as an HTML table, comma-separated values and in tab-separated values. The comparative statistics section uses different sources than the country statistics section, making data comparisons possible.

946　**European marketing data and statistics.** European Research
　　　Consultants. London: European Research Consultants, 1962–.
　　　ISSN: 0071-2930.
338.094　　　　　　　　　　　　　　　　　　　　　　　　　HA1107.E87

Demographic trends and forecasts, and economic statistics for 44 European countries. Includes 24 years of data on advertising, cultural indicators, consumer market sizes and expenditures, labor force, foreign trade, health, energy, environment, IT and telecommunications, literacy and education, crime, retailing, travel and tourism, and consumer prices. Sources include the International Monetary Fund, United Nations, national statistical offices, and national trade associations. Companion volume to *International marketing data and statistics* (187).

947　**Eurostat yearbook.** Statistical Office of the European
　　　Communities. ill. Luxembourg, [Belgium]: Office for Official
　　　Publications of the European Communities, 1995–. ISSN: 1681-
　　　4789.
314.05　　　　　　　　　　　　　　　　　　　　　　　　　HA1107.E89

Economic, social, business, and environmental data for the European Union and its Member States, as well as major trade partners. In seven chapters: Statisticians for Europe; People in Europe; The economy (national accounts, prices and wages, balance of payments, international trade in goods); The environment; Science and technology; Sectors and enterprises (business structures at a glance, industry and construction, distributive trade, financial markets, transport, tourism, energy); and Agriculture, forestry, and fisheries. Appendixes include a glossary, geonomenclature, classification of economic activities, classification of commodities, and a list of abbreviations and acronyms. The most recent edition is available online (http://epp.eurostat.ec.europa.eu/).

**948**  **Foreign government resources on the web.** University of Michigan. [Ann Arbor, Mich.]: Documents Center, University of Michigan Library. http://www.lib.umich.edu/govdocs/foreign.html.
ZA5050

Websites of foreign governments arranged by region, then by country. For each country, links to main home page and websites of major agencies. Also contains links to sites compiling background information, embassy listings, constitutions and other legal material, news, and statistics, either for countries worldwide or in a particular region.

**949**  **Global development finance.** World Bank. 2 v. Washington: World Bank, 1997–. ISSN: 1020-5454.
336.3435091724                                                   HJ8899.W672

External debt and financial flow data for 136 countries. Vol. 1 is *Analysis and outlook*, with financial flows to developing countries. Vol. 2 is *Summary and country tables* and includes summary data for regions and income groups. Indicators include external debt stocks and flows, major economic aggregates, key debt ratios, average terms of new commitments, and currency composition of long-term debt. Also available online and on CD-ROM, with data from 1970.

**950**  **The index of economic freedom.** Heritage Foundation. maps. Washington: The Heritage Foundation, 1995–. ISSN: 1095-7308.
338.9005                                                          HB95.I48

Uses 50 independent variables to rank 161 countries, including Hong Kong, on the level of government involvement in the economy. The more that a government is involved in constraint in the production, distribution, or consumption of goods and services, the less freedom the editors believe is present. In addition to the score, 2-page long country profiles discuss trade policy, fiscal burden, government intervention, monetary policy, foreign investment, banking and finance, wages and prices, property rights, regulation, and informal market. The 2007 ed. adds a chapter on regions. The current version is available for free at http://www.heritage.org/research/.

**951    Inter-university consortium for political and social research.** University of Michigan. [1997–.] Ann Arbor, Mich.: Institute for Social Research, University of Michigan. http://www.icpsr.umich.edu/.

Archive of international social science data, with a large collection of economic data. Thematic collections are Census Enumerations; Community and Urban Studies; Conflict, Aggression, Violence, Wars; Economic Behavior and Attitudes; Education; Elites and Leadership; Geography and Environment; Government Structures, Policies, and Capabilities; Health Care and Facilities; Instructional Packages; International Systems; Legal Systems; Legislative and Deliberative Bodies; Mass Political Behavior and Attitudes; Organizational Behavior; Social Indicators; Social Institutions and Behavior; Publication-Related Archive; and External Data Resources. Data, which can be downloaded for SAS, SPSS, and STATA, are available to the 500 member institutions, but some is also available to the public.

**952    NationMaster.com.** 2003–. NationMaster.com. http://www.nationmaster.com/index.php.

HA154

Uses data from government and international organizations to present comparative statistics between nations. Some of the topics covered include economy, education, health issues, immigration, industry, labor, taxation, and transportation. Data is displayed in easy-to-read graphs. The source of the data is also cited. This is a companion to StateMaster.com (Brooklyn, N.Y.: StateMaster.com, 2006–).

**953    Nordic statistical yearbook = Nordisk statistisk årsbok.** Nordic Council of Ministers. ill. Copenhagen, [Denmark]: Nordic Council of Ministers, 1997–. ISSN: 1398-0017.

HA1461.N67

Provides comprehensive statistics of various aspects of life in the five Nordic countries, i.e., Denmark, Finland, Iceland, Norway, and Sweden, as well as independent Greenland, Faroe Islands, and the Åland Islands. Chapters cover area, climate, population, labor, industry, trade, and finance. Published in English and Swedish.

954    **Political risk yearbook online.** PRS Group. 1999–. East Syracuse,
       N.Y.: PRS Group. https://www.prsgroup.com/prsgroup_
       shoppingcart/pc-48-7-political-risk-yearbook.aspx.

Political and economic risk analysis for 106 countries. Reports are PDF
files with a country forecast (highlights, current data, comments and
analysis, forecast scenarios, political players), and country conditions
(investment climate, climate for trade including political violence and
legal framework, background on geography, history, social conditions,
government, political conditions, and environmental trends). Includes
forecasts for GDP growth, current account, inflation, political turmoil,
investment and trade restrictions, and domesic and international economic problems. Also has statistics for foreign direct investment flows by
source country and sector.

955    **Russia and Eurasia facts and figures annual.** Gulf Breeze, Fla.:
       Academic International Press, 1998–. ISSN: 1074–1658.

Covers individual countries from the former USSR with tables on key
areas of public finances, trade, economy, health, energy, industry, etc.
Major sections are preceded by overview of key personnel and events.
Continues the series *USSR facts and figures* (Gulf Breeze, Fla.: Academic
International Press, v. 1–17, 1977–92).

956    **SourceOECD.** Organisation for Economic Co-operation and
       Development. [Paris, France]: OECD. http://new.sourceoecd.org/.

A subscription database containing OECD books, reports, working papers,
serials, and statistical databases on economic and social topics, as well as
the environment, energy, and technological development. Focuses mainly
on the 30 OECD member states and major nonmember developing
countries.

   Serials include journals; the OECD Factbook (Paris: OECD, 2005–)
and other statistical works; and titles that forecast and analyze trends,
such as the OECD Economic Outlook (Paris: Organisation for Economic
Co-operation and Development, 1967–), *African economic outlook* (Paris:
African Development Bank, Development Centre of the Organisation
for Economic Co-operation and Development, 2002–), International
Migration Outlook (Paris: Organisation for Economic Co-operation and
Development, 2006–), and OECD-FAO Agricultural Outlook (Paris:
Organisation for Economic Co-operation and Development; Food and
Agriculture Organization, 2005–).

Current, themed databases include the OECD Economic Outlook Database (Paris: Organisation for Economic Co-operation and Development, 2002–), SourceOECD Main Economic Indicators (Paris: Organisation for Economic Co-operation and Development, 2002–), Banking Statistics, Education Statistics, Globalisation, Indicators of Industry and Services, Insurance, International Development, International Direct Investment Statistics, International Migration Statistics, the ITCS International Trade by Commodity Database, Monthly Statistics of International Trade, the National Accounts Database, OECD Health Data, OECD Statistics on International Trade in Services, the Revenue Statistics of OECD Member Countries Database, the Science and Technology Database, the Social Expenditure Database, Structural and Demographic Business Statistics, Taxing Wages Statistics, and the Telecommunications Database. Statistical databases of the International Energy Agency are also available via this source. OECD.Stat enables users to query multiple databases simultaneously and to export search results in several formats.

Also incorporates Future Trends, an index of published and unpublished sources in more than a dozen languages covering issues affecting the public and private sectors. Glossary.

**957**   **Statistical sites on the World Wide Web.** U.S. Bureau of Labor Statistics. Washington: U.S. Bureau of Labor Statistics. http://www. bls.gov/bls/other.htm.

Links to official government statistical offices all over the world, including more than 130 countries and some international agencies. Also links to sites of nearly 70 U.S. federal statistical agencies. Excellent starting point for researchers.

**958**   **Statistical yearbook: Annuaire statistique.** United Nations. 37 v. New York: United Nations. ISSN: 0082-8459.

310.5                                                                                          HA12.5.U63

A summary of international statistics to continue the *Statistical yearbook of the League of Nations.* Covers population, agriculture, mining, manufacturing, finance, trade, social statistics, education, etc., of the various countries of the world, the tables usually covering a number of years. References are given to sources. A world summary was introduced beginning with v. 15 (1963), summarizing tables appearing in various chapters. The *Monthly bulletin of statistics online* (New York: U.N. Statistical Div., Dept. of Economic and Social Development, 1992–) complements this resource by providing current information.

**959** **STAT-USA Internet.** STAT-USA. [1994–.] [Washington, D.C.?]: STAT-USA, U.S. Dept. of Commerce. http://www.stat-usa.gov/.

382     HF1379

Business and economic information compiled mainly from federal agencies. There are two main sections, "State of the Nation" and "Globus & NTDB."

"State of the Nation" concentrates on current U.S. information, with 2,500 files on general economic indicators (consumer price index, producer price index, gross domestic product, national income and product accounts), regional economic statistics (by NAICS sector, state personal income, metropolitan personal income) housing and construction (housing starts and building permits, new construction, new home sales), employment (employment cost index, local area employment and unemployment, weekly unemployment claims report), manufacturing and industry (retail sales, manufacturing inventories and sales, industrial production and capacity utilization, current industry reports), monetary statistics (interest rates, foreign exchange rates, bank credit), and economic policy (Beige Book, Treasury Statements).

"Globus & NTDB" is useful for current exchange rates (weekly, monthly, and annual), current and historical trade leads (United Nations trade leads, Defense Logistics Agency leads, FedBizOpps, commercial trade leads), international trade (Asia Development Bank, World Bank, Inter-American Development Bank, and European Bank Business Opportunities, country reports on terrorism, Country Studies Program reports, *International trade update newsletter, National trade estimates report on foreign trade barriers, World bank commodity price data*—"PinkSheets"—and *World factbook*), market and country research (*Country background notes, Country commercial guides, Industry sector analysis reports,* Global Agriculture Information Network [GAIN], *AgWorld attaché reports, International market insight (IMI) reports,* and Multilateral Development Bank), contacts (*NTDB global trade directory, National export directory,* Foreign Trade Offices), and current press releases (U.S. international trade in goods and services, FT900 supplemental tables, U.S. Export Sales—USDA, U.S. import and export price indexes, U.S. international transactions, and additional press releases).

**960**   **United Nations common database (UNCDB).** United Nations Statistic Division. New York: United Nations Statistic Division. http://unstats.un.org/unsd/cdb/cdb_help/cdb_quick_start.asp.

Provides socioeconomic data from 55 sources on 274 countries and areas, with coverage from 1948–2050. Allows comparison of data from 10 countries at a time, and data can be downloaded to Excel. Formerly a fee-based database but now free.

Covers 31 topics: agriculture, forestry, and fishing; communication and culture; construction; development assistance; economically active/not economically active population; education and learning; energy; environment; financial statistics; health, health services, impairment, disabilities, nutrition; households and families, marital status, fertility; human settlements, housing, geographical distribution of population; income, consumption and wealth; industrial production; international finance; international tourism; international trade; millennium development goals (MDG); mining and quarrying; national accounts; population composition and change; prices; public order and safety; science and technology, intellectual property; services industries; social security and welfare services; socioeconomic groups and social mobility; statistical yearbook; transport; and women and men.

**961 VIBES.** Jeanie M. Welch, J. Murrey Atkins Library (University of North Carolina at Charlotte). [199?–.] Charlotte, N.C.: University of North Carolina at Charlotte, J. Murrey Atkins Library. http://library.uncc.edu/vibes/.

025.04; 382; 330; 650

Links to over 3,000 free Internet sources with international business and economic information in English. Organized into three categories: comprehensive, regional, and national. Coverage includes agricultural and forest products; banking and finance (includes insurance); business news, business practices and company information (includes labor); country information; emerging markets; foreign exchange rates; foreign stock markets; international electronic commerce; international statistics (general and economic); international tourism; international trade law; marketing and advertising; patents (includes other intellectual property); petroleum, energy, mining, and construction; portals (web meta pages with several international links); taxation in foreign countries (includes social security); trade issues and statistics; and business and economics for Africa, Asia-Pacific, Eastern Europe, Western Europe, Latin America and the Caribbean, Middle East, and NAFTA (U.S., Canada, and Mexico).

# Great Britain

**962** **British historical statistics.** B. R. Mitchell. xi, 886 p. Cambridge, [Cambridgeshire]; New York: Cambridge University Press, 1988. ISBN: 0521330084.

314.1                                                      HA1134.M58

A cumulation and expansion of Mitchell's *Abstract of British historical statistics* and Mitchell and H. G. Jones's *Second abstract of British historical statistics.* Emphasizes social and economic history, including population and vital statistics, transportation and communications, public finance, and financial institutions. Each of the 16 chapters contains information on sources and coverage. Includes some of the earliest available data; most tables cover to about 1980.

**963** **Country briefings.** Economist.com. [199?–.] London: Economist Newspaper. http://www.economist.com/countries/.

909.83                                                      HC59.15

News from *The economist* (151) print edition, country profiles, forecasts, statistics, political outlook, economic policy outlook, economic forecast, and economic structure for 60 countries. Ten key economic statistics can be downloaded into Excel (GDP per head, GDP, government consumption, budget balance, consumer prices, public debt, labour costs per hour, recorded unemployment, current-account balance, and foreign-exchange reserves). Links to some subscription-based materials and free external related websites, such as governmental and news websites.

**964** **Economic history services.** EH.Net. 2004–. [Oxford, Ohio]: EH.Net. http://eh.net/.

                                                      HC21.E25

Owned by the Economic History Association and intended primarily for economic historians, historians of economics, economists, and historians, EH.net has research abstracts and book reviews, course syllabi, directory of economic historians, Encyclopedia of Economic and Business History, historical economic data sets (such as Global Financial Data, 1880–1913 and historic labor statistics), links to economic history websites, and a section called "How Much Is That?"

"How Much Is That?" gives comparative values of money, including five ways to compare the worth of a U.S. dollar, 1790–2005; the price of gold for 1257–2005; annual Consumer Price Index for the United States for 1774–2005; the purchasing power of the British pound, 1264–2005; annual real and nominal GDP for the United States, 1790–2005; annual real and nominal GDP for the United Kingdom, 1086–2005; interest rate series for the United Kingdom and the United States, 1790–2001; and daily closing values of the Dow Jones Industrial Average (DJIA) from 1896.

**965   EIU.com.** Economist Intelligence Unit (Great Britain). 2005–.
[London?]: Economist Intelligence Unit. http://www.eiu.com/.

Covers political, economic, and business information for 201 countries. Access to Economist Intelligence Unit publications: *Country finance, Country commerce, Country monitor, Business Africa, Business Asia, Business China, Business Eastern Europe, Business Europe, Business India intelligence, Business Latin America,* and *Business Middle East.* Country reports similar to Political Risk Yearbook (192), but with more frequent updates. Key data include GDP, forecast GDP, exports, imports, inflation, exchange rates, interest rates, consumer and producer prices, deposit rate, lending rate, money market rate, select commodity prices, and select industry data. Many numbers can be downloaded into Excel. Archives available from 1992.

**966   EIU country data.** Bureau van Dijk Electronic Publishing. 2002–.
[s.l.]: Bureau van Dijk. http://countrydata.bvdep.com/ip/.

HB3730

Annual, quarterly, and monthly economic indicators and forecasts. 278 series from 1980 to the present for 117 countries and 40 regional aggregates (e.g., ASEAN, Australasia, Balkans, Economies in Transition, Sub-Saharan Africa, Oil Exporters, Central America). Series have seven general categories: gross domestic product, fiscal and monetary indicators, demographics and income, foreign payments, external debt stock, external debt service, and external trade. Key forecast series include real GDP growth, GDP per head, consumer price inflation, exchange rate and current-account balance/GDP, with forecasts to 2030.

**967   Europa world plus.** Europa Publications Limited, Routledge, Taylor & Francis Group. 2003–. New York: Routledge; Taylor & Francis Group. http://www.europaworld.com/pub/about/.

D443.E87

Economic and political information for more than 250 countries and territories. Includes *Europa world year book* (145) and the *Europa regional surveys of the world* series:

- *Africa south of the Sahara* (London; New York: Routledge, 1971–)
- *Central and south-eastern Europe* (London: Europa Publications, 2000–)
- *Eastern Europe, Russia and Central Asia* (London; New York: Routledge, 2000–)
- *The Far East and Australasia* (London: Europa, 1969–)
- *The Middle East and North Africa* (991)
- *South America, Central America and the Caribbean* (London: Europa, 1985–)
- *South Asia* (London; New York: Routledge, 2003–)
- *The USA and Canada* (London; New York: Routledge, 1989–)
- *Western Europe* (London; New York: Routledge, 1988–)

Country entries include country profile, geography, chronology, history, economy, country statistics, government and politics directory, society and media directory, business and commerce directory, and bibliography.

Unique to the online version is the comparative statistics section, which generates five years of multinational statistics on area and population, agriculture, industry, finance, external trade, and education in tables and charts downloaded as an HTML table, comma-separated values and in tab-separated values. The comparative statistics section uses different sources than the country statistics section, making data comparisons possible.

**968**  **Foreign government resources on the web.** University of Michigan. [Ann Arbor, Mich.]: Documents Center, University of Michigan Library. http://www.lib.umich.edu/govdocs/foreign.html.

ZA5050

Websites of foreign governments arranged by region, then by country. For each country, links to main home page and websites of major agencies. Also contains links to sites compiling background information, embassy listings, constitutions and other legal material, news, and statistics, either for countries worldwide or in a particular region.

**969**  **Global development finance.** World Bank. 2 v. Washington: World Bank, 1997–. ISSN: 1020-5454.

336.3435091724                                                    HJ8899.W672

External debt and financial flow data for 136 countries. Vol. 1 is *Analysis and outlook*, with financial flows to developing countries. Vol. 2 is *Summary and country tables* and includes summary data for regions and income groups. Indicators include external debt stocks and flows, major economic aggregates, key debt ratios, average terms of new commitments, and currency composition of long-term debt. Also available online and on CD-ROM, with data from 1970.

**970    The index of economic freedom.** Heritage Foundation. maps. Washington: The Heritage Foundation, 1995–. ISSN: 1095-7308.
338.9005                                                                    HB95.I48

Uses 50 independent variables to rank 161 countries, including Hong Kong, on the level of government involvement in the economy. The more that a government is involved in constraint in the production, distribution, or consumption of goods and services, the less freedom the editors believe is present. In addition to the score, 2-page long country profiles discuss trade policy, fiscal burden, government intervention, monetary policy, foreign investment, banking and finance, wages and prices, property rights, regulation, and informal market. The 2007 ed. adds a chapter on regions. The current version is available for free at http://www.heritage.org/research/.

**971    International historical statistics: Europe, 1750–2000.** 5th ed. B. R. Mitchell. xvii, 960 p. Houndmills, Basingstoke, Hampshire, [England]; New York: Palgrave Macmillan, 2003. ISBN: 0333994116.
314                                                              HA1107.M5; R220.2

A companion to the author's *International historical statistics: The Americas* (904). Official and unofficial statistical sources were used to provided comparative data for European countries. Data for more than two centuries are arranged in ten sections that cover population and vital statistics, labor force, agriculture, industry, external trade, transport, and communications. Recently updated.

**972    Inter-university consortium for political and social research.** University of Michigan. [1997–.] Ann Arbor, Mich.: Institute for Social Research, University of Michigan. http://www.icpsr.umich.edu/.

Archive of international social science data, with a large collection of economic data. Thematic collections are Census Enumerations; Community and Urban Studies; Conflict, Aggression, Violence, Wars; Economic Behavior and Attitudes; Education; Elites and Leadership; Geography and Environment; Government Structures, Policies, and Capabilities; Health Care and Facilities; Instructional Packages; International Systems; Legal Systems; Legislative and Deliberative Bodies; Mass Political Behavior and

Attitudes; Organizational Behavior; Social Indicators; Social Institutions and Behavior; Publication-Related Archive; and External Data Resources. Data, which can be downloaded for SAS, SPSS, and STATA, are available to the 500 member institutions, but some is also available to the public.

**973**   **NationMaster.com.** 2003–. NationMaster.com. http://www. nationmaster.com/index.php.

HA154

Uses data from government and international organizations to present comparative statistics between nations. Some of the topics covered include economy, education, health issues, immigration, industry, labor, taxation, and transportation. Data is displayed in easy-to-read graphs. The source of the data is also cited. This is a companion to StateMaster.com (Brooklyn, N.Y.: StateMaster.com, 2006–).

**974**   **Political risk yearbook online.** PRS Group. 1999–. East Syracuse, N.Y.: PRS Group. https://www.prsgroup.com/prsgroup_ shoppingcart/pc-48-7-political-risk-yearbook.aspx.

Political and economic risk analysis for 106 countries. Reports are PDF files with a country forecast (highlights, current data, comments and analysis, forecast scenarios, political players), and country conditions (investment climate, climate for trade including political violence and legal framework, background on geography, history, social conditions, government, political conditions, and environmental trends). Includes forecasts for GDP growth, current account, inflation, political turmoil, investment and trade restrictions, and domesic and international economic problems. Also has statistics for foreign direct investment flows by source country and sector.

**975**   **SourceOECD.** Organisation for Economic Co-operation and Development. [Paris, France]: OECD. http://new.sourceoecd.org/.

A subscription database containing OECD books, reports, working papers, serials, and statistical databases on economic and social topics, as well as the environment, energy, and technological development. Focuses mainly on the 30 OECD member states and major nonmember developing countries.

Serials include journals; the OECD Factbook (Paris: OECD, 2005–) and other statistical works; and titles that forecast and analyze trends, such as the OECD Economic Outlook (Paris: Organisation for Economic

Co-operation and Development, 1967–), *African economic outlook* (Paris: African Development Bank, Development Centre of the Organisation for Economic Co-operation and Development, 2002–), International Migration Outlook (Paris: Organisation for Economic Co-operation and Development, 2006–), and OECD-FAO Agricultural Outlook (Paris: Organisation for Economic Co-operation and Development; Food and Agriculture Organization, 2005–).

Current, themed databases include the OECD Economic Outlook Database (Paris: Organisation for Economic Co-operation and Development, 2002–), SourceOECD Main Economic Indicators (Paris: Organisation for Economic Co-operation and Development, 2002–), Banking Statistics, Education Statistics, Globalisation, Indicators of Industry and Services, Insurance, International Development, International Direct Investment Statistics, International Migration Statistics, the ITCS International Trade by Commodity Database, Monthly Statistics of International Trade, the National Accounts Database, OECD Health Data, OECD Statistics on International Trade in Services, the Revenue Statistics of OECD Member Countries Database, the Science and Technology Database, the Social Expenditure Database, Structural and Demographic Business Statistics, Taxing Wages Statistics, and the Telecommunications Database. Statistical databases of the International Energy Agency are also available via this source. OECD.Stat enables users to query multiple databases simultaneously and to export search results in several formats.

Also incorporates Future Trends, an index of published and unpublished sources in more than a dozen languages covering issues affecting the public and private sectors. Glossary.

976   **Statistical sites on the World Wide Web.** U.S. Bureau of Labor Statistics. Washington: U.S. Bureau of Labor Statistics. http://www.bls.gov/bls/other.htm.

Links to official government statistical offices all over the world, including more than 130 countries and some international agencies. Also links to sites of nearly 70 U.S. federal statistical agencies. Excellent starting point for researchers.

977   **Statistical yearbook: Annuaire statistique.** United Nations. 37 v. New York: United Nations. ISSN: 0082-8459.

310.5                                                          HA12.5.U63

A summary of international statistics to continue the *Statistical yearbook of the League of Nations.* Covers population, agriculture, mining, manufacturing, finance, trade, social statistics, education, etc., of the various countries of the world, the tables usually covering a number of years. References are given to sources. A world summary was introduced beginning with v. 15 (1963), summarizing tables appearing in various chapters. The *Monthly bulletin of statistics online* (New York: U.N. Statistical Div., Dept. of Economic and Social Development, 1992–) complements this resource by providing current information.

**978    STAT-USA Internet.** STAT-USA. [1994–.] [Washington, D.C.?]: STAT-USA, U.S. Dept. of Commerce. http://www.stat-usa.gov/.
382                                                                        HF1379

Business and economic information compiled mainly from federal agencies. There are two main sections, "State of the Nation" and "Globus & NTDB."

"State of the Nation" concentrates on current U.S. information, with 2,500 files on general economic indicators (consumer price index, producer price index, gross domestic product, national income and product accounts), regional economic statistics (by NAICS sector, state personal income, metropolitan personal income) housing and construction (housing starts and building permits, new construction, new home sales), employment (employment cost index, local area employment and unemployment, weekly unemployment claims report), manufacturing and industry (retail sales, manufacturing inventories and sales, industrial production and capacity utilization, current industry reports), monetary statistics (interest rates, foreign exchange rates, bank credit), and economic policy (Beige Book, Treasury Statements).

"Globus & NTDB" is useful for current exchange rates (weekly, monthly, and annual), current and historical trade leads (United Nations trade leads, Defense Logistics Agency leads, FedBizOpps, commercial trade leads), international trade (Asia Development Bank, World Bank, Inter-American Development Bank, and European Bank Business Opportunities, country reports on terrorism, Country Studies Program reports, *International trade update newsletter, National trade estimates report on foreign trade barriers, World bank commodity price data—"PinkSheets"—and World factbook*), market and country research (*Country background notes, Country commercial guides, Industry sector analysis reports,* Global Agriculture Information Network [GAIN], *AgWorld attaché reports, International market insight (IMI) reports,* and Multilateral Development Bank), contacts (*NTDB global trade directory, National export directory,* Foreign Trade Offices), and current press releases (U.S. international trade in goods and services, FT900 supplemental tables, U.S. Export Sales—USDA,

U.S. import and export price indexes, U.S. international transactions, and additional press releases).

**979    United Nations common database (UNCDB).** United Nations Statistic Division. New York: United Nations Statistic Division. http://unstats.un.org/unsd/cdb/cdb_help/cdb_quick_start.asp. Provides socioeconomic data from 55 sources on 274 countries and areas, with coverage from 1948–2050. Allows comparison of data from 10 countries at a time, and data can be downloaded to Excel. Formerly a fee-based database but now free.

Covers 31 topics: agriculture, forestry, and fishing; communication and culture; construction; development assistance; economically active/ not economically active population; education and learning; energy; environment; financial statistics; health, health services, impairment, disabilities, nutrition; households and families, marital status, fertility; human settlements, housing, geographical distribution of population; income, consumption and wealth; industrial production; international finance; international tourism; international trade; millennium development goals (MDG); mining and quarrying; national accounts; population composition and change; prices; public order and safety; science and technology, intellectual property; services industries; social security and welfare services; socioeconomic groups and social mobility; statistical yearbook; transport; and women and men.

**980    The value of a pound: Prices and incomes in Britain 1900–1993.** Oksana Newman, Allan Foster. xiv, 306 p. New York; London: Gale Research International, 1995. ISBN: 1873477317.

338.5280210941

A similar format to *The value of a dollar*, with statistics on earnings and employment, consumer expenditures, finance and economics, a chronology of events, and historic introduction to provide context. Chapters are arranged by decade, beginning in 1900 and ending in 1993. For an interesting look at life and economic value in 19th-century England, see Daniel Pool's *What Jane Austen ate and Charles Dickens knew.*

## Middle East

**981    The Arab world competitiveness report 2005.** Augusto Lopez-Claros, World Economic Forum. xiv, 352 p. New York: Palgrave MacMillan, 2005. ISBN: 1403948011.

320.9174927

Discussion of the economic issues facing the Arab world, with articles and statistics. Pt. 1 contains articles on reform, competitiveness, labor markets, politics, economic freedom, and women in the Arab world. Pt. 2 contains country profiles for Algeria, Bahrain, Egypt, Jordan, Kuwait, Lebanon, Libya, Libyan Arab Jamahiriya, Morocco, Oman, Qatar, Saudi Arabia, Syria, Syrian Arab Republic, Tunisia, United Arab Emirates, and Yemen. Profiles include key economic indicators, human development indicators, infrastructure and technology diffusion indicators, economic trends, export profiles, and competitiveness rankings. Pt. 3 contains data tables, compiling data for all the countries, with coverage of the macroeconomic climate, infrastructure and technology diffusion indicators, human resources (education, labor, and health), infrastructure, public institutions, domestic competition, cluster development, environment, and company operations and strategy.

**982  Consumer Middle East.** Euromonitor PLC. London: Euromonitor PLC, 1998–.

658.834C7583                                   HC415.15.Z9C616

Market-size time series for last five years and forecasted time series for upcoming five years for over 330 consumer markets, as well as economic, demographic, lifestyle, and purchasing data and analysis. Also lists manufacturer and brand shares for major consumer goods sectors. Covers Algeria, Egypt, Israel, Jordan, Kuwait, Morocco, Saudi Arabia, Tunisia, Turkey, United Arab Emirates, with information on political structure, main industries, and the economy. Tables rank per capita consumer market sizes by country.

**983  Country briefings.** Economist.com. [199?–.] London: Economist Newspaper. http://www.economist.com/countries/.

909.83                                               HC59.15

News from *The economist* (151) print edition, country profiles, forecasts, statistics, political outlook, economic policy outlook, economic forecast, and economic structure for 60 countries. Ten key economic statistics can be downloaded into Excel (GDP per head, GDP, government consumption, budget balance, consumer prices, public debt, labour costs per hour, recorded unemployment, current-account balance, and foreign-exchange reserves). Links to some subscription-based materials and free external related websites, such as governmental and news websites.

**984  EIU.com.** Economist Intelligence Unit (Great Britain). 2005–. [London?]: Economist Intelligence Unit. http://www.eiu.com/.

Covers political, economic, and business information for 201 countries. Access to Economist Intelligence Unit publications: *Country finance, Country commerce, Country monitor, Business Africa, Business Asia, Business China, Business Eastern Europe, Business Europe, Business India intelligence, Business Latin America,* and *Business Middle East.* Country reports similar to Political Risk Yearbook (192), but with more frequent updates. Key data include GDP, forecast GDP, exports, imports, inflation, exchange rates, interest rates, consumer and producer prices, deposit rate, lending rate, money market rate, select commodity prices, and select industry data. Many numbers can be downloaded into Excel. Archives available from 1992.

**985   EIU country data.** Bureau van Dijk Electronic Publishing. 2002–. [s.l.]: Bureau van Dijk. http://countrydata.bvdep.com/ip/.

HB3730

Annual, quarterly, and monthly economic indicators and forecasts. 278 series from 1980 to the present for 117 countries and 40 regional aggregates (e.g., ASEAN, Australasia, Balkans, Economies in Transition, Sub-Saharan Africa, Oil Exporters, Central America). Series have seven general categories: gross domestic product, fiscal and monetary indicators, demographics and income, foreign payments, external debt stock, external debt service, and external trade. Key forecast series include real GDP growth, GDP per head, consumer price inflation, exchange rate and current-account balance/GDP, with forecasts to 2030.

**986   Europa world plus.** Europa Publications Limited, Routledge, Taylor & Francis Group. 2003–. New York: Routledge; Taylor & Francis Group. http://www.europaworld.com/pub/about/.

D443.E87

Economic and political information for more than 250 countries and territories. Includes *Europa world year book* (145) and the *Europa regional surveys of the world* series:

- *Africa south of the Sahara* (London; New York: Routledge, 1971–)
- *Central and south-eastern Europe* (London: Europa Publications, 2000–)
- *Eastern Europe, Russia and Central Asia* (London; New York: Routledge, 2000–)
- *The Far East and Australasia* (London: Europa, 1969–)
- *The Middle East and North Africa* (991)
- *South America, Central America and the Caribbean* (London: Europa, 1985–)

- *South Asia* (London; New York: Routledge, 2003–)
- *The USA and Canada* (London; New York: Routledge, 1989–)
- *Western Europe* (London; New York: Routledge, 1988–)

Country entries include country profile, geography, chronology, history, economy, country statistics, government and politics directory, society and media directory, business and commerce directory, and bibliography.

Unique to the online version is the comparative statistics section, which generates five years of multinational statistics on area and population, agriculture, industry, finance, external trade, and education in tables and charts downloaded as an HTML table, comma-separated values and in tab-separated values. The comparative statistics section uses different sources than the country statistics section, making data comparisons possible.

**987 Foreign government resources on the web.** University of Michigan. [Ann Arbor, Mich.]: Documents Center, University of Michigan Library. http://www.lib.umich.edu/govdocs/foreign.html.

ZA5050

Websites of foreign governments arranged by region, then by country. For each country, links to main home page and websites of major agencies. Also contains links to sites compiling background information, embassy listings, constitutions and other legal material, news, and statistics, either for countries worldwide or in a particular region.

**988 Global development finance.** World Bank. 2 v. Washington: World Bank, 1997–. ISSN: 1020-5454.

336.3435091724                                                     HJ8899.W672

External debt and financial flow data for 136 countries. Vol. 1 is *Analysis and outlook*, with financial flows to developing countries. Vol. 2 is *Summary and country tables* and includes summary data for regions and income groups. Indicators include external debt stocks and flows, major economic aggregates, key debt ratios, average terms of new commitments, and currency composition of long-term debt. Also available online and on CD-ROM, with data from 1970.

**989 The index of economic freedom.** Heritage Foundation. maps. Washington: The Heritage Foundation, 1995–. ISSN: 1095-7308.

338.9005                                                              HB95.I48

Uses 50 independent variables to rank 161 countries, including Hong Kong, on the level of government involvement in the economy. The more that a government is involved in constraint in the production, distribution, or consumption of goods and services, the less freedom the editors believe is present. In addition to the score, 2-page long country profiles discuss trade policy, fiscal burden, government intervention, monetary policy, foreign investment, banking and finance, wages and prices, property rights, regulation, and informal market. The 2007 ed. adds a chapter on regions. The current version is available for free at http://www.heritage.org/research/.

**990    Inter-university consortium for political and social research.** University of Michigan. [1997–.] Ann Arbor, Mich.: Institute for Social Research, University of Michigan. http://www.icpsr.umich. edu/.

Archive of international social science data, with a large collection of economic data. Thematic collections are Census Enumerations; Community and Urban Studies; Conflict, Aggression, Violence, Wars; Economic Behavior and Attitudes; Education; Elites and Leadership; Geography and Environment; Government Structures, Policies, and Capabilities; Health Care and Facilities; Instructional Packages; International Systems; Legal Systems; Legislative and Deliberative Bodies; Mass Political Behavior and Attitudes; Organizational Behavior; Social Indicators; Social Institutions and Behavior; Publication-Related Archive; and External Data Resources. Data, which can be downloaded for SAS, SPSS, and STATA, are available to the 500 member institutions, but some is also available to the public.

**991    The Middle East and North Africa.** Europa Publications Limited. ill., maps. London: Europa Publications, 1964–. ISSN: 0076-8502.
DS49.M5

Annual. Covers Algeria, Bahrain, Cyprus, Egypt, Iran, Iraq, Israel, Jordan, Kuwait, Lebanon, Libya, Morocco and Western Sahara, Oman, Qatar, Saudi Arabia, Syria, Tunisia, Turkey, United Arab Emirates, and Yemen. Each country includes sections on physical and social geography, recent history, and economy, along with a statistical survey, directory, and bibliography. Many statistics are reproduced from the United Nations, International Monetary Fund, and other organizations. The introductory general survey consists of signed essays on regional history, economic trends, and social and political reforms. Includes organizations and commodities. Bibliography. Index. Also available online at Europa World Plus (144) with additional features and more current content.

**992**   **NationMaster.com.** 2003–. NationMaster.com. http://www. nationmaster.com/index.php.

HA154

Uses data from government and international organizations to present comparative statistics between nations. Some of the topics covered include economy, education, health issues, immigration, industry, labor, taxation, and transportation. Data is displayed in easy-to-read graphs. The source of the data is also cited. This is a companion to StateMaster.com (Brooklyn, N.Y.: StateMaster.com, 2006–).

**993**   **Political risk yearbook online.** PRS Group. 1999–. East Syracuse, N.Y.: PRS Group. https://www.prsgroup.com/prsgroup_ shoppingcart/pc-48-7-political-risk-yearbook.aspx. Political and economic risk analysis for 106 countries. Reports are PDF files with a country forecast (highlights, current data, comments and analysis, forecast scenarios, political players), and country conditions (investment climate, climate for trade including political violence and legal framework, background on geography, history, social conditions, government, political conditions, and environmental trends). Includes forecasts for GDP growth, current account, inflation, political turmoil, investment and trade restrictions, and domesic and international economic problems. Also has statistics for foreign direct investment flows by source country and sector.

**994**   **Statistical sites on the World Wide Web.** U.S. Bureau of Labor Statistics. Washington: U.S. Bureau of Labor Statistics. http://www. bls.gov/bls/other.htm. Links to official government statistical offices all over the world, including more than 130 countries and some international agencies. Also links to sites of nearly 70 U.S. federal statistical agencies. Excellent starting point for researchers.

**995**   **Statistical yearbook: Annuaire statistique.** United Nations. 37 v. New York: United Nations. ISSN: 0082-8459.

310.5                                                                    HA12.5.U63

A summary of international statistics to continue the *Statistical yearbook of the League of Nations.* Covers population, agriculture, mining, manufacturing, finance, trade, social statistics, education, etc., of the various countries of the world, the tables usually covering a number of years.

References are given to sources. A world summary was introduced beginning with v. 15 (1963), summarizing tables appearing in various chapters. The *Monthly bulletin of statistics online* (New York: U.N. Statistical Div., Dept. of Economic and Social Development, 1992–) complements this resource by providing current information.

**996    STAT-USA Internet.** STAT-USA. [1994–.] [Washington, D.C.?]: STAT-USA, U.S. Dept. of Commerce. http://www.stat-usa.gov/.

382    HF1379

Business and economic information compiled mainly from federal agencies. There are two main sections, "State of the Nation" and "Globus & NTDB."

"State of the Nation" concentrates on current U.S. information, with 2,500 files on general economic indicators (consumer price index, producer price index, gross domestic product, national income and product accounts), regional economic statistics (by NAICS sector, state personal income, metropolitan personal income) housing and construction (housing starts and building permits, new construction, new home sales), employment (employment cost index, local area employment and unemployment, weekly unemployment claims report), manufacturing and industry (retail sales, manufacturing inventories and sales, industrial production and capacity utilization, current industry reports), monetary statistics (interest rates, foreign exchange rates, bank credit), and economic policy (Beige Book, Treasury Statements).

"Globus & NTDB" is useful for current exchange rates (weekly, monthly, and annual), current and historical trade leads (United Nations trade leads, Defense Logistics Agency leads, FedBizOpps, commercial trade leads), international trade (Asia Development Bank, World Bank, Inter-American Development Bank, and European Bank Business Opportunities, country reports on terrorism, Country Studies Program reports, *International trade update newsletter, National trade estimates report on foreign trade barriers, World bank commodity price data*—"PinkSheets"—and *World factbook*), market and country research (*Country background notes, Country commercial guides, Industry sector analysis reports,* Global Agriculture Information Network [GAIN], *AgWorld attaché reports, International market insight (IMI) reports,* and Multilateral Development Bank), contacts (*NTDB global trade directory, National export directory,* Foreign Trade Offices), and current press releases (U.S. international trade in goods and services, FT900 supplemental tables, U.S. Export Sales—USDA, U.S. import and export price indexes, U.S. international transactions, and additional press releases).

**997**    **United Nations common database (UNCDB).** United Nations
Statistic Division. New York: United Nations Statistic Division.
http://unstats.un.org/unsd/cdb/cdb_help/cdb_quick_start.asp.
Provides socioeconomic data from 55 sources on 274 countries and areas,
with coverage from 1948–2050. Allows comparison of data from 10 countries at a time, and data can be downloaded to Excel. Formerly a fee-based
database but now free.

Covers 31 topics: agriculture, forestry, and fishing; communication
and culture; construction; development assistance; economically active/
not economically active population; education and learning; energy; environment; financial statistics; health, health services, impairment, disabilities, nutrition; households and families, marital status, fertility; human
settlements, housing, geographical distribution of population; income,
consumption and wealth; industrial production; international finance;
international tourism; international trade; millennium development goals
(MDG); mining and quarrying; national accounts; population composition and change; prices; public order and safety; science and technology, intellectual property; services industries; social security and welfare
services; socioeconomic groups and social mobility; statistical yearbook;
transport; and women and men.

**998**    **VIBES.** Jeanie M. Welch, J. Murrey Atkins Library (University of
North Carolina at Charlotte). [199?–.] Charlotte, N.C.: University
of North Carolina at Charlotte, J. Murrey Atkins Library. http://
library.uncc.edu/vibes/.
025.04; 382; 330; 650

Links to over 3,000 free Internet sources with international business
and economic information in English. Organized into three categories:
comprehensive, regional, and national. Coverage includes agricultural
and forest products; banking and finance (includes insurance); business
news, business practices and company information (includes labor);
country information; emerging markets; foreign exchange rates; foreign
stock markets; international electronic commerce; international statistics
(general and economic); international tourism; international trade law;
marketing and advertising; patents (includes other intellectual property);
petroleum, energy, mining, and construction; portals (web meta pages
with several international links); taxation in foreign countries (includes
social security); trade issues and statistics; and business and economics for
Africa, Asia-Pacific, Eastern Europe, Western Europe, Latin America and
the Caribbean, Middle East, and NAFTA (U.S., Canada, and Mexico).

# Pacific Area

**999   EIU.com.** Economist Intelligence Unit (Great Britain). 2005–. [London?]: Economist Intelligence Unit. http://www.eiu.com/. Covers political, economic, and business information for 201 countries. Access to Economist Intelligence Unit publications: *Country finance, Country commerce, Country monitor, Business Africa, Business Asia, Business China, Business Eastern Europe, Business Europe, Business India intelligence, Business Latin America,* and *Business Middle East.* Country reports similar to Political Risk Yearbook (192), but with more frequent updates. Key data include GDP, forecast GDP, exports, imports, inflation, exchange rates, interest rates, consumer and producer prices, deposit rate, lending rate, money market rate, select commodity prices, and select industry data. Many numbers can be downloaded into Excel. Archives available from 1992.

**1000   EIU country data.** Bureau van Dijk Electronic Publishing. 2002–. [s.l.]: Bureau van Dijk. http://countrydata.bvdep.com/ip/.

HB3730

Annual, quarterly, and monthly economic indicators and forecasts. 278 series from 1980 to the present for 117 countries and 40 regional aggregates (e.g., ASEAN, Australasia, Balkans, Economies in Transition, Sub-Saharan Africa, Oil Exporters, Central America). Series have seven general categories: gross domestic product, fiscal and monetary indicators, demographics and income, foreign payments, external debt stock, external debt service, and external trade. Key forecast series include real GDP growth, GDP per head, consumer price inflation, exchange rate and current-account balance/GDP, with forecasts to 2030.

**1001   Europa world plus.** Europa Publications Limited, Routledge, Taylor & Francis Group. 2003–. New York: Routledge; Taylor & Francis Group. http://www.europaworld.com/pub/about/.

D443.E87

Economic and political information for more than 250 countries and territories. Includes *Europa world year book* (145) and the *Europa regional surveys of the world* series:

- *Africa south of the Sahara* (London; New York: Routledge, 1971–)
- *Central and south-eastern Europe* (London: Europa Publications, 2000–)

- *Eastern Europe, Russia and Central Asia* (London; New York: Routledge, 2000–)
- *The Far East and Australasia* (London: Europa, 1969–)
- *The Middle East and North Africa* (991)
- *South America, Central America and the Caribbean* (London: Europa, 1985–)
- *South Asia* (London; New York: Routledge, 2003–)
- *The USA and Canada* (London; New York: Routledge, 1989–)
- *Western Europe* (London; New York: Routledge, 1988–)

Country entries include country profile, geography, chronology, history, economy, country statistics, government and politics directory, society and media directory, business and commerce directory, and bibliography.

Unique to the online version is the comparative statistics section, which generates five years of multinational statistics on area and population, agriculture, industry, finance, external trade, and education in tables and charts downloaded as an HTML table, comma-separated values and in tab-separated values. The comparative statistics section uses different sources than the country statistics section, making data comparisons possible.

**1002 Foreign government resources on the web.** University of Michigan. [Ann Arbor, Mich.]: Documents Center, University of Michigan Library. http://www.lib.umich.edu/govdocs/foreign.html.

ZA5050

Websites of foreign governments arranged by region, then by country. For each country, links to main home page and websites of major agencies. Also contains links to sites compiling background information, embassy listings, constitutions and other legal material, news, and statistics, either for countries worldwide or in a particular region.

**1003 Global development finance.** World Bank. 2 v. Washington: World Bank, 1997–. ISSN: 1020-5454.

336.3435091724                                      HJ8899.W672

External debt and financial flow data for 136 countries. Vol. 1 is *Analysis and outlook*, with financial flows to developing countries. Vol. 2 is *Summary and country tables* and includes summary data for regions and income groups. Indicators include external debt stocks and flows, major economic aggregates, key debt ratios, average terms of new commitments, and currency composition of long-term debt. Also available online and on CD-ROM, with data from 1970.

1004 **The index of economic freedom.** Heritage Foundation. maps. Washington: The Heritage Foundation, 1995–. ISSN: 1095-7308.
338.9005                                                    HB95.I48

Uses 50 independent variables to rank 161 countries, including Hong Kong, on the level of government involvement in the economy. The more that a government is involved in constraint in the production, distribution, or consumption of goods and services, the less freedom the editors believe is present. In addition to the score, 2-page long country profiles discuss trade policy, fiscal burden, government intervention, monetary policy, foreign investment, banking and finance, wages and prices, property rights, regulation, and informal market. The 2007 ed. adds a chapter on regions. The current version is available for free at http://www.heritage.org/research/.

1005 **International historical statistics: Africa, Asia and Oceania, 1750–2000.** 4th ed. B. R. Mitchell. xix, 1113 p, 29 cm. Houndmills, Basingstokes, Hampshire, [U.K.]; New York: Palgrave Macmillan, 2003. ISBN: 0333994124; 9780333994122.
310                                                        HA4675

Gives key economic and social indicators in this companion to the author's *International historical statistics: The Americas* (904). Official and unofficial statistical sources were used to provide comparative data for the included countries. Data for more than two centuries are arranged in ten sections that cover population and vital statistics, labor force, agriculture, industry, external trade, transport, and communications.

1006 **Inter-university consortium for political and social research.** University of Michigan. [1997–.] Ann Arbor, Mich.: Institute for Social Research, University of Michigan. http://www.icpsr.umich. edu/.

Archive of international social science data, with a large collection of economic data. Thematic collections are Census Enumerations; Community and Urban Studies; Conflict, Aggression, Violence, Wars; Economic Behavior and Attitudes; Education; Elites and Leadership; Geography and Environment; Government Structures, Policies, and Capabilities; Health Care and Facilities; Instructional Packages; International Systems; Legal Systems; Legislative and Deliberative Bodies; Mass Political Behavior and Attitudes; Organizational Behavior; Social Indicators; Social Institutions and Behavior; Publication-Related Archive; and External Data Resources. Data, which can be downloaded for SAS, SPSS, and STATA, are available to the 500 member institutions, but some is also available to the public.

**1007 Key indicators of developing Asian and Pacific countries.**
Economics and Development Resource Center. Manila,
Philippines; Hong Kong, [China]: ADB; Oxford University Press,
1970–. ISSN: 0116-3000.

HC411

Presents economic and financial statistics from 1998–2005 for Asian
and Pacific countries. Each year's publication also has a specific focus
(*Measuring policy effectiveness in health and education, Labor markets
in Asia: Promoting full, productive, and decent employment, Poverty in
Asia: Measurement, estimates, and prospects,* etc.). Categories for data
include: poverty, inequality, and human development; education indicators; environment indicators; health and nutrition indicators; mortality
and reproductive health; population; population by age group; labor
and employment by gender and economic activity; land use; agriculture
production; total and per capita GNI; shares of major sectors in GDP;
expenditure shares in GDP; domestic saving, capital formation, and
resource gap; growth rates of GDP and major sectors; inflation rates;
growth rates of merchandise exports and imports; foreign trade indicators; direction of trade: merchandise exports and imports; government
finance indicators; money supply indicators; foreign direct investment,
net inflows; international reserves indicators; external debt and debt service payments; debt indicators; official flows from all sources to DMC's;
net private flows from all sources to DMC's; and aggregate net resource
flows from all sources to DMC's. Also available online.

**1008 NationMaster.com.** 2003–. NationMaster.com. http://www.
nationmaster.com/index.php.

HA154

Uses data from government and international organizations to present
comparative statistics between nations. Some of the topics covered include
economy, education, health issues, immigration, industry, labor, taxation,
and transportation. Data is displayed in easy-to-read graphs. The source of
the data is also cited. This is a companion to StateMaster.com (Brooklyn,
N.Y.: StateMaster.com, 2006–).

**1009 Political risk yearbook online.** PRS Group. 1999–. East Syracuse,
N.Y.: PRS Group. https://www.prsgroup.com/prsgroup_
shoppingcart/pc-48-7-political-risk-yearbook.aspx.

Political and economic risk analysis for 106 countries. Reports are PDF
files with a country forecast (highlights, current data, comments and

analysis, forecast scenarios, political players), and country conditions (investment climate, climate for trade including political violence and legal framework, background on geography, history, social conditions, government, political conditions, and environmental trends). Includes forecasts for GDP growth, current account, inflation, political turmoil, investment and trade restrictions, and domesic and international economic problems. Also has statistics for foreign direct investment flows by source country and sector.

**1010 Statistical sites on the World Wide Web.** U.S. Bureau of Labor Statistics. Washington: U.S. Bureau of Labor Statistics. http://www. bls.gov/bls/other.htm.

Links to official government statistical offices all over the world, including more than 130 countries and some international agencies. Also links to sites of nearly 70 U.S. federal statistical agencies. Excellent starting point for researchers.

**1011 Statistical yearbook: Annuaire statistique.** United Nations. 37 v. New York: United Nations. ISSN: 0082-8459.

310.5                                                                HA12.5.U63

A summary of international statistics to continue the *Statistical yearbook of the League of Nations.* Covers population, agriculture, mining, manufacturing, finance, trade, social statistics, education, etc., of the various countries of the world, the tables usually covering a number of years. References are given to sources. A world summary was introduced beginning with v. 15 (1963), summarizing tables appearing in various chapters. The *Monthly bulletin of statistics online* (New York: U.N. Statistical Div., Dept. of Economic and Social Development, 1992–) complements this resource by providing current information.

**1012 STAT-USA Internet.** STAT-USA. [1994–.] [Washington, D.C.?]: STAT-USA, U.S. Dept. of Commerce. http://www.stat-usa.gov/.

382                                                                      HF1379

Business and economic information compiled mainly from federal agencies. There are two main sections, "State of the Nation" and "Globus & NTDB."

"State of the Nation" concentrates on current U.S. information, with 2,500 files on general economic indicators (consumer price index, producer price index, gross domestic product, national income and product accounts), regional economic statistics (by NAICS sector, state personal income, metropolitan personal income) housing and construction (housing starts and building permits, new construction, new home sales), employment (employment cost index, local area employment and unemployment, weekly unemployment claims report), manufacturing and industry (retail sales, manufacturing inventories and sales, industrial production and capacity utilization, current industry reports), monetary statistics (interest rates, foreign exchange rates, bank credit), and economic policy (Beige Book, Treasury Statements).

"Globus & NTDB" is useful for current exchange rates (weekly, monthly, and annual), current and historical trade leads (United Nations trade leads, Defense Logistics Agency leads, FedBizOpps, commercial trade leads), international trade (Asia Development Bank, World Bank, Inter-American Development Bank, and European Bank Business Opportunities, country reports on terrorism, Country Studies Program reports, *International trade update newsletter, National trade estimates report on foreign trade barriers, World bank commodity price data*— "PinkSheets"— and *World factbook*), market and country research (*Country background notes, Country commercial guides, Industry sector analysis reports,* Global Agriculture Information Network [GAIN], *AgWorld attaché reports, International market insight (IMI) reports,* and Multilateral Development Bank), contacts (*NTDB global trade directory, National export directory,* Foreign Trade Offices), and current press releases (U.S. international trade in goods and services, FT900 supplemental tables, U.S. Export Sales—USDA, U.S. import and export price indexes, U.S. international transactions, and additional press releases).

**1013  United Nations common database (UNCDB).** United Nations Statistic Division. New York: United Nations Statistic Division. http://unstats.un.org/unsd/cdb/cdb_help/cdb_quick_start.asp.

Provides socioeconomic data from 55 sources on 274 countries and areas, with coverage from 1948–2050. Allows comparison of data from 10 countries at a time, and data can be downloaded to Excel. Formerly a fee-based database but now free.

Covers 31 topics: agriculture, forestry, and fishing; communication and culture; construction; development assistance; economically active/not economically active population; education and learning; energy; environment; financial statistics; health, health services, impairment, disabilities, nutrition; households and families, marital status, fertility; human settlements, housing, geographical distribution of population; income, consumption and wealth; industrial production; international finance;

international tourism; international trade; millennium development goals (MDG); mining and quarrying; national accounts; population composition and change; prices; public order and safety; science and technology, intellectual property; services industries; social security and welfare services; socioeconomic groups and social mobility; statistical yearbook; transport; and women and men.

**1014 VIBES.** Jeanie M. Welch, J. Murrey Atkins Library (University of North Carolina at Charlotte). [199?–.] Charlotte, N.C.: University of North Carolina at Charlotte, J. Murrey Atkins Library. http://library.uncc.edu/vibes/.
025.04; 382; 330; 650

Links to over 3,000 free Internet sources with international business and economic information in English. Organized into three categories: comprehensive, regional, and national. Coverage includes agricultural and forest products; banking and finance (includes insurance); business news, business practices and company information (includes labor); country information; emerging markets; foreign exchange rates; foreign stock markets; international electronic commerce; international statistics (general and economic); international tourism; international trade law; marketing and advertising; patents (includes other intellectual property); petroleum, energy, mining, and construction; portals (web meta pages with several international links); taxation in foreign countries (includes social security); trade issues and statistics; and business and economics for Africa, Asia-Pacific, Eastern Europe, Western Europe, Latin America and the Caribbean, Middle East, and NAFTA (U.S., Canada, and Mexico).

# United States

**1015 Almanac of the 50 states.** Information Publications. Burlington, Vt.: Information Publications, 1985–. ISSN: 0887-0519.
317.3                                                                   HA203.A5

Subtitle: *Basic data profiles with comparative tables.* Place of publication varies. In two parts: 1) statistical and demographic profiles of each of the 50 states, the District of Columbia, and the entire U.S., with tables of vital statistics, health, education, housing, government finance, etc.; 2) tables that rank the same areas according to 54 selected criteria such as population, households, doctors, hospitals, crime rate, etc. Sources of data are cited.

**1016  American factfinder.** U.S. Census Bureau. [1999–.] Washington, D.C.: U.S. Census Bureau. http://factfinder.census.gov/.
317.3                                                                        HA181

U.S. population, housing, economic, and geographic data from the Economic Census, the American Community Survey, the 1990 Census, Census 2000 and the latest Population Estimates. Details range from national, state, county, county subdivision, census tract, block group, place, consolidated city, congressional district, American Indian and Alaska Native areas, metropolitan areas, urbanized area, region, and division. With maps, statistical data, geographic comparison tables, useful for researchers in various areas of business and economics.

Marketers find it useful for demographics; economists enjoy the easy search for Economic Census data, data from the Survey of Business Owners, Business Expenses Survey, Nonemployer Statistics, Annual Survey of Manufacturers, and County Business Patterns.

**1017  Business statistics of the United States.** Cornelia J. Strawser. ill. Lanham, Md.: Bernan Press, 1996–. ISSN: 1086-8488.
338.12                                                                  HC101.A13122

Compiles data from other sources. Part I contains economic data; pt. II, industry profiles; pt. III, historical data. Highlights are more than 150 tables, 30 years of annual data and four years of monthly data, and information by ciy, state, region, and country. A good general source to start with, if the *Statistical abstract of the United States* (678) does not have what is needed. Available as an e-book.

**1018  Consumer USA.** Euromonitor Publications Limited. London: Euromonitor Publications Limited, 1988–. ISSN: 0952-9543.
339.47097305                                                              HC101.C744

Market-size time series for last five years and forecasted time series for upcoming five years for over 330 consumer markets, as well as economic, demographic, lifestyle, and purchasing data and analysis. Also lists manufacturer and brand shares for major consumer goods sectors.

**1019  Country briefings.** Economist.com. [199?–.] London: Economist Newspaper. http://www.economist.com/countries/.
909.83                                                                     HC59.15

News from *The economist* (151) print edition, country profiles, forecasts, statistics, political outlook, economic policy outlook, economic forecast, and economic structure for 60 countries. Ten key economic statistics can be downloaded into Excel (GDP per head, GDP, government consumption, budget balance, consumer prices, public debt, labour costs per hour, recorded unemployment, current-account balance, and foreign-exchange reserves). Links to some subscription-based materials and free external related websites, such as governmental and news websites.

**1020 County and city data book.** U.S. Bureau of the Census, U.S. Census Bureau. ill. Washington: U.S. Dept. of Commerce, Bureau of the Census, 1949–. ISSN: 0082-9455.

317.3                                                                    HA202.A36

A supplement to *Statistical abstract of the United States* (678); continues in part *Cities supplement* and also *County data book.* Presents the latest available census figures for each county, and for the larger cities in the United States. Also has summary figures for states, geographical regions, urbanized areas, standard metropolitan areas, and unincorporated places. The 14th ed., dated 2007, is the latest at this time. Also available online at http://www.census.gov/statab/www/ccdb.html.

**1021 CRSP databases.** Chicago: Center for Research in Security Prices, 1989–.

One of the best sources for current and historical security data for the NYSE (daily from July 1962; monthly from Dec. 1925), AMEX (daily from July 1962; monthly from July 1962), and NASDAQ (daily from July 1972; monthly from Dec. 1972) Stock Markets. Data subsets include: CRSP U.S. Stock Database (NYSE, AMEX, NASD, S&P, annual/quarterly/monthly/daily); CRSP U.S. Government Bond Fixed Term Index Series: monthly and daily; CRSP U.S. Treasury Risk-Free Rates File; and CRSP Fama-Bliss Discount Bond Files for prices and yields. Delivered by DVD or CD-ROM. Also available through Wharton Research Data Services (WRDS).

**1022 Economic history services.** EH.Net. 2004–. [Oxford, Ohio]: EH.Net. http://eh.net/.

HC21.E25

Owned by the Economic History Association and intended primarily for economic historians, historians of economics, economists, and historians, EH.net has research abstracts and book reviews, course syllabi, directory of economic historians, Encyclopedia of Economic and Business History, historical economic data sets (such as Global Financial Data, 1880–1913 and historic labor statistics), links to economic history websites, and a section called "How Much Is That?"

"How Much Is That?" gives comparative values of money, including five ways to compare the worth of a U.S. dollar, 1790–2005; the price of gold for 1257–2005; annual Consumer Price Index for the United States for 1774–2005; the purchasing power of the British pound, 1264–2005; annual real and nominal GDP for the United States, 1790–2005; annual real and nominal GDP for the United Kingdom, 1086–2005; interest rate series for the United Kingdom and the United States, 1790–2001; and daily closing values of the Dow Jones Industrial Average (DJIA) from 1896.

**1023  Economic indicators.** United States Council of Economic Advisers. Washington: United States G.P.O., 1948–. ISSN: 0013-0125.
330.973005                                                    HC101.A186

Basic statistical series on U.S. prices, wages, production, business activity, purchasing power, credit, money and Federal finance, as well as international statistics like industrial production and consumer prices for major industrial countries. Monthly data is online from 1998 to the present at http://purl.access.gpo.gov/GPO/LPS1458/.

**1024  Economic report of the President transmitted to the Congress.** Council of Economic Advisers. ill. Washington: G.P.O., 1950–. ISSN: 0193-1180.
330.973                                                      HC106.5.A272

Review of the nation's economic condition, documented by statistics. Special attention is paid to economic trends, the state of employment and production, real income, and Federal budget outlays. Reports are available online at http://origin.www.gpoaccess.gov/eop/and http://fraser. stlouisfed.org/publications/ERP/ and select statistical data from 1997 to the present are available for download at http://www.gpoaccess.gov/eop/ download.html.

**1025  EIU.com.** Economist Intelligence Unit (Great Britain). 2005–. [London?]: Economist Intelligence Unit. http://www.eiu.com/.

Covers political, economic, and business information for 201 countries. Access to Economist Intelligence Unit publications: *Country finance, Country commerce, Country monitor, Business Africa, Business Asia, Business China, Business Eastern Europe, Business Europe, Business India intelligence, Business Latin America,* and *Business Middle East.* Country reports similar to Political Risk Yearbook (192), but with more frequent updates. Key data include GDP, forecast GDP, exports, imports, inflation, exchange rates, interest rates, consumer and producer prices, deposit rate, lending rate, money market rate, select commodity prices, and select industry data. Many numbers can be downloaded into Excel. Archives available from 1992.

**1026  EIU country data.** Bureau van Dijk Electronic Publishing. 2002–. [s.l.]: Bureau van Dijk. http://countrydata.bvdep.com/ip/.

HB3730

Annual, quarterly, and monthly economic indicators and forecasts. 278 series from 1980 to the present for 117 countries and 40 regional aggregates (e.g., ASEAN, Australasia, Balkans, Economies in Transition, Sub-Saharan Africa, Oil Exporters, Central America). Series have seven general categories: gross domestic product, fiscal and monetary indicators, demographics and income, foreign payments, external debt stock, external debt service, and external trade. Key forecast series include real GDP growth, GDP per head, consumer price inflation, exchange rate and current-account balance/GDP, with forecasts to 2030.

**1027  Europa world plus.** Europa Publications Limited, Routledge, Taylor & Francis Group. 2003–. New York: Routledge; Taylor & Francis Group. http://www.europaworld.com/pub/about/.

D443.E87

Economic and political information for more than 250 countries and territories. Includes *Europa world year book* (145) and the *Europa regional surveys of the world* series:

- *Africa south of the Sahara* (London; New York: Routledge, 1971–)
- *Central and south-eastern Europe* (London: Europa Publications, 2000–)
- *Eastern Europe, Russia and Central Asia* (London; New York: Routledge, 2000–)
- *The Far East and Australasia* (London: Europa, 1969–)
- *The Middle East and North Africa* (991)
- *South America, Central America and the Caribbean* (London: Europa, 1985–)
- *South Asia* (London; New York: Routledge, 2003–)
- *The USA and Canada* (London; New York: Routledge, 1989–)
- *Western Europe* (London; New York: Routledge, 1988–)

Country entries include country profile, geography, chronology, history, economy, country statistics, government and politics directory, society and media directory, business and commerce directory, and bibliography.

Unique to the online version is the comparative statistics section, which generates five years of multinational statistics on area and population, agriculture, industry, finance, external trade, and education in tables and charts downloaded as an HTML table, comma-separated values and in tab-separated values. The comparative statistics section uses different sources than the country statistics section, making data comparisons possible.

**1028 Federal Reserve bulletin.** Board of Governors of the Federal Reserve System. Washington: G.P.O., 1915–. ISSN: 0014-9209.

332.110973                                                     HG2401.A5

The most complete current information, including statistics, on financial conditions in the United States. Includes bank asset quality, bank assets and liabilities, bank structure data, business finance, exchange rates, flow of funds accounts, household finance, industrial activity, interest rates, and money stock and reserve balances. Also reports on financial developments in foreign countries. No longer published quarterly in print. Current *Bulletins* are available at: http://www.federalreserve.gov/pubs/bulletin/default.htm.

**1029 The Federal Reserve System: An encyclopedia.** R. W. Hafer. xxxii, 451 p., ill. Westport, Conn.: Greenwood Press, 2005. ISBN: 0313328390.

332.11097303                                                   HG2563.H235

Contains 250 well-written articles explaining the somewhat mysterious Federal Reserve System, its structure, process, and policies. Entries also cover people and key events related to the Federal Reserve. Appendixes provide the text of The Federal Reserve Act, Federal Reserve Regulations, and a list of the Membership of the Board of Governors: 1913–2004. Available as an e-book.

**1030 FRED.** Federal Reserve Bank of St. Louis. 1997–. St. Louis: Federal Reserve Bank of St. Louis. http://research.stlouisfed.org/fred2/.

330.973                                                        HC106

More than 3,000 U.S. economic time series, organized into topics: banking, business/fiscal, consumer price indexes (Cpis), employment and popula- tion, exchange rates, gross domestic product (GDP) and components, interest rates, monetary aggregates, producer price indexes (Ppis), reserves and monetary base, U.S. trade and international transactions, U.S. financial data, and regional data. Data varies in frequency (daily, weekly, biweekly, monthly, quarterly, annual) and some are seasonally adjusted. Data are from the mid 1990s. For older data, use ALFRED®: ArchivaL Federal Reserve Economic Data (http://alfred.stlouisfed.org/), which covers vintage data in the same areas from 1927.

**1031  Handbook of U.S. labor statistics: Employment, earnings, prices, productivity, and other labor data.** Bernan Press. Lanham, Md.: Bernan Press, 1997–. ISSN: 1526-2553.
331.0973021                                             HD8051.H36

While this data can be found in other Bureau of Labor Statistics sources, this conveniently places the most useful labor statistics in one source. Includes statistics on employment (status, earnings, characteristics, experience, contingent and alternative work arrangements), projections by industry and occupation, productivity and costs, compensation, prices and living conditions, consumer expenditures, safety and health, labor management relations, and foreign labor and prices. Available as an e-book.

**1032  Harmonized tariff schedule of the United States.** U.S. International Trade Commission. [1987–.] Washington, D.C.: International Trade Commission. ISSN: 1066–0925. http://www. usitc.gov/tata/hts/bychapter/index.htm.
343.73056; 347.30356                                   KF6654.599.U55

Approximately 5,000 six- to ten-digit product-based numbers arranged into over 95 chapters. The schedule classifies imported merchandise for rate of duty and for statistical purposes and is used by most countries. Three statistical appendixes are Schedule C, Classification of Country and Territory Designations for U.S. Import Statistics; International Standard Country Codes; and Customs District and Port Codes.

**1033  Historical statistics of the United States.** Richard Sutch, Susan B. Carter. New York: Cambridge University Press. http://hsus. cambridge.org/.

Standard source for American historical data. No uniform end date for tables, but many end in the late 1990s. Examples of tables include population, work, labor, education, health, and government finance. Tables are easily searched and can be downloaded into Excel or CSV formats. Also in print as a 5 v. set.

**1034  The index of economic freedom.** Heritage Foundation. maps. Washington: The Heritage Foundation, 1995–. ISSN: 1095-7308.
338.9005                                                                      HB95.I48

Uses 50 independent variables to rank 161 countries, including Hong Kong, on the level of government involvement in the economy. The more that a government is involved in constraint in the production, distribution, or consumption of goods and services, the less freedom the editors believe is present. In addition to the score, 2-page long country profiles discuss trade policy, fiscal burden, government intervention, monetary policy, foreign investment, banking and finance, wages and prices, property rights, regulation, and informal market. The 2007 ed. adds a chapter on regions. The current version is available for free at http://www.heritage.org/research/.

**1035  International historical statistics: The Americas, 1750–2000.** 5th ed. B. R. Mitchell. xv, 830 p. Houndmills, Basingstoke, Hampshire, [England]; New York: Palgrave Macmillan, 2003. ISBN: 0333994108.
317                                                                      HA175.M55

A companion to the author's *International historical statistics: Europe* (971) and *International historical statistics: Africa and Asia* (862). Presents comparative statistics for 26 North, Central, and South American countries from the early 19th century to the late 20th century for most. Tables are grouped in 11 broad subject areas.

**1036  Inter-university consortium for political and social research.** University of Michigan. [1997–.] Ann Arbor, Mich.: Institute for Social Research, University of Michigan. http://www.icpsr.umich.edu/.

Archive of international social science data, with a large collection of economic data. Thematic collections are Census Enumerations; Community and Urban Studies; Conflict, Aggression, Violence, Wars; Economic Behavior and Attitudes; Education; Elites and Leadership; Geography and Environment; Government Structures, Policies, and Capabilities; Health Care and Facilities; Instructional Packages; International Systems; Legal Systems; Legislative and Deliberative Bodies; Mass Political Behavior and

Attitudes; Organizational Behavior; Social Indicators; Social Institutions and Behavior; Publication-Related Archive; and External Data Resources. Data, which can be downloaded for SAS, SPSS, and STATA, are available to the 500 member institutions, but some is also available to the public.

1037 **National compensation survey.** U.S. Dept. of Labor, Bureau of Labor Statistics. 1998–. Washington, D.C.: Bureau of Labor Statistics. http://www.bls.gov/ncs/home.htm.

HD4976.A735N38

Summarizes wages, earnings, and hours for cities, regions, and the nation. "Wage data are shown by industry, occupational group, full-time and part-time status, union and nonunion status, establishment size, time and incentive status, and job level." —*Summary*. Also includes benefits and the Employment Cost Index, which is released quarterly.

1038 **NationMaster.com.** 2003–. NationMaster.com. http://www.nationmaster.com/index.php.

HA154

Uses data from government and international organizations to present comparative statistics between nations. Some of the topics covered include economy, education, health issues, immigration, industry, labor, taxation, and transportation. Data is displayed in easy-to-read graphs. The source of the data is also cited. This is a companion to StateMaster.com (Brooklyn, N.Y.: StateMaster.com, 2006–).

1039 **Political risk yearbook online.** PRS Group. 1999–. East Syracuse, N.Y.: PRS Group. https://www.prsgroup.com/prsgroup_shoppingcart/pc-48-7-political-risk-yearbook.aspx.

Political and economic risk analysis for 106 countries. Reports are PDF files with a country forecast (highlights, current data, comments and analysis, forecast scenarios, political players), and country conditions (investment climate, climate for trade including political violence and legal framework, background on geography, history, social conditions, government, political conditions, and environmental trends). Includes forecasts for GDP growth, current account, inflation, political turmoil, investment and trade restrictions, and domesic and international economic problems. Also has statistics for foreign direct investment flows by source country and sector.

**1040 Small business economic trends.** NFIB Education Foundation. 1993–. Washington, D.C.: NFIB Education Foundation. http://www.nfib.com/page/sbet/.

Monthly report with economic indicators such as optimism, earnings, sales, prices, employment, compensation, credit conditions, inventories, and capital outlays. Information comes from a survey of members of the National Federation of Independent Business. Online from 10/03/2001.

**1041 The small business economy.** U.S. Government Printing Office. 2004–. Washington, D.C.: U.S. Government Printing Office. ISSN: 1932-3573. http://purl.access.gpo.gov/GPO/LPS1196/.

338.7                                                                     HD2346.U5S78

Annual review, including small business trends, demographics, financing, federal procurement, women in business, regulations, and data. Data includes U.S. Business Counts and Turnover Measures for 1980–2005, Macroeconomic Indicators for 1995–2005, Business Turnover by State, Opening and Closing Establishments for 1992–2005, and Characteristics of Self-Employed Individuals for 1995–2004.

**1042 SourceOECD.** Organisation for Economic Co-operation and Development. [Paris, France]: OECD. http://new.sourceoecd.org/.

A subscription database containing OECD books, reports, working papers, serials, and statistical databases on economic and social topics, as well as the environment, energy, and technological development. Focuses mainly on the 30 OECD member states and major nonmember developing countries.

Serials include journals; the OECD Factbook (Paris: OECD, 2005–) and other statistical works; and titles that forecast and analyze trends, such as the OECD Economic Outlook (Paris: Organisation for Economic Co-operation and Development, 1967–), *African economic outlook* (Paris: African Development Bank, Development Centre of the Organisation for Economic Co-operation and Development, 2002–), International Migration Outlook (Paris: Organisation for Economic Co-operation and Development, 2006–), and OECD-FAO Agricultural Outlook (Paris: Organisation for Economic Co-operation and Development; Food and Agriculture Organization, 2005–).

Current, themed databases include the OECD Economic Outlook Database (Paris: Organisation for Economic Co-operation and

Development, 2002–), SourceOECD Main Economic Indicators (Paris: Organisation for Economic Co-operation and Development, 2002–), Banking Statistics, Education Statistics, Globalisation, Indicators of Industry and Services, Insurance, International Development, International Direct Investment Statistics, International Migration Statistics, the ITCS International Trade by Commodity Database, Monthly Statistics of International Trade, the National Accounts Database, OECD Health Data, OECD Statistics on International Trade in Services, the Revenue Statistics of OECD Member Countries Database, the Science and Technology Database, the Social Expenditure Database, Structural and Demographic Business Statistics, Taxing Wages Statistics, and the Telecommunications Database. Statistical databases of the International Energy Agency are also available via this source. OECD.Stat enables users to query multiple databases simultaneously and to export search results in several formats.

Also incorporates Future Trends, an index of published and unpublished sources in more than a dozen languages covering issues affecting the public and private sectors. Glossary.

**1043 State and local government finances.** U.S. Bureau of the Census. Washington: U.S. Census Bureau. http://www.census.gov/govs/www/estimate.html.

A census of U.S. state and local gov. finances is taken every five years, with an annual survey for the intervening years. The statistics in spreadsheet format cover gov. financial activity in four broad categories of revenue, expenditure, debt, and assets. A print version is also available.

**1044 State and metropolitan area data book.** U.S. Dept. of Commerce, Bureau of the Census. ill. Washington: U.S. Dept. of Commerce, Bureau of the Census, 1980–. ISSN: 0276-6566.

317.3                                                                        HA202.S84

A supplement to *Statistical abstract of the United States* (678).

In three main parts. First part is data for individual states and for the United States as a whole. Statistical items include population and vital statistics, health, education, employment, income, government, social welfare, crime, construction, housing, banking, elections, energy, transportation, natural resources, trade, and services. Second part is similar data for metropolitan areas arranged alphabetically. Third part is data for metropolitan areas ranked by population-size categories. Five appendixes provide information on standard metropolitan statistical areas ranked by population size, effects of population change, estimates of states and congressional districts population and voting age population, etc.

Latest edition is 2006; find the previous 5th ed. of 1997–8 online at http://www.census.gov/statab/www/smadb.html.

**1045  The state of working America.** Economic Policy Institute. ill. Washington: Economic Policy Institute, 1988–. ISSN: 1054-2159. 330.973008623                                                    HD8051.S73

Biennial covering family incomes, wages, taxes, unemployment, wealth, and poverty. Includes data and commentary. Commentary places the numbers in context, as well as explains how the data could be interpreted and used.

**1046  Statistical abstract of the United States.** U.S. Dept. of the Treasury, Bureau of Statistics, U.S. Dept. of Commerce and Labor, Bureau of Statistics, U.S. Bureau of Foreign and Domestic Commerce, U.S. Bureau of the Census, U.S. Census Bureau. ill. Washington: U.S. G.P.O., 1878–. ISSN: 0081-4741.

317.3                                                              HA202

A single-volume work presenting quantitative summary statistics on the political, social, and economic organization of the United States. Statistics given in the tables cover a period of several years. Indispensable in any library: it serves not only as a first source for statistics of national importance but also as a guide to further information, as references are given to the sources of all tables. Includes a table of contents arranged by broad subject areas and a detailed alphabetical index. Also available online from the Census Bureau at http://www.census.gov/compendia/statab/.
Supplement: *County and city data book* (1020).

**1047  Statistical sites on the World Wide Web.** U.S. Bureau of Labor Statistics. Washington: U.S. Bureau of Labor Statistics. http://www.bls.gov/bls/other.htm.

Links to official government statistical offices all over the world, including more than 130 countries and some international agencies. Also links to sites of nearly 70 U.S. federal statistical agencies. Excellent starting point for researchers.

**1048  Success by the numbers: Statistics for business development.** Ryan Womack, Reference and User Services Association. vii, 59 p., ill. Chicago: American Library Association; Reference and User Services Association, 2005. ISBN: 0838983278.

HF54.56.S832

A guide to U.S. statistical resources, with information on how the data is gathered, as well as where to find it. Chapters on: Federal business statistics and the 2002 economic census; Finding Florida statistical resources and data; Demographics and marketing; Economic forecasts; Industry statistics; Financial statistics; Labor, employment, and wages statistics; and Trade statistics. State and national sources are provided and sources are both free and fee-based.

**1049 United Nations common database (UNCDB).** United Nations Statistic Division. New York: United Nations Statistic Division. http://unstats.un.org/unsd/cdb/cdb_help/cdb_quick_start.asp.

Provides socioeconomic data from 55 sources on 274 countries and areas, with coverage from 1948–2050. Allows comparison of data from 10 countries at a time, and data can be downloaded to Excel. Formerly a fee-based database but now free.

Covers 31 topics: agriculture, forestry, and fishing; communication and culture; construction; development assistance; economically active/not economically active population; education and learning; energy; environment; financial statistics; health, health services, impairment, disabilities, nutrition; households and families, marital status, fertility; human settlements, housing, geographical distribution of population; income, consumption and wealth; industrial production; international finance; international tourism; international trade; millennium development goals (MDG); mining and quarrying; national accounts; population composition and change; prices; public order and safety; science and technology, intellectual property; services industries; social security and welfare services; socioeconomic groups and social mobility; statistical yearbook; transport; and women and men.

**1050 United States business history, 1602–1988: A chronology.** Richard Robinson. xii, 643 p. New York: Greenwood Press, 1990. ISBN: 0313260958.

338.0973                                                                 HC103.R595

"Designed to provide a basic calendar of representative events. in the evolution of U.S. business."—*Pref.* Contains descriptive historical data, arranged by year, then under categories of general news and business news. Significant individuals, specific companies, inventions, trade unions, and key business, economic, and social developments are included. Brief bibliography; detailed index. Complemented by *Robinson's business history of the world: A chronology.*

**1051** The value of a dollar: Colonial era to the Civil War, 1600–1865. Scott Derks, Tony Smith. 436 p., ill. Millerton, N.Y.: Grey House, 2005. ISBN: 1592370942.

338.520973                                              HB235.U6D47

Similar to *The value of a dollar, 1860–2004* (1052), each chapter covers a different period of time. Each chapter includes background, historical snapshots, currency, selected incomes, services and fees, financial rates and exchanges, commodities, selected prices, and miscellany. Slave trades are included through chapter four, 1800–1824. Useful for historical research, as well as an interesting glimpse into history.

**1052** The value of a dollar: Prices and incomes in the United States, 1860–2004. 3rd ed. Scott Derks. xvii, 664 p., ill. Millerton, N.Y.: Grey House, 2004. ISBN: 1592370748.

338.520973                                              HB235.U6V35

Illustrates trends in prices. Each chapter covers a different period of time and includes background, historical snapshots, currency, selected incomes, services and fees, financial rates and exchanges, commodities, selected prices, and miscellany. Also has composite consumer price index with the value of an 1860 dollar from 1860–2003. Data is by city, county, or state.

For earlier information, see *The value of a dollar: Colonial era to the Civil War, 1600–1865* (1051).

**1053** VIBES. Jeanie M. Welch, J. Murrey Atkins Library (University of North Carolina at Charlotte). [199?–.] Charlotte, N.C.: University of North Carolina at Charlotte, J. Murrey Atkins Library. http://library.uncc.edu/vibes/.

025.04; 382; 330; 650

Links to over 3,000 free Internet sources with international business and economic information in English. Organized into three categories: comprehensive, regional, and national. Coverage includes agricultural and forest products; banking and finance (includes insurance); business news, business practices and company information (includes labor); country information; emerging markets; foreign exchange rates; foreign stock markets; international electronic commerce; international statistics (general and economic); international tourism; international trade law; marketing and advertising; patents (includes other intellectual property);

petroleum, energy, mining, and construction; portals (web meta pages with several international links); taxation in foreign countries (includes social security); trade issues and statistics; and business and economics for Africa, Asia-Pacific, Eastern Europe, Western Europe, Latin America and the Caribbean, Middle East, and NAFTA (U.S., Canada, and Mexico).

# 8 > SPECIALIZED INDUSTRY INFORMATION

## Agribusiness

### Additional Reference Sources

1054 **Elsevier's dictionary of agriculture, in English, German, French, Russian and Latin.** T. Tosheva, M. Djarova, Boriána Deliĭska. 777, [1] p. New York: Elsevier Science B.V., 2000. ISBN: 0444500057.

630.3                                                        S411.T64

Contains 9,389 terms "commonly used in agriculture science, practice and education" covering "all fields related to agriculture."—*Pref.* The first part lists English terms followed by their German, French, and Russian equivalents. Latin names are also provided for plants, animals, epizootic diseases, and pests. Chemical formulas are given where appropriate. The second section includes separate indexes for the French, German, Russian, and Latin terms, referring back to the first part.

1055 **Encyclopedia of agricultural science.** Charles J. Arntzen, Ellen M. Ritter. 4 v., ill. San Diego, Calif.: Academic Press, 1994. ISBN: 0122266706.

630.3                                                        S411.E713

"Intended for a broad international audience of . . . students, . . . faculty, . . . research scientists, extension specialists and development workers; agricultural producers, . . . as well as advanced high school students and the general reader with a background in science."—*Pref.*

   This four-volume encyclopedia covers plant, animal, forest, soil, and range sciences; entomology; horticulture; natural resources; agricultural engineering; agricultural economics; food and fiber processing and industries; agricultural organizations; and social issues in agriculture. Two hundred ten articles averaging ten pages each are arranged alphabetically. Each article is organized with an outline, glossary, essay, and bibliography. Numerous illustrations, charts, and tables. Index. Appendixes list U.S. colleges and universities granting degrees in agriculture and U.N. organizations concerned with agriculture.

**1056  Technical conversion factors for agricultural commodities.** 2000 Rome: Food and Agricultural Organization of the United Nations. http://www.fao.org/es/ess/tcf.asp. 1st ed., 1960; 2nd draft ed., 1972.

"This latest electronic publication updates two earlier printed versions of the publication produced in 1960 and revised in 1972, by the Statistics Division of FAO. It is an extremely useful and necessary compendium for both statisticians and economists to follow the commodity product sequence (referred to as 'the commodity tree') and allows one the possibility of using the information presented to convert product data from primary equivalent to secondary equivalent and/or vice versa. Also, it is an essential tool in building up supply utilization accounts, food balance sheets and calculating derived agricultural statistics. The document shows, inter alia, data per country for crop seeding rates, waste rates, extraction rates, the average live weight of animals, birth rates, take-off rates, as well as yield per animal for a number of major livestock products."—*Introd.*

The current digital edition is published as a PDF file. Released in 2000, the site description indicates that the content is continuously updated. Searchable by keyword. Also, the information is organized by continent and country, and a clickable world map speeds navigation through the file. Ends with 61 commodity tree graphics that illustrate the commodity product extraction sequence. This digital edition does not include the data collection forms found in the 1972 edition. Also missing are simple conversion factors, such as bushel into kilograms.

Published in English, French, and Spanish. A majority of the country descriptions are written in English, with less frequent French and Spanish descriptions associated with Francophone and Hispanophone nations.

## Definition of the Industry

**1057  IBISWorld United States.** IBISWorld. New York: IBISWorld. http://www.ibisworld.com/.

HC103 .I247

700 reports on the following industries: agriculture, forestry, fishing and hunting; mining; utilities; construction; manufacturing; wholesale trade; retail trade; transportation and warehousing; information; finance and insurance; real estate and rental and leasing; professional, scientific, and technical services; administrative and support and waste management and remediation services; educational services; health care and social assistance; arts, entertainment, and recreation; accommodation and food services; and other services. Setting this database apart are reports on small industries, such as parking lots and garages.

Reports include industry definition; key statistics; segmentations (products and services segmentation, major market segments, industry concentration, geographic spread); market characteristics (market size, demand determinants, domestic and international markets, basis of competition, life cycle); industry conditions (barriers to entry, taxation, industry assistance, regulation and deregulation, cost structure, capital and labor intensity, technology and systems, industry volatility, globalization); key factors (sensitivities and success factors); key competitors; and industry performance (current and historical).

## Internet Resources

1058  **AAEA on-line.** Agricultural Economics Association. 2001–. [Ames, Iowa]: Agricultural Economics Association. http://www.aaea.org/.

An association for those interested in the economics of agriculture, rural communities, and natural resources. The website includes Career Central, Continuing Education Opportunities, the American Agricultural Economics Association Foundation, Information Central (publ.: *American journal of agricultural economics, Review of agricultural economics, Choices, AAEA newsletter; C-FARE review of the census of agriculture; News & developments; Resources & links; Upcoming events*), link to AgEcon Search (with citations and abstracts from literature on agricultural economics), and AAEA sections.

1059  **Agletter.** Federal Reserve Bank of Chicago. 1996–. Chicago: Federal Reserve Bank of Chicago. ISSN: 1080-8639. http://www.chicagofed. org/economic_research_and_data/ag_letter.cfm.

Information on credit conditions at Seventh Federal Reserve District agricultural banks, agricultural economic indicators (prices received by farmers, consumer prices, exports, farm machinery, production, or stocks), and farmland value.

**1060 Agricultural retailers association.** Agricultural Retailers Association. 2006–. Washington, D.C.: Agricultural Retailers Association. http://www.aradc.org/.

Includes issue briefs (Agricultural Business Security Tax Credit, Chemical Site Security, Natural Gas, etc.), a newsletter, and annual reports, as well as links to state associations, Congress, government offices, and the media. This advocacy group's site is useful for news, some statistics, and for viewing what is important to agribusiness retailers and distributors.

**1061 National agri-marketing association.** National Agri-Marketing Association. [Overland Park, Kans.]: National Agri-Marketing Association. http://www.nama.org/.

The organization focuses on the marketing of agribusiness and its associated products. It holds an annual conference and an annual forum. The website has a calendar of events, a membership directory (accessible to members only), links to member company websites, and industry news from their publication *AgriMarketing*.

**1062 National grain and feed association.** National Grain and Feed Association. 2001–. Washington: National Grain and Feed Association. http://www.ngfa.org/.

The trade association's website has news, a calendar of events, trade rules and arbitration, facts, career information, and history. Covers corn, wheat, soybeans, sunflower, barley, rye, oats, and flaxseed.

**1063 Technical conversion factors for agricultural commodities.** 2000 Rome: Food and Agricultural Organization of the United Nations. http://www.fao.org/es/ess/tcf.asp.

1st ed., 1960; 2nd draft ed., 1972.

"This latest electronic publication updates two earlier printed versions of the publication produced in 1960 and revised in 1972, by the Statistics Division of FAO. It is an extremely useful and necessary compendium for both statisticians and economists to follow the commodity product sequence (referred to as 'the commodity tree') and allows one the possibility of using the information presented to convert product data from primary equivalent to secondary equivalent and/or vice versa. Also, it is an essential tool in building up supply utilization accounts, food balance sheets and calculating derived agricultural statistics. The document shows, inter alia, data per country for crop seeding rates, waste rates, extraction rates, the average live weight of animals, birth rates, take-off rates, as well as yield per animal for a number of major livestock products."—*Introd.*

The current digital edition is published as a PDF file. Released in 2000, the site description indicates that the content is continuously updated. Searchable by keyword. Also, the information is organized by continent and country, and a clickable world map speeds navigation through the file. Ends with 61 commodity tree graphics that illustrate the commodity product extraction sequence. This digital edition does not include the data collection forms found in the 1972 edition. Also missing are simple conversion factors, such as bushel into kilograms.

Published in English, French, and Spanish. A majority of the country descriptions are written in English, with less frequent French and Spanish descriptions associated with Francophone and Hispanophone nations.

## Organizations and Associations

**1064  AAEA on-line.** Agricultural Economics Association. 2001–. [Ames, Iowa]: Agricultural Economics Association. http://www.aaea.org/.

An association for those interested in the economics of agriculture, rural communities, and natural resources. The website includes Career Central, Continuing Education Opportunities, the American Agricultural Economics Association Foundation, Information Central (publ.: *American journal of agricultural economics, Review of agricultural economics, Choices, AAEA newsletter; C-FARE review of the census of agriculture; News & developments; Resources & links; Upcoming events*), link to AgEcon Search (with citations and abstracts from literature on agricultural economics), and AAEA sections.

**1065  Agricultural retailers association.** Agricultural Retailers Association. 2006–. Washington, D.C.: Agricultural Retailers Association. http://www.aradc.org/.

Includes issue briefs (Agricultural Business Security Tax Credit, Chemical Site Security, Natural Gas, etc.), a newsletter, and annual reports, as well as links to state associations, Congress, government offices, and the media. This advocacy group's site is useful for news, some statistics, and for viewing what is important to agribusiness retailers and distributors.

**1066  National agri-marketing association.** National Agri-Marketing Association. [Overland Park, Kans.]: National Agri-Marketing Association. http://www.nama.org/.

The organization focuses on the marketing of agribusiness and its associated products. It holds an annual conference and an annual forum. The website has a calendar of events, a membership directory (accessible to members only), links to member company websites, and industry news from their publication *AgriMarketing*.

**1067 National grain and feed association.** National Grain and Feed Association. 2001–. Washington: National Grain and Feed Association. http://www.ngfa.org/.
The trade association's website has news, a calendar of events, trade rules and arbitration, facts, career information, and history. Covers corn, wheat, soybeans, sunflower, barley, rye, oats, and flaxseed.

**1068 USDA.** U.S. Dept. of Agriculture. Washington, D.C.: U.S. Dept. of Agriculture. http://www.usda.gov/.
Among the duties of the USDA is monitoring agribusiness. The agribusiness portion of the website covers biotechnology; commodity standards and grades; data and statistics; exporting goods; food distribution; food labeling and packaging; food quality; food safety; importing goods; marketing assistance; organic certification; price support; quality assurance; safety inspections; trade policy and procedures; and transportation and distribution.

## Periodicals

**1069 Agletter.** Federal Reserve Bank of Chicago. 1996–. Chicago: Federal Reserve Bank of Chicago. ISSN: 1080-8639. http://www.chicagofed. org/economic_research_and_data/ag_letter.cfm.
Information on credit conditions at Seventh Federal Reserve District agricultural banks, agricultural economic indicators (prices received by farmers, consumer prices, exports, farm machinery, production, or stocks), and farmland value.

**1070 Chemical economics handbook.** Stanford Research Institute. looseleaf, charts. Stanford, Calif.: Stanford Research Institute, 1983–.

HD9651.4

Reports on 300 chemical products (such as acetaldehyde) or product groups (acrylic resins and plastics), with information on manufacturing processes, environmental issues, and supply and demand by region (producing companies, statistics, consumption, price and trade). Coverage is for the United States, Western Europe, and Japan. Also available online.

# Specialized Sources of Industry Data

**1071 Agletter.** Federal Reserve Bank of Chicago. 1996–. Chicago: Federal Reserve Bank of Chicago. ISSN: 1080-8639. http://www.chicagofed. org/economic_research_and_data/ag_letter.cfm.

Information on credit conditions at Seventh Federal Reserve District agricultural banks, agricultural economic indicators (prices received by farmers, consumer prices, exports, farm machinery, production, or stocks), and farmland value.

**1072 Agricultural prices.** U.S. Dept. of Agriculture, Crop Reporting Board. Washington, D.C.: U.S. Dept. of Agriculture, National Agricultural Statistics Service, 1942–. ISSN: 0002-1601.
338.130973                                            HD9004.U523a

The annual summary of indexes of prices received and paid by U.S. farmers: prices received for farm commodities by states and prices paid for production items by region and the U.S. over the past year and earlier years. Also available online at http://usda.mannlib.cornell.edu/MannUsda/viewDocumentInfo.do?documentI D=1003/.

**1073 Agricultural prices: Price indices and absolute prices, quarterly statistics = Prix agricoles: Indices de prix et prix absolus, statistiques trimestrielles.** Statistical Office of the European Communities. Luxembourg: Office des publications officielles des Communautés européennes, 1990–. ISSN: 1015-9924.
338.13094021                                          HD1920.5.A17

An annual compilation of both price indexes and absolute prices during the ten-year span 1989–99 for all member states of the European Union. Explanations and tables are in English, French, and German.

**1074 The CRB commodity yearbook.** Commodity Research Bureau (U.S.). ill. New York: Wiley, 1994–. ISSN: 1076-2906.
332.6328                                              HF1041.C56

Provides background information and statistical data on 100 domestic and international agricultural and industrial commodities, and on financial and stock index futures. Includes seasonal patterns and historical data from the prior ten years, with some tables going back 100 years. Organized alphabetically by commodity, with articles on each commodity that describe the commodity and give pricing trends and factors affecting price. Data sources are primarily U.S. official publications, with some from U.N., trade association, and international organization publications. Includes feature articles discussing current issues. Also available on CD-ROM.

**1075 Hoover's online.** Reference Press. 1996–. Austin, Tex.: Reference Press. http://www.hoovers.com/.

338.7                                    HG4057

Nearly 18 million records describing public and private companies primarily in the United States, but including Canada, United Kingdom, Europe, and Asia/Pacific. Profiles have an overview, history, family tree, industry information, products/operations, top competitors, competitive landscape, top executives with biographies, news, significant developments, and financial data (summary; income statement; balance sheet; cash flow; historical financials such as five years of P/E and per share; stock quote; interactive stock chart; market data; earnings estimates; this year's ratios for the company, industry, and market; SEC filings; and industry watch).

Covers 600 industries, organized into the following categories: Aerospace and Defense; Agriculture; Automotive and Transport; Banking; Beverages; Business Services; Charitable Organizations; Chemicals; Computer Hardware; Computer Services; Computer Software; Construction; Consumer Products Manufacturers; Consumer Services; Cultural Institutions; Education; Electronics; Energy and Utilities; Environmental Services and Equipment; Financial Services; Food; Foundations; Government; Health Care; Industrial Manufacturing; Insurance; Leisure; Media; Membership Organizations; Metals and Mining; Pharmaceuticals; Real Estate; Retail; Security Products and Services; Telecommunications Equipment; Telecommunications Services; and Transportation Services.

Coverage can be brief, but generally includes a fact sheet, overview, selected companies, industry watch with video interviews, news from the last 90 days, and web resources for terminology, associations, and organizations, and online publications. Includes Hoover's print publications (*Hoover's handbook of American business* [35], *Hoover's handbook of private companies* [36]).

**1076 IBISWorld United States.** IBISWorld. New York: IBISWorld. http://www.ibisworld.com/.

HC103 .I247

700 reports on the following industries: agriculture, forestry, fishing and hunting; mining; utilities; construction; manufacturing; wholesale trade; retail trade; transportation and warehousing; information; finance and insurance; real estate and rental and leasing; professional, scientific, and technical services; administrative and support and waste management and remediation services; educational services; health care and social assistance; arts, entertainment, and recreation; accommodation and food services; and other services. Setting this database apart are reports on small industries, such as parking lots and garages.

Reports include industry definition; key statistics; segmentations (products and services segmentation, major market segments, industry concentration, geographic spread); market characteristics (market size, demand determinants, domestic and international markets, basis of competition, life cycle); industry conditions (barriers to entry, taxation, industry assistance, regulation and deregulation, cost structure, capital and labor intensity, technology and systems, industry volatility, globalization); key factors (sensitivities and success factors); key competitors; and industry performance (current and historical).

**1077 Statistical highlights of U.S. agriculture.** U.S. Dept. of Agriculture, National Agricultural Statistics Service. ill. Washington, D.C.: U.S. Dept. of Agriculture, National Agricultural Statistics Service, [1996–].

S411.S714

"[B]rings together the most important economic and statistical information in agriculture in a single summary report."—*Opening letter*

Provides a timely snapshot of American agricultural production and consumption. Each basic measured segment of the agricultural sector receives a brief descriptive summary followed by a set of data tables. Geographic scope is state and national level. Chronological span is the most recent five years. Not indexed.

Aggregated data used in the publication are collected by the USDA Economic Research Service, National Agricultural Statistics Service, and World Agricultural Outlook Board. Missing from this report is data from the Agricultural Marketing Service and Foreign Agricultural Service.

Published as part of the USDA Statistical Bulletin series. 2004/2005, no. 1003; 2002/2003, no. 1000; 2001/2002, no. 976; 2000/2001, no. 971; 1999/2000, 967; 1996/1997, no. 936.

Also available online at http://purl.access.gpo.gov/GPO/LPS3899.

# Biotechnology

## *Internet Resources*

1078 **BIO.** Biotechnology Industry Association. 2007. Washington, D.C.: Biotechnology Industry Association. http://www.bio.org/.

A relatively new association, BIO was founded in 1993. Its website has news and media, coverage of national issues (health care, food and agriculture, industrial and environmental, bioethics, intellectual property, regulatory, tax and financial), state and local initiatives, letters, testimony and comments, speeches and publications, industry at a glance (statistics, guide, timeline, reports), events and conferences, and business and finance.

1079 **Biotechnology industry organization.** Biotechnology Industry Organization. Washington, D.C.: Biotechnology Industry Organization. http://www.bio.org/.

Coverage of national issues (health care, food and agriculture, industrial and environmental, bioethics, intellectual property, regulatory, tax and financial), state and local issues, government testimony and comments, speeches and publications, independent reports, BIO reports, conferences and events, and capital formation.

1080 **Biotechnology information directory.** Cato Research. 1995–. Durham, N.C.: Cato Research. http://biotech.cato.com/.

3,500 links to organizations, databases and bioinformatics, research institutes and universities, RSS news feeds and blogs, publications, product catalogs, data standards and glossaries, directories, clinical trials, pharmaceutical companies, careers, and education.

1081 **Ernst and Young.** Ernst and Young. 2007. London: Ernst and Young. http://www.ey.com/global/content.nsf/International/Industry_Overview/.

Ernst and Young provides "accounting and auditing, tax reporting and operations, tax advisory, business risk services, technology and security risk services, transaction advisory, and human capital services." The site is useful for articles on financial management, corporate governance, initial public offerings (IPOs), and industry reports (asset management, automotive, banking and capital markets, biotechnology, consumer products, insurance, media and entertainment, mining and metals, oil and gas, pharmaceuticals, real estate and construction, hospitality and leisure, technology, telecommunications, utilities).

1082 **Technology review.** Massachusetts Institute of Technology. 1998–. Cambridge, Mass.: Association of Alumni and Alumnae of the Massachusetts Institute of Technology. ISSN: 1099-274X. http://www.technologyreview.com/.

620                                                                                      T171.M47

Covers trends and developments in business technology, especially as they affect the energy, nanotech, biotech, and infotech industries. Includes annual list of the top emerging technologies. For many years, it included an annual R&D Scorecard, published each fall, which now is useful for tracking historical research and development expenditures.

## Organizations and Associations

1083 **BIO.** Biotechnology Industry Association. 2007 Washington, D.C.: Biotechnology Industry Association. http://www.bio.org/.
A relatively new association, BIO was founded in 1993. Its website has news and media, coverage of national issues (health care, food and agriculture, industrial and environmental, bioethics, intellectual property, regulatory, tax and financial), state and local initiatives, letters, testimony and comments, speeches and publications, industry at a glance (statistics, guide, timeline, reports), events and conferences, and business and finance.

1084 **Biotechnology industry organization.** Biotechnology Industry Organization. Washington, D.C.: Biotechnology Industry Organization. http://www.bio.org/.
Coverage of national issues (health care, food and agriculture, industrial and environmental, bioethics, intellectual property, regulatory, tax and financial), state and local issues, government testimony and comments, speeches and publications, independent reports, BIO reports, conferences and events, and capital formation.

1085 **USDA.** U.S. Dept. of Agriculture. Washington, D.C.: U.S. Dept. of Agriculture. http://www.usda.gov/.
Among the duties of the USDA is monitoring agribusiness. The agribusiness portion of the website covers biotechnology; commodity standards

and grades; data and statistics; exporting goods; food distribution; food labeling and packaging; food quality; food safety; importing goods; marketing assistance; organic certification; price support; quality assurance; safety inspections; trade policy and procedures; and transportation and distribution.

## Periodicals

1086  **Technology review.** Massachusetts Institute of Technology. 1998–. Cambridge, Mass.: Association of Alumni and Alumnae of the Massachusetts Institute of Technology. ISSN: 1099-274X. http://www.technologyreview.com/.

620                                                                      T171.M47

Covers trends and developments in business technology, especially as they affect the energy, nanotech, biotech, and infotech industries. Includes annual list of the top emerging technologies. For many years, it included an annual R&D Scorecard, published each fall, which now is useful for tracking historical research and development expenditures.

## Specialized Sources of Industry Data

1087  **Bioscan.** Phoenix, Ariz.: Oryx Press, 1987–. ISSN: 0887-6207.
338.76208025                                         HD9999.B44B56

Information on some 2,000 U.S. and foreign companies, giving contact information, company history, number of employees, facilities, very brief financial highlights (sales, net income, earnings per share, shares outstanding, total assets), business strategy, alliances, mergers and acquisitions, principal investors, and products in development, and products on the market. Available online through *BioWorld*.

1088  **CorpTech directory of technology companies.** U.S. ed. Corporate Technology Information Services. maps. Woburn, Mass.: Corporate Technology Information Services, 1995–.
338.7402573                                          HG4057.A16

Describes more than 50,000 U.S. companies that manufacture or develop high-technology products. Company profiles generally include company name and address, telephone and fax numbers, executives and their departments (including research and development, marketing, purchasing, and personnel), type of ownership, date established, annual sales, number of employees, corporate history, and product codes. Indexed by firm and by product. A table converts SIC codes to CorpTech codes. Also available online and on CD-ROM.

**1089 Forrester research.** Forrester Research. [1999–2003.] Cambridge, Mass.: Forrester. http://www.library.hbs.edu/forrester.htm.

HF5548.32T174

Nearly 17,000 original reports on technology's effect on business and the consumer in the United States, Canada, Europe, and Asia Pacific. Research is in two categories, technology and industry.

Topics in technology are application development, business intelligence, computing systems, consumer devices and access, content and collaboration, customer experience, enterprise applications, enterprise mobility, IT management, IT services, networking, portals and site technology, security, software infrastructure, and tech sector economics.

Topics in industry are brand strategy, brand tactics, consumer electronics, consumer products, customer insight, emerging marketing channels, energy and utilities, financial services, government, healthcare and life sciences, high tech, industry insight, manufacturing, marketing and advertising, marketing planning, media and entertainment, mobile services, professional services, relationship marketing, retail, telecommunications, television advertising, transportation and logistics, and travel.

Reports typically range from 3–20 pages, and some are available as videos.

**1090 Hoover's online.** Reference Press. 1996–. Austin, Tex.: Reference Press. http://www.hoovers.com/.

338.7 HG4057

Nearly 18 million records describing public and private companies primarily in the United States, but including Canada, United Kingdom, Europe, and Asia/Pacific. Profiles have an overview, history, family tree, industry information, products/operations, top competitors, competitive landscape, top executives with biographies, news, significant developments, and financial data (summary; income statement; balance sheet; cash flow; historical financials such as five years of P/E and per share; stock quote; interactive stock chart; market data; earnings estimates; this year's ratios for the company, industry, and market; SEC filings; and industry watch).

Covers 600 industries, organized into the following categories: Aerospace and Defense; Agriculture; Automotive and Transport; Banking;

Beverages; Business Services; Charitable Organizations; Chemicals; Computer Hardware; Computer Services; Computer Software; Construction; Consumer Products Manufacturers; Consumer Services; Cultural Institutions; Education; Electronics; Energy and Utilities; Environmental Services and Equipment; Financial Services; Food; Foundations; Government; Health Care; Industrial Manufacturing; Insurance; Leisure; Media; Membership Organizations; Metals and Mining; Pharmaceuticals; Real Estate; Retail; Security Products and Services; Telecommunications Equipment; Telecommunications Services; and Transportation Services.

Coverage can be brief, but generally includes a fact sheet, overview, selected companies, industry watch with video interviews, news from the last 90 days, and web resources for terminology, associations, and organizations, and online publications. Includes Hoover's print publications (*Hoover's handbook of American business* [35], *Hoover's handbook of private companies* [36]).

**1091 Marketresearch.com academic.** Kalorama Information. 1999–. Bethesda, Md.: Kalorama Information. http://www.marketresearch. com/.

HF5415.2.K35

Market research reports from various sources (Icon Group, Kalorama, BizMiner, etc.) for Consumer Goods (apparel, cosmetics and personal care, house and home, pet services and supplies, travel services), Food and Beverage (alcoholic beverages, coffee and tea, soft drinks, confectionery, dairy products, food processing), Heavy Industry (energy, mining, utilities, construction, machines and parts, manufacturing, metals, paper and forest products, plastics, automotive, aviation & aerospace, logistics and shipping), Service Industries (accounting and finance, corporate services, banking and financial services, insurance), Public Sector (associations/nonprofits, education, government), Life Science (biotechnology, agriculture, genomics, proteomics, medical imaging, healthcare facilities, managed care, regulation and policy, cardiovascular devices, equipment and supplies, wound care, pharmaceuticals, diseases and conditions, prescription drugs, therapeutic area), Technology & Media (computer equipment, electronics, networks, e-commerce and IT outsourcing, software, telecommunications, wireless), and Demographics (age, lifestyle and economics, multicultural).

Reports range in length, with some over 300 pages long, and give a variety of information (definition of industry, consumer demographics, consumer shopping habits, spending patterns, sales, establishments, employment, forecasts, trends, market size, market share, and market segmentation). Some company information is also included.

# Chemical

## Additional Reference Sources

**1092  Global market information database.** Euromonitor. [1999–.]
[London]: Euromonitor. http://www.gmid.euromonitor.com/.

HD2755.5.G56

Market reports, company profiles, and demographic, economic, and marketing statistics for 205 countries. Market reports are for 16 consumer markets (food and drink, tobacco, toys, etc.) and 14 industrial and service markets (accountancy, broadcasting, chemicals, property services, etc.).

Reports have market size, market sectors, share of market, marketing activity, research and development, corporate overview, distribution, consumer profiles, market forecasts, sector forecasts, sources, and definitions. Additional reports are available for market segments, such as baby food. Company profiles have background, recent news, competitive environment, and outlook. Consumer lifestyle reports and very useful marketing background analyze the consumer by country, gender, age, marital status, educational attainment, ethnicity, religion, home ownership, household profile, employment, income, health, eating and personal grooming habits, leisure activities, personal finance, communication, transport, and travel.

Search for data, which can be exported into Excel or browse for reports. Data are available from 1977 through 2016 and include inflation, exchange rates, GDP, GNI, government expenditures, government finance, income, labor, and money supply.

**1093  Harris U.S. manufacturers directory.** National ed. Harris
InfoSource. Twinsburg, Ohio: Harris InfoSource, 2000–. ISSN:
1531-8273.

338

HF5035.H37

Entries for U.S. companies include location, contact information, industry descriptions, Standard Industrial Classification (SIC) or NAICS codes, executive names, and size. Indexed by company name, geography, product or service category, and SIC code. Libraries receiving questions about local companies may want to invest in the regional and state directories also published by Harris. Available in an online version.

**1094  Major chemical and petrochemical companies of the world.**
Graham and Whiteside. London: Graham and Whiteside, 2000–.
ISSN: 1369-5444; ISBN: 1860991920.
658.0029; 661.804                                                                    HD9650.3

Lists over 7,000 companies, giving contact information, executive names, business description, brand names and trademarks, subsidiaries, principal bank, principal law firm, ticker symbol, date established, number of employees, auditors, and two years of very brief financial information (sales turnover, profit before tax, profit after tax, dividend per share, earnings per share, share capital, shareholders' equity).

## Internet Resources

**1095  Manufacturing.net.** Advantage Business Media. 2000s–. [s.l.]:
Reed Business Information. http://www.manufacturing.net/.
Covers manufacturing for aerospace, automotive, chemical, food, material handling, pharmaceuticals, and utilities. Includes design and development; case studies; electrical and electronics; energy; environmental; facilities and operations; labor relations; manufacturing technology; materials; quality control; safety; and supply chain management. Has international focus.

## Organizations and Associations

**1096  Americanchemistry.com.** American Chemistry Council.
2007. [Arlington, Va.]: American Chemistry Council. http://
americanchemistry.com/s_acc/index.asp.
Founded in 1872, the American Chemistry Council represents chemical companies, including chlorine and plastics companies. The site includes policy issues, security, environment, product stewardship, tax and trade, news, initiatives, and industry statistics (chemistry in economy, chemistry-dependent economy, chemistry-dependent jobs, consumer chemFactor, industrial chemFactor, packaging chemFactor, economic impact, industry profile, industry facts, business of chemistry, jobs and wages). Additional associations exist for various segments of the chemical industry, including the National Paint & Coatings Association, the Adhesive and Sealant Council, and the Synthetic Organic Chemical Manufacturers Association.

## Specialized Sources of Industry Data

**1097 Chemical economics handbook.** Stanford Research Institute. loose-leaf, charts. Stanford, Calif.: Stanford Research Institute, 1983–.

HD9651.4

Reports on 300 chemical products (such as acetaldehyde) or product groups (acrylic resins and plastics), with information on manufacturing processes, environmental issues, and supply and demand by region (producing companies, statistics, consumption, price and trade). Coverage is for the United States, Western Europe, and Japan. Also available online.

**1098 Hoover's online.** Reference Press. 1996–. Austin, Tex.: Reference Press. http://www.hoovers.com/.

338.7                                                                    HG4057

Nearly 18 million records describing public and private companies primarily in the United States, but including Canada, United Kingdom, Europe, and Asia/Pacific. Profiles have an overview, history, family tree, industry information, products/operations, top competitors, competitive landscape, top executives with biographies, news, significant developments, and financial data (summary; income statement; balance sheet; cash flow; historical financials such as five years of P/E and per share; stock quote; interactive stock chart; market data; earnings estimates; this year's ratios for the company, industry, and market; SEC filings; and industry watch).

Covers 600 industries, organized into the following categories: Aerospace and Defense; Agriculture; Automotive and Transport; Banking; Beverages; Business Services; Charitable Organizations; Chemicals; Computer Hardware; Computer Services; Computer Software; Construction; Consumer Products Manufacturers; Consumer Services; Cultural Institutions; Education; Electronics; Energy and Utilities; Environmental Services and Equipment; Financial Services; Food; Foundations; Government; Health Care; Industrial Manufacturing; Insurance; Leisure; Media; Membership Organizations; Metals and Mining; Pharmaceuticals; Real Estate; Retail; Security Products and Services; Telecommunications Equipment; Telecommunications Services; and Transportation Services.

Coverage can be brief, but generally includes a fact sheet, overview, selected companies, industry watch with video interviews, news from the

last 90 days, and web resources for terminology, associations, and organizations, and online publications. Includes Hoover's print publications
(*Hoover's handbook of American business* [35], *Hoover's handbook of private
companies* [36]).

# Computers

## *Internet Resources*

**1099  IEEE computer society.** IEEE Computer Society. 2007. Washington,
    D.C.: IEEE Computer Society. http://www.computer.org/.
The society was founded in 1946 to serve computer professionals. Its
website has publications (technical magazines, journals, letters, tutorials,
books), abstracts and tables of contents of the conference publications,
career development and educational activities, communities, and a volunteer center.

## *Organizations and Associations*

**1100  IEEE computer society.** IEEE Computer Society. 2007. Washington,
    D.C.: IEEE Computer Society. http://www.computer.org/.
The society was founded in 1946 to serve computer professionals. Its
website has publications (technical magazines, journals, letters, tutorials,
books), abstracts and tables of contents of the conference publications,
career development and educational activities, communities, and a volunteer center.

## *Specialized Sources of Industry Data*

**1101  Directory of top computer executives.** East ed. Applied Computer
    Research. Phoenix: Applied Computer Research, 1985–. ISSN:
    1936-4202.
338.4.700402574                       HD9696.C63U516313
Lists information technology information for companies with minimum gross revenues of $50 million or a minimum of 250 employees in
manufacturing and service, banking, diversified finance, insurance, retail,
transportation, utilities, education, health service, federal government,
state government, and local government. Entries give company name,
contact information, top computer executive names, subsidiary divisions,

type of industry, second level manager names, major computer systems used, number of PCs deployed throughout the organization, and number of information system employees. Arranged geographically and indexed by company name and industry classification. Available in print and pdf editions for the Eastern U.S., Western U.S., and Canada. Also available online.

**1102 FACCTS.** Faulkner Information Services. 1995–. Pennsauken, N.J.: Faulkner Information Services. ISSN: 1082-7471. http://www. faulkner.com/showcase/faccts.htm.

005                                                                                      QA76.753

Over 1,200 reports on trends, issues, market conditions, implementation guides, companies, products, and services in information technology. Arranged into 14 categories: enterprise data networking, broadband, information security, electronic government, electronic business, content management, IT asset management, application development, Website management, converging communications, telecom and global network services, mobile business strategies, wireless communications, and Internet strategies. Especially useful for the up-to-date technology trend reports.

**1103 Forrester research.** Forrester Research. [1999–2003.] Cambridge, Mass.: Forrester. http://www.library.hbs.edu/forrester.htm.

HF5548.32T174

Nearly 17,000 original reports on technology's effect on business and the consumer in the United States, Canada, Europe, and Asia Pacific. Research is in two categories, technology and industry.

Topics in technology are application development, business intelligence, computing systems, consumer devices and access, content and collaboration, customer experience, enterprise applications, enterprise mobility, IT management, IT services, networking, portals and site technology, security, software infrastructure, and tech sector economics.

Topics in industry are brand strategy, brand tactics, consumer electronics, consumer products, customer insight, emerging marketing channels, energy and utilities, financial services, government, healthcare and life sciences, high tech, industry insight, manufacturing, marketing and advertising, marketing planning, media and entertainment, mobile services, professional services, relationship marketing, retail, telecommunications, television advertising, transportation and logistics, and travel.

Reports typically range from 3–20 pages, and some are available as videos.

**1104 Gartneradvisory intraweb.** Gartner Group. 2000–. [Stamford, Conn.]: Gartner Group. http://www.gartner.com/.

The database is made from Gartner Research and Advisory Services, Datapro, and Dataquest Research. Especially useful for reports that discuss strategy within the IT industry. Also has company profiles, trends, developments, and product reports.

**1105 Hoover's online.** Reference Press. 1996–. Austin, Tex.: Reference Press. http://www.hoovers.com/.

338.7                                                    HG4057

Nearly 18 million records describing public and private companies primarily in the United States, but including Canada, United Kingdom, Europe, and Asia/Pacific. Profiles have an overview, history, family tree, industry information, products/operations, top competitors, competitive landscape, top executives with biographies, news, significant developments, and financial data (summary; income statement; balance sheet; cash flow; historical financials such as five years of P/E and per share; stock quote; interactive stock chart; market data; earnings estimates; this year's ratios for the company, industry, and market; SEC filings; and industry watch).

Covers 600 industries, organized into the following categories: Aerospace and Defense; Agriculture; Automotive and Transport; Banking; Beverages; Business Services; Charitable Organizations; Chemicals; Computer Hardware; Computer Services; Computer Software; Construction; Consumer Products Manufacturers; Consumer Services; Cultural Institutions; Education; Electronics; Energy and Utilities; Environmental Services and Equipment; Financial Services; Food; Foundations; Government; Health Care; Industrial Manufacturing; Insurance; Leisure; Media; Membership Organizations; Metals and Mining; Pharmaceuticals; Real Estate; Retail; Security Products and Services; Telecommunications Equipment; Telecommunications Services; and Transportation Services.

Coverage can be brief, but generally includes a fact sheet, overview, selected companies, industry watch with video interviews, news from the last 90 days, and web resources for terminology, associations, and organizations, and online publications. Includes Hoover's print publications (*Hoover's handbook of American business* [35], *Hoover's handbook of private companies* [36]).

1106  **Infotech trends.** Data Analysis Group. 1999. Cloverdale, Calif.: Data Analysis Group. http://www.infotechtrends.com/.

Indexes 65 periodicals (*Business week, Computer world, PC week, KM world, Forbes, Internet week*) with coverage of computers, computer peripherals, software, storage, the Internet, and communications equipment. Includes forecast sales and shipments, market share, installed base, and industry trends. Coverage begins in 1984. Results can be downloaded to Excel.

1107  **Jupiterresearch.** Jupiter Communications. New York: Jupiter Communications. http://www.jupiterresearch.com/bin/item.pl/ home.

Combines proprietary primary research with secondary research to give trends, statistics, forecasts, and best practices on information technology and its effects on industries and consumers. In seven categories: Personal Technologies; Marketing & Media; Web Technologies & Operations; European Focus; Industry Focus; Jupiter Data (statistics); and Hot Topics.

1108  **Plunkett's e-commerce and Internet business almanac.** Jack W. Plunkett, Plunkett Research, Ltd. ill. Houston, Tex.: Plunkett Research, 2000–. ISSN: 1548-5447.

004                                          HF5548.325.U6P59

Like all the Plunkett almanacs, contains data on 300 major companies. Company profiles include types of business, brands and affiliates, contacts, employee benefits and top salaries, sales and profit numbers, growth plans, and competitive advantage. Especially useful for the industry statistics and rankings at the front of the volume. Also contains a glossary of key words and phrases. Available as an e-book.

# Construction

## Additional Reference Sources

1109  **The dictionary of real estate appraisal.** 4th ed. Appraisal Institute. xii, 448 p., ill. Chicago: Appraisal Institute, 2002. ISBN: 0922154724.

333.33203                                    HD1387.D435

Combines definitions of terms with examples of usage and investor advice. Where useful, contains formulas, charts, and figures. Additional addenda to this edition include: property types and subtypes; business valuation glossary; international valuation glossary; real estate organizations and professional designations; federal agencies, legislation, programs, and court cases; information technology glossary; measures and conversions; and architecture and construction glossary. Contains cross-references.

## Definition of The Industry

**1110  IBISWorld United States.** IBISWorld. New York: IBISWorld. http://www.ibisworld.com/.

HC103 .I247

700 reports on the following industries: agriculture, forestry, fishing and hunting; mining; utilities; construction; manufacturing; wholesale trade; retail trade; transportation and warehousing; information; finance and insurance; real estate and rental and leasing; professional, scientific, and technical services; administrative and support and waste management and remediation services; educational services; health care and social assistance; arts, entertainment, and recreation; accommodation and food services; and other services. Setting this database apart are reports on small industries, such as parking lots and garages.

Reports include industry definition; key statistics; segmentations (products and services segmentation, major market segments, industry concentration, geographic spread); market characteristics (market size, demand determinants, domestic and international markets, basis of competition, life cycle); industry conditions (barriers to entry, taxation, industry assistance, regulation and deregulation, cost structure, capital and labor intensity, technology and systems, industry volatility, globalization); key factors (sensitivities and success factors); key competitors; and industry performance (current and historical).

## Internet Resources

**1111  Associated general contractors of America.** Associated General Contractors of America. 2007–. Washington, D.C.: Associated General Contractors of America. http://www.agc.org/index.ww.
The association was founded in 1918 as a trade association. The site has information on safety and risk management, contract documents, supervisory training, labor and human resources, the environment, construction economics, marketing, careers, legislative and public affairs, and news.

1112  **The blue book of building and construction.** Contractors
Register. [1997–.] Jefferson Valley, N.Y.: Contractors Register.
http://www.thebluebook.com/.

Search by state to find companies, contact information, geographical area
served, year established, types of projects, typical project size, labor affiliation, license number, recent projects completed, manufacturers certifica-
tions, and brands used. Also available for specific states in print.

1113  **Ernst and Young.** Ernst and Young. 2007. London: Ernst and
Young. http://www.ey.com/global/content.nsf/International/
Industry_Overview/.

Ernst and Young provides "accounting and auditing, tax reporting and
operations, tax advisory, business risk services, technology and security
risk services, transaction advisory, and human capital services." The site is
useful for articles on financial management, corporate governance, initial
public offerings (IPOs), and industry reports (asset management, automotive, banking and capital markets, biotechnology, consumer products,
insurance, media and entertainment, mining and metals, oil and gas, pharmaceuticals, real estate and construction, hospitality and leisure, technology, telecommunications, utilities).

## *Organizations and Associations*

1114  **Associated general contractors of America.** Associated General
Contractors of America. 2007–. Washington, D.C.: Associated
General Contractors of America. http://www.agc.org/index.ww.

The association was founded in 1918 as a trade association. The site has
information on safety and risk management, contract documents, supervisory training, labor and human resources, the environment, construction
economics, marketing, careers, legislative and public affairs, and news.

## *Specialized Sources of Industry Data*

1115  **Global financial data.** Global Financial Data. [2003–.] Los
Angeles: Global Financial Data. http://www.globalfinancialdata.
com/.

20,000 financial and economic data series for some 200 countries, dating from the 1600s to the present. Categories are daily stock market data
from 1962 (open, high, low, close, volume, available in split adjusted or

unadjusted format); state, national, and international real estate market data from 1830 (includes Median New Home Prices—United States, Winans International U.S. Real Estate Index—Price Only, Austria ATX Real Estate Index, Shanghai SE Real Estate Index); international bond indices from 1862; central bank interest yields; commercial paper yields; commodity indices; commodity prices; consumer price indices; U.S and European corporate bond yields, some from 1857; international deposit rates; international exchange rates, some from 1660; futures contracts; government bond yields; gross domestic product; international interbank interest rates from the 1980s; interest rate swaps from 1988 (United States, Europe, Japan); U.S. intraday data, daily from January 1933 to May 2007; international lending rates, some from 1934; overnight and call money rates, some from 1857 (monthly, weekly, daily); international population; sector indices (consumer discretionary, consumer staples, energy, finance, health care, industrials, information technology, materials, telecommunications, transports, utilities), stock indices—preferred stocks; stock indices—composites; stock indices—size and style; stock market—AMEX; stock market—NASDAQ; stock market—NYSE; stock market—OTC; stocks (capitalization, volume, dividend yields and P/E ratios, technical indicators); total return indices—bills; total return indices—bonds; total return indices—stocks; international treasury bill yields; international unemployment rates, some from 1890; and international wholesale price indices.

**1116  Hoover's online.** Reference Press. 1996–. Austin, Tex.: Reference Press. http://www.hoovers.com/.

338.7                                                                    HG4057

Nearly 18 million records describing public and private companies primarily in the United States, but including Canada, United Kingdom, Europe, and Asia/Pacific. Profiles have an overview, history, family tree, industry information, products/operations, top competitors, competitive landscape, top executives with biographies, news, significant developments, and financial data (summary; income statement; balance sheet; cash flow; historical financials such as five years of P/E and per share; stock quote; interactive stock chart; market data; earnings estimates; this year's ratios for the company, industry, and market; SEC filings; and industry watch).

Covers 600 industries, organized into the following categories: Aerospace and Defense; Agriculture; Automotive and Transport; Banking; Beverages; Business Services; Charitable Organizations; Chemicals;

Computer Hardware; Computer Services; Computer Software; Construction; Consumer Products Manufacturers; Consumer Services; Cultural Institutions; Education; Electronics; Energy and Utilities; Environmental Services and Equipment; Financial Services; Food; Foundations; Government; Health Care; Industrial Manufacturing; Insurance; Leisure; Media; Membership Organizations; Metals and Mining; Pharmaceuticals; Real Estate; Retail; Security Products and Services; Telecommunications Equipment; Telecommunications Services; and Transportation Services.

Coverage can be brief, but generally includes a fact sheet, overview, selected companies, industry watch with video interviews, news from the last 90 days, and web resources for terminology, associations, and organizations, and online publications. Includes Hoover's print publications (*Hoover's handbook of American business* [35], *Hoover's handbook of private companies* [36]).

**1117  IBISWorld United States.** IBISWorld. New York: IBISWorld. http://www.ibisworld.com/.

HC103 .I247

700 reports on the following industries: agriculture, forestry, fishing and hunting; mining; utilities; construction; manufacturing; wholesale trade; retail trade; transportation and warehousing; information; finance and insurance; real estate and rental and leasing; professional, scientific, and technical services; administrative and support and waste management and remediation services; educational services; health care and social assistance; arts, entertainment, and recreation; accommodation and food services; and other services. Setting this database apart are reports on small industries, such as parking lots and garages.

Reports include industry definition; key statistics; segmentations (products and services segmentation, major market segments, industry concentration, geographic spread); market characteristics (market size, demand determinants, domestic and international markets, basis of competition, life cycle); industry conditions (barriers to entry, taxation, industry assistance, regulation and deregulation, cost structure, capital and labor intensity, technology and systems, industry volatility, globalization); key factors (sensitivities and success factors); key competitors; and industry performance (current and historical).

**1118  Marketresearch.com academic.** Kalorama Information. 1999–. Bethesda, Md.: Kalorama Information. http://www.marketresearch. com/.

HF5415.2.K35

Market research reports from various sources (Icon Group, Kalorama, BizMiner, etc.) for Consumer Goods (apparel, cosmetics and personal care, house and home, pet services and supplies, travel services), Food and Beverage (alcoholic beverages, coffee and tea, soft drinks, confectionery, dairy products, food processing), Heavy Industry (energy, mining, utilities, construction, machines and parts, manufacturing, metals, paper and forest products, plastics, automotive, aviation & aerospace, logistics and shipping), Service Industries (accounting and finance, corporate services, banking and financial services, insurance), Public Sector (associations/nonprofits, education, government), Life Science (biotechnology, agriculture, genomics, proteomics, medical imaging, healthcare facilities, managed care, regulation and policy, cardiovascular devices, equipment and supplies, wound care, pharmaceuticals, diseases and conditions, prescription drugs, therapeutic area), Technology & Media (computer equipment, electronics, networks, e-commerce and IT outsourcing, software, telecommunications, wireless), and Demographics (age, lifestyle and economics, multicultural).

Reports range in length, with some over 300 pages long, and give a variety of information (definition of industry, consumer demographics, consumer shopping habits, spending patterns, sales, establishments, employment, forecasts, trends, market size, market share, and market segmentation). Some company information is also included.

# Consulting

## Additional Reference Sources

**1119** **Plunkett's consulting industry almanac.** Jack W. Plunkett, Plunkett Research, Ltd. Houston, Tex.: Plunkett Research, 2003–. ISSN: 1552-2288.

331                                                                HD69.C6P58

Data on nearly 300 leading public and private companies. Company profiles include types of business, brands and affiliates, contacts, employee benefits and top salaries, sales and profit numbers, growth plans, and competitive advantage. Especially useful for the industry trends, statistics and rankings at the front of the volume (Employment in management and technical consulting services, U.S. 1995–2005; Largest computer and Internet consulting companies 2004–2005; Largest human resources consulting companies 2004–2005; Largest management consulting companies 2004–2005), and information on the main associations and organizations in the back of the volume. Available as an e-book.

## Definition of the Industry

1120  **IBISWorld United States.** IBISWorld. New York: IBISWorld.
http://www.ibisworld.com/.

HC103.I247

700 reports on the following industries: agriculture, forestry, fishing and hunting; mining; utilities; construction; manufacturing; wholesale trade; retail trade; transportation and warehousing; information; finance and insurance; real estate and rental and leasing; professional, scientific, and technical services; administrative and support and waste management and remediation services; educational services; health care and social assistance; arts, entertainment, and recreation; accommodation and food services; and other services. Setting this database apart are reports on small industries, such as parking lots and garages.

Reports include industry definition; key statistics; segmentations (products and services segmentation, major market segments, industry concentration, geographic spread); market characteristics (market size, demand determinants, domestic and international markets, basis of competition, life cycle); industry conditions (barriers to entry, taxation, industry assistance, regulation and deregulation, cost structure, capital and labor intensity, technology and systems, industry volatility, globalization); key factors (sensitivities and success factors); key competitors; and industry performance (current and historical).

## Organizations and Associations

1121  **Association of management consulting firms.** Association of
Management Consulting Firms. 2007. New York: Association of
Management Consulting Firms. http://www.amcf.org/.

The association was founded in 1929 for consultants. The site provides benchmarking data, member polls, annual operating survey (reports on annual billing revenues, size of professional staff, typical project size, number of domestic offices), news, and an event calendar, mostly available to members. There are similar associations for different types of consultants (Independent Computer Consultants Association, Association of Consultants to Nonprofits, Association of Consulting Foresters, etc.).

## Periodicals

1122  **Plunkett's consulting industry almanac.** Jack W. Plunkett,
Plunkett Research, Ltd. Houston, Tex.: Plunkett Research, 2003–.

ISSN: 1552-2288.

331                                                    HD69.C6P58

Data on nearly 300 leading public and private companies. Company profiles include types of business, brands and affiliates, contacts, employee
benefits and top salaries, sales and profit numbers, growth plans, and
competitive advantage. Especially useful for the industry trends, statistics
and rankings at the front of the volume (Employment in management
and technical consulting services, U.S. 1995–2005; Largest computer and
Internet consulting companies 2004–2005; Largest human resources consulting companies 2004–2005; Largest management consulting companies
2004–2005), and information on the main associations and organizations
in the back of the volume. Available as an e-book.

## Specialized Sources of Industry Data

1123  Hoover's online. Reference Press. 1996–. Austin, Tex.: Reference
      Press. http://www.hoovers.com/.

338.7                                                   HG4057

Nearly 18 million records describing public and private companies primarily in the United States, but including Canada, United Kingdom, Europe,
and Asia/Pacific. Profiles have an overview, history, family tree, industry
information, products/operations, top competitors, competitive landscape, top executives with biographies, news, significant developments,
and financial data (summary; income statement; balance sheet; cash flow;
historical financials such as five years of P/E and per share; stock quote;
interactive stock chart; market data; earnings estimates; this year's ratios
for the company, industry, and market; SEC filings; and industry watch).

Covers 600 industries, organized into the following categories:
Aerospace and Defense; Agriculture; Automotive and Transport; Bank-
ing; Beverages; Business Services; Charitable Organizations; Chemi-
cals; Computer Hardware; Computer Services; Computer Software;
Construction; Consumer Products Manufacturers; Consumer Services;
Cultural Institutions; Education; Electronics; Energy and Utilities;
Environmental Services and Equipment; Financial Services; Food;
Foundations; Government; Health Care; Industrial Manufacturing;
Insurance; Leisure; Media; Membership Organizations; Metals and
Mining; Pharmaceuticals; Real Estate; Retail; Security Products and Ser-
vices; Telecommunications Equipment; Telecommunications Services;
and Transportation Services.

Coverage can be brief, but generally includes a fact sheet, overview,
selected companies, industry watch with video interviews, news from the

last 90 days, and web resources for terminology, associations, and organizations, and online publications. Includes Hoover's print publications (*Hoover's handbook of American business* [35], *Hoover's handbook of private companies* [36]).

**1124 IBISWorld United States.** IBISWorld. New York: IBISWorld. http://www.ibisworld.com/.

HC103.I247

700 reports on the following industries: agriculture, forestry, fishing and hunting; mining; utilities; construction; manufacturing; wholesale trade; retail trade; transportation and warehousing; information; finance and insurance; real estate and rental and leasing; professional, scientific, and technical services; administrative and support and waste management and remediation services; educational services; health care and social assistance; arts, entertainment, and recreation; accommodation and food services; and other services. Setting this database apart are reports on small industries, such as parking lots and garages.

Reports include industry definition; key statistics; segmentations (products and services segmentation, major market segments, industry concentration, geographic spread); market characteristics (market size, demand determinants, domestic and international markets, basis of competition, life cycle); industry conditions (barriers to entry, taxation, industry assistance, regulation and deregulation, cost structure, capital and labor intensity, technology and systems, industry volatility, globalization); key factors (sensitivities and success factors); key competitors; and industry performance (current and historical).

**1125 Marketresearch.com academic.** Kalorama Information. 1999–. Bethesda, Md.: Kalorama Information. http://www.marketresearch. com/.

HF5415.2.K35

Market research reports from various sources (Icon Group, Kalorama, BizMiner, etc.) for Consumer Goods (apparel, cosmetics and personal care, house and home, pet services and supplies, travel services), Food and Beverage (alcoholic beverages, coffee and tea, soft drinks, confectionery, dairy products, food processing), Heavy Industry (energy, mining, utilities, construction, machines and parts, manufacturing, metals, paper and forest products, plastics, automotive, aviation & aerospace, logistics and shipping), Service Industries (accounting and finance, corporate services, banking and financial services, insurance), Public Sector (associations/ nonprofits, education, government), Life Science (biotechnology, agriculture, genomics, proteomics, medical imaging, healthcare facilities, managed care, regulation and policy, cardiovascular devices, equipment and supplies, wound care, pharmaceuticals, diseases and conditions, prescription drugs, therapeutic area), Technology & Media (computer equipment, electronics, networks, e-commerce and IT outsourcing, software, telecommunications, wireless), and Demographics (age, lifestyle and economics, multicultural).

Reports range in length, with some over 300 pages long, and give a variety of information (definition of industry, consumer demographics, consumer shopping habits, spending patterns, sales, establishments, employment, forecasts, trends, market size, market share, and market segmentation). Some company information is also included.

**1126 Plunkett's consulting industry almanac.** Jack W. Plunkett, Plunkett Research, Ltd. Houston, Tex.: Plunkett Research, 2003–. ISSN: 1552-2288.

331                                                                    HD69.C6P58

Data on nearly 300 leading public and private companies. Company profiles include types of business, brands and affiliates, contacts, employee benefits and top salaries, sales and profit numbers, growth plans, and competitive advantage. Especially useful for the industry trends, statistics and rankings at the front of the volume (Employment in management and technical consulting services, U.S. 1995–2005; Largest computer and Internet consulting companies 2004–2005; Largest human resources consulting companies 2004–2005; Largest management consulting companies 2004–2005), and information on the main associations and organizations in the back of the volume. Available as an e-book.

# Financial Services

**1127 The bankers' almanac.** Reed Information Services Ltd. West Sussex, England: Reed Information Services, 1993–. ISSN: 1462-4125.

HG2984.B3

International coverage of over 4,000 banks, with information on executives, bank owners and their percentage of shares, bank correspondents, bank name changes, liquidations, balance sheet figures, profits and loss statements, world and country rankings, credit ratings, national bank and SWIFT codes. Also available, for a fee at http://www.bankersalmanac.com/.

**1128 Best's insurance reports. Internat. ed.** A. M. Best Company. Oldwick, N.J.: A. M. Best, 1985–. ISSN: 0884-4313.

368.0025                                                                 HG8021.B47

The best known guide to insurance companies. Includes Best's ratings (indicates financial stength of a company), business reviews (includes where company is licensed, what lines of business it writes), management information, and financial information for 3,400 U.S. and Canadian companies. Use not only for the ratings, but for the capitalization analysis.

## Additional Reference Sources

**1129 Banking information index.** American Bankers Association. Ann Arbor, Mich.: UMI, 1994–. ISSN: 1075-282X.

016.3321                                             Z7164.F5A53; HG1501

Indexes over 200 periodicals of interest to the financial services industry, especially banking. Also available through *Banking information source* (427).

**1130 Banking information source.** ProQuest Information and Learning Company. Ann Arbor, Mich.: ProQuest Information and Learning. http://il.proquest.com/products_pq/descriptions/pq_banking_info. shtml.

Indexes nearly 450 journals and trade publications in banking and finance, many of which also appear in full-text. Indexing is from ABA's *Banking information index* (1129) and FINIS (Financial Industry Information Service). About half of the publications are unique to Banking Information Source and not covered in ABI/Inform Global (788) or Complete. These unique titles include: *ABA bank directors briefing, ABA trust & investments, American banker, American bankruptcy law journal, Bank accounting & finance, Bank of America journal of applied corporate finance, Compliance reporter, Credit union journal, Financial adviser, Financial markets, institutions & instruments, Private asset management, School of Bank Marketing papers, Stonier Graduate School of Banking theses,* and *Internal revenue bulletin.* Coverage is from 1971 to the present. Also available through Dialog (Stamford, Conn.: Thomson Corporation, 2002–).

1131 **Business insights.** Datamonitor (Firm). [London?]: Reuters. http://www.globalbusinessinsights.com/autologin.asp.

HF54.7

Reports on energy, consumer goods, finance, health care, and technology. Reports, typically over 100 pages long, cover new product innovations, marketing strategies, market drivers, key players, trends, forecast business opportunities, and industry interviews. International focus, especially strong for European coverage.

1132 **The corporate finance sourcebook.** New Providence, N.J.: National Register, 1979–. ISSN: 0163-3031.

332.02573                                                    HG4057.A1565

Directory of firms involved in capital investments and financial services (e.g., venture capital, private lenders, commercial and financial factors, business intermediaries, leasing companies and corporate real estate, commercial, U.S.-based foreign, and investment banks and trusts, securities analysts and CPA/auditing firms). Entries include personnel, financial information, type of investor or service, minimum investment, funds available, average number of deals completed annually, industry preferences, and exit criteria. Indexed by name of company, personnel, and geography.

1133 **The credit union directory.** Accuity. Duluth, Ga.: Accuity, 1900–. ISSN: 0196-3678.

334.2202573                                                    HG2037.R28

Organized by state and then by city, the Directory gives contact information, date founded, number of employees, charter, CUNA ID, route number, Fedwire status, one year of financial information (asset rank, assets, shares, loans), number of members, ROA, executive names, and branches.

1134 **Dictionary of banking terms.** 5th ed. Thomas P. Fitch. viii, 534 p. Hauppauge, N.Y.: Barron's, 2006. ISBN: 9780764132636.

332.103                                                          HG151.F57

Contains 3,000 succint definitions about banking terms, practices, laws, and regulations. Good cross-references.

1135 **Elsevier's banking dictionary in seven languages: English, American, French, Italian, Spanish, Portuguese, Dutch, and German.** 3rd rev. and enl. ed. Julio Ricci. 359 p. Amsterdam, [The Netherlands]; New York: Elsevier, 1990. ISBN: 0444880674.

A polyglot dictionary for banking and finance arranged on an English-language base with equivalent terms in the other languages. The third revision of Elsevier's banking dictionary in seven languages, adding Portuguese to the list of languages. More than 2,400 terms; indexed by terms in the other languages.

**1136 Encyclopedia of American business history and biography.** Facts On File. ill. New York: Facts On File, 1988–. ISBN: 0816013713.

HE2751.R143

Combines biographical entries with articles discussing major companies, government and labor organizations, inventions, and legal decisions for various industries. The signed entries range in length from one-half to ten or more pages; most include photographs or other illustrations, and list publications and references, archives, and unpublished documents. Each volume is available separately. Volumes include: *The airline industry; The automobile industry, 1896–1920; The automobile industry, 1920–1980; Banking and finance to 1913; Banking and finance, 1913–1989; Iron and steel in the nineteenth century; Iron and steel in the twentieth century; Railroads in the nineteenth century;* and *Railroads in the age of regulation, 1900–1980.*

**1137 Global market information database.** Euromonitor. [1999–.] [London]: Euromonitor. http://www.gmid.euromonitor.com/.

HD2755.5.G56

Market reports, company profiles, and demographic, economic, and marketing statistics for 205 countries. Market reports are for 16 consumer markets (food and drink, tobacco, toys, etc.) and 14 industrial and service markets (accountancy, broadcasting, chemicals, property services, etc.).

Reports have market size, market sectors, share of market, marketing activity, research and development, corporate overview, distribution, consumer profiles, market forecasts, sector forecasts, sources, and definitions. Additional reports are available for market segments, such as baby food. Company profiles have background, recent news, competitive environment, and outlook. Consumer lifestyle reports and very useful marketing background analyze the consumer by country, gender, age, marital status, educational attainment, ethnicity, religion, home ownership, household profile, employment, income, health, eating and personal grooming habits, leisure activities, personal finance, communication, transport, and travel.

ECONOMICS & BUSINESS

Search for data, which can be exported into Excel or browse for reports. Data are available from 1977 through 2016 and include inflation, exchange rates, GDP, GNI, government expenditures, government finance, income, labor, and money supply.

**1138** **Mergent bank and finance manual.** Mergent, Inc. New York: Mergent, Inc., 2001–. ISSN: 1539-6444.

332.13                                                                                    HG4961.M65

Covers banks, insurance companies, investment trusts, and financial institutions. Has basic company financials, company description, list of properties and subsidiaries, report of independent auditors, annual meeting date, capital stock, dividends and long-term debt information, and contact information. Included in Mergent Online (19).

**1139** **North American financial institutions directory.** North American ed. Thomson Financial Publishing. maps. Skokie, Ill.: Thomson Financial, 2000–. ISSN: 1529-1367.

332.10257                                                                              HG1536.P635

Covers Canada, the U.S., Central America, the Caribbean, and Mexico. Entries vary in length from very brief to extensive, the latter providing information about branches and corporate and financial structure. A separate section lists banks by name and gives ranked lists of banks, commercial banks, savings and loan banks, and credit unions. Includes directories of associations, the Federal Reserve System, pertinent government organizations (e.g., the Secret Service), and a limited directory of the largest international banks.

**1140** **The savings directory.** Accuity. ill., maps. Duluth, Ga.: Accuity, 2005–. ISSN: 1931-8839.

332.3202573                                                                            HG2150.U18

Lists savings and loans institutions by state and city, then gives type of charter, type of institution, membership code, type of insurance for deposits, type of ownership, year established, number of employees, officers, brief financial data, routing number, mortgage portfolios, and other operational information. Also available in LexisNexis.

**1141** **Thomson bank directory.** 5 v. Thomson Financial Publishing. maps. Skokie, Ill.: Thomson Financial, 2000–. ISSN: 1529-1375.

332.102573                                                                             HG2441.R3

The best known bank directory, it provides information primarily for U.S. banks, but coverage includes international banks and government banking agencies and officials. Information includes national routing codes, personnel, basic financials, credit ratings, standard settlement instructions, and industry statistics and rankings. Also available through various aggregator databases. A similar resource, with much wider international coverage, is the *World bank directory* (Skokie, Ill.: Accuity, 2005–).

1142 **Thorndike encyclopedia of banking and financial tables.** [4th ed.] [David] [Thorndike], [A.S. Pratt and Sons], Thomson Financial Publishing. Arlington, Va.; [Skokie, Ill.]: A.S. Pratt and Sons; [Thomson Financial], [2007].

Tables for loan payment and amortization, compound interest and annuity, simple interest, savings and withdrawals, installment loans, and investment. A companion Yearbook (Boston: Warren, Gorham, and Lamont) is also published.

## Definition of the Industry

1143 **IBISWorld United States.** IBISWorld. New York: IBISWorld. http://www.ibisworld.com/.

HC103.I247

700 reports on the following industries: agriculture, forestry, fishing and hunting; mining; utilities; construction; manufacturing; wholesale trade; retail trade; transportation and warehousing; information; finance and insurance; real estate and rental and leasing; professional, scientific, and technical services; administrative and support and waste management and remediation services; educational services; health care and social assistance; arts, entertainment, and recreation; accommodation and food services; and other services. Setting this database apart are reports on small industries, such as parking lots and garages.

Reports include industry definition; key statistics; segmentations (products and services segmentation, major market segments, industry concentration, geographic spread); market characteristics (market size, demand determinants, domestic and international markets, basis of competition, life cycle); industry conditions (barriers to entry, taxation, industry assistance, regulation and deregulation, cost structure, capital and labor intensity, technology and systems, industry volatility, globalization); key factors (sensitivities and success factors); key competitors; and industry performance (current and historical).

## Internet Resources

**1144 Credit union directory.** National Credit Union Administration. Alexandria, Va.: National Credit Union Administration. http://purl.access.gpo.gov/GPO/LPS208.

Information from NCUA on U.S. credit unions, except "state-chartered natural person credit unions that are either uninsured or covered by private insurance corporations."—*Pref.* Gives charter number, address, name of CEO/manager, telephone number, assets, loans, net worth ratio, percent share growth, percent loan growth, loans/assets ratio, investments/assets ratio, number of members, and number of full-time employees. Also includes national statistics.

**1145 Ernst and Young.** Ernst and Young. 2007. London: Ernst and Young. http://www.ey.com/global/content.nsf/International/Industry_Overview/.

Ernst and Young provides "accounting and auditing, tax reporting and operations, tax advisory, business risk services, technology and security risk services, transaction advisory, and human capital services." The site is useful for articles on financial management, corporate governance, initial public offerings (IPOs), and industry reports (asset management, automotive, banking and capital markets, biotechnology, consumer products, insurance, media and entertainment, mining and metals, oil and gas, pharmaceuticals, real estate and construction, hospitality and leisure, technology, telecommunications, utilities).

**1146 Federal deposit insurance corporation.** Federal Deposit Insurance Corporation. [1996–.] [Washington, D.C.]: Federal Deposit Insurance Corporation. http://www.fdic.gov/.

HG2441

The site is organized into: Deposit Insurance, Consumer Protection, Industry Analysis, Regulation & Examinations, Asset Sales, and News & Events. Includes Call Reports and Thrift Financial Reports from 1998 to the present; an institution directory for federally insured institutions;

Summary of Deposits; Quarterly Banking Profile from December 31, 1994; statistics on banking and depository institutions; and laws and regulations.

## Organizations and Associations

1147 **American bankers association.** American Bankers Association. 2007. Washington, D.C.: American Bankers Association. http:// www.aba.com/default.htm.
Organized into the following areas: benchmarking and survey research; conferences/schools; consumer connection; economic perspective; job bank; press room; products (books, fingerprint products, periodicals, surveys/statistics); state associations; solutions and resources; training; affiliates; and members services.

1148 **National association of mutual insurance companies.** National Association of Mutual Insurance Companies. 2007. Indianapolis, Ind.: National Association of Mutual Insurance Companies. http:// www.namic.org/default.asp.
Founded in 1895, the association serves mutual (non–publicly traded) insurance companies. The site has a registered user access member directory, news, discussion forums, podcasts, *IN magazine*, seminars, event calendar, and government affairs (includes reports).

## Specialized Sources of Industry Data

1149 **Banking and monetary statistics, 1941–1970.** Board of Governors of the Federal Reserve System. vii, 1168 p. Washington: Board of Governors of the Federal Reserve System, 1976.
332.0973                                                                        HG2493.U54
Reprint of pt. 1 of the Board's 1943 publication of the same title; it includes "data on the condition and operation of all banks.statistics of bank debits, bank earnings, bank suspensions, branch, group, and chain banking, currency, money rates, security markets, Treasury finance, production and movement of gold, and international financial developments." *Pref.* Some statistical series predate 1914. Part 2 of the 1943 work, giving member bank statistics for each Federal Reserve district, was not reprinted. Volume 2, 1941–70, amends and updates v. 1. Available online in PDF at http:// fraser.stlouisfed.org/publications/bms2/.

**1150  Banking information index.** American Bankers Association. Ann Arbor, Mich.: UMI, 1994–. ISSN: 1075-282X.

016.3321                                                        Z7164.F5A53; HG1501

Indexes over 200 periodicals of interest to the financial services industry, especially banking. Also available through *Banking information source* (427).

**1151  Bank quarterly.** Sheshunoff Rating Services, Inc. Austin, Tex.: Sheshunoff Rating Services.

332.10973021                                                        HG2401.B34

Data on liquidity, earnings, loan exposure, capital adequacy, and other ratios for specific banks and savings and loans. Available online as BankFocus.

**1152  Bankscope.** Bureau van Dijk Electronic Publishing. [199?–.] [Brussels, Belgium]: Bureau van Dijk Electronic Publishing. http://scope.bvdep.com/.

Financial information on 25,000 public and private banks worldwide. Provides standardized reports, ratings, ownership data, financial analysis, security and price information, scanned images of the bank's annual or interim accounts, and country risk reports. Most data goes back eight years. Data sources include Fitch Ratings. Standardized reports contain detailed consolidated and/or unconsolidated balance sheet and income statement, as well as 36 pre-calculated ratios. Data can be downloaded to Excel. Also available on DVD-ROM or through WRDS (115).

**1153  Best's aggregates and averages.** A. M. Best Company. Oldwick, N.J.: A. M. Best, 1998–. ISSN: 1099-3592.

362.104258                                                        RA413.5.U5B476

Available for Property/Casualty, as well as Life/Health, with summary data on the insurance industry. Includes balance sheet and summary of operations, annual statements, quantitative analysis, insurance expenses, time series, premiums written, industry underwriting, leading companies and groups (with assets, policyholders surplus, reserves, premiums written, underwriting gain/loss, net investment income, realized capital gains, underwriting expense ratio, etc.), rankings, and composite listings. Coverage is for Canada and the United States.

**1154  Credit union directory.** National Credit Union Administration. Alexandria, Va.: National Credit Union Administration. http://purl.access.gpo.gov/GPO/LPS208.

Information from NCUA on U.S. credit unions, except "state-chartered natural person credit unions that are either uninsured or covered by private insurance corporations."—*Pref.* Gives charter number, address, name of CEO/manager, telephone number, assets, loans, net worth ratio, percent share growth, percent loan growth, loans/assets ratio, investments/assets ratio, number of members, and number of full-time employees. Also includes national statistics.

1155 **Federal deposit insurance corporation.** Federal Deposit Insurance Corporation. [1996–.] [Washington, D.C.]: Federal Deposit Insurance Corporation. http://www.fdic.gov/.

HG2441

The site is organized into: Deposit Insurance, Consumer Protection, Industry Analysis, Regulation & Examinations, Asset Sales, and News & Events. Includes Call Reports and Thrift Financial Reports from 1998 to the present; an institution directory for federally insured institutions; Summary of Deposits; Quarterly Banking Profile from December 31, 1994; statistics on banking and depository institutions; and laws and regulations.

1156 **The financial services fact book.** Insurance Information Institute. ill. New York: Insurance Information Institute [and] Financial Services Roundtable, 2002–. ISSN: 1537-6257.

658                                                                           HG181.F643465

Current information on insurance, banking, securities, and the financial services industry as a whole. Includes statistics on U.S. savings, investment and debt ownership, consumer fraud and identity theft, convergence of financial services companies, IT spending, and the growth of online commerce. The most current fact book is available at http://www.financialservicesfacts.org/financial/.

1157 **Forrester research.** Forrester Research. [1999–2003.] Cambridge, Mass.: Forrester. http://www.library.hbs.edu/forrester.htm.

HF5548.32T174

Nearly 17,000 original reports on technology's effect on business and the consumer in the United States, Canada, Europe, and Asia Pacific. Research is in two categories, technology and industry.

Topics in technology are application development, business intelligence, computing systems, consumer devices and access, content and collaboration, customer experience, enterprise applications, enterprise mobility, IT management, IT services, networking, portals and site technology, security, software infrastructure, and tech sector economics.

Topics in industry are brand strategy, brand tactics, consumer electronics, consumer products, customer insight, emerging marketing channels, energy and utilities, financial services, government, healthcare and life sciences, high tech, industry insight, manufacturing, marketing and advertising, marketing planning, media and entertainment, mobile services, professional services, relationship marketing, retail, telecommunications, television advertising, transportation and logistics, and travel.

Reports typically range from 3–20 pages, and some are available as videos.

**1158  Hoover's online.** Reference Press. 1996–. Austin, Tex.: Reference Press. http://www.hoovers.com/.

338.7                                                                 HG4057

Nearly 18 million records describing public and private companies primarily in the United States, but including Canada, United Kingdom, Europe, and Asia/Pacific. Profiles have an overview, history, family tree, industry information, products/operations, top competitors, competitive landscape, top executives with biographies, news, significant developments, and financial data (summary; income statement; balance sheet; cash flow; historical financials such as five years of P/E and per share; stock quote; interactive stock chart; market data; earnings estimates; this year's ratios for the company, industry, and market; SEC filings; and industry watch).

Covers 600 industries, organized into the following categories: Aerospace and Defense; Agriculture; Automotive and Transport; Banking; Beverages; Business Services; Charitable Organizations; Chemicals; Computer Hardware; Computer Services; Computer Software; Construction; Consumer Products Manufacturers; Consumer Services; Cultural Institutions; Education; Electronics; Energy and Utilities; Environmental Services and Equipment; Financial Services; Food; Foundations; Government; Health Care; Industrial Manufacturing; Insurance; Leisure; Media; Membership Organizations; Metals and Mining; Pharmaceuticals; Real Estate; Retail; Security Products and Services; Telecommunications Equipment; Telecommunications Services; and Transportation Services.

Coverage can be brief, but generally includes a fact sheet, overview, selected companies, industry watch with video interviews, news from the last 90 days, and web resources for terminology, associations, and organizations, and online publications. Includes Hoover's print publications

(*Hoover's handbook of American business* [35], *Hoover's handbook of private companies* [36]).

**1159 IBISWorld United States.** IBISWorld. New York: IBISWorld. http://www.ibisworld.com/.

HC103.I247

700 reports on the following industries: agriculture, forestry, fishing and hunting; mining; utilities; construction; manufacturing; wholesale trade; retail trade; transportation and warehousing; information; finance and insurance; real estate and rental and leasing; professional, scientific, and technical services; administrative and support and waste management and remediation services; educational services; health care and social assistance; arts, entertainment, and recreation; accommodation and food services; and other services. Setting this database apart are reports on small industries, such as parking lots and garages.

Reports include industry definition; key statistics; segmentations (products and services segmentation, major market segments, industry concentration, geographic spread); market characteristics (market size, demand determinants, domestic and international markets, basis of competition, life cycle); industry conditions (barriers to entry, taxation, industry assistance, regulation and deregulation, cost structure, capital and labor intensity, technology and systems, industry volatility, globalization); key factors (sensitivities and success factors); key competitors; and industry performance (current and historical).

**1160 Marketresearch.com academic.** Kalorama Information. 1999–. Bethesda, Md.: Kalorama Information. http://www.marketresearch.com/.

HF5415.2.K35

Market research reports from various sources (Icon Group, Kalorama, BizMiner, etc.) for Consumer Goods (apparel, cosmetics and personal care, house and home, pet services and supplies, travel services), Food and Beverage (alcoholic beverages, coffee and tea, soft drinks, confectionery, dairy products, food processing), Heavy Industry (energy, mining, utilities, construction, machines and parts, manufacturing, metals, paper and forest products, plastics, automotive, aviation & aerospace, logistics and shipping), Service Industries (accounting and finance, corporate services, banking and financial services, insurance), Public Sector (associations/

nonprofits, education, government), Life Science (biotechnology, agriculture, genomics, proteomics, medical imaging, healthcare facilities, managed care, regulation and policy, cardiovascular devices, equipment and supplies, wound care, pharmaceuticals, diseases and conditions, prescription drugs, therapeutic area), Technology & Media (computer equipment, electronics, networks, e-commerce and IT outsourcing, software, telecommunications, wireless), and Demographics (age, lifestyle and economics, multicultural).

Reports range in length, with some over 300 pages long, and give a variety of information (definition of industry, consumer demographics, consumer shopping habits, spending patterns, sales, establishments, employment, forecasts, trends, market size, market share, and market segmentation). Some company information is also included.

**1161  Securities industry fact book.** Securities Industry Association. New York: SIA, 1993–. ISSN: 1933-7043.

Information on capital markets, the securities industry, market activity, investor participation, global markets, and savings and investment. Good for finding statistics on corporate underwriting and private placements, capital raised for U.S. business, initial public offerings by state, total U.S. mergers and acquisitions, securities industry employment by firm category, securities industry profitability, pre-tax profit margins and return on equity, stock market capitalization, stock exchange activity, compound annual rates of return by decade for stocks, bonds and treasuries, and value of international securities offerings. Some data goes back to 1965.

# Food and Beverage

**1162  Plunkett's food industry almanac.** Jack W. Plunkett, Plunkett Research, Ltd. Houston, Tex.: Plunkett Research, 2003–. ISSN: 1547-6308.

338.1                                                              HD9003.P57

Data on 300 major companies including in retail, distribution, and specialty products. Company profiles include types of business, brands and affiliates, contacts, employee benefits and top salaries, sales and profit numbers, growth plans, and competitive advantage. Especially useful for the industry statistics and rankings at the front of the volume. Available as an e-book.

## Additional Reference Sources

**1163** **Global market information database.** Euromonitor. [1999–.] [London]: Euromonitor. http://www.gmid.euromonitor.com/.

HD2755.5.G56

Market reports, company profiles, and demographic, economic, and marketing statistics for 205 countries. Market reports are for 16 consumer markets (food and drink, tobacco, toys, etc.) and 14 industrial and service markets (accountancy, broadcasting, chemicals, property services, etc.).

Reports have market size, market sectors, share of market, marketing activity, research and development, corporate overview, distribution, consumer profiles, market forecasts, sector forecasts, sources, and definitions. Additional reports are available for market segments, such as baby food. Company profiles have background, recent news, competitive environment, and outlook. Consumer lifestyle reports and very useful marketing background analyze the consumer by country, gender, age, marital status, educational attainment, ethnicity, religion, home ownership, household profile, employment, income, health, eating and personal grooming habits, leisure activities, personal finance, communication, transport, and travel.

Search for data, which can be exported into Excel or browse for reports. Data are available from 1977 through 2016 and include inflation, exchange rates, GDP, GNI, government expenditures, government finance, income, labor, and money supply.

**1164** **The Oxford encyclopedia of food and drink in America.** Andrew F. Smith. 2 v., ill. Oxford; New York: Oxford University Press, 2004. ISBN: 0195154371.

641.3003                                                                 TX349.E45

Contains 770 articles, written by some 200 authors, on the social and economic history of food and beverages in the U.S. Arranged alphabetically, the articles are well written and engaging, many with illustrations. The articles range from events (Thanksgiving), personalities (Julia Childs), companies (Burger King), advertising (Aunt Jemima), to issues (biotechnology). Provides a welcome context for the industry. Available in online form.

**1165** **Thomas food and beverage market place.** Grey House Publishing, Inc. Millerton, N.Y.: Grey House, 2001–. ISSN: 1544-6344.

338                                                                      HD9003.T48

Combines *Food and beverage market place, Food and beverage market place—suppliers guide,* and *Thomas food industry register,* to form a comprehensive directory for companies in the industry. The 40,000 company profiles include contact information, executive titles, company description, parent company name, company divisions, number of employees, size of facility, sales volume, Standard Industrial Classification (SIC) codes, company type, and other locations. Published in three volumes. Vol. 1 lists food and beverage manufacturers and has indexes for brand names and ethnic foods. Vol. 2, products, equipment, and services, is arranged alphabetically by product or service. Indexes for brand name, transportation region, transportation type, and wholesale product type. Vol. 3, brokers, importers, exporters, consumer catalogs, and industry resources, with indexes for each. Also available online.

## Organizations and Associations

1166 **American beverage association.** American Beverage Association. Washington, D.C.: American Beverage Association. http://www.ameribev.org/index.aspx.

The site is full of useful statistics and background. Sections include All about Beverages (What America Drinks, Who Makes What?, History of Beverages, America's Beverages, Memorabilia); Industry Issues; News & Resources (Beverage Industry Market Research, Membership Directory); and Straight Talk about Beverage Products.

1167 **Food and drug administration.** Food and drug administration. [2005]. [Washington, D.C.]: The Office. http://www.fda.gov/.

The FDA's site has a wide range of information for the consumer and the researcher, including: Enforcement Activities (clinical trials, enforcement report, product recalls and alerts); Products Regulated by FDA (animal drugs and food, aquaculture, bioengineered food, biologics, gene therapy, mobile phones, sunlamps, tattoos, food, drugs, xenotransplantation); news; hot topics; publications; major initiatives/activities (advisory committees, bar coding, buying medical products online, Data Council, Facts@ FDA) and Food Industry (Prior Notice of Imports, Registration of Food Facilities).

1168 **International dairy foods association.** International Dairy Foods Association. 2007. Washington, D.C.: International Dairy Foods Association. http://www.idfa.org/.

The association represents the dairy industry, including milk, cheese, and ice cream. The site has industry facts, regulations, legislation, economic analysis, product marketing, meetings and training, and products and publications. Most useful for the statistics on the industry, links to butter and cheese cash prices, butter and milk futures and options, and federal milk marketing order data/prices. There are similar associations for various areas of the food industry, including the Chocolate Manufacturers Association, Natural Products Association, and the Foodservice and Packaging Institute.

**1169 Snack food association.** Snack Food Association. 2006 Alexandria, Va.: Snack Food Association. http://www.sfa.org/.

The association was founded in 1937 and is international in scope. The SFA website has information for consumers and the press, a calendar of events, and reports.

## Periodicals

**1170 Beverage industry annual manual.** Magazines for Industry. ill., some col. Cleveland, Ohio: Magazines for Industry, 1972/3–. ISSN: 8755-0717.

338.476630973                                      HD9348.U5B63

Entries for over 750 companies, nearly 1,200 products, and 750 resources, such as industry associations. Also has information on marketing, distribution, trends, consumption, and production.

## Specialized Sources of Industry Data

**1171 Beverage industry annual manual.** Magazines for Industry. ill., some col. Cleveland, Ohio: Magazines for Industry, 1972/3–. ISSN: 8755-0717.

338.476630973                                      HD9348.U5B63

Entries for over 750 companies, nearly 1,200 products, and 750 resources, such as industry associations. Also has information on marketing, distribution, trends, consumption, and production.

**1172 Hoover's online.** Reference Press. 1996–. Austin, Tex.: Reference Press. http://www.hoovers.com/.

338.7                                              HG4057

Nearly 18 million records describing public and private companies primarily in the United States, but including Canada, United Kingdom,

Europe, and Asia/Pacific. Profiles have an overview, history, family tree, industry information, products/operations, top competitors, competitive landscape, top executives with biographies, news, significant developments, and financial data (summary; income statement; balance sheet; cash flow; historical financials such as five years of P/E and per share; stock quote; interactive stock chart; market data; earnings estimates; this year's ratios for the company, industry, and market; SEC filings; and industry watch).

Covers 600 industries, organized into the following categories: Aerospace and Defense; Agriculture; Automotive and Transport; Banking; Beverages; Business Services; Charitable Organizations; Chemicals; Computer Hardware; Computer Services; Computer Software; Construction; Consumer Products Manufacturers; Consumer Services; Cultural Institutions; Education; Electronics; Energy and Utilities; Environmental Services and Equipment; Financial Services; Food; Foundations; Government; Health Care; Industrial Manufacturing; Insurance; Leisure; Media; Membership Organizations; Metals and Mining; Pharmaceuticals; Real Estate; Retail; Security Products and Services; Telecommunications Equipment; Telecommunications Services; and Transportation Services.

Coverage can be brief, but generally includes a fact sheet, overview, selected companies, industry watch with video interviews, news from the last 90 days, and web resources for terminology, associations, and organizations, and online publications. Includes Hoover's print publications (*Hoover's handbook of American business* [35], *Hoover's handbook of private companies* [36]).

1173 **Hospitality and tourism index.** EBSCO Publishing. [Ipswich, Mass.]: EBSCO Publishing. http://search.epnet.com/login.aspx?authtype=ip,uid&profile=ehost/.

Indexes scholarly research and industry news relating to all areas of hospitality and tourism, including culinary arts, hotel management, and travel. Formed from the now ceased Cornell University's hospitality database, the Universities of Surrey and Oxford Brookes Articles in Hospitality and Tourism, and Purdue University's Lodging, Restaurant, and Tourism Index. Coverage from 1965.

1174 **Marketresearch.com academic.** Kalorama Information. 1999–. Bethesda, Md.: Kalorama Information. http://www.marketresearch.com/.

HF5415.2.K35

Market research reports from various sources (Icon Group, Kalorama, BizMiner, etc.) for Consumer Goods (apparel, cosmetics and personal care, house and home, pet services and supplies, travel services), Food and Beverage (alcoholic beverages, coffee and tea, soft drinks, confectionery, dairy products, food processing), Heavy Industry (energy, mining, utilities, construction, machines and parts, manufacturing, metals, paper and forest products, plastics, automotive, aviation & aerospace, logistics and shipping), Service Industries (accounting and finance, corporate services, banking and financial services, insurance), Public Sector (associations/nonprofits, education, government), Life Science (biotechnology, agriculture, genomics, proteomics, medical imaging, healthcare facilities, managed care, regulation and policy, cardiovascular devices, equipment and supplies, wound care, pharmaceuticals, diseases and conditions, prescription drugs, therapeutic area), Technology & Media (computer equipment, electronics, networks, e-commerce and IT outsourcing, software, telecommunications, wireless), and Demographics (age, lifestyle and economics, multicultural).

Reports range in length, with some over 300 pages long, and give a variety of information (definition of industry, consumer demographics, consumer shopping habits, spending patterns, sales, establishments, employment, forecasts, trends, market size, market share, and market segmentation). Some company information is also included.

**1175  Thomas food and beverage market place.** Grey House Publishing, Inc. Millerton, N.Y.: Grey House, 2001–. ISSN: 1544-6344.

338                                                                    HD9003.T48

Combines *Food and beverage market place, Food and beverage market place—suppliers guide,* and *Thomas food industry register,* to form a comprehensive directory for companies in the industry. The 40,000 company profiles include contact information, executive titles, company description, parent company name, company divisions, number of employees, size of facility, sales volume, Standard Industrial Classification (SIC) codes, company type, and other locations. Published in three volumes. Vol. 1 lists food and beverage manufacturers and has indexes for brand names and ethnic foods. Vol. 2, products, equipment, and services, is arranged alphabetically by product or service. Indexes for brand name, transportation region, transportation type, and wholesale product type. Vol. 3, brokers, importers, exporters, consumer catalogs, and industry resources, with indexes for each. Also available online.

# Health care

## *Additional Reference Sources*

1176  **AHA guide to the health care field.** American Hospital
    Association. v. Chicago: Healthcare Infosource, Inc., 1997–.
    RA977.A1 A46|RA977.A44

Title varies: 1949–71, pt. 2 of Aug. issue (called "Guide issue," 1956–70)
of *Hospitals,* which superseded *American hospital directory* (1945–48);
1972–73, *The AHA guide to the health care field*; 1974–96, *American Hospital Association guide to the health care field.*
    "America's directory of hospitals and health care systems."—*Cover.*
Description based on 2006–07 ed.
    "Provides basic data reflecting the delivery of health care in the United
States and associated territories."—*Introd.* Four major sections, each with
table of contents and explanatory information: (A) Hospitals, institutional,
and associate members; (B) networks, health care systems, and alliances;
(C) lists of health organizations, agencies, and providers; and (D) indexes.
Current edition also available in CD-ROM format.
    Statistical information concerning hospitals is published in *AHA hos-
pital statistics* (Chicago: Health Forum, 2005–).

1177  **The dictionary of health economics.** Anthony J. Culyer.
    Northampton, Mass: Edward Elgar, 2005. ISBN: 1843762080.
362.103                                                    RA410.A3C85

Definitions of terms, concepts, and methods from the field of health
economics and related fields, such as epidemiology, pharmacoeconomics,
medical sociology, medical statistics, and others. Alphabetical arrangement. Personal names are included only when they are part of a headword.
Also includes health economists' professional organizations, but no government agencies or research groups in universities (cf. *Pref.*). For health
services researchers and professionals. Also available as an e-book. A similar title is *Dictionary of health economics and finance* (1178).

1178  **Dictionary of health economics and finance.** David E. Marcinko,
    Hope R. Hetico. 436 p. New York: Springer Publ., 2006. ISBN:
    0826102549.
338.4/7362103                                              RA410.A3D53

Definitions, abbreviations and acronyms, and eponyms of medical economics and health care sector terminology. Bibliography. A similar title is *The dictionary of health economics* (1177).

**1179 Dictionary of health insurance and managed care.** David Edward Marcinko. New York: Springer, 2006. ISBN: 0826149944.
368.382003 RA413.D53

Up-to-date health insurance, managed care plans and programs, health care industry terminology and definitions, abbreviatons, and acronyms. Available online via netLibrary.

**1180 Encyclopedia of biostatistics.** 2nd ed. P. Armitage, Theodore Colton. 8 v. Chichester [England]; West Sussex [England]: John Wiley, 2005. ISBN: 047084907X.
610.21 RA409.E53

First edition, 1998 (6 v.). Description based on rev. and enl. ed., 2005 (8 v.).
Contents: v. 1, A–Chap; v. 2, Char–Dos; v. 3, Dou–Gre; v. 4, Gro–Mar; v. 5, Mas–Nui; v. 6, Nul–Ran; v. 7, Rao–Str; v. 8, Stu–Z, index.
Biostatistics can be defined as the application of statistical methods to the life sciences, medicine, and the health sciences. Clinical epidemiology, clinical trials, disease modeling, epidemiology, statistical computing, and vital and health statistics are some examples of the areas covered. This edition contains more than 1,300 articles, with approximately 300 revised and 182 new entries. New topics include, for example, applications of biostatistics to bioinformatics, study of the human genome, and outbreaks of infectious-disease epidemics. Bibliographies, many cross-references, author index, and a selected list of review articles. Available both in print and online through http://www.interscience.wiley.com.

**1181 Encyclopedia of health care management.** Michael J. Stahl. xxxvii, 621 p., ill. Thousand Oaks, Calif.: Sage, 2004. ISBN: 0761926747.
362.1068 RA971.E52

Alphabetical list of entries at the beginning of the book provides an overview of the terminology and variety of subject areas covered in this resource including business and economics, statistics, law, clinical research, informatics, and others. A reader's guide with the following major headings is provided: Accounting and activity-based costing, Economics, Finance, Health policy, Human resources, Information technology, Institutions and organizations, International health care issues, Legal and regulatory issues, Managed care, Marketing and customer value, Operations and decision making, Pharmaceuticals and clinical trials, Quality, Statistics and data mining, and Strategy. The main section, consisting of approximately 650 entries, is alphabetically arranged. Each entry contains the term's definition, background, and other relevant information. Includes tables on health care acronyms, medical degrees, medical legislation, and others. Cross-references, list of further readings, and websites. Index. Also available online from Sage eReference (http://www.sage-ereference.com/public/browse.php).

**1182  Essentials of managed health care.** 5th ed. Peter R. Kongstvedt. xxi, 841 p., ill. Sudbury, Mass.: Jones and Bartlett, 2007. ISBN: 9780763739836.

362.104258                                                      RA413.E87

1st ed., 1989; 4th ed., 2001 had title *The managed health care handbook.* 5th ed., 2007 is the rev. ed. of two different titles by the same author: *The managed health care handbook,* 4th ed., 2001, and rev. ed. of *Essentials of managed health care,* 4th ed., 2001. Contents: section 1: Introduction to managed health care (ch. 1–4); section 2: The health care delivery system (ch. 5–8); section 3: Medical management (ch. 9–16); section 4: Operational management and marketing (ch. 17–25); section 5: Special markets (ch. 26–29); section 6: Legal and regulatory issues (ch. 30–33); glossary; index. Intended as a guide and a resource to the managed health care system, with information on types of managed care plans and integrated healthcare delivery systems, physician networks in managed health care, prescription drug benefits in managed health care, etc.

**1183  Global market information database.** Euromonitor. [1999–.] [London]: Euromonitor. http://www.gmid.euromonitor.com/.

HD2755.5.G56

Market reports, company profiles, and demographic, economic, and marketing statistics for 205 countries. Market reports are for 16 consumer markets (food and drink, tobacco, toys, etc.) and 14 industrial and service markets (accountancy, broadcasting, chemicals, property services, etc.).

Reports have market size, market sectors, share of market, marketing activity, research and development, corporate overview, distribution, consumer profiles, market forecasts, sector forecasts, sources, and definitions. Additional reports are available for market segments, such as baby food. Company profiles have background, recent news, competitive

environment, and outlook. Consumer lifestyle reports and very useful marketing background analyze the consumer by country, gender, age, marital status, educational attainment, ethnicity, religion, home ownership, household profile, employment, income, health, eating and personal grooming habits, leisure activities, personal finance, communication, transport, and travel.

Search for data, which can be exported into Excel or browse for reports. Data are available from 1977 through 2016 and include inflation, exchange rates, GDP, GNI, government expenditures, government finance, income, labor, and money supply.

**1184 Health care reform around the world.** Andrew C. Twaddle. xiii, 419 p., ill. Westport, Conn: Auburn House, 2002. ISBN: 0865692882.

362.1                                                RA394.H4145

Describes health care reform efforts and trends in different countries, with roughly comparable information for the countries included. Ch. 1 is an international comparison of health care system reforms—United Kingdom, Eastern and Western Europe, United States, the Middle East, Latin America, Asia, and Oceania. Online edition available via Greenwood Digital Collection (ebooks.greenwood.com/browse/index.jsp) and netLibrary.

**1185 Health care systems around the world: Characteristics, issues, reforms.** Marie L. Lassey, William R. Lassey, Martin J. Jinks. xiii, 370 p., ill., maps. Upper Saddle River, N.J.: Prentice Hall, 1997. ISBN: 0131042335.

362.1                                                RA393.L328

Contents: Introduction, basic issues and concepts; The countries and their characteristics; The United States, high-technology and limited access; Canada, challenges to public payment for universal care; Japan, preventive health care as cultural norm; Germany, a tradition of universal health care; France, centrally controlled and locally managed; The Netherlands, gradual adaptation; Sweden, decentralized comprehensive care; The United Kingdom, the economy model; The Czech Republic, a new mixture of public and private services; Hungary, creating a remodeled system; Russia, transition to market and consumer orientation; China, privatizing socialist health care; Mexico, modernizing structure and expanded rural services; Organization variations and reforms; Economic organization of health care, comparative perspectives;

Expectations for reform, a glimpse at the future. Description and analysis of health care systems in different countries, addressing demographic, social, and economic characteristics, also health promotion, prevention of disease, and health care. Includes bibliographical references and index.

**1186 Health care systems of the developed world: How the United States' system remains an outlier.** Duane A. Matcha. x, 198 p., ill. Westport, Conn: Praeger, 2003. ISBN: 027597992X.

362.10973                                                          RA441.M38

Contents: ch. 1, Introduction; ch. 2, The United States; ch. 3, Canada; ch. 4, United Kingdom; ch. 5, Germany; ch. 6, Sweden; ch. 7, Japan; ch. 8, Conclusion. Provides an introduction to selected major healthcare systems, with consideration of their historical and political basis. Provides a framework for analysis and comparison of the different systems. Various tables and figures related to health insurance, personal health care expenditures, self-rated health status, future concerns, and others. Includes bibliographical references and index. *World health systems: Challenges and perspectives* (1189) presents profiles of health systems in 28 countries. A 1997 publication, *Health care systems around the world: Characteristics, issues, reforms* (1185), provides additional information in this area. Milton I Roemer's *National health systems of the world*, publ. 1991–93, remains an important title. It consists of a comprehensive study and analysis of national health systems in 68 industrialized, middle-income, and very poor countries, with a cross-national analysis of the major health care issues within different systems.

**1187 Hospital and health administration index.** American Hospital Association., American Hospital Association.; Resource Center., National Library of Medicine (U.S.). Chicago: American Hospital Association, 1995–1999. ISSN: 1077-1719.

016.36211                                              Z6675.H75H67; RA963

1945–54, *Index of current hospital literature*; 1955–57, *Hospital periodical literature index*; 1957–94, *Hospital literature index*, cumulated at five-year intervals for the 1945–77 volumes as *Cumulative index of hospital literature*. Discontinued; last published in 1999. Described as a "primary guide to literature on hospital and other health care facility administration, including multi-institutional systems, health policy and planning, and the administrative aspects of health care delivery. . . . Special emphasis is given to the theory of health care systems in general; health care in industrialized countries, primarily in the United States; and provision of health care both inside and outside of health care facilities"—*Introd.* A separate online database, HealthSTAR (Health Services Technology, Administration, and Research) for this literature, previously maintained by NLM, is no longer available (cf. list of NLM's retired databases at http://www.nlm.nih.gov/services/pastdatabases.html). Relevant content is available via MEDLINE (1188)/PubMed (Bethesda, Md.: U.S. National Center for Biotechnology Information, 1996–) or HealthSTAR (Ovid) (1199), and also CINAHL (Ipswich, Mass.: EBSCO, 1982–)

**1188  MEDLINE.** National Library of Medicine (U.S.). 1900s–. Bethesda, Md: National Library of Medicine (U.S.). http://purl.access.gpo.gov/GPO/LPS4708.

MEDLINE®—Medical Literature Analysis and Retrieval System Online (National Library of Medicine®—NLM), primary subset of PubMed® (Bethesda, Md.: U.S. National Center for Biotechnology Information, 1996–) and part of the Entrez (Bethesda, Md.: National Library of Medicine, 2004–) databases provided by the National Center for Biotechnology Information (NCBI). Coverage extends back to 1950, with some older material (cf. http://www.nlm.nih.gov/services/oldmed.html).

Bibliographic database, providing comprehensive access to the international biomedical literature from the fields of medicine, nursing, dentistry, veterinary medicine, allied health, and the preclinical sciences. It is also a primary source of information from the international literature on biomedicine, including the following topics as they relate to biomedicine and health care: Biology, environmental science, marine biology, plant and animal science, biophysics, and chemistry. For indexing articles, NLM uses Medical Subject Headings MeSH® (Bethesda, Md.: U.S. National Library of Medicine, 1975–), a controlled vocabulary of biomedical terms. MEDLINE can also be searched via the NLM Gateway (Bethesda, Md.: National Library of Medicine, 2000–). An increasing number of MEDLINE citations contain a link to the free full-text articles.

The MEDLINE database is the electronic counterpart of *Index Medicus®* (Bethesda, Md.: U.S. Dept. of Health, Education and Welfare; Public Health Service; National Institutes of Health; National Library of Medicine, 1960–2004), *Index to dental literature* (Chicago: American Dental Association, 1962–1999), and the *International nursing index* (New York: American Journal of Nursing Company, 1966–2000).

For detailed information, see the MEDLINE fact sheet at http://www. nlm.nih.gov/pubs/factsheets/medline.html

**1189 World health systems: Challenges and perspectives.** Bruce Fried, Laura M. Gaydos. xii, 563 p., ill. Chicago: Health Administration Pr., 2002. ISBN: 0585426422.

362.1                                                              RA441.W676

Contents: pt. I, Current issues facing global health systems; pt. II, Profiled countries: the wealthy countries (ch. 4–15); The transitional countries (ch. 16–28); The very poor countries (ch. 29–31); glossary of terms; index. Presents profiles of health systems in 28 countries. Organized in three categories by the wealth of each nation: wealthy, transitional, and very poor. Addresses the various challenges health services face, how they are organized, and how they are financed. Each chapter includes disease patterns and health system financing, also the "history, present status and future challenges of their health systems"—*Pref.* Available online via netLibrary.

## *Internet Resources*

**1190 Agency for healthcare research and quality (AHRQ).** Agency for Healthcare Research and Quality (U.S.). 1990s Rockville, Md: Agency for Healthcare Research and Quality. http://www.ahrq.gov.

"The Agency for Healthcare Research and Quality (AHRQ) is the lead Federal agency charged with improving the quality, safety, efficiency, and effectiveness of health care for all Americans. As one of 12 agencies within the Department of Health and Human Services, AHRQ supports health services research that will improve the quality of health care and promote evidence-based decision making."—*AHRQ at a glance (http://www.ahrq. gov/about/ataglance.htm)*

Searchable website ("search AHRQ" and "A–Z Quick Menu") provides access to a variety of resources, with links to clinical and consumer health information, research findings, funding opportunities, data and surveys, quality assessment, specific populations (minorities, women, elderly, and others), and public health preparedness (bioterrorism and response). Links to a large number of full-text documents, including links to the tools, literature, and news in patient safety (e.g., *AHRQ patient safety network*) and tips on how to prevent medical errors.

1191 **American hospital association.** American Hospital Association. Chicago: American Hospital Association. http://www.aha.org/ aha_app/index.jsp.

Founded in 1898, the association represents hospitals, health care networks, and their consumers. The website provides "Fast Facts on U.S. Hospitals," reports and studies, trends, testimony, regulations, and a section for members only. Some information is only available for a fee.

1192 **Centers for Medicare and Medicaid services (U.S.).** Centers for Medicare and Medicaid Services (U.S.), U.S. Health Care Financing Administration. 2001–. Baltimore, Md.: Centers for Medicare and Medicaid Services, U.S. Dept. of Health and Human Services. http://cms.hhs.gov/.

Centers for Medicare and Medicaid Services (CMS), formerly Health Care Financing Administration.

Detailed information on Medicare, the federal health insurance program for people 65 years and older and for younger people with certain disabilities, providing details on enrollment, benefits, and other data; Medicaid, a joint federal and state program (state programs vary from state to state) that helps with medical costs for people with low income and limited means; SCHIP (State Children's Health Insurance Program); regulation and guidance manuals and Health Insurance Portability and Accountability Act (HIPAA), research, statistics, data and systems. Also provides various tools and resources helpful in navigating this website (http://www.cms.hhs.gov/home/tools.asp), for example a "participating physician directory," a "glossary tool" and an "acronym lookup tool."

1193 **The Dartmouth atlas of health care.** Dartmouth Institute for Health Policy and Clinical Practice, Dartmouth Medical School, American Hospital Association. Lebanon, N.H.: Dartmouth Institute for Health Policy and Clinical Practice. http://www. dartmouthatlas.org/atlases.shtm.

The Dartmouth Atlas Project started as a series of books and is now accessible via a web-based resource, providing access to the *Dartmouth atlas of health care* series (national editions, specialty-specific editions, state editions, and regional editions). Describes and illustrates quality, cost, and delivery of healthcare services in the U.S. and geographic variations in practice patterns, with description of the physician workforce and distribution of resources. Written for health policy analysts and other health professionals. The home page at http://www.dartmouthatlas.org/index. shtm provides additional information.

**1194 Department of health and human services.** U.S. Department of Health and Human Services. 1997–. [Washington, D.C.]: U.S. Dept. of Health and Human Services. http://www.hhs.gov/.

The U.S. Department of Health and Human Services is responsible for "protecting the health of all Americans and providing essential human services, especially for those who are least able to help themselves."—*HHS What We Do.* To that end, their website provides a rich source of information on aging, disasters and emergencies, diseases and conditions, drug and food information, families and children, grants and funding, policies and regulations, reference collections (dictionaries and glossaries, various indexes, clinical trials database, food additive database, statistics, reports), resource locators, safety and wellness, and specific populations.

**1195 European health for all database (HFA-DB).** World Health Organization Regional Office for Europe. 2000s–. Copenhagen, Denmark: World Health Organization Regional Office for Europe. http://data.euro.who.int/hfadb/.

Description based on Jan. 2007 version.

Provides basic health statistics and health trends for the member states of the WHO European Region, with approximately 600 health indicators, including basic demographic and socioeconomic indicators; some lifestyle- and environment-related indicators; mortality, morbidity, and disability; hospital discharges; and health care resources, utilization, and expenditures. Can be used as a tool for international comparison and for assessing the health situation and trends in any European country.

**1196 Faststats A to Z.** National Center for Health Statistics (NCHS). Hyattsville, Md: U.S. Dept. of Health and Human Services, Centers for Disease Control and Prevention, National Center for Health Statistics. http://www.cdc.gov/nchs/fastats/Default.htm.

Provides topic-appropriate public health statistics (e.g., birth data, morbidity and mortality statistics, and health care use) and relevant links to further information and publications. Includes state and territorial data, with clickable map for individual state data. Also includes data derived from the "Behavioral Risk Factor Surveillance System (BRFSS)," which compiles data for 16 negative behaviors.

1197  **Federation of American hospitals.** Federation of American
       Hospitals. Washington, D.C.: Federation of American Hospitals.
       http://www.fahs.com/.

The federation represents privately owned and managed community
hospitals and health systems. The website has testimony, congressional
communications, health and economic statistics, list of member facilities,
*Hospital outlook* (bimonthly newsletter), information on the annual meeting, and a members only section.

1198  **Health in the Americas.** Pan American Sanitary Bureau. v.,
       ill. Washington, D.C: Pan American Health Organization, Pan
       American Sanitary Bureau, Regional Office of the World Health
       Organization, 1998–.

610.8s; 362.1091812                                              RA10.P252

Published by Pan American Health Organization (PAHO) (Washington:
Pan American Health Organization, 1990s–); "Salud en las Américas."
    Title varies: Previously had title *Summary of reports on the health con-
ditions in the Americas* and *Health conditions in the Americas*. Description
based on 2007 ed. (2 v.): v. 1, Regional analysis; v. 2, Country-by-country
assessment.
    Health data, facts, health trends, and related information for Central and
South America, with emphasis on health disparities. Provides a vision for the
future of health and health challenges in the Americas. Also available online
through netLibrary; both print and online versions in English or Spanish.
    A complement to this publication is *Health statistics from the Ameri-
cas*, publ. in print format 1991–98, and now online (2003 ed. http://www.
paho.org/english/dd/pub/SP_591.htm and 2006 ed. http://www.paho.org/
English/DD/AIS/HSA2006.htm).

1199  **HealthSTAR (Ovid).** National Library of Medicine (U.S.). 2000–.
       Sandy, Utah: Ovid Technologies. http://www.ovid.com/site/
       products/ovidguide/hstrdb.htm.

Ovid HealthSTAR (HSTR); HealthSTAR (Health Services Technology,
Administration, and Research).
    "Comprised of data from the National Library of Medicine's (NLM)
MEDLINE and former HealthSTAR databases . . . contains citations to the
published literature on health services, technology, administration, and
research. It focuses on both the clinical and non-clinical aspects of health
care delivery. . . . Offered by Ovid as a continuation of NLM's now-defunct

HealthSTAR database. Retains all existing backfile citations and is updated with new journal citations culled from MEDLINE. Contains citations and abstracts (when available) to journal articles, monographs, technical reports, meeting abstracts and papers, book chapters, government documents, and newspaper articles from 1975 to the present."—*Publ. notes.* A list of NLM's retired databases, including the original HealthSTAR database, can be found at http://www.nlm.nih.gov/services/pastdatabases.html .

Relevant content on health services research, health technology, health administration, health policy, health economics, etc., can also be found in MEDLINE® (1189)/PubMed® (Bethesda, Md.: U.S. National Center for Biotechnology Information, 1996–), NLM® Gateway (Bethesda, Md.: National Library of Medicine, 2000–), and also CINAHL® (Ipswich, Mass.: EBSCO, 1982–).

**1200  International health data reference guide.** National Center for Health Statistics (U.S.), National Center for Health Statistics (U.S.)., National Center for Health Statistics (U.S.). ill. Hyattsville, Md.: U.S. Dept. of Health and Human Services, Public Health Service, National Center for Health Statistics, [1984?]–.

362.1021                                                                                      RA407.A58

Description based on 11th ed., 2003.

"Provides information collected in 2003 on the availability of selected national vital, hospital, health personnel resources, and population-based health survey statistics. Information for 40 nations. . . . Main purpose is to provide information not readily available in published form. It is not designed to provide information on the availability of measures such as crude birth and death rates or life expectancy at birth"—*Pref.* Biennial. Also available online on the National Center for Health Statistics (NCHS) (Hyattsville, Md.: Centers for Disease Control and Prevention, 1990s–) website at http://purl.access.gpo.gov/GPO/LPS24629.

**1201  MEDLINE.** National Library of Medicine (U.S.). 1900s–. Bethesda, Md: National Library of Medicine (U.S.). http://purl.access.gpo. gov/GPO/LPS4708.

MEDLINE®—Medical Literature Analysis and Retrieval System Online (National Library of Medicine®—NLM), primary subset of PubMed® (Bethesda, Md.: U.S. National Center for Biotechnology Information, 1996–) and part of the Entrez (Bethesda, Md.: National Library of Medicine, 2004–) databases provided by the National Center for Biotechnology

Information (NCBI). Coverage extends back to 1950, with some older material (cf. http://www.nlm.nih.gov/services/oldmed.html).

Bibliographic database, providing comprehensive access to the international biomedical literature from the fields of medicine, nursing, dentistry, veterinary medicine, allied health, and the preclinical sciences. It is also a primary source of information from the international literature on biomedicine, including the following topics as they relate to biomedicine and health care: Biology, environmental science, marine biology, plant and animal science, biophysics, and chemistry. For indexing articles, NLM uses Medical Subject Headings MeSH® (Bethesda, Md.: U.S. National Library of Medicine, 1975–), a controlled vocabulary of biomedical terms. MEDLINE can also be searched via the NLM Gateway (Bethesda, Md.: National Library of Medicine, 2000–). An increasing number of MEDLINE citations contain a link to the free full-text articles.

The MEDLINE database is the electronic counterpart of *Index Medicus*® (Bethesda, Md.: U.S. Dept. of Health, Education and Welfare; Public Health Service; National Institutes of Health; National Library of Medicine, 1960–2004), *Index to dental literature* (Chicago: American Dental Association, 1962–1999), and the *International nursing index* (New York: American Journal of Nursing Company, 1966–2000).

For detailed information, see the MEDLINE fact sheet at http://www.nlm.nih.gov/pubs/factsheets/medline.html

**1202 MEPS Medical expenditure panel survey.** U.S. Agency for Healthcare Research and Quality. 1996–. Bethesda, Md: Agency for Healthcare Research and Quality. http://www.meps.ahrq.gov/mepsweb/.

RA408.5

Produced by Agency for Healthcare Research and Quality (AHRQ) (1190).

"Set of large-scale surveys of families and individuals, their medical providers (doctors, hospitals, pharmacies, etc.), and employers across the United States. MEPS collects data on the specific health services that Americans use, how frequently they use them, the cost of these services, and how they are paid for, as well as data on the cost, scope, and breadth of health insurance held by and available to U.S. workers" (*Website*). Provides information on health expenditures, utilization of health services, health insurance, and nursing homes, and reimbursement mechanisms. MEPS topics include access to health care, children's health, children's insurance coverage, health care disparities, mental health, minority health, the uninsured, and other topics. Further details concerning the survey background, data overview, and frequently asked questions are provided at the website. Provides full-text access to MEPS publications: highlights, research findings, statistical briefs, etc.

**1203 Partners in information access for the public health workforce.** U.S. National Library of Medicine. 2003–. Bethesda, Md.: U.S. National Library of Medicine, National Institutes of Health, Dept. of Health and Human Services. http://phpartners.org/.

"Collaboration of U.S. government agencies, public health organizations, and health sciences libraries which provides timely, convenient access to selected public health resources on the Internet . . . [with the mission of] helping the public health workforce find and use information effectively to improve and protect the public's health."—*Website*

Provides links to the individual partner websites, such as Agency for Healthcare Research and Quality (AHRQ) (1190), American Public Health Association (APHA), Association of Schools of Public Health (ASPH), Association of State and Territorial Health Officials (ASTHO), Centers for Disease Control and Prevention (CDC) (Atlanta: Centers for Disease Control and Prevention, U.S. Dept. of Health and Human Services, 1998–), Medical Library Association (MLANET) (Chicago: Medical Library Association [MLA], 1998–), National Library of Medicine (Bethesda, Md.: National Library of Medicine, 1993–), and several other organizations. Provides extensive information on several public health topics (currently to bioterrorism, environmental health, and HIV/AIDS). For additional information and links see the Partners in Information Access for the Public Health Workforce fact sheet at http://www.nlm.nih.gov/nno/partners.html.

**1204 State snapshots.** Agency for Healthcare Research and Quality. 2007–. Rockville, Md: Agency for Healthcare Research and Quality. http://statesnapshots.ahrq.gov/statesnapshots/index.jsp.

Based on data collected from the *National healthcare quality report* (http://purl.access.gpo.gov/GPO/LPS62498). Also called *NHRQ state snapshots*. Linked Agency for Healthcare Research and Quality (1190) website.

Provides "state-specific health care quality information including strengths, weaknesses, and opportunity for improvement . [to] better understand healthcare quality and disparities" (*Website*). A "state selection map" (http://statesnapshots.ahrq.gov/statesnapshots/map.jsp?menuID=2&state=) allows users to choose a particular state and compare it to other states in terms of healthcare quality, types of care (preventive, acute, and chronic), settings of care (hospitals, ambulatory care, nursing home, and home health), several specific conditions, and clinical preventive services. Provides help with interpretation of results and a methods section.

The Kaiser Family Foundation (Menlo Park, Calif.: Henry J. Kaiser Family Foundation, 2000–) makes a comparable website available: "State Health Facts" (http://www.statehealthfacts.org). Provides statistical data and health policy information on various health topics, with a standardized menu for information about each state ("individual state profiles" tab) and to find out how it compares to the U.S. overall ("50 state comparisons" tab). Categories include demography and the economy, health status, health coverage & the uninsured, Medicaid and SCHIP, health costs & budgets, Medicare, managed care and health insurance, providers and service use, minority health, women's health, and HIV/AIDS.

**1205 WHOSIS.** World Health Organization. [1994]–. Geneva, [Switzerland]: World Health Organization. http://www.who.int/ whosis/.

Published by World Health Organization (WHO).

Provides description and online access to statistical and epidemiological information, data, and tools available from WHO and other sites: mortality and health status, disease statistics, health systems statistics, risk factors and health services, and inequities in health. Provides links to several databases: WHOSIS database, with the latest "core health indicators" from WHO sources (including *The world health report* [Geneva: World Health Organization, 1995–] and *World health statistics* [1206]), which make it possible to construct tables for any combination of countries, indicators and years, Causes of Death database, WHO Global InfoBase Online, Global Health Atlas, and Reproductive Health Indicators database.

**1206 World health statistics.** World Health Organization. 2005–. Geneva, Switzerland: World Health Organization. http://www.who. int/healthinfo/statistics/en/.

1939/46–96 publ. as *World health statistics annual = Annuaire de statistiques sanitaires mondiales* (print version).

Part of WHOSIS: WHO Statistical Information System (Geneva, Switzerland: World Health Organization, 1994).

Description based on online 3rd ed., 2007 ed. (http://www.who.int/whosis/whostat2007.pdf ).

Contents: pt. 1, "Ten statistical highlights in global public health." Pt. 2, "World health statistics": "Health status: Mortality"; "Health status: Morbidity"; "Health services coverage"; "Risk factors"; "Health systems"; "Inequities in health"; "Demographic and socioeconomic statistics."

"Presents the most recent health statistics for WHO's 193 Member States . . . collated from publications and databases produced by WHO's technical programmes and regional offices . . . selected on the basis of their relevance to global health, the availability and quality of the data, and the accuracy and comparability of estimates. The statistics for the indicators are derived from an interactive process of data collection, compilation, quality assessment and estimation occurring among WHO's technical programmes and its Member States"—*Introd.* Print version also available.

## *Organizations and Associations*

**1207  Agency for healthcare research and quality (AHRQ).** Agency for Healthcare Research and Quality (U.S.). 1990s Rockville, Md: Agency for Healthcare Research and Quality. http://www.ahrq.gov.

"The Agency for Healthcare Research and Quality (AHRQ) is the lead Federal agency charged with improving the quality, safety, efficiency, and effectiveness of health care for all Americans. As one of 12 agencies within the Department of Health and Human Services, AHRQ supports health services research that will improve the quality of health care and promote evidence-based decision making."—*AHRQ at a glance (http://www.ahrq.gov/about/ataglance.htm)*

Searchable website ("search AHRQ" and "A–Z Quick Menu") provides access to a variety of resources, with links to clinical and consumer health information, research findings, funding opportunities, data and surveys, quality assessment, specific populations (minorities, women, elderly, and others), and public health preparedness (bioterrorism and response). Links to a large number of full-text documents, including links to the tools, literature, and news in patient safety (e.g., *AHRQ patient safety network*) and tips on how to prevent medical errors.

**1208  American hospital association.** American Hospital Association. Chicago: American Hospital Association. http://www.aha.org/aha_app/index.jsp.

Founded in 1898, the association represents hospitals, health care networks, and their consumers. The website provides "Fast Facts on U.S. Hospitals," reports and studies, trends, testimony, regulations, and a section for members only. Some information is only available for a fee.

**1209 American public health association (APHA).** American Public Health Association. 1998–. Washington: American Public Health Association. http://www.apha.org/.

RA421

Searchable website of the American Public Health Association (APHA), an organization representing public health professionals, with the mission to protect Americans and their communities from health threats. Provides links to 24 sections (http://www.apha.org/membergroups/sections/aphasections/) representing major public health disciplines or public health programs and selected links to a wide variety of public health topics and resources (e.g., A–Z Health Topics at http://www.apha.org/advocacy/health / and Public Health Links at http://www.apha.org/about/Public+Health+Links/). Includes a Health Disparities Projects and Interventions database, sponsored by APHA (http://www.apha.org/programs/disparitiesdb/). APHA participates in Partners in Information Access for the Public Health Workforce (1203), a collaborative project to provide public health professionals with access to information resources to help them improve the health of the American public.

**1210 Department of health and human services.** U.S. Department of Health and Human Services. 1997–. [Washington, D.C.]: U.S. Dept. of Health and Human Services. http://www.hhs.gov/.

The U.S. Department of Health and Human Services is responsible for "protecting the health of all Americans and providing essential human services, especially for those who are least able to help themselves."—*HHS What We Do.* To that end, their website provides a rich source of information on aging, disasters and emergencies, diseases and conditions, drug and food information, families and children, grants and funding, policies and regulations, reference collections (dictionaries and glossaries, various indexes, clinical trials database, food additive database, statistics, reports), resource locators, safety and wellness, and specific populations.

**1211 Federation of American hospitals.** Federation of American Hospitals. Washington, D.C.: Federation of American Hospitals. http://www.fahs.com/.

The federation represents privately owned and managed community hospitals and health systems. The website has testimony, congressional communications, health and economic statistics, list of member facilities, *Hospital outlook* (bimonthly newsletter), information on the annual meeting, and a members only section.

## Periodicals

1212  **Federation of American hospitals.** Federation of American Hospitals. Washington, D.C.: Federation of American Hospitals. http://www.fahs.com/.

The federation represents privately-owned and managed community hospitals and health systems. The website has testimony, congressional communications, health and economic statistics, list of member facilities, *Hospital outlook* (bimonthly newsletter), information on the annual meeting, and a members only section.

## Specialized Sources of Industry Data

1213  **American hospital association.** American Hospital Association. Chicago: American Hospital Association. http://www.aha.org/aha_app/index.jsp.

Founded in 1898, the association represents hospitals, health care networks, and their consumers. The website provides "Fast Facts on U.S. Hospitals," reports and studies, trends, testimony, regulations, and a section for members only. Some information is only available for a fee.

1214  **Business insights.** Datamonitor (Firm). [London?]: Reuters. http://www.globalbusinessinsights.com/autologin.asp.

HF54.7

Reports on energy, consumer goods, finance, health care, and technology. Reports, typically over 100 pages long, cover new product innovations, marketing strategies, market drivers, key players, trends, forecast business opportunities, and industry interviews. International focus, especially strong for European coverage.

1215  **The Dartmouth atlas of health care.** Dartmouth Institute for Health Policy and Clinical Practice, Dartmouth Medical School, American Hospital Association. Lebanon, N.H.: Dartmouth

Institute for Health Policy and Clinical Practice. http://www. dartmouthatlas.org/atlases.shtm.

The Dartmouth Atlas Project started as a series of books and is now accessible via a web-based resource, providing access to the *Dartmouth atlas of health care* series (national editions, specialty-specific editions, state editions, and regional editions). Describes and illustrates quality, cost, and delivery of healthcare services in the U.S. and geographic variations in practice patterns, with description of the physician workforce and distribution of resources. Written for health policy analysts and other health professionals. The home page at http://www.dartmouthatlas.org/index. shtm provides additional information.

**1216 Department of health and human services.** U.S. Department of Health and Human Services. 1997–. [Washington, D.C.]: U.S. Dept. of Health and Human Services. http://www.hhs.gov/.

The U.S. Department of Health and Human Services is responsible for "protecting the health of all Americans and providing essential human services, especially for those who are least able to help themselves."—*HHS What We Do.* To that end, their website provides a rich source of information on aging, disasters and emergencies, diseases and conditions, drug and food information, families and children, grants and funding, policies and regulations, reference collections (dictionaries and glossaries, various indexes, clinical trials database, food additive database, statistics, reports), resource locators, safety and wellness, and specific populations.

**1217 Faststats A to Z.** National Center for Health Statistics (NCHS). Hyattsville, Md: U.S. Dept. of Health and Human Services, Centers for Disease Control and Prevention, National Center for Health Statistics. http://www.cdc.gov/nchs/fastats/Default.htm.

Provides topic-appropriate public health statistics (e.g., birth data, morbidity and mortality statistics, and health care use) and relevant links to further information and publications. Includes state and territorial data, with clickable map for individual state data. Also includes data derived from the "Behavioral Risk Factor Surveillance System (BRFSS)," which compiles data for 16 negative behaviors.

**1218 Health and healthcare in the United States: County and metro area data.** NationsHealth Corporation. 2 v., maps. Lanham, Md: Bernan Press, c1999–c2001. ISSN: 1526-1573.

RA407.3.H415

1st ed., 1999–2nd ed., 2000; 2nd ed. technical consultant, Russell G. Bruce. Compendium of health-related statistics and reference maps for each of the 3,000 counties and the 80 metropolitan areas in the U.S.—demographics, vital statistics, healthcare resources, and Medicare data. Based on information from the National Center for Health Statistics (Hyattsville, Md.: Centers for Disease Control and Prevention, 1990s–) and the U.S. Bureau of the Census. Accompanying CD-ROMs make it possible to manipulate the data.

**1219 Health care state rankings.** Morgan Quitno Corporation. v. Lawrence, Kans: Morgan Quitno Corp, c1993–. ISSN: 1065-1403. 362.10973                                                          RA407.3.H423

Description based on 15th ed., 2007. Subtitle: *Health care in the 50 United States.* Contains data relating to medical care, delivery of health care, and health status indicators, which are derived from federal and state government sources, and from professional and private organizations. Presented in tabular form, with tables arranged in seven categories: Birth and reproductive health; Deaths; Facilities (hospitals, nursing homes, etc.); Finance; Incidence of disease; Personnel; Physical fitness. Appendix (with 2005 and 2006 charts), sources, and index. Another title, *Health care state perspectives*, includes state-specific reports for each of the 50 states.

**1220 Health in the Americas.** Pan American Sanitary Bureau. v., ill. Washington, D.C: Pan American Health Organization, Pan American Sanitary Bureau, Regional Office of the World Health Organization, 1998–. 610.8s; 362.1091812                                          RA10.P252

Published by Pan American Health Organization (PAHO) (Washington: Pan American Health Organization, 1990s–); "Salud en las Américas."

Title varies: Previously had title *Summary of reports on the health conditions in the Americas* and *Health conditions in the Americas.* Description based on 2007 ed. (2 v.): v. 1, Regional analysis; v. 2, Country-by-country assessment.

Health data, facts, health trends, and related information for Central and South America, with emphasis on health disparities. Provides a vision for the future of health and health challenges in the Americas. Also available online through netLibrary; both print and online versions in English or Spanish.

A complement to this publication is *Health statistics from the Americas*, publ. in print format 1991–98, and now online (2003 ed. http://www .paho.org/english/dd/pub/SP_591.htm and 2006 ed. http://www.paho .org/English/DD/AIS/HSA2006.htm).

**1221  HealthSTAR (Ovid).** National Library of Medicine (U.S.). 2000–. Sandy, Utah: Ovid Technologies. http://www.ovid.com/site/products/ovidguide/hstrdb.htm.

Ovid HealthSTAR (HSTR); HealthSTAR (Health Services Technology, Administration, and Research).

"Comprised of data from the National Library of Medicine's (NLM) MEDLINE and former HealthSTAR databases . . . contains citations to the published literature on health services, technology, administration, and research. It focuses on both the clinical and non-clinical aspects of health care delivery. . . . Offered by Ovid as a continuation of NLM's now-defunct HealthSTAR database. Retains all existing backfile citations and is updated with new journal citations culled from MEDLINE. Contains citations and abstracts (when available) to journal articles, monographs, technical reports, meeting abstracts and papers, book chapters, government documents, and newspaper articles from 1975 to the present."—*Publ. notes.* A list of NLM's retired databases, including the original HealthSTAR database, can be found at http://www.nlm.nih.gov/services/pastdatabases.html.

Relevant content on health services research, health technology, health administration, health policy, health economics, etc., can also be found in MEDLINE® (1188)/PubMed® (Bethesda, Md.: U.S. National Center for Biotechnology Information, 1996–), NLM® Gateway (Bethesda, Md.: National Library of Medicine, 2000–), and also CINAHL® (Ipswich, Mass.: EBSCO, 1982–).

**1222  Hoover's online.** Reference Press. 1996–. Austin, Tex.: Reference Press. http://www.hoovers.com/.

338.7                                                                    HG4057

Nearly 18 million records describing public and private companies primarily in the United States, but including Canada, United Kingdom, Europe, and Asia/Pacific. Profiles have an overview, history, family tree, industry information, products/operations, top competitors, competitive landscape, top executives with biographies, news, significant developments, and financial data (summary; income statement; balance sheet; cash flow; historical financials such as five years of P/E and per share; stock quote; interactive stock chart; market data; earnings estimates; this year's ratios for the company, industry, and market; SEC filings; and industry watch).

Covers 600 industries, organized into the following categories: Aerospace and Defense; Agriculture; Automotive and Transport; Banking;

Beverages; Business Services; Charitable Organizations; Chemicals; Computer Hardware; Computer Services; Computer Software; Construction; Consumer Products Manufacturers; Consumer Services; Cultural Institutions; Education; Electronics; Energy and Utilities; Environmental Services and Equipment; Financial Services; Food; Foundations; Government; Health Care; Industrial Manufacturing; Insurance; Leisure; Media; Membership Organizations; Metals and Mining; Pharmaceuticals; Real Estate; Retail; Security Products and Services; Telecommunications Equipment; Telecommunications Services; and Transportation Services.

Coverage can be brief, but generally includes a fact sheet, overview, selected companies, industry watch with video interviews, news from the last 90 days, and web resources for terminology, associations, and organizations, and online publications. Includes Hoover's print publications (*Hoover's handbook of American business* [35], *Hoover's handbook of private companies* [36]).

**1223 International health data reference guide.** National Center for Health Statistics (U.S.), National Center for Health Statistics (U.S.)., National Center for Health Statistics (U.S.). ill. Hyattsville, Md.: U.S. Dept. of Health and Human Services, Public Health Service, National Center for Health Statistics, [1984?]–.

362.1021            RA407.A58

Description based on 11th ed., 2003.

"Provides information collected in 2003 on the availability of selected national vital, hospital, health personnel resources, and population-based health survey statistics. Information for 40 nations. . . . Main purpose is to provide information not readily available in published form. It is not designed to provide information on the availability of measures such as crude birth and death rates or life expectancy at birth"—*Pref.* Biennial. Also available online on the National Center for Health Statistics (NCHS) (Hyattsville, Md.: Centers for Disease Control and Prevention, 1990s–) website at http://purl.access.gpo.gov/GPO/LPS24629.

**1224 Marketresearch.com academic.** Kalorama Information. 1999–. Bethesda, Md.: Kalorama Information. http://www.marketresearch.com/.

                     HF5415.2.K35

Market research reports from various sources (Icon Group, Kalorama, BizMiner, etc.) for Consumer Goods (apparel, cosmetics and personal care, house and home, pet services and supplies, travel services), Food and Beverage (alcoholic beverages, coffee and tea, soft drinks, confectionery, dairy products, food processing), Heavy Industry (energy, mining, utilities, construction, machines and parts, manufacturing, metals, paper and forest products, plastics, automotive, aviation & aerospace, logistics and shipping), Service Industries (accounting and finance, corporate services, banking and financial services, insurance), Public Sector (associations/nonprofits, education, government), Life Science (biotechnology, agriculture, genomics, proteomics, medical imaging, healthcare facilities, managed care, regulation and policy, cardiovascular devices, equipment and supplies, wound care, pharmaceuticals, diseases and conditions, prescription drugs, therapeutic area), Technology & Media (computer equipment, electronics, networks, e-commerce and IT outsourcing, software, telecommunications, wireless), and Demographics (age, lifestyle and economics, multicultural).

Reports range in length, with some over 300 pages long, and give a variety of information (definition of industry, consumer demographics, consumer shopping habits, spending patterns, sales, establishments, employment, forecasts, trends, market size, market share, and market segmentation). Some company information is also included.

**1225  MEPS Medical Expenditure panel survey.** U.S. Agency for Healthcare Research and Quality. 1996–. Bethesda, Md: Agency for Healthcare Research and Quality. http://www.meps.ahrq.gov/mepsweb/.

RA408.5

Produced by Agency for Healthcare Research and Quality (AHRQ) (1190).

"Set of large-scale surveys of families and individuals, their medical providers (doctors, hospitals, pharmacies, etc.), and employers across the United States. MEPS collects data on the specific health services that Americans use, how frequently they use them, the cost of these services, and how they are paid for, as well as data on the cost, scope, and breadth of health insurance held by and available to U.S. workers" (*Website*). Provides information on health expenditures, utilization of health services, health insurance, and nursing homes, and reimbursement mechanisms. MEPS topics include access to health care, children's health, children's insurance coverage, health care disparities, mental health, minority health, the uninsured, and other topics. Further details concerning the survey background, data overview, and frequently asked questions are provided at the website.

Provides full-text access to MEPS publications: highlights, research findings, statistical briefs, etc.

**1226 Partners in information access for the public health workforce.**
U.S. National Library of Medicine. 2003–. Bethesda, Md.: U.S.
National Library of Medicine, National Institutes of Health, Dept.
of Health and Human Services. http://phpartners.org/.

"Collaboration of U.S. government agencies, public health organizations, and health sciences libraries which provides timely, convenient access to selected public health resources on the Internet . . . [with the mission of] helping the public health workforce find and use information effectively to improve and protect the public's health."—*Website*

Provides links to the individual partner websites, such as Agency for Healthcare Research and Quality (AHRQ) (1190), American Public Health Association (APHA), Association of Schools of Public Health (ASPH), Association of State and Territorial Health Officials (ASTHO), Centers for Disease Control and Prevention (CDC) (Atlanta: Centers for Disease Control and Prevention, U.S. Dept. of Health and Human Services, 1998–), Medical Library Association (MLANET) (Chicago: Medical Library Association [MLA], 1998–), National Library of Medicine (Bethesda, Md.: National Library of Medicine, 1993–), and several other organizations. Provides extensive information on several public health topics (currently to bioterrorism, environmental health, and HIV/AIDS). For additional information and links see the Partners in Information Access for the Public Health Workforce fact sheet at http://www.nlm.nih.gov/nno/partners .html.

**1227 WHOSIS.** World Health Organization. [1994]–. Geneva,
[Switzerland]: World Health Organization. http://www.who.int/
whosis/.

Published by World Health Organization (WHO).

Provides description and online access to statistical and epidemiological information, data, and tools available from WHO and other sites: mortality and health status, disease statistics, health systems statistics, risk factors and health services, and inequities in health. Provides links to several databases: WHOSIS database, with the latest "core health indicators" from WHO sources (including *The World health report* [Geneva: World Health Organization, 1995–] and *World health statistics* [1206]), which make it possible to construct tables for any combination of countries, indicators and years, Causes of Death database, WHO Global InfoBase Online, Global Health Atlas, and Reproductive Health Indicators database.

1228 **World health statistics.** World Health Organization. 2005–. Geneva, Switzerland: World Health Organization. http://www.who. int/healthinfo/statistics/en/.

1939/46–96 publ. as *World health statistics annual = Annuaire de statistiques sanitaires mondiales* (print version).

Part of WHOSIS: WHO Statistical Information System (Geneva, Switzerland: World Health Organization, 1994).

Description based on online 3rd ed., 2007 ed. (http://www.who.int/ whosis/whostat2007.pdf ).

Contents: pt. 1, "Ten statistical highlights in global public health." Pt. 2, "World health statistics": "Health status: Mortality"; "Health status: Morbidity"; "Health services coverage"; "Risk factors"; "Health systems"; "Inequities in health"; "Demographic and socioeconomic statistics."

"Presents the most recent health statistics for WHO's 193 Member States . . . collated from publications and databases produced by WHO's technical programmes and regional offices . . . selected on the basis of their relevance to global health, the availability and quality of the data, and the accuracy and comparability of estimates. The statistics for the indicators are derived from an interactive process of data collection, compilation, quality assessment and estimation occurring among WHO's technical programmes and its Member States"—*Introd.* Print version also available.

# Leisure

## Additional Reference Sources

1229 **Bibliography of tourism and travel research studies, reports, and articles.** Charles R. Goeldner, Karen Duea Travel Reference Center, University of Colorado, Boulder . 9 v. (v, 762 leaves). Boulder, Colo.; [Salt Lake City, Utah]: Business Research Division, Graduate School of Business Administration, University of Colorado; Travel Research Association, 1980. ISBN: 0894780522.

016.3801459104                                    Z6004.T6G63; G155.A1

Contents: v. 1, *Information sources*; v. 2, *Economics*; v. 3, *International tourism*; v. 4, *Lodging*; v. 5, *Recreation*; v. 6, *Transportation*; v. 7, *Advertising-Planning*; v. 8, *Statistics-Visitors*; v. 9, *Index*.

Earlier ed.: *Travel research bibliography*, 1976.
Aims "to provide a ready source of research references on travel, recreation, and tourism for use in business, government, and academic fields."—*Pref.* Entries are mainly for post-1970 publications.

**1230 Hoover's online.** Reference Press. 1996–. Austin, Tex.: Reference Press. http://www.hoovers.com/.

338.7                                     HG4057

Nearly 18 million records describing public and private companies primarily in the United States, but including Canada, United Kingdom, Europe, and Asia/Pacific. Profiles have an overview, history, family tree, industry information, products/operations, top competitors, competitive landscape, top executives with biographies, news, significant developments, and financial data (summary; income statement; balance sheet; cash flow; historical financials such as five years of P/E and per share; stock quote; interactive stock chart; market data; earnings estimates; this year's ratios for the company, industry, and market; SEC filings; and industry watch).

Covers 600 industries, organized into the following categories: Aerospace and Defense; Agriculture; Automotive and Transport; Banking; Beverages; Business Services; Charitable Organizations; Chemicals; Computer Hardware; Computer Services; Computer Software; Construction; Consumer Products Manufacturers; Consumer Services; Cultural Institutions; Education; Electronics; Energy and Utilities; Environmental Services and Equipment; Financial Services; Food; Foundations; Government; Health Care; Industrial Manufacturing; Insurance; Leisure; Media; Membership Organizations; Metals and Mining; Pharmaceuticals; Real Estate; Retail; Security Products and Services; Telecommunications Equipment; Telecommunications Services; and Transportation Services.

Coverage can be brief, but generally includes a fact sheet, overview, selected companies, industry watch with video interviews, news from the last 90 days, and web resources for terminology, associations, and organizations, and online publications. Includes Hoover's print publications (*Hoover's handbook of American business* [35], *Hoover's handbook of private companies* [36]).

**1231 Marketresearch.com academic.** Kalorama Information. 1999–. Bethesda, Md.: Kalorama Information. http://www.marketresearch.com/.

HF5415.2.K35

Market research reports from various sources (Icon Group, Kalorama, BizMiner, etc.) for Consumer Goods (apparel, cosmetics and personal care, house and home, pet services and supplies, travel services), Food and Beverage (alcoholic beverages, coffee and tea, soft drinks, confectionery, dairy products, food processing), Heavy Industry (energy, mining, utilities, construction, machines and parts, manufacturing, metals, paper and forest products, plastics, automotive, aviation & aerospace, logistics and shipping), Service Industries (accounting and finance, corporate services, banking and financial services, insurance), Public Sector (associations/nonprofits, education, government), Life Science (biotechnology, agriculture, genomics, proteomics, medical imaging, healthcare facilities, managed care, regulation and policy, cardiovascular devices, equipment and supplies, wound care, pharmaceuticals, diseases and conditions, prescription drugs, therapeutic area), Technology & Media (computer equipment, electronics, networks, e-commerce and IT outsourcing, software, telecommunications, wireless), and Demographics (age, lifestyle and economics, multicultural).

Reports range in length, with some over 300 pages long, and give a variety of information (definition of industry, consumer demographics, consumer shopping habits, spending patterns, sales, establishments, employment, forecasts, trends, market size, market share, and market segmentation). Some company information is also included.

1232 **Plunkett's airline, hotel, and travel industry almanac.** Jack W. Plunkett, Plunkett Research, Ltd. ill. Houston, Tex.: Plunkett Research, 2002–. ISSN: 1554-1215.

387.7                                    HE9803.A2P58; G155.U6P58

Data on 324 major companies, both public and private. Company profiles include types of business, brands and affiliates, contacts, employee benefits and top salaries, sales and profit numbers, growth plans, and competitive advantage. Especially useful for the industry trends, statistics and rankings (forecasts to 2020, top destinations worldwide, top airlines, top tourism nations, etc.) at the front of the volume and information on the main associations and organizations in the back of the volume. Most information is for the U.S., but some international coverage is provided. Available as an e-book.

## Definition of The Industry

1233 **Dictionary of travel, tourism and hospitality.** 3rd ed. S. Medlik. ix, 273 p., maps. Oxford [England]; Boston: Butterworth-Heinemann, 2003. ISBN: 0750656506.

338.479103                                    G155.A1M397

Divided into seven parts. The largest (Pt. 1) is a dictionary of over 4,000 terms. Pts. 2 and 3 are definitions of international and national organizations. Pt. 4 is a biographical dictionary of people associated with the travel industry. Pt. 5 is a list of abbreviations. Pt. 6 is a table giving information on countries of the world. Pt. 7 is a bibliography of dictionaries, journals, directories, manuals, sources of statistics, and other books. Available as an e-book.

**1234  IBISWorld United States.** IBISWorld. New York: IBISWorld. http://www.ibisworld.com/.

HC103.I247

700 reports on the following industries: agriculture, forestry, fishing and hunting; mining; utilities; construction; manufacturing; wholesale trade; retail trade; transportation and warehousing; information; finance and insurance; real estate and rental and leasing; professional, scientific, and technical services; administrative and support and waste management and remediation services; educational services; health care and social assistance; arts, entertainment, and recreation; accommodation and food services; and other services. Setting this database apart are reports on small industries, such as parking lots and garages.

Reports include industry definition; key statistics; segmentations (products and services segmentation, major market segments, industry concentration, geographic spread); market characteristics (market size, demand determinants, domestic and international markets, basis of competition, life cycle); industry conditions (barriers to entry, taxation, industry assistance, regulation and deregulation, cost structure, capital and labor intensity, technology and systems, industry volatility, globalization); key factors (sensitivities and success factors); key competitors; and industry performance (current and historical).

## Internet Resources

**1235  Ernst and Young.** Ernst and Young. 2007. London: Ernst and Young. http://www.ey.com/global/content.nsf/International/ Industry_Overview/.

Ernst and Young provides "accounting and auditing, tax reporting and operations, tax advisory, business risk services, technology and security risk services, transaction advisory, and human capital services." The site is useful for articles on financial management, corporate governance, initial public offerings (IPOs), and industry reports (asset management, automotive, banking and capital markets, biotechnology, consumer products, insurance, media and entertainment, mining and metals, oil and gas, pharmaceuticals, real estate and construction, hospitality and leisure, technology, telecommunications, utilities).

**1236 ITA.** International Trade Administration. 2007. Washington, D.C.: International Trade Administration. http://tinet.ita.doc.gov/.
The Office of Travel & Tourism Industries is "the sole source for characteristic statistics on international travel to and from the United States"— *About the OTTI.* The site bears this out, with historical tables on inbound travelers to the United States (data beginning in 1987), as well as current statistics, divided into national (visitors to the United States and U.S. travelers abroad), state/city/territory (visitors to U.S. states, territories, and cities), and country (country and region level data for visitors to the United States and U.S. travel abroad).

**1237 Sports business research network.** SBRnet. Princeton, N.J.: SBRnet. http://www.sbrnet.com/.

HD9992.U52

Gives articles and statistics for apparel, baseball/softball, basketball, billiards/bowling, boxing, camping, cheerleading, climbing, equestrian, exercise/fitness, eyewear, field hockey, fishing, football, footwear, golf, gymnastics, hunting/target shooting, ice hockey, lacrosse, martial arts, motorsports, paintball, racquet sports, running/track and field, soccer, sports medicine; volleyball; water sports; wheel sports; winter sports, wrestling, broadcasting, careers, college sports, disabled, endorsement, facilities, financial, licensing, new media, Olympics, sponsorship, sport management education, total sporting goods market, women's sports, and youth/amateur. Includes a U.S. and Canadian college sports program directory, a website directory for some 10,000 sports organizations, and a trade show and meeting calendar.

## *Organizations and Associations*

**1238 American hotel and lodging association.** American Hotel and Lodging Association. 2007. Washington, D.C.: American Hotel and Lodging Association. http://www.ahla.com/.
The AHLA represents "individual hotel property members, hotel companies, student and faculty members, and industry suppliers."—*About.* The site is organized into Membership; Hotel Hospitality News; Governmental Affairs; Hotel Meetings and Events; Hotel Hospitality Products; Hospitality Sponsorships; AH&LA Information Center; Hospitality Publications; Careers in Hospitality; Hotel Press Room; AH&LA Membership; Feature

Hospitality Program; and Insurance Center. Free highlights on the site include a history of lodging, Lodging Industry Profile, Top 50 Hotel Companies (gives number of domestic and international rooms and properties for each company), and industry links.

1239 **Plunkett's airline, hotel, and travel industry almanac.** Jack W. Plunkett, Plunkett Research, Ltd. ill. Houston, Tex.: Plunkett Research, 2002–. ISSN: 1554-1215.
387.7 HE9803.A2P58; G155.U6P58

Data on 324 major companies, both public and private. Company profiles include types of business, brands and affiliates, contacts, employee benefits and top salaries, sales and profit numbers, growth plans, and competitive advantage. Especially useful for the industry trends, statistics and rankings (forecasts to 2020, top destinations worldwide, top airlines, top tourism nations, etc.) at the front of the volume and information on the main associations and organizations in the back of the volume. Most information is for the U.S., but some international coverage is provided. Available as an e-book.

## Periodicals

1240 **Trends in the hotel industry.** U.S. ed. Pannell, Kerr, Forster. ill. New York: Pannell, Kerr, Forster, 1980–. ISSN: 0276-5357.
338.47647947301 TX909.A1H3

Gives trends and financial performance (revenue, expense, and profit information) for U.S. hotels. Arranged by property type, location, rate, and size. Also lists franchise fees, payroll costs by dollars per available room, percentage of occupancy, utility costs, marketing, and departmental costs and expenses (rooms, food, beverage, telecommunications). Also available in online format.

## Specialized Sources of Industry Data

1241 **American hotel and lodging association.** American Hotel and Lodging Association. 2007. Washington, D.C.: American Hotel and Lodging Association. http://www.ahla.com/.

The AHLA represents "individual hotel property members, hotel companies, student and faculty members, and industry suppliers."—*About.* The site is organized into Membership; Hotel Hospitality News; Governmental Affairs; Hotel Meetings and Events; Hotel Hospitality Products; Hospitality Sponsorships; AH&LA Information Center; Hospitality Publications;

Careers in Hospitality; Hotel Press Room; AH&LA Membership; Feature Hospitality Program; and Insurance Center. Free highlights on the site include a history of lodging, Lodging Industry Profile, Top 50 Hotel Companies (gives number of domestic and international rooms and properties for each company), and industry links.

1242 **Hospitality and tourism index.** EBSCO Publishing. [Ipswich, Mass.]: EBSCO Publishing. http://search.epnet.com/login.aspx?authtype=ip,uid&profile=ehost/.

Indexes scholarly research and industry news relating to all areas of hospitality and tourism, including culinary arts, hotel management, and travel. Formed from the now ceased Cornell University's hospitality database, the Universities of Surrey and Oxford Brookes Articles in Hospitality and Tourism, and Purdue University's Lodging, Restaurant, and Tourism Index. Coverage from 1965.

1243 **IBISWorld United States.** IBISWorld. New York: IBISWorld. http://www.ibisworld.com/.

HC103.I247

700 reports on the following industries: agriculture, forestry, fishing and hunting; mining; utilities; construction; manufacturing; wholesale trade; retail trade; transportation and warehousing; information; finance and insurance; real estate and rental and leasing; professional, scientific, and technical services; administrative and support and waste management and remediation services; educational services; health care and social assistance; arts, entertainment, and recreation; accommodation and food services; and other services. Setting this database apart are reports on small industries, such as parking lots and garages.

Reports include industry definition; key statistics; segmentations (products and services segmentation, major market segments, industry concentration, geographic spread); market characteristics (market size, demand determinants, domestic and international markets, basis of competition, life cycle); industry conditions (barriers to entry, taxation, industry assistance, regulation and deregulation, cost structure, capital and labor intensity, technology and systems, industry volatility, globalization); key factors (sensitivities and success factors); key competitors; and industry performance (current and historical).

1244 **ITA.** International Trade Administration. 2007. Washington, D.C.: International Trade Administration. http://tinet.ita.doc.gov/.

The Office of Travel & Tourism Industries is "the sole source for characteristic statistics on international travel to and from the United States" —*About the OTTI.* The site bears this out, with historical tables on inbound travelers to the United States (data beginning in 1987), as well as current statistics, divided into national (visitors to the United States and U.S. travelers abroad), state/city/territory (visitors to U.S. states, territories, and cities), and country (country and region level data for visitors to the United States and U.S. travel abroad).

**1245  Plunkett's airline, hotel, and travel industry almanac.** Jack W. Plunkett, Plunkett Research, Ltd. ill. Houston, Tex.: Plunkett Research, 2002–. ISSN: 1554-1215.

387.7                                        HE9803.A2P58; G155.U6P58

Data on 324 major companies, both public and private. Company profiles include types of business, brands and affiliates, contacts, employee benefits and top salaries, sales and profit numbers, growth plans, and competitive advantage. Especially useful for the industry trends, statistics and rankings (forecasts to 2020, top destinations worldwide, top airlines, top tourism nations, etc.) at the front of the volume and information on the main associations and organizations in the back of the volume. Most information is for the U.S., but some international coverage is provided. Available as an e-book.

**1246  Trends in the hotel industry.** U.S. ed. Pannell, Kerr, Forster. ill. New York: Pannell, Kerr, Forster, 1980–. ISSN: 0276-5357.

338.47647947301                                        TX909.A1H3

Gives trends and financial performance (revenue, expense, and profit information) for U.S. hotels. Arranged by property type, location, rate, and size. Also lists franchise fees, payroll costs by dollars per available room, percentage of occupancy, utility costs, marketing, and departmental costs and expenses (rooms, food, beverage, telecommunications). Also available in online format.

# Media

## Additional Reference Sources

**1247  Global market information database.** Euromonitor. [1999–.] [London]: Euromonitor. http://www.gmid.euromonitor.com/.

HD2755.5.G56

Market reports, company profiles, and demographic, economic, and marketing statistics for 205 countries. Market reports are for 16 consumer markets (food and drink, tobacco, toys, etc.) and 14 industrial and service markets (accountancy, broadcasting, chemicals, property services, etc.).

Reports have market size, market sectors, share of market, marketing activity, research and development, corporate overview, distribution, consumer profiles, market forecasts, sector forecasts, sources, and definitions. Additional reports are available for market segments, such as baby food. Company profiles have background, recent news, competitive environment, and outlook. Consumer lifestyle reports and very useful marketing background analyze the consumer by country, gender, age, marital status, educational attainment, ethnicity, religion, home ownership, household profile, employment, income, health, eating and personal grooming habits, leisure activities, personal finance, communication, transport, and travel.

Search for data, which can be exported into Excel or browse for reports. Data are available from 1977 through 2016 and include inflation, exchange rates, GDP, GNI, government expenditures, government finance, income, labor, and money supply.

**1248 Hoover's online.** Reference Press. 1996–. Austin, Tex.: Reference Press. http://www.hoovers.com/.

338.7 HG4057

Nearly 18 million records describing public and private companies primarily in the United States, but including Canada, United Kingdom, Europe, and Asia/Pacific. Profiles have an overview, history, family tree, industry information, products/operations, top competitors, competitive landscape, top executives with biographies, news, significant developments, and financial data (summary; income statement; balance sheet; cash flow; historical financials such as five years of P/E and per share; stock quote; interactive stock chart; market data; earnings estimates; this year's ratios for the company, industry, and market; SEC filings; and industry watch).

Covers 600 industries, organized into the following categories: Aerospace and Defense; Agriculture; Automotive and Transport; Banking; Beverages; Business Services; Charitable Organizations; Chemicals; Computer Hardware; Computer Services; Computer Software; Construction; Consumer Products Manufacturers; Consumer Services; Cultural Institutions; Education; Electronics; Energy and Utilities; Environmental Services and Equipment; Financial Services; Food; Foundations; Government; Health

Care; Industrial Manufacturing; Insurance; Leisure; Media; Membership Organizations; Metals and Mining; Pharmaceuticals; Real Estate; Retail; Security Products and Services; Telecommunications Equipment; Telecommunications Services; and Transportation Services.

Coverage can be brief, but generally includes a fact sheet, overview, selected companies, industry watch with video interviews, news from the last 90 days, and web resources for terminology, associations, and organizations, and online publications. Includes Hoover's print publications (*Hoover's handbook of American business* [35], *Hoover's handbook of private companies* [36]).

**1249 IBISWorld United States.** IBISWorld. New York: IBISWorld. http://www.ibisworld.com/.

HC103.I247

700 reports on the following industries: agriculture, forestry, fishing and hunting; mining; utilities; construction; manufacturing; wholesale trade; retail trade; transportation and warehousing; information; finance and insurance; real estate and rental and leasing; professional, scientific, and technical services; administrative and support and waste management and remediation services; educational services; health care and social assistance; arts, entertainment, and recreation; accommodation and food services; and other services. Setting this database apart are reports on small industries, such as parking lots and garages.

Reports include industry definition; key statistics; segmentations (products and services segmentation, major market segments, industry concentration, geographic spread); market characteristics (market size, demand determinants, domestic and international markets, basis of competition, life cycle); industry conditions (barriers to entry, taxation, industry assistance, regulation and deregulation, cost structure, capital and labor intensity, technology and systems, industry volatility, globalization); key factors (sensitivities and success factors); key competitors; and industry performance (current and historical).

**1250 Magazine dimensions.** Media Dynamics, Inc. New York: Media Dynamics, 1993–. ISSN: 1074-7419.

659.132                                  HF6105.U5M23

Statistical information mixed with narrative, providing a picture of the magazine industry. Chapters include: General dimensions (history of magazines from 1740–2006, trends in magazines published and ad revenues, changing face of editorial content, magazine CPM's), Magazine audiences (audience definitions, circulation trends, subscriber profiles, reader profiles by magazine, total audience by magazine, website audiences, reading diet by genre, median age and income trends, reader-per-copy, reach and frequency, and accumulation patterns), and Qualitative factors (reader attitudes and intensity of exposure, location and timing of reading, advertising receptivity, comparison to TV), and Information sources (circulation audits, subscriber/panel studies, syndicated audience/marketing research).

**1251 This business of television.** Rev. and updated 3rd ed. Howard J. Blumenthal, Oliver R. Goodenough. xxiv, 568 p. New York: BillBoard Books, 2006. ISBN: 0823077632.

HE8700.8.B58

In 11 sections this comprehensive updated edition covers the basics of television (broadcast, cable, satellite, and home video), such as marketing, distribution, and production. Sections include: Distribution, Regulation of distribution, Audience measurement and advertising, Programming business (market segments, economics of production, sales), Big media, Broader definition of television (public television, home shopping, religious television), Programming and program development, Regulation of programming, Production, Legal and business affairs, and Television outside the U.S. Appendixes provide various contract forms.

**1252 World radio TV handbook.** Nielsen Business Publications. ill., maps, music, ports. New York: Nielsen Business Publications, 1947–. ISSN: 0144-7750.

TK6540.W67

"A complete directory of international radio and television." Published Copenhagen, Denmark: O. Lund Johansen, 1961–82; London; New York: Billboard Publications, 1982–2002. Continues *World radio handbook for listeners including world-wide radio who's who*, *World-radio-television handbook*, and *World radio handbook*. Currently divided into the following sections: Features (product reviews, articles, interviews), National radio, International radio, Frequency lists, Television, and Reference. Listing of worldwide radio and TV services; world satellite broadcasts; short, medium, and long wave frequency tables; list of official international broadcasting organizations; Internet resources; and users clubs.

## *Definition of the Industry*

**1253  IBISWorld United States.** IBISWorld. New York: IBISWorld.
http://www.ibisworld.com/.

HC103.I247

700 reports on the following industries: agriculture, forestry, fishing and
hunting; mining; utilities; construction; manufacturing; wholesale trade;
retail trade; transportation and warehousing; information; finance and
insurance; real estate and rental and leasing; professional, scientific, and
technical services; administrative and support and waste management
and remediation services; educational services; health care and social
assistance; arts, entertainment, and recreation; accommodation and food
services; and other services. Setting this database apart are reports on small
industries, such as parking lots and garages.

Reports include industry definition; key statistics; segmentations
(products and services segmentation, major market segments, industry
concentration, geographic spread); market characteristics (market size,
demand determinants, domestic and international markets, basis of
competition, life cycle); industry conditions (barriers to entry, taxation,
industry assistance, regulation and deregulation, cost structure, capital
and labor intensity, technology and systems, industry volatility, globalization); key factors (sensitivities and success factors); key competitors; and
industry performance (current and historical).

## *Internet Resources*

**1254  Ernst and Young.** Ernst and Young. 2007. London: Ernst and
Young. http://www.ey.com/global/content.nsf/International/
Industry_Overview/.

Ernst and Young provides "accounting and auditing, tax reporting and
operations, tax advisory, business risk services, technology and security
risk services, transaction advisory, and human capital services." The site is
useful for articles on financial management, corporate governance, initial
public offerings (IPOs), and industry reports (asset management, automotive, banking and capital markets, biotechnology, consumer products,
insurance, media and entertainment, mining and metals, oil and gas, pharmaceuticals, real estate and construction, hospitality and leisure, technology, telecommunications, utilities).

## Organizations and Associations

**1255 Federal communications commission.** U.S. Superintendent of Documents. 2007. Washington, D.C.: U.S. Government Printing Office, Superintendent of Documents. http://www.fcc.gov/.

The FCC was founded in 1923 and regulates interstate and international communications by radio, television, wire, satellite and cable. The website contains a treasure trove of information, including reports, statistics, trends, rules and regulations, and more. Examples include annual reports on cable industry prices, periodic reviews of the radio industry, the statistics of communications common carriers, statistical trends in telephony, local and long distance telephone industries, local telephone competition and broadband deployment, telephone industry infrastructure and service quality, federal-state joint board monitoring reports, telephone numbering facts, and international traffic data.

## Specialized Sources of Industry Data

**1256 Broadcasting and cable yearbook.** ill. New Providence, N.J.: R. R. Bowker, 1993–. ISSN: 0000-1511.

384.540973                                                    HE8689.B77

Profiles of 4,825 AM radio stations, 9,000 FM radio stations, and 2,180 television stations in the U.S., and 1,100 Canadian TV and radio stations. Includes call letters, frequency or channel, contact information, ownership, programming information, and key personnel. Industry overview has market rankings, business rankings, television advertising shares, history of broadcasting and cable, chronology of electronic media, and FCC's rules of broadcasting. Also contains directory information for over 5,100 service companies, such as law firms, engineers, marketing consultants, and industry associations.

**1257 Federal communications commission.** U.S. Superintendent of Documents. 2007. Washington, D.C.: U.S. Government Printing Office, Superintendent of Documents. http://www.fcc.gov/.

The FCC was founded in 1923 and regulates interstate and international communications by radio, television, wire, satellite and cable. The website contains a treasure trove of information, including reports, statistics, trends, rules and regulations, and more. Examples include annual reports on cable industry prices, periodic reviews of the radio industry, the statistics of communications common carriers, statistical trends in telephony, local and long distance telephone industries, local telephone competition and broadband deployment, telephone industry infrastructure and service quality, federal-state joint board monitoring reports, telephone numbering facts, and international traffic data.

**1258  International television and video almanac.** 32nd ed. Quigley Publishing Company. ill. New York: Quigley, 1987–. ISSN: 0895-2213.

384.5505                                                HE8700.I57

Brief biographies and obituaries, review of the year with statistics, awards, and Nielsen ratings, and lists of: current series; movies and miniseries from 1999–2004; stations and network affiliates; producers and distributors of TV programs; cable networks; wireless cable; interactive television; production services; DVD producers; wholesalers; retailers and distributors, as well as revenues; and professional organizations. Briefly covers the industry internationally.

**1259  Kagan's media trends.** Paul Kagan Associates. Carmel, Calif.: Paul Kagan Associates, 1992–. ISSN: 1070-6917.

384.04105220                                            P96.E252U645

Reports on trends, and gives projections and data for broadcast TV, radio stations, cable MSOs, cable networks, consumer entertainment, direct broadcast satellite, digital TV, interactive TV, Internet, motion pictures, newspapers, pay TV, pay-per-view, video-on-demand and DVR, satellite radio, television programming, video and DVD, video games, and wireless telecommunications. Includes consumer spending, ad spending, revenues, consumer confidence, consumer expectations, and market penetration. Some data are for 30 years.

**1260  Magazine dimensions.** Media Dynamics, Inc. New York: Media Dynamics, 1993–. ISSN: 1074-7419.

659.132                                                 HF6105.U5M23

Statistical information mixed with narrative, providing a picture of the magazine industry. Chapters include: General dimensions (history of magazines from 1740–2006, trends in magazines published and ad revenues, changing face of editorial content, magazine CPM's), Magazine audiences (audience definitions, circulation trends, subscriber profiles, reader profiles by magazine, total audience by magazine, website audiences, reading diet by genre, median age and income trends, reader-per-copy, reach and frequency, and accumulation patterns), and Qualitative factors (reader attitudes and intensity of exposure, location and timing of reading, advertising receptivity, comparison to TV), and Information sources (circulation audits, subscriber/panel studies, syndicated audience/marketing research).

**1261 Marketresearch.com academic.** Kalorama Information. 1999–. Bethesda, Md.: Kalorama Information. http://www.marketresearch. com/.

HF5415.2.K35

Market research reports from various sources (Icon Group, Kalorama, BizMiner, etc.) for Consumer Goods (apparel, cosmetics and personal care, house and home, pet services and supplies, travel services), Food and Beverage (alcoholic beverages, coffee and tea, soft drinks, confectionery, dairy products, food processing), Heavy Industry (energy, mining, utilities, construction, machines and parts, manufacturing, metals, paper and forest products, plastics, automotive, aviation & aerospace, logistics and shipping), Service Industries (accounting and finance, corporate services, banking and financial services, insurance), Public Sector (associations/ nonprofits, education, government), Life Science (biotechnology, agriculture, genomics, proteomics, medical imaging, healthcare facilities, managed care, regulation and policy, cardiovascular devices, equipment and supplies, wound care, pharmaceuticals, diseases and conditions, prescription drugs, therapeutic area), Technology & Media (computer equipment, electronics, networks, e-commerce and IT outsourcing, software, telecommunications, wireless), and Demographics (age, lifestyle and economics, multicultural).

Reports range in length, with some over 300 pages long, and give a variety of information (definition of industry, consumer demographics, consumer shopping habits, spending patterns, sales, establishments, employment, forecasts, trends, market size, market share, and market segmentation). Some company information is also included.

**1262 Radio dimensions.** Media Dynamics, Inc. ill. New York: Media Dynamics, 2005–. ISSN: 1931-4795.

659                                                         HF6146.R3R323

Uses data from MRI, Simmons, Scarborough Research, and Radio Recall to show who listens to radio. Augmented by narratives that give context to the data. Chapters on: History of radio, Radio basics (trends in ownership, radio's penetration from 1925–present, ad revenue and profits from 1935–present), Radio audiences (Arbitron's PPM, average number of stations listened to per week, listening trends, daypart audiences, radio usage, Internet radio, satellite radio), Reach and frequency patterns, SQAD's CPP estimates, and Qualitative factors.

1263 **SRDS TV and cable source.** Standard Rate and Data Service. maps. Wilmette, Ill.: Standard Rate and Data Service, 1994–. ISSN: 1071-4596.

Lists broadcast, cable, syndicated and alternative television outlets, organized by state. Entries give contact information, executives, corporate owner, system background, coverage, insertion networks, traffic specifications, and special features. Each market includes a profile, with sales rankings by merchandise, SQAD cost per point levels, top daily newspapers and newspaper groups, metro radio stations by county, and a demographic profile of the market. Also available online.

## Motor Vehicles

### Additional Reference Sources

1264 **Branham automobile reference book, showing in illustrated form the location of motor and serial numbers on all passenger cars and trucks.** Branham Publishing Company. illus. Chicago: Branham Printing, 1922–.

629.2085                                                      TL151.B75

Provides "type of body, weight of each type by model and year with actual N.A.C.C. and S.A.E. horsepower rating, cubic inch displacement, bore and stroke in inches, the factory advertised price or list price on passenger cars and factory list price on trucks."—*Pref.* Supplements issued between editions.

1265 **Encyclopedia of American business history and biography.** Facts On File. ill. New York: Facts On File, 1988–. ISBN: 0816013713.

HE2751.R143

Combines biographical entries with articles discussing major companies, government and labor organizations, inventions, and legal decisions for various industries. The signed entries range in length from one-half to ten or more pages; most include photographs or other illustrations, and list publications and references, archives, and unpublished documents. Each volume is available separately. Volumes include: *The airline industry; The automobile industry, 1896–1920; The automobile industry, 1920–1980; Banking and finance to 1913; Banking and finance, 1913–1989; Iron and steel in the nineteenth century; Iron and steel in the twentieth century; Railroads in the nineteenth century;* and *Railroads in the age of regulation, 1900–1980.*

**1266  Hoover's online.** Reference Press. 1996–. Austin, Tex.: Reference Press. http://www.hoovers.com/.

338.7                                                                                    HG4057

Nearly 18 million records describing public and private companies primarily in the United States, but including Canada, United Kingdom, Europe, and Asia/Pacific. Profiles have an overview, history, family tree, industry information, products/operations, top competitors, competitive landscape, top executives with biographies, news, significant developments, and financial data (summary; income statement; balance sheet; cash flow; historical financials such as five years of P/E and per share; stock quote; interactive stock chart; market data; earnings estimates; this year's ratios for the company, industry, and market; SEC filings; and industry watch).

Covers 600 industries, organized into the following categories: Aerospace and Defense; Agriculture; Automotive and Transport; Banking; Beverages; Business Services; Charitable Organizations; Chemicals; Computer Hardware; Computer Services; Computer Software; Construction; Consumer Products Manufacturers; Consumer Services; Cultural Institutions; Education; Electronics; Energy and Utilities; Environmental Services and Equipment; Financial Services; Food; Foundations; Government; Health Care; Industrial Manufacturing; Insurance; Leisure; Media; Membership Organizations; Metals and Mining; Pharmaceuticals; Real Estate; Retail; Security Products and Services; Telecommunications Equipment; Telecommunications Services; and Transportation Services.

Coverage can be brief, but generally includes a fact sheet, overview, selected companies, industry watch with video interviews, news from the last 90 days, and web resources for terminology, associations, and organizations, and online publications. Includes Hoover's print publications (*Hoover's handbook of American business* [35], *Hoover's handbook of private companies* [36]).

**1267  Publications and thought leadership from the automotive industry sector.** PricewaterhouseCoopers. 2000–. New York:

PricewaterhouseCoopers. http://www.pwc.com/gx/en/automotive/ industry-publications-and-thought-leadership.jhtml.

Includes reports on the global automative industry, analyst notes, and mergers and acquisitions. Individual reports vary annually. Reports are free, full of data, trends and analysis, and are international in scope.

## Internet Resources

**1268** **Automotive aftermarket industry association (AAIA).** Automotive Aftermarket Industry Association. 1997–. Bethesda [Md.]: Automotive Aftermarket Industry Association. http://www. aftermarket.org/Home.asp.

The association represents manufacturers, distributors and retailers for "motor vehicle parts, accessories, service, tools, equipment, materials and supplies."—*About.* The site includes events, press releases, *Aftermarket insider magazine*, facts, newsletters, education, government affairs, international trade, market research, member services, and standards and technology.

**1269** **Ernst and Young.** Ernst and Young. 2007. London: Ernst and Young. http://www.ey.com/global/content.nsf/International/ Industry_Overview/.

Ernst and Young provides "accounting and auditing, tax reporting and operations, tax advisory, business risk services, technology and security risk services, transaction advisory, and human capital services." The site is useful for articles on financial management, corporate governance, initial public offerings (IPOs), and industry reports (asset management, auto-motive, banking and capital markets, biotechnology, consumer products, insurance, media and entertainment, mining and metals, oil and gas, phar-maceuticals, real estate and construction, hospitality and leisure, technol-ogy, telecommunications, utilities).

**1270** **Publications and thought leadership from the automotive industry sector.** PricewaterhouseCoopers. 2000–. New York: PricewaterhouseCoopers. http://www.pwc.com/gx/en/automotive/ industry-publications-and-thought-leadership.jhtml.

Includes reports on the global automative industry, analyst notes, and mergers and acquisitions. Individual reports vary annually. Reports are free, full of data, trends and analysis, and are international in scope.

## Organizations and Associations

1271 **Automotive aftermarket industry association (AAIA).**
Automotive Aftermarket Industry Association. 1997–. Bethesda
[Md.]: Automotive Aftermarket Industry Association. http://www.
aftermarket.org/Home.asp.

The association represents manufacturers, distributors and retailers for
"motor vehicle parts, accessories, service, tools, equipment, materials and
supplies."—*About*. The site includes events, press releases, *Aftermarket
insider magazine*, facts newsletters, education, government affairs, international trade, market research, member services, and standards and
technology.

## Periodicals

1272 **Automotive news.** ill. Detroit: Crain Automotive Group. ISSN:
0005-1551.
338.4762922205                                                    TL1.A865

Reports trends, developments, and economic impacts for the automotive
industry. An annual supplement to *Automotive News* is the *Market Data
Book*, which has production (North America car and truck production
history and forecast, five-year history by country, production by assembly
plant, car and light-truck production by platform, car and truck production by model and by month), dealer (J.D. Power and Assoc. data,
dealer census data, financial data, ad spending data, used-car prices and
volumes), and sales data (North America light-vehicle sales history and
forecast, U.S. light-vehicle sales summary by make, North America car
and truck sales, five-year history by make, U.S. car and light-truck sales by
model and by month, Canada sales by month, Mexico sales by model and
by month). Available through LexisNexis Academic Universe and through
the Automotive News Data Center.

1273 **Branham automobile reference book, showing in illustrated
form the location of motor and serial numbers on all passenger
cars and trucks.** Branham Publishing Company. illus. Chicago:
Branham Printing, 1922–.
629.2085                                                          TL151.B75

Provides "type of body, weight of each type by model and year with actual
N.A.C.C. and S.A.E. horsepower rating, cubic inch displacement, bore and

stroke in inches, the factory advertised price or list price on passenger cars and factory list price on trucks."—*Pref.* Supplements issued between editions.

**1274  Ward's world motor vehicle data.** Ward's Communications Inc. ill. Southfield, Mich.: Ward's Communications, 2000–. ISSN: 1553-8176.

629.222                                                      HD9710.A1W373

Contains 30 years of data on production and sales for passenger cars and commercial vehicles for 47 countries. Also has production by manufacturer, sales by manufacturer, total vehicles in operation by country and vehicle type, and assembly plant locations by manufacturer and region. Information derived from government agencies, trade associations, and private sources. The CD-ROM provides time series in Excel.

## Specialized Sources of Industry Data

**1275  Automotive aftermarket industry association (AAIA).** Automotive Aftermarket Industry Association. 1997–. Bethesda [Md.]: Automotive Aftermarket Industry Association. http://www. aftermarket.org/Home.asp.

The association represents manufacturers, distributors and retailers for "motor vehicle parts, accessories, service, tools, equipment, materials and supplies."—*About.* The site includes events, press releases, *Aftermarket insider magazine,* facts, newsletters, education, government affairs, international trade, market research, member services, and standards and technology.

**1276  Automotive news.** ill. Detroit: Crain Automotive Group. ISSN: 0005-1551.

338.4762922205                                                 TL1.A865

Reports trends, developments, and economic impacts for the automotive industry. An annual supplement to *Automotive News* is the *Market Data Book,* which has production (North America car and truck production history and forecast, five-year history by country, production by assembly plant, car and light-truck production by platform, car and truck production by model and by month), dealer (J.D. Power and Assoc. data, dealer census data, financial data, ad spending data, used-car prices and volumes), and sales data (North America light-vehicle sales history and forecast, U.S. light-vehicle sales summary by make, North America car and truck sales, five-year history by make, U.S. car and light-truck sales by model and by month, Canada sales by month, Mexico sales by model and by month). Available through LexisNexis Academic Universe and through the Automotive News Data Center.

1277 **Census of transportation.** United States Dept. of Commerce, Bureau of the Census. 54 v. Washington: U.S. Dept. of Commerce, Bureau of the Census, 1963–2003.

380.50973                                                                    HE203.C44

Begun in 1963 and continued through 1997 (now part of the *Economic Census*). Includes the results of the truck inventory and use survey, commodity transportation survey, vehicle inventory and use survey, and national travel survey. Available online through the U.S. Census (http://www.census.gov/prod/www/abs/transpor.html/).

1278 **Marketresearch.com academic.** Kalorama Information. 1999–. Bethesda, Md.: Kalorama Information. http://www.marketresearch.com/.

HF5415.2.K35

Market research reports from various sources (Icon Group, Kalorama, BizMiner, etc.) for Consumer Goods (apparel, cosmetics and personal care, house and home, pet services and supplies, travel services), Food and Beverage (alcoholic beverages, coffee and tea, soft drinks, confectionery, dairy products, food processing), Heavy Industry (energy, mining, utilities, construction, machines and parts, manufacturing, metals, paper and forest products, plastics, automotive, aviation & aerospace, logistics and shipping), Service Industries (accounting and finance, corporate services, banking and financial services, insurance), Public Sector (associations/nonprofits, education, government), Life Science (biotechnology, agriculture, genomics, proteomics, medical imaging, healthcare facilities, managed care, regulation and policy, cardiovascular devices, equipment and supplies, wound care, pharmaceuticals, diseases and conditions, prescription drugs, therapeutic area), Technology & Media (computer equipment, electronics, networks, e-commerce and IT outsourcing, software, telecommunications, wireless), and Demographics (age, lifestyle and economics, multicultural).

Reports range in length, with some over 300 pages long, and give a variety of information (definition of industry, consumer demographics, consumer shopping habits, spending patterns, sales, establishments, employment, forecasts, trends, market size, market share, and market segmentation). Some company information is also included.

**1279** **Plunkett's automobile industry almanac.** Jack W. Plunkett, Plunkett Research, Ltd. ill. Houston, Tex.: Plunkett Research, 2003–. ISSN: 1552-3004.

381                                                    HD9710.U5P58

Data on 300 major companies including manufacturing, retailing and financial services. Company profiles include types of business, brands and affiliates, contacts, employee benefits and top salaries, sales and profit numbers, growth plans, and competitive advantage. Especially useful for the industry trends, statistics, and rankings at the front of the volume. Available as an e-book.

**1280** **Publications and thought leadership from the automotive industry sector.** PricewaterhouseCoopers. 2000–. New York: PricewaterhouseCoopers. http://www.pwc.com/gx/en/automotive/industry-publications-and-thought-leadership.jhtml.

Includes reports on the global automative industry, analyst notes, and mergers and acquisitions. Individual reports vary annually. Reports are free, full of data, trends and analysis, and are international in scope.

**1281** **Ward's motor vehicle facts and figures.** Ward's Communications Inc. ill. Southfield, Mich.: Ward's Communications, 1999–. ISSN: 1553-8184.

629.222 13; 629.2222                               HD9710.U5W323

Annual data for the U.S. automotive industry. The data are presented in the following categories: production/factory sales, retail sales, registrations, automotive trade, materials, transportation expenditures, travel trends, automotive businesses (including corporate profits, R&D, and expenditures), environment/regulations, and traffic fatalities. Includes international data.

**1282** **Ward's world motor vehicle data.** Ward's Communications Inc. ill. Southfield, Mich.: Ward's Communications, 2000–. ISSN: 1553-8176.

629.222                                            HD9710.A1W373

Contains 30 years of data on production and sales for passenger cars and commercial vehicles for 47 countries. Also has production by manufacturer, sales by manufacturer, total vehicles in operation by country and vehicle type, and assembly plant locations by manufacturer and region. Information derived from government agencies, trade associations, and private sources. The CD-ROM provides time series in Excel.

# Pharmaceutical

## *Additional Reference Sources*

**1283** **Burger's medicinal chemistry and drug discovery.** 6th ed. Alfred
Burger, Donald J. Abraham. 6 v., ill. (some color). Hoboken, N.J.:
Wiley, 2003. ISBN: 0471370320.

615.19                                                                                   RS403.B8

1st ed., 1951, to 4th ed., 1980–1, had title *Medicinal chemistry*. 5th ed.,
1995–7.

Contents: v. 1, "Drug discovery"; v. 2, "Drug discovery and drug
development"; v. 3, "Cardiovascular agents and endocrines"; v. 4, "Auto-
coids, diagnostics, and drugs from new biology"; v. 5, "Chemotherapeutic
agents"; v. 6, "Nervous system agents."

Updated and expanded ed. Comprehensive resource for information
on drug studies and drug research, with the latest developments in medicinal drug research and drug development. Includes high priority areas and
subjects, such as molecular modeling in drug design, virtual screening,
bioinformatics, chemical information computing systems in drug discovery,
structural biology of drug action, etc. Includes bibliographical references and
index. For medical and science libraries. Also available in electronic format.

**1284** **A dictionary of pharmacology and allied topics.** 2nd ed.
D. R. Laurence, John Carpenter. xi, 373 p. Amsterdam, [The
Netherlands]; New York: Elsevier, 1998.

615.103                                                                                  RS51.L38

First edition, 1994, had title *A dictionary of pharmacology and clinical drug
evaluation.*

Includes currently accepted usage for pharmacological terms and
relevant terminology from other disciplines (e.g., ethics, law, social policy,
statistics), with etymology for most terms, as well as terms used by official
regulatory authorities. Does not include individual drugs. Intended for
basic and clinical pharmacologists and others involved in clinical drug
evaluation.

**1285** **Dictionary of pharmacy.** Dennis B. Worthen, Julian H. Fincher.
xiii, 528 p. New York: Pharmaceutical Products Press, 2004.
ISBN: 0789023288.

615.103                                                                                 RS51.D482

Comprehensive list of terms from pharmacy and also terminology relevant to pharmacy from several other disciplines. A–Z arrangement; cross-references (see, see also, contrast, and compare). In separate sections, includes abbreviations; Latin and Greek terms; weights and measures; practice standards; the code of ethics for pharmacists; and lists of professional associations, organizations, and colleges and schools of pharmacy in the United States and Canada. Resource for pharmacy students, faculty, and practicing pharmacists.

**1286  Hoover's online.** Reference Press. 1996–. Austin, Tex.: Reference Press. http://www.hoovers.com/.

338.7                                                          HG4057

Nearly 18 million records describing public and private companies primarily in the United States, but including Canada, United Kingdom, Europe, and Asia/Pacific. Profiles have an overview, history, family tree, industry information, products/operations, top competitors, competitive landscape, top executives with biographies, news, significant developments, and financial data (summary; income statement; balance sheet; cash flow; historical financials such as five years of P/E and per share; stock quote; interactive stock chart; market data; earnings estimates; this year's ratios for the company, industry, and market; SEC filings; and industry watch).

Covers 600 industries, organized into the following categories: Aerospace and Defense; Agriculture; Automotive and Transport; Banking; Beverages; Business Services; Charitable Organizations; Chemicals; Computer Hardware; Computer Services; Computer Software; Construction; Consumer Products Manufacturers; Consumer Services; Cultural Institutions; Education; Electronics; Energy and Utilities; Environmental Services and Equipment; Financial Services; Food; Foundations; Government; Health Care; Industrial Manufacturing; Insurance; Leisure; Media; Membership Organizations; Metals and Mining; Pharmaceuticals; Real Estate; Retail; Security Products and Services; Telecommunications Equipment; Telecommunications Services; and Transportation Services.

Coverage can be brief, but generally includes a fact sheet, overview, selected companies, industry watch with video interviews, news from the last 90 days, and web resources for terminology, associations, and organizations, and online publications. Includes Hoover's print publications (*Hoover's handbook of American business* [35], *Hoover's handbook of private companies* [36]).

1287  **International pharmaceutical abstracts.** Thomson Scientific.
199?–. Philadelphia: Thomson Scientific. http://scientific.thomson.
com/products/ipa/.

615                                                                                    RS1

Also called IPA. Published in print since 1964. Launched and distributed
electronically in 1970, with coverage back to 1964. The Thomson Corporation, already involved in the production of the IPA database since 2001,
assumed ownership of IPA in 2005 from the American Society of Health-
System Pharmacists (ASHP), its previous publisher. Currently available in
print (semimonthly) and in a variety of electronic formats from several
vendors.

Indexes the international literature in applied pharmacology, including state pharmacy journals, abstracts of presentations at major pharmacy
meetings, related health and medical journals, and journals of alternative
and herbal medicine. Approximately 18,000 records annually. Each IPA
record includes an English-language abstract. Intended for pharmacists
and life science researchers.

1288  **Red book.** Thomson Healthcare. ill. Montvale, N.J.: Thomson
Healthcare, 2004–. ISSN: 1556-3391.

338                                                                     HD9666.1.D75

Volumes in 1941/42–1943/44 had title *Drug topics price book* (continues
the "Red book price list section" of the *Druggists' circular,* issues semian-
nually 1897–1940); 1944–92 had title *Drug topics red book*; 1993–94, *Red
book*; 1995–2003, *Drug topics red book.*

*Red book* description based on 2006 ed.

Product, pricing, and clinical and pharmaceutical reference information for prescription and over-the-counter (OTC) drugs, many with
full-color photographs. Provides nationally recognized average wholesale
prices and direct and federal upper-limit prices for prescription drugs.
Also includes prices for reimbursable medical supplies and, for example,
a vitamin comparison table of popular multivitamin products, a guide to
herbal/alternative medicines, a list of FDA-approved new drugs, generics,
and OTC products, and also a list of "Websites worth watching." Includes
poison control centers and manufacturers, pharmaceutical wholesalers,
and third-party administrator directories. Intended for pharmacists and
other health care professionals. For electronic delivery options, see http://
www.micromedex.com/products/redbook.

# Internet Resources

**1289  Drugs@FDA.** U.S. Food and Drug Administration, Center for Drug and Evaluation Research. Washington: U.S. Food and Drug Administration, Center for Drug and Evaluation Research. http://www.accessdata.fda.gov/scripts/cder/drugsatfda.

RM300

Includes FDA-approved brand-name and generic drug products. Searchable by drug name, active ingredient, new drug application number (NDA), abbreviated new drug application (ANDA), and biologics license application (BLA). Provides a drug's FDA history and helps with finding labels for approved drug products. Also provides monthly drug approval reports. Further information and answers to questions relating to this website can be found at http://www.fda.gov/Drugs/InformationOnDrugs/ucm075234.htm.

**1290  Ernst and Young.** Ernst and Young. 2007. London: Ernst and Young. http://www.ey.com/global/content.nsf/International/Industry_Overview/.

Ernst and Young provides "accounting and auditing, tax reporting and operations, tax advisory, business risk services, technology and security risk services, transaction advisory, and human capital services." The site is useful for articles on financial management, corporate governance, initial public offerings (IPOs), and industry reports (asset management, automotive, banking and capital markets, biotechnology, consumer products, insurance, media and entertainment, mining and metals, oil and gas, pharmaceuticals, real estate and construction, hospitality and leisure, technology, telecommunications, utilities).

**1291  Industry profile.** Pharmaceutical Research and Manufacturers of America. 1996–. Washington, D.C.: Pharmaceutical Research and Manufacturers of America. ISSN: 1934-8231. http://www.phrma.org/.

338.7616151

Formerly a print serial, this report has research and development spending, information on incentives, partnerships, Medicare and Medicaid, and industry approaches to innovation. The Pharmaceutical Research and Manufacturers of America website also has reports on the U.S. health care system, the cost of prescription drugs, and drug discovery and development.

1292 **International pharmaceutical abstracts.** Thomson Scientific.
199?–. Philadelphia: Thomson Scientific. http://scientific.thomson.
com/products/ipa/.
615                                                                                                            RS1

Also called IPA. Published in print since 1964. Launched and distributed electronically in 1970, with coverage back to 1964. The Thomson Corporation, already involved in the production of the IPA database since 2001, assumed ownership of IPA in 2005 from the American Society of Health-System Pharmacists (ASHP), its previous publisher. Currently available in print (semimonthly) and in a variety of electronic formats from several vendors.

Indexes the international literature in applied pharmacology, including state pharmacy journals, abstracts of presentations at major pharmacy meetings, related health and medical journals, and journals of alternative and herbal medicine. Approximately 18,000 records annually. Each IPA record includes an English-language abstract. Intended for pharmacists and life science researchers.

1293 **Manufacturing.net.** Advantage Business Media. 2000s–. [s.l.]:
Reed Business Information. http://www.manufacturing.net/.

Covers manufacturing for aerospace, automotive, chemical, food, material handling, pharmaceuticals, and utilities. Includes design and development; case studies; electrical and electronics; energy; environmental; facilities and operations; labor relations; manufacturing technology; materials; quality control; safety; and supply chain management. Has international focus.

1294 **WHO drug information.** World Health Organization. Geneva,
Switzerland: World Health Organization. ISSN: 1010-9609. http://
www.who.int/druginformation.

RS189.W47

Quarterly journal, available since 1987 in print and also online since 1996.

Provides an overview of topics relating to drug development and regulation that are of current relevance, with the latest international news, prescribing and access of medicines worldwide. Also introduces newly released guidance documents. Includes lists of proposed and recommended International Nonproprietary Names for Pharmaceutical Substances (INN). For health professionals and policy makers. Further information and links to INNs, the current 16th ed. (March 2009 and March 2010 update) of the *WHO model list of essential medicines*, and other related WHO publications can be found at http://www.who.int/ medicines/publications/en/.

## Organizations and Associations

1295 **Food and drug administration.** Food and drug administration. [2005]. [Washington, D.C.]: The Office. http://www.fda.gov/. The FDA's site has a wide range of information for the consumer and the researcher, including: Enforcement Activities (clinical trials, enforcement report, product recalls and alerts); Products Regulated by FDA (animal drugs and food, aquaculture, bioengineered food, biologics, gene therapy, mobile phones, sunlamps, tattoos, food, drugs, xenotransplantation); news; hot topics; publications; major initiatives/activities (advisory committees, bar coding, buying medical products online, Data Council, Facts@ FDA) and Food Industry (Prior Notice of Imports, Registration of Food Facilities).

1296 **Industry profile.** Pharmaceutical Research and Manufacturers of America. 1996–. Washington, D.C.: Pharmaceutical Research and Manufacturers of America. ISSN: 1934-8231. http://www.phrma.org/.
                                                                                    338.7616151

Formerly a print serial, this report has research and development spending, information on incentives, partnerships, Medicare and Medicaid, and industry approaches to innovation. The Pharmaceutical Research and Manufacturers of America website also has reports on the U.S. health care system, the cost of prescription drugs, and drug discovery and development.

## Specialized Sources of Industry Data

1297 **Industry profile.** Pharmaceutical Research and Manufacturers of America. 1996–. Washington, D.C.: Pharmaceutical Research and Manufacturers of America. ISSN: 1934-8231. http://www.phrma.org/.
                                                                                    338.7616151

Formerly a print serial, this report has research and development spending, information on incentives, partnerships, Medicare and Medicaid, and industry approaches to innovation. The Pharmaceutical Research and Manufacturers of America website also has reports on the U.S. health care system, the cost of prescription drugs, and drug discovery and development.

1298 **Marketresearch.com academic.** Kalorama Information. 1999–.
Bethesda, Md.: Kalorama Information. http://www.marketresearch.
com/.

HF5415.2.K35

Market research reports from various sources (Icon Group, Kalorama,
BizMiner, etc.) for Consumer Goods (apparel, cosmetics and personal
care, house and home, pet services and supplies, travel services), Food and
Beverage (alcoholic beverages, coffee and tea, soft drinks, confectionery,
dairy products, food processing), Heavy Industry (energy, mining, utilities, construction, machines and parts, manufacturing, metals, paper and
forest products, plastics, automotive, aviation & aerospace, logistics and
shipping), Service Industries (accounting and finance, corporate services,
banking and financial services, insurance), Public Sector (associations/
nonprofits, education, government), Life Science (biotechnology, agriculture, genomics, proteomics, medical imaging, healthcare facilities, managed care, regulation and policy, cardiovascular devices, equipment and
supplies, wound care, pharmaceuticals, diseases and conditions, prescription drugs, therapeutic area), Technology & Media (computer equipment,
electronics, networks, e-commerce and IT outsourcing, software, telecommunications, wireless), and Demographics (age, lifestyle and economics,
multicultural).

Reports range in length, with some over 300 pages long, and give a
variety of information (definition of industry, consumer demographics, consumer shopping habits, spending patterns, sales, establishments,
employment, forecasts, trends, market size, market share, and market segmentation). Some company information is also included.

## Restaurants

### *Additional Reference Sources*

1299 **Hoover's online.** Reference Press. 1996–. Austin, Tex.: Reference
Press. http://www.hoovers.com/.

338.7                                                                HG4057

Nearly 18 million records describing public and private companies primarily in the United States, but including Canada, United Kingdom, Europe,
and Asia/Pacific. Profiles have an overview, history, family tree, industry
information, products/operations, top competitors, competitive landscape,

top executives with biographies, news, significant developments, and financial data (summary; income statement; balance sheet; cash flow; historical financials such as five years of P/E and per share; stock quote; interactive stock chart; market data; earnings estimates; this year's ratios for the company, industry, and market; SEC filings; and industry watch).

Covers 600 industries, organized into the following categories: Aerospace and Defense; Agriculture; Automotive and Transport; Banking; Beverages; Business Services; Charitable Organizations; Chemicals; Computer Hardware; Computer Services; Computer Software; Construction; Consumer Products Manufacturers; Consumer Services; Cultural Institutions; Education; Electronics; Energy and Utilities; Environmental Services and Equipment; Financial Services; Food; Foundations; Government; Health Care; Industrial Manufacturing; Insurance; Leisure; Media; Membership Organizations; Metals and Mining; Pharmaceuticals; Real Estate; Retail; Security Products and Services; Telecommunications Equipment; Telecommunications Services; and Transportation Services.

Coverage can be brief, but generally includes a fact sheet, overview, selected companies, industry watch with video interviews, news from the last 90 days, and web resources for terminology, associations, and organizations, and online publications. Includes Hoover's print publications (*Hoover's handbook of American business* [35], *Hoover's handbook of private companies* [36]).

## Internet Resources

1300 **National restaurant association.** National Restaurant Association. 2007. Washington, D.C.: National Restaurant Association. http://www.restaurant.org/.

Founded in 1919, the association represents 935,000 restaurant and foodservice companies. The website has news, community outreach, food safety and nutrition, careers and education, policy and politics, events, tips for running a business, and industry research. The industry research portion of the site has Industry Overviews (at a glance, forecast, state and local statistics), Research by Topic (H/R, operations, consumer, economy), links to resources for company research, and current industry trends. A great resource for locating demographic trends, consumer food-and-beverage preferences, cost of sales, gross profits, and employee turnover. Some data is available for free.

## Organizations and Associations

1301 **National restaurant association.** National Restaurant Association. 2007. Washington, D.C.: National Restaurant Association. http://www.restaurant.org/.

Founded in 1919, the association represents 935,000 restaurant and food-service companies. The website has news, community outreach, food safety and nutrition, careers and education, policy and politics, events, tips for running a business, and industry research. The industry research portion of the site has Industry Overviews (at a glance, forecast, state and local statistics), Research by Topic (H/R, operations, consumer, economy), links to resources for company research, and current industry trends. A great resource for locating demographic trends, consumer food-and-beverage preferences, cost of sales, gross profits, and employee turnover. Some data is available for free.

## Specialized Sources of Industry Data

1302 **National restaurant association.** National Restaurant Association. 2007. Washington, D.C.: National Restaurant Association. http://www.restaurant.org/.

Founded in 1919, the association represents 935,000 restaurant and food-service companies. The website has news, community outreach, food safety and nutrition, careers and education, policy and politics, events, tips for running a business, and industry research. The industry research portion of the site has Industry Overviews (at a glance, forecast, state and local statistics), Research by Topic (H/R, operations, consumer, economy), links to resources for company research, and current industry trends. A great resource for locating demographic trends, consumer food-and-beverage preferences, cost of sales, gross profits, and employee turnover. Some data is available for free.

## Retail Trade

## Additional Reference Sources

1303 **Business insights.** Datamonitor (Firm). [London?]: Reuters. http://www.globalbusinessinsights.com/autologin.asp.

HF54.7

Reports on energy, consumer goods, finance, health care, and technology. Reports, typically over 100 pages long, cover new product innovations, marketing strategies, market drivers, key players, trends, forecast business opportunities, and industry interviews. International focus, especially strong for European coverage.

**1304  Directory of apparel specialty stores.** Business Guides, Inc. Tampa, Fla.: Business Guides, 1997–. ISSN: 1092-4442.
381.45687029473                                    HD9940.U3D459

Entries for retailers with a minimum of $500,000 in annual sales. Arranged by category (women's, men's, children's, and family apparel, accessory retailers, sporting goods retailers, and resident buyers). Provides contact information, year founded, total sales, product sales, number of units, trade names, total selling square feet, average check-outs, product lines carried, apparel price lines, key personnel, and geographic areas of operation. Indexed by product, name of company, and exclusion.

**1305  Directory of department stores.** Chain Store Guide. ill. Tampa, Fla.: Business Guides, 1998–. ISSN: 1097-7023.
                                                   HF5465.U4D47

Lists companies with a minimum $250,000 sales volume, including department stores, shoe stores, jewelry stores, leather/luggage stores, and optical stores. Listings give contact information, year founded, total sales, breakdown of type of sales (footwear, apparel, etc.), customer sales (breakdown of sales channels, Internet, catalog, retail), private label, Internet orders, mail order, catalog names, total units, trade names, total selling square feet, average check outs, product lines, price lines, areas of operation, and key personnel. Also lists resident buyers, with contact information, stores served, and key personnel representing those stores.

**1306  Hoover's online.** Reference Press. 1996–. Austin, Tex.: Reference Press. http://www.hoovers.com/.
338.7                                              HG4057

Nearly 18 million records describing public and private companies primarily in the United States, but including Canada, United Kingdom, Europe, and Asia/Pacific. Profiles have an overview, history, family tree, industry information, products/operations, top competitors, competitive landscape, top executives with biographies, news, significant developments, and financial data (summary; income statement; balance sheet; cash flow; historical financials such as five years of P/E and per share; stock quote; interactive stock chart; market data; earnings estimates; this year's ratios for the company, industry, and market; SEC filings; and industry watch).

Covers 600 industries, organized into the following categories: Aerospace and Defense; Agriculture; Automotive and Transport; Banking; Beverages; Business Services; Charitable Organizations; Chemicals; Computer Hardware; Computer Services; Computer Software; Construction; Consumer Products Manufacturers; Consumer Services; Cultural Institutions; Education; Electronics; Energy and Utilities; Environmental Services and Equipment; Financial Services; Food; Foundations; Government; Health Care; Industrial Manufacturing; Insurance; Leisure; Media; Membership Organizations; Metals and Mining; Pharmaceuticals; Real Estate; Retail; Security Products and Services; Telecommunications Equipment; Telecommunications Services; and Transportation Services.

Coverage can be brief, but generally includes a fact sheet, overview, selected companies, industry watch with video interviews, news from the last 90 days, and web resources for terminology, associations, and organizations, and online publications. Includes Hoover's print publications (*Hoover's handbook of American business* [35], *Hoover's handbook of private companies* [36]).

**1307  The retail market research yearbook.** Richard K. Miller and
Associates. Loganville, Ga.: Richard K. Miller and Associates,
2005–. ISSN: 1930-966X.

381

An overview of the retail market, with information on companies, consumers, and resources for each retail industry segment. Chapters include: Market summary; Current and future trends; Industry profile; Department stores; Discount stores and supercenters; Warehouse clubs; Supermarkets; Variety and dollar stores; Drug stores; Apparel; Footwear; Jewelry; Health, beauty, and cosmetics; Consumer electronics; Home decor and furnishings; Home centers and hardware; Housewares and home textiles; Book stores; Music and video; Office products; Sporting goods; Toys and video games; Pet supplies; Crafts and fabrics; Photography; Closeout and off-price chains; Convenience stores; Military post exchanges; Resale and thrift stores; E-commerce; Catalog and mail-order retail; Television home shopping; Christmas holiday shopping; Back-to-school; Holiday markets; and The bridal and wedding market.

**1308 RN and WPL encyclopedia.** Salesman's Guide, Inc. New York: Salesman's Guide, 1984–. ISSN: 1526-3851.

338.768702573                                    HD9940.U3R5

Over 121,500 entries for registered numbers (RN's) and wool product labels (WPL's) for over 31,500 U.S. textile manufacturers. Gives name of manufacturer and contact information.

## Definition of the Industry

**1309 IBISWorld United States.** IBISWorld. New York: IBISWorld. http://www.ibisworld.com/.

HC103.I247

700 reports on the following industries: agriculture, forestry, fishing and hunting; mining; utilities; construction; manufacturing; wholesale trade; retail trade; transportation and warehousing; information; finance and insurance; real estate and rental and leasing; professional, scientific, and technical services; administrative and support and waste management and remediation services; educational services; health care and social assistance; arts, entertainment, and recreation; accommodation and food services; and other services. Setting this database apart are reports on small industries, such as parking lots and garages.

Reports include industry definition; key statistics; segmentations (products and services segmentation, major market segments, industry concentration, geographic spread); market characteristics (market size, demand determinants, domestic and international markets, basis of competition, life cycle); industry conditions (barriers to entry, taxation, industry assistance, regulation and deregulation, cost structure, capital and labor intensity, technology and systems, industry volatility, globalization); key factors (sensitivities and success factors); key competitors; and industry performance (current and historical).

## Specialized Sources of Industry Data

**1310 IBISWorld United States.** IBISWorld. New York: IBISWorld. http://www.ibisworld.com/.

HC103.I247

700 reports on the following industries: agriculture, forestry, fishing and hunting; mining; utilities; construction; manufacturing; wholesale trade; retail trade; transportation and warehousing; information; finance and

insurance; real estate and rental and leasing; professional, scientific, and technical services; administrative and support and waste management and remediation services; educational services; health care and social assistance; arts, entertainment, and recreation; accommodation and food services; and other services. Setting this database apart are reports on small industries, such as parking lots and garages.

Reports include industry definition; key statistics; segmentations (products and services segmentation, major market segments, industry concentration, geographic spread); market characteristics (market size, demand determinants, domestic and international markets, basis of competition, life cycle); industry conditions (barriers to entry, taxation, industry assistance, regulation and deregulation, cost structure, capital and labor intensity, technology and systems, industry volatility, globalization); key factors (sensitivities and success factors); key competitors; and industry performance (current and historical).

## Telecommunications

### Additional Reference Sources

**1311  Desktop encyclopedia of telecommunications.** 3rd ed. Nathan
J. Muller. xx, 1250 p., ill. New York: McGraw-Hill, 2002. ISBN:
0071381481.

621.38203                                                    TK5102.M85

Written for nontechnical professionals, the *Encyclopedia* explains local and wide-area networking, equipment and services, network applications, regulations, standards, industry trends, and covers industry organizations. Articles can be thorough, with information on the evolution of a technology or a regulation. The second edition is available as an e-book through NetLibrary.

**1312  Encyclopedia of wireless telecommunications.** Francis Botto.
1 v. (various pagings), ill. Boston: McGraw-Hill, 2002. ISBN:
0071390251.

621.38203                                                    TK5103.2.B68

While no print source can keep up with the pace of technological advances, this source provides a solid background on architectures, devices and handsets, free space communications technology, globalization, infrastructure, LAN technologies, local communication technologies

(Bluetooth, Piano, IrDA, etc.), principles of radio and light, services and products, e-business, and standards and protocols.

**1313 Global market information database.** Euromonitor. [1999–.] [London]: Euromonitor. http://www.gmid.euromonitor.com/.

HD2755.5.G56

Market reports, company profiles, and demographic, economic, and marketing statistics for 205 countries. Market reports are for 16 consumer markets (food and drink, tobacco, toys, etc.) and 14 industrial and service markets (accountancy, broadcasting, chemicals, property services, etc.).

Reports have market size, market sectors, share of market, marketing activity, research and development, corporate overview, distribution, consumer profiles, market forecasts, sector forecasts, sources, and definitions. Additional reports are available for market segments, such as baby food. Company profiles have background, recent news, competitive environment, and outlook. Consumer lifestyle reports and very useful marketing background analyze the consumer by country, gender, age, marital status, educational attainment, ethnicity, religion, home ownership, household profile, employment, income, health, eating and personal grooming habits, leisure activities, personal finance, communication, transport, and travel.

Search for data, which can be exported into Excel or browse for reports. Data are available from 1977 through 2016 and include inflation, exchange rates, GDP, GNI, government expenditures, government finance, income, labor, and money supply.

**1314 The Irwin handbook of telecommunications.** 5th ed. James H. Green. xxxviii, 770 p., ill. New York: McGraw-Hill, 2006. ISBN: 0071452222.

621.382                                  TK5102.3.U6G74

Serves almost as a textbook for telecommunications, with background information, trends, definitions, and applications for telecommunications. Parts of the book include: Principles of telecommunications, Switching systems, Transmission technologies, Customer premise systems, Telecommunications networks. Appendix A: Telecommunications acronym dictionary; Appendix B: Glossary. Bibliography. Available as an e-book.

**1315 Major telecommunications companies of the world.** Graham and Whiteside. London: Graham and Whiteside, 1998–. ISSN: 1369-5460.

Entries for 3,500 companies from around the world, giving contact information, executives' names, principal activities, parent company, subsidiaries, status (public/private), number of employees, and principal shareholders. Useful for libraries that do not have good international business directories.

## Definition of the Industry

1316  **Desktop encyclopedia of telecommunications.** 3rd ed. Nathan J. Muller. xx, 1250 p., ill. New York: McGraw-Hill, 2002. ISBN: 0071381481.

621.38203                                                                TK5102.M85

Written for nontechnical professionals, the *Encyclopedia* explains local and wide-area networking, equipment and services, network applications, regulations, standards, industry trends, and covers industry organizations. Articles can be thorough, with information on the evolution of a technology or a regulation. The second edition is available as an e-book through NetLibrary.

1317  **Encyclopedia of wireless telecommunications.** Francis Botto. 1 v. (various pagings), ill. Boston: McGraw-Hill, 2002. ISBN: 0071390251.

621.38203                                                              TK5103.2.B68

While no print source can keep up with the pace of technological advances, this source provides a solid background on architectures, devices and handsets, free space communications technology, globalization, infrastructure, LAN technologies, local communication technologies (Bluetooth, Piano, IrDA, etc.), principles of radio and light, services and products, e-business, and standards and protocols.

## Internet Resources

1318  **Cellular telecommunications industry association.** Cellular Telecommunications Industry Association. 2007 Washington, D.C.: CITA.org. http://www.ctia.org/.

Founded in 1984, the association represents "all sectors of wireless communications—cellular, personal communication services and enhanced specialized mobile radio."—*About us.* The website is divided into six sections: Media (press releases, industry info, publications, multimedia library), Advocacy (policy topics, position papers, FCC filings, research, federal and state affairs), Consumer Info, Membership, Conventions and Events, and Business Resources (Wireless Internet Caucus, certification, common short code, industry directory, career center). Most useful for the industry statistics (total number of wireless subscribers, roaming revenues, average monthly bill, number of U.S. cell sites) and glossary.

**1319** **Ernst and Young.** Ernst and Young. 2007. London: Ernst and Young. http://www.ey.com/global/content.nsf/International/Industry_Overview/.

Ernst and Young provides "accounting and auditing, tax reporting and operations, tax advisory, business risk services, technology and security risk services, transaction advisory, and human capital services." The site is useful for articles on financial management, corporate governance, initial public offerings (IPOs), and industry reports (asset management, automotive, banking and capital markets, biotechnology, consumer products, insurance, media and entertainment, mining and metals, oil and gas, pharmaceuticals, real estate and construction, hospitality and leisure, technology, telecommunications, utilities).

**1320** **Federal communications commission.** U.S. Superintendent of Documents. 2007. Washington, D.C.: U.S. Government Printing Office, Superintendent of Documents. http://www.fcc.gov/.

The FCC was founded in 1923 and regulates interstate and international communications by radio, television, wire, satellite and cable. The website contains a treasure trove of information, including reports, statistics, trends, rules and regulations, and more. Examples include annual reports on cable industry prices, periodic reviews of the radio industry, the statistics of communications common carriers, statistical trends in telephony, local and long distance telephone industries, local telephone competition and broadband deployment, telephone industry infrastructure and service quality, federal-state joint board monitoring reports, telephone numbering facts, and international traffic data.

**1321** **International telecommunication union.** International Telecommunication Union. 2007. Genève [Geneva, Switzerland]: International Telecommunication Union. http://www.itu.int/.

HE8675.I7233

The ITU is a trade association focusing on radio communications, standardization, and development in the information and communication technology industry. Their website has news, events, and publications. Recent publications include: *ITU Internet reports 2006: digital.life; World information society report; World telecommunication standardization assembly; Measuring the information society ICT opportunity index and world telecommunication/ICT indicators; Radio regulations;* and *Telecommunications industry at a glance.* Most publications are available for a fee, but often a free executive summary is provided online.

**1322 Telelcommunications industry association.** Telelcommunications Industry Association. 2007. Arlington, Va.: Telelcommunications Industry Association. http://www.tiaonline.org/.

Founded in 1924, the association is an advocate for the information, communications, and entertainment technology industries. Its website has information on standards, numbering resources (Electronic Serial Number Assignment, Mobile Equipment IDentifier, System Operator Code), publications (*Industry Playbook* and *Technology and Policy Primer,* letters, filings, policy trackers, legislative-regulatory call agendas), Market Review and Forecast (available for a fee), news, events, and a section for members only.

## *Organizations and Associations*

**1323 Cellular telecommunications industry association.** Cellular Telecommunications Industry Association. 2007. Washington, D.C.: CITA.org. http://www.ctia.org/.

Founded in 1984, the association represents "all sectors of wireless communications—cellular, personal communication services and enhanced specialized mobile radio."—*About us.* The website is divided into six sections: Media (press releases, industry info, publications, multimedia library), Advocacy (policy topics, position papers, FCC filings, research, federal and state affairs), Consumer Info, Membership, Conventions and Events, and Business Resources (Wireless Internet Caucus, certification, common short code, industry directory, career center). Most useful for the industry statistics (total number of wireless subscribers, roaming revenues, average monthly bill, number of U.S. cell sites) and glossary.

**1324 Federal communications commission.** U.S. Superintendent of Documents. 2007. Washington, D.C.: U.S. Government Printing Office, Superintendent of Documents. http://www.fcc.gov/.

The FCC was founded in 1923 and regulates interstate and international communications by radio, television, wire, satellite and cable. The website contains a treasure trove of information, including reports, statistics, trends, rules and regulations, and more. Examples include annual reports on cable industry prices, periodic reviews of the radio industry, the statistics of communications common carriers, statistical trends in telephony, local and long distance telephone industries, local telephone competition and broadband deployment, telephone industry infrastructure and service quality, federal-state joint board monitoring reports, telephone numbering facts, and international traffic data.

1325  **International telecommunication union.** International
       Telecommunication Union. 2007. Genève [Geneva, Switzerland]:
       International Telecommunication Union. http://www.itu.int/.

                                                        HE8675.I7233

The ITU is a trade association focusing on radio communications, standardization, and development in the information and communication technology industry. Their website has news, events, and publications. Recent publications include: *ITU Internet reports 2006: digital.life*; *World information society report*; *World telecommunication standardization assembly*; *Measuring the information society ICT opportunity index and world telecommunication/ICT indicators*; *Radio regulations*; and *Telecommunications industry at a glance*. Most publications are available for a fee, but often a free executive summary is provided online.

1326  **Telelcommunications industry association.** Telelcommunications
       Industry Association. 2007. Arlington, Va.: Telelcommunications
       Industry Association. http://www.tiaonline.org/.

Founded in 1924, the association is an advocate for the information, communications, and entertainment technology industries. Its website has information on standards, numbering resources (Electronic Serial Number Assignment, Mobile Equipment IDentifier, System Operator Code), publications (*Industry Playbook* and *Technology and Policy Primer*, letters, filings, policy trackers, legislative-regulatory call agendas), Market Review and Forecast (available for a fee), news, events, and a section for members only.

## *Specialized Sources of Industry Data*

1327  **Cellular telecommunications industry association.** Cellular
       Telecommunications Industry Association. 2007. Washington,
       D.C.: CITA.org. http://www.ctia.org/.

Founded in 1984, the association represents "all sectors of wireless communications—cellular, personal communication services and enhanced specialized mobile radio."—*About us*. The website is divided into six sections: Media (press releases, industry info, publications, multimedia library), Advocacy (policy topics, position papers, FCC filings, research, federal and state affairs), Consumer Info, Membership, Conventions and Events, and Business Resources (Wireless Internet Caucus, certification, common short code, industry directory, career center). Most useful for the industry statistics (total number of wireless subscribers, roaming revenues, average monthly bill, number of U.S. cell sites) and glossary.

**1328  Forrester research.** Forrester Research. [1999–2003.] Cambridge, Mass.: Forrester. http://www.library.hbs.edu/forrester.htm.

HF5548.32T174

Nearly 17,000 original reports on technology's effect on business and the consumer in the United States, Canada, Europe, and Asia Pacific. Research is in two categories, technology and industry.

Topics in technology are application development, business intelligence, computing systems, consumer devices and access, content and collaboration, customer experience, enterprise applications, enterprise mobility, IT management, IT services, networking, portals and site technology, security, software infrastructure, and tech sector economics.

Topics in industry are brand strategy, brand tactics, consumer electronics, consumer products, customer insight, emerging marketing channels, energy and utilities, financial services, government, healthcare and life sciences, high tech, industry insight, manufacturing, marketing and advertising, marketing planning, media and entertainment, mobile services, professional services, relationship marketing, retail, telecommunications, television advertising, transportation and logistics, and travel.

Reports typically range from 3–20 pages, and some are available as videos.

**1329  Hoover's online.** Reference Press. 1996–. Austin, Tex.: Reference Press. http://www.hoovers.com/.

338.7                                                                       HG4057

Nearly 18 million records describing public and private companies primarily in the United States, but including Canada, United Kingdom, Europe, and Asia/Pacific. Profiles have an overview, history, family tree, industry information, products/operations, top competitors, competitive landscape, top executives with biographies, news, significant developments, and financial data (summary; income statement; balance sheet; cash flow; historical financials such as five years of P/E and per share; stock quote; interactive stock chart; market data; earnings estimates; this year's ratios for the company, industry, and market; SEC filings; and industry watch).

Covers 600 industries, organized into the following categories: Aerospace and Defense; Agriculture; Automotive and Transport; Banking; Beverages; Business Services; Charitable Organizations; Chemicals; Computer Hardware; Computer Services; Computer Software; Construction; Consumer Products Manufacturers; Consumer Services; Cultural Institutions; Education; Electronics; Energy and Utilities; Environmental Services and Equipment; Financial Services; Food; Foundations; Government; Health Care; Industrial Manufacturing; Insurance; Leisure; Media; Membership Organizations; Metals and Mining; Pharmaceuticals; Real Estate; Retail; Security Products and Services; Telecommunications Equipment; Telecommunications Services; and Transportation Services.

Coverage can be brief, but generally includes a fact sheet, overview, selected companies, industry watch with video interviews, news from the last 90 days, and web resources for terminology, associations, and organizations, and online publications. Includes Hoover's print publications (*Hoover's handbook of American business* [35], *Hoover's handbook of private companies* [36]).

## Transportation

### Additional Reference Sources

**1330  Directory of United States exporters.** New York: Journal of Commerce, 1990–. ISSN: 1057-6878.

HF3011.D63

Describes U.S. cargo shippers and the products they export. Gives contact information, SIC code, top executives, TEU's (twenty-foot equivalent unit container size) and metric tonnage, estimated value, ports of exit, and products. Arranged by state and indexed by company and product (uses Harmonized Commodity Codes). Also provides contact information for: export assistance centers, U.S. and foreign commercial service international posts, trade commissions, foreign embassies and consulates, U.S. foreign trade zones, world ports, and banks and other financial services. Companion to *Directory of United States importers* (60).

1331 **Directory of United States importers.** Journal of Commerce, Inc. ill. New York: Journal of Commerce, 1991–. ISSN: 1057-5111.
382.502573                                                    HF3012.D53

A geographical listing of importers to the U.S., indexed by products (Harmonized Commodity Codes) and industry (Standard Industrial Classification [SIC] codes). Gives contact information, SIC code, top executives, TEU's (Twenty-foot Equivalent Unit container size) and metric tonnage, estimated value, ports of exit, and products. Also provides contact information for: trade commissions, foreign embassies and consulates in the U.S., U.S. foreign trade zones, world ports, and banks and other financial services. Companion to the *Directory of United States exporters* (59).

1332 **Handbook of transportation science.** 2nd ed. Randolph W. Hall. vi, 741 p., ill. Boston: Kluwer Academic Publishers, 2003. ISBN: 1402072465.
388                                                            HE192.5.H36

Provides information on transportation fundamentals. Includes: human elements in transportation, flows and congestion, spatial models, routing and network models, and economic models. Each chapter contains a lengthy list of references. Available as an e-book.

1333 **Harris U.S. manufacturers directory.** National ed. Harris InfoSource. Twinsburg, Ohio: Harris InfoSource, 2000–. ISSN: 1531-8273.
338                                                            HF5035.H37

Entries for U.S. companies include location, contact information, industry descriptions, Standard Industrial Classification (SIC) or NAICS codes, executive names, and size. Indexed by company name, geography, product or service category, and SIC code. Libraries receiving questions about local companies may want to invest in the regional and state directories also published by Harris. Available in an online version.

1334 **Hoover's online.** Reference Press. 1996–. Austin, Tex.: Reference Press. http://www.hoovers.com/.
338.7                                                          HG4057

Nearly 18 million records describing public and private companies primarily in the United States, but including Canada, United Kingdom, Europe, and Asia/Pacific. Profiles have an overview, history, family tree, industry information, products/operations, top competitors, competitive landscape, top executives with biographies, news, significant developments, and financial data (summary; income statement; balance sheet; cash flow; historical financials such as five years of P/E and per share; stock quote; interactive stock chart; market data; earnings estimates; this year's ratios for the company, industry, and market; SEC filings; and industry watch).

Covers 600 industries, organized into the following categories: Aerospace and Defense; Agriculture; Automotive and Transport; Banking; Beverages; Business Services; Charitable Organizations; Chemicals; Computer Hardware; Computer Services; Computer Software; Construction; Consumer Products Manufacturers; Consumer Services; Cultural Institutions; Education; Electronics; Energy and Utilities; Environmental Services and Equipment; Financial Services; Food; Foundations; Government; Health Care; Industrial Manufacturing; Insurance; Leisure; Media; Membership Organizations; Metals and Mining; Pharmaceuticals; Real Estate; Retail; Security Products and Services; Telecommunications Equipment; Telecommunications Services; and Transportation Services.

Coverage can be brief, but generally includes a fact sheet, overview, selected companies, industry watch with video interviews, news from the last 90 days, and web resources for terminology, associations, and organizations, and online publications. Includes Hoover's print publications (*Hoover's handbook of American business* [35], *Hoover's handbook of private companies* [36]).

**1335 Lloyd's maritime directory.** Lloyd's of London Press. ill. Colchester, Essex, [U.K.]: Lloyd's of London Press, 1982–. ISSN: 0268-327X.

387.2025                                                          HE951.L56

Lists shippers, shipowners, towage, salvage, ship management services, builders, and repairers worldwide. Gives contact information, main personnel, services, and repair facilities.

**1336 Plunkett's airline, hotel, and travel industry almanac.** Jack W. Plunkett, Plunkett Research, Ltd. ill. Houston, Tex.: Plunkett Research, 2002–. ISSN: 1554-1215.

387.7                                            HE9803.A2P58; G155.U6P58

Data on 324 major companies, both public and private. Company profiles include types of business, brands and affiliates, contacts, employee benefits and top salaries, sales and profit numbers, growth plans, and competitive advantage. Especially useful for the industry trends, statistics and rankings (forecasts to 2020, top destinations worldwide, top airlines, top tourism nations, etc.) at the front of the volume and information on the main associations and organizations in the back of the volume. Most information is for the U.S., but some international coverage is provided. Available as an e-book.

**1337  Register of ships.** Lloyd's Register of Shipping. London: Lloyd's Register of Shipping, 1966–. ISSN: 0141-4909.

623.82405                                                                                    HE565.A3L7

Published under varying titles since 1760 and by Lloyd's since 1834. Merged with *Underwriters' registry for iron vessels* in 1885. Recent issues in four or more volumes, with some variation in contents. The "Register of ships" gives the names, classes, and general information concerning the ships classed by Lloyd's register, together with particulars of all known ocean-going merchant ships in the world of 100 tons gross and upwards. It also lists lighters carried on board ship, floating docks, liquefied gas carriers, ships carrying refrigerated cargo, refrigerated cargo containers, refrigerated stores and container terminals, and offshore drilling rigs. The "Register" is updated by means of cumulative monthly supplements containing the latest survey records for all classed ships, and changes of name, ownership, flag, tonnage, etc., for all ships, whether classed or not. The "Shipowners" section gives a list of owners and managers of the ships recorded in the "Register" with their fleets, as well as lists of former and compound names of ships. An appendix contains a list of shipbuilders with existing ships they have built, marine engine builders and boilermakers, dry and wet docks, telegraphic addresses and codes used by shipping firms, marine insurance companies and marine associations.

## Definition of the Industry

**1338  Glossary of transport: English, French, Italian, Dutch, German, Swedish.** Gordon Logie. xxvii, 296 p. Amsterdam, [The Netherlands]; New York: Elsevier Scientific, 1980. ISBN: 0444417311.

380.503                                                                                    HE141.L63

Gives equivalent terms in the broad subject areas of transport and transportation studies, roads and road traffic, parking and road vehicles, railways, waterborne transport, and aviation. Indexes in all six languages.

1339  **IBISWorld United States.** IBISWorld. New York: IBISWorld.
http://www.ibisworld.com/.

HC103.I247

700 reports on the following industries: agriculture, forestry, fishing and hunting; mining; utilities; construction; manufacturing; wholesale trade; retail trade; transportation and warehousing; information; finance and insurance; real estate and rental and leasing; professional, scientific, and technical services; administrative and support and waste management and remediation services; educational services; health care and social assistance; arts, entertainment, and recreation; accommodation and food services; and other services. Setting this database apart are reports on small industries, such as parking lots and garages.

Reports include industry definition; key statistics; segmentations (products and services segmentation, major market segments, industry concentration, geographic spread); market characteristics (market size, demand determinants, domestic and international markets, basis of competition, life cycle); industry conditions (barriers to entry, taxation, industry assistance, regulation and deregulation, cost structure, capital and labor intensity, technology and systems, industry volatility, globalization); key factors (sensitivities and success factors); key competitors; and industry performance (current and historical).

## Internet Resources

1340  **Annual report.** International Air Transport Association. 1990–.
[Geneva, Switzerland]: International Air Transport Association.
http://www.iata.org/.
387.70601                                      HE9761.1.I58a

The IATA represents 260 airlines and the annual report gives statistics on the prior year, as well as providing a chapter on the state of the industry, with prospects and trends.

1341  **ITS/operations resource guide.** U.S. Dept. of Transportation.
[Washington, D.C.]: U.S. Dept. of Transportation, Federal Highway Administration. http://www.resourceguide.its.dot.gov/.

TE228.3.I883

Lists some 400 resources. Categories are Points of Contact; Software Tools and Databases; Training, Workshops, and Seminars; Videos; Websites; and Documents for Intelligent Transportation Systems. Entries are annotated, with URLs, contact information, and pricing. Many of the listed resources are free.

**1342 National transportation library.** National Transportation Library (U.S.). Washington, D.C.: U.S. Dept. of Transportation. http://ntl. bts.gov/.

Provides links to many government transportation resources, including a State Department of Transportation (DOT) Google search, TRB Research in Progress (RIP) Database, International Transport Research Documentation (ITRD) Database, National Technical Information Service Database (indexes government-funded documents published since 1990), TranStats (statistical data), Rural and Agricultural Transportation: Data & Information Resources, as well as resources the library created (bibliographies, Transportation Libraries Directory, and information about their reference service).

**1343 National transportation safety board.** U.S. National Transportation Safety Board. 2007. Washington, D.C.: National Transportation Safety Board. http://www.ntsb.gov/.

TE153.N364

The NTSB examines the safety of aviation, highways, marine, pipeline and hazardous materials, railroad, and transportation disaster assistance, and issues reports and recommendations. Reports include Accident Reports, Annual Review of Aircraft Accident Data, reports in the Aviation Accident Database, Legal Matters, and Opinions & Orders. Some online reports date back to the early 1970s.

**1344 TRIS online.** National Transportation Library (U.S.). [1999?–.] Washington, D.C.: National Transport Library, Bureau of Transportation Statistics and Transportation Research Board. http://purl.access.gpo.gov/GPO/LPS17946/.

HE151

Index of over half a million technical reports, books, websites, and articles on transportation. Covers aviation, economics and finance, energy and environment, freight, geographic information services, highway/road transportation, intelligent transportation systems, laws and regulations, maritime/waterways, operations and traffic control, pedestrians and bicycles, planning and policy, public transportation, rail transportation, references and directories, and safety and security.

# Organizations and Associations

**1345  National transportation library.** National Transportation Library (U.S.). Washington, D.C.: U.S. Dept. of Transportation. http://ntl. bts.gov/.

Provides links to many government transportation resources, including a State Department of Transportation (DOT) Google search, TRB Research in Progress (RIP) Database, International Transport Research Documentation (ITRD) Database, National Technical Information Service Database (indexes government-funded documents published since 1990), TranStats (statistical data), Rural and Agricultural Transportation: Data & Information Resources, as well as resources the library created (bibliographies, Transportation Libraries Directory, and information about their reference service).

**1346  National transportation safety board.** U.S. National Transportation Safety Board. 2007. Washington, D.C.: National Transportation Safety Board. http://www.ntsb.gov/.

TE153.N364

The NTSB examines the safety of aviation, highways, marine, pipeline and hazardous materials, railroad, and transportation disaster assistance, and issues reports and recommendations. Reports include Accident Reports, Annual Review of Aircraft Accident Data, reports in the Aviation Accident Database, Legal Matters, and Opinions & Orders. Some online reports date back to the early 1970s.

**1347  Plunkett's airline, hotel, and travel industry almanac.** Jack W. Plunkett, Plunkett Research, Ltd. ill. Houston, Tex.: Plunkett Research, 2002–. ISSN: 1554-1215.

387.7                                    HE9803.A2P58; G155.U6P58

Data on 324 major companies, both public and private. Company profiles include types of business, brands and affiliates, contacts, employee benefits and top salaries, sales and profit numbers, growth plans, and competitive advantage. Especially useful for the industry trends, statistics and rankings (forecasts to 2020, top destinations worldwide, top airlines, top tourism nations, etc.) at the front of the volume and information on the main associations and organizations in the back of the volume. Most information is for the U.S., but some international coverage is provided. Available as an e-book.

## *Periodicals*

**1348 Annual report.** International Air Transport Association. 1990–. [Geneva, Switzerland]: International Air Transport Association. http://www.iata.org/.

387.70601                                                            HE9761.1.I58a

The IATA represents 260 airlines and the annual report gives statistics on the prior year, as well as providing a chapter on the state of the industry, with prospects and trends.

**1349 Lloyd's maritime directory.** Lloyd's of London Press. ill. Colchester, Essex, [U.K.]: Lloyd's of London Press, 1982–. ISSN: 0268-327X.

387.2025                                                              HE951.L56

Lists shippers, shipowners, towage, salvage, ship management services, builders, and repairers worldwide. Gives contact information, main personnel, services, and repair facilities.

**1350 Plunkett's airline, hotel, and travel industry almanac.** Jack W. Plunkett, Plunkett Research, Ltd. ill. Houston, Tex.: Plunkett Research, 2002–. ISSN: 1554-1215.

387.7                                                    HE9803.A2P58; G155.U6P58

Data on 324 major companies, both public and private. Company profiles include types of business, brands and affiliates, contacts, employee benefits and top salaries, sales and profit numbers, growth plans, and competitive advantage. Especially useful for the industry trends, statistics and rankings (forecasts to 2020, top destinations worldwide, top airlines, top tourism nations, etc.) at the front of the volume and information on the main associations and organizations in the back of the volume. Most information is for the U.S., but some international coverage is provided. Available as an e-book.

**1351 Railroad facts.** Association of American Railroads. ill. Washington: Office of Information and Public Affairs, Association of American Railroads, 1983–. ISSN: 0742-1850.

385.0973                                                              HE2713Y4

Continues *Yearbook of railroad facts* (1965–82). Summary of railroad operations throughout the year. Includes statistics on employment, financial results, traffic, plant and equipment, fuel consumption and cost, etc.

ECONOMICS & BUSINESS

**1352  Register of ships.** Lloyd's Register of Shipping. London: Lloyd's
Register of Shipping, 1966–. ISSN: 0141-4909.

623.82405                                                    HE565.A3L7

Published under varying titles since 1760 and by Lloyd's since 1834.
Merged with *Underwriters' registry for iron vessels* in 1885. Recent issues
in four or more volumes, with some variation in contents. The "Register
of ships" gives the names, classes, and general information concerning the
ships classed by Lloyd's register, together with particulars of all known
ocean-going merchant ships in the world of 100 tons gross and upwards.
It also lists lighters carried on board ship, floating docks, liquefied gas
carriers, ships carrying refrigerated cargo, refrigerated cargo containers,
refrigerated stores and container terminals, and offshore drilling rigs.
The "Register" is updated by means of cumulative monthly supplements
containing the latest survey records for all classed ships, and changes of
name, ownership, flag, tonnage, etc., for all ships, whether classed or not.
The "Shipowners" section gives a list of owners and managers of the ships
recorded in the "Register" with their fleets, as well as lists of former and
compound names of ships. An appendix contains a list of shipbuilders
with existing ships they have built, marine engine builders and boilermakers, dry and wet docks, telegraphic addresses and codes used by shipping
firms, marine insurance companies and marine associations.

**1353  Transportation statistics annual report.** Bureau of
Transportation Statistics. 1994–. Washington, D.C.: Bureau
of Transportation Statistics, U.S. Dept. of Transportation.
ISSN: 1932-3700. http://www.bts.gov/publications/
transportation_statistics_annual_report/.

380                                                    HE202.5.T747

Presents transportation indicators and statistics. Covers traffic flows (passenger border crossings, Amtrak station boardings, domestic freight ton-
miles, etc.), condition of the transportation system (highways, bridges,
airport runways, transit fleet vehicles, and rail, aircraft, and maritime vessel fleets), accidents (fatalities and injuries by means of transportation),
variables influencing traveling behavior (travel time, vehicle availability,
distance, income, ethnicity), travel times, availability of mass transit and
number of passengers served, travel costs of intracity commuting and
intercity trips, productivity in the transportation sector, transportation
and economic growth, government transportation finance (revenues,
expenditures, investment, subsidies), transportation-related variables that

influence global competitiveness, frequency of vehicle and transportation facility repairs, vehicle weights, transportation energy, and collateral damage to the human and natural environment. Data is normally for one year or ten years.

## Specialized Sources of Industry Data

**1354 Aerospace facts and figures.** Aerospace Industries Association of America. ill. Los Angeles: Aero Publishers, 1945–. ISSN: 0898-4425.
629.105                                                                           TL501.A818

Includes sections for aerospace summary, aircraft production (sales, orders, production), missile programs (orders, sales, outlays), space programs (orders, sales, outlays), air transportation (operating expenses, revenues, traffic and passenger statistics, jet fuels costs and consumption, air cargo statistics), research and development (federal outlays, Department of Defense outlays), foreign trade (U.S. imports and exports), employment and finance (income statement, balance sheet, operating ratios, capital expenditures). Data are drawn from both government and commercial sources.

**1355 The airline encyclopedia, 1909–2000.** Myron J. Smith. 3 v., ill. Lanham, Md.: Scarecrow Press, 2002. ISBN: 0810837900.
387.703                                                                           HE9780.S65

Provides annual operational and statistical information for global airlines companies. Useful for finding historic information on international companies and for details like terrorism and in-flight crime, accidents and incidents, natural disasters, and literary or film references. Appendixes include a list of acronyms and abbreviations and a list of sources. Indexed by regional name of carrier and by name and subject.

**1356 Census of transportation.** United States Dept. of Commerce, Bureau of the Census. 54 v. Washington: U.S. Dept. of Commerce, Bureau of the Census, 1963–2003.
380.50973                                                                         HE203.C44

Begun in 1963 and continued through 1997 (now part of the *Economic Census*). Includes the results of the truck inventory and use survey, commodity transportation survey, vehicle inventory and use survey, and national travel survey. Available online through the U.S. Census (http://www.census.gov/prod/www/abs/transpor.html/).

1357 **IBISWorld United States.** IBISWorld. New York: IBISWorld. http://www.ibisworld.com/.

HC103.I247

700 reports on the following industries: agriculture, forestry, fishing and hunting; mining; utilities; construction; manufacturing; wholesale trade; retail trade; transportation and warehousing; information; finance and insurance; real estate and rental and leasing; professional, scientific, and technical services; administrative and support and waste management and remediation services; educational services; health care and social assistance; arts, entertainment, and recreation; accommodation and food services; and other services. Setting this database apart are reports on small industries, such as parking lots and garages.

Reports include industry definition; key statistics; segmentations (products and services segmentation, major market segments, industry concentration, geographic spread); market characteristics (market size, demand determinants, domestic and international markets, basis of competition, life cycle); industry conditions (barriers to entry, taxation, industry assistance, regulation and deregulation, cost structure, capital and labor intensity, technology and systems, industry volatility, globalization); key factors (sensitivities and success factors); key competitors; and industry performance (current and historical).

1358 **Marketresearch.com academic.** Kalorama Information. 1999–. Bethesda, Md.: Kalorama Information. http://www.marketresearch. com/.

HF5415.2.K35

Market research reports from various sources (Icon Group, Kalorama, BizMiner, etc.) for Consumer Goods (apparel, cosmetics and personal care, house and home, pet services and supplies, travel services), Food and Beverage (alcoholic beverages, coffee and tea, soft drinks, confectionery, dairy products, food processing), Heavy Industry (energy, mining, utilities, construction, machines and parts, manufacturing, metals, paper and forest products, plastics, automotive, aviation & aerospace, logistics and shipping), Service Industries (accounting and finance, corporate services, banking and financial services, insurance), Public Sector (associations/ nonprofits, education, government), Life Science (biotechnology, agriculture, genomics, proteomics, medical imaging, healthcare facilities, managed care, regulation and policy, cardiovascular devices, equipment and supplies, wound care, pharmaceuticals, diseases and conditions, prescription drugs, therapeutic area), Technology & Media (computer equipment, electronics, networks, e-commerce and IT outsourcing, software, telecommunications, wireless), and Demographics (age, lifestyle and economics, multicultural).

Reports range in length, with some over 300 pages long, and give a variety of information (definition of industry, consumer demographics, consumer shopping habits, spending patterns, sales, establishments, employment, forecasts, trends, market size, market share, and market segmentation). Some company information is also included.

1359  **National transportation library.** National Transportation Library (U.S.). Washington, D.C.: U.S. Dept. of Transportation. http://ntl.bts.gov/.

Provides links to many government transportation resources, including a State Department of Transportation (DOT) Google search, TRB Research in Progress (RIP) Database, International Transport Research Documentation (ITRD) Database, National Technical Information Service Database (indexes government-funded documents published since 1990), TranStats (statistical data), Rural and Agricultural Transportation: Data & Information Resources, as well as resources the library created (bibliographies, Transportation Libraries Directory, and information about their reference service).

1360  **National transportation safety board.** U.S. National Transportation Safety Board. 2007. Washington, D.C.: National Transportation Safety Board. http://www.ntsb.gov/.

TE153.N364

The NTSB examines the safety of aviation, highways, marine, pipeline and hazardous materials, railroad, and transportation disaster assistance, and issues reports and recommendations. Reports include Accident Reports, Annual Review of Aircraft Accident Data, reports in the Aviation Accident Database, Legal Matters, and Opinions & Orders. Some online reports date back to the early 1970s.

1361  **Plunkett's airline, hotel, and travel industry almanac.** Jack W. Plunkett, Plunkett Research, Ltd. ill. Houston, Tex.: Plunkett Research, 2002–. ISSN: 1554-1215.

387.7                                        HE9803.A2P58; G155.U6P58

Data on 324 major companies, both public and private. Company profiles include types of business, brands and affiliates, contacts, employee benefits and top salaries, sales and profit numbers, growth plans, and competitive advantage. Especially useful for the industry trends, statistics and rankings (forecasts to 2020, top destinations worldwide, top airlines, top tourism nations, etc.) at the front of the volume and information on the main associations and organizations in the back of the volume. Most information is for the U.S., but some international coverage is provided. Available as an e-book.

**1362  Railroad facts.** Association of American Railroads. ill. Washington: Office of Information and Public Affairs, Association of American Railroads, 1983–. ISSN: 0742-1850.

385.0973                                                               HE2713Y4

Continues *Yearbook of railroad facts* (1965–82). Summary of railroad operations throughout the year. Includes statistics on employment, financial results, traffic, plant and equipment, fuel consumption and cost, etc.

**1363  Transportation statistics annual report.** Bureau of Transportation Statistics. 1994–. Washington, D.C.: Bureau of Transportation Statistics, U.S. Dept. of Transportation. ISSN: 1932-3700. http://www.bts.gov/publications/transportation_statistics_annual_report/.

380                                                                HE202.5.T747

Presents transportation indicators and statistics. Covers traffic flows (passenger border crossings, Amtrak station boardings, domestic freight ton-miles, etc.), condition of the transportation system (highways, bridges, airport runways, transit fleet vehicles, and rail, aircraft, and maritime vessel fleets), accidents (fatalities and injuries by means of transportation), variables influencing traveling behavior (travel time, vehicle availability, distance, income, ethnicity), travel times, availability of mass transit and number of passengers served, travel costs of intracity commuting and intercity trips, productivity in the transportation sector, transportation and economic growth, government transportation finance (revenues, expenditures, investment, subsidies), transportation-related variables that influence global competitiveness, frequency of vehicle and transportation facility repairs, vehicle weights, transportation energy, and collateral damage to the human and natural environment. Data is normally for one year or ten years.

# Utilities

## Additional Reference Sources

**1364 Hoover's online.** Reference Press. 1996–. Austin, Tex.: Reference Press. http://www.hoovers.com/.

338.7 HG4057

Nearly 18 million records describing public and private companies primarily in the United States, but including Canada, United Kingdom, Europe, and Asia/Pacific. Profiles have an overview, history, family tree, industry information, products/operations, top competitors, competitive landscape, top executives with biographies, news, significant developments, and financial data (summary; income statement; balance sheet; cash flow; historical financials such as five years of P/E and per share; stock quote; interactive stock chart; market data; earnings estimates; this year's ratios for the company, industry, and market; SEC filings; and industry watch).

Covers 600 industries, organized into the following categories: Aerospace and Defense; Agriculture; Automotive and Transport; Banking; Beverages; Business Services; Charitable Organizations; Chemicals; Computer Hardware; Computer Services; Computer Software; Construction; Consumer Products Manufacturers; Consumer Services; Cultural Institutions; Education; Electronics; Energy and Utilities; Environmental Services and Equipment; Financial Services; Food; Foundations; Government; Health Care; Industrial Manufacturing; Insurance; Leisure; Media; Membership Organizations; Metals and Mining; Pharmaceuticals; Real Estate; Retail; Security Products and Services; Telecommunications Equipment; Telecommunications Services; and Transportation Services.

Coverage can be brief, but generally includes a fact sheet, overview, selected companies, industry watch with video interviews, news from the last 90 days, and web resources for terminology, associations, and organizations, and online publications. Includes Hoover's print publications (*Hoover's handbook of American business* [35], *Hoover's handbook of private companies* [36]).

## Definition of the Industry

**1365 IBISWorld United States.** IBISWorld. New York: IBISWorld. http://www.ibisworld.com/.

HC103.I247

700 reports on the following industries: agriculture, forestry, fishing and hunting; mining; utilities; construction; manufacturing; wholesale trade; retail trade; transportation and warehousing; information; finance and insurance; real estate and rental and leasing; professional, scientific, and technical services; administrative and support and waste management and remediation services; educational services; health care and social assistance; arts, entertainment, and recreation; accommodation and food services; and other services. Setting this database apart are reports on small industries, such as parking lots and garages.

Reports include industry definition; key statistics; segmentations (products and services segmentation, major market segments, industry concentration, geographic spread); market characteristics (market size, demand determinants, domestic and international markets, basis of competition, life cycle); industry conditions (barriers to entry, taxation, industry assistance, regulation and deregulation, cost structure, capital and labor intensity, technology and systems, industry volatility, globalization); key factors (sensitivities and success factors); key competitors; and industry performance (current and historical).

## Internet Resources

**1366  BP statistical review of world energy.** BP Amoco. 1999–. London: BP Amoco. http://www.bp.com/statisticalreview/.

Information, analysis, and historical data on energy markets worldwide. Organized into five parts: group chief executives introduction; 2005 in review; review by energy type (oil, natural gas, coal, nuclear energy, hydroelectricity, primary energy, renewable energy, and electricity); downloads; using the review; and energy charting tool.

Historical data include oil: proved reserves; oil: proved reserves—barrels (from 1980); oil: production—barrels (from 1965); oil: production—tonnes (from 1965); oil: consumption—barrels (from 1965); oil: consumption—tonnes (from 1965); oil: regional consumption—by product group (from 1965); oil: spot crude prices; oil: crude prices since 1861; oil: refinery capacities (from 1965); oil: refinery throughputs (from 1980); oil: regional refining margins (from 1992); oil: trade movements (from 1980); oil: inter-area movements; oil: imports and exports; gas: proved reserves—bcm (from 1980); gas: production—bcm (from 1970); gas: production—bcf (from 1970); gas: production—Mtoe (from 1970); gas: consumption—bcm (from 1965); gas: consumption—bcf (from 1965); gas: consumption—Mtoe (from 1965); gas: trade movements pipeline; gas:

trade movements LNG; gas: prices; coal: reserves; coal: production—tonnes (from 1981); coal: production—Mtoe (from 1981); coal: consumption—Mtoe (from 1965); coal: prices; nuclear energy: consumption—TWh (from 1965); nuclear energy: consumption—Mtoe (from 1965); hydroelectricity: consumption—TWh (from 1965); hydroelectricity: consumption—Mtoe (from 1965); primary energy: consumption—Mtoe (from 1965); primary energy: consumption by fuel type—Mtoe; electricity generation—TWh (from 1990); and approximate conversion factors.

**1367  Edison electric institute.** Edison Electric Institute. 2003–. Washington, D.C.: Edison Electric Institute. http://www.eei.org/.

The institute represents shareholder-owned electric companies. Its website has industry information (electricity policy, energy infrastructure, environmental issues, retail services and delivery, reliability issues, and accounting issues), industry overview and statistics, meetings, news, and their magazine *ElectricPerspectives.*

**1368  Energy information administration.** Energy Information Administration. 2007. Washington, D.C.: Energy Information Administration. http://www.eia.doe.gov/.

The EIA is the statistical agency of the U.S. Department of Energy. The website has energy statistics for petroleum, natural gas, electricity, coal, nuclear energy, and renewable and alternative fuels. Also has detailed international country energy information, forecasts and analyses, state and national historical data, households, buildings and industry, and an Energy Kid's Page.

**1369  Ernst and Young.** Ernst and Young. 2007. London: Ernst and Young. http://www.ey.com/global/content.nsf/International/Industry_Overview/.

Ernst and Young provides "accounting and auditing, tax reporting and operations, tax advisory, business risk services, technology and security risk services, transaction advisory, and human capital services." The site is useful for articles on financial management, corporate governance, initial public offerings (IPOs), and industry reports (asset management, automotive, banking and capital markets, biotechnology, consumer products, insurance, media and entertainment, mining and metals, oil and gas, pharmaceuticals, real estate and construction, hospitality and leisure, technology, telecommunications, utilities).

1370 **Manufacturing.net.** Advantage Business Media. 2000s–. [s.l.]: Reed Business Information. http://www.manufacturing.net/.

Covers manufacturing for aerospace, automotive, chemical, food, material handling, pharmaceuticals, and utilities. Includes design and development; case studies; electrical and electronics; energy; environmental; facilities and operations; labor relations; manufacturing technology; materials; quality control; safety; and supply chain management. Has international focus.

1371 **Technology review.** Massachusetts Institute of Technology. 1998–. Cambridge, Mass.: Association of Alumni and Alumnae of the Massachusetts Institute of Technology. ISSN: 1099-274X. http://www.technologyreview.com/.

620                                                                T171.M47

Covers trends and developments in business technology, especially as they affect the energy, nanotech, biotech, and infotech industries. Includes annual list of the top emerging technologies. For many years, it included an annual R&D Scorecard, published each fall, which now is useful for tracking historical research and development expenditures.

## *Organizations and Associations*

1372 **Edison electric institute.** Edison Electric Institute. 2003–. Washington, D.C.: Edison Electric Institute. http://www.eei.org/.

The institute represents shareholder-owned electric companies. Its website has industry information (electricity policy, energy infrastructure, environmental issues, retail services and delivery, reliability issues, and accounting issues), industry overview and statistics, meetings, news, and their magazine *ElectricPerspectives*.

1373 **Energy information administration.** Energy Information Administration. 2007. Washington, D.C.: Energy Information Administration. http://www.eia.doe.gov/.

The EIA is the statistical agency of the U.S. Department of Energy. The website has energy statistics for petroleum, natural gas, electricity, coal, nuclear energy, and renewable and alternative fuels. Also has detailed international country energy information, forecasts and analyses, state and national historical data, households, buildings and industry, and an Energy Kid's Page.

## Periodicals

1374 **Technology review.** Massachusetts Institute of Technology. 1998–. Cambridge, Mass.: Association of Alumni and Alumnae of the Massachusetts Institute of Technology. ISSN: 1099-274X. http://www.technologyreview.com/.

620                                                    T171.M47

Covers trends and developments in business technology, especially as they affect the energy, nanotech, biotech, and infotech industries. Includes annual list of the top emerging technologies. For many years, it included an annual R&D Scorecard, published each fall, which now is useful for tracking historical research and development expenditures.

## Specialized Sources of Industry Data

1375 **Basic petroleum data book.** American Petroleum Institute. Washington: American Petroleum Institute, 1981–. ISSN: 0730-5621.

338.2728021                                     HD9564.B37

Worldwide petroleum statistics from 1947. "Oil and natural gas data on worldwide reserves, exploration and drilling, production, refining, transportation, historical prices, product demand, imports, exports and environmental information."—*Pref.* Includes a glossary and source list.

1376 **BP statistical review of world energy.** BP Amoco. 1999–. London: BP Amoco. http://www.bp.com/statisticalreview/.

Information, analysis, and historical data on energy markets worldwide. Organized into five parts: group chief executives introduction; 2005 in review; review by energy type (oil, natural gas, coal, nuclear energy, hydroelectricity, primary energy, renewable energy, and electricity); downloads; using the review; and energy charting tool.

    Historical data include oil: proved reserves; oil: proved reserves—barrels (from 1980); oil: production—barrels (from 1965); oil: production—tonnes (from 1965); oil: consumption—barrels (from 1965); oil: consumption—tonnes (from 1965); oil: regional consumption—by product group (from 1965); oil: spot crude prices; oil: crude prices since 1861; oil: refinery capacities (from 1965); oil: refinery throughputs (from 1980); oil: regional refining margins (from 1992); oil: trade movements (from 1980); oil: inter-area movements; oil: imports and exports; gas: proved reserves—bcm (from 1980); gas: production—bcm (from 1970); gas:

production—bcf (from 1970); gas: production—Mtoe (from 1970); gas: consumption—bcm (from 1965); gas: consumption—bcf (from 1965); gas: consumption—Mtoe (from 1965); gas: trade movements pipeline; gas: trade movements LNG; gas: prices; coal: reserves; coal: production—tonnes (from 1981); coal: production—Mtoe (from 1981); coal: consumption— Mtoe (from 1965); coal: prices; nuclear energy: consumption—TWh (from 1965); nuclear energy: consumption—Mtoe (from 1965); hydroelectricity: consumption—TWh (from 1965); hydroelectricity: consumption—Mtoe (from 1965); primary energy: consumption—Mtoe (from 1965); primary energy: consumption by fuel type—Mtoe; electricity generation—TWh (from 1990); and approximate conversion factors.

**1377  Energy information administration.** Energy Information Administration. 2007. Washington, D.C.: Energy Information Administration. http://www.eia.doe.gov/.

The EIA is the statistical agency of the U.S. Department of Energy. The website has energy statistics for petroleum, natural gas, electricity, coal, nuclear energy, and renewable and alternative fuels. Also has detailed international country energy information, forecasts and analyses, state and national historical data, households, buildings and industry, and an Energy Kid's Page.

**1378  IBISWorld United States.** IBISWorld. New York: IBISWorld. http://www.ibisworld.com/.

HC103.I247

700 reports on the following industries: agriculture, forestry, fishing and hunting; mining; utilities; construction; manufacturing; wholesale trade; retail trade; transportation and warehousing; information; finance and insurance; real estate and rental and leasing; professional, scientific, and technical services; administrative and support and waste management and remediation services; educational services; health care and social assistance; arts, entertainment, and recreation; accommodation and food services; and other services. Setting this database apart are reports on small industries, such as parking lots and garages.

Reports include industry definition; key statistics; segmentations (products and services segmentation, major market segments, industry concentration, geographic spread); market characteristics (market size, demand determinants, domestic and international markets, basis of competition, life cycle); industry conditions (barriers to entry, taxation, industry assistance, regulation and deregulation, cost structure, capital and labor intensity, technology and systems, industry volatility, globalization); key factors (sensitivities and success factors); key competitors; and industry performance (current and historical).

**1379 Marketresearch.com academic.** Kalorama Information. 1999–. Bethesda, Md.: Kalorama Information. http://www.marketresearch. com/.

HF5415.2.K35

Market research reports from various sources (Icon Group, Kalorama, BizMiner, etc.) for Consumer Goods (apparel, cosmetics and personal care, house and home, pet services and supplies, travel services), Food and Beverage (alcoholic beverages, coffee and tea, soft drinks, confectionery, dairy products, food processing), Heavy Industry (energy, mining, utilities, construction, machines and parts, manufacturing, metals, paper and forest products, plastics, automotive, aviation & aerospace, logistics and shipping), Service Industries (accounting and finance, corporate services, banking and financial services, insurance), Public Sector (associations/nonprofits, education, government), Life Science (biotechnology, agriculture, genomics, proteomics, medical imaging, healthcare facilities, managed care, regulation and policy, cardiovascular devices, equipment and supplies, wound care, pharmaceuticals, diseases and conditions, prescription drugs, therapeutic area), Technology & Media (computer equipment, electronics, networks, e-commerce and IT outsourcing, software, telecommunications, wireless), and Demographics (age, lifestyle and economics, multicultural).

Reports range in length, with some over 300 pages long, and give a variety of information (definition of industry, consumer demographics, consumer shopping habits, spending patterns, sales, establishments, employment, forecasts, trends, market size, market share, and market segmentation). Some company information is also included.

**1380 Plunkett's energy industry almanac.** Jack W. Plunkett, Plunkett Research, Ltd. ill. Houston, Tex.: Plunkett Research, 1999–. ISSN: 1542-5061.

338

HD9502.U5P58

Data on nearly 500 leading companies, both public and private. Company profiles include types of business, brands and affiliates, contacts, employee benefits and top salaries, sales and profit numbers, growth plans, and competitive advantage. Especially useful for the industry background (definition of the industry, deregulation, technology's impact on the industry), trends, statistics and rankings at the front of the volume (U.S. energy imports and exports: selected years 1950–2005, U.S. energy consumption and expenditures indicators: selected years 1950–2005, Renewable energy consumption in the transportation and electric power sectors: 2000–2005, U.S. energy production, Total and by renewable energy power sources: 1950–2005), and information on the main associations and organizations in the back of the volume. Most information is for the U.S., but some international coverage is provided. Available as an e-book.

# INDEX

Department of health and human
services, **1194, 1210, 1216**
Derivatives dictionary, **372, 436**
*Desktop encyclopedia of
telecommunications. 3rd ed.,* **306,
1311, 1316**
*A dictionary of accounting. 3rd ed.,* **219**
*Dictionary of banking terms. 5th ed.,*
**1134**
*A dictionary of business. 3rd ed., New
ed.,* **741**
*A dictionary of business and
management. 4th ed.,* **742**
*A dictionary of business quotations,* **805**
*Dictionary of business terms,* **743**
*Dictionary of e-business: A definitive
guide to technology and business
terms. 2nd ed.,* **304**
*Dictionary of finance and investment
terms. 7th ed.,* **373**
*Dictionary of financial abbreviations,*
**374**
*The dictionary of health economics,*
**1177**
*Dictionary of health economics and
finance,* **1178**
*Dictionary of health insurance and
managed care,* **1179**
*A dictionary of human resource
management* **269, 523**
*Dictionary of international business
terms. 3rd ed.,* **479, 744**
*Dictionary of international economics
terms,* **127, 480, 745**
*Dictionary of international trade,* **128**
*Dictionary of international trade:
Handbook of the global trade
community includes 21 key
appendixes. 7th ed.,* **129, 481**
*Dictionary of labour biography,* **120**
*The dictionary of marketing,* **582**
*Dictionary of marketing
communications,* **583**

*A dictionary of pharmacology and
allied topics. 2nd ed.,* **1284**
*Dictionary of pharmacy,* **1285**
*The dictionary of real estate appraisal.
4th ed.,* **1109**
*Dictionary of social and market
research,* **584**
*Dictionary of trade policy terms. 4th
ed.,* **130**
*Dictionary of travel, tourism and
hospitality. 3rd ed.,* **1233**
*The direct marketing market place,*
**592, 661**
*Direction of trade statistics,* **178**
*Directory of American firms operating
in foreign countries,* **56, 58**
*Directory of apparel specialty stores,*
**1304**
*Directory of corporate archives in the
United States and Canada,* **57, 92**
*Directory of department stores,* **1305**
*The directory of executive recruiters,*
**819**
*Directory of foreign firms operating in
the United States,* **56, 58**
Directory of members, **719, 751**
*Directory of obsolete securities,* **391**
*Directory of registered investment
advisors,* **398**
*Directory of top computer executives.
East ed.,* **551, 1101**
*The directory of trade and
professional associations in the
European Union: = Ré pertoire
de. associations professionnelles et
commerciales dans l'Union europé
enne,* **486, 752**
*Directory of United States exporters,*
**59**, 60,**1330**, 1331
*Directory of United States importers,*
59, **60**, 1330, **1331**
*Directory of U.S. labor organizations,*
**135, 753**

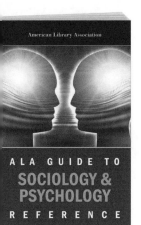
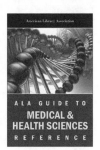

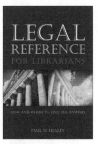